STUBBORN STRUCTURES

NOT ADDED BY
UNIVERSITY OF MICHIGAN

NOT ADDED BY
UNIVERSITY OF MICHIGAN

STUBBORN STRUCTURES

Reconceptualizing Post-Communist Regimes

Edited by
BÁLINT MAGYAR

with an introduction by
HENRY E. HALE

Central European University Press
Budapest–New York

Copyright © by Bálint Magyar 2019

Published in 2019 by

Central European University Press

Nádor utca 11, H-1051 Budapest, Hungary
Tel: +36-1-327-3138 or 327-3000
Fax: +36-1-327-3183
E-mail: ceupress@press.ceu.edu
Website: www.ceupress.com

224 West 57th Street, New York NY 10019, USA
Tel: +1-732-763-8816
E-mail: ceupress@press.ceu.edu

All rights reserved. No part of this publication may be reproduced, stored in a retrieval system, or transmitted, in any form or by any means, without the permission of the Publisher.

ISBN 978-963-386-214-8

Library of Congress Control Number: 2019934918

Printed in Hungary by
Prime Rate Kft., Budapest

Table of Contents

List of Figures vii
List of Tables xi
Editor's Preface 1

I. CONCEPTUAL FRAMEWORKS

HENRY E. HALE: Freeing Post-Soviet Regimes from the Procrustean Bed of Democracy Theory 5

JÁNOS KORNAI: The System Paradigm Revisited: Clarification and Additions in the Light Of Experiences in the Post-Communist Region 21

OLEKSANDR FISUN: Neopatrimonialism in Post-Soviet Eurasia 75

BÁLINT MAGYAR: Towards a Terminology for Post-communist Regimes 97

II. ACTORS OF POWER

NIKOLAY PETROV: Putin's Neo-Nomenklatura System and its Evolution 179

MIKHAIL MINAKOV: Republic of Clans: The Evolution of the Ukrainian Political System 217

ULADZIMIR ROUDA: Is Belarus a Classic Post-Communist Mafia State? 247

LÁSZLÓ NÁNDOR MAGYARI: The Romanian Patronal System of
Public Corruption 275

III. TECHNIQUES AND TOOLS

ZOLTÁN SZ. BÍRÓ: The Russian Party System 319

ANDREI KAZAKEVICH: The Belarusian Non-Party Political System:
Government, Trust and Institutions, 1990–2015 353

MIKLÓS HARASZTI: Illiberal State Censorship: A Must-have
Accessory for Any Mafia State 371

DUMITRU MINZARARI: Disarming Public Protests in Russia:
Transforming Public Goods into Private Goods 385

IV. WEALTH AND OWNERSHIP

ANDREY RYABOV: The Institution of Power&Ownership in the
Former USSR: Origin, Diversity of Forms, and Influence on
Transformation Processes 415

ILJA VIKTOROV: Russia's Network State and Reiderstvo Practices:
The Roots to Weak Property Rights Protection after the post-
Communist Transition 437

BÁLINT MAGYAR: From Free Market Corruption Risk to the
Certainty of a State-Run Criminal Organization (using Hungary
as an example) 461

V. CONTRASTS AND CONNECTIONS

ALEXEI PIKULIK: Belarus, Russia, and Ukraine as Post-Soviet Rent-
Seeking Regimes 489

SARAH CHAYES: The Structure of Corruption: A Systemic Analysis . 507

KÁLMÁN MIZSEI: The New East European Patronal States and the
Rule-of-Law 531

BÁLINT MAGYAR: Parallel System Narratives—Polish and
Hungarian Regime Formations Compared 611

List of Contributors 657
Index 659

List of Figures

Figure 2.1.	Interactions between the primary and secondary characteristics	28
Figure 2.2.	World map, 2013–2015. Categories of post-socialist countries according to the "capitalist vs. socialist" typology	30
Figure 2.3.	World map, 2013–2015. Categories of post-socialist countries according to the "democracy – autocracy – dictatorship" typology	44
Figure 4.1.	Traditional religions in Europe by country (2014)	99
Figure 4.2.	Inglehart–Welzel Cultural Map	101
Figure 4.3.	Ruling elites in a liberal democracy—autonomous elites	120
Figure 4.4.	Ruling elite of the communist regime—the nomenklatura	121
Figure 4.5.	Ruling elite of the post-communist single pyramid patronal network—adopted political family	122
Figure 4.6.	Disaggregation of political regimes by various dimensions of democracy	133
Figure 14.1.	Corporate raiding (*reiderstvo*)	438
Figure 15.1.	Corruption risk in public procurements, 2009–2015	467
Figure 15.2.	Proportion of public procurements without advertised tenders as a percentage of all public procurements, 2009–2015	468

Figure 15.3. Price distortion of Hungarian public procurements for each type, 2009–2015 469

Figure 15.4. Price distortions for Hungarian public procurements, 2009–2015 469

Figure 15.5. Number of public tenders awarded to Lajos Simicska (S), and to István Garancsi, Lőrinc Mészáros and István Tiborcz (G+M+T), 2013–2015 (no.) 472

Figure 15.6. Ranking according to selected institutional competitiveness indicators in a world ranking of 168 countries (2015) 476

Figure 15.7. Is "petty corruption" or "grand corruption" more dominant in Hungary? (percentage of respondents, broken down by party affiliation) 479

Figure 15.8. Proportion of those who chose categories related to grand corruption to describe corruption (percentage of respondents, broken down by party affiliation) 480

Figure 15.9. To what extent do voters in each party consider it likely that the Prime Minister is enriching himself through front men? (percentage) 481

Figure 15.10. Characterization of the present Hungarian political system by voters in each party (percentage) 483

Figure 19.1. The intersecting cycles of economic growth in Poland and Hungary (in percentage of annual growth of GDP) .. 631

Infograpics following page 516

Figure A.1. Infographic: The Structure of Kleptocracy in Azerbaijan
Figure A.2. Government Elements
Figure A.3. Private Sector Elements
Figure A.4. Criminal Elements
Figure A.5. Active Facilitators
Figure A.6. External Enablers
Figure A.7. Enabling Condition
Figure A.8. Revenue Streams

Figure B.1. Infographic: The Structure of Kleptocracy in Kyrgyzstan
Figure B.2. Government Elements
Figure B.3. Private Sector Elements
Figure B.4. Criminal Elements

List of Figures

Figure B.5. Active Facilitators
Figure B.6. External Enablers
Figure B.7. Enabling Condition
Figure B.8. Revenue Streams

Figure C.1. Infographic: The Structure of Kleptocracy in Moldova
Figure C.2. Government Elements
Figure C.3. Private Sector Elements
Figure C.4. Criminal Elements
Figure C.5. Active Facilitators
Figure C.6. External Enablers
Figure C.7. Enabling Condition
Figure C.8. Revenue Streams

List of Tables

Table 2.1.	Characteristics of the capitalist and socialist systems	27
Table 2.2.	Characteristics of democracy, autocracy, and dictatorship	38
Table 2.3.	Relation between the two kinds of typology	42
Table 2.4.	Distribution of alternative forms of politics and government in the post-socialist region	48
Table 4.1.	The proportion of Muslim and ethnic Russian population in the former states of the Soviet Republic in Central Asia after 2010	100
Table 4.2.	Legacies of Patronalism at the End of Communist Rule	105
Table 4.3.	Post-communist countries of Eurasia by political institutional system	108
Table 4.4.	State – society relationships in three ideal-type political regimes	114
Table 4.5.	Formal Constitutions and Patronalism in Post-Communist Countries since the Mid-1990s	115
Table 4.6.	Organizational connections of people to power institutions in three ideal-type political regimes	117
Table 4.7.	The formal position of the chief patron, the decision making "body" and the type of patronal networks in Russia	118
Table 4.8.	Key system components and political processes in three ideal-type political regimes	135

Table 4.9.	Interpretative layers of categories to describe the mafia state	137
Table 4.10.	Typology of relationships between state and organized crime	140
Table 4.11.	Some dimensions for defining the mafia state	144
Table 4.12.	Model differences in the positions of the ideal typical major entrepreneurs and oligarchs	147
Table 4.13.	Main types of political and economic actors in three ideal-type political regimes	154
Table 4.14.	Primary characteristics of state and private property relations in three ideal-type political regimes	156
Table 4.15.	Features of ownership in three ideal-type political regimes	157
Table 4.16.	Types and certain features of *reiderstvo* in post-communist regimes	162
Table 4.17.	The nature of nationalization, deprivatization, renationalization in three ideal-type political regimes	166
Table 4.18.	Patterns of corruption in three ideal-type political regimes	171
Table 4.19.	Role of law and legality in three ideal-type political regimes	172
Table 5.1.	Major substitutions and proxies, beginning in 2014	189
Table 5.2.	The "planet system" of Putin's elites, as of January 2017	198
Table 6.1.	Rulers of Soviet Ukraine since 1957	227
Table 6.2.	Clans of Dnipropetrovs'k regional group	234
Table 6.3.	Clans of Donets'k regional group	237
Table 15.1.	The World Bank control of corruption (the ability of a state to curtail corruption) percentile ranking (Country rank among all countries of the world: 0=lowest; 100=highest)	474
Table 15.2.	Support for particular corruption-related statements according to type of settlement (in percentage)	484
Table 16.1.	Rents in Russia, Ukraine, and Belarus	503

Editor's Preface

The publishing of *Post-Communist Mafia State* and its twin volume, *Twenty-Five Sides of a Post-Communist Mafia State* has generated comments and discussions among scholars involved in the analysis of the post-communist realities. It is from this communication and cooperation that studies that aim to go beyond the generalities of political systems analysis and grasp the specific essential features of the post-communist societies could be assembled into the present volume. This endeavor managed to be realized owing to the Open Society Fellowship grant that the editor received for the 2015-2016 year. Thanks should go to Krisztina Kiss for her work as research assistant, and to the editorial team of the Central European University Press.

I.
CONCEPTUAL FRAMEWORKS

HENRY E. HALE

Introduction: Freeing Post-Soviet Regimes from the Procrustean Bed of Democracy Theory

Ever since the communist systems of Europe and Eurasia started to crumble, observers have primarily understood what came next through a conceptual framework based on distinguishing between democratic and nondemocratic regimes, sometimes identifying a spectrum running between these two poles.[1] The conceptual apparatus of "democracy" has anchored this framework, as even those regimes near the more authoritarian pole are frequently studied for what democratic attributes they lack (e.g., as "failed" democratic transitions) and what their prospects are for becoming democratic.[2] One offshoot has been a voluminous body of work on popular protest, often interpreted as the potentially democratizing mobilization of civil society in nondemocratic systems, and on political opposition more generally.[3] For some countries and purposes, this has been appropriate and productive. For example, a logic of democracy goes a long way in explaining political dynamics and outcomes in countries like Estonia, and is sometimes useful in identifying the different ways in which a country like Russia falls short of the democratic ideal. Similarly, where protests break out and even overthrow a regime, making them important to understand, this logic is useful in investigating how a regime's opponents are faring. But in other cases and for other purposes, we may also want to know how nondemocratic regimes *actually function*, and a wealth of insightful country studies now make crystal clear that the conceptual framework of democracy (including studies focusing on what democratic attributes a country lacks) is woefully inadequate for this task.[4]

The present volume represents a major step forward in the effort to understand post-communist politics in ways that escape the procrustean bed of theory oriented primarily to the democratization research agenda. This is not the first step taken along this road, of course. A growing comparative literature has supplied many useful insights for understanding post-Soviet politics by proceeding from the logic not of democracy but from its opposite, authoritarianism.[5] Steven Levitsky and Lucan Way have helped pioneer one particularly influential effort, which explores relatively democratic outcomes in countries like Ukraine or Georgia as the result of "weak" authoritarianism.[6] Other work has sought to build theory on "hybrid regimes" that are not treated simply as examples of weak democracy/authoritarianism, but have unique political dynamics of their own.[7] Some have argued, however, that we need to go even further, that even these theories of authoritarianism and hybrid regimes tend to rely on concepts that seem natural in democracies but miss much of what we actually observe when looking up close at post-communist politics. These concepts include a tendency to focus on the formal institutions of autocracy, such as dominant parties and secret services, and readily understandable practices such as jailing dissenters and manipulating the content of state-owned media.

What such an approach to "authoritarianism" or "hybrid regimes" can miss are elements often found to be central to the logic of post-communist non-democracies, in particular highly complex *informal* (not officially codified) understandings and arrangements that often penetrate formal institutions and give them meanings that can be easily misunderstood if formalities are taken too literally. To redress this problem in scholarship is not simply a matter of paying attention to the informal aspects of politics. While several studies, including those mentioned above, have begun to address the importance of informal understandings and arrangements, it would appear that at least two major obstacles currently inhibit our making such phenomena more central to how we conceptualize post-Soviet politics. First, these practices and understandings are inherently hard to study precisely because they are informal and not officially codified in texts that are readily accessible to researchers. Moreover, since many of these practices are illicit, they are often intentionally hidden or disguised. As if that were not enough, important informal arrangements can be extremely complex and protean, hard to grasp in their entirety at any one moment yet also ever-changing, adapting to new developments in their environments and innovating as actors apply their human creativity to the pursuit of their goals. Second, largely thanks to these limitations, we lack a robust vocabulary for describing and discussing these phenomena. Some studies venture to coin a few new terms for what they describe, but only a few seem to have caught on. The absence of lexical convergence in our studies stunts the ability of accumulated research to develop robust theory.

This book does not claim to achieve this lexical convergence, but it does provide a major service by bringing together contributions that explicitly aim in this direction. Since contributing authors generally agree that convergence is best achieved through intensive research-based interaction rather than coercion, no requirement has been made that this volume's authors adopt a given vocabulary or theoretical framework. Each chapter therefore follows the approach that is most comfortable for the author, making the most sense for the author's particular subject and purpose. What the reader will gain is thus not a dictionary with examples, but a kind of conceptual cornucopia, an intellectual feast. The resulting variety, however, is not random but reflects a larger harmony of purpose that we believe significantly advances our understanding of post-communist regimes.

The volume thus begins by addressing the need for a larger theoretical framework and vocabulary capable of powering research forward into the "real politics" of post-communist countries, with several perspectives being proposed on what this framework and vocabulary might look like. Subsequent chapters examine more specific topics, evaluating the usefulness of different frameworks and often proposing topic-specific conceptual advances of their own. Importantly, the vast majority of authors come from East-Central Europe and Eurasia, the set of countries on which this book focuses. They are thus writing about topics with which they are intimately familiar, privy to highly nuanced local understandings that can often escape even the best-trained outside observers. While this book does not offer the final word on the subject, it is a crucial intermediate step along the road to conceptual consensus, resulting in what may be the most ambitious attempt yet to advance a new vocabulary of post-communist regimes.

**

Without discounting the utility of the more standard "democratic" and "authoritarian" conceptual frameworks,[8] I have found in my own research that understanding post-communist politics is well served by a framework that builds from the ground up—proceeding from a fundamental social context that these countries share to varying degrees—as opposed to concepts derived from a vision of what these countries might become. This context is *patronalism*, "a social equilibrium in which individuals organize their political and economic pursuits primarily around the personalized exchange of concrete rewards and punishments, and not primarily around abstract, impersonal principles such as ideological belief or categorizations that include many people one has not actually met in person."[9] All societies are to some extent patronal; connections matter everywhere, including in the most developed democracies.[10] In some countries, however, connections matter far more than others, unconstrained by the need to observe formalities that facilitate a robust role for collective political action along impersonal social lines.

Patronalistic practices can include a wide variety of behaviors linked to politics that involve extended chains of actual personal acquaintance. Some of these have a negative connotation, such as nepotism, bribery, a reluctance to trust strangers (including in consideration for jobs) without a personal connection of some kind, disregard for formal law, patronage politics, the abuse of public office for personal material or political gain, and inefficiency. But patronalism also has a morality of its own that many see as positive, including a high valuation put on deep personal relationships, strong bonds of mutual commitment among family and friends, robust embeddedness in larger communities, the capacity to mobilize large numbers of people quickly for the pursuit of larger goals, and flexibility. It also has the potential to avoid senseless "red tape" when something needs to get done, and can even open up opportunities for people on the lower end of the social totem pole to call on larger networks of extended family or acquaintances to improve their position or defend themselves. Patronalism is thus not meant to connote negative associations, but to serve as a neutral term for a social condition that has wider implications for politics.

Indeed, to the extent that patronalism dominates, it has several important implications for the practice of politics. One is that the chief actors in politics are likely to be best understood as extended, roughly hierarchical networks of actual political acquaintance—entities that might be called simply "patronal networks." Thus instead of privileging formal institutional actors like "parties" or "parliament"—or even specific individuals—in our descriptions of politics (not to mention in our theory), the logic of patronalism would lead us instead to identify, map out, and emphasize the roles of major patronal networks and to think about what governs their behavior.

This includes recognizing that the most important patronal networks are likely *not to reduce to* but instead to *interpenetrate* (cut across) many different formal institutions, including political parties (perhaps multiple parties at the same time), the legislature, the executive branch, private sector firms, mass media, and even "civil society" organizations.

Another implication is that political systems might be understood less by the formal institutions they contain and more by how a country's patronal networks are (at a given time) arranged vis-à-vis each other and, by implication, their leading patrons. A *single-pyramid system* is thus a system in which a country's main patronal networks are glommed together, coordinating their most consequential activities around a single center of authority. In the current era, this is typically a "president" who is the chief patron of the most powerful network, though as this volume's chapter by Kálmán Mizsei makes clear, the chief patron need not hold such a lofty formal title. In a *competing-pyramid system*, by contrast, the most influential patronal networks are not coordinated around the authority of any single patron or network, instead they compete outright for power and resources. This competition can take place through both formal channels (e.g., seeking to win elections) and informal ones (e.g., campaigns to discredit each other in media or efforts to seize each other's resources).

While there can be some overlap between these two Weberian idealtype systems and the concepts of "authoritarianism" and "democracy," the patronal politics perspective's emphasis on elite networks' configurations makes it better able both to capture the actual practice of politics in these systems and to accommodate theories of regime *dynamics*. Indeed, if the logic of "democracy" is about an ideal-typical "regime" that is by definition institutionalized and stable in nature, then the logic of patronal politics is about patterns of complex interaction among potentially rival patronal networks that is constantly subject to change. In fact, one of the chief arguments advanced in favor of the patronal politics approach is that it is better able to account for the regime dynamics observed in the post-communist space, with many states seemingly oscillating back and forth between relatively authoritarian and democratic systems in regular patterns that are not captured by terms like democratic/authoritarian "weakness" or "lack of consolidation."[11]

The patronal politics perspective thus places emphasis on factors that drive the behavior of patronal networks, including what sustains them, what changes them, what leads them to relate to each other in different ways, how one might achieve dominance over the others, and the different forms that both domination and non-domination might take. Among some of the general propositions it generates are that networks generally need direct, personal access to power in order to gain or at least protect their resources.[12] In addition, leaders tend to govern and rule (exercising and maintaining power) by working through patronal networks in their coalition in ways that often overshadow their reliance on the straightforward use of the formal institutions of state. And among the chief challenges a leader faces in doing so is network coordination: if the coordination of networks within his or her single-pyramid system starts to falter (for example, if they all agree on supporting the current president but cannot agree on what would happen with an anticipated succession) a competing-pyramid situation can quickly emerge.

The theory of patronalism is still at an early stage, with my own theoretical work to date primarily addressing certain broad patterns that leave a great deal to be explained. One of the larger questions left unanswered in my previous work is whether we can usefully identify different types of patronal networks and different types of single- and competing-pyramid systems, and, linking the two, whether different types of networks can be expected to produce different types of single—or competing—pyramid systems, or something in between. Another question involves what the relationship is between patronal politics and concepts like legitimacy. Related to this, what are the actual goals of patrons and their networks, and how do different assumptions about motives shape their behavior and configurations? The origins of patronalism itself also constitute an important area for research, including the sources of possible social transformations away from it or even back toward it in a given country.

* * *

Taken together, the contributions of this volume go a long way toward supplying us with some potential answers to questions like these that I have encountered in my work on patronalism, and they more generally break important new ground in understanding a quarter century of post-communism. The first part of the book features three chapters that each present distinct and elaborate theoretical contributions. Addressing them in the order in which they appear, János Kornai's is the most "traditional" in the sense described above, explicitly using the terms "democracy" and "autocracy" (along with "capitalism" and "socialism") while innovatively adapting them to the reality he observes in the post-communist world. His chapter is an example of how these terms can be profitably employed despite the problems discussed above. Indeed, Kornai is interested less in the specific workings of post-communist regimes than in what precisely distinguishes them from their totalitarian "starting point" when the old communist regimes began to soften or simply collapse, and how one might therefore categorize today's Hungary, in light of its widely reported democratic backsliding.

For Kornai, the starting point is "dictatorship," which effectively represents a terror-ridden and completely closed society without any meaningful institutions on which citizens can rely to exercise their rights or power, and no organized opposition. "Democracy" is its opposite, with "autocracy" being defined as a middle category where democratic forms exist (i.e., opposition parties) but are weak and manipulated by an overarching central authority, which "cannot be removed through a peaceful and civilized procedure," yet which refrains from exercising the most systematic forms of terror. By developing a more conventional distinction between capitalism and socialism, this framework shows nicely how today's Hungary relates to the communist regimes of years past as well as to the most clearly democratic, capitalist countries of Europe: Hungary is a capitalist autocracy, though "a special kind of capitalism, and a specific kind of autocracy."

Oleksandr Fisun's contribution also draws upon pedigreed theoretical constructs, particularly that of neopatrimonialism, which is perhaps the most elaborate preexisting alternative framework to those oriented to the notions of democracy and autocracy. This conceptual apparatus has been extensively applied to African politics, but rarely to the post-Soviet world, a gap that Fisun's pioneering work is now addressing.[13] If traditional Weberian "patrimonialism" refers to a form of legitimate domination through which public office and private wealth are fused, the addition of "neo-" refers to the fact that this basic principle holds informally even in the presence of key elements of modernity, notably a substantial state bureaucracy. Fisun's development of the theory builds on the core insight that state actors are first and foremost rent-seekers, seeking material gain through the use of their official positions and façade institutions while working through patron-client relations.

I regard neopatrimonialism as essentially a subtype of patronal politics theory, a subtype that specifies the key behavioral assumption as being rent-seeking and then explores the implications that follow from this. The broader concept of patronalism also allows for other behavioral assumptions—indeed, not everything done in this part of the world can be explained as a product of rent-seeking, such as anti-smoking initiatives in Russia. But Fisun's work shows that theory built on this assumption can explain a great deal of post-communist behavior, allowing for novel contributions like "neopatrimonial democracy" that help explain how a country like Ukraine can simultaneously meet standard definitions of "democratic" yet be highly corrupt. This makes the neopatrimonial model one of the most productive directions researchers can take within the broader framework of patronalism. Fisun locates the origin of post-Soviet neopatrimonialism in the sequencing of modernization: marketization and democratization preceded national consolidation.

Rounding out the most explicitly conceptual part of this book, Bálint Magyar's chapter is the most ambitious and trailblazing, essentially forming the heart of this volume. Here, Magyar systematically introduces a completely new grammar developed specifically to convey understandings about post-communist politics that our existing lexicon and linguistic norms miss or tend to distort. A sweeping historical analysis explains why some (primarily more Western) countries in this region experienced a crucial separation of three categories of social action: political activities, market activities, and communal activities. Where this happened, the conceptual toolbox of democracy may be adequate in ways noted by Kornai. Where this did not occur to the same extent, we are more likely to witness the patterns of patronal politics that I describe above, including the neopatrimonial forms of rent-seeking that Fisun discusses. Magyar also observes, however, that dynamism is possible even among countries where the separation of politics, markets, and communal activities has prevailed, as circumstances can arise in which powerful actors erode the barriers keeping them apart. Hungary is the most prominent post-communist example of such a case, and Georgia may represent a case of a country moving in the opposite direction.

The bulk of Magyar's chapter is devoted to creating a new terminology for understanding politics when the separation of the political, the market, and the communal is unrealized. Proceeding from some of the basic terminology from patronalism theory, including the centrality of patronal networks and the distinction between single- and multiple-pyramid systems, Magyar considers different realms of politics step by step and supplies a vocabulary adequate to each one. For example, he makes a number of important contributions concerning how we should conceptualize and talk about single-pyramid systems. One of his central innovations is the notion of the "adopted political family" through which the chief patron exercises power, a concept that frees us from having to use ill-fitting terms like "inner circle," "team," "administration," "service gentry," or "nomenklatura." The term "adopted political family" effectively conveys an informal institution that unites different networks and their resources, extends across formal institutions, is based on patronal rather than organizational loyalty (no free entry or exit), is hierarchical, and follows cultural patterns associated with "clans" or a patriarchal family. Magyar also incorporates some terms specific to post-communist regimes that have made their way into broader discourse, such as "oligarch," though refines them usefully by introducing the notions of "poligarch" (a politician wielding an economic empire) and "minigarch" (a local, or otherwise scale-limited, oligarch).

Importantly, Magyar's grammar covers not only nouns but also verbs. For example, if a central action of liberal democracy is about "governing" and the corresponding action in communist dictatorships was of "commanding," the analogous action in post-communist single-pyramid systems is "arranging." Similarly, democracy's "joining" and communist dictatorship's "enrollment" correspond with post-communist autocracy's "cooptation/adoption."

Magyar also introduces a very useful new typology of states themselves, clarifying the relationship among different concepts that have emerged. For example, just as a "patronal state" is only one of many types of "states," a "clan state" is a particular kind of patronal state (one in which the elite is structured as an adopted political family). Magyar also explicitly introduces the notion of legitimacy to the theory of patronal politics, an innovative development: clan states can be both legitimate and illegitimate, and an illegitimate clan state is a "mafia state."[14] The idea of a mafia state, therefore, cannot be dismissed as simply a pejorative term for a regime one does not like. Instead, it represents a theory about how clan politics functions in the absence of legitimacy and about how this politics does in fact display behaviors widely associated with classic mafia, a concept well enough known to justify its usage in the type's name, which he argues has advantages over the increasingly common but less theoretically grounded notion of "kleptocracy." Of course, observers may disagree on whether a given regime is in fact illegitimate, but this is exactly the kind of debate that Magyar's conceptualization intends to promote and set on a solid theoretical footing. The concept of the mafia state also generates a number of terms well suited to Magyar's new grammar of post-communist politics, including the notion of an "organized upperworld" to accompany the familiar "organized underworld" and the idea of "stooges" as the "front men" for the regime's illicit activities.

* * *

The volume's remaining chapters provide the proverbial meat for the intellectual feast, addressing specific topics in post-communist politics and engaging the concepts discussed above while making additional theoretical contributions of their own. Some of the chapters examine specific countries (or sets of countries) and explain the particular regime dynamics that we witness there. Mikhail Minakov's chapter develops the concept of "clan state" as it applies to Ukraine, explaining how largely regionally based patronal networks rose to political dominance. This was not a simple process of clans capturing power, however, as the transition process and power struggles altered the clans themselves, the most powerful of which are now sophisticated, multi-layered organizations that compete with one another in the political and economic arenas. Uladzimir Rouda examines the very different patterns of politics to be observed in neighboring Belarus. Belarus, he argues, does resemble Magyar's notion of a mafia state (which he also relates to the Weberian concept of sultanism, a form of patrimonial rule). But Rouda also identifies several Belarusian deviations from the ideal-type mafia state model, in particular its absence of any formal party of power and the domination of state ownership of the economy.

Alexei Pikulik takes a comparative approach, explaining why Belarus, Ukraine, and Russia have tended to display different dynamics over the past quarter century. Pikulik's theory, which resembles Fisun's neopatrimonialism but adopts the term "rent-seeking regime" and builds on theories of the rentier state, argues that the key driver of regime dynamics is change in the availability of large-scale external rents to the regime in question. The ruling "business-administrative groups" in Russia and Belarus have held power for years largely because such rents became available toward the outset of their single-pyramid rule—in Russia this was the hydrocarbon boom of the 2000s and for Belarus this was the supply of subsidies and transit revenue from Russia. This reinforced the status quo. For Ukraine, rents arrived when Ukraine was in a competing-pyramid situation, with multiple pyramids having access to the incoming rents, the result being reinforced political competition.

The following chapters direct readers' attention to Romania, Hungary, and Poland. The contribution by Magyar, in conversation with Kornai's chapter, makes the case for contemporary Hungary as a classic mafia state, discussing the institutional changes that helped bring this about. While Poland has also undergone a movement away from classic democracy, Magyar contends that it does not appear to be becoming a mafia state. The key difference lies in the role of ideology. While the Hungarian adopted political family *uses* ideology for its own purposes, including wealth accumulation, Poland's dominant party is instead *driven* by a particular ideological vision. In the Polish case, its central leadership displays little inclination to amass riches for itself and rewards its supporters with positions in power rather than individual wealth. Nándor László Magyari examines Romania, identifying several factors that have served as barriers to its developing a single-pyramid system. These include a divided-executive constitution that keeps patronal network coordination centered around at least two rather than a single patron, a proportional representation election system that promotes coalition-building among groups aspiring to power, and a very active civil society and media sphere that has proven capable of mobilizing enough people to thwart efforts to concentrate power.

Following Magyari's work is another set of chapters that establish the importance of specific institutions of rule in different countries, arguing for their centrality in building and sustaining mafia states and other kinds of single-pyramid systems in the post-communist space. Nikolay Petrov coins the notion of a "neo-nomenklatura" system, arguing that Russian President Vladimir Putin has restored—but crucially in a new form—this fundamental feature of the Soviet regime to sustain a solid and loyal elite through which to govern. Andrei Kazakevich contends that Belarus' lack of a ruling party, described by Rouda as a deviation from the ideal-type mafia state model, has been a central part of Alyaksandr Lukashenka's regime, growing out of his confrontation with political parties, a confrontation that resonated with the population's widespread lack of trust in political institutions. Miklós Haraszti calls attention to the ways in which mafia states can control the media through what he calls "quasi-democratic state censorship," eschewing outright bans on criticism but employing a wide array of informal pressures through channels such as licensing authorities and libel laws. Kálmán Mizsei highlights the importance of prosecutors and the secret services in building single-pyramid systems, examining cases in Moldova and Ukraine. Andrey Ryabov develops the broader notion of "power&ownership" and its centrality to the politics of many post-communist regimes. This term captures the expectation that those who occupy positions of political power will also control large-scale material assets. Similarly, Dumitru Minzarari's chapter shows how the Russian state's (largely informal) control over jobs desired by the middle class has helped it weather crises that might otherwise have led to the mass defection of the same middle class and potentially revolution.

The remaining chapters examine one of the core features of mafia states: corruption. Bálint Magyar's chapter on this subject pioneers the use of quantitative analysis in studying mafia states, identifying certain telltale features on which statistics can be available, as illustrated in the case of Hungary (for example, contract overpricing). Sarah Chayes presents an elaborate dissection of the specific structures of kleptocracy in multiple post-Soviet cases, blazing a trail in the visual representation of corrupt networks in single-pyramid systems. Ilja Viktorov's contribution examines patterns of corruption that do not necessarily originate from the state's chief patron, those that fall under the category of *reiderstvo*, or "raiding" typically involving some sort of nefarious scheme to seize someone else's property and that may or may not be initiated by state actors.

* * *

Overall, the chapters that follow significantly deepen our understanding of post-communist politics, containing useful detail and conceptual innovations that cannot be found elsewhere and that almost all originate from the region itself. While this book is dedicated to understanding East-Central Europe and Eurasia, I am confident that it will also prove helpful to those who study other regions of the globe where patronal politics is prominent. This volume is thus likely to stimulate further comparative research that pushes and applies the concepts developed here to different regions and contexts.

NOTES

[1] Valerie Bunce, "Should Transitologists Be Grounded?," *Slavic Review* 54, no. 1 (1995): 111–27; Timothy J. Colton, "Politics," in *After the Soviet Union: From Empire to Nations* (New York: Norton, 1992), 17–48; Terry Lynn Karl and Philippe C. Schmitter, "Modes of Transition in Latin America, Southern and Eastern Europe," *International Social Science Journal* 43 (June 1991): 269–84; Herbert Kitschelt et al., *Post-Communist Party Systems: Competition, Representation and Inter-Party Cooperation* (New York: Cambridge University Press, 1999); Michael McFaul, *Russia's Unfinished Revolution* (Ithaca, NY: Cornell University Press, 2001).

[2] Ian Bremmer and Cory Welt, "The Trouble with Democracy in Kazakhstan," *Central Asian Survey* 15, no. 2 (1996): 179–99; Timothy J. Colton and Henry E. Hale, "Putin's Uneasy Return and Hybrid Regime Stability: The 2012 Russian Election Studies Survey," *Problems of Post-Communism* 61, no. 2 (April 2014): 3–22; M. Steven Fish, *Democracy Derailed in Russia: The Failure of Open Politics* (New York: Cambridge University Press, 2005); Vladimir Gel'man, *Authoritarian Russia: Analyzing Post-Soviet Regime Changes* (Pittsburgh: University of Pittsburgh Press, 2015); Stephen E. Hanson, *Post-Imperial Democracies: Ideology and Party Formation in Third Republic France, Weimar Germany, and Post-Soviet Russia* (New York: Cambridge University Press, 2010); Martha Brill Olcott, *Tajikistan's Difficult Development Path* (Washington: Carnegie Endowment, 2012); Thomas F. Remington, *Politics in Russia* (Boston: Longman, 2010); Philip G. Roeder, "Varieties of Post-Soviet Authoritarian Regimes," *Post-Soviet Affairs* 10, no. 1 (January 1994): 61–101; Daniel Treisman, *The Return: Russia's Journey from Gorbachev to Medvedev* (New York: Simon and Schuster, 2012).

[3] Debra Lynn Javeline, *Protest and the Politics of Blame: The Russian Response to Unpaid Wages* (Ann Arbor: University of Michigan Press, 2003); Tomila Lankina and Alisa Voznaya, "New Data on Protest Trends in Russia's Regions," *Europe-Asia Studies* 67, no. 2 (February 7, 2015): 327–42; Graeme Robertson, "Protesting Putinism," *Problems of Post-Communism* 60, no. 2 (April 3, 2013): 11–23; Regina Smyth and Sarah Oates, "Mind the Gaps: Media Use and Mass Action in Russia," *Europe-Asia Studies* 67, no. 2 (2015): 285–305; Stephen Crowley, "Why Protests Keep Putin Up at Night," *Foreign Affairs*, April 19, 2017, https://www.foreignaffairs.com/articles/russian-federation/2017-04-19/why-protests-keep-putin-night; Mikhail Dmitriev, "Lost in Transition? The Geography of Protests and Attitude Change in Russia," *Europe-Asia Studies* 67, no. 2 (February 7, 2015): 224–43; Olga Onuch, *Mapping Mass Mobilizations: Understanding Revolutionary Moments in Argentina and Ukraine* (London: Palgrave Macmillan, 2014); Valerie J. Bunce and Sharon L. Wolchik, *Defeating Authoritarian Leaders in Postcommunist Countries* (New York: Cambridge University Press, 2011); Vladimir Gel'man, "Political Opposition in Russia: A Dying Species?," *Post-Soviet Affairs* 21, no. 3 (January 1, 2005): 226–46; Eugene Huskey and Gulnara Iskakova, "The Barriers to Intra-Opposition Cooperation in the Post-Communist World: Evidence from Kyrgyzstan," *Post-Soviet Affairs* 26, no. 3 (2010): 228–62; Jody

LaPorte, "Hidden in Plain Sight: Political Opposition and Hegemonic Authoritarianism in Azerbaijan," *Post-Soviet Affairs* 31, no. 4 (July 4, 2015): 339–66.

4   Jessica Allina-Pisano, *The Post-Soviet Potemkin Village: Politics and Property Rights in the Black Earth* (New York: Cambridge University Press, 2008); Andrew Scott Barnes, *Owning Russia: The Struggle Over Factories, Farms, and Power* (Cornell University Press, 2006); Venelin I. Ganev, *Preying on the State: The Transformation of Bulgaria after 1989* (Ithaca: Cornell University Press, 2007); Marlene Laruelle, "Discussing Neopatrimonialism and Patronal Presidentialism in the Central Asian Context," *Demokratizatsiya: The Journal of Post-Soviet Democratization* 20, no. 4 (2012): 301–24; Alena Ledeneva, *How Russia Really Works* (Ithaca: Cornell University Press, 2006); Bálint Magyar, *Post-Communist Mafia State: The Case of Hungary* (Budapest–New York: Central European University Press and Noran Libro, 2016); Stanislav Markus, *Property, Predation, and Protection: Piranha Capitalism in Russia and Ukraine* (New York: Cambridge University Press, 2015); Edward A. D. Schatz, *Modern Clan Politics: The Power of "Blood" in Kazakhstan and Beyond* (Seattle: University of Washington Press, 2004); Andrew Wilson, *Virtual Politics: Faking Democracy in the Post-Soviet World* (New Haven, CT: Yale University Press, 2005).

5   Ora John Reuter and Graeme B. Robertson, "Subnational Appointments in Authoritarian Regimes: Evidence from Russian Gubernatorial Appointments," *The Journal of Politics* 74, no. 4 (2012): 1023–37; Ora John Reuter, *The Origins of Dominant Parties: Building Authoritarian Institutions in Post-Soviet Russia* (Cambridge University Press, 2017); William Zimmerman, *Ruling Russia: Authoritarianism from the Revolution to Putin* (Princeton: Princeton University Press, 2014).

6   Steven Levitsky and Lucan Way, "The Rise of Competitive Authoritarianism," *Journal of Democracy* 13, no. 2 (April 2002): 51–65; Steven Levitsky and Lucan A. Way, *Competitive Authoritarianism: Hybrid Regimes after the Cold War* (New York: Cambridge University Press, 2010); Lucan A. Way, *Pluralism by Default: Weak Autocrats and the Rise of Competitive Politics* (Baltimore, MD: Johns Hopkins University Press, 2015).

7   Larry Diamond, "Thinking about Hybrid Regimes," *Journal of Democracy* 13, no. 2 (April 2002): 21–35; J. Paul Goode, "Nationalism in Quiet Times: Ideational Power and Post-Soviet Hybrid Regimes," *Problems of Post-Communism* 59, no. 3 (June 2012): 6–16; Henry E. Hale, "Eurasian Polities as Hybrid Regimes: The Case of Putin's Russia," *Journal of Eurasian Studies* 1, no. 1 (January 2010): 33–41; Luke March, "Managing Opposition in a Hybrid Regime: Just Russia and Parastatal Opposition," *Slavic Review* 68, no. 3 (2009): 504–27; Graeme B. Robertson, *The Politics of Protest in Hybrid Regimes: Managing Dissent in Post-Communist Russia* (New York: Cambridge University Press, 2011); Daniel S. Treisman, "Presidential Popularity in a Hybrid Regime: Russia under Yeltsin and Putin," *American Journal of Political Science* 55, no. 3 (July 2011): 590–609.

8   Indeed, I adopt them myself for addressing different kinds of questions.

9   Henry E. Hale, *Patronal Politics: Eurasian Regime Dynamics in Comparative Perspective* (New York, NY: Cambridge University Press, 2015), 20.

10 Richard Lachmann, "American Patrimonialism: The Return of the Repressed," *The Annals of the American Academy of Political and Social Science* 636 (July 2011): 204–30.

11 Henry E. Hale, "Regime Cycles: Democracy, Autocracy, and Revolution in Post-Soviet Eurasia," *World Politics* 58, no. 1 (October 2005): 133–65.
12 This is not to say they have no other strategies for protecting their assets. One work that establishes an important research agenda on this topic is Markus, *Property, Predation, and Protection.*
13 Michael Bratton and Nicolas Van de Walle, *Democratic Experiments in Africa: Regime Transitions in Comparative Perspective* (New York: Cambridge University Press, 1997); Gero Erdmann and Ulf Engel, "Neopatrimonialism Reconsidered: Critical Review and Elaboration of an Elusive Concept," *Commonwealth and Comparative Politics* 45, no. 1 (February 2007): 95–119; Oleksandr Fisun, "Rethinking Post-Soviet Politics from a Neopatrimonial Perspective," *Demokratizatsiya: The Journal of Post-Soviet Democratization* 20, no. 2 (Spring 2012): 87–96; Aleksandr A. Fisun, *Demokratiia, Neopatrimonializm I Global'nye Transformatsii* (Kharkiv, Ukraine: Konstant, 2007).
14 Magyar, *Post-Communist Mafia State.*

JÁNOS KORNAI

The System Paradigm Revisited: Clarification and Additions in the Light of Experiences in the Post-Socialist Region*

INTRODUCTION

What prompted this study? What type of readers am I addressing? My prime motivation in my academic life has been to discover what kind of society we live in, what its characteristics may be. As any researcher does, I have taken a conceptual apparatus and methodology as a point from which to view my subject matter. Still, as most researchers, I have rarely chosen the method itself, the outlook or approach driving my research, as

---

* This chapter is a slightly revised version of the text originally published under the same title in *Acta Oeconomica* 66, no. 4 (2016): 547–596. Let me express my gratitude here first of all to my wife, Zsuzsa Dániel, who encouraged me to write this study despite all hardships; she was the first reader of several earlier drafts, supporting my progress with several thoughtful suggestions. I also owe my thanks to all the people who read the manuscript and supported me with their recommendations, helped me to collect data and explore the literature. I would like to emphasize Ádám Kerényi's role, who helped me most with his initiatives and exceptional working capacity. It would be really hard to compare the invaluable support from the other contributors, therefore I simply list their names: Dóra Andrics, Réka Branyiczki, Rita Fancsovits, Péter Gedeon, Péter Mihályi, Quang A. Nguyen, Ildikó Pető, Andrea Reményi, Eszter Rékasi, Miklós Rosta, András Simonovits, Ádám Szajkó, Zoltán Sz. Bíró, Judit Ványai and Chenggang Xu. I am grateful to Brian McLean, my friend and permanent translator for many decades, for the faithful and well readable translation. I would also like to thank Corvinus University of Budapest for providing me the conditions of undisturbed work and "By Force of Thought" Foundation for its contribution to research funding.

the subject of a separate paper. The primary aim of my article "The System Paradigm" was to summarize my principles in the *theory of science*.[1] Seventeen years have passed since and I have been much influenced by new experiences: the changes that have occurred in China, the consolidation of the Putin regime, and most strongly of all, the events in Hungary under the political group headed by Viktor Orbán, the prime minister since the election in 2010. It is high time to review the conceptual framework, along with some other matters underlying comparative systems theory.

This study is intended above all for past and future readers studying my works, whether many or few. Apart from them, I target researchers in comparative economics, comparative political science and comparative sociology, and historians of the present-day period; researchers working at universities, research institutes, international bodies, financial institutions, and think tanks, or more specifically, those who professionally analyze the changes occurring in the post-socialist region.

One aim is to sum up, more thoroughly than my first study of the system paradigm did, some elements of my conceptual and analytical apparatus. I do not offer a survey of the literature on the problem. Were I to do so I would need to deal proportionately with views, concepts and methodological principles I agree with, and those I consider incorrect. I am not setting out to do that, I am simply setting out to describe my own paradigm. I mention others' works only if I wish to stress my agreement with them, or the fact of adopting something from theirs into my own thinking—or if I dispute their statements. In that sense the study is not balanced or impersonal, and cannot be so.[2]

Although these aims have motivated me, I hope the study will go beyond my message concerning the theory of science, and as a side-product assist the reader in understanding some major phenomena of our time. For example, Huntington spoke of democracy's "third wave."[3] Where has it gone? Is it moving on or has it retreated? Or what place does Viktor Orbán's Hungary hold in comparative systems theory? Is it a specific Hungarian model, a "Hungaricum," or does it have close or distant relatives?[4]

1. THE CAPITALIST VERSUS THE SOCIALIST SYSTEM

System

The word "system" in everyday language and in many sciences occurs in several different senses, from the universe to living organisms, man-made machinery to various human communities, existing, directly observable systems to notional, intellectual ones. In all cases this term conveys the meaning that several lesser parts form a coherent whole. These parts interact. They are not separate items thrown together, for there are comprehensible relations among them organizing them into a structure. The first part of the study uses the term "system" with two meanings. I compare the *socialist* and the *capitalist systems*. On occasions I add an attribute, calling them the two *great* systems,[5] but the attribute contains no value judgment: I am not bowing before the greatness of either.

A distinct, *specific system* may emerge in a country over a shorter or longer period, as far as a distinct combination of forms of political power, dominant ideology, ownership relations, and coordination of social activities are concerned. In this sense it has become customary to refer even colloquially to the Putin system or Orbán system. The use of the word *system* here has an important clarifying force: it points to the mutual effects of various elements in the public state of affairs, operation of the country, and structure of the machinery of power.

I use the capitalism *versus* socialism pair of concepts purely in a *descriptive, positive* sense. I am not referring to an imaginary socialism—not to conditions that socialists or communists think should pertain under a socialist system—but to *existing* socialism (to fall back on an old communist party jargon). Likewise, I am not examining an imaginary capitalism—not what uncritical devotees of capitalism think should be present—but *existing* capitalism, as it is.

I obviously did not invent the two terms. Historians of ideas report that both expressions antedate Marx, "capitalism" appearing in Louis Blanc and Pierre-Joseph Proudhon, and "socialism" in the works of Henri de Saint-Simon. However, they became widespread through Marx's main work *Capital*,[6] and not simply among Marxists, believers in socialism and antagonists of capitalism. They are used by several moderate or radical opponents of socialism as well, such as Ludwig von Mises and Joseph Schumpeter.[7]

These days they are heard constantly from politicians and the media, and have been taken up in everyday speech, as well.

However, it must be said that many people avoid this pair of concepts. With "capitalism" there are several reasons. Former reform communists were ashamed to find formations of capitalism appearing out of their efforts. German economic politicians after the Second World War, sensing anti-capitalist feelings among broad swathes of voters, thought it wise to give the long-standing system a new name: "social market economy."[8] Nor are conservative populists fond of calling their institutional creation capitalism, as they wish to be seen as anti-profit, anti-bank, anti-capitalists.

There are several considerations behind the avoidance of the term "socialist" as well. Marxists reserve the word "communist" for the Marxian vision, where people share goods according to their needs. Existing socialism was seen as a transitional state that would last only until communism appeared.[9] Meanwhile many Westerners, including politicians, scholars and journalists, referred consistently to the Soviet Union and other countries controlled by communist parties as "communist countries," and do so to this day. The same people would reserve the term "socialist" for the welfare states created by social democratic parties.

It is vital in the theory of science to distinguish sharply between the content of a concept and the name it bears. Many terms in the social sciences and the political sphere have a political slant—associations redolent of value judgments and *Weltanschauung*. In this respect, it is *impossible* to reach a consensus on terms. My experience, especially in the academic world, is that people cling more tightly to their vocabularies than to the views they express with the words included in those vocabularies. Their compulsive insistence is upon a vocabulary which have been hammered into their heads, or to use a more elegant term, which has become imprinted in their minds by the reading matter and lectures that have affected them most. If that is how it was put by Marx, Max Weber or Polányi (or whoever made the biggest impression on them), it cannot be put otherwise. Or it may happen that the favored term is one they invented themselves and wish to establish as their own terminological innovation.

I abandoned long ago my efforts to end the conceptual confusions. I acknowledged that an absence of conceptual consensus often leads to a dialogue of the deaf. This applies not only to the *capitalism* versus *socialism* pair of concepts, but to many other expressions, on which this study touches later (e. g., *democracy* versus *dictatorship*). I am attempting only to ensure that readers of my works will understand clearly what one expression or another means in my vocabulary.

Types and their characteristics

The capitalist system and the socialist system represent two *types* of sociopolitical formation in the recent past and in the present.

The creation of a typology is among the major steps in scientific examination. It has played a big part in developing many disciplines (e.g., biology, genetics, medicine, linguistics, cognitive sciences, anthropology or psychology).[10] A type is a *theoretical* construct. *Actual,* individual historical constructs such as Hitler's Germany or Churchill's UK differ from each other in important respects. Nonetheless, I describe, within my own conceptual apparatus, both of them as capitalist countries. Similarly different in their essential characteristics were Stalin's Soviet Union, Kádár's Hungary and Ceaușescu's Romania. Still, I call all three socialist countries. To distinguish the types within a typology calls for describing their *characteristics,* which may differ sharply.[11] Here the task is to find the characteristics which, on the one hand, *distinguish* the two types, the capitalist and socialist systems; and on the other hand, they show what is *common* to the many individual phenomena occurring in each country belonging to the same type in a given period.

Although a type is a theoretical construct existing only in researchers' minds, it is based on the observation of reality and underlines important common features of past and present structures. Given the specific realizations of the "great system" that vary between countries and periods, the type is created to embody their common characteristics in a theoretical generalization.[12] So the usable, operable typology is based on observation of the historical reality. Social science distils it from experience.

In the rest of this study I employ the pairs capitalist system/capitalism and socialist system/socialism as synonymous.[13]

In creating types, the method here is to pick out the various characteristics in which each type differs *markedly* from the others. The aim is not profuse description. On the contrary, it is to grasp the relatively few, highly characteristic, conspicuous features. The best would be to list as few as possible—simply those necessary and sufficient for differentiation.[14] I do not claim that the number of such characteristics should be exactly nine;

I would be open to altering *Table 2.1* if there were convincing arguments for doing so.

It is essential to list among the characteristics only those that are *system-specific*. The comparative table should by no means include phenomena which are found frequently in both great systems, important and influential though they may be to the operation of certain institutions or the lives of citizens. For example, repression cannot appear as a system characteristic because it does not appear exclusively under the socialist system. Ruthless examples have occurred and continue to occur under the capitalist system as well: in Hitler's Germany, in Hungary under the Horthy and the Nazi Arrow-Cross regime, Franco's Spain, and many Latin American military dictatorships. Under both systems it may happen that incompetent people gain leading positions. In both, the major economic indicators fluctuate strongly. However great the effects of these phenomena, they are not system-specific.

I do not want to give an impression of exactitude. In describing the characteristics, I have to allow myself to use umbrella terms such as "state ownership" and "private ownership," although I know that both categories can take many different legal forms.[15] There appear repeatedly in the table words like "dominant" and "largely," without mention of a quantitative value for them. If it is 70 per cent, then it is dominant but if it is 69 per cent, it is not? I content myself with not describing the system in terms of quantification but in a qualitative fashion, and relying on the intuition of those using the conceptual apparatus, in the hope that they will likewise sense the meaning of these inadequately precise words. My professional conscience is quieted by knowing that many scientific typologies do the same. Taking that into account, caution must be shown in using such typologies: there are some analytical tasks to which they are fitted and some to which they are not.

Another reason I tend to use expressions like "dominant" and "largely" is because I know that there can appear in a given type of country phenomena that differ from, or are even contrary to, the dominant phenomenon. For example, while the Soviet or Polish economy was tormented by the shortage economy there were still unsold goods in the stores and warehouses. In the western world with its typical surplus economy, there are long queues of consumers waiting for tickets to a new and exciting film.

Is there not a discrepancy of size in comparing capitalism, which has been around for centuries and will probably continue to exist for several

Table 2.1. Characteristics of the capitalist and socialist systems

No.	Capitalist system	Socialist system
Primary characteristics		
1.	The ruling political group ensures the dominance of private property and market coordination	The ruling political group, i.e., the Communist Party, enforces the dominance of public property and bureaucratic coordination
2.	Dominant form of property: private ownership	Dominant form of property: state ownership
3.	Dominant form of coordination mechanism: market coordination	Dominant form of coordination mechanism: bureaucratic coordination
Secondary characteristics		
4.	Surplus economy, i.e., the buyers' market, is the dominant state of the market for goods and services	Shortage economy, i.e., the sellers' market, is the dominant state of the market for goods and services
5.	Labor surplus is the dominant state of the labor market	Labor shortage is the dominant state of the labor market
6.	Fast technical progress; the system often generates revolutionary innovation	Slow technical progress; the system rarely generates revolutionary innovation
7.	High income inequality	Low income inequality
8.	Hard budget constraint for organizations in a quite broad sphere	Soft budget constraint for organizations in a quite broad sphere
9.	Direction of corruption: it is mostly the seller who bribes the buyer	Direction of corruption: it is mostly the buyer who bribes the seller

more, with socialism, which existed historically for only a few decades and then collapsed? Is my reason for bringing the latter up not that I was a citizen under the socialist system for much of my life? I firmly answer both questions in the negative. Now, 25 years after the collapse, I am convinced that such a comparison has great explanatory power. History, at a price of suffering for millions of people, set up a laboratory experiment by bringing into being a system markedly different from capitalism. Comparing them yields a better understanding of what capitalism is. Such randomly generated experiments also teach a lot in other branches of science. Examining the victim of an accident marked an important step in neurology. Part of the patient's brain was damaged and researchers knew precisely which part, and from that they could deduce what functions that part of the brain played.

What is to be understood by a *hierarchy* of characteristics? How do *primary* and *secondary* characteristics differ?[16] In my line of thought, primary characteristics determine the system as a whole, including secondary characteristics. The joint presence of the primary characteristics is a *necessary and sufficient condition* for the appearance of the secondary ones. It could also be said that primary characteristics form the *minimum conditions* for the existence of the capitalist or the socialist system. A sensible first stage when beginning to study a country is to concentrate on these primary characteristics. The results of doing so will then have predictive force. However, the primary characteristics do not generate all the secondary ones in a deterministic way. The effect is stochastic. There is a very good chance of finding the secondary characteristics in a country examined if the primary characteristics have already been identified.

Figure 2.1. Interactions between the primary and secondary characteristics

Primary Characteristics

1. Relation of the political sphere to property forms and coordination mechanisms
2. Dominant form of property
3. Dominant coordination mechanism

Secondary Characteristics

4. Power relations between the two sides of the market for goods and services
5. Power relations between the two sides of the labor market
6. Speed and qualitative features of technical progress
7. Income distribution
8. Softness/hardness of the budget constraint
9. Direction of corruption

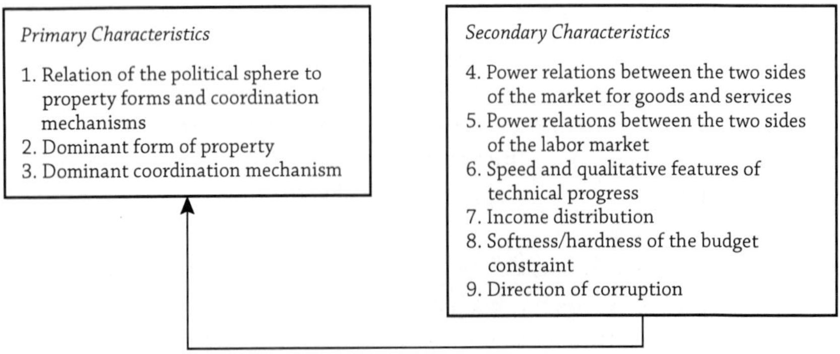

This relationship is shown in *Figure 2.1*. The figure shows mutual effects: the primary and secondary characteristics have mutual influences on each other. The thick arrow denotes that the primary characteristics are the *decisive* ones, and the thin arrow in the opposite direction that the reactive influence is less strong.

The expression "decisive," as I have noted already, shows a *tendency*, not full determination. Many people whose forebears have suffered from heart disease will inherit that susceptibility. But whether the disease actually emerges depends to a large extent on the patients' way of life—if they drink alcohol, smoke, fail to exercise, or find themselves in stressful situations, they are more likely to suffer acute heart disease than if they live moderate, cautious lives, do sports and live calmly. All socialist systems are inclined to develop a shortage economy, but the intensity of shortage was very strong in the 1980s in the Soviet Union, Poland and Romania, but less so in East Germany.[17]

Within the two blocs shown in *Figure 2.1* there are also interactions among the characteristics. To simplify the explanation, these are ignored in the figure and in this textual commentary on it.

Classifying the post-socialist region's countries by the typology of capitalist versus socialist systems

Let us apply the conceptual apparatus introduced above to the countries which qualified as socialist countries in 1987.[18] Altogether 47 countries belong here; let us call the area they occupied the *post-socialist region*.[19] The word "region" is not applied in a geographical sense, as this is not a group of adjacent countries; most are in Europe and Asia, but some in Africa and Latin America also belong here.[20]

The locations of the post-socialist region on the world map appear in *Figure 2.2*. The countries of the post-socialist region are marked with various non-white shades in the figure. The other parts of the world, marked in white, never went through a socialist-system phase of rule by a communist party.

Rule under the socialist system is marked in black.[21] The whole region would be black if the map showed the situation in 1987. Now the only spot of black on the world map is the territory of one country, North Korea—a tiny dot on the map of the world. Countries in transition from

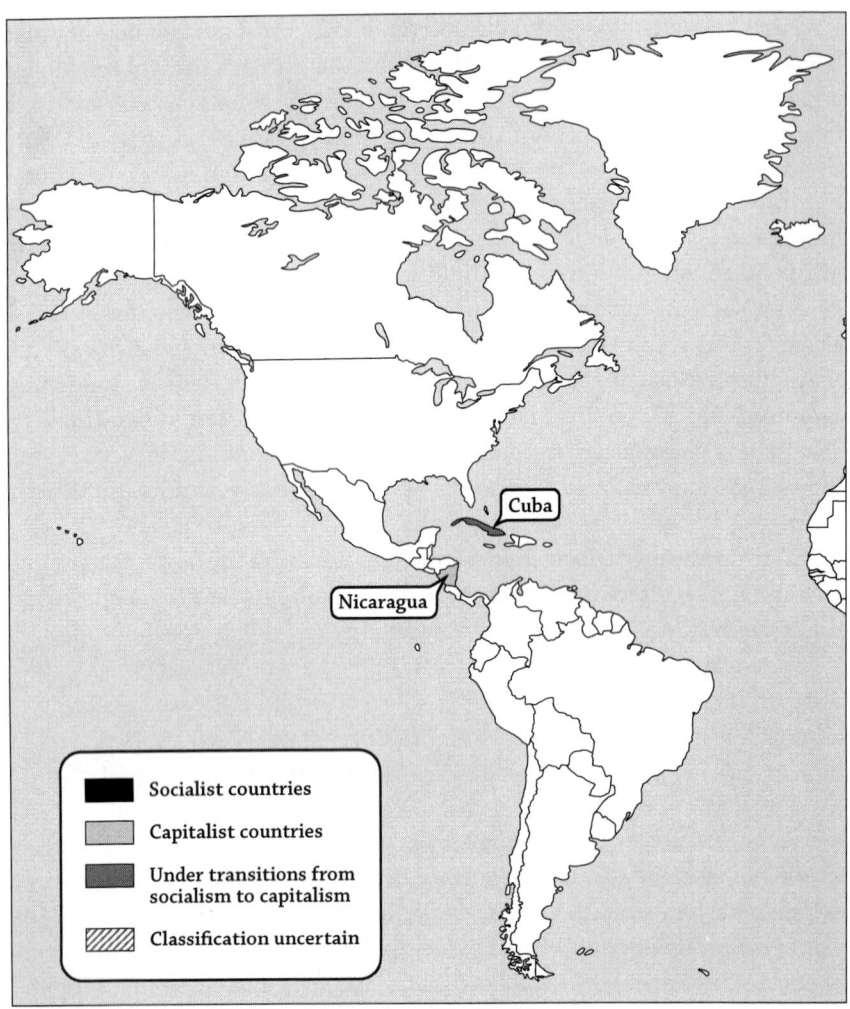

socialism to capitalism are marked in dark grey. Again, this applies to only one country, Cuba, making a single spot of dark grey at a global scale. Most of the region is colored light grey: these are the countries where the capitalist system operates.[22]

A sizeable part of the region has a diagonally striped pattern. This denotes uncertainty: I am uncertain whether these countries should be marked black, light grey or dark grey.

The sources for placing the countries in these categories are considered again in the comments on another world map (*Figure 2.3*). There I will

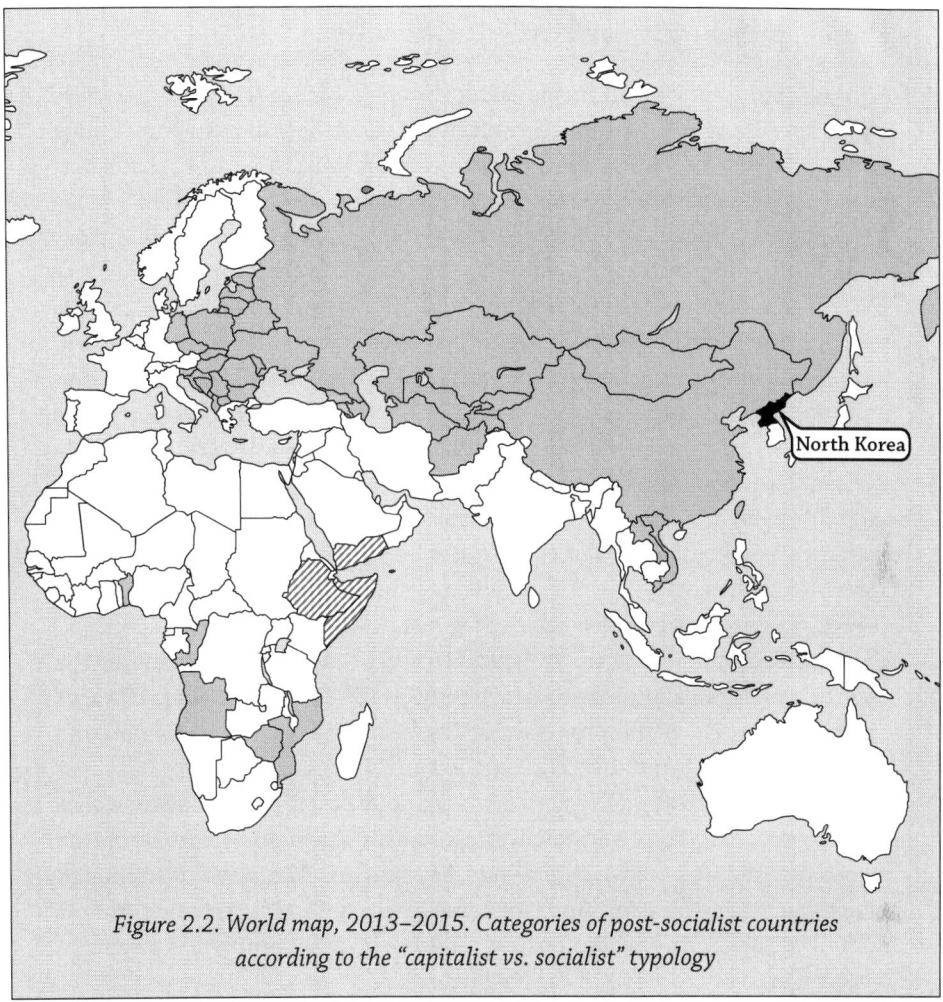

Figure 2.2. World map, 2013–2015. Categories of post-socialist countries according to the "capitalist vs. socialist" typology

shed light on the relation between the two world maps and the background materials accessible on my website.[23]

There is a broad if not full consensus among experts as to when the *change of system* occurred in the countries affected. This expression, often used in political jargon and everyday speech, gains considerable content in the conceptual and analytical framework already discussed. With a few exceptions, the countries in the group qualifying as socialist in 1987 all have undergone a transition from socialism to capitalism.

Static representation and the transformations

Figure 2.2 presents a still image, as if a snapshot were taken of the world and a specific group of countries within it. The shot shows a *static* state of the present, but if a motion picture camera were to be used instead, it would show the *dynamics* of the changes of system as well.

The map conveys the presence of the two systems at a point in history when both are operating according to the characteristics apparent in *Table 2.1*.[24] It does not depict the *creation phase* of the system. I draw attention to this primarily in connection with Characteristic 1. The initiatory role in the genesis of the socialist system is played by the political sphere; the communist party makes very rapid moves in historical terms to impose state ownership and centralized bureaucratic coordination on society. By comparison, the transitions in most countries from pre-capitalist forms to the capitalist system were very slow. Initially, the political authorities only tolerated and took advantage of the services and resources of the bourgeoisie. The relation of the political forces to capitalism changed gradually until they had become active defenders of private ownership, market coordination and enforcer of private contract. Different again was the role of the political sphere in the route back after 1989–1990 from socialism towards capitalism, in which the processes of transformation were instigated and headed by the pro-capitalist political forces.

Only one country in *Figure 2.2* is marked in dark grey, to show that it is in transition from socialism to capitalism. As mentioned before, the one country I put here when writing this study in 2016 was Cuba. Though a member of the Castro family remains at the pinnacle of power, this is no longer the Cuba of Fidel Castro. Cautiously, the country has begun to display the characteristics of capitalism.

To continue the earlier comparison, of using a motion picture camera instead of taking a still image, many more countries would appear as dark grey in the squares representing the 1990s and 2000s. The speed of change and the pace of the transformation of certain characteristics varied from country to country.

Historians and historical recollections like to focus on a particular calendar date for the beginning or end of a historical period. The October Revolution in 1917 Tsarist Russia is often understood to have been started by the blank shot from the Aurora cruiser signaling the attack on the Winter Palace in St. Petersburg. In fact, most period changes are more blurred in time.

Figure 2.2 shows the world-historical defeat of socialism through the lens of my conceptual apparatus. Three decades earlier, the socialist system prevailed over 34.7 per cent of the world's population and 30.7 per cent of its area.[25] Nowadays, when the socialist system persists only in North Korea, the proportions have shrunk to 0.3 per cent of the population and 0.1 per cent of the area.[26]

The explanatory power of a capitalist-versus-socialist typology

When examining a complex historico-social phenomenon, it is rare to find a convincing *single-factor explanation* to account for its appearance and/or long-term duration. Complex phenomena are complex indeed and call for a *multi-factor explanation*.

Both under capitalism and socialism appear several important complex phenomena, explained by several factors; *one* of them is the system. I emphasize the word *one* because not for a moment do I claim that a full explanation of a certain complex phenomenon can be gained by simply pinpointing the great system in which it appears. But there can often be found within a larger ensemble of explanatory factors some that are system-specific. Indeed, one or two may turn out to be the most important elements of explanation. Here are two examples.

One is the speed and quality attributes of technical progress, which is affected by several factors, e. g., the country's level of economic development, the state of its education system, and the size of its state support for research. Alongside these, the system-specific effects are notably important. It can be shown how large numbers of *revolutionary innovations* have appeared under capitalism, which deeply affect production and people's lives, whereas the socialist system could produce just one outside the arms industry.[27] Promising inventions that appeared in a socialist country could find no innovator able to spread it on a mass scale; this function would be usurped by a capitalist innovator instead. One well-known example is Ernő Rubik's invention, Rubik's Cube. In then-socialist Hungary, Rubik had no luck touting his creation round the industrial leaders. Rubik's Cube began its worldwide conquest when its manufacture and mass marketing were taken over by capitalist firms abroad. Even the distribution process for this first pioneering innovation was immeasurably swifter under capitalist conditions than under the socialist system.

The other example is the labor-market situation. Search processes take place under all systems: employees seek employers that meet their needs and vice versa. The search process is accompanied by ubiquitous frictions: everywhere there are temporarily unfilled jobs and ready workers unable to find jobs. This is a complex matter explainable by many concurrent factors. One example is the flexibility of knowledge generated by the education system. Does it facilitate quick adjustment to the rapidly changing demand for labor? Other factors include legal constraints on dismissing employees, the effectiveness of labor recruitment agencies, and so on. But some basic explanatory factors are system-specific. What are the general labor-market proportions of supply to demand? Does it tend towards excess supply (capitalism) or excess demand (socialism in its mature, relatively developed stage)? That determines to what extent employees are at the mercy of employers. An employee is under constant threat of dismissal and unemployment, they feel more defenseless than those who find jobs easily. Here we have arrived at deep-rooted system-specific effects, namely the relative power of employers and employees.[28]

The two examples enhance in a further way the argument for the explanatory power of the capitalism-versus-socialism typology. The nine system-specific factors listed in *Table 2.1* were compiled with a *positive* approach. They do not reflect the author's desires or choices of values. These are the characteristics of countries considered socialist or capitalist, an observable group from which the list of characteristics in *Table 2.1* can be "distilled." Those who acknowledge this as a positive description, and shift to the *normative* approach, can append to them their views on the capitalism-versus-socialism pair, based on their own system of values. For my part, I do not reach any summary moral conclusion. By my system of values, dynamism and rapid technical advance form a great virtue in capitalism, but I see the risks and drawbacks of such development. For one, I see the vulnerability of the workforce as a repugnant characteristic of capitalism. As for the socialist system, it did not just have repulsive characteristics. Many of them were attractive: upward social mobility for the poor, some reduction in social distances, and employee security stemming from the labor shortage. The typology described above offers methodological assistance to evaluating the great systems. Value judgments should be based upon considering the whole set of characteristics for the system in question.

It is not unlike the marking system in education. Let us assume that the individual marks reflect each student's attainments. Then it is up to the teachers, the parents, the classmates or the personnel department of a future workplace to decide what configuration of the marks to take as a basis for forming an opinion of each student: the simple average of the marks, or the mark in some successful subject taken by the evaluator to be the most important. I will return to this question later, but before discussing the value judgments about the great systems, let me present the typology I use for the alternative forms of politics and government.

2. VARIETIES OF THE TWO GREAT SYSTEMS, ALTERNATIVE FORMS OF POLITICS AND GOVERNMENT

The varieties of the great systems

Although the idea had a long theoretical history behind it, much attention was rightly paid in comparative systems theory to the work of Peter A. Hall and David Soskice on the varieties of capitalism.[29] This was a seminal idea which generated a school of thought; by now it is possible to talk of a broad and viable *research program* for examining the varieties of capitalism.[30]

Although this ground-breaking work discussed the varieties of the capitalist system only, it can be applied by analogy to those of the socialist system as well. The lively and complex debate that arose before the change of system, about socialism's alternative "economic mechanisms," the various models of socialism, and the many possible forms that reform might take, can certainly be called a discourse on the varieties of socialism, although the word "variety" was not used in this sense. Here I see much of my own work as part of a research program into "varieties of systems," though the works I can list did not use that term before the appearance of the works of Hall and Soskice, or for a long time after. Now, in this study, I too will apply this useful and operable expression.

There are several kinds of criteria on which to base the typology of varieties for each of the great systems. For instance, it is possible to produce a typology whose types represent the characteristic distribution of income and wealth. Another angle would be to measure how much the state intervenes in the operation of the economy and in what ways. Hall and Soskice brought these criteria to the fore in their study, which created and contrasted two main varieties: liberal market economies and coordinated market economies. The prime example of the first is the economy of the United States and of the second that of Germany.

William J. Baumol, Robert E. Litan, and Carl J. Schramm employed other criteria in defining types of varieties: whether private initiative and the spirit of enterprise are strong or weak. They therefore named their varieties entrepreneurial capitalism versus oligarchic or state-run capitalism.[31]

Dorothee Bohle and Béla Greskovits likewise came up with a new typology: capitalism is neo-liberal or embedded neo-liberal or neo-corporatist.[32]

Daron Acemoglu and James A. Robinson's book has had great influence.[33] The authors put the exciting question of what explains why some nations fail at a turning point and others succeed. They see as the major explanatory factor whether their social organisms are inclusive or exclusive. This is a typology with great explanatory power, although it does not preclude attention to other influential factors as well.

In the rest of this study I use another typology of varieties, not to replace those mentioned but to complement them. The main organizing criterion here is the *politico-governmental form*. This is not my invention. Both political scientists and political philosophers—beginning with ancient Greek philosophers, continuing with Machiavelli and concluding with present-day researchers—attach huge importance to analyzing the alternative forms of political power. This has been seminal throughout in political science and political philosophy. Sadly, the other social sciences, including economics (with estimable exceptions), have largely broken off from political science. My first study entitled "The System Paradigm," appearing in 2000, merely touched on the relations of politics and the economy. The almost two decades since have taught me much, among other things, what a huge effect political structures and political ideas have, and how vital it is to examine in detail the course of history for an understanding of the transformations of society. It is necessary when analyzing the "great" change of system not only to dissect it, but to know *how* the great change, the shift from socialism to capitalism, occurred, and what kind of formation it brought into being. Understanding that shift would have been sufficient motivation to write this second study on the system paradigm.

Democracy, autocracy and dictatorship

Political science has given rise to a great many typologies of politico-governmental forms. In this discipline too there appears the phenomenon mentioned earlier whereby authors cling tightly to their own conceptual systems or to those of some school of scholars to which they subscribe. The subject being politics, concept creation and interpretation are permeated by the differences of political opinion. In this respect this study is not meant to impose its system of concepts on anyone. I would like above all to clarify my own words. Having done so, I cannot go on here and there without arguing in their favor, pointing out the advantages of the phraseology I chose.[34]

The typology of varieties that I employ distinguishes three types: democracy, autocracy and dictatorship. The characteristics of these types appear in *Table 2.2*.

The structure and logic of *Table 2.2* follow *Table 2.1* in distinguishing two great blocs: the primary and the secondary characteristics. Repetition is tiring, but let me stress again: the ensemble of primary characteristics contains the minimum conditions for distinguishing the three forms. It does not attempt a detail-rich description. On the contrary, it shows here solely the characteristics which jointly are sufficient and necessary for one or the other form to exist.

Characteristics 1 and 2 were expressed first by Schumpeter in *Capitalism, Socialism and Democracy*, and then utilized and developed further by Dahl and Huntington.[35] This approach singles out the *procedural* side of the processes of politics and exercising power as the main characteristic of democracy. Democracy has no need for the annihilation of a tyrant, for a military coup or a bloody uprising. There exists a bloodless, peaceful, civilized procedure for ousting the government: competition among several parties, then elections according to legally endorsed procedures. The loser in a democracy concedes defeat and congratulates the winner.

The simultaneous presence of Characteristics 1 and 2 in *Table 2.2* is necessary and sufficient to demarcate democracy and autocracy at one end of the political spectrum. Characteristics 3 and 4 are not needed for that purpose as there is no difference between the two in this respect. However, all four primary characteristics must be weighed to distinguish autocracy and dictatorship at the other end of the political spectrum. Here Characteristic 3 comes to the fore: an autocracy has a legal opposition, albeit a weak one; an autocracy allows for a multi-party system, while a dictatorship rests on a one-party system.[36] Here Characteristic 4 becomes decisive: terror and bloodshed reign under dictatorship, claiming millions of lives. By comparison, power is exercised almost without bloodshed under the orderly conditions of an autocracy.[37]

Table 2.2. Characteristics of democracy, autocracy, and dictatorship

No.	Democracy	Autocracy	Dictatorship
Primary characteristics			
1.	The government can be removed through a peaceful and civilized procedure	The government cannot be removed through a peaceful and civilized procedure	The government cannot be removed through a peaceful and civilized procedure
2.	Institutions which jointly guarantee the conditions of removing the government are strong	Institutions which could jointly guarantee the conditions of removing the government are either formal or weak	Institutions which could jointly guarantee the conditions of removing the government do not exist
3.	Legal parliamentary opposition exists; multiple parties run for elections	Legal parliamentary opposition exists; multiple parties run for elections	No legal parliamentary opposition; only one party runs for elections
4.	No terror (large-scale detention in forced-labor camps and executions)	No terror (large-scale detention in forced-labor camps and executions), but various means of coercion are occasionally used against political adversaries (imprisonment with false allegation, or even politically motivated murder)	Terror (large-scale detention in forced-labor camps and executions)
Secondary characteristics			
5.	No repressive means are used against parliamentary opposition	Repressive means are used against parliamentary opposition	No parliamentary opposition
6.	Institutions of "checks and balances" are active and independent	Institutions functioning as "checks and balances" are weak and non-independent	No institutions have been created to act as "checks and balances"
7.	Relatively few officials are appointed by the ruling political group	The ruling political group appoints its own cadres to virtually all important offices	The ruling political group appoints its own cadres to all important offices
8.	No legal constraints against civil protest; strong civil society	No legal constraints against civil protest; weak civil society	Civil protest against the government is prohibited by law
9.	Interested persons and their organizations take part in many forms and to relevant degrees in preparations for decision-making (significant levels of participation)	There are legal frameworks for participation but they are practically not applied	Participation is not even formally prescribed
10.	Freedom of the press is guaranteed by law, and is actually enforced	Freedom of the press is constrained by legal and economic means	No freedom of the press

Absent from the primary characteristics is the question of how far a form expresses the wishes of the populace. This is excluded from the criteria on two grounds. One is the strong difference between the *positive* and the *normative* approaches. The enquiry here is not into what the desirable characteristics of a democracy might be. Nor is it claimed that regimes lacking such characteristics do not merit the label democracy. It is simply what characteristics distinguish the existing alternative politico-governmental forms. To remain within the positive realm of analysis, are the democracies the ones that invariably express the will of the people? Sadly, it is not rare for an autocratic tyrant or a dictator to enjoy sincere support from a large majority. Think of the masses of Germans, disillusioned by Weimar republic and sincerely supporting Hitler.

Two criteria applied when compiling the list of four primary characteristics and six secondary ones (as in *Table 2.1*). Each characteristic should appear in each case belonging to the type. In other words, it should be a characteristic *common* to all specific historical instances of some politico-governmental form. The other criterion is that a characteristic should distinguish one alternative type strongly from at least another. It may be that there are one or two more characteristics which satisfy both criteria. It may be that some characteristic should be described differently. I am open to all proposals that point in this direction. What I cannot abandon is the well-articulated connection between the primary and secondary concept pairs. Within this interaction the effect of the primary characteristics is stronger than the force in the opposite direction—the primary characteristics are the ones that set the course of each country in a decisive way.

Autocracy, in this paradigm, is no blurred "middle way" between democracy and dictatorship, but a sharply identifiable *type* in the sense Max Weber termed an "ideal type."[38] It is a theoretical construct that in my approach is distinct from two other types: democracy and dictatorship.

When I began to apply this typology in earlier writings, several people questioned why I was isolating exactly three types. I replied that the number three has no special attraction for me. I gladly accept other typologies involving two or four types. I am concerned solely with discerning markedly different formations.

I appreciate that many social scientists can work more easily with a concept "system" that sees current politico-governmental forms as a "mixture"—each regime displaying elements of democracy and dictatorship in different proportions. I do not want to dissuade them. I see this is more convenient for their ideas, but mine call for the use of strongly outlined types.

This study deals only with politico-governmental forms prevalent in the post-socialist region, but if it extended to the whole world, it would be clear that autocracy as a type can be used profitably to analyze other regions as well.

There are vital aspects, with huge effects on the destinies of nations and individuals, which I have not accounted for in the politico-governmental forms of the triple typology. Here is one example: the concept of nationalism and policy governed thereby. Democracy gives no protection here either: think of the horrific First World War. Before it broke out, most politicians on both sides had fuelled the insurgent tensions, including the leading statesmen of French and British democracies, and then the outbreak sent a wave of nationalistic fervor over most people in both democracies. Nor were socialist countries immunized from nationalistic politics by the internationalist idea that workers of all lands should unite. Note, for example, the inter-socialist Sino-Vietnamese war of 1979. I believe in democracy but do not find it ideal. To quote Churchill's classic remark, "It has been said that democracy is the worst form of government except for all those other forms that have been tried from time to time."[39] I see it as an especially important virtue that while it lasts, the government can be removed in a civilized way.

The hardness and softness of autocracy and dictatorship

The common characteristic of autocracy and dictatorship is control from above. The hierarchical pyramid has one person at its peak—a leader, autocrat or dictator whom no one orders around. Moving down from the peak, those at each level behave in two ways: obedient upwards and domineering downwards. Only at the bottom do people obey orders, but have no one to domineer.

There is a strong *centralizing tendency* that applies in both autocracy and dictatorship. Both systems are liable to subject to the central will as many activities and spheres as possible.

There are many means of asserting the central will: reward and punishment, primarily the actual award of recompense and the actual imposition of penalties, but promises and threats have their place too. People's actions are strongly influenced by the hope that unconditional loyalty will win favor and the fear that disloyalty will lead to reprisals.

Softness or *hardness* of political power refers overall to the nature of the means of coercion applied from above. Let us look at Characteristic 4 in *Table 2.2*. One of the factors distinguishing autocracy and dictatorship is that the former does not use bloodthirsty terror or other brutal means of oppression. My generation experienced both in the Stalinist period, when citizens feared any noise in the night: was there a black car coming to take them for torture or forced labor or to the scaffold? Here is a simple litmus test: if our lives are dominated by such fears, we are living in a dictatorship, but if they do not face fears of that kind from the regime, the politico-governmental form is "merely" autocracy.

It is also worth looking at *degrees of softness and hardness* at various phases of a certain politico-governmental form. The succession in history may be of several kinds. Communist dictatorship under Stalin was especially hard, but the period of Brezhnev and Andropov was more of a soft dictatorship: all the characteristics of dictatorship were present, but with less use of bloodshed or brutality in repression.

Many people in Hungary feel that life was easier in the final phase of the Kádár regime than it is now, under the third Fidesz government, which started in 2014. Certainly, for people avoiding politics, soft, decaying dictatorship is more pleasant and easier to bear than hard autocracy. It is more important, however, for the comparative theory of systems to point out the boundary between autocracy and dictatorship.

Autocracies are inclined to turn into dictatorships. If my study were not limited to snapshots, if it could depict the dynamics of history as a motion picture, it could show that autocracy can turn into dictatorship rapidly or slowly. However, the purpose of this study is not to write history, but to create types through a Weberian approach. Within these bounds it is worth making a pronounced distinction between autocracy and dictatorship.

The relation between the two typologies

This study has applied two kinds of typology. The relation between them appears in *Table 2.3*.[40]

Table 2.3 illustrates two vital statements. Democracy does not make society immune from autocracy or even dictatorship, into which it may be turned by a combination of unfortunate circumstances, as several historical examples show. To mention only the most tragic, Weimar democracy proved defenseless against the forces of Nazi dictatorship. There are more recent examples too. Russia's short-lived democracy gave way after a few years to the autocracy of Putin.

Table 2.3. Relation between the two kinds of typology

Forms of government	Great systems	
	Capitalist	Socialist
Democracy	feasible	unfeasible
Autocracy	feasible	feasible
Dictatorship	feasible	feasible

As said earlier, capitalism can operate without democracy, but the statement cannot be reversed. Democracy cannot operate without capitalism—"democratic socialism" is impossible.[41]

Of course this pronouncement depends on the interpretation put on words: the "impossibility" applies if the expressions capitalism and socialism are interpreted as described in *Table 2.1*, and that of democracy as in *Table 2.2*.

It is not right to say that establishing the capitalist system suffices or in time produces democracy of itself. Capitalism is a *necessary but not sufficient* condition for democracy. Of course, the statement about the impossibility of democratic socialism depends on what is meant by "in time." Does it mean years, decades, even centuries? China in my view can be seen now as having a capitalist system, while its politico-governmental form remains a dictatorship. It has a one-party system with no legal opposition. The transition from socialism to capitalism began decades ago, but there is no sign that the country is any nearer to democracy.

The theory of a *totalitarian system* is associated with the work and name of Hannah Arendt.[42] Her underlying idea can only be partly fitted into my system of concepts. The last line of *Table 2.3* can be attuned to her use of words. Hitler's Germany and Stalin's Russia are dictatorships of the cruelest, hardest kind. To that extent it is right to use the same term for them. Both were totalitarian in that the holders of power did not shrink from any means of exerting it. Both were also totalitarian in seeking to invade all dimensions of life, including the private sphere, people's most personal affairs: child-bearing, family life, personal sexual preferences, and matters of religious faith. Yet there were essential differences between them. In this analytical context I do not see as the most important differences the question of which of the two ideologies was ethically more acceptable or from the outset more disgraceful. Nor do I measure the difference in the number of millions of victims they had. The essential difference is that one operated under a capitalist system and the other under a socialist one. This is important not only for comparative systems theory, but for the huge difference it made in people's lives.

Classification of post-socialist countries by the typology of politico-governmental forms

Let us now apply the conceptual apparatus outlined above to the countries which counted as socialist in 1987, i.e., to the post-socialist region. *Figure 2.3* presents another world map.

Democracies appear in light grey, autocracies in dark grey, dictatorships in black, while countries of uncertain classification have a diagonally striped pattern.[43]

Before commenting on the content of the map, let me mention the sources from which the two world maps *(Figures 2.2 and 2.3)* were drawn.

Use was made of the classifications in several well-known international reports.[44] We placed far-reaching, but not uncritical reliance on these classifications, so that ours differ from those in one international report or another. The other source is the vast literature analyzing single countries or groups of countries. It was only possible to consult a fraction of these.[45]

This world map, like *Figure 2.2*, gives a *static* snapshot of the present, not a dynamic, film-like account showing when or how some country moved from one politico-governmental form to another. The transition in some was quite rapid and in others slow and gradual. Nor was the direction immutable; sometimes it doubled back. It would clearly be instructive to show the pace of change, but that would far exceed the scope of this study, calling for a sizeable handbook, or lengthier still, a book on each country or smaller or larger groups of countries. I regret not having the strength for that, but hope others will undertake such huge tasks.

I would like to say a separate word on some countries. Russia, as mentioned, developed procedurally in the few years after the collapse of the Soviet Union a real multi-party system and operated as a liberal parliamentary democracy. But at one point it turned back and became an autocracy that does not shrink from tough repression.[46] Of the Soviet successor coun-

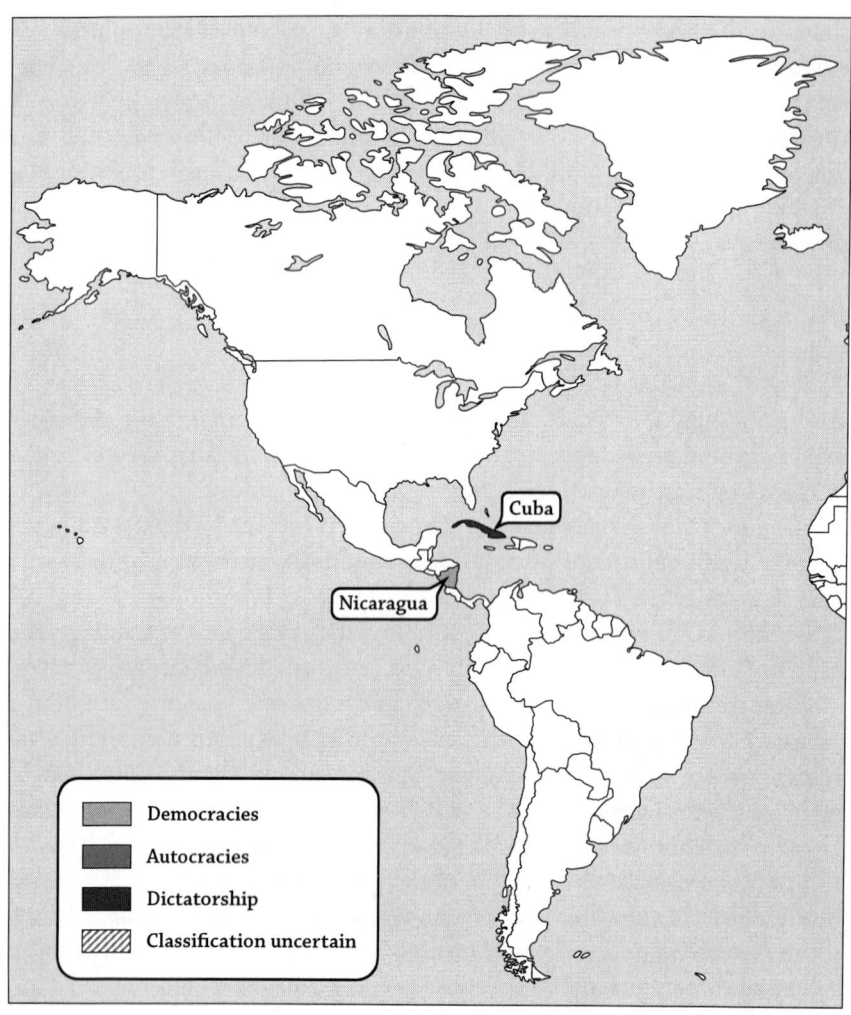

tries, the three Baltic states, Georgia, Moldova and Ukraine can be classified as democracies. The other Soviet successor states can be seen as autocracies, with two exceptions. Turkmenistan counts as a dictatorship, while Kyrgyzstan's classification is uncertain. The country is in the process of shifting from autocracy to dictatorship, or might have even passed the threshold and became an outright dictatorship.

There is broad and thorough debate taking place on China's politico-governmental form and economy, with contributions from the West and from outside the People's Republic (Mainland China), including some from

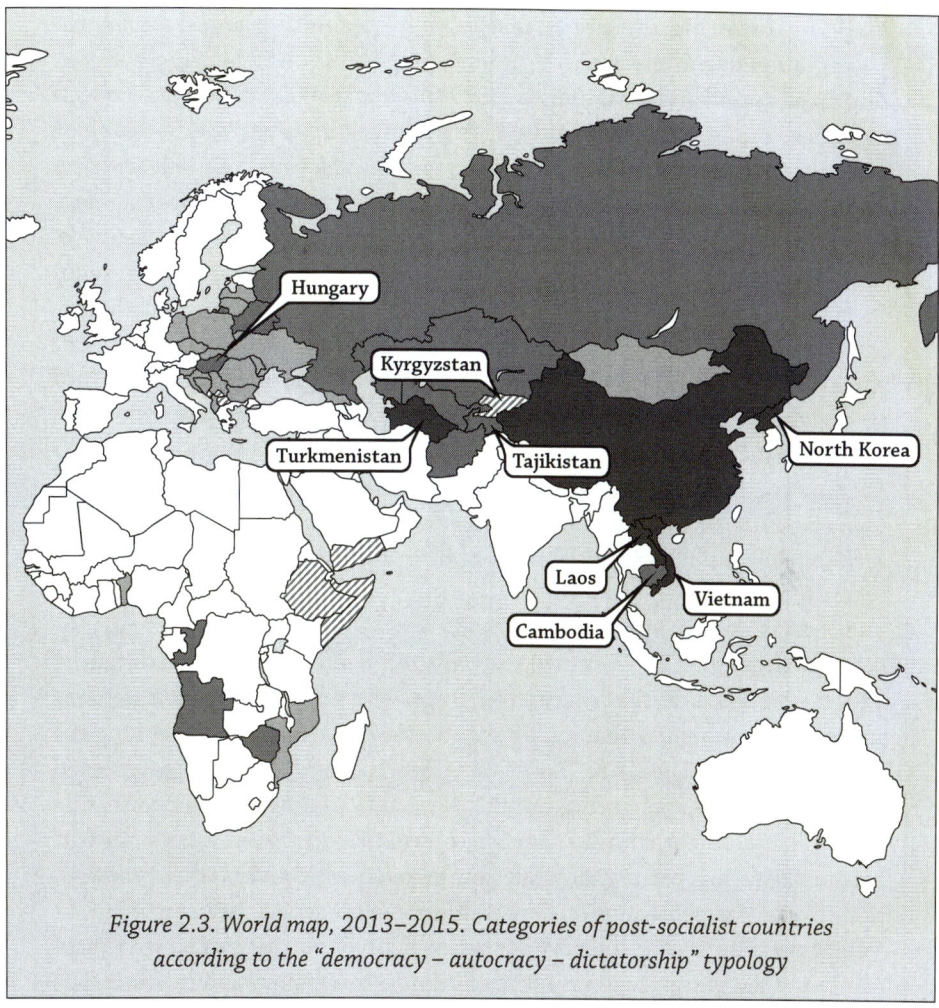

Figure 2.3. World map, 2013–2015. Categories of post-socialist countries according to the "democracy – autocracy – dictatorship" typology

Taiwan and from Hong Kong, which is not fully incorporated into the People's Republic. Sporadically and within the limits of censorship and self-censorship come voices of those still living within the People's Republic.[47]

According to some, China has for a long time possessed the main characteristics of the capitalist system, although the size of the state-owned sector remains very great. In politico-governmental form it is clearly a dictatorship in all respects. For a while the dictatorship softened somewhat, but in recent years it has hardened again. The leading political force still styles itself the communist party, but it abandoned long ago the Leninist program of forcing the dominance of state ownership and bureaucratic coordination on society. Another view is that China long ago began a transition from socialism to capitalism and from dictatorship to democracy, but did so very slowly and cautiously. It will take a long time, but there will be a capitalist system in the end. This interpretation does not exclude the possibility of a slow transition towards less repressive politico-governmental forms. Indeed, the most optimistic expect the transition to end in democracy. Finally, a third view taken is that China is a unique formation, semi-socialist and semi-capitalist. All this is led by a new kind of politico-governmental form, whose characteristics differ from the standard ones of autocracy or dictatorship—China as the main manifestation of the "third road." For my part I accept the first view and China has been marked on the two world maps accordingly.[48]

The two maps reflect the same view of Vietnam and Laos. However, the scarce amount of information available for Cambodia suggests that having suffered an especially ruthless form of dictatorship, it has since become an autocracy.[49]

In *Figure 2.2*, showing the "socialism *versus* capitalism" typology, Cuba was classified as a country in transition from socialism to capitalism, although it was still taking the first steps. The one-party system remains and no opposition can operate legally, so that it has been placed among the dictatorships in *Figure 2.3*. The dictatorship is still there, though softened and somewhat less repressive, but the possibility cannot be excluded that its politico-governmental form will move towards autocracy or even democracy. Yet there is a big chance that while private ownership and market coordination spread, the politico-governmental form will remain a dictatorship.

Some countries of the post-socialist region has been marked with diagonally striped pattern, to signify the author's uncertainty about which type to place it in. This may have several reasons:

(a) The country has undergone or is undergoing armed conflict. The politico-governmental form may be varying between democracy, autocracy, and even dictatorship. These cases can be found on my website in Background material 5.[50]

(b) Islam is the most prevalent religion in many of the countries. In some it leaves no mark on the operation of the economy or politico-governmental form, but in others a specific theocratic form of politics and government emerges. This could be seen as a sub-type of autocracy. Information again appears in Background Material 5. I do not feel conversant enough with the Islamic world, so these countries remain problematic and I have marked them with the diagonally striped pattern.

(c) Finally, there are some post-socialist countries that do not belong to either (a) or (b) (cannot be characterized with armed conflicts or the increased political power of Islam), but insufficient information precludes me from placing them in my own typology, and I have marked them with the diagonally striped pattern for that reason.

In defense of the term autocracy

Between the extreme types of democracy and dictatorship there is a middle type which cannot be termed as either. There is a large measure of consensus about this among political scientists and exponents of comparative system theory. However, there is no such consensus on the criteria for separating democracy and the intermediate type. Similarly, it is hard to gauge whether a country is a case of the intermediate type or a dictatorship. All I can do in this study is what I did in my earlier works: present readers with my own criteria for distinguishing the three types. These criteria are summed up in *Table 2.2*. Whether readers agree or not, let it at least be clear how the author has defined the three forms.

The choice of types ties in closely with their names. Many of the terms used in the political sphere have a political ring to them, which means we have left the realm of positive, value-free description for that of normative analysis that engenders value judgments. I do not want to shut my eyes to this phenomenon.

My use of autocracy for the middle type arises partly from my system of values and political convictions. I am a democrat devoid of illusions. Despite its shortcomings and dangers I rate this political form best. It would be a big mistake for believers in democracy to let the word be used for forms of government whose fundamental characteristics are not democratic, and I am wholly against doing so. The problem cannot be avoided by qualifying what to me stands for something so valuable. I dismiss for normative reasons such combinations as "illiberal democracy" or "leader democracy" and judge the use of them as harmful.[51] I distinguish the characteristics of democracy and autocracy as types in *Table 2.2* in such a way as to exclude any kind of "illiberal" or "leader democracy" from the former category.

Many people no longer recall the official nomenclature of communist ideology. That too used a qualifier. The dictatorship under the socialist system was known as "people's democracy." This was advanced as true democracy, as opposed to "bourgeois democracy," which was dismissed as mere verbal democracy, for it served the bourgeoisie, not the people. My conceptual apparatus defines the characteristics of democracy in a way that requires no grammatical attributes.

The declining "third wave" of democratization

I was strongly influenced by the work of Samuel P. Huntington, especially *The Third Wave*.[52] Were he to read this study he would probably fault me for putting mere static snapshots on the two world maps. History in his view could only be conveyed dynamically. If only I had the strength to create a book to include, along with other things, a dynamic description of the transformation processes in each post-socialist country. This study cannot attempt that. As shown earlier, I am imparting static snapshots, which I see as important, useful and workable despite their limitations. They provide handgrips for the analysis by distinguishing each type *sharply:* the capitalist system from the socialist, the democratic politico-governmental form from autocracy, and autocracy from dictatorship. In my view, it is the absence of such sharp distinctions that leads to strongly debatable or even erroneous placement of the post-socialist countries in Huntington's figure.[53]

Table 2.4. Distribution of alternative forms of politics and government in the post-socialist region

| | Percentage of ||
	Region's population	Region's area
Democracy	10.3	11.3
Autocracy	14.8	56.7
Dictatorship	68.4	26.1

Note: Data, rounded off to one decimal place, were drawn from Background Material 4, available on my website, and were calculated on the basis of Background Materials 1 and 3, published on the same site. The totals of the two columns are less than 100 by 6.5 and 5.9 percent, respectively. This difference comes from the fact that some countries listed in Background Material 3 were not assigned to any of the three groups—their classification was considered uncertain.

According to the typology of this study, there was communist dictatorship in East-Central Europe and the Baltic before the events in 1989–92, although the repression had eased somewhat in some countries. The winds were blowing towards democracy, but according to my strict criteria, the minimum conditions for democracy were not met. Huntington, however, lists Hungary, Poland, East Germany and the three Baltic states as countries where the first wave of democratization took place,[54] while he places Bulgaria and Mongolia among those involved in the third wave of democratization.

An often quoted metaphor is the glass half-full or half-empty. Huntington rejoiced (as did millions, I among them) that wave after wave of countries joined those with democracy. We are glad that there is a little more water in the glass after some decades. But looking at *Figure 2.3*, the world map of the distribution of politico-governmental forms, it is a bitter sight to see the countries with glasses half or three quarters empty. The Soviet Union collapsed, Mao Zedong's reign of terror ended, yet only a tenth of the inhabitants and area of the post-socialist region live in countries that can be classified as democracies. The proportions appear in a little more detail in *Table 2.4*.[55]

There are no serious signs that democratization is continuing—Huntington's third wave has ceased. In fact, Hungary has undergone what Huntington calls a "reverse wave": a democracy that worked better or worse for a decade or two has relapsed into autocracy.[56] There have been plenty of signs of this. Since the general elections in 2016, Poland has started along the Hungarian road by destroying important institutions serving as checks and balances and moving away from democracy and the rule of law. And who knows how many other countries will be subjected to the reverse wave.[57]

Empirical support for the maps

The main purpose of this study is to review my own conceptual apparatus, and in that connection, outline two typologies, and present the criteria that distinguish various types. There are no "proving" concepts or typologies. They are *no statements* whose truth can be confirmed or refused empirically. The conceptual apparatus and typology of a work belong among the tools of the researcher. They are expected to be *workable* and assist in understanding the truth. I consider that the apparatus outlined here fulfils that purpose, and I hope to convince as many readers as possible of the same.

On the other hand, the qualifications made on the basis of my own system of concepts and typology (the two maps, *Figures 2.2* and *2.3* in this text, Background Material 2 and the table shown in Background Material 3 on my website) are *propositions,* susceptible to refusal. Any of the presentations of countries on the map may reflect the truth rightly or wrongly (given the criteria for placing them). The assertions made by the grey and black tones may be true or false, confirmable or dismissible and replaceable by a different assertion.

Several international organizations are engaged in preparing comparative reports to show how countries fare in building up the institutions for their capitalist market economies, in ensuring civil rights, or to what extent their forms of government can be considered as democracies, dictatorships, or other formations. Each report follows a distinct methodology with differing typologies and classifications. Unfortunately, I am not aware of any study designed to compare such reports with each other or look critically at their methodologies. My assistants and I have mainly used the materials of two organizations: Bertelsmann and Freedom House.[58] While I rate highly the huge, conscientious research effort in them and appreciate that the reports are available free of charge to politicians, media people and academics, I do not agree with their methodologies, conceptual frameworks and criteria in many respects.[59] Let me mention a few of these.[60]

My study categorizes in a different way to produce a typology of politico-governmental forms. As mentioned, a *central* place is held by Schumpeter's procedural approach: reflecting on whether the government can be voted out of office in well-defined, civilized, multi-party elections. This embraces the stability of the system of checks and balances and effective intervention, the degree of independence of civil society and lower-level organizations from central government, the relative strength of centralizing and decentralizing tendencies, and so on.

What I miss most from the reports mentioned is one of the main ideas in this study: they do not sufficiently perceive whether the interaction between constituent anti-market or anti-democratic phenomena produces *a coherent system*. To use an old-fashioned Hegelian expression, the reports in the study of several countries did not perceive the critical point where many small quantitative changes turn into a qualitative change. It is as if a student were having a given performance rated by several different teachers. In many cases I rate more strictly than a Bertelsmann or Freedom House report.[61]

Let me recall here *Table 2.2*, which compares the characteristics of the three politico-governmental forms, notably Characteristic 7: Which positions does the ruling political group occupy for its own people? To what extent does a degree of civil-service autonomy cease? What proportion do "political appointees" represent of all the functionaries? On paper an institution is seemingly independent, but in fact it is wholly controlled by people subordinate to the central will. This phenomenon is ill-considered or underestimated by the organizations making international comparisons, vital though it is to the transformation of democracy into autocracy, or even dictatorship. They are impressed by the rules expressed in formal, public words, while unaware of the background selection processes whereby the top leader and his subservient underlings place their own people in all important positions.

Here I have merely compared the rigor or indulgence in handing out grades, without considering the empirical grounding of the judgments. Both Bertelsmann and Freedom House reports make strong, careful assessments with armies of specialists, huge piles of documents and vast data banks behind them. There are no such armies behind my two world maps, just research by a few assistants and my own analyses. It is with due modesty and caution that I put forward these compilations, knowing that the rating of each country is debatable. To return to the earlier metaphor: I feel I am not authorized to dispense grades against which there is no appeal.

3. HUNGARY'S PLACE ACCORDING TO THE TWO TYPOLOGIES

Applying the general methodological frame to the experience gained in Hungary

This part of the study does not aim to supplement the picture drawn about the nature and power structure of the political force ruling Hungary since 2010. There are many shelves full of such studies already.[62] Each day brings new twists, critical reports of which can be found in the press. Nor will I attempt here to make all my earlier writings "up-to-date" with the present study.

Hungary is the post-socialist country I know best. I would like to apply the analytic apparatus offered in this study—primarily the conceptual framework and the two typologies—to the specific Hungarian experience. Can Hungary be fitted into the two typologies, or is it a single, unique case? This application tests the viability of the analytical apparatus, the conceptual framework, and the typologies. It also presents an opportunity to go beyond the specific Hungarian case and add some further thoughts of more general validity.

Hungary's capitalism

Let us turn back to *Table 2.1*. All three primary and all six secondary characteristics of capitalism apply in Hungary. It is not on any "third road." It cannot be classed as a non-capitalist, non-socialist system.

Capitalism is a very strong system, capable of significant achievements even under inimical conditions. Its strength has been apparent in Hungary, above all in acceleration of technical progress. Achievements of the high-technology period spread at a rapid pace, and the country itself contributed more than one revolutionary innovation. Despite many mistakes and omissions in economic policy, the economy has climbed out of its trough. GDP is rising, although the growth rate is modest: it is not as fast as the acceleration usually manifesting during rapid growth after a crisis. This is true capitalism, although the beneficial aspects of it have been weaker and the repugnant ones stronger than those experienced in many more favorable variants.

The ruling politico-governmental system exerts a strong influence on the Hungarian economy, but I do not find it apposite to call it "state capitalism."[63] That term is surrounded by utter confusion. Many use it to assert that the state has adopted functions of capitalist private ownership, or that the state itself has turned capitalist. That is certainly not the case. However strong the desire of those in power may be to increase their wealth, it is wrong to see this as a single motivating force. The machinery of the state is not being operated according to the rules of the capitalist market economy.

All kinds of capitalism display *entwining* of the political sphere (the state apparatus run by ruling parties, legislators and the government leadership) with the business sphere. This entwining is unusually strong in Hungary, and occurs along many strands and by many means. All kinds of capitalism bring *corruption*. This is unusually common in Hungary, involves huge sums of money, and appears in many different forms. This entwining and corruption appear at first glance as a proliferating jungle, but further examination of it reveals a few characteristic features:

1. The state sector is spreading again, if only to a modest extent.[64] The form it takes is usually not confiscation of privately owned firms, banks or other organizations, though that too occurs. The methods are more refined. The state often buys up hitherto privately owned firms, banks or other organizations at depressed prices, having first used state powers to impede their operation and turn them into lossmakers. It then places its own loyal people at the head of such a state-owned firm or financial organization. This gains it strong positions in business life.

2. Often a business unit on the verge of collapse is bought by the state at a negligible price, then boosted from public funds, rendered viable again, and reprivatized. The selling price will not be high and the gains will be made by new owners close to Fidesz, the ruling party.

3. A very high proportion of state expenditure goes on financing the current operation of the governmental machinery, and on investments financed wholly or partly out of public funds. To the latter can be added as a source the large contributions for structural transformation of the country received from the European Union (EU), whose allocation rests with the Hungarian government. All these state expenditures are spent in a biased way. Where loopholes in the law allow, the procedures for public procurement are circumvented. Where there is no way of avoiding them, they are bent to ensure that firms close to the governing party make the winning bids. This allows giant firms or empires of companies to expand at great speed, and it can be that some of the extra profits find their way back into the pockets of those who eased the path to winning the competitive bidding. Normally the police and the state prosecution show no inclination to seek evidence of such apparent corruption.[65] Decision-makers are often led by political bias and personal advantage in matters of public procurement, careers in state service, pay of leaders, bail-outs of endangered firms and other organizations, and softening of budget constraints. The beneficiaries become loyal supporters of the ruling group; a patron-client relation develops between holders of political power and those to whom they give preference. There spreads the repugnant phenomenon known in the literature as *clientelism* and *crony capitalism*.

4. To the cases just described can be added all-too-common ones where beneficiaries have family or kinship ties with decision-makers. Such immoral occurrences have long been known as *nepotism*.

5. The arsenal includes not only reward, but dissuasive punishment. If the head of a capitalist group aims too high or moves too close to the

pyramid of power, there is retaliation: procurement bids and business takeovers will fail, administrative penalties will be imposed, and regulations will appear that restrict activity.

6. The expression *state capture* has joined the vocabulary of political studies and is not rare in Hungary either: legislation and other regulations are tailored to the needs of specific capitalist groups. The opposite effect is at least as common: the state captures the business realm. State leaders appoint and dismiss the oligarchs. Such intervention by politicians and bureaucrats extends from the top of the business hierarchy down to the middle management levels. They decide who gets rich quick, sometimes with lightning speed, and whose wealth diminishes.

This particular Hungarian variant of collaboration of the ruling political group and the business realm, with dominance of the former and widespread corruption, has led to the term *mafia state,* coined by Bálint Magyar and now widespread in political parlance.[66] There is certainly a strong similarity between what happens in Hungary and in the mafias of Italy, the United States, Russia and many other places. Luckily for us, there are essential differences. The "godfather" or small group ruling a mafia punish insubordination not with dismissal or employment in a less powerful but still comfortable position, but with execution. A death threat ensures unconditional obedience. It is a stronger disciplinary method than demotion and/or deprival of fat earnings.[67]

Most of Characteristics 1 to 6, elucidated above, are not fuelled merely by motives of power or money. There can be discerned in them also a *nationalist tendency*. Where possible, preference goes to businesses in Hungarian, rather than foreign or multinational ownership.[68] This is one normative principle when judging public procurement bids. The nationalist government may also resort to other weapons, such as manipulating the foreign exchange rate. A falling Hungarian forint will make imports more costly and thereby improve the sales chances of more expensive Hungarian producers, at the expense of consumers.

Leading government politicians are often heard to make anti-capitalist remarks. This should not mislead people. The system under which Hungarians live is a capitalist one.

Hungary's autocracy

Let us turn back to *Table 2.2*. All four primary and all six secondary characteristics of autocracy are met in Hungary. I am aware that the state of affairs in Hungary is still a matter of debate among critical domestic and foreign analysts: Can Hungary be called a democracy even though many chances have ensued that are alien to democracy? As I noted earlier, there is no consensus among specialists, politicians or politically minded citizens on how to interpret the concept of democracy, and so I am not expecting this study to convince anybody that it is wrong to qualify Hungary as such. I trust only that for those who have followed the study so far it is plain and clear that Hungary is an autocracy according to the typology presented here.

Let me stress the minimum conditions for autocracy: a government that *cannot* be voted out by the customary democratic processes; a system of institutions (introduction of electoral regulations advantageous to the incumbent political force, reduction of the funds required for the opposition to function effectively; drastic curtailment of the influence of the opposition press and media, etc.) that almost guarantees Fidesz electoral victory.[69] The ruling party fills leading positions at all levels with its trusty people. It has installed its own "checks and balances" even for the unlikely event that the opposition wins the elections, assuring that the reliable people appointed by the present ruling group will remain in key posts and impede the normal operation of a new government.

It came as no surprise to those who looked at likely events without wishful thinking.[70] True democrats can accept it if they lose an election. Viktor Orbán could not accept his defeat in 2002 and 2006 and resolved it should never happen to him again. In his famous speech at Kötcse in 2009 he announced in advance that Hungary needed a right-wing regime that could stay in place for at least 15–20 years.[71] I count myself among those who took Orbán's determination seriously. The first signs of him building an autocracy were clear a few months after he took power.

Unfortunately, the first signs of danger had little effect. Years went by before the full danger to democracy became clear to Hungarian and foreign observers. The reactions of the EU and other international bodies were slow and feeble. Democracy is a fragile and vulnerable politico-governmental system, since its very liberalism makes it grant freedom of expression and assembly also to enemies of democracy. The EU, built on democratic principles, had, and it seems still has, no effective means of halting anti-democratic actions.

Autocracy, as I said earlier, may be softer or harder. In Hungary, the signs of hardening are appearing, but I still would not class the present situation as dictatorship. It suffices to look at *Table 2.2*. Among the primary characteristics of a dictatorship is a one-party system with a total absence of legal opposition. Likewise a primary characteristic is terror: mass arrests, grim forced labor camps, mass political murders, death sentences imposed under arbitrary rules devised by the dictatorship, or exceeding even its own laws, investigators who torture their victims or shoot them dead.

Memories of dictatorship are still strong in the older generations, and they can distinguish between autocracy and dictatorship at a glance. A false distinction may arise not only from wishful thinking, but from fear (perhaps not unfounded) of a bad future that has penetrated our thinking. Autocracy, as the middle politico-governmental form in the typology, must be distinguished from democracy on the one hand and dictatorship on the other.[72]

Nor is the *leadership cult* a specific characteristic among the three types in my typology. The admiration for Viktor Orbán that has arisen, in part spontaneously and in part artificially, is not an exceptional phenomenon, not one apparent only in Hungary. It appears in almost all autocracies and dictatorships, either in an extreme form almost of worship of the leader, or more soberly. More rarely, charismatic figures may appear in democracies as well: the aura around Churchill, or later De Gaulle or Roosevelt, in the critical periods of the Second World War. I avoid the widespread term "authoritarian" regime or "authoritarianism" for blurring the distinctions, because in a democracy, an autocracy or a dictatorship alike there can appear a person at the peak of power who has high prestige and authority, whether to serve good purposes successfully or evil ones cruelly, whether the admiration is voluntary or thrust upon the people, and whether the person on the peak is worthy or unworthy of respect.

The foreign policy of the Hungarian government

Mention has already been made of *strong nationalist tendencies* in the autocracy of Hungary, but only in domestic affairs, for the benefit of Hungarian producers and entrepreneurs, at the expense of foreign-owned or multinational companies in Hungary. To this has been attached a well-known "national" economic policy: making imports harder, for instance through monetary policy that pushes up their prices. Let us now extend the examination to foreign policy.

Memories of the catastrophes and bloodshed of the two world wars, careful study of how the conflicts arose, and the conclusions drawn prompted Western European statesmen to found the association of countries which evolved into today's European Union. Let there be no more war among the great countries of Europe, not least because such war had burgeoned into world war twice in the last century. Also behind this was a community of economic and political interests, but the prime purpose was to ensure peace in Europe: peaceful coordination of their countries' interests and a common approach in support of European ideas, rather than threats and armed conflicts. From the outset there were internal antagonisms to contend with: integration to the degree found in the United States was out of the question in a region of European countries deeply affected by centuries of national traditions. Within every member state there is rivalry between political forces ready to concede more sovereignty and those not prepared to do so and wanting to move back to the fullest degree of sovereignty.

Although these two forces exist in all EU countries, it is specific to Hungary to find such methodical efforts to weaken EU powers, ignore its regulations, exploit legal loopholes, and make anti-Brussels rhetoric integral to official government policy. This approach has been taken by Prime Minister Orbán in a small member state dependent on imports and foreign investment and on the EU funds available for free. He is becoming known increasingly abroad as a leading light in nationalism and rebellion against European cohesion.

Of assistance to the ruling Hungarian political force in this was the wave of refugees from war-torn countries that reached Hungary in 2015: people by the hundred thousand, mainly Muslim adults, seeking the security and higher living standards of developed European countries. Many of them lack the ability or will to assimilate. There begins to appear a case of what Huntington described in a 1992 lecture as a clash of civilizations.[73] The wave of refugees found the leaders of the most developed countries unprepared. They responded with human empathy, as humanism dictates and all true democrats can only agree with that. But they did so without a plan for containing an unending stream, or organizing and financing the coexistence with the people streaming in. The words and acts of the European political leaders were hasty and inconsistent. The confusion, impatience or even xenophobia arising in several countries was enhanced by bloody acts of terrorism, and by the terror and threats of ISIS. Orbán from the outset refused decisively and clearly to grant any migrants refuge. He expressed crude outrage against the volunteers who displayed humanitarian sympathy towards them. His rough words stirred an outrage among people who expressed humane empathy for the suffering, but enthralled members of the Hungarian public who were already inclined to xenophobia. Hungary became the first country in Europe to erect a razor-wire fence along its southern borders. This act was initially condemned, but later imitated by foreign politicians.

I will not detail the further problems arising from the migration wave and acts of terrorism, or conflicts between national sovereignty and European cohesion. I simply want to indicate these factors and place them in the thematic field of this study. Nationalism and xenophobia are not specifically Hungarian, but the methods chosen by the ruling party and government for addressing these ambiguous problems are constituting a Hungaricum.[74] There is a danger that Hungarian policy will make waves beyond the country's borders and attract adherents. Hungary, sadly, has a tradition of policy swings. The group in power likes to call its rule democracy and claim Hungary a place in the culture of European Christianity. Meanwhile there are heard repeated speeches that belittle Western democracy and talk of the decline of the West, while lauding many Eastern versions of despotism, citing the tyrannical regimes of Russia, Kazakhstan and Azerbaijan, the hard-liner government of Singapore, the semi-feudal Islamic autocracies of the Arab sheikdoms, and the ever-hardening dictatorship in China. Clearly there are also economic intentions behind this: the Eastern orientation is expected to yield investment, loans and big orders. But there are other motives too: affinity felt between its own autocracy and the methods of Afro-Asian despotism. This double game is also unique to Hungary: it is not a common characteristic of all autocracies.

A Hungarian hybrid?

Some decades ago I gave a lecture taking issue with those who sought an "optimal" system, a combination of the best rules of the game. Let me quote what I said: "Those aiming for this somehow imagine themselves in a big supermarket. There on the shelves can be seen the various mechanism constituents, embodiments of various beneficial system characteristics. . . .

Those designing a system have nothing to do but gather up 'optimal elements' into a shopping cart and go home to fit up an 'optimal system'. Except that this is a naive dream. History does not maintain any such supermarket from which we can choose at will. . . . The only choice for those deciding what system to adopt is between various pre-packaged 'tie-ins'."[75]

So when Viktor Orbán and his political partners built up their power, were they refuting, through their deeds, my assertion of 36 years before? Has it rendered the metaphor of history's supermarket offering system elements erroneous?

Many people see the actual Hungarian system of today as a particular mix of the socialist and capitalist systems, containing elements of both, as a half-socialist, half-capitalist hybrid. It is also thought widely that Hungary's politico-governmental form is a particular mix of democracy and dictatorship, it is a hybrid, obtained by the cross-fertilizing of a democracy-plant and a dictatorship-plant.

My study rejects this system-theoretical innovation. The Hungary we inhabit is no hybrid. It is a special kind of capitalism, and a specific kind of autocracy. The conceptual frame and analytical apparatus of my study lead directly to this conclusion.

I must not omit to say that the supermarket metaphor only defines the sharp contours of the social formations. Beside other experiences, the changes in Hungary also point to a need to refine my earlier theory.

There appear in the capitalism of present-day Hungary and other countries *islands* that resemble socialism. Foremost is the health-care sector, where the state dominates the supply side in many countries, while on the demand side free or almost free provision is offered. This generates a secondary socialist characteristic: a shortage economy. Symptoms can be seen: actual queuing in out-patient clinics or virtual queuing on arbitrarily long waiting lists. Concomitant is a grey or black economy of gratuities to medics that ease frictions in by lubricating the machinery of the official supply. Yet such socialism is literally an island in a capitalist sea.

The transition to capitalism is largely over in Hungary and the other post-socialist countries, but much of the *legacy* of socialism remains, above all in people's mentality. Far from disliking the paternalism of the state, many dispute their responsibility to see to themselves and expect the country's leader to guide and look after them. That is one reason why Hungary underwent such a smooth turn away from the rule of law, the enforcement of contracts, and broad local self-governance. Centralization has strengthened. However, the ruling political power has no intention of returning to the starting point, to the position before the change of system by restoring socialism. After carrying out the turn, they halted on the road which leads away from democracy, rule of law, decentralization, and respect for private ownership. The regime has every reason to maintain the autocratic capitalism in its particular Hungarian form. As mentioned before, the intention is far from ending the dominance of private ownership. What the regime really wants is reinforcing the links between the ruling political force, leading bureaucrats and the business realm, and thus strengthening the position of political power holders therein. The aim is not to abolish the market, simply to intervene in populist manner (such as arbitrarily reducing certain utility charges below the market price), and/or to interfere crudely in the fine machinery of market coordination for selfish financial gain. Since the primary characteristics of capitalism have survived, the Hungarian system of institutions is not semi-socialist and semi-capitalist. Capitalism persists, but in a specifically Hungarian form where its repugnant characteristics are particularly strong.

The present politico-governmental form in Hungary was not brought into being by a leading politician pushing a shopping cart round and filling it with elements of democracy and dictatorship, in order to aptly assemble their "optimal" combination. It was more a question of selecting various specific elements of the system sitting on the shelves like different loaves in the supermarket bakery department or different cold cuts in the delicatessen department. Those who devised the present Hungarian system of institutions chose alternative elements throughout the system of institutions. For instance, when dividing up the branches of the state, choosing and assigning powers to the so-called independent institutions (central bank, audit office, budgetary council, etc.), and setting out how judges were to be appointed. The main selection criterion was how to make their power stronger and less easy to remove. From the UK's democracy they adopted perhaps the worst characteristic, i.e., a disproportionate distribution of mandates after general elections. The British "winner takes all" principle in single-round elections makes it almost impossible for a coalition of several opposition parties to emerge. From the US democracy, they took over the idea that supreme court members could stay in their posts for a very long time if they wished. So a constitutional court judge chosen and appointed by Fidesz would remain in his/her position and maintain loyalty to the political group which appointed him even if the opposition should win the next parliamentary elections.

Government propaganda has it that the country took politically a specifically Hungarian "third road." In truth, when the government took over, its starting point was democracy; one with many faults—more corruption and incompetence than Western democracies matured over long periods—but still a democracy. This impeded the main aim of the new power holders: to stay in power through several parliamentary terms while maintaining outward signs of democracy. They took another course: building autocracy fast and decisively. They were not taking a well-worn path, as various countries at various times arrived at autocracy in various ways. There was much improvisation and many unawaited developments, but they reached full autocracy quite soon.

The Peron type of autocracy in Argentina started out from the trade-union movement, and it gained wide support by introducing regulations that benefited the workers and lower classes. By contrast, the moves of the present Hungarian variant serve to benefit the well-to-do strata of society to the detriment of the poor, the dispossessed, the handicapped, the ill and the old.

To sum up, in terms of primary and secondary characteristics (see *Tables 2.1* and *2.2*), my answer to the question raised in the title of this section—Is there a Hungarian hybrid?—is a decisive no. To use the reference frame of the system paradigm presented in the study, the specific Hungarian characteristics are "merely" tertiary, although by that I am not trying to belittle the notably harmful effects of the specific Hungarian form, which cause much suffering to a high proportion of the population.

The Orbán system

The socio-historical formation that has emerged in Hungary is indeed unique to the same extent only as all other socio-historical constructs. Present-day Albania, Mongolia and Vietnam are also "unique" in this sense. This statement is compatible logically with the fact that each concrete system is a historical realization of a certain type according to the criteria defined by some typology. The same type has other historical realizations as well.

The present form of Hungarian society is a specific instance of a broader category: autocratic capitalism. Viewing this through the eyeglasses of comparative system-theory, it can be seen that Hungary's system has characteristics in common with other autocratic capitalist formations, but also attributes that distinguish it from all other countries belonging to the same type.

It is right to speak of an Orbán *system*. As noted in the introduction to the study, the word "system" applies to a wide variety of formations. The characteristics of Orbán's Hungary amount to a system because they affect and reinforce each other. Each serves a common purpose: to boost, solidify and render irremovable the power of its leadership and its head, Viktor Orbán.

Many aspects of the system are stamped with Orbán's personality. I am not one to belittle the effect personality traits in leading politicians have on the course of history. Their individual traits is one of the powerful factors explaining for the differences between the autocracies of Horthy, the head of the Hungarian state in the period 1920–1944, and Orbán: the two differ in social background, family and educational upbringing, military experience, system of value, culture and psyche.

In Orbán's case there has emerged a stratum of tens of thousands whom he has placed in high posts and enriched. They defend the *status quo* vigorously out of self-interest, not just because they are loyal to their leader but to retain their power and wealth.

Once the Orbán system took shape, it began to develop its own operating mechanisms and evolutionary and selective attributes. Institutions appear or give way to others that better serve the main purpose of strengthening power. People rise to fame and power, only to fall again (usually into still cozy, well paid, but less powerful posts). More new faces appear, yet more enthusiastic and anxious to serve the leader. There is no need for central commands in lesser matters: faithful subordinates can even read their superiors' thoughts. Of course, the smooth operation of this machinery requires that all the others, the subordinates of the few thousand people grasping power in their hands, i.e. the millions of ordinary citizens accept the current situation unresistingly and silently. Their silent passivity is also a unique Hungaricum, embedded in centuries of Hungarian history. The dynamics of resignation and patience, or protest and rebellion, present researchers with politically relevant and intellectually stimulating problems, to which this study cannot extend.

Although it is quite clear to me that social formations constantly change, this study compares the types mainly through static pictures. It would be good to take things further to show the typologies of *change*, the types through which great social transformations occur: slow or fast, by revolutions or reforms, through shocks or in small steps, bloodily or bloodlessly. For instance, there could be compiled a typology for the rise and fall of great worldwide empires, from ancient times to the present day, including those of Germany, the Soviet Union or Britain.

That brings us to the difference between the approaches in two groups of disciplines: history and the modern social sciences (economics, sociology, political science). The main body of historians see historical processes as unique successions of differing situations. Only a few scholars attempt to create philosophies or theories of history. Those of Marx, Spengler and Toynbee differ strongly, but they share an aim of pinpointing *regularities* within the complex processes of history. Among social scientists this approach is not exceptional, but general, I could even say, mandatory. While business schools are busy with case studies, and economic historians may chart the course of a specific bank or manufacturer, most members of university departments of economics build models and introduce their students to apply them. There is no sense in discussing which discipline has the more important standard approach. Both are needed, both must remain. I hope this study will reach a few historians, especially those of them who study the contemporary period. Perhaps their ideas can also be enriched by a paradigm that recognizes alternative systems, characteristic formations and types, where they see only details of a unique and never-recurrent process.

CLOSING REMARKS

This study makes recommendations to researchers analyzing and comparing various social systems, as to how they can approach such subjects. Although inspired by experience of the post-socialist region, I am sure its underlying ideas can be applied to analyzing countries elsewhere.

I have advanced an updated version of the system paradigm described in my earlier work, as *one* of the possible approaches. I have discussed closely two typologies (capitalism versus socialism and democracy–autocracy–dictatorship) as *two* of the possible alternative typologies. My emphases convey that the paradigm and two typologies I put forward are not exclusive. In doing so I am not seeking peace or avoiding controversies, simply expressing my conviction that no single, universally applicable methodology can suffice to analyze society. No single paradigm, no single system of concepts and no single typology can claim a monopoly on solving every problem.

Let us imagine a formation of several materials with a complex structure, in a three-dimensional space. Such things are exhibited by sculptors or "visual artists."

The creation is a lively spectacle if seen from afar. That is how we sense the creation as a whole. The sight of it constantly changes as it is approached. (For example, we can perceive the outlines of the politico-governmental forms if only three types are distinguished, as this study has done. The picture becomes more subtle if sub-types are added to each category, or still finer distinctions are made by breaking it down into sub-sub-types.) For understanding it, there is no perfect distance between the observer and the observed artifact. All perspectives have their useful role to play.

Imagine that several spotlights have been fixed to the walls and the ceiling, each giving off light of a different color. The spectator sees the artifact differently depending on which spotlight is on and which color shines. And if the museum allows us to take various sections of the artifact, crosswise and lengthways, in all directions, again there will be various patterns to see. No view, no section offers the "true" shape. All views are "true," if the spotlight's shine is strong; all sections are "true" if studied by expert eyes.

This study had the modest aim of proposing one or two spotlights and one or two possible sections for analysts. I am open to understanding and applying other approaches and typologies as well.

Notes

[1] János Kornai, "The System Paradigm," in *Paradigms of Social Change: Modernization, Development, Transformation, Evolution*, ed. Waltraud Schekle, et al. (Frankfurt and New York: Campus Verlag – St. Martin's, 2000).

[2] With most subjects it is thought immodest for authors to quote their own works repeatedly and thus to crowd the bibliography, but many such references are inevitable if the subject is an author's own work. This study is aimed primarily at those who have read my works, whom I am trying to assist in the "maintenance" of their ideas evoked by those works.

[3] Samuel P. Huntington, *The Third Wave: Democratization in the Late Twentieth Century* (Norman and London: University of Oklahoma Press, 1991).

4 The term "Hungaricum" was used originally to mark goods which are produced in Hungary and became worldwide known as "Tokaji aszú," a desert wine called "The King of Wines" already in the Middle Ages, or "barackpálinka," a brandy made from apricot.

5 What I call a *great system* is related, but not identical, to the Marxist "mode of production" or the neo-Marxist concept of "social formation." I stand aloof from the simplified, primitive theory that political economy lecturers of the socialist period would drum into seminar students, citing in a deterministic, ostensibly "progressive" order of primitive communism, slave-owning society, feudalism, capitalism, and finally, victorious socialism or its full-fledged version, communism.

6 Karl Marx, *Capital: A Critique of Political Economy*, 3 vols. (London: Penguin Books, 1990–1992). Individual volumes originally published in 1867, 1885, and 1894, respectively.

7 Ludwig von Mises, *Socialism: An Economic and Sociological Analysis* (Indianapolis: Liberty, 1981); Joseph. A. Schumpeter, *Capitalism, Socialism and Democracy* (London and New York: Routledge, 2010).

8 Nowadays, when the use of the term "varieties of capitalism" is widespread, we could say: they wanted to create a variety of capitalism with strong welfare-state characteristics. This intention was inherent in the term "social market economy," dissociating the capitalism of Northern and Western Europe from its Anglo-American counterpart.

9 While the socialist system existed, no country in the bloc ever termed itself communist. That is why I entitled my work *The Socialist System*, not the "Communist," which many would have recognized more easily. It can be disputed whether the decision was apt, but it left no room for misunderstanding, as I wrote down clearly what I meant by "socialist system" in János Kornai, *The Socialist System: The Political Economy of Communism* (Princeton: Princeton University Press, 1992).

10 Of special interest are the typologies of modern psychology and the cognitive sciences. Studying these could be very useful to comparative system theory in the social sciences.

11 There are several synonyms for the word "characteristic" in this context: trait, feature or attribute, for example.

12 In my phraseology, I employ the unqualified word "type." It has the same meaning as what Max Weber calls an "ideal type." Yet I avoid Weber's term, since I find that the attribute "ideal" has a distractingly normative ring. However, Weber too used the expression "ideal type" to denote an abstract theoretical mapping of existing systems. See Max Weber, *Economy and Society* (Berkeley: University of California Press, 2007).

13 The second term in each pair (capitalism and socialism, respectively) denotes, for many authors, a system of ideas rather than a formation that exists or has existed. It should be clear from the context that I am discussing the latter: "capitalism" denotes the capitalist system as it exists or has existed, "socialism" likewise.

14 *Table 2.1* contains many expressions I have taken over from my earlier works, where I discussed their meanings in detail. They include coordination mecha-

nism, market and bureaucratic coordination, shortage economy, surplus economy, labor shortage, labor surplus, revolutionary innovation, soft and hard budget constraints. For space reasons I cannot go into these again here.

15 The category of state ownership includes both central- and local-government ownership. This needs mentioning as the Hungarian vernacular often inaccurately confines state ownership to central-government ownership. If a school, say, or a hospital passes from local-government into central-government hands, this is labelled "nationalization," while it means only that the execution/implementation of the state's ownership rights has been centralized, important though that change may be as well.

16 *Basic* and *fundamental* are commonly used synonyms for "primary" in this context.

17 János Kornai, *Economics of Shortage* (Amsterdam: North-Holland, 1980); Kornai, *Dynamism, Rivalry, and the Surplus Economy: Two Essays on the Nature of Capitalism* (Oxford: Oxford University Press, 2014).

18 Kornai, *The Socialist System*.

19 Like many authors, I apply the epithet "post-socialist" to the countries that were under the control of the communist party in 1989–90. Here again there appears a conceptual mix-up: many politicians and political analysts apply the labels "post-socialist" or "post-communist," usually with a pejorative ring, to parties that emerged from the former ruling communist party after the change of system, taking over many officials of the previous party and most of its assets. This they do regardless of what changes have occurred in the leadership or membership or in its ideology.

20 A list of the post-socialist countries appears on my website (http://www.kornai-janos.hu/Kornai2016-SP-revisited.html), as *Tables 1* and *2* in Background Material 1.

21 Background Material 2, appearing on my website shows the two world maps, *Figure 2.2* and *2.3*, not in black-and-white but in various colors. The colors might help in recognizing the distribution of various types in the region.

22 Empirical support for the classifications would be much clearer if there were reliable statistics on the developments in ownership relations and the spread of the market mechanism. Unfortunately, the data available are only partial and sporadic. All countries prepare statistics on production and added value, broken down by industries, geographical regions, occupations, or output produced, but nowhere do national statistical offices calculate or publish regularly any breakdown of output data by form of ownership, or the proportion of total production sold at administratively set prices. It is surprising to find that only non-state institutions in a handful of countries concern themselves with ownership relations and the radical transformation of coordination mechanisms, although these were among the basic requirements for the change of system. Prestigious international organizations regularly publish comparative figures on production, foreign trade, or financial affairs, but—in my view—they pay insufficient attention to the transformation of ownership relations and the relative weights of bureaucratic and market coordination.

23 See Background Material 2 and 3 on my website.

24 Cuba is an exception. It has been qualified here as a country at a transitional stage.
25 Kornai, *The Socialist System*.
26 See Background Material 4 on my website.
27 Kornai, *Dynamism, Rivalry, and the Surplus Economy*, 3–24.
28 Kornai, *Economics of Shortage*; Kornai, *Dynamism, Rivalry, and the Surplus Economy*.
29 For their first comprehensive volume of studies, see Peter A. Hall and David Soskice, eds., *Varieties of Capitalism: The Institutional Foundations of Comparative Advantage* (Oxford: Oxford University Press, 2001).
30 The expression "research program" was introduced into the theory of science by Imre Lakatos, and it is used here in the sense applied by Lakatos. See Imre Lakatos, *The Methodology of Scientific Research Programmes*, vol. 1 Philosophical Papers (Cambridge: Cambridge University Press, 1978).
31 William J. Baumol, Robert E. Litan, and Carl J. Schramm, *Good Capitalism, Bad Capitalism, and the Economics of Growth and Prosperity* (New Haven and London: Yale University Press, 2007).
32 Dorothee Bohle and Béla Greskovits, *Capitalist Diversity on Europe's Periphery* (Ithaca and London: Cornell University Press, 2012).
33 Daron Acemoglu and James A. Robinson, *Why Nations Fail: The Origins of Power, Prosperity, and Poverty*, 1st ed. (New York: Crown Publishers, 2012).
34 As I stated earlier, I am not expecting others to adopt my conceptual apparatus. But at this point Don Quixote begins to tilt at the windmill of conceptual clarification, in the vain hope that others will be convinced of the advantages of the concepts and expressions I recommend.
35 Schumpeter, *Capitalism, Socialism and Democracy*; Robert A. Dahl, *Dilemmas of Pluralist Democracy: Autonomy versus Control* (New Haven: Yale University Press, 1983); Huntington, *The Third Wave*. Quoting these authors, I took this approach in my study of the change in politico-governmental forms that occurred in 1989–90, at a time when few people in Hungary saw the possibility of voting out the government as an important criterion of democracy. János Kornai, "The Great Transformation of Central and Eastern Europe: Success and Disappointment," *Economics of Transition* 14, no. 2 (2006).
36 Here I ignore a few parties surviving from the former multi-party systems in socialist Poland, East Germany and China. They retained their party nature only in a formal sense, while supporting the power of the communist party and operating under its control.
37 Putin has imprisoned several political opponents, but he has not used torture to extract confessions. Arresting and sentencing to many years of imprisonment was done "legally," based on the laws and legal forms of the regime. There is a ghastly suspicion that those in power may have ordered the murders of some opposition politicians and journalists, but unfeeling though it may sound, the figures must be considered when making comparisons. The number of murders committed in secret by the Russian autocracy may have been in the tens or hundreds, but the number who lost their lives in Stalin's terror was measured in millions, and those condemned to merciless forced labor in tens of millions.

38 See the earlier footnote 12.
39 Quoted from Churchill's speech of November 11, 1947, in Richard Langworth, ed. *Churchill by Himself: The Definitive Collection of Quotations* (London and New York: PublicAffairs, 2013).
40 The relation between the market and democracy is analyzed by Péter Gedeon. His conceptual apparatus differs from mine in several respects and there is no space here for comparing the two, but his conclusions and those of this study overlap in many ways. See Péter Gedeon, "Piac és demokrácia: Barátok vagy ellenségek?," *Politikatudományi Szemle* 23, no. 1 (2014).
41 This idea appeared in writings about socialism several decades ago. I was influenced especially by Charles E. Lindblom, *Politics and Markets: The World's Political Economic Systems* (New York: Basic Books, 1977). His use of concepts differs from the one in this study, but the ultimate conclusion is the same: the democratic form of political power cannot operate under a socialist system.
42 Hannah Arendt, *The Origins of Totalitarianism* (New York: Schocken Books, 2004). Originally published in 1951.
43 Background Material 3 on my website shows in table form the classifications applied on the two world maps, *Figure 2.2* and *2.3* in the main text, furthermore, Background Material 2 on my website. It could be said that the two maps convey in color what the table conveys in words.
44 Bertelsmann Stiftung, *Transformation Index Methodology* (2016), http://www.bti-project.org/en/index/methodology/; *Codebook for Country Assessments* (2016), https://www.bti-project.org/fileadmin/files/BTI/Downloads/Zusaetzliche_Downloads/Codebook_BTI_2016.pdf; *Bertelsmann Transformation Index Country Reports* (2016), http://www.bti-project.org/fileadmin/files/BTI/Downloads/Zusaetzliche_Downloads/BTI_2016_Scores.xlsx; European Bank of Reconstruction and Development, *Transition Indicators Methodology* (2015), http://www.ebrd.com/cs/Satellite?c=Content&cid=1395237866249&d=&pagename=EBRD%2FContent%2FContentLayout; *Country-level Transition Indicators* (2015), http://www.ebrd.com/what-we-do/economicresearch-and-data/data/forecasts-macro-data-transition-indicators.html; *Tic: Transition Indicators by Countries* (2015), www.ebrd.com/cs/Satellite?c=Content&cid=1395245467784&d=&pagename=EBRD%2FContent%2FDownloadDocument; Freedom House, *Methodology* (2016), https://freedomhouse.org/report/nations-transit-2015/methodology; *Nations in Transit – Country Reports* (2016), https://freedomhouse.org/report/nations-transit-2016/nit-2016-table-country-scores; World Economic Forum, *Appendix: Methodology and Computation of the Global Competitiveness Index 2015–2016* (2016), http://reports.weforum.org/global-competitiveness-report-2015-2016/appendix-methodology-and-computation-of-the-global-competitiveness-index-2015-2016/; *Global Competitiveness Report* (2016), http://reports.weforum.org/global-competitiveness-report-2015-2016/; *The Global Competitiveness Index Historical Dataset, 2005–2015* (2016), www3.weforum.org/docs/gcr/2015-2016/GCI_Dataset_2006-2015.xlsx. The classifications of postsocialist countries in the reports appear as Background Material 4 on my website. I am grateful to Ádám Kerényi for his hard, circumspect work in processing these

inclusive materials and his useful proposals for incorporating the information gathered from such rich data banks into the line of thought in my study.

[45] Selected reference lists of the huge literature for individual countries or country groups and conclusions drawn from the study of a part of this literature are on record in the author's archives.

[46] Zoltán Sz. Bíró, *Oroszország: válságos évek* [Russia: Critical years] (Budapest: Russica Pannonicana, 2012).

[47] Let me pick a few from the varied literature: Minxin Pei, *China's Trapped Transition: The Limits of Developmental Autocracy* (Cambridge, MA: Harvard University Press, 2006); Kellee S. Tsai, *Capitalism without Democracy: The Private Sector in Contemporary China* (Ithaca: Cornell University Press, 2007); Jie Chen and Bruce J. Dickson, "Allies of the State: Democratic Support and Regime Support among China's Private Entrepreneurs," *China Quarterly* 196 (2008); Yasheng Huang, *Capitalism with Chinese Characteristics: Entrepreneurship and the State* (New York: Cambridge University Press, 2008); David. L. Schambaugh, *China's Communist Party: Atrophy and Adaptation* (Berkeley: University of California Press, 2008); Chenggang Xu, "The Fundamental Institutions of China's Reforms and Development," *Journal of Economic Literature* 49, no. 4 (2011); James McGregor, *No Ancient Wisdom, No Followers: The Challenges of Chinese Authoritarian Capitalism* (Westport: Prosepacta Press, 2012); Gary King, Jennifer Pan, and Margaret E. Roberts, "How Censorship in China Allows Government Criticism but Silences Collective Expression," *American Political Science Review* 107, no. 2 (2013); Nicholas R. Lardy, *Markets over Mao: The Rise of Private Business in China* (Washington, D.C.: Peterson Institute for International Economics, 2014); Michael A. Witt and Gordon Redding, "China: Authoritarian Capitalism," in *The Oxford Handbook of Asian Business Systems*, ed. Michael A. Witt and Gordon Redding (Oxford: Oxford University Press, 2014); András Székely-Doby, "A kínai reformfolyamat politikai gazdaságtani logikája," *Közgazdasági Szemle* 61, no. 12 (2014); Barry Naughton and Kellee S. Tsai, eds., *State Capitalism, Institutional Adaptation and the Chinese Miracle* (New York: Cambridge University Press, 2015); Mária Csanádi, *China in between Varieties of Capitalism and Communism* (Budapest: Institute of Economics, Centre for Economics and Regional Studies, Hungarian Academy of Sciences, 2016); Orville Schell, "Crackdown in China: Worse and Worse," *New York Review of Books*, April 21, 2016.

[48] János Kornai, "Példaképünk: Kína?," in *Társadalmi riport 2014*, ed. Tamás Kolosi and István György Tóth (Budapest: TÁRKI, 2014); Kornai, "Threatening Dangers," available online: http://www.kornai-janos.hu/Kornai2014 Threatening dangers.pdf. Original in Hungarian: "Fenyegető veszélyek," *Élet és Irodalom* 58, no. 21, May 23, 2014: 5.

[49] As in China, classifying the system in the three Indo-Chinese countries is in dispute. See, for example, Jonathan D. London, ed. *Politics in Contemporary Vietnam: Party, State, and Authority Relations* (Houndmills: Palgrave-Macmillan, 2014) and Benedict J. Tria Kerkvliet, "Democracy and Vietnam," in *Handbook of Southeast Asian Democratization*, ed. William Coase (Abington-on-Thames: Routledge, 2015).

50 I am grateful to Andrea Reményi for researching Background Material 5 and compiling *Table 2*.
51 The expression "illiberal democracy" was coined by Fareed Zakaria in 1997, but when Viktor Orbán used it to characterize his own Hungarian politico-governmental form, there was widespread protest and Zakaria himself dissociated himself from such usage in an article. See Fareed Zakaria, "The Rise of Illiberal Democracy," *Foreign Affairs* 76, no. 6 (1997); Zakaria, "The Rise of Putinism," *Washington Post*, July 31, 2014. http://www.washingtonpost.com/opinions/fareed-zakaria-the-rise-of-putinism/2014/07/31/2c9711d6-18e7-11e4-9e3b-7¬f2f110c6265_story.html. The term "leader democracy" occurs even in the title of a study by András Körösényi. See András Körösényi, "Political Representation in Leader Democracy," *Government and Opposition* 40, no. 3 (2003). The antecedents in theoretical history go back to Max Weber and Karl Schmitt, see Weber, *Economy and Society*; Carl Schmitt, *The Concept of the Political* (Chicago: University of Chicago Press, 1996). For some further notable contributions to the debate on the boundaries and variants of democracy, see Ivan Krastev and Stephen Holmes, "An Autopsy of Managed Democracy," *Journal of Democracy* 23, no. 3 (2012); András Körösényi and Veronika Patkós, "Liberális és illiberális populizmus: Berlusconi és Orbán politikai vezetése," *Politikatudományi Szemle* 24, no. 2 (2015); Ivan Szelényi and Tamás Csillag, "Drifting from Liberal Democracy: Neo-Conservative Ideology of Managed Illiberal Democratic Capitalism in Post-Communist Europe," *Intersections: East European Journal of Society and Politics* 1, no. 1 (2015).
52 Huntington, *The Third Wave*.
53 Ibid., 11. (Figure 1.1)
54 I suspect that the six countries were entered on Huntington's diagram in the wrong place. It emerges from the context that, according to *his own periodization*, these countries set out on the path of democratization not in the first wave, but in the second, which reached its zenith in 1962.
55 For more detailed summary figures, see Background Material 4 on my website.
56 The image of a reverse wave is vivid, but not accurate enough. When the wave moving towards democracy and a capitalist market economy reverses, it does not arrive where it began. There is no sign of the communist system being restored. It was a common remark among the transition specialists of the 1990s that you can scramble eggs, but not unscramble them again.
57 It is thought-provoking to read an article by Katalin Balog, a US-based philosophy professor born in Hungary, pointing to similarities between the changes in Hungary and the "Trump phenomenon" in the United States. Katalin Balog, "An Inconsistent Triad: Trump, Sanders, Clinton, and the Radical Mismatch in the Theater of Politics," *Quarks Daily* (2016), http://www.3quarksdaily.com/3quarksdaily/2016/06/an-inconsistent-triad-trump-sanders-clinton-and-the-radical-mismatch-in-the-theater-of-politics-by-k.html. What is shared most closely is the change in political discourse: it has become acceptable in speech and writing, social discussion, political speeches and press articles, to proclaim racism, xenophobia, and national supremacy. These prepare the ground for turning away from democracy. Balog points to a study by Amanda Taub,

which examines the strengthening of American authoritarianism. Amanda Taub, "The Rise of American Authoritarianism," *Vox* (2016), http://www.vox.com/2016/3/1/11127424/trump-authoritarianism.

[58] See Bertelsmann, *Transformation Index Methodology* (2016); *Codebook for Country Assessments* (2016); *Bertelsmann Transformation Index Country Reports* (2016); and Freedom House, *Methodology* (2016); *Nations in Transit – Country Reports* (2016).

[59] For an overview of reports compiled by international organizations see Background Material 6 on my website. Both Bertelsmann and Freedom House reports use quantitative indicators and qualitative denotations concurrently to convey the state of the country examined. Freedom House's qualitative classifications are tied wholly to quantitative indices. Certain ranges of democracy scores (DS) are translated into a qualitative description (e.g., a DS score between 6.00 and 7.00 counts as a "consolidated authoritarian regime"). So the entirety of Freedom House's verbal expressions does not amount to a typology, for as I have mentioned, a typology emphasizes strong, shared qualitative characteristics. Instead, a Freedom House report undertakes a complete *classification* of each country, giving each class a name. This is justified methodologically, but differs from what this study sets out to do. That is why I have dealt with this in a footnote, not the text, where I will put down my reservations and critical observations.

[60] I fully understand the desire of the international comparative reports to add quantitative indicators to their qualitative types, but I cannot cover the advantages and drawbacks of using them in this study, which is already too long as it is.

[61] Bertelsmann reports make no use of the term dictatorship in their qualitative ratings, preferring to talk of "hard-line autocracy." Of course they have a right to name things as they will, but it is unfortunate to omit from their vocabulary such a graphic, widespread expression as dictatorship. No doubt my regret at this omission is due to my sterner value judgments.

[62] Prior to the victory of this political force at the 2010 general elections, József Debreczeni managed to predict the likely developments in several fields, see József Debreczeni, *Arcmás* [Image] (Budapest: Noran Libro, 2009). First after the assumption of power to show the radical changes and processes occurring was a study by Gábor Halmai, followed by my own study, "Taking Stock," which pointed out a radical transformation, i.e., that the government had already dismantled some essential institutions of democracy and begun to build up its autocratic rule. See Gábor Halmai, "Búcsú a jogállamtól," *Élet és Irodalom*, July 22, 2010; János Kornai, "Taking Stock," *CESifo Forum* 12, no. 2 (2011). Apart from a huge number of press articles examining the matter there were several academic studies, of which I should highlight here the following: Attila Ágh, "Bánatos regionális körkép," *Élet és Irodalom* 60, no. 12 (2016); Tamás Bauer, "Szabadságharc – az első lépések," in *Manuscript* (Budapest: Institute of Economics, Centre for Economics and Regional Studies, Hungarian Academy of Sciences, 2016); András Bozóki, "Van félnivalójuk," *Népszabadság, Weekend supplement*, April 9, 2016; János Kornai, "Centralization and the Capitalist Market

Economy," *Economics of Transition* 20, no. 4 (2012); Kornai, "Hungary's U-turn," *Journal of Democracy* 26, no. 3 (2015); András Körösényi, ed. *A magyar politikai rendszer – negyedszázad után* (Budapest: Osiris-MTA Társadalomtudományi Kutatóközpont Politikatudományi Intézet, 2015); Bálint Magyar, *Post-Communist Mafia-State: The Case of Hungary* (Budapest: CEU Press and Noran Libro, 2016); Bálint Magyar and Júlia Vásárhelyi, *Magyar polip: A posztkommunista maffiaállam* [Hungarian octopus: Post-communist mafia state], 3 vols. (Budapest: Noran Libro, 2013–2015).

[63] The term "state capitalism" has been used by politicians and political analysts of various persuasions (from shades of the socialist and communist movements through liberals to fascists). Some apply it to a formation congenial to them, others to one they oppose. A serviceable account of its history appears in Wikipedia [https://en.wikipedia.org/wiki/State_capitalism]. One interesting branch of Hungarian discourse on the subject was the 2005 debate between János Kis and Gáspár Miklós Tamás (two philosophers) on socialism, capitalism and state capitalism. See Gáspár Miklós Tamás, "Lassú válasz Kis Jánosnak," *Népszabadság*, October 1, 2005.; the 2005 article by Kis was published again in the author's volume of collected writings in János Kis, *Mi a liberalizmus?* [What is liberalism?] (Bratislava: Kalligram, 2014), 429–439.

[64] Péter Mihályi, *A privatizált vagyon visszaállamosítása Magyarországon 2010–2014* [Renationalization of private wealth in Hungary, 2010–2014] (Budapest: Institute of Economics, Centre for Economics and Regional Studies, Hungarian Academy of Sciences, 2015).

[65] To an extent the task of investigating corruption is taken up by non-governmental media, research groups and opposition politicians. (To pick an example, a report of the Corruption Research Center Budapest produced comprehensive data based on a very large sample. Corruption Research Center Budapest, *Competitive Intensity and Corruption Risks. Statistical Analysis of Hungarian Public Procurement – 2009–2015* (2016), http://www.crcb.eu/wp-content/uploads/2016/05/hpp_2016_crcb_report1_en_160513_.pdf) But revealing corruption is only a first step. Its effects are limited unless published suspicions are followed by police investigations, criminal charges, court procedures, and penal sentences on the guilty. That is all a state monopoly. Not even the most impartial judge can sentence those against whom police and prosecutors have not made impartial investigations and filed charges.

[66] Bálint Magyar began using the expression in the early 2000s. For details on this term, see Magyar, *Post-Communist Mafia-State*, 1–55, and Magyar and Vásárhelyi, *Magyar polip*, vol. 1: 8–95. See furthermore volume 2 (2014) and 3 (2015) of the same book.

[67] Albert Hirschman pointed out in a brilliant essay that there are two organizations against which there is and can be no opposition, either by voice or by exit: Stalinist power and the mafia. See Albert O. Hirschman, *Exit, Voice, and Loyalty* (Cambridge MA: Harvard University Press, 1970). Under today's Hungarian system it is possible to protest by word of mouth or by exit, or if all else fails, by the extreme form of exit, leaving the country.

68 There are exceptions. A strong, prestigious multinational firm with a "strategic agreement" with the government may receive special treatment. Where two priorities clash—strengthening central power and nationalist bias in favor of Hungarian capital, the former usually proves stronger.

69 If need be Fidesz will enter into open or secret coalition with the far-right party Jobbik. The nightmare memory looms of the fall of Weimar democracy: the coalition of former Chancellor Franz von Papen and other conservative politicians with the Nazi party.

70 "Wishful thinking" describes well the particularly distorted, biased outlook on future events: individual desires and hopes are embedded in rational and objective thinking, which unavoidably blurs the boundary between a positive aspect (what is) and a normative aspect (what should be).

71 Orbán's speech was heard a few months before he took power. An edited version appeared in the weekly *Nagyítás* early in 2010. The references to this study include the URL for the text at the Fidesz website, see Viktor Orbán, "Megőrizni a létezés magyar minőségét" [To Maintain the Hungarian standard of existence]. http://www.fidesz.hu/hirek/2010-02-17/meg337rizni-a-letezes-magyar-min337seget/.

72 I understand the horror at the danger of fascism, but disagree with those who term, like Rudolf Ungváry in his otherwise excellent volume of analyses, the Hungarian politico-governmental formation "fascistoid." Rudolf Ungváry, *A láthatatlan valóság* [Invisible reality] (Bratislava: Kalligram, 2014).

73 Samuel P. Huntington, *The Clash of Civilizations and the Remaking of World Order* (New York: Simon and Schuster, 1996).

74 The nationalism of the political group in power has deep roots and traditions which date back hundreds of years. On this topic see Péter Agárdi, *Nemzeti értékviták és kultúrafelfogások 1847–2014* [Reflections on national values and cultural attitudes, 1847–2014] (Budapest: Napvilág Kiadó, 2015); Péter Kende, *Államiság a kommunizmus után* [Statehood after Communism] (Bratislava: Kalligram, 2013); János Rainer M., ed. *Búvópatakok – a feltárás* (Budapest: 1956 Institute, 2012); Rainer M., ed. *Búvópatakok – széttekintés* (Budapest: 1956 Institute, 2013); Ungváry, *A láthatatlan valóság*.

75 János Kornai, "The Dilemmas of a Socialist Economy: The Hungarian Experience," *Cambridge Journal of Economics* 4, no. 2 (1980): 290.

OLEKSANDR FISUN

Neopatrimonialism in post-Soviet Eurasia*

Thirty years of transformation in post-Soviet Eurasia make it possible to draw some conclusions regarding politics and regime development. Recent scholarship has done much to further our understanding of the complicated and contradictory singularity of the democratization processes in the post-Soviet space. It has gone far in revealing the distinctiveness of the region's democratic transitions as well as the new political regimes that are forming in the new independent states of the former USSR. The growing multiplicity of the forms and models of the post-Soviet type political regimes that manifested towards the end of the 1990s–mid-2000s has stimulated revision and correction of the many established conceptual blueprints and approaches to the analysis of post-communist development.

---

* It is a great pleasure to acknowledge that the present chapter is a result of beneficial support and extraordinary fruitful environment of several organizations and institutions: the Canadian Institute of Ukrainian Studies at University of Alberta and the John Kolasky Memorial Endowment Fund; the Aleksanteri Institute at University of Helsinki; the Fulbright Scholar Program, Kennan Institute and Woodrow Wilson International Center for Scholars in Washington DC; and the Netherlands Institute for Advanced Study in the Humanities and Social Sciences (NIAS-KNAW) in Amsterdam. I would like to extend my gratitude also to the members of the Program on New Approaches to Research and Security in Eurasia (PONARS Eurasia) at the Institute for European, Russian and Eurasian Studies (IERES) at the Elliott School of International Affairs, the George Washington University, for their contributions and comments at various conferences and meetings during past several years.

Initially, political scientist Samuel P. Huntington's theory of a global third wave of democratization[1] urged the majority of researchers to analyze post-Soviet developments in the context of democratic transitions in other parts of the world—particularly Latin America and Southern, Central and Eastern Europe. Today, skepticism and disappointment have replaced the euphoria that emerged after the downfall of the USSR. Researchers talk about the development of various types of post-Soviet hybrid regimes whose nature and "machinery" are very far from liberal standards.[2] These insights are useful but incomplete for solving the puzzle of post-Soviet politics. Today, we have a consensus in understanding that 25 years of the post-Soviet political transformations gave birth to a variety of new political regimes that can be identified as hybrids, which combine elements of democratic and non-democratic regimes.

What are the inner workings of hybrid regimes in post-Soviet Eurasia? What are the distinctive characteristics of the political regimes, which have arisen in the former Soviet area? How are they different from similar hybrid regimes in Asia, Africa, and Latin America? Is a hybrid regime a stage on the road to a competitive democracy or does it turn into something else? What do we understand and what do we not understand after thirty years?

A significant obstacle to developing conceptual clarity in our understanding of post-Soviet politics is the dominating tendency to study these hybrid regimes in terms of the traditional dichotomies of "democracy versus authoritarianism," which brings researchers to theoretical dead ends, best exemplified by the various efforts to define "democracies" and "authoritarianisms" with adjectives. The scholastic search for battles between democracy and authoritarianism in the post-Soviet political space—conflicts between good and bad, or democrats and non-democrats—is not an adequate tool for understanding post-Soviet societies. It discourages an understanding of the real meaning of political struggle—the dynamics of elite contestation and its consequences for political and regime development in post-Soviet societies.

Current research clearly shows that the model of democratic elite pact-making, which was peculiar to Central and Eastern Europe, proved to be irrelevant for post-Soviet development. Post-Soviet elites made pacts in one form or another, but instead of establishing democracy, these pacts instead stabilized and consolidated different variants of non-democratic or semi-democratic regimes.[3] The post-Soviet intra-elite consolidations resulted in cartel agreements for restricting competition and excluding "outsiders" from exploiting public resources. Thus, post-Soviet pacts did not facilitate democratization, but instead led to informal arrangements of state capture and monopolistic appropriation of public, political, and economic functions.

So, what are the distinctive characteristics of the political regimes in the former Soviet area? The central thesis of this chapter is that the *key idiosyncrasies of post-Soviet states' political development and regime dynamics is best understood through the concept of neopatrimonialism*. Despite a large number of viable theories explaining what is happening, it appears that many post-Soviet political developments are leading to a renewal, modification, and rationalization of the patrimonial systems of domination, but by no means to the establishment of Western-style, rational-legal competitive democracies. This concept allows for the most precise description of the post-Soviet reality.[4]

The German political scientist Max Weber widely used the concept of "patrimonialism" in his fundamental work *Economy and Society*, which he contrasted with both feudal and bureaucratic rational-legal forms of government.[5] In its initial form, a patrimonial set-up derives from the household administrations of a chief, especially from the separation of clients from their chief's household and the granting to them of fiefs, benefices, preferences, tax-farming opportunities and so on.[6] According to Weber, "in the pure type, patrimonial domination, especially of the estate-type, regards all governing powers and the corresponding economic rights as privately appropriated economic advantages."[7]

One should point out, that the concept of "patrimonialism" itself is based on the word *patrimonium*, which was mentioned for the first time in Roman law to mean inherited, family property. In this context, the concept of *patrimonial kingdom* was used by Grotius, Hobbes, and Pufendorf to identify a special dominant form of power (dominion), implying the possession of the body politic on the basis of full ownership, obtained, for example, as a result of acquisition or conquest. The independent status of the patrimonialism concept was first developed by a conservative Swiss legal scholar, Karl Ludwig von Haller, in his work, *Restoration of the Science of the State* (1816–1834). Haller, in counterweight to the concept of the "social contract," proposed a patrimonial theory of the state's power originating from the private property of the ruler. In his opinion, property is not a result of the existence of the state, but the opposite, the state and power appear as means through which to realize private property rights. Functions of the state (primarily, in enforcing the law, collecting taxes and ensuring security) grow from the administration of the private properties of the ruler, i.e. from his own economy and personal system of enforcement. The concept of patrimonialism was broadly used by many German historians and legal scholars (Robert von Mohl, Georg Jellinek, Otto von Gierke, Georg von Below), whose works Weber knew well, and some of whom were his direct colleagues and friends. Patrimonialism, as a rule, was viewed in German political-historical theory as a special form of governance, based on the private ownership and governing of the state as private property, much like how a landowner disposes of his estate (*Grundherrschaft*). This stands in contrast to other forms of power that are limited by contracts, various agreements, traditional liberties, and so forth.

While further developing these theoretical insights, Max Weber pointed out and stressed the *political* dimension of the patrimonial state. Weber assigned a special meaning to the *private appropriation of the judicial and military functions of the state*, which often "tends to be treated as a legal basis for a privileged status position of those appropriating them, as compared to the appropriation of purely economic advantages having to do with the income from domains, from taxes, or perquisites."[8] In his letter to Georg von Below of June 21, 1914, Weber stressed that he used the concept of patrimonialism explicitly for designating specific types of *political domination*, that postulated appropriation of the public authority and connected to it judicial and military powers: "I must limit the concept of patrimonialism to certain kinds of *political* domination. I hope you will find that I have sufficiently emphasized the absolute distinction between domestic, personal and manorial authority, on the one hand, and political *Herrschaft* on the other, which is none of these but rather military and judicial authority."[9]

In that sense, Max Weber takes a significant step forward from previous interpretations, which situated patrimonialism in the various forms of personal patriarchal relations within the family, and ultimately equated patrimonialism with the expression of the private legal aspects of patrimonial land ownership. Having stressed the public-political dimension of patrimonialism, and its distinction from both patriarchal relations within the household and the estate relations within the framework of *Grunderrschaft*, Weber not only significantly reassessed this concept, but also introduced new possibilities for its use in comparative analysis.

One of Weber's most important conclusions is that a patrimonial way of exercising power can occur within very different economic and political systems. The term "patrimonial" state, in his opinion, is justified whenever judicial power and other rights of political origin are viewed as privately appropriated powers. "The patrimonial office," notes Weber, "lacks above all the bureaucratic separation of the 'private' and the 'official' sphere. For the political administration, too, is treated as a purely personal affair of the ruler, and political power is considered part of his personal property, which can be exploited by means of contributions and fees."[10] Although the degree of patrimonialization in different types of societies and systems can vary, "for our terminology," writes Weber, "the decisive fact is that, regardless of content, governing powers and the related emoluments are treated as private rights."[11]

Therefore, the main feature of patrimonialism is the private appropriation of a governmental sphere by those who hold political power, and the indivisibility of the public and private spheres of society. In the neopatrimonial system, the ruling groups regard society as their own private domain, and the fulfillment of public functions as a legitimate means to their own personal enrichment. As Reinhard Bendix, one of the prominent researchers of Weber's works, writes, "under patrimonialism the ruler treats all political administration as his personal affairs in same way in which he exploits his possession of political power as a useful adjunct of his private property."[12]

Guenther Roth from the Berkeley school of historical sociology was the first scholar to point out the rise of new modernized forms of patrimonial domination, especially in the new post-colonial states of Africa and Asia. In his opinion, it is entirely evident that very important legal-rational elements of the modern state are absent in new post-colonial states and instead, even after the disappearance of forms of traditional legitimacy, there is continuing reproduction of existing forms of administrative practice. Instead of turning to Weber's juxtaposition of the bureaucratic with charismatic, Roth proposes using another Weberian concept, that of patrimonialism, as one that can better describe the conditions of post-traditional society. In his opinion, two forms of patrimonialism should be distinguished: first, the traditional patrimonial regimes, which are based on the traditional legitimacy and hereditary authority (Imperial Ethiopia is a typical example); second, modern forms of patrimonialism, which postulate "personal rulership on the basis of loyalties that do not require any belief in the ruler's unique personal qualification, but are inextricably linked to material incentives and rewards."[13] If traditional patrimonialism is, to a larger degree, becoming a "dying" type of regime, then the institutional matrix of post-colonial states encourages "de-traditionalizing" of personal rule, which much more often takes the patrimonial, rather than the charismatic, form of domination, implementing material interests. Personal patrimonial regimes differ "from charismatic rulership in that the patrimonial ruler need have neither personal charismatic appeal nor a sense of mission; they differ from legal-rational bureaucracies in that neither constitutionally regulated legislation nor advancement on the basis of training and efficiency need be predominant in public administration."[14]

In addition, Roth specifically points out that patrimonial type personal domination should not be equated to, or mixed up with, authoritarianism. Many authoritarian regimes do indeed have many features of both modern and traditional patrimonialism, and these features could be even more important than the elements of charisma or legal-rationalist practices that they possess. "Typologically, however," notes Roth, "it would be inadvisable to equate 'patrimonial' with 'authoritarian.' The latter term has been useful in establishing a continuum ranging from pluralist democracy to totalitarianism; the former category properly belongs to a typology of beliefs *and* organizational practices that can be found at any point of such a continuum."[15] Which is to say that patrimonialism can be observed in various forms of the modern state and be completely compatible with certain forms of capitalism, as well as socialism.

Shmuel Eisenstadt has taken further steps in developing a complex theory of *neopatrimonialism*. Traditional patrimonialism, in his opinion, was typical for various societies in antiquity and during the middle ages. The emergence of fundamentally new neopatrimonial structures, in contrast, is a product of the modernization of contemporary postcolonial societies in Asia, Africa, and Latin America, conditioned by the formation of the modern state's political institutions and characterized by a symbiosis of diverse elements that takes place within the framework of a distinctive regime "synthesis" between the traditional and the modern.[16] This synthesis is not "transitional," but the opposite: it has significant stability and its own developmental logic, which leads to a change in the "understanding" of the functioning of modern-type formal political institutions—parliament, parties, the bureaucratic and the judicial-legal spheres. According to Eisenstadt, the emergence of neopatrimonial regimes is explained in significant degree by the failures of modernization and of the politics of nation- and state-building. As he wrote:

The use of the term "patrimonial" in the depicting of these various regimes implied a reaction to the inadequacies of the central assumption of the basic studies of modernization, as well as later concepts such as "breakdown," "political decay" or "transitional" societies. It emphasized the inadequacy of these assumptions by indicating first, that many of these societies and states did not develop into the direction of some modern nation-states or revolutionary societies; second, that these regimes did not necessarily constitute a "transitory," "transitional," passing phase towards an inevitable path to one type of modernity; third, by indicating that there was yet some internal "logic" in their development; and, last, by emphasizing that part at least of this logic or pattern could be derived from some aspects of the traditions of these societies and understood in terms of these aspects.[17]

Unlike Roth, Eisenstadt connected patrimonialism to a lesser degree with personal domination and the various forms of personalistic rulership, but most of all with the dominating pattern of relations between the center and the periphery of the system, i.e. with a specific structure of relations within the framework of the whole social system and the methods for its reproduction. As Eisenstadt wrote, "the most important characteristics of neopatrimonial society were to be found in the structure of centers and in center-periphery relations. In the majority of cases the center increasingly came to monopolize power and political resources, allowing little independent access by broader groups to such resources and to the positions controlling them. Such growing monopolization was associated with only minimal attempts by the centers to restructure the periphery (above all, center-periphery relations) or to create social institutions based on new constellations of ground rules and new structural principles."[18]

The novelty of Eisenstadt's approach was that he not only determined the limits of the modernization of postcolonial societies but also convincingly demonstrated which socio-political systems arose as a result of modernization and to what degree the result was at odds with initial optimistic expectations. As Eisenstadt explains, neopatrimonialism was characterized by "a continuous crystallization of several political syndromes: the monopolization of central power and political resources by the center; the minimization of independent access by broader groups to such resources and to the positions controlling them, but at the same time only a minimal degree of creation by the centers or by the society of new, more differentiated, types of social organizations and institutions."[19]

One can identify three main principles of the neopatrimonial systems' functionality:

1) The political center is separated and independent from the periphery, it concentrates the political, economic and symbolic resources of the authority, while simultaneously closing access to all other groups and levels of the society to these resources and positions of control over them;
2) The state is managed as a private possession (*patrimonium*) of the ruling groups—holders of the state authority, which privatize various social functions and institutions, making them sources of own private profit;
3) Ethnic, clan, regional and family/relative ties do not disappear, but are reproduced in the modern political and economic relations, determining methods and principals of their functioning.

The most important "working" principle for the functioning of the neopatrimonial system is *clientelism* or the *patron-client relationship*.[20] In its most common form, clientelism can be defined as personal dependence relations, which grow from an asymmetric exchange of favors and status positions between parties with unequal resources. A patron protects his clients, while the latter offer him various favors. The economic and power resources of the former is exchanged for the political and electoral loyalty of the latter. As Robin Theobald stresses, practically all researchers of patrimonialism consider "the essential feature of patrimonial regimes to be the exchange of resources (jobs, promotions, titles, contracts, licenses, immunity from the law, etc.) between key figures in government and strategically located individuals: trade union leaders, businessmen, community leaders, and so forth. In return for these resources, the government or heads of state receive economic and political support."[21] In other words, when the channels of rational-legal type official interaction are underdeveloped, the transmission and mutual accommodation of particular interests is achieved through the mechanism of patron-client relations, which asymmetrically "re-distribute" the benefits according to the status and position of each participant involved in such interactions.

Another significant aspect of neopatrimonial political regimes is the degree of *personalization of power*. As a rule, personalized types of power and control in neopatrimonial societies are connected to a weak rationalization of the political process, which leads to the dominance of traditional ideas about power (chief, tzar, prince, ruler) and their projection on contemporary reality. Therefore, the head of state in such a society unavoidably becomes the embodiment of the political system, its symbolic center and main nerve, tying together formal and informal threads of government into a single system; all other political institutions are secondary from the start and are only means for the realization of his (or her) political strategy. Personalization of power presumes the self-identification of the masses not with political programs (which can change overnight), but with the personality of the leader, loyalty to whom means also loyalty to the political regime that he embodies. This type of value determinations reflects the domination of the patron-client type social ties in neopatrimonial societies.

Modern researchers determine neopatrimonialism as "a form of organization in which relationships of a broadly patrimonial type pervade political and administrative system which is formally constructed on rational-legal lines. Officials hold positions in bureaucratic organizations with powers which are formally defined, but exercise those powers, so far as they can, as a form not of public service but of private property. Relationships with others likewise fall into the patrimonial pattern of vassal and lord, rather than the rational-legal one of subordinate and superior, and behavior is correspondingly devised to display personal status rather than to perform an official function."[22]

Besides neopatrimonialism, a growing number of scholars have been attracted to the Weberian concept of sultanism, especially in the context of analysis of personalist dictatorships and various regimes of personified authority. Weber views sultanism as an extreme form of patrimonialism, which "tend to arise whenever traditional domination develops an administration and a military force which are purely personal instruments of the master.... By controlling these instruments the ruler can broaden the range of his arbitrary power and put himself in a position to grant grace and favor at the expense of the traditional limitations of patriarchal and gerontocratic structures. Where domination is primarily traditional, even though it is exercised by virtue of ruler's personal autonomy, it will be called *patrimonial authority*; where it indeed operates primarily in the basis of discretion, it will be called *sultanism*."[23] Weber, however, also notes that in the case of pure sultanism, "it is fiscal arbitrariness which is likely to be most important."[24]

The time is ripe for a theoretical synthesis and conceptual reformulation of the problems, features and peculiarities of post-Soviet development that do not fit into the mainstream paradigm of democratic transition—as has already been noted by a number of insightful researchers.[25] Successful democratic transitions in Western Europe and other parts of the world during the earlier waves of democratization, as a rule, took place already after *rational bureaucratization* and *national state building* processes. For example, the third wave of democratization in Southern Europe and Latin America was preceded by a lengthy period of nineteenth-century oligarchic democracies, followed by the authoritarian developments of the 1920s–1930s. By contrast, democratization in the majority of post-Soviet states began before the fairly complex and dramatic processes of rational-bureaucratic modernization and national consolidation were completed.[26] Taras Kuzio wrote, "Post-Soviet states . . . launched into democratisation and marketization without the many state and national attributes commonly assumed to be necessary for the success of a market economic and liberal democratic project."[27] This *inversion development logic*, in my opinion, determines the fundamental differences in the political trajectories, as well as final results of the democratic transition in Latin America, Southern and Central Europe on the one hand, and post-Soviet transformations on the other.

The fact that post-Soviet development was taking place under conditions of incomplete national building and the unfinished rational-bureaucratic transformation of the state led to the situation that, in the majority of cases, the political developments in a number of successor states after the disintegration of the Soviet Union *led to the emergence of a neopatrimonial domination system, rather than the establishment of democracy*. The thesis of the neopatrimonial nature of post-Soviet transformations offers a conceptual foundation for reinterpreting the reversive trends that marked this (defined often as the fourth) wave of democratization.[28] It is the framework provided by the theory of neopatrimonialism that most precisely captures, in my view, the essence of post-Soviet development and is able to integrate within a single approach those characteristics and idiosyncrasies that constitute this development's historic distinctness.

The main characteristics of the post-Soviet neopatrimonial model are:
- the formation of the class of rent-seeking political entrepreneurs, who use political capabilities deriving from merging authority and property for achieving their own economic goals;[29]

- private use of state-administrative resources, primarily the power and fiscal functions of the state, which are exploited mainly for the suppression of political opposition and the elimination of economic competitors;
- the key role of client-patron relations and ties in structuring the political-economic process as well as the arena of real political struggle.

In this context, and seen from a larger historical perspective, *perestroika* and the collapse of communism should be viewed, on the one hand, as a qualitatively new stage of rationalization tied to the transition to new, democratic methods of legitimization and the formal establishment of legal-bureaucratic forms of domination. On the other hand, it should also be viewed as a process of direct patrimonial appropriation by the ruling elites (party/management; second and third level nomenclature; and regional, republic-level sub-elites) of the state control machinery. The democratization and economic reforms of the 1990s modernized and strengthened administrative-political market mechanisms, while at the same time also reinforced the workings of the patron-client exchange of resources between the different segments of the center and periphery. This process transformed the elements of patrimonial domination of the semi-traditional type that existed in the depths of the Soviet system into a system of an updated and "modernized" neopatrimonialism, one in which these patrimonial relations lose their traditionalist character and acquire a modern economic dimension. This kind of transformation becomes the precondition for the formation of a system of *political capitalism* (to use Max Weber's term, which in modern terminology could be described as a "capitalism of friends and relatives," or "crony capitalism") based on some degree of partimonialization of state, society and economy.[30]

It should be noted, however, that the post-Soviet transformations of the 1990s did not recreate a traditional patrimonial system (and thus constituted a significant break with previous semi-traditional forms of patrimonialism that marked the Soviet experience). The neopatrimonial system that emerged instead stimulated the development of post-Soviet political capitalism and endowed the workings of democratic mechanisms with a neopatrimonial logic, one in which the actors' behavior is guided less by *traditional and/or not ideological motives than by financial incentives of the rent-seeking type.*

In his analysis of the various forms of patrimonialism, Weber specifically draws attention to those that can exist within the framework of sufficiently modernized social and political institutions. Patrimonialism, for example,

> can resort to monopolistic want satisfaction, which in part may rely on profit-making enterprises, fee-taking or taxation. In this case, the development of markets is, according to the type of monopolies involved, more or less seriously limited by irrational factors. The important openings for profit are in the hands of the ruler and of his administrative staff. Capitalism is thereby either directly obstructed, if the ruler maintains his own administration, or is diverted into political capitalism, if there is tax farming, leasing or sale of offices, and capitalist provision for armies and administration.[31]

Therefore, the concept of post-Soviet neopatrimonialism justifies the Weberian idea that patrimonialism is completely compatible with, and even stimulates the development of certain types of capitalism. These types, according to Weber, are:

> a) capitalist trading, b) capitalist tax farming, lease and sale of offices, c) capitalist provision of supplies for the state and the financing of wars, d) under certain circumstances, capitalist plantations and other colonial enterprises. All these forms are indigenous to patrimonial regimes and often reach a very high level of development. This is not, however, true of the type of profit-making enterprise with heavy investments in fixed capital and a rational organization of free labor which is oriented to the market purchases of private consumers. This type of capitalism is altogether too sensitive to all sorts of irrationalities in the administration of law, administration and taxation, for these upset the basis of *calculability*.[32]

The post-Soviet version of neopatrimonial structures is distinguished by the formal installation of modern state institutions (a parliamentary and multi-party system, electoral mechanisms and modern constitution), which—while serving as legitimate façades of the system—are overall *internally subordinated to the "patrimonial logic" of their functioning*. The key role in the working of post-Soviet neopatrimonial systems is played not by rational-legal relations within the system of official interactions, but by *client-patron ties* that regulate the access of the neopatrimonial players to various types of resources based on relationships of personal dependence that derive from the asymmetrical exchange of capital. *Accordingly, the formation of economic capital happens not through the appropriation of the means of production, but primarily through the appropriation of the public administrative means of governance.*

Despite all the variety of social-economic and state-legal forms, and despite all the political and ideological orientations, political process in post-Soviet neopatrimonial systems has a set of common, and at the same time fundamental, features.

The leading place in the system of neopatrimonial rule is occupied by the representatives of *neopatrimonial bureaucracy,* which to a significant degree combines the functional roles of administrative, political and economic elites. In this sense, neopatrimonial bureaucracy acts in these kinds of systems as *the main agent of political and economic process.* The foundation for this is the functional independence of the neopatrimonial bureaucracy from the rest of society. As a leading political-economic force and a real "party of power," neopatrimonial bureaucracy is based on regional, clan and family/relative ties and constitutes a complex pyramid of various patronages, linked together through a mechanism of client relations by the presidential authority (sometimes, such patron-client network is indeed institutionalized in the form of a formal "party of power"). As before, the economic function of coordinating general interests in a neopatrimonial society merges with the function of governing it, which in turn intertwines with the function of the symbolic and ideological integration of society as a whole.

Patrimonial bureaucracy is a term used by Weber to analyze combined or transitional types of domination: "We shall be compelled again and again to form expressions like 'patrimonial bureaucracy' in order to make the point that the characteristic traits of the respective phenomenon belong in part to the rational form of domination, whereas other traits belong to a traditionalist form of domination, in this case to that of estates."[33] Using a familiar Weberian differentiation of methods to live "for politics" and "from politics," neopatrimonial bureaucracy can be defined as a specialized administrative-management layer, whose main source of existence is based to one or another degree on various prebendal incomes deriving from the capitalization of public offices rather than on fixed salaries.

According to Weber, the "professional politician living *from* politics can be a pure 'prebendary' or a salaried 'official.' Either he draws an income from charges and fees for particular services—gratuities and bribes are only an irregular and formally illegal variant of this category of income—or he draws a fixed remuneration in kind or a salary in money, or a combination of both. He can assume the character of an 'entrepreneur,' like the condottiere or the holder of a leased or purchased office in the past, or like the American 'boss' who regards his expenses as a capital investment from which he will derive a yield by exploiting his influence."[34]

Within the neopatrimonial bureaucracy, central positions are occupied by the "president's people," namely a patron-client network formed around the head of state figure; its top is occupied by those personally loyal to him (or her), who take up key positions in state and party apparatuses and oversee enforcement ministries and key sectors of the economy. The main structural element of the patron-client network is *a system of personal connections, ending with the president and based, first of all on regional, family-clan or ethnic commonality, as well as the commonality of current political and business interests. This informal institution plays a directing, organizing, and mobilizing role both within the actual "party of power," and in the political development of the society overall, which renders the issue of leadership of any party or state in such a society to be of secondary importance.*

All other components of the political field (parliament, parties, interest groups, trade unions and other public organizations) in neopatrimonial society do not become a full-scale element of the "political game." On the contrary, the latter as a rule is dominated by parties whose function is not to ensure the competitiveness of the political process, but rather to ensure support for the ruling group. Which is to say that the real mechanism of party politics, as it is understood in the modern paradigm of democracy, does not in fact exist in the neopatrimonial political system: the relationship between the party and state institutions in this case turns out to be upside down. It is not the parties that control the formation and the functioning of the government and other state agencies. Rather, it is the ruling patron-client network that directs and controls the activities of the parties and other public organizations, turning them into an appendage of the state apparatus, into political agencies of the neopatrimonial bureaucracy. At the same time, the ruling party of power becomes a sort of variation of the presidential administration, while party bureaucracy effectively dissolves in the state bureaucracy.

The formal organization of a party of power is viewed by a ruler as the means for creating a network of patron-client relations in different levels of society, which form the basis for the domination of the presidential patron-client network among others. One can point out the following main functions of the ruling parties in the neopatrimonial political system (independent of the existence, or absence, of other parties). First, they exercise control over the selection and nomination of the leading cadres in the state apparatus, and also over the formation of the representative organs of all levels. The second function is the organization of mass support for goals set by the authority, generating popular support for certain decisions (through social meetings, rallies, demonstrations and referendums). The third is the political upbringing and ideological conditioning of the masses in accordance with one or another official doctrine. The fourth function is the control and leadership over mass organizations. The real task of the party mechanism (and this can be noted as the fifth function) is most often the *private distribution* of the public offices, ministries, positions in national and regional administration, as well as state corporations and banks *among the members of the ruling group,* that is, the patrimonial privatization of the state. Party mechanism based on the principle of patron-client relations recruits new members to the "party of power," "shuffles" those already in the deck, while simultaneously distributing and re-distributing profitable government positions and "feeding" spheres.

In many variations of neopatrimonial systems, parliamentary bodies evolved into sorts of "registration chambers," which do not play an independent role in the decision making process. Parliament, formed primarily from the members of the ruling (or dominant semi-government) parties, does not possess practically any rights in such systems and does not oversee state activity. In fact, parliamentary bodies become one of the methods for institutionalizing patron-client relations between the "power holders" (nowadays, instead of the royal administration it is patron-client network headed by the president) and other social forces. Comprised of multiple patronages, joined into the hierarchical system, parliament becomes an element of the *singular* power system and not one of the branches of power in the European understanding. For the ruler's patron-client network, this mechanism becomes an important resource for assuring the loyalty and integration of potential counter-elites into its own system of authority. Parliamentarians, caught between the grinding wheels of "representative clientelism" accept defined rules of the game, since the acquisition and preservation of the parliamentary seat, and therefore, of all the material benefits and advantages connected with it, depend to a much larger degree on the predisposition of the ruling clan patron, than on the voters.

Post-Soviet type political systems reproduce the logic of the neopatrimonial political process: this is not the struggle of party-political alternatives in the framework of parliamentary competition, but a *struggle of neopatrimonial bureaucracy's various factions for the monopolization of one or another segment of client-patronage networks, for their change and redistribution*. As Shmuel Eisenstadt states, parliamentary elections in the neopatrimonial systems, as a rule, are used for the conquest of positions of control over resource distribution and in establishing control over the sections of client-patronage networks. Political struggle, as well as state policy, revolves more around competition for access to resources, dominant positions and offices, rather than support for new types of economic activity and new forms of status and class relations. The interconnection of the neopatrimonial center and various politico-economic elites was established not through electoral democratic mechanisms and political participation, but through entering into client-patronage networks, various corporative formations and the formal "party of power." Rent-seeking entrepreneurs who appeared as a result of post-Soviet economic reforms, as a rule, did not strive for autonomous political activity outside the existing patron-client network, very rarely supported alternative political forces and in a large measure, did not show interest in restructuring the political sphere. On the contrary, under the conditions of unfinished rational-bureaucratic transformation and an incomplete separation of politics and economy, entrance into the clientele's chains of resources and capital trade became the most advantageous and "inexpensive" strategy of rent-seeking groups. Neopatrimonial systems minimize the independent access of the autonomous social groups to the center and to the positions of control over the resources distribution, while stimulating rent-seeking entrepreneurs to join the system of resource redistribution within the framework of patron-client networks. As a result, the dependence of various social groups on the patrimonial center grows and their autonomy is minimized.[35] Neopatrimonial ruling groups attempt to "control and regulate the political process in such a way that it would not threaten their monopoly on central political power and would not enable the development among various groups of independent access to sources of society-wide power."[36]

Transplanted to the post-Soviet soil, the main elements of the modern democratic system (political parties, elections, and parliament) are subjected to significant transformation in the neopatrimonial society, becoming a casing that covers patrimonial and semi-patrimonial social ties. Joint together in a significant measure not by modern, legal-rational ties of the civic type, but by the patron-client relations, modern political institutions become a convenient substructure under which the reproduction of the various forms of neopatrimonial domination takes place.

Therefore, unlike the democratization models in Latin America, Southern and East-Central Europe, in the post-Soviet states neopatrimonial elites are divided and compete among themselves—first of all, for the client-patronage network, in the center of which is the leader of the state. *Post-Soviet elitist-party cleavages can be determined exactly through the positioning either within or outside the "state partition" system.* Instead of the classical division between the moderate and radical, liberals and conservatives, left and right, post-Soviet neopatrimonial regimes can be characterized by the sub-elite fragmentation that grows from the competition for the best position in the hierarchal clientelistic distribution of "favors and privileges." In this sense *the essence of the political struggle in the neopatrimonial system, consist of the struggle for positioning and patronage from the head of state, but not for potential voters.* All members and detachments of the post-Soviet elite are, in one form or another, involved in the competition and struggle for a share of the "public pie," which is regulated by the supreme state leader, who acts as the arbiter above the party (above the fraction). If the key to the modern democratic state's stability is the rulers' ability to sustain effective communication and rapidly react to the various social layers' demands, then stability in a neopatrimonial system is based on the ability of various elites to obtain and keep patron-client ties to various segments of the society, as well as keeping a low level of conflict in competition with each other for better positioning in the patron-client network.

Depending on the model of elite consolidation, it is possible to delineate a few basic forms of neopatrimonialism within the post-Soviet regime:

Sultanistic Neopatrimonialism—characterized by an extreme concentration of power, pure personal rulership, sham elections, and clan-based models of voting (e.g., Turkmenistan, Uzbekistan, Tajikistan).[37]

Oligarchic Neopatrimonialism—linked with the formation of a wide strata of oligarchic and/or regional rent-seeking actors, acting together with, or in place of, weak governmental institutions primarily via clientistic networks of patronage and pork barrel rewards (e.g., Yeltsin's Russia, Kuchma's Ukraine).

Bureaucratic Neopatrimonialism—based on state-bureaucratic monopolies and semi-coercive centralization of neopatrimonial domination under super-presidentialism, operating via law enforcement/fiscal structures; and utilizing populist/patriotic mobilization and plebiscites (e.g., Belarus, Russia, Georgia).

Neopatrimonial Democracy—where political actors compete through formal electoral mechanisms for different branches of government in a divided executive constitutional setting, but their goals are still focused on state capture as the primary gain of power-sharing (Ukraine, Moldova, Kyrgyzstan).[38]

Notes

[1] Samuel P. Huntington, *The Third Wave: Democratization in the Late Twentieth Century* (Norman: University of Oklahoma Press, 1991).

[2] Among seminal works, see Michael McFaul, "The Fourth Wave of Democracy and Dictatorship: Noncooperative Transitions in the Postcommunist World," *World Politics* 54, no. 2 (2002): 212–44; Thomas Carothers, "The End of the Transition Paradigm," *Journal of Democracy* 13, no. 1 (2002): 5–21; Steven Levitsky and Lucan A. Way, "The Rise of Competitive Authoritarianism," *Journal of Democracy* 13, no. 2 (2002): 51–65; Larry Diamond, "Thinking About Hybrid Regimes," *Journal of Democracy* 13, no. 2 (2002): 21–35; Steven Levitsky and Lucan A. Way, *Competitive Authoritarianism: Hybrid Regimes after the Cold War* (New York: Cambridge University Press, 2010); Lucan A. Way, *Pluralism by Default: Weak Autocrats and the Rise of Competitive Politics* (Baltimore, MD: Johns Hopkins University Press, 2015); Henry Hale, *Patronal Politics: Eurasian Regime Dynamics in Comparative Perspective* (New York: Cambridge University Press, 2015). For recent summaries of the democratization debate, see Larry Diamond, Marc F. Plattner, and Philip J. Costopoulos, eds., *Debates on Democratization* (Baltimore, MD: Johns Hopkins University Press, 2010); Kathryn Stoner and Michael McFaul, eds., *Transitions to Democracy: A Comparative Perspective* (Baltimore, MD: Johns Hopkins University Press, 2013); Larry Diamond and Marc F. Plattner, eds., *Democracy in Decline?* (Baltimore, MD: Johns Hopkins University Press, 2015). Stephan Haggard and Robert R. Kaufman, "Democratization during the Third Wave," *Annual Review of Political Science* 19, no. 1 (2016): 125–44.

[3] Vladimir Gel'man, "Post-Soviet Transitions and Democratization: Towards Theory-Building," *Democratization* 10, no. 2 (2003): 95.

[4] For a review of the relevant growing literature on neopatrimonialism, see Aleksandr Fisun, *Demokratiia, neopatrimonializm i global'nye transformatsii* [Democracy, neopatrimonialism, and global transformations], (Kharkiv: Konstanta, 2006), 154–63. For recent reviews of the concept, see Gero Erdmann and Ulf Engel, "Neopatrimonialism Reconsidered: Critical Review and Elaboration of an Elusive Concept," *Commonwealth & Comparative Politics* 45, no. 1 (2007): 95–119; Anne Pitcher, Mary H. Moran, and Michael Johnston, "Rethinking Patrimonialism and Neopatrimonialism in Africa," *African Studies Review* 52, no. 1 (2009):

125–56; Daniel C. Bach, "Patrimonialism and Neopatrimonialism: Comparative Trajectories and Readings," *Commonwealth & Comparative Politics* 49, no. 3 (2011): 275–94. See also important developments of the concept in Jean Francois Medard, "The Underdeveloped State in Tropical Africa: Political Clientelism or Neo-Patrimonialism," in *Private Patronage and Public Power*, ed. Christopher Clapham (New York: St. Martin's Press, 1982): 162–92; Michael Bratton and Nicholas van de Walle, *Democratic Experiments in Africa: Regime Transitions in a Comparative Perspective* (Cambridge: Cambridge University Press, 1997); Julia Adams and Mounira M. Charrad, eds., *Patrimonial Power in the Modern World* (Thousand Oaks, CA: Sage, 2011); Daniel C. Bach and Mamoudou Gazibo, eds., *Neopatrimonialism in Africa and Beyond* (London: Routledge, 2012).

[5] Max Weber, *Economy and Society: An Outline of Interpretive Sociology*, ed. Guenther Roth and Claus Wittich (Berkeley: University of California Press, 1978), 226–41, 1010–1110.

[6] Robin Theobald, "Patrimonialism," *World Politics* 34, no. 4 (1982): 555.

[7] Weber, *Economy and Society*, 236.

[8] Weber, *Economy and Society*, 236–37.

[9] Guenther Roth, "Introduction," in Weber, *Economy and Society*, xcv.

[10] Weber, *Economy and Society*, 1028–29.

[11] Weber, *Economy and Society*, 237. The way Weber characterizes the process of patrimonialization is *the degree of which in different societies can be very different*: "By virtue of conferment, the prebendary or the vassal has as a rule had a personal *right* to the office bestowed upon him. Like the artisan who possessed the economic means of production, the prebendary possessed the means of administration. He had to bear the costs of administration out of his office fees or other income, or he passed on to the lord only part of the taxes gathered from the subjects, retaining the rest. In the extreme case he could bequeath and alienate his office like other possession." In Max Weber, "The Social Psychology of the World Religions," in *From Max Weber: Essays in Sociology*, edited and translated by H. H. Gerth and C. Wright Mills (New York: Oxford University Press, 1946), 297–98.

[12] Reinhard Bendix, *Max Weber: An Intellectual Portrait* (London: Methuen, 1966), 345.

[13] Guenther Roth, "Personal Rulership, Patrimonialism, and Empire-Building in the New States," *World Politics* 20, no. 2 (1968): 196.

[14] Ibid.

[15] Ibid., 197.

[16] Shmuel Eisenstadt, *Traditional Patrimonialism and Modern Neopatrimonialism* (London: Sage, 1973), 7–30; Idem, *Revolutions and the Transformation of Societies: A Comparative Study of Civilizations* (New York: The Free Press, 1978), 274–310.

[17] Eisenstadt, *Traditional Patrimonialism*, 10.

[18] Eisenstadt, *Revolutions and the Transformation of Societies*, 276.

[19] Eisenstadt, *Traditional Patrimonialism*, 18.

[20] On clientelism and patronage, see Shmuel Eisenstadt and Rene Lemarchand, eds., *Political Clientelism: Patronage and Development* (London: Sage, 1981); Carl H. Landé, "Political Clientelism in Political Studies: Retrospect and Prospects,"

International Political Science Review 4, no. 4 (1983): 435–54; Shmuel Eisenstadt and Luis Roniger, *Patrons, Clients and Friends: Interpersonal Relations and the Structure of Trust in Society* (Cambridge: Cambridge University Press, 1984); Simona Piattoni, ed., *Clientelism, Interests, and Democratic Representation: The European Experience in Historical and Comparative Perspective* (Cambridge: Cambridge University Press, 2001); Herbert Kitschelt and Steven I. Wilkinson, *Patrons, Clients, and Policies: Patterns of Democratic Accountability and Political Competition* (Cambridge: Cambridge University Press, 2007); Allen Hicken, "Clientelism," *Annual Review of Political Science* 14, no. 1 (2011): 289–310.

21 Theobald, "Patrimonialism," 552.

22 Christopher Clapham, *Third World Politics* (Madison: University of Wisconsin Press, 1985), 48. See growing literature on informal polities and informal governance: Hans-Joachim Lauth, "Informal Institutions and Democracy," *Democratization* 7, no. 4 (2000): 21–50; Gretchen Helmke and Steven Levitsky, "Informal Institutions and Comparative Politics: A Research Agenda," *Perspectives on Politics* 2, no. 4 (2004): 725–40; Steven Levitsky and Gretchen Helmke, eds., *Informal Institutions and Democracy: Lessons from Latin America* (Baltimore, MD: Johns Hopkins University Press, 2006); Thomas Christiansen and Christine Neuhold, eds., *The International Handbook on Informal Governance* (Cheltenham: Edward Elgar, 2012).

23 Weber, *Economy and Society*, 231–32.

24 Ibid., 240.

25 A sophisticated, innovative analysis suggested, for example, by Georgi Derluguian, implements a comprehensive reconstruction the dynamics of the collapse of state socialism and the subsequent post-Soviet development paths. His interpretation of "nationalization provincial revolutions" in 1990 is based on the idea of the neo-patrimonial nature of post-Soviet Eurasia states. See Georgi Derluguian, *Bourdieu's Secret Admirer in the Caucasus: A World-System Biography* (Chicago: University of Chicago Press, 2005), 15–16, 222–28; Georgi Derluguian and Timothy Earle, "Strong Chieftaincies Out of Weak States, or Elemental Power Unbound," in *Troubled Regions and Failing States: The Clustering and Contagion of Armed Conflicts*, ed. Kristian Berg Harpviken (Bingley: Emerald Group Publishing, 2010), 51–76.

26 Valerie Bunce, "Comparative Democratization: Big and Bounded Generalizations," *Comparative Political Studies* 33, nos. 6–7 (2000): 703–34; Taras Kuzio, "Transition in Post-Communist States: Triple or Quadruple?" *Politics* 21, no. 3 (2001): 168–77; Anna Grzymala-Busse and Pauline Jones Luong, "Reconceptualizing the State: Lessons from Post-Communism," *Politics & Society* 30, no. 4 (2002): 529–54; Grzegorz Ekiert and Stephen E. Hanson, eds., *Capitalism and Democracy in Central and Eastern Europe: Assessing the Legacy of Communist Rule* (Cambridge: Cambridge University Press, 2003); Jeffrey Kopstein, "Post-Communist Democracy: Legacies and Outcomes," *Comparative Politics* 35, no. 1 (2003): 231–50.

27 Taras Kuzio, "Transition in Post-Communist States: Triple or Quadruple?" *Politics* 21, no. 3 (2001): 171.

[28] Indeed, elements of patrimonial practices have been repeatedly noted by many researchers in various aspects of post-Soviet political development. For examples, see Vladimir Shlapentokh, "Early Feudalism—the Best Parallel for Contemporary Russia," *Europe-Asia Studies* 48, no. 3 (1996): 393–411; Donald N. Jensen, "How Russia Is Ruled – 1998," *Demokratizatsiya: The Journal of Post-Soviet Democratization* 7, no. 3 (1999): 341–69; Steven Solnick, "Russia's 'Transition': Is Democracy Delayed Democracy Denied?" *Social Research* 66, no. 3 (1999): 789–824; Kimitaka Matsuzato, "From Communist Boss Politics to Post-Communist Caciquismo—the Meso-Elite and Meso-Governments in Post-Communist Countries," *Communist and Post-Communist Studies* 34, no. 2 (2001): 175–201; William Tompson, "Putin's Challenge: The Politics of Structural Reform in Russia," *Europe-Asia Studies* 54, no. 6 (2002): 933–57; Allen Lynch, *How Russia is Not Ruled: Reflections on Russian Political Development* (Cambridge: Cambridge University Press, 2005); Vadim Volkov, *Violent Entrepreneurs: The Use of Force in the Making of Russian Capitalism* (Ithaca, NY: Cornell University Press, 2002); Alena V. Ledeneva, *Can Russia Modernise? Sistema, Power Networks and Informal Governance* (Cambridge: Cambridge University Press, 2013). Yet neither the Weberian theory of patrimonialism, nor modern neopatrimonialistic conceptions have attracted serious attention from post-Soviet researchers in the 1990s. The only exception is the work of Mikhail V. Maslovski, which examines the Weberian treatment of patrimonialism for the first time in a post-Soviet setting, as well as its applicability to an interpretation of the Soviet past. See Mikhail Maslovski, "Max Weber's Concept of Patrimonialism and the Soviet System," *Sociological Review* 44, no. 2 (1996): 294–308. Among the most interesting recent revivals of the concept as a leading framework for understanding the post-Soviet politics, society, and regime developments, see: Vladimir Gel'man, "The Vicious Circle of Post-Soviet Neopatrimonialism in Russia," *Post-Soviet Affairs* 32, no. 5 (2016): 455–73; for more wider scope of *patronal politics*, see Henry Hale, *Patronal Politics: Eurasian Regime Dynamics in Comparative Perspective* (New York: Cambridge University Press, 2015).

[29] Political science implies that political entrepreneurs are to be perceived as people, who invest various kinds of resources into politics, counting on the future returns in the form of the state policy that would be beneficial to them. In modern political-economic literature, rent-seeking in the broad sense is determined as struggle for the politically based provision of favors and privileges. In the more narrow sense, this means "striving for the direct nonproductive profit" i.e. privatization not of the real, but of politically derived margin in the form of rent. Rent-seeking to a significant degree is one of the elements of Weberian political capitalism and is a consequence of the partimonialization of the state public policy. In our context, reference to rent-seeking specifies the neopatrimonial version of such methods for capital accumulation.

[30] See Weber, *Economy and Society*, 164–66.

[31] Ibid., 238.

[32] Weber, *Economy and Society*, 240; see also 199, 1091.

[33] Weber, "The Social Psychology of the World Religions," 300.

34 Max Weber, "The Profession and Vocation of Politics," in *Political Writings*, ed. Peter Lassman and Ronald Speirs (Cambridge: Cambridge University Press, 1994), 320.

35 Eisenstadt, *Revolutions and the Transformation of Societies*, 276–78; Id., *Traditional Patrimonialism*, 14–17.

36 Eisenstadt, *Revolutions and the Transformation of Societies*, 288.

37 H. E. Chehabi and Juan J. Linz, eds., *Sultanistic Regimes* (Baltimore, MD: Johns Hopkins University Press, 1998); Farid Guliyev, "Post-Soviet Azerbaijan: Transition to Sultanistic Semiauthoritarianism? An Attempt at Conceptualization," *Democratizatsiya* 13, no. 3 (2005): 393–435. Marlene Laruelle, "Discussing Neopatrimonialism and Patronal Presidentialism in the Central Asian Context," *Democratizatsiya: The Journal of Post-Soviet Democratization* 20, no. 4 (2012): 301–24.

38 On sources of competitive politics in post-Soviet Eurasia, see Henry Hale, "Regime cycles: Democracy, Autocracy, and Revolution in Post-Soviet Eurasia," *World Politics* 58, no. 1 (2005): 133–65; Hale, "Democracy or Autocracy on the March? The Colored Revolutions as Normal Dynamics of Patronal Presidentialism," *Communist & Post-Communist Studies* 39, no. 3 (2006): 305–29; Hale, "Formal Constitutions in Informal Politics: Institutions and Democratization in Eurasia," *World Politics* 63, no. 4 (2011): 581–617; Lucan A. Way, "Authoritarian State Building and the Sources of Regime Competitiveness in the Fourth Wave: The Cases of Belarus, Moldova, and Ukraine," *World Politics* 57, no. 2 (2005): 231–51. On neopatrimonial democracy in Ukraine, see Oleksandr Fisun, "Ukrainian Teeter-Totter: Vices and Virtues of a Neopatrimonial Democracy," *PONARS Eurasia Policy Memo*, no. 120 (October 2010); Oleksandr Fisun. "The Future of Ukraine's Neopatrimonial Democracy," *PONARS Eurasia Policy Memo*, no. 394 (October 2015).

BÁLINT MAGYAR

Towards a terminology for post-communist regimes

I. Regime change stranded in historical legacy

The formula for regime change following the collapse of the East European communist regimes in 1989–1990 seemed clear: to take the step from **one-party communist dictatorship** with a state monopoly on property to a multi-party parliamentary democracy based on private property ownership and a market economy. This model, established by the Western democracies, is called liberal democracy, which can take either presidential or parliamentary forms. The institutional guarantees at the heart of liberal democracy are: in political terms, the separation of powers, provisions for removing incumbent authorities, and a competitive process for gaining power; and, in the economic sphere, guarantees for the preeminence of private property, free market competition, and the security provided by property rights.

When legal norms are violated in a **liberal democracy**, mechanisms of institutional control and the division of powers will—more or less—correct such deviations. If these mechanisms work properly, deviations of this sort do not achieve a critical mass, and so do not pose a threat to the system. However, if the deviations from the legal standards of liberal democracy are not only present in great number, but form the mainstream goals and values of government, then we can speak of a new system, with dominant characteristics that set it apart from other type of regimes.

At the same time, it could also be observed that the more east a newly established post-communist regime is located, the more likely it is for it to escape (or never enter) the gravitational pull of Western liberal democracies, and thus create its own fields of power and continue on a separate orbit. Yet it would be a mistake to describe these countries merely in terms of their "deficiencies" with respect to the ideals of liberal democracy. We must face the fact that there exist deeply influential, historically constituted value structures and cultural patterns that limit the possibility of social-political transformation.

During the Cold War era, Hungarian historian Jenő Szűcs spoke of three historically defined regions of Europe,[1] arguing that long before the World War II, a East-Central European region existed but was a part of what was then the Soviet Bloc. He discerned the eastern perimeter of East-Central Europe as the border between Western and Orthodox Christianity. The territory of the post-World War II Soviet Union only deviated from this border in two places: on the one hand, it re-annexed the Catholic and Protestant Baltic states Russia had once already conquered under the Czars, while on the other, the Balkan states that were largely or wholly within the dominion of Orthodox Christianity (Bulgaria, Romania and parts of Yugoslavia) did not belong to the Soviet Union. But after the failure of the communist system and the breakdown of the USSR the socially determined, centuries-old cultural and religious borders sprang once again to life and are, in some measure, associated with geographic patterns of political development.

This has implications for Western illusions regarding the democratization of former communist countries. After all, even after the 2004 expansion of the EU, it gradually became clear that it was a major question whether the democratic institutional system established in Western Europe could be extended, and if so, whether it would take root. Is it possible to cross the divide of Western value systems along the "distinctly marked border splitting Europe along the southern reaches of the Elbe-Saale, the Leitha, and further along the western border of ancient Pannonia"? For it was along this line, "the eastern border of the Carolingian Empire around 800 AD," that the "organic symbiosis of late Antique Christianity and barbarian Germanic elements had taken place over the previous three centuries."[2]

But it is the dismantling not only of the border between cultures and value systems that the Leitha represents at issue here, but also of the border dividing East-Central Europe from Eastern Europe—**Western Christianity from the Orthodox.** Even under the relatively uniform rule of communist dictatorship, this socio-cultural border held strong. A team of East-Central European scholars has branded the form of communism present on the eastern side of this border **patrimonial communism.**[3]

There, formal state structures were permeated by extended, hierarchical power networks led by patrons who plied patronage and selective punishments to keep both elites and masses in line while subtly competing for power within the regime—a phenomenon that Henry E. Hale calls *patronalism*. Such features were particularly evident in the USSR, Albania, Bulgaria, Macedonia and Romania, with patronalistic (patrimonial) elements only slightly weaker in the Baltic republics and Serbia. Other states featured a more **formal-rational type of communism**, including the Czech Republic, East Germany, Poland, Hungary, Slovenia, and Croatia.[4]

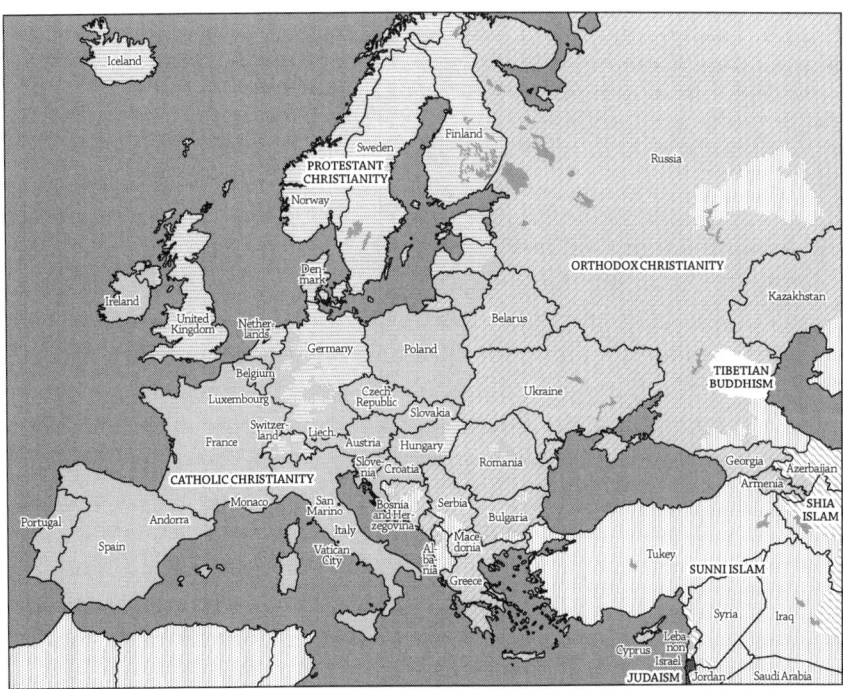

Figure 4.1. *Traditional religions in Europe by country (2014)*

Among the former Soviet states, furthest afield from Western Europe we find Central Asia representing a distinct region of its own in terms of this social makeup and value system. Today this region is characterized by the revitalization of Islam, the presence of relatively few ethnic Russians, and a correspondingly small Orthodox Christian population (Kazakhstan had the largest proportion of ethnic Russians in Central Asia, but since 1989 that percentage has dropped from 38 to 20 percent of the total population).

Table 4.1. *The proportion of Muslim and ethnic Russian population in the former states of the Soviet Republic in Central Asia after 2010*

	Muslim (%)	Ethnic Russian (%)
Azerbaijan	97	1.3
Kazakhstan	70	20
Kyrgyzstan	88	6
Tajikistan	97	0.5
Turkmenistan	93	2
Uzbekistan	96	4

Source: Pew Research Center, "Religious Composition by Country, 2010–2050," http://www.pewforum.org/2015/04/02/religious-projection-table/2010/percent/all/; Sebastien Peyrouse, *The Russian Minority in Central Asia: Migration, Politics, and Language*, (Woodrow Wilson International Center for Scholars, 2008), 3–5; and https://en.wikipedia.org/wiki/Ethnic_Russians_in_post-Soviet_states, accessed August 28, 2017.

The argument that a value system shaped by religious affiliation simultaneously carries an imprint, and provides a coherent framework for other "secular" values as well, is demonstrated by Inglehart and Welzel's cultural map, in which the dimensions of survival versus self-expression can equally be interpreted as the scale of closed versus open societies.

The illusion that liberal democracy could be exported, the idea of its "Drang nach Osten" (Eastwards push), was grounded in the presumption that after the collapse of communist power the political system of liberal democracy could be raised over its ruins. The assumption was that, irrespective of prevalent value structures, such an undertaking would be merely a question of a propitious historical moment and political will. But these autonomously shifting "tectonic plates" of historically predetermined value structures do not support just any odd political construction one might want to establish.

The evaporation of the confidence placed in the democratization of autocracies within the former communist bloc was followed not much later by the fizzling out of democratic hopes vested in the "Arab Spring." Where the failure of the democratic experiments did not obliterate stateness, nations faced either the restoration of an autocratic system similar to what preceded the democratic upheavals (as in Egypt) or the rise of a different

Figure 4.2. Inglehart–Welzel Cultural Map

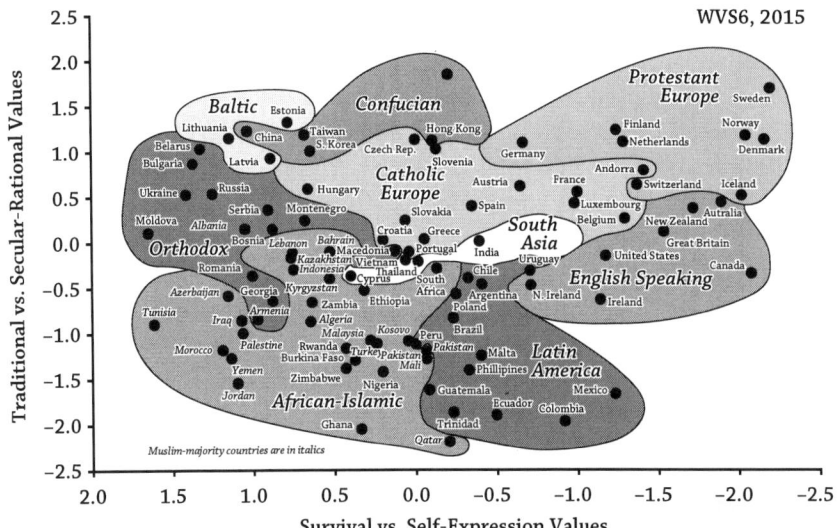

Analysis of World Values Survey data made by political scientists Ronald Inglehart and Christian Welzel asserts that there are two major dimensions of cross cultural variation in the world: **Traditional values** versus **Secular-rational values** and **Survival values** versus **Self-expression values**. The global cultural map (below) shows how scores of societies are located on these two dimensions. Moving upward on this map reflects the shift from Traditional values to Secular-rational and moving rightward reflects the shift from Survival values to Self–expression values.

- *Traditional values* emphasize the importance of religion, parent-child ties, deference to authority and traditional family values. People who embrace these values also reject divorce, abortion, euthanasia and suicide. These societies have high levels of national pride and a nationalistic outlook. *Secular-rational values* have the opposite preferences to the traditional values. These societies place less emphasis on religion, traditional family values and authority. Divorce, abortion, euthanasia and suicide are seen as relatively acceptable. (Suicide is not necessarily more common.)
- *Survival values* place emphasis on economic and physical security. It is linked with a relatively ethnocentric outlook and low levels of trust and tolerance. *Self-expression values* give high priority to environmental protection, growing tolerance of foreigners, gays and lesbians and gender equality, and rising demands for participation in decision-making in economic and political life.

Source: World Values Survey wave 6 2010–2014, 2015

"nationalist" autocratic form (as in a significant majority of the former Soviet member states). Moreover, presently we are witnesses to the dismantling of a secular state (Turkey), and thereby a pillar of the democratic setup. However, where stateness was practically erased in the course of civil wars that erupted during the democratic transition (e.g., Libya, Syria), a political-social disaster has obtained that reaches far beyond these countries themselves. In the wake of these crises, the burning issue for liberal democracies has become less how to maintain democracy export and more how to avoid "autocracy import." This question, however, falls beyond the purview of this chapter.

The three "historical regions" of the former Soviet Empire—firstly the socialist countries outside the Soviet Union, secondly the European member states of the Soviet Union, and thirdly the former member states of the Soviet Union in Central Asia—have varying potential for adapting to the institutional system of liberal democracy.[5]

The former East-Central European socialist countries (now including the Baltic states) are bound to the economies of the EU member states through innumerable ties after having entered the gravitational field of the European Union. The change of direction in foreign trade had already begun by the seventies and only intensified after the change of regimes and the transition crisis. The dissolution of Comecon in 1991 was only a post-hoc acknowledgement of what had already de facto taken place. Economic reorientation was only further entrenched by the privatization of a decisive portion of state property, bringing Western capital into a favorable position everywhere (though to varying degrees). Then the expansion of the European Union between 2004 and 2013 also incorporated a decisive majority of those former socialist countries that had been outside of the Soviet Union, and all those that had historically belonged to a Western Christian Church.

A precondition for accession was the establishment of a liberal democratic institutional system. Therefore, the only question for these countries was who would win the inner struggle between an imported and more or less domesticated Western institutional system and what many perceived as an Eastern culture weighed down by a communist past. Those optimistic in the outcome believed that shortcomings in the operation of the democratic institutional system, the provisions for human rights, or the proper managing of public finances were only temporary difficulties that could be handled through the control of EU institutions (the stick) and the desired access to of EU resources (the carrot). In terms of traditional corruption, Romania and Bulgaria seemed to be the most infected countries, but the consecutive governments of each state upheld their strong commitments to the EU. In contrast, the Hungarian autocratic attempt of 2010 signifies both a new standard of corruption (on par with a centrally directed state criminal organization) and a challenge to those EU leaders trying to implant EU values in a state that its own leaders see as a "resource cow" there to be milked.

For the European Soviet republics, the change of regime meant only a collapse of the communist power structure. This was followed not by the consistent development of liberal democratic institutions but rather a presidential system that gave only limited rein to democratic institutions. Even the development of such presidentialism was in some instances preempted—or accompanied during various crises—by the weakening of stateness and the appearance of a sort of oligarchic anarchy in the wake of massive privatization. For them, the gravitational pull of the EU was faint, and where present—as in Moldova and Ukraine—it was used more to defend against what they saw as renewed Russian expansionism and empire-building than as part of any attempt to actually adopt the EU's liberal socio-structural values.

In the former Soviet republics of Central Asia, it was typically old communist structures themselves (especially the top levels of the party and secret service nomenklatura) that turn directly into the "reformed" national centers of power.

II. Underlying structural determinants of the major types of the post-communist regimes

The following pages will focus on three structural elements that had a deep impact and, I argue, historically determined the development of different post-communist regime types, providing a framework that they could not easily escape.

Claus Offe divides the field of possible social activities into three categories: **political, market, and communal activities**. As he explains,

> political action is embedded in a state structure and framed within features such as the acquisition and use of legitimate authority, accountability, hierarchy, and the use of rule-bound power for giving orders and extracting resources. Its intrinsic standard of goodness is

legality. Market action is recognized by the contract-based pursuit of acquisitive interests within the framework of legal rules that specify, among other things such as property rights, the universe of items that can be "for sale," and which cannot. Its standard of goodness is success or *profitability*. Finally, communal action is defined by a sense of reciprocal obligation among persons who share significant markers of identity and cultural belonging, that is, belonging to the same family, religious group, locality, and so on. The standard of goodness of communal action is shared *values and shared notions of virtue*. Now, in each of these three realms of social action, we can distinguish "appropriate," or consistent modes from "hybrid" and inappropriate ones.[6]

The separation of these three spheres of social action—a centuries-long development—is peculiar to European society. The fulfillment of the separation is achieved in liberal democracies, where not only does the institutional system map the separation of these spheres, but specific regulations and a series of guarantees excluding conflicts of interest regulate the manner in which these spheres interact and diverge. Proceeding from the West towards the East, it can be observed that this separation of the spheres of social action has either not, or only rudimentarily, been realized. And the communist regimes rising to power in 1917 (and after 1945) not only halted this process where it had begun or been developed, but reversed it. The framework of totalitarian communist ideology and established order liquidated the three spheres of social action, private property, the private sphere, and autonomous communities, uniting them in a single neo-archaic form. If this change impacted Central Eastern Europe as a regression, going further east it meant that the process of separation was arrested and frozen.

As a result of the Western separation of these three categories of social action, social relations not only within the spheres in question but within the whole political-economic sphere progress in a fundamentally formalized, impersonal system. Where the separation of social activities is rudimentary, or not in evidence, one typically sees informal and personal relations dominating instead of formalized, impersonal networks. These relations tend to be organized into patron-client patterns of subservience, into **patronal networks**.[7]

The differentiation of communist regimes as described above—**formal-rational communist regimes** and **patrimonial communist regimes**—reflects the peculiarity of these regimes. In other words, if societies that are characterized by an advanced level of separation between different types of social activities are taken over by a communist regime, the resulting system, the inevitable regression in this regard notwithstanding, will still maintain some characteristics of the earlier bureaucratic-rational rule (as defined by Max Weber). These countries can be categorized as the least patronalistic, formal-rational communist regimes.

Table 4.2. Legacies of Patronalism at the End of Communist Rule

Most Patronalistic	Albania, Armenia, Azerbaijan, Belarus, Bulgaria, Georgia, Kazakhstan, Kyrgyzstan, Macedonia, Moldova, Romania, Russia, Tajikistan, Turkmenistan, Ukraine, Uzbekistan
Moderately Patronalistic	Estonia, Latvia, Lithuania, Serbia, Slovakia
Least Patronalistic	Croatia, Czech Republic, East Germany (DDR), Hungary, Poland, Slovenia

Source: Henry E. Hale, *Patronal Politics: Eurasian Regime Dynamics in Comparative Perspective* (Cambridge University Press, 2015), 60

We can observe that the more informal and personal matters affect the way public power is wielded through patronal networks, the less a separation will be observed between the rulers and the ruled assets—to use Weber's terminology.[8] By these means the **administrative powers of their public offices are appropriated for private use**. These networks

> break the frame of accountability, legal rules, and so on, and employ the powers of office for private and self-serving ends; they act in rent-seeking ways rather than according to their rules of office. That is to say, they tyrannize citizens, steal or embezzle public assets, and impose arbitrary taxes in order to increase their personal income. . . . In such societies, which lack standards of differentiation between political, economic, and communal modes of action, it is only from an external perspective of observers applying such standards that corruption becomes visible as such.[9]

In the post-communist regimes where the **appropriation of public authority for private interests** (in other words corruption, and especially grand corruption) is typical, these are not the objectionable and superficial concomitant phenomena of the established system, but constituent factors of the regime.

If analyses of post-communist regimes do not tackle the three definitive factors mentioned above (the extent to which the spheres of social action are separated, public authority is organized into a patron-client system, and public authority is appropriated for private interests), they will fall into the trap of simply considering the regimes as different levels of deviation from liberal democracy, thereby ruling out the possibility of hypothesizing their existence as independent systems. Analyses expounding this approach usually only focus on the political institutional system and the ideologies used in practice, and treat the otherwise decisive role of ownership relations rather offhandedly. It ought to be clear that a number of post-communist regimes, having come under the influence (and into the institutional circle) of the European Union, may thus be described using the conceptual framework applicable to liberal democracies. But it should be equally clear that an attempt to do so with the rest of the post-communist regimes is misleading because it does not allow for the obvious possibility that these may not be temporary stages on the path towards democracy, but the "terminus" of another type of regime.

III. The end of the "transition paradigm" and the inadequacy of the conceptual framework used to describe liberal democracy in characterizing post-communist regimes

In the decades following the change of regimes, one of the first illusions that had to be overcome was the unlimited extendibility of liberal democracy. But this did not constitute a break with the vocabulary and grammar that presupposed post-communist regimes could be described with the categories used to characterize the institutional systems of liberal democracy, reflecting the measure of deviance from the expected by applying the appropriate privative suffix. This has two damaging consequences from the perspective of gaining an understanding of post-communist regimes. Firstly, if unintentionally, it relegates constituent phenomena of the system (such as the mutually reliant concentration of power and property) to a secondary category of importance. Secondly, it still considers the conditions characteristic of liberal democracies as the organizational principles of the regimes in question, and marks the defining traits out as mere deviancies that are surmountable and are to be surmounted. Efforts to break out of this linguistic trap took two directions.

III/1. An interpretation along the democracy–dictatorship axis

Interpreting the democratic deficit and functional disorders that followed the dissolution of the communist regimes in Eastern Europe presents a scene of great variety. Attempts at description usually try to interpret the political processes that took place in the post-communist states **along the liberal democracy-dictatorship axis**. The post-communist countries set off in the direction of the liberal democratic world, but had not yet arrived. Alternatively: though they had progressed a great deal along this path, they stalled, perhaps turned around. Transitology appears not only as a transformation of social systems, but also as a reference to its own literal meaning: these systems are underway, and form different models according to the rate of their distance or deviation from liberal democracy.

Some analysts label the systems in transition with specific phrases, **adding a restrictive qualifier or a privative suffix to the term of democracy**: illiberal, controlled, restricted, quasi, partial, etc. democracy—trying to determine the level of deviance on the basis of various institutional indicators, and they assess whether the respective system passes the democracy test in light of such aggregated scores.

Others have come to feel that a more accurate impression is offered by describing these systems as versions of **autocracies or dictatorships with the addition of softening adjectives**—semi-autocratic regime, soft dictatorship or for that matter, competitive, electoral autocracy.

Terms like **hybrid regimes** or related labels are also indicative of **attempts to place the systems along the democracy-dictatorship scale**, but these no longer seek to define the respective establishment in correlation to one or the other end of the scale.

What is common to these approaches is that the various ruling establishments are defined by formal and technical features rather than in a substantive sense. One intrinsic weakness of these scaling attempts along the democracy-dictatorship axis is that they reduce the institutional distortions of liberal democracies to mere quantitative indicators. Moreover, they do not treat them as sovereign systems, but as sets of isolated, uncorrelated indicators. Of course, scaling seems to allow for a quantitative comparison of various autocratic regimes, but at the same time it excludes specific systemic differences from the analysis. So these—otherwise politically useful and orienting—procedures and aggregates of democratic deficit indicators allow for a perception of the degree of deviation from the "ideal" state of affairs, but they are no help in terms of the specific, systemic nature of the deviation.

A study by János Kornai also signifies a break with the transition paradigm, when in providing the **typology of the institutional system of post-communist regimes**, he divides the types of **democracy, autocracy and dictatorship** along primary and secondary traits.[10] These types are presented not as stations of a strictly linear development, but as marking independent, stable political systems. Crossing from one to the other is therefore not unidirectional, but possible both ways (See Table 2.2 in this volume).

The post-communist countries of Eurasia can be categorized according to the above as observed in their political institutional systems in the following way:

Table 4.3. *Post-communist countries of Eurasia by political institutional system (based on János Kornai)*

Democracies	Autocracies	Dictatorships
Albania, Bulgaria, Croatia, Czech Republic, Estonia, Georgia, Latvia, Lithuania, Macedonia, Moldova, Poland, Romania, Serbia, Slovakia, Slovenia, Ukraine	Armenia, Azerbaijan, Belarus, Hungary, Kazakhstan, Kyrgyzstan*, Russia, Tajikistan, Uzbekistan	China, North Korea, Turkmenistan, Vietnam

* In the process of shifting from autocracy to dictatorship.

In perusing the lists, in spite of the clear-cut criteria, a sense of uncertainty nevertheless is bound to prevail. This stems partly from the fact that if approached in their dynamic reality the regimes' seemingly stable categorizations may change. Though generally, a majority of the countries in question do find a stable place in one of the categories, changes do occur. The most spectacular shifts in this sense were those of Georgia in the direction of the democracies, and that of Hungary towards autocracy. Similarly, the categorization of certain Central Asian post-soviet regimes may give cause for some indecision, as they—among them Turkmenistan—teeter on the brink between being an autocracy and being a dictatorship. In fact, this shift between autocracy and democracy may take place repeatedly in the post-regime-change history of a country, as in the cases of Ukraine and Moldova.

Another reason for a sense of unease with regard to the categorization of these countries is that though the Western post-communist countries may be called democracies when compared to the post-communist autocratic regimes, if they are pitted against the Western liberal democracies it becomes palpably clear that the nature of the democracies in question is not the same. The grounds on which the difference can be established is to be found in the prevalent level of patronalism. An axis can be drawn within the category of democratic countries from **liberal democracies** to **patronal democracies** on this basis. In liberal democracies, the above-cited traits of democracies as set out by Kornai serve to balance the formally defined civil institutions, while in patronal democracies they strike a balance between the informal, competing patronal networks. Along these lines Slovenia and Estonia would be found at the end of the scale closest to Western liberal democracies, while Moldova and Ukraine would be closest to the autocracies. In the latter two countries, what separates them from the post-communist autocracies with a single-pyramid arrangement of power networks is that no patronal network has succeeded in securing a permanently dominant, monopoly position in either country. Though attempts were made to establish one, social resistance limited the positions of the patronal networks claiming a monopoly on power and established a new dynamic balance between the various competing patronal networks. As will be discussed later, anti-corruption government action declared the liquidation of the different informal patronal networks as their goal. However there is a significant difference between an intention to shift in a politically neutral manner from a system built on patron-client relations to the formalized transparent institutions of liberal democracy grounded in equal rights, and the mere use of the anti-corruption campaign by a dominant patronal network to undermine or liquidate the rival patronal networks in the framework of a politically selective law-enforcement action.

So it is apparent that the formalized political institutions and the authority invested in them may cover wholly divergent types of collective actors.

III/2. Moving on to the substantive—sociological, anthropological—concepts of description

Other analytical approaches refer to **types of systems** that challenge liberal democracy, such as "majoritarian democracy," "dominant-party system," "one-party system," or "authoritarian democracy." These notions do not directly link issues of power concentration and wealth accumulation. This linkage is partly made by labels alluding to the **illegitimate beneficiaries of the regime**, including "clientelist regime," "crony capitalism," or "kleptocracy." These definitions reflect fertile perceptual shifts in the explanation of post-communist regimes, but the adjectives used as complex categories provide only a limited understanding due to their presuppositions and underlying subtext. **Clientelist**, as an adjective, does not express the illegitimacy of the relationship, for example. And the term **crony**, in the context of corrupt transactions, assumes parties or partners of equal rank (even if acting in different roles) and implies voluntary transactions—occasional, though repeatable—that can be terminated or continued by either party at their will and without consequences.

As for the arrangement connoted by the term **kleptocratic**, it does not reflect the real nature of most post-communist regimes in a number of ways. First, the notion of kleptocracy does not generally imply an aggressive takeover of property but rather the simple hijacking of current revenue through classical mechanisms of corruption. Second, the kleptocratic regime does not establish a system based on permanent patron-client relations of subservience. Third, the kleptocratic system is not necessarily centralized or monopolized; it could also be decentralized, or even anarchic. Fourth, the notion of kleptocracy does not well capture coercion, instead highlighting mainly the exploitation of opportunities offered up by circumstance.

The conceptual framework we desire for post-communist regimes should not only highlight deviation from the norms of liberal democracy and emphasize the appropriate techniques of power concentration, but should also depict the underlying nature and structure of the ruling elite. This is the aim of the authors of this volume who, breaking with the hybrid regime paradigm, attempt to convey the sui generis traits of post-communist regimes through the adaptation and reformulation of Max Weber's typology for systems of rule. It is with this ambition in mind that some observers of the change in the praxis of power and administration—attentive to the expansion of informal, personal chains of command and the growing distance from liberal democracy—sometimes describe the resulting regimes as featuring the characteristics of a reincarnated **feudal system of vassalage**, which is often labeled a **neopatrimonial** system.[11] "Where domination is primarily traditional, even though it is exercised by virtue of the ruler's personal autonomy, it will be called *patrimonial authority*," writes Weber. He continues, "where it indeed operates primarily on the basis of discretion, it will be called *sultanism*. The transition is definitely continuous. Both forms of domination are distinguished from *elementary* patriarchalism by the presence of a personal *staff*."

One might thus ask: If this description fits the administrative practices of the single-pyramid patronal networks and the mafia states in evidence in the post-communist world, why cannot the system simply be considered patrimonial? Because even as the term is suitable to spotlight the historical regression taking place in public administration and the professional apparatus—if it had previously existed at all—it does not describe the system as a whole. This can be seen in three ways.

First, the (neo)patrimonial term cannot be used, because a patrimonial system inherently carries its own legitimation: The lord does not require reaffirmation from his underlings; he is not chosen. The case of the mafia state, examined later in this volume, illustrates the problem. The sociological nature of rule in the mafia state (indeed based on personal discretion rather than normative decisions and generally on patron-client relations) and the legitimacy of the system (absent in the case of mafia states) are not in harmony with one another, failing to coincide. More generally, whereas in the case of the feudal states of old, the real nature of power and its legitimacy overlapped in a kind of natural harmony and required no illegitimate mechanisms for alignment, this is not the case most post-communist regimes.

Second, the mafia state does not permeate the entire administration, but only those of its parts and levels that are important from the point of view of ideology, power, and wealth accumulation. In other areas (those not important in terms of the above considerations), it is enough for the leadership to ensure the option of intervention as it pleases and the loyalty of the apparatus, as well as—if it is deemed worthwhile—the possibility of rewarding its clients through the distribution of employment positions. The complete disruption of the complex system of professional administration required by modern society would not even be in its interest. The possibilities of intervention are all-inclusive, but they are only applied when necessary.

Third—though for different reasons—neither democracies nor classic autocracies nor dictatorships necessitate the institution of "stooges," or "front men," an important type of actor that will be discussed later in this volume. According to these standard existing conceptions of regimes, everyone is simply who they are, be it as defined by the rule of law or by compulsion. As we will see, this assumption is unwarranted and misleading in the post-communist world.

III/3. Patronal politics—post-communist mafia state

In terms of the analytical tools appropriate for analyzing post-communist mafia states and other kinds of regimes, Henry E. Hale's set of categories comes closest. "Patronal politics," he writes, refers to "politics in societies where individuals organize their political and economic pursuits primarily around the personalized exchange of concrete rewards and punishments through chains of actual acquaintance, and not primarily around abstract, impersonal principles such as ideological belief or categorizations like economic class that include many people one has not actually met in person." Politics, therefore, tends to revolve heavily around individualized punishments and awards, and those who can "mete these out" most effectively and organize informal patron-client hierarchies tend to dominate. The main actors in post-Soviet politics, he argues, thus tend to be extensive, hierarchical networks of actual personal acquaintance. How these patronal networks coordinate their activities vis-à-vis each other drives whether a country appears to be more or less democratic at any given point in time. When networks coordinate political activities around a single chief patron a "single-pyramid" system results that can appear highly autocratic. Networks can also arrange themselves in multiple "competing pyramids," with none dominating the other and hence underpinning a much more open form of politics.[12] Hale argues that this conceptual framework applies not only to post-Soviet politics but also to earlier eras in the history of Eurasian societies. As such, it is a broader concept than "post-communist mafia state," which describes a specific form of patronal politics commonly seen in the post-Soviet historical period. In particular, "post-communist mafia state" connotes the combination of two things: first, a particular organizational form developed by the "adopted political family" (the conveyor of the single-pyramid arrangement, so named to capture an aspect of its ruling culture); and second, its illegitimacy, even according to the legal norms it has itself declared.

IV. A comparative conceptual terminology of liberal democracies, post-communist autocracies and communist regimes—the main collective actors

At this point in the discussion of post-communist regimes, there is no getting around the problem that if one wants to break away from the underlying presuppositions of the transition paradigm, it is scarcely enough to change the words used to label the regimes. After all, it would be self-defeating to rename the typical post-communist regime while failing to follow through and conceptually reestablish its component elements accordingly. Such a failure would simply carry mistaken presumptions forward regarding how these elements operate (and even regarding what they really are).

The proposed new conceptual framework must be built upon, and correspond with, the three fundamental ideas outlined earlier:
- rudimentary or no separation of spheres of social action;
- organization of executive power according to a patron-client system;
- privatization of public authority.

My attempt to refresh the conceptual framework rests essentially on Hale's *Patronal Politics* and my own *Post-Communist Mafia State*.[13] It is based on contrasting the conceptual categories of **ideal-typical liberal democracy** with conceptual categories found useful for describing post-communist regimes. Using these categories as the two extremes at either end of a scale, one can place the praxis found in a given post-communist regime depending on their position in the three areas described above. In what follows, I use the term of **ideal-typical post-communist autocracy** for those regimes that fall outside the gravitational pull of Western liberal democracies. The success or failure of particular policies can of course override "historical determinism" to a limited degree. That is to say—as previously mentioned—even an EU member state, such as Hungary, may swerve markedly towards being an autocratic post-communist regime, and, vice-versa, countries historically belonging to the latter category may incorporate characteristics of liberal democracy. For example, Georgia constantly improved its position on the World Bank "control of corruption" ranking from 1996 to 2014, going from the most corrupt formerly Soviet state to the least, achieving equal status with Slovenia.[14] This means that while Georgia was effective in limiting the activity of informal patronal networks and forcing its political system into more formalized, impersonal institutions, Hungary went in the opposite direction. It did away with individual and institutional autonomy supported by formalized regulations and built informal patron-client relations that span increasingly large swaths of society. In using the term **communist regime**, I refer to its "classical" historical form.

Table 4.4. *State – society relationships in three ideal-type political regimes*

Liberal democracy	Post-communist autocracy	Communist regime
democracy	autocracy	dictatorship
constitutional state (*Rechtstaat*)	criminal state / mafia state	party state
separation of powers	connected powers	merger of powers
separation of church and state	client church	church repressed by state
conflict of public and private interests	fusion of public and private interests	repression of private interests
transparent / regulated *cooperation* and *connections* between public and private spheres	non-transparent / informal *collusion* of public and private spheres	*subordination* of private interests to state sphere

IV/1. Main collective actors: ruling elite of patronal networks—adopted political family

In the ideal-typical liberal democracy, formally defined institutions, imagined communities and horizontal political organizations are the main collective actors. In the ideal-typical post-communist regime, in contrast, the main collective actors are patronal, informal, hierarchical networks of clients that extend far beyond any single formal institution. If one of the patronal networks is dominant in a country and gains a monopoly for itself or a coalition of networks that it leads, we can speak of a **single-pyramid patronal system**. On the other hand, if some sort of a balance between competing patronal networks evolves, that would be a multi-pyramid or **competing-pyramid system**. The nature of a given political establishment may favor the development of a single-pyramid patronal system or may deter its coming about.

Table 4.5. Formal Constitutions and Patronalism in Post-Communist Countries since the Mid-1990s

Degree of Patro-nalism	Type of Executive Power		
	Presidentialism	Divided Executive	Parliamentarism
High	Azerbaijan*, Belarus*, Georgia*, Kazakhstan*, Kyrgyzstan (until 2010*), Moldova (until 2000*), Russia*, Tajikistan*, Turkmenistan*, Ukraine* (1991–2006; 2010–2014), Uzbekistan*	Armenia*, Ukraine (2006–2010*; 2014–*), Kyrgyzstan (2010–*), Moldova (2016–*), Romania*	Albania, Bulgaria*, Hungary (2010–), Macedonia*, Moldova (2000–2016)
Moderate			Estonia, Latvia, Lithuania*, Hungary (1998–2010), Serbia*, Slovakia*
Low		Croatia (until 2000*), Poland*	Croatia (2001–*), Czech Republic (2012–*), Hungary (until 1998), Slovenia*

* Countries having direct presidential elections.
Source: based on Hale, *Patronal Politics*, 459, but revised and modified in some particulars.

This does not merely signify that a parliamentary system tends to work against the dominance of a single patronal network. It also means that in contrast to the purely presidential setup, a system with divided executive power can offer more institutional possibilities for competing patronal networks to keep each other in check, establishing "more democratic" conditions as they settle around the positions of president and prime minister as key seats of executive power. It is no coincidence that when a patronal network strives for a dominant role in a regime characterized by such divided executive power; it usually attempts to switch to a purely presidential system. And similarly, when such attempts fail, the other patronal networks fight for the reintroduction of divided executive power. Events proceeded in this fashion both in Ukraine and in Moldova.

A high degree of patronalism and presidentialism go hand in hand in the formation of single-pyramid systems, and the direct election of presidents is taken as a matter of fact. This does not, however, mean that where there are direct presidential elections, a presidentialist system must develop on all accounts. Constitutional arrangements may allow, for example, a strong mandate for a directly elected president while giving that same president only a narrow scope of executive power. We can speak of a presidentialist system in effect when the person of the prime minister depends not on a parliamentary majority, but the president. Meanwhile, in countries where the competencies of executive power are substantially shared between the president and the prime minister, there is once again only the direct election of presidents. In parliamentary systems, the impediment to the formation of single-pyramid patronal networks can basically be provided by the proportionality of the electoral system, which is normally able to make sure that no single political actor acquires a constitutional majority, or the exclusive opportunity to decide who staffs the key institutions guaranteeing the system of checks and balances. Wherever the electoral system is disproportionate, a monopoly on political power may come about even in a parliamentary system, opening the gates to the formation of a single-pyramid patronal system, as observed in the case of Hungary in 2010.

The head of the single-pyramid system is the chief patron, whose power rests basically on access to resources, power of enforcement, and a capacity to monitor subpatrons and clients. On these grounds, it is evident that the positions of the **chief patron**, **subpatron** and **client** can be differentiated within a patronal network. These three categories in their own neutral way define the actors of patronal networks from various eras. However, they may appear in different forms over the course of history.

Table 4.6. *Organizational connections of people to power institutions in three ideal-type political regimes*

Liberal democracy	Post-communist autocracy	Communist regime
multi-pyramid system	single-pyramid system	single-pyramid system
non-patronal networks	patronal networks	patronal networks
dominance of formal institutions	dominance of informal institutions	dominance of formal institutions

The transformation of patronal networks can most easily be followed in the example of Russia, where the tsar wielded the most power before the 1917 Russian Revolution, and the elite of his patronal network were formed from the service gentry and the feudal estates. The Revolution of 1917 eventually ushered in a new form of patronal network led by the party general secretary and populated largely by the party nomenklatura. In the presidential system that followed the collapse of the communist system and that stabilized by the end of the nineties, the elite of the patronal network takes the form of the adopted political family. The term **ruling elite** is a neutral expression, which in itself neither refers to the organizational makeup, structure, or internal relations within the elite, or even its legitimation. However, when we speak of the ruling elite of a patronal network, this implicitly includes its immediate hierarchical nature.

In Russia under the tsars, members of the ruling elite were part of the elite on the basis of birth, by virtue of their status as nobles. The prerogatives of elites were invested in the elite individual. It was possible to lift someone into this circle, to adopt persons into it, but no one could be stripped of their status because of disloyalty. For the disloyal, law enforcement could mean the loss of life, freedom, or property, but not status. In the case of the communist nomenklatura, the relationship was the reverse: the elite consisted of what might be called an impersonal register of positions of power. Here it was the position, and not the person's status, that was fixed; the person in the position could be changed at the whim of the party general secretary. Yet the ruling elite of both tsarist and communist patronal networks—whether by virtue of personal status or the register of impersonal positions—had a formalized set of rules for incorporation and expulsion. Not so in the case of the post-communist patronal network's elite, in which formal and informal roles and positions churn in an opaque, untraceable conglomeration.

Table 4.7. *The formal position of the chief patron, the decision making "body" and the type of patronal networks in Russia*

	before 1917	1917–1991	after 1991
The formal position of chief patron (as the head of executive power)	tsar	party general secretary	president
The ruling "body" (the decision making center)	court	politburo	patron's court
Ruling elite according to the type of patronal networks	service gentry, feudal "orders"	nomenklatura	adopted political family
Type of the patronal state	feudal state	party state	mafia state

For this reason, the ruling elite of the post-communist patronal network that structures the adopted political family cannot be related to either its feudal or its communist precursors. The difference can be summed up as follows:

**The patronal network in a post-communist single-pyramid system
(a) does not resemble the service gentry or (feudal) order** (as in pre-revolutionary Russia) because in the adopted political family:
- there is no corporate-type organization, no rank order-type separate positions in relation to the chief patron, no corporate self-consciousness;
- the client/vassal does not have the legal status of a vassal but only the vassal's social position; while equal rights are not de jure eliminated, the social position of vassals is created en masse;

- there is no "contractual" relation to the chief patron;
- the client/vassal does not possess property as an unquestionable consequence of its orderly status; subpatrons and clients can be deprived of their property by arbitrary means;

(b) does not resemble the nomenklatura (as in the USSR, because the adopted political family:
- extends the network of political and bureaucratic administration beyond its formal institutions;
- is not necessarily the adoption of a person, but of a "family," whereas individuals belonged to the nomenklatura;
- has privileges that may bring not only extra consumption and income, but property as well; and the privileges gained in property are not restricted for the duration of being in "service," but can be kept and inherited;

(c) can be characterized as an adopted political family, because:
- different networks of extended personal acquaintance are organized into a single adopted political family;
- not only individuals, but families / adopted families are incorporated;
- it is informal, without formal membership;
- it extends over formal institutions;
- it is based on patronal, and not organizational loyalty (there is no free entrance into or free exit from it);
- it is hierarchical;
- the position within the adopted political family does not converge necessarily with the formal administrative positions;
- its power was based on the merger of political and economic "resources";
- it follows the cultural patterns of rule by the patriarchal family or clan.

IV/1.1 Autonomous elites

In the ideal-typical liberal democracy, the above-mentioned separation of social activities (political, economic, communal), and the division of powers within the political sphere result in societies in which no single, uniform elite can be named. Individual **fragmented, autonomous elites** are related neither in a legal, nor—in ideal cases—in an illegal chain of command.

Figure 4.3. Ruling elites in a liberal democracy—autonomous elites

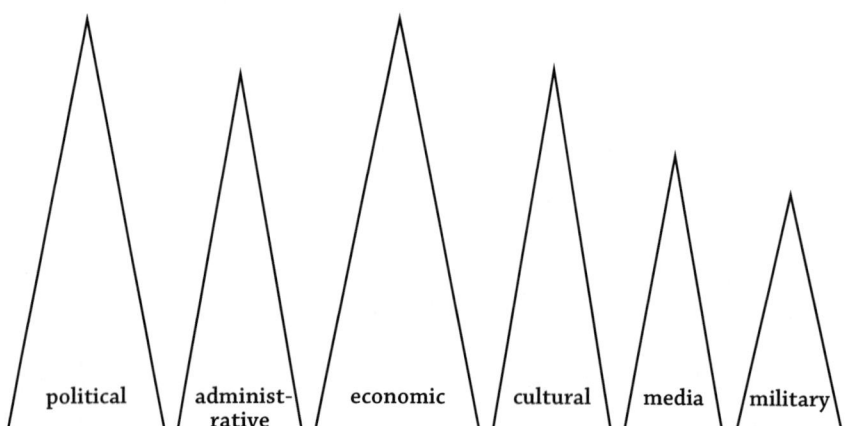

IV/1.2 The nomenklatura

In the case of communist regimes, the communist party radically eliminated boundaries between the various types of social action, as well as the division between the branches of power—wherever these existed in the first place. The elites ideal-typically had no form of autonomy; they could only be placed through a unified nomenklatura ruled by the communist party.

Sub-elite organizations (labor unions, women's association, academia etc.) were the carriers of the will of the communist party; organizationally speaking, they were the party's transmission belts. Only the leading figures among these "partial elites" could normally hope to make it into the broad governing body of the true political elite, the central committee of the communist party, while only the leaders of the secret service and military elite were on occasion included in the smaller, actual decision-making bodies, the political committees. The system of privileged personal benefits serves as a guide in deciphering the hierarchical relationships between positions within the partial elites of the nomenklatura. In communist Hungary, for example, the exchange rate between positions occupied by the partial elites took the form of sophisticated consumer and prestige benefits. These included a hierarchy-based access to goods and services including party hotel resorts, the number of stags and the size of their antlers licensed for shooting at a state hunt, different levels of privileged health care, or the hierarchy of license plate numbers for official cars and more. The range of privileges was tied strictly to position, and not to persons.

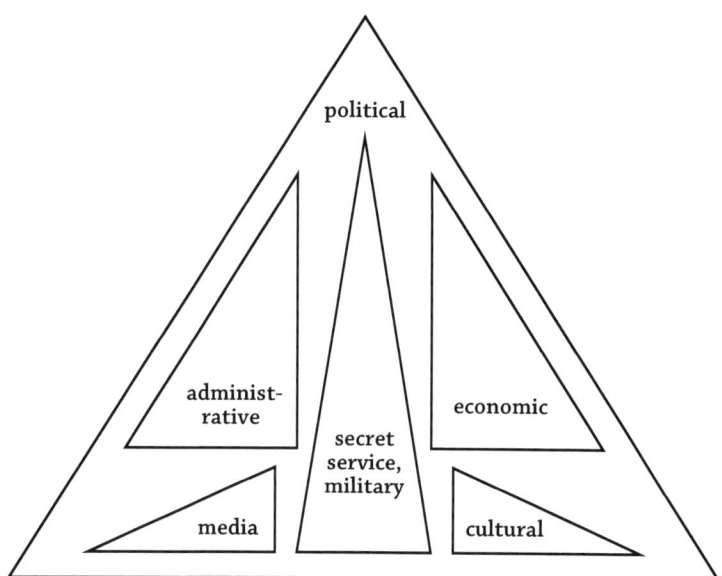

Figure 4.4. Ruling elite of the communist regime—the nomenklatura

IV/1.3 The adopted political family

In post-communist regimes, the process of sub-elites becoming relatively autonomous began during the early regime-change process. But soon the alignment of individual autonomous elites into rival political-economic patronal networks followed, despite conditions that would have been typical for liberal democracies. In those post-communist regimes where the rotation of rival political forces persisted over time, there was a better chance for autonomous economic, cultural, media and other elites to take a hold, or at least attach themselves to competing patronal networks that are unable to secure power exclusively, finding subsistence under their wings. This latter scenario, however, is perhaps the best outcome for countries further outside the EU's gravitational pull.

In post-communist regimes where a single-pyramid patronal system is established, parallel to the removal of the balance and autonomy of political institutions, the autonomy of economic organizations and social institutions is also eliminated. The amalgamation of the autocratic political rulers, combined with curtailed economic opportunities, also means that in such regimes the subjugation is not total; some segments of certain elites at lower levels (certainly in no position to shape the regime) may remain outside the single-pyramid system's dominant network's chain of command.

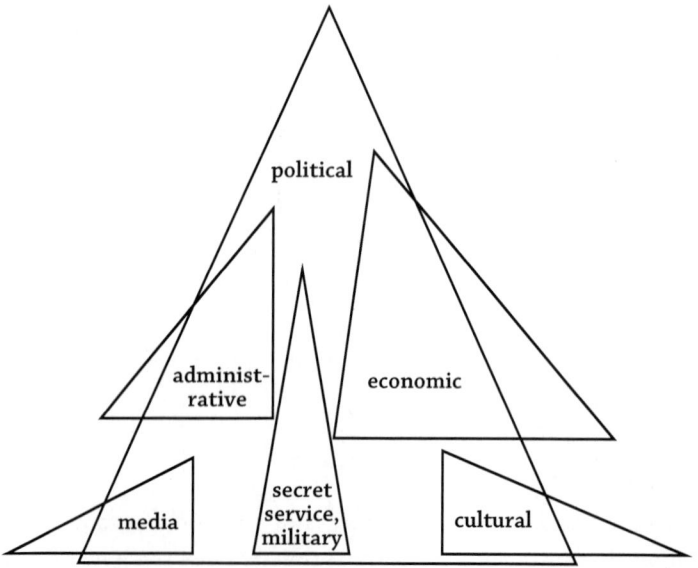

Figure 4.5. Ruling elite of the post-communist single pyramid patronal network—adopted political family

In contrast to the communist nomenklatura's fixed, super-formalized system of positions, the elite, defined as the adopted political family, is a formation composed of an aggregate of formal and informal positions ordered into a patronal network. Of course the key positions of political power belong to it. Which is to say that executive power forcibly subjugates the legislative and enforcement branches to its authority and joins the formal positions of the political elite with positions in the economic elite and other legally undefined, informal positions—to be addressed later— through the appropriation of the state in the service of private interests. Organizational loyalty is replaced by personal loyalty.

In Western-style democracies a list of the most influential people usually means the ranking of people disconnected in terms of hierarchy, or chains of command, simply on the basis of their presumed social influence (reflecting the separation of the different spheres of social action). Influence in a single-pyramid post-communist regime ruled by a dominant patronal network however, is measured not by power over society but by proximity to the chief patron. The list of influential[15] people compiled by political scientists annually in Hungary since 2014, for example, rarely shows anyone but people who have won their positions of "social influence" through the favor of the chief patron—and who might just as well lose it at any moment—among the first 40–50 top positions. They include hardly anyone who has taken such an influential position through their own independent efforts.

By the directly merging authority over the circumstances of political and economic activity, the dominant patronal network forming the adopted political family establishes conditions in which political and economic power are heavily reliant on one another. There is no economic power without political power (or at least a stake in the political hinterland) and political power—having been privatized—presumes command of market positions in the economy. Russian analysts use the expression *vlast'-sobstvennost'* (power&ownership) to describe this interwoven state of affairs as an independent category.[16]

IV/2. Main collective actors: decision-making center of patronal networks—the patron's court

In liberal democracies it is not only political action that is kept apart from forms of economic and communal action. Within the sphere of political activity, through the division of the branches of power, there is a boundary drawn between the branches of power that regulate (legislative), govern (executive), and control political action (law enforcement). The decision-making team, in a narrow sense, is the **government in power**, which normally includes politicians of the party (or parties) that have won free elections.

The decision-making center of the nomenklatura in communist regimes is the top leading body of the ruling communist party, the **political committee** (politburo) consisting of only a handful of people. The elite of the nomenklatura, the communist party, is the "leading force of society" as set out in the constitution. In corresponding organizational terms, the partial elites are doubled, because each of the leading positions throughout the hierarchy is controlled by an individual political commissar. This is what makes it possible, on the one hand, to keep the independent movement of the partial elites within bounds, and on the other, to switch the bureaucratic functionality of the partial elites temporarily into a campaign mode, when such mobilization is initiated through various campaigns directed from above. The classical literature of Kremlinology, while studying differences in the level of power between those in positions of power that are formally on an identical level, cannot disregard the fact that even the very question of informal power makes only sense within a formalized party structure. For without being a member of the political committee no one can exercise real power and influence decision-making. Being dropped from the political committee was concomitant with the complete loss of all prerogatives of power: in Stalinist times, this meant the Gulag and death, while later, in communism's "humanized" form, it entailed sinecure without any access to power, a pension, and a partial continuation of consumer privileges.

The decision-making center of post-communist regimes operating in single-pyramid patronal systems is the small circle of the chief patron at the top of the adopted political family: the **patron's court**. This occasionally changing small circle is composed of actors with formal positions of executive power and others with informal positions. It is rather difficult to keep track of the bureau's membership because changes are not limited to changes among people in formal positions. The actors of the patron's court—to be described later—are: poligarchs, oligarchs, counsellors, corruption brokers and the political family's secret service and security guard.

Since the patron's court does not constitute a formalized body, it shows a great variety of forms as it appears in different post-communist regimes. This concerns both its origins and its structure. In the case of the newly emerged **Hungarian patronal regime**, the family VIP box by the football pitch paints the clearest picture of the country's real power center, as the chief patron cheers in the awkward intimacy of his circle, with people who are in their civil roles under a rule of law (minister, mayor, chief prosecutor, president of the State Audit Office, bank chairman, leaders of NGOs, businessmen, and so on) together with the people of his court and household. No liberal principles like the separation of powers or conflict of interests can be allowed to disturb the national-fraternal unity, the harmony of the VIP box. The cultural modes of the head of the adopted political family, the features of his rule, differ vastly from the modes of other 20th century autocrats and dictators. He does not show his power in parades or party congresses. The manifestations of his rule—as a pater familias—bear the characteristics of relations within a patriarchal family.

In **Putin's Russia**, the patron's court is "identified as an 'inner circle' of people who take part in practically all of Putin's meetings," according to Olga Kryshtanovskaya's classic study on the subject.[17] She describes this inner circle as the joined network of three "tables."[18]

- The Monday meetings are—in effect—meetings of the president with members of the **government**, that is, a decision-making body reflecting the pattern of the formalized government structure. The media deals extensively with these meetings.
- The circle of participants at the Saturday meetings is more closed, and its composition does not coincide with bureaucratic boundaries. The people participating in the meeting of the body called the **Security Council** have formal political positions (in the presidential cabinet, government, secret service organizations or the prosecutor's office), are confidants of Putin, and are key figures in executive authority and law enforcement. All that the media reports in this case is that at the meetings "various questions of domestic and foreign policy" were discussed.
- "There is also a third group, which might be called the **'tea-drinking group'**. This consists of Putin's personal friends, who meet informally at his official residence. Nothing is known of the frequency of such meetings, and every precaution is taken to ensure that even the names of those who are admitted into this inner circle are not made public. . . . These patterns of interaction are underpinned by less formal patterns of informal association, or 'clans'."[19]

Referring to countries further east, this type of center of power is described as clan structure.[20] It is worthwhile to deflate a common misunderstanding here, where a description of the structure of power is confused with the question of the origins of the informal, personal relations that compose it. The clan can in itself be considered an adopted political family—when analyzing political systems—where the meaning of the latter, more general category is supplied by a weave of personal and informal relations whose dominant and cultural patterns derive from the patriarchal large family. In the combination of the three words—adopted political family—the signifier **adopted** refers to acceptance into the family, which is not necessarily based on ties of blood. What the word **family** conveys is not only the transformation of personal relationships into quasi family ties, but also that this generally goes beyond individuals and extends to families and (sub)patronal networks that had been excluded until then. Of course, these personal relationships of dependence and mutuality may equally be either hierarchical or horizontal. The signifier **political** gives expression to the fact that the given patronal network rules as a single-pyramid system over state authority as a whole, and the legitimate means of state enforcement are within its powers to deploy.

Naturally, informal patronal networks can grow out of various types of personal networks of acquaintance, the signs of which they may continue to bear later to some degree. In some of the post-communist regimes, such as **Russia**, the decision-making power center of the adopted political family is grounded in the relationships that developed on the lower levels of the former party and secret service nomenklatura. The necessarily restricted circle and locality of these relationships provides grounds on which the power center ruled by Putin, considered a quasi clan structure, can be called the St. Petersburg Clan. However, the acquaintances within this "clan" is formal, not familiar, revolving mainly around the positions in the Mayoral cabinet in St. Petersburg. It is denoted as a clan simply as an allusion to the fact that the formal relations take on clan-type patterns, made up of informal networks and the patriarchal extended family.

In the post-communist regimes of Central Asia, on the other hand, it is the top positions of the communist party and the secret service that switched directly into informal patronal networks. These post-Soviet republics, however, also bear the signs of ethnic and clan divisiveness. Yet the ruling elite of the Russian post-communist regime still cannot be called a neo-nomenklatura, nor can the Central Asian regime be called a clan structure in the traditional sense. And the individual Central Asian autocracies also differ from one another in terms of the relationship between the ruling elite and the clan structure. The clans mostly come together to form tribes, and at times the tribes will form tribal unions, which in Kazakhstan are called *zhuz*. The chief patron will sometimes be balancing between a few such larger *zhuzs*; elsewhere the clans will form six-seven regional groups, and one or two stronger regional groupings will rise to more-or-less monopolizing the available positions (Tajikistan, Turkmenistan, Uzbekistan). At other times nonaligned *local tribes* of a hundred or so drive the political system towards a parliamentary bargain-mechanism (Kyrgyzstan).[21] In what follows, however, when we speak of a **political-economic clan**,[22] we mean not the traditional clan, but the adopted family as defined above. That is, a system of relationships in which informal, personal networks are only like a clan in terms of their ruling and cultural patterns, but have no history of the clan type.

In **Hungary**, it was the former alternative liberal party Fidesz, founded originally as a youth organization, that changed directly into a patronal network, grounded in early friendships from student fraternities at university. A transformation of the party and its subsequent achievement of a two-thirds parliamentary majority during the elections of 2010, resulted in Orbán and his inner circles acquiring unlimited political power. This enabled them to eliminate individual and institutional autonomies as well as the system of checks and balances within the parliamentary system, and to arrange members of society into a single-pyramid patronal system dominated by its network. This did not of course happen on the basis of the former communist party and secret service nomenklatura, though those who surrendered were accepted, and the secret service apparatus was domesticated for the purposes of the adopted political family.

The adopted political family's sources of recruitment can be based on different types of personal acquaintances: kinship, ethnicity, region, friendship, patronage, or service in formal institutions (army, party, secret service, youth organization, etc.).[23] But there can be no equating the new forms of the post-communist ruling elite's internal structure with the informal networks of acquaintances of past eras. This difference cannot be dissolved even by adding the prefix "neo" to earlier systems (neo-nomenklatura, neo-patrimonial, neo-feudal).

IV/3. Quasi collective actors of post-communist autocracies— patronal parties

As opposed to the foregoing, political parties are considered the main collective political actors in liberal democracies. When it comes to its commonplace definition, Wikipedia, for example defines "political party" as "a group of people who come together to contest elections and hold power in the government. The party agrees on some policies and programs for the society with a view to promote the collective good or to further their supporters' interests."[24] If we seek to examine a party's functions in greater detail, we may do so—quoting Wilhelm Hofmeister and Karsten Grabow[25]—as follows:

- **political opinion-making function**: articulating and aggregating social interests by expressing public expectations and demands of social groupings to the political system;
- **selection function**: recruiting political personnel and nurturing future generations of politicians;
- **integration function**: integrating various interests into a general political project and transforming it into a political program, and campaigning to receive the consent and support of a majority;
- **socialization and participation function**: promoting the political socialization and participation of citizens by creating a link between them and the political system;
- **political power exercising function**: participating in elections to occupy political charges, organizing the government;
- **legitimating function**: contributing to the legitimacy of the political system and anchoring the political order in the consciousness of the citizens and in social forces.

Post-communist regimes also have numerous political parties, yet the definition above is best applied to parties in the new EU member countries in Central Eastern Europe. But even in their case, questions immediately arise, including whether these parties operate in close concert with dominant patronal networks (which developed in the course of the disposal of state property and occasional reallocation) or independently of them. Moving on to the second (East European, Christian Orthodox) and third (Central Asian, Muslim) historical regions of post-communist regimes, it becomes obvious that the definition of parties developed for liberal democracies can only be applied in a very limited sense. In their case we could rather speak of **patronal parties**, which ensure the patronal networks a formal (though nonexclusive) framework to grant them legitimacy in a restricted competition.

IV/3.1. Types of patronal party: centralized party, vassal party, transmission belt party

The obvious reason why leading parties of post-communist autocracies do not endorse the democratic internal organization of liberal parties is that it would be incompatible with the autocratic nature of these regimes if their governing parties operated upon democratic principles. The "democratic centralism" of the communist parties before regime change took the form of **centralized parties**, where the topmost organ of the pyramid-like, hierarchically constructed party, the politburo, had a monopoly on power. In communist regimes, the chief overseeing body of the party did not wholly lose its importance even in parallel with the authority of the first secretary. For example, anyone who counted as a current confidant, or favorite, of Stalin was at the same time a member of the formal decision-making body, the politburo. This is why one of the favorite subjects of the Kremlinology literature was the analysis of the composition and changes of this body, focusing on informal coalitions therein.

Though the role of the number-one leader of the party (the general secretary) remained to be decisive, his powers were no longer as unlimited as during the classical Stalinist period, with the collective decisions of Political Committee gaining a much more important role in the changes of power within the party.

The governing parties of post-communist autocracies however, can now be considered **vassal parties**. The party chair at their helm—usually chief patron of the dominant patronal network—is no longer subject to decisions of any formal body. Appointments to positions of power within the party, as well as outside of the party, depend on the president's personal, discretionary decision. The party hierarchy is no longer the broadest frame of power like that which structured the communist nomenklatura. Instead, it is just a part of the patronal network. In the case of the "leading force" of the post-communist autocracies, the actual decisions are taken away from the—nevertheless strictly controlled—bodies of the party, and are transferred by the chief patron to the decision-making pool of the inner circle of minions, the adopted political family, without formal structure and legitimacy.

When vassal parties cease to function as the center of decision making, and merely mediate between informal/personal and formal/institutional competencies and positions, it is possible to call them **transmission belt parties**. Before regime change, the communist party, as the center of power, did have "transmission belt" organizations (labor unions, popular front-like organizations, communist youth organizations, cultural associations, women's organization etc.) in the sense that they transmitted the will of the topmost body of the communist party to various segments of society. In post-communist autocracies, the governing party becomes the transmission belt of the patronal network, that is, of the adopted political family. In other words, the adopted political family becomes real center of power, which gains formal legitimacy through the party that meditates the adopted political family's will toward the formal, legitimate political institutions. After all, it functions behind the scenes of a staged democracy, where the party itself is the political stooge (a concept developed below) for the adopted political family. The chief patron, if in the position of president of the republic, standing above the parties, may at times (as in, for example, Russia) not even formally be a "member" of the delegating party even as this same patron controls the party's cadre and policy matters.

IV/3.2. Non-party system, dominant party system, multi-party system

A more democratic system among the post-communist regimes could also be called a **multiparty system**—from the perspective of the formalized, competing political actors. A multiparty system is characterized by the rotation of political actors and ruling parties, and no single party monopoly over the branches of power. Opposition parties are potentially ready to replace the party in government, and are not forced to submit to, or be dependent upon, the governing party. Post-communist dictatorships are obviously **one-party** formations.

Post-communist autocracies are the focus of the study at present, and their party composition—a single pyramid patronal system—can usually be described as a **dominant party system**. In their case the dominant parties are clearly patronal parties, which are, in terms of their internal setup, vassal parties, and in terms of their function, transmission belt parties.

With regard to its origin, the **dominant party** can be:
- **an inherited or transformed communist party**: this is most typical of those post-communist autocracies—especially Turkmenistan and Uzbekistan—where the member republics broke away from the Soviet Union practically without any real democratic transition, under the leadership of the local communist party and secret service elite. A similar story seemed to unfold initially in the Republic of Moldova as well. Such inherited parties, however, only seem to hold out temporarily, and usually lose their significance, disappear, or change into "nationalist" parties.

- in other cases, the dominant party is formed from the **party or party conglomerate backing the chief patron**—originating from the opposition to the communist party in the democratic transition.
- the most prevalent formation in long-standing post-communist autocracies, however, is the **dominant party set up by the chief patron**. The party may have been set up by the former local communist party chief who, having stabilized his power through a presidential system, rid himself of his skin like a snake. Having shed the communist patronal network (and former nomenklatura), he has brought about a presidential dominant party with a new, or reformed, patronal network in its place, dependent on himself alone. If the establishment of the single-pyramid system came after a longer transition through patronal democracy, as with the Yeltsin-Putin turn in Russia, the new patronal network is recast as a political party founded by the chief patron independently of the communist party, which endures in opposition.

In contrast to the political parties of liberal democracies, patronal parties are naturally characterized by not serving as political institutions with an interest in channeling and formulating the grassroots desires of the electorate. Instead, they act as one of the necessary formal institutions (which can be necessary even in autocracies) for the top-down extension of the patronal network. That is, it is not the population that chooses party leaders with the aim of seizing political power based on ideologies, programs or personal interests, but chief patrons who integrate clients into the patronal network they rule over. The dominant parties operate as a sort of HR-organization, through which it is not those who believe in similar ideals, but those who swear loyalty to the same chief patron who are recruited: it is not the members who get the people aspiring to lead them to compete, but the leaders who have potential clients competing for their favor.

It is easiest to create new dominant parties based on patron-client relationships headed by the chief patron, from the top executive position of the presidential system. The history of the dominant party in Hungary, Fidesz, is of special interest in this regard, because it grew into a major party in the parliamentary system and shifted from the western to a vassal party phase of party development while still in opposition. Another exception is the Belarusian post-communist autocratic regime, in which no dominant party supporting the president can be found. The Belarusian chief patron,

Lukashenka, runs a **non-party system**, in which the constitutive parliamentary majority is ensured by "independent" members of parliament without any party ties who are selected through the state bureaucracy and elected, as a matter of course. In this regime lacking a dominant party, the functions of the dominant party are served by the state bureaucracy itself and the order of appointments overseen by the president.

In the post-communist autocracies characterized by a dominant party system, **opposition parties** cannot gain a rotational party role. In terms of their relationships to the dominant parties, they can be grouped as follows:
- **marginalized party**: this type is not dependent on the chief patron, but is forced into a marginalized position without prospects by being financially incapacitated and through the centralization of power, restricted media access, discrimination against activists, criminalization, and politically selective law enforcement.
- **domesticated party**: a party that is formally in opposition, but informally and in the trap of deals and blackmail it acts out the role of an opposition incapable of ever winning against the dominant party. Nevertheless, its leading cadres may be well served by this in the form of some financial and political career opportunities.
- **liquidated party**: an opposition party that was threatening for the dominant party, and was banned by the regime, or liquidated through the imprisonment or perhaps even murder of its leaders, after unsuccessful attempts to force it into a domesticated position.
- **virtual opposition party launched by the chief patron**: at times when brushing the opposition parties off the party structure has been too successful, the central power may itself launch "opposition parties" under its control, but fitting well into the democratic scene.

IV/3.3. Free elections versus managed actions demonstrating loyalty

The presentation of political regimes on a scale of democracy-autocracy-dictatorship can also be shown on a scale spanning fair elections to the complete lack of elections. The connection between the level of freedom in various electoral systems and political regimes is demonstrated by the following figure from Marc Howard and Philip Roessler (amended by the definitions discussed before).

Figure 4.6. Disaggregation of political regimes by various dimensions of democracy

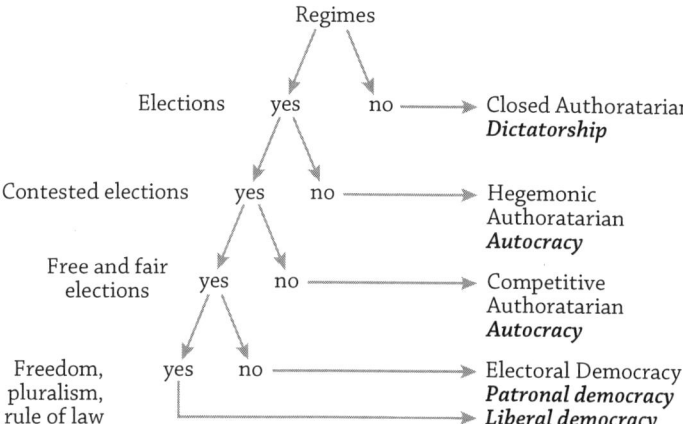

Note: "Elections" refers to the election of leaders in the offices of executive power or the parliament that elect them. Source: Marc Howard and Philip Roessler, "Liberalizing Electoral Outcomes in Competitive Authoritarian Regimes," *American Journal of Political Science* 50, no. 2 (2006): 367. Terms in bold italics were added by me.

The focus of the present study is on post-communist autocracy and patronal democracies. Both contested elections and unfree-unfair elections may occur in autocracies. On the basis of electoral practice, the line between the two may be drawn according to the following indicators:

- Elections should be considered to be **not free and fair**, if the governing party: manipulates the electoral law to its own advantage through its positions in public office; uses government resources for its campaign and mobilizes the apparatus of public administration; allows unequal access to the media; threatens the opposition parties or its candidates with politically selective law enforcement; and excludes them from competition. The tax authorities, police, and the prosecutor's office operate as part of the governing party's campaign staff. Of course, the degree to which such instruments are used can be very different, and on a very wide scale. There is still however, no direct electoral fraud in the counting of ballots.
- In the case of **contested elections**, the votes are not "counted" and instead the desired "results" are simply announced, and the measures described above are also present in their extreme forms. The attrition

of political actors is at times replaced by their liquidation, literally: the bans on opposition parties, imprisonment of their candidates, forced exile or physical liquidation of their charismatic figures.

Even in the case of the post-communist patronal democracies, curbs on free and fair elections are a matter worth considering. But the real dividing line in its comparison to autocratic practices is whether the removal or liquidation of political rivals through politically selective law enforcement does occur, or whether the advantage of government forces in the course of the election campaigns (in terms of electoral law, material resources and access to media) is "only" ensured, as it were, by legal means.

In the case of post-communist patronal democracies, elections take place between competing patronal networks, with a new balance resulting between them (in regimes that can be described as parliamentary and as having divided executive power). The question of what role elections serve in post-communist autocracies is, however, very valid, especially where more drastic cases are concerned. What is the actual function of the elections if the results are predetermined? Following earlier work by Hale,[26] the **functions of the contested elections** can be grouped as follows:

- **loyalty demonstration:** in the case of contested elections, a profane, electoral act becomes a sacred demonstration of loyalty. The "elections" are a show of subservience on the part of patronal networks and their members, an occasion for the rulers to mobilize supporters.
- **controlled renewing of formal, political positions of the patronal network:** elections can provide a useful mechanism for coopting other networks, distributing patronage, or facilitating powersharing among the important elite groups. Furthermore, they can test the quality of new cadres to staff the autocratic regime, discovering new potentially valuable cadres. Indeed, the cadres of the adopted political family who are assigned public functions must be endowed with certain abilities in order to complete the tasks expected of them by the patronal network in such a way as to minimalize the violent mechanisms of coercion.
- **stabilisation, risk minimalization:** regimes that do not allow regular, contested elections do face crises and revolutions, but these tend to be highly unpredictable for the ruler. This risk gives rulers an interest in channeling public challenges through more predictable mechanisms.

In so doing, rulers structure the political struggle according to ground rules that they themselves design, that enable them to prepare long in advance, and that reduce the chances of losing power.
- **legitimation:** chief patrons derive legitimation even from unfair elections. Such victories tell everyone that the officially winning chief patron in fact does possess the raw power to carry on contested elections and orchestrate a win, creating incentives for society's networks to coordinate around the winners' networks, reinforcing or moving closer toward a single-pyramid arrangement. (The question of legitimacy will have a key role in the—later elaborated—denomination of the regime and state that keeps it in operation.)

As Hale writes, contested national elections enable patronal power networks to communicate their relative strength, with the dominant ones making clear that they are capable of following through on their promises to deliver resources or carry out punishments in the future. This is essential for keeping potentially opportunistic elites in line.[27]

Table 4.8. Key system components and political processes in three ideal-type political regimes

Liberal democracy	Post-communist autocracy	Communist regime
head of the executive power (president/PM)	chief patron (patronal presidentialism)	general party secretary
govern (within formal authorization)	dispose (beyond formal authorization)	command (within formal authorization)
government	patron's court	politburo
autonomous elites	adopted political family	nomenklatura
multi-party system	dominant-party system	one-party system
free and fair election	manipulated election	uncontested election

Liberal democracy	Post-communist autocracy	Communist regime
assessment of political alternatives	loyalty demonstration	enforced ritual action
real choice	constrained choice	no choice
marketing campaign	monopolizing campaign	right suspending campaign
governing party politicians' party democratic party	transmission belt party vassal party patron's party	state party cadre party centralized party
joining	cooptation / adoption	enrollment
opposition party	liquidated / marginalized / domesticated / fake party	n.a.

V. The comparative conceptual array for liberal democracies and post-communist regimes—The distinctive character of state in post-communist autocracies: the mafia state

The wide variety in names for post-communist regimes is also reflected in the variety of definitions found for the states that are typical of them. The diversity of designations found in the literature mostly aims at the deviancies as compared with liberal democracies even in naming the states established in post-communist autocracies. Let us try to clear up the relationship between these different layers of meaning, keeping in mind that our discussion centers on post-communist autocracies.

The various names for the states set up in post-communist regimes can be interpreted along the lines of a number of dimensions. The point of departure is of course Max Weber's classical definition, according to which the state is defined as exercising a monopoly on the legitimate use of violence.[28]

The first dimension of categorization that we may address concerns the **nature of the ruling elite that holds state power in its grips** (See Table 4.9).

Table 4.9. Interpretative layers of categories to describe the mafia state

	The type of state	Interpretive features of the category	To which features of the state the category refers
1.	State ↓	Monopoly on the right to authorize the legitimate use of violence	Institutions by which the ruling elite exercises legitimate coercion
2.	Network state ↓	1st feature + increasing informal character of the connections within and between the units of the state	The ruling elite's exercising power through mainly informal power networks
3.	Patronal state ↓	1st + 2nd features + the personal, patronal, hierarchically dependent character of the ruling elite	The ruling elite's internal dependency, patron-client relations (patronal power network)
4	Clan state ↓	1st + 2nd + 3rd features + the adopted political family (political-economic clan) structure of the ruling elite	The ruling elite's anthropological structure and cultural patterns
5	Mafia state	1st + 2nd + 3rd + 4th features + the illegitimate character of the ruling elite's practice of power	The legality of the ruling elite's actions

Along this dimension the signifier **network** should be attached to the state, if the functions of the state organization are—upholding the basic definition—dominated by informal networks of the ruling elite, rather than being institutionalized, formalized, and realized through impersonal relations. If the state is characterized by an informal network structured by a patronal network, and if the command structure is of the patron-client type, then we can speak of a **patronal state**. If the given patronal network forms a clan type of adopted political family, we can use the designation of **clan state** to signify its being not simply patronal. The adopted political family—as discussed earlier—differs from the bureaucratic, military, or nomenklatura versions of patronal networks. The adoption of the client consecrates neither an organizational ethos nor ties of blood or actual kinship, in keeping with a large family cultural pattern, but of loyalty towards the chief patron. We can speak of a **mafia state**, if—on the basis of the way the patronal network operates—the state cannot be considered legitimate even by its own standards. Such states are identifiable structurally by the institution of the stooge (see below) and centrally managed anti-corruption campaigns actually aimed at subjugating or liquidating competing patronal networks in the pursuit of (or retention of) monopolized political power. This is not about a conflict between principles and praxis of anti-corruption and corruption, but the intent to monopolize opportunities for corruption. By these means, the ideology of the anti-corruption campaigns covers intentions that stand directly opposed to these campaigns' declared goals: the "nationalization" of the corruption "market" or, in other words, its cleansing of competitors. The discrepancy between the declared goal and the real intentions delegitimizes the regime and make the financial growth of the adopted political family something that ought to be hidden.

Patriarchal family—classical mafia—mafia state: The expansion of the entitlements of the head of the family

It is possible to arrive at the concept of the post-communist mafia state through the historical switch in the function of the head of the patriarchal family, the narrowest patronal network, when the norms accepted within the patriarchal family confront the modern norms of social organization: The **classical mafia**—as a form of the **organized criminal underworld**—is no more than a violent, illegitimate attempt at giving sanction to the pre-modern powers vested in the patriarchal head of the family in a society established along the lines of modern equality of rights. This attempt is at the same time being thwarted, as far as possible, by state organs of public authority. The mafia is an adopted family, "the form of artificial kinship, which implied the greatest and most solemn obligations of mutual help on the contracting parties."[29] **The classical mafia is an illegitimate neo-archaism**.

Though two types of mafia have developed historically, this is not relevant in terms of the line of argument advanced here, concerning the illegitimate extension of the authority of the patriarchal head of the family. Nevertheless, it is worth noting that though the Sicilian mafia had aspired to the handling of quasi state functions in the face of Italian ambitions of unification, the American mafia was merely the unorthodox tool of advancement and social mobility for recently arrived Italian immigrants. A number of new groups of immigrants invested efforts in "making it" by means of organized crime, among others.

The **mafia state** on the other hand—as the **organized criminal upper-world**—is a project to sanction the authority of the patriarchal head of the family, the chief patron on the level of a country, among the scenes of the democratic institutional system, with an invasion of the powers of state and its set of tools. All that was achieved by the classical mafia by means of threats, blackmail, and—if necessary—violent bloodshed, in the mafia state is ensured through the bloodless, illegitimate coercion of the state ruled by the adopted political family. **The mafia state is the business venture of the adopted political family managed through the instruments of public authority.** In terms of patterns of leadership, the exercise of sovereign power by the chief patron, the head of the executive power, the patriarchal family, the household, the estate, and the country are isomorphous concepts. On all these levels, the same cultural patterns of applying power are followed. In the same manner as the patriarchal head of the family is decisive in instances disposing of personal and property matters, also defining status (the status that regulates all aspects of the personal roles and competencies among the "people of his household"), so the head of the adopted political family is leader of the country, where the reinterpreted nation signifies his "household." Such a head does not appropriate, only disposes. He or she has a share, dispenses justice, and imparts some of this share and justice on the "people of his household," his or her nation, to all according to their status and merit.

In the same way that the classical mafia eliminates "private banditry,"[30] the mafia state also sets out to end partisan, anarchic corruption, which is replaced by a centralized, largely legalized enforcement of tribute organized from the top.

State—partially appropriated state—fully appropriated state: Degree of appropriation of the state by private interests

When certain organs of the state and their scopes of activity are subjected systematically and at length to private interests, we can speak of a partially appropriated state. This is no different from the phenomenon of **state capture**. This may equally occur through the actions of actors in external (economic, criminal) or internal (political and administrative) spheres.

The degree of relations between the state and criminal groups under state capture, and the differentiation within those relations with regard to who is the dominant party are made palpable as described in Table 4.10.

Table 4.10. Typology of relationships between state and organized crime

The state's relation to organized crime	The initiator of state – organized crime connection	
	Criminal organizations (organized underworld)	The state
State combating corruption and criminal organizations	Crime groups avoiding or attacking the state	Crime groups, gangs under attack by the state
Partial state capture	Organized crime groups developing corrupting and collusive relations with elites	Elites seeking services from organized crime
	Organized crime groups coopting state institutions	Elites monopolizing control over organized crime activities
Criminal state (organized upperworld)		Elites creating or taking over the role of organized crime

Source: modified version of a table from Alexander Kupatadze, "'Transitions after transitions': Coloured revolutions and organized crime in Georgia, Ukraine and Kyrgyzstan" (PhD thesis, University of St. Andrews, 2010), 36. http://hdl.handle.net/10023/1320.

The logical end of the series would however be the situation in which the state itself acts as a criminal organization, that is, as a criminal state. According to Janine R. Wedel's distinction, the "differences between the 'partially appropriated state' and the 'clan-state' appear to lie in (1) the degree of penetration of state bodies and authorities and the nature of vertical linkages and (2) the degree to which politics is dominated by groups such as institutional nomads and clans and has become merely a means for them to access state resources for themselves. The partially appropriated state and the clan-state fall along a continuum—from substantial appropriation of the state by private actors to sweeping appropriation and from considerable use of politics to access state resources to a near wholesale intertwining of state resources and politics."[31]

Organizational crime—state crime—criminal state

In the field of organizational crime David O. Friedrichs has systematized criminal acts according to the type of organization that commits them.[32] The concept of the criminal state, and within that, the mafia state can also be explored along the lines of this criminal organization logic. He differentiates between corporate crimes and state crimes. However, government and business may occasionally collaborate, and even directly encourage and assist each other in committing certain crimes. Three separate categories follow from this: state-facilitated corporate crime, corporate-facilitated state crime, and state-corporate crime, which occurs when the former two act together on an equal basis. "**Governmental crime**—or crime that occurs within the context of government—is the principal cognate form of white-collar crime. **State crime** (or crime of the state) is macro-level harm carried out on behalf of the state or its agencies; **political white-collar crime** is crime carried out by individuals or networks of individuals who occupy governmental positions and seek economic or political advantage for themselves or their party."[33]

Not only does **state crime** exist, but so too does the concept of a **criminal state**: a state that systematically, deliberately, and perniciously violates and impairs the fundamental rights of its citizens. Within such a state, both the various economic entities that depend on public procurements and tenders, and the civil society organizations—that in reality function as political puppets and serve the interests of power—are interwoven very tightly within the state and government. In such cases, those involved in corrupt activities and those in a repressive regime are connected to each other in manifold ways.[34] Nevertheless, it is worth classifying these potential states according to their main criminal activity. Consequently, one can differentiate between a "**criminal state**, with a central project of a crime against humanity;" a "**repressive state**, with a core project of systematic denial of basic rights to citizens or some group of citizens;" a "**corrupt**

state, with systematic looting of the state for the benefit of the leadership and relatives or associates of the leadership;" and finally a **"negligent state**, characterized by a basic failure to alleviate forms of suffering that the state could address."[35] A criminal state, of course, may exhibit different combinations of the "state projects" listed above.

The central figure in the criminal state is not an arbitrarily-structured power elite with an incidental culture. It is the adopted political family with powers granted by the chief patron, which are then extended to the entire nation through illegitimate means from a supreme, narrow group of decision-makers, working as a non-formalized, non-legitimate body. Typically a dozen or two dozen individuals make up the patron's court of the mafia state. The criteria for a **criminal organization** according to the Palermo Protocols[36]—defined by the Council of Europe's Group of specialists on organized crime (PC-S-CO)—applies to the chief patron and his circles: "three or more people," "a group formed for an extended period of time and acting in concert" that has a "hierarchy" and "mutually-reinforcing effects on those acting in it," and includes "the objective of perpetrating criminal offenses," "dividing up tasks" required for this, and if necessary, "contracting" persons outside of the criminal organization.

From amongst isolated violations of the law, the contours of relationships in the mafia state are outlined by the **linked actions** of organized crime. These include acts that are unlawful in and of themselves (such as extortion, fraud and financial fraud, embezzlement, misappropriation, money laundering, insider trading, agreements that limit competition in a public procurement or concession procedure, bribery, bribery of officials, both the active and passive forms of these last two criminal acts, abuse of authority, abuse of a public service position, buying influence, racketeering, etc.) combined with acts that are not unlawful in and of themselves (such as motions submitted by independent Parliamentary representatives, instigating tax audits, etc.).

While earlier the term post-communist autocracy applied to the concentration of political power, the term post-communist mafia state includes both the concentration of power and the personal, or familial, accumulation of wealth. Though all three composites of the criminal state (repressive, corrupt, and negligent) are present in the case of post-communist autocracy, this analysis places emphasis on the trait of corruption. This is because the emergence of corruption presupposes the presence in different measures of the two other traits.

Criminal state—gangster state—mafia state

Those who at times would prefer to use the term gangster state instead of criminal state, seek to find an expression alluding to the criminal group that directs the state. Yet the expression gangster leaves the anthropological nature of the criminal group an open question, while the term mafia state suggests the adopted family, clan aspect of the criminal group.

Rent-seeking state—kleptocratic state—predatory state

In the case of post-communist autocracies, among the terms used there are also those referring to one of the supposedly determinant goals of the appropriation of the state, the appropriation of public revenues for private purposes. But while the signifier used, rent-seeking, is a sort of neutral, technical term, the word kleptocratic alludes to the criminal activity of the ruling elite. The phrase predatory state, in contrast, indicates the violence that accompanies this activity. What makes the term mafia state more specific is that it also implies the anthropological structure of the perpetrator, the patron's court and the adopted political family.

Resource state

The term "resource state" shifts the emphasis to the sources tapped by the rent-seeking activity of the patron's court. But the name may also be compared with the expression "developmental state." It is a shared characteristic of both designations that they may be addressing the over-taxation of citizens, the overuse of their resources without suitable justification, usually lacking legitimacy. Meanwhile, as "developmental" indicates the voluntarist communal goals of the state, "resource state" expresses appropriation for private purposes as the goal of the ruling elite. Naturally, development goals may also mask, in major part, motivations for the private accumulation of wealth.

The resource state could even be seen as the inverse of the **welfare state** in liberal democracies. While in the case of the latter the state increases responsibility towards citizens in terms of social support and the creation of opportunities through taxation, the resource state does exactly the opposite, neglecting the needs and security of those who do not belong to the adopted political family while appropriating the resources of the community for private purposes. **The mafia state is the privatized form of a parasite state.**

Table 4.11. Some dimensions for defining the mafia state

	The basis for the term used	Alternative terms used for the description of the mafia state
1.	Actor	network / patronal / clan / mafia state
2.	Action	rent-seeking / kleptocratic / predatory state
3.	Legality	corrupt / partially captured / criminal state

As the foregoing has clearly shown, the names given to post-communist autocracies with the help of substantive categories do not exclude each other, but lay stress on different degrees and dimensions of the same group of phenomena.

VI. The comparative conceptual array for liberal democracies and post-communist autocracies—The main individual actors of post-communist patronal networks

VI/1. Politician versus poligarch

People in political roles in post-communist autocracies cannot largely be considered politicians, at least, not in the Western sense of people managing public affairs from positions of public authority they have obtained directly or indirectly through elections. In the autocratic case, strict rules of conflict of interest to separate public and private interests do not apply. To the contrary, to paraphrase Max Weber, they handle their authority as economic opportunities they appropriated in their private interest. While the political power of the poligarchs is public, the underlying economic power remains hidden. Although their personal wealth is secured from their political position and decisions, their illegitimate financial advantages overstep the limits of privileged allowances that could be related to his position and revenues from classical corruption. Managing the family business in the form of a political venture, the poligarch also establishes land leases, real estate possessions and a network of companies through **stooges**, front men, who legally stand for his illegally acquired property and authority. At times poligarchs pile up private fortunes in the frame of pseudo-civil organizations or foundations sourced from billions in public funds where they have informal decision-making competencies over the money.

VI/2. Public servant versus patronal servant

Within the administrative system of the mafia state the patterns of traditional autocratic rule increasingly emerge. The patriarchal head of the adopted political family governs in circumstances that do not adhere to the law. Rather, he gives commands personally, or through his confidants, thereby diluting and adjusting the traits of the bureaucratic administration typical in the modern state to his own demands. While the public servant's motive is to adhere to legal procedures, the patronal servant proves his loyalty to the (chief) patron of the patronal network.

What follows for the professional bureaucratic administration (as described by Weber) from this is:[37]

- the normative system of *"a regular system of appointment on the basis of free contract, and orderly promotion"* is disassembled;
- the *"clearly defined sphere of competence subject to impersonal rules"* are loosened. The political appointees handle a great variety of roles in the adopted political family, within the legitimate sphere of administration: stooge, governor, commissar, steward, treasurer, etc., expressions that describe the real functions of their roles more accurately in sociological terms, than would the official definitions of the administrative positions;
- the *"rationally established hierarchy"* is disrupted. The affiliates of the adopted political family traverse the lower and higher regions of public administration freely; the centralization of decisions pertaining to promotions by subjective mechanisms increases as the normative system of promotion is replaced by discretional decision-making mechanisms driven by political interests. If the elastic laws are still too tight for the implementation of the preferences of the adopted political family with regard to personnel, the "normative" environment is shaped to fit demands through regulations tailored to fit;
- *"technical training as a regular requirement"* is relativized. When necessary, peculiar exemptions pave the way for the positions that previously had strict prerequisites in terms of professional training;

- allowances and property entitlements are added on to *"fixed salaries"* as one rises through the hierarchy, reaching domains well beyond legal sources of income.

The Weberian traits of the professional bureaucratic administration either regress—if they could even be found in the post-communist autocracies in the first place—or never take form.

VI/3. Entrepreneur versus oligarch

Contrary to the ideal-typical western entrepreneur, the oligarch of the post-communist autocracy uses his legitimate fortune not only to build economic power, but political power or influence as well. His economic power is public, but his political power is kept hidden.

A distinction has to be made between the ideal types of the major entrepreneur, the organized criminal underworld's entrepreneur, and the oligarch. The **major entrepreneur** undertakes **legitimate economic activity, and his access to this activity is also legitimate**, meaning it is conducted according to accepted social norms: he secures both market and state contracts through transparent competition. The political authorities do not infringe on his autonomous position, which is guaranteed by law. In contrast, **the entrepreneur of the organized underworld** mainly carries on **illegal economic activities** (drug trade, prostitution, oil bleaching, extortion, protection racket, etc.) **under illegal conditions**. He stands in conflict with representatives of public authority and seeks to draw them under his influence by illegitimate means (bribery, threats, blackmail, and occasionally physical violence). The **oligarch of the post-communist systems** however, seeks to secure **illegal support for otherwise legal economic activity** by means of corruption. Until a single political force wholly takes over political power, he is assured relative autonomy, a bargaining position and a competitive edge.

A post-communist autocracy reduces the autonomy of the major entrepreneur, while restricting, domesticating, or eliminating the organized underworld. Drawing upon its monopoly of power, it destroys the relative autonomy of the oligarchs, and aims to integrate them into its own chain of command. The patron-client relationship also turns around in the mafia state: basically it is no longer the economic players who approach the political sphere with their claims, but it is the political regime that milks the economic actors as well as the taxpayers, by way of contracts and privileges issued to its subjugated oligarchs. A network of subcontractors and suppliers then extends this patron-client relationship to the lower reaches of the economy.

The oligarch is not only distinguished from the ideal type of the major entrepreneur by the advantages the regime ensures, but also by the measure of vulnerability to power, the degree to which the oligarch's particular economic activity and existential conditions make it possible to force him into a patron-client type of relationship.

Table 4.12. Model differences in the positions of the ideal typical major entrepreneurs and oligarchs

	Major entrepreneur	**Oligarch**
Relationship to the adopted political family	not embedded	embedded
Economic activity	legitimate	legitimate
Economic activity ordered on basis of	competition, market terms, legitimate	personal contacts, illegitimate or "legalized" illegitimate practices
Business performance	dependent primarily on performance in the market	dependent primarily on political relationships
Target group for products and services	largely not domestic consumers	largely local, domestic consumers
Mobility of activity	geographically mobile	place-bound, immobile
Nature of activity	difficult, or impossible to monopolize by the state	easily monopolized by the state
Conditions for the business venture	not directly under the influence, or hardly influenced by state arbitrariness, thus not easy to blackmail, less vulnerable to political decisions	established by state arbitrariness and therefore wholly prone to state influence, even to the extent of liquidation, and therefore open to blackmail

	Major entrepreneur	Oligarch
Source of wealth accumulation	mainly market, though also possibly competitive privatization	mainly directed privatization, state concessions, state procurement, guided bid for tenders
Nature of risk	independent of the state, market dependent	under influence of the state, based on patron-client relationship
Utilization of profit	utilized in transparent fashion, largely reinvested	drawn out of the venture, utilized in other (less transparent) fashion
Status of business	autonomous	kept, tribute-bound
Type of venture	profit oriented by market, innovative	tribute exacting through non-market tools, non-innovative

In the full-fledged post-communist autocracy, one can identify different **types of oligarchs**:
- The **inner circle oligarchs** did not have significant wealth to begin with. They manage to secure their start-up capital from positions weaving through politics—building on what would be called greenfield investments. Their wealth can be compared to that of those who made it as a result of the chaotic, spontaneous privatizations following the regime-change. Forming the inner circle of oligarchs with ties to political ventures, most of them belong to the **top spheres of the adopted political family, and also play active roles in shaping politics without legitimate position in public office.**
- The **adopted oligarchs** accumulated their wealth in the period of "oligarchic anarchy." Their admission into the political family only stabilizes their position and protects them in the world of politically motivated, violent redistributions of wealth. They can access opportunities offered by the adopted political family, and provide benefits in return: their contributions are exacted as the economic or political demands

of the political family would have it, at any given time. Their account balance nevertheless remains in the black by a wide margin.
- The **surrendered oligarchs** earlier enjoyed relative autonomy or had "played for the rival team." Reasons for their surrender may include contracts petering out under the mafia state, or non-market tools of state coercion—tax authorities, prosecutor's office, police—enforcing the change indirectly. Since they are struggling to survive economically, with a lot to lose but no protected bargaining position with the regime, they are compelled to find their place in the chain of command under the political family. They enjoy privileges, but pay their corruption taxes to the political family as required, meeting all expectations.
- **Escort oligarchs** are basically not beholden for their wealth to the political business venture of the mafia state. Rather, their network reaches back to the period before or around the regime change. They are the greatest oligarchs of the transition, whose favors were courted by different political sides for support. They were further reinforced by this mutual dependence. However, the position of "equal accommodation and equal distance" towards rival political forces by patronal networks is undermined by the disruption of the political balance between competing patronal networks. The encroaching advance of the adopted political family tipped the previously autonomous oligarchs out of their balancing act between various political forces, and in the first round, forced them into the roles of committed adjuncts in the venture. Though as allied oligarchs they have not been included in the political family's chain of command, they had to end any supportive ties with rival political forces or patronal clans.
- The **autonomous oligarchs** do not commit themselves permanently to any political force. While attempting to establish corrupt business relations with actors in the political sphere, they try to keep their integrity. This, however, is only possible if no patronal network manages to monopolize all political power. Their freedom of maneuver becomes sharply limited by conditions under the mafia state: they are either forced to surrender or, if they balk at this solution and come to be considered rival oligarchs, they become the targets of efforts at economic annihilation. Their relationships with any political force rivaling the adopted political family are criminalized and used as a pretext for their destruction—by means of politically selective law enforcement.

- The adopted political family of the mafia state considers **rival oligarchs** the most dangerous, those who clearly have their own political ambitions. They are meted out direct state coercion (as in the Khodorkovsky model in Russia). Those who don't have personal political ambitions and only support alternative political forces can count on more peaceful forms of expulsion (the Berezovsky model). In addition, those who try to resist the efforts of the adopted political family to make them surrender will also find themselves in the status of a rival oligarch.

Under a regime of competing patronal networks it can still be an open question as to who among those with partial political power, on the one hand, and economic power, on the other, is the leader, who depends on whom, who gives orders and who executes them. In a single-pyramid patronal system, and especially in a post-communist mafia state, however, the chief patron is evidently the one who can outlaw his rival by means of the legislature, the tax authorities, the prosecutor's office or the police. The one who can eject the other from the game using state powers is the winner who takes all. Those who argue that in post-communist autocracies oligarchs have captured the state fail to recognize that the reverse is true. In the tight political venture that is the mafia state, the adopted political family appoints its own oligarchs and gives them power. The oligarch cannot blackmail the chief patron here, since the classical mafia technique assumes publicity and the institutions of democracy, which can be activated when wrongdoing is unveiled. The indebted politician is blackmailed not with the threat of physical violence, but with that of disclosure. As the tax authorities, the prosecutor's office, the parliament, and so on, belong to the chief patron in the mafia state of the organized upperworld, the chances of an oligarch blackmailing him are rather thin.

Independent oligarchs only exist temporarily. In the mafia state, everyone works to fill the same family purse, from which everyone receives their share according to the rules of the political family.

While the term "oligarch" conjures images of vast wealth and national—even regional—influence, there are some local "oligarchs" who, if their local embeddedness, influence and wealth are to be considered, would better be called "**minigarchs**."[38] Though the size and scale are different in the case of oligarchs and minigarchs, their structural attributes are similar.

VI/4. The real holder of a public authority or owner of property versus the stooge

The stooge has no real power: his formal position, legal standing—whether in the field of politics or that of the economy—serves only to bridge the gap between the legitimate and illegitimate spheres. The political stooges are "governors," while the stooges of the business ventures are "stewards," so far as their sociological function is concerned.

Those who can be considered **political stooges** do not use the authority vested in them on the basis of their public office autonomously. In other words, their formal authorizations contradict their actual scope of action. The **economic stooges** represent poligarchs in the economic sphere, and especially in the fields dependent on the state. But oligarchs might also have economic stooges, when they do not wish to reveal the full gamut of their economic activities resulting from their political contacts. The economic stooges of the poligarchs can be either "friends of the family," insignificant businessmen, or oligarchs of the adopted family of the inner circle. Not only an individual, but an institution may also act as a "stooge," e.g., private or public foundations.

It is this institution of the stooge, among others, that separates the classical mafia and, by the same token, the mafia state from those systems where the nature of power and its legitimation coincide. In an ideal-typical liberal democracy, the stooge is not a structural component of the system. But neither is he in the various historical predecessors of patronal systems: after all, the feudal landlord does not hang upon the acknowledgment of his vassals, and he could as a matter of course hold his goods and estate publicly to be his own. In the communist regimes, people in the positions defined by the nomenklatura were exactly what the official, formal position said. Neither one nor the other system had any need for the presence of stooges in order to bridge the gap between the formal position and the actual competencies.

VI/5. Lobbyist versus corruption broker

The lobbyist of Western democracies is a legitimate mediator between the spheres of politics and the market. It is precisely the institutionally guaranteed separation of political and market activities that requires a regulated and transparent mode of contact between the two spheres, with the legally authorized lobbyist in one of these roles, helping along **cooperation** between the two spheres. In stark contrast, the corruption broker of the post-communist mafia state is no transparent actor of the power&ownership system, but rather an actor in the **collusion** between the two spheres. The corruption broker[39] connects participants of a corrupt transaction as a mediator, or legitimizes the illegitimate business deal as a judicial expert. His activities and position have changed a great deal during the two decades following the regime change. Under the conditions of the socialist shortage economy, the "business client" and the "corrupt service provider" would connect directly in almost all walks of life. The end of the post-regime-change shortage economy eliminated the market foundations of these corrupt relations in such dimensions. At the same time, forms of more robust corrupt transactions demanding greater expertise came into being. This created the situation in which the mediator's position was established, whereby the main fields of activity, apart from the expected reliance on a network of contacts, were organized around the writing of bids for tenders, legal advocacy, and the preparation of draft laws.

In the fluid conditions following the initial regime change from communism, corruption brokers could simultaneously be at the service of clients with different political or patronal network ties. Later, with the stabilization of the party structure, the more constant bonds of corruption brokers in a mercenary role under one or another patron were established, and the party's own financial network was built and operated with these corruption brokers. Personnel did not normally mix or match between different patronal networks. With a monopoly on political power, in a single-pyramid system the dominant patronal network assembled its own corruption brokers under the adopted political family in strict order, and also employs a number of them in the roles of political stooges.

In parallel to this, naturally, while seeking to liquidate the financial background of rival political and economic forces, it also eliminates their network of corruption brokers. On the new grounds of the mafia state's monopoly on power the proportions of fields of activity among its own corruption brokers also changes internally: with the systemic legalization of the adopted political family's channels of corruption, the field of planning draft laws and decrees makes it into the foreground of their activities, and the services provided by the writers of bids is also largely taken over by the now essentially unchecked state. In the same way that legislation and preparation of draft laws and regulations are in the mafia state no longer the tools of creating normative regulation applicable to everyone, and the normative status of equality before the law is undermined by laws arbitrarily tailored to individuals and businesses.

Under the conditions created by the mafia state, there are two types of lower-level, day-to-day corruption brokers[40] that gain vast importance and simultaneously go through a strange metamorphosis. One of these is the **gatekeeper**, who ensures the bureaucratic background and protection of the illegitimate deal within the public administration. In the earlier stage he is the official of the bureaucracy as posited by Max Weber, who is led astray by an occasional commission. With the establishment of the single-pyramid patronal system, however, not only does the appointment of the official in charge come from above, but so too do the orders for his continued activity as a corruption broker. The entry of the political stooge indicates that the transformation of public good to private benefit has turned from an occasional deviance into a systemic operation. The other type is the **representative broker**, who under the mafia state, in a role as deputy for poligarchs, may even give his name to the ownership of major corporations. In terms of the size of his wealth, his business, he may even be considered an oligarch, and yet is not, only an economic stooge. Of course it is also frequent that an oligarch and stooge are embodied in one and the same person.

VI/6. The state's security forces versus the family security guards and secret services

In communist regimes, the secret services and the state enforcement organizations were under the control of the small, topmost body of the party. Loyalty to the chairman of the party was indivisible from the formal position, and in case of a downfall the loyalty of the secret services transferred to the new leader. In post-communist autocracies, the personal attachment and dependence on the chief patron and his "family" becomes stronger. Though it is not possible to test how loyalty survived in the wake of the death of autocrats and the fall of variously colored revolutions, Hungary's example is illustrative in a number of respects. After the electoral defeat of Fidesz following its term in government between 1998 and 2002, the chief patron withdrew some of the secret service cadres from the formal institutions and established an alternative, private secret service and security capacity, and then placed these at the head of the reformed secret service and security organs after Fidesz' 2010 election victory. The newly established Counter Terrorism Center (TEK), which was invested with secret service, counterintelligence, police and investigative functions as well, is directed by Viktor Orbán's former personal bodyguard. On a larger scale, the situation is the same in the case of the recently established Russian National Guard, with Putin's personal bodyguard also becoming it leader. Essentially, the cadre policy of the secret service and enforcement organizations centered around the chief patron is primarily to break away from

Table 4.13. Main types of political and economic actors in three ideal-type political regimes

Liberal democracy	Post-communist autocracy	Communist regime
citizen	client / servant	subject
politician	poligarch (political entrepreneur) / political stooge	high level party cadre / functionary
trustee	smotryaschiy, "holder"	(middle and low level) party cadre/ functionary
public servant	patronal servant	administrative cadre, apparatchik (bureaucratic functionary)
state's security services	patron's security services	party's security services
entrepreneur	oligarch/minigarch	state enterprise leader
lobbyist	corruption broker	tolkach, "pusher"
business interest representation	facilitating corrupt exchange	plan or barter bargain
n.a.	front man, stooge, "strohmann"	n.a.

the formalized order of advancement established by the former communist nomenklatura that regulated and somewhat limited the number of candidates who could be considered for a given position. In the mafia state, the chief criterion for filling a position of real power—independent of advancement and position on the formal table of rank—is a close personal connection and a relationship of trust with the chief patron.

The state enforcement function of communist regimes was handled by formalized organs of the state. In post-communist autocracies, however, there is a great predilection for the use of paramilitary organizations, of various "spontaneous" groups that are sympathetic to the regime and that are supported, as well as partly directed, by it (e.g., football hooligans, skinheads etc.), or even of criminal groups on occasion, all extraneous to the formal institutional system but useful against politicians, journalists, or movements that become inconvenient or unmanageable for the regime.

VII. Coordination of the political and economic spheres

On the basis of the primary characteristics of the two "great" systems, the capitalist and the socialist, János Kornai places post-communist regimes in the category of the capitalist system: "There is a broad if not full consensus among experts as to when the *change of system* occurred in the countries affected. . . . With a few exceptions, the countries in the group qualifying as socialist in 1987 all have undergone a transition from socialism to capitalism."[41]

Though in terms of their characteristics it seems that the post-communist autocracies and dictatorships could be adjusted to the capitalist model with the appendage of the epithet "dominant," it still would make sense to propose that an attempt be made to also define an intermediate status that is not a transition from "socialism" to "capitalism," but an independent, stable entity.

Under capitalism, following the separation of political and market activities, the political sphere is called upon to ensure the competitively neutral operation of the market dominated by private property. In contrast, in post-communist autocracies the political sphere does not guarantee, but rather controls, the economy, tolerating its free operation in economic areas that are difficult to access or of no interest to the ruling elite. It expropriates and operates the economy for private gains in areas that can

Table 4.14. Primary characteristics of state and private property relations in three ideal-type political regimes

Liberal democracies	Post-communist autocracy	Communist regime
The political group in power **ensures** the dominance of private property and market coordination	The political group in power **controls and partially appropriates** private property and coordination of the market	The political group in power, the communist party **imposes** dominance of state property and bureaucratic coordination
Private property is the dominant form of property	*Power&ownership (vlast'-sobstvennost')* is the determinative form of ownership	*State property* is the dominant form of property
Market coordination is the dominant mechanism of coordination *(competitive market)*	*Relational coordination*: the determinative coordinating mechanism overseen and directed by the adopted political family *(relational market-redistribution)*	*Bureaucratic coordination* is the dominant coordinating mechanism *(bureaucratic resource-redistribution)*

be drawn into its sphere of influence—through the instruments of power. The means of relation based operation of power&ownership encompass the whole range of legitimate to illegitimate tools, including the legislature, top-down corruption, and the distribution or redistribution of property.

If we wish to delineate the economies of the three types in ideal-typical terms, this may be achieved by defining them as **market economy, relational economy** and **command economy**, where the coordination is impersonal-formal, personal-informal, and bureaucratic-formal in each ideal-type respectively.

VIII. Power&ownership: distribution and expropriation of property in post-communist autocracies

It is useful to analyze post-communist regimes as a separate category within the set that frequently feature single-pyramid patronal network arrangements. First and foremost, their economies were determined almost exclusively by state ownership. The power struggle after the collapse of the communist system was then inevitably tied up with competition for property and rent-seeking positions. The dismantling of state property took various courses in different post-communist regimes. In most, where the collapse of the communist ruling elite did take place, as a result of privatization, the private sector's share of GDP ranged between 60 and 80 percent by the 2000s. A low private sector share (25 to 55 percent) could be found

Table 4.15. Features of ownership in three ideal-type political regimes

Liberal democracy	Post-communist autocracy	Communist regime
private property	power&ownership	state property
competitive market	relational market	administrative market
market economy	relational economy	command economy
trading and taxing	taking (taxation, rents, tribute, plunder) and rent-seeking (administrative, budgetary, natural resources)	centralised allocation: (re)distributing
privatization	*prikhvatizatsiya*, "grabitization"	n.a.
nationalization	deprivatization, renationalization, patrimonialization	nationalization / collectivization
hostile takeover	*reiderstvo* (centrally led corporate raiding)	expropriation

only in those Central Asian republics (Turkmenistan, Uzbekistan, Tadzhikistan) where the last communist party leaders saved and held on to their power in the long term. Only Belarus remains an exception to the rule, where the private sector made up only 30 percent of GDP as late as 2010.[42] The form of distribution was privatization.

VIII/1. Privatization versus *prikhvatizatsiya*

In Western democracies, state corporations work in a market environment dominated by private property. This means management has to stand its ground in market competition. The property and income of these corporations can be expropriated neither by corporate management nor by the ruling elite. A state-owned corporation could be privatized in cases of inefficient or ineffective operation or if public policy goals were not served by state management. However, privatization in such a case is a transparent market transaction that involves not only setting a price as favorable as possible for the public budget but also guarantees that the services provided by the state corporation will continue. This is a change of ownership rather than a (politically motivated) distribution of property. At the same time, in Western societies there is usually market demand with strong enough capital to make possible the competitive market acquisition of state companies. In the West, therefore, privatization is a market transaction that does not establish a new social strata of wealth but that constitutes an alternative field of investment for the existing wealthy strata.

In post-communist regimes however, this is a matter of **creating the property owners**. Yet the waves of privatization that took place in these countries were not usually conducted through a transparent, legitimate process. This is evident in a Russian term widely used to describe the phenomenon: *prikhvatizatsiya*. This term is a conflation of the Russian word for privatization and the Russian verb "to acquire, to grab." A literal translation into English would yield something like "grabitization,"[43] which also alludes to the arbitrary, aggressive aspect of the process.

Fours aspects of the post-communist environment made it almost inevitable that the distribution of property would be politically motivated:
- A **suitable legal environment was absent** at the time of regime change—with a few Central European exceptions—that could have satisfactorily ensured the protection of private property and guar-

anteed appropriate and transparent rules of transition from state to private ownership.
- The collapse of the communist power structure usually went hand in hand with the **breakdown of functions of state control**, with the result being that decisions about the distribution of state property were made through a political machinery and state apparatus that were neither stable nor conscious of their temporary position. This impacted post-communist regimes in two ways: countries either had a relatively cultured, *legally continuous transition* (e.g., Hungary, Poland), or (especially in the Central Asian former Soviet republics) a *command continuous transition*.
- A market transaction in the Western sense was impossible simply because there was **no financially sound internal demand**. By definition, this was not possible: under the conditions of state monopoly and the command economy, no one could have accumulated assets close to what would have been needed.
- When an administrative market and command economy are collapsing, it is **impossible to determine the exact value of a former state corporation** in a market environment that has not even been established. After all, neither the price of the products nor the costs of production—nor for that matter supply and demand—had been shaped by market forces. Of course, it could be suspected that the raw materials industry, which had been selling at depressed rates compared to international rates, would bring significant profits to those who managed to grab it.

These features of the early post-communist environment inevitably undermined the legitimacy and social acceptance of the changes in ownership. Indeed, even if the authorities at the time had eschewed their own interests, they would still have found themselves largely trapped, facing only a choice among lesser evils:
- If they treated state property as **belonging in a way to society as a whole**, the logical next step would be a process of **coupon privatization**, by which a large share of the most productive state property would be distributed among the population as a whole and among any former owners (or their descendants) in the form of vouchers (as in the Czech Republic) or **compensation notes** (as was done for some confiscated property in Hungary). However, this resulted in a high

degree of fragmentation in ownership rights and thus did not result in any substantial individual growth in wealth. The market price of the properties dropped, enabling a few individuals to take advantage of downwardly spiraling prices to concentrate property in their own hands and then, later, politicize their assets.
- If they attempted to **distribute ownership of state corporations to employees,** the resulting allocation of shares generally favored management. In this case, the process typically resulted in "red" and "green" barons emerging within the corporations who would either buy out existing management or remove the masses of the corporations' workers. This process usually coincided with the diversion of certain units or corporate stocks into new businesses tied to the management, often leading to the collapse of the large state (mostly industrial) corporations and the layoff of a significant share of their workers.
- If the primary concern for privatizers was to **draw in working capital**, this was in effect only possible by letting foreign corporations in, which was not always a desirable or popular solution.

Thus even if we presume that privatizers would have wished to manage the distribution of property in some sort of normative manner—be it providing some sort of social justice, acting on a romantic ideal of labor self-management, or acting on a professional rationale—privatization would have come with a serious legitimacy deficit. Citizens' sense of justice would not have been compatible with (in the first two scenarios) the wealth accumulation of leaders connected to the previous regime or (in the third scenario) the arrival of foreign owners en-masse, which would have been seen as the country being sold off. But the patterns we see show that the rise of a new propertied strata in the process of regime change was mainly determined by inherited or new relational powers (network capital).

In the former communist system, state property belonged to the political body and thus was owned and managed by the nomenklatura. As a result of their positions as handlers, they disposed of it like bureaucrats rather than like private owners. In the course of privatization, the spheres of politics and the market were separate only in appearance. Not only did the political sphere designate and provide for the first private owners, but coupled with the economic sphere, members of the political sphere held each other hostage in the following sense: In post-soviet autocracies, the administrative economies did not turn into market economies in the Western sense, but got entrenched along the way in a **relational economy**. The system of **power&ownership** was reproduced in a new form.

VIII/2. Hostile takeover versus corporate raiding (*reiderstvo*)[44]

Because post-communist privatization featured a legitimacy deficit, the coercive redistribution of private property that was won from the state began almost immediately. It would be misleading to try and apply the term "hostile takeover" to this process, at least, as this term is used in the West. While a "hostile takeover" is widely considered immoral in Western democracies, the term usually refers to actions that are legal, including: the use of a minority block of shares in ways running counter to the interest of the corporation; decisions that set back the company; or destructive labor union tactics. Hostile takeovers in the West are rarely characterized by the illegal use of public authority, and physical violence is even rarer.

Corporate raiding, or corporate asset-grabbing as it has come to be practiced in post-communist regimes (colloquially called *reiderstvo* in Russia), always bears the marks of one form of coercion or other. Whether the coercion takes a physical form or is conducted in one of the many other ways the public authorities practice it, we can differentiate between black, gray and white raiding. The table below presents different forms of *reiderstvo*, its initiators-conductors, and the correlation of its practice with some other post-communist regime traits.

In the categorical differentiation displayed in Table 4.16, what is meant by **black raiding** is essentially the illegal acquisition of property by means of physical violence. From the early 1990s, "shadow privatization led quickly to the spread of violent crime that was a by-product of the first wave of ownership redistribution throughout Russia. A considerable part of the male population was involved in that wave of criminal redistribution. Considering the extent of the violence and killing, that initial wave of 'black raiding' was comparable in some respects to a civil war, and affected most of Russia's industrially developed regions."[45] The agents of black raiding are typically underworld criminal persons or groups. But even in this phase, some entrepreneurs appear as clients, who invest their capital in criminal groups that carry out black raiding. In this sense, black raiding may to a limited degree involve criminal clients par excellence as well as lower-level public officials.

Table 4.16. Types and certain features of reiderstvo in post-communist regimes

Strength of the state	"Legitimacy" of raiding	The initiator or client of the corporate raiding			
		Organized upper-world: chief patron (top level public authority)	Low or middle level public authority	Rival entrepreneurs or oligarchs	Organized underworld: criminal groups
Strong state	White raiding				
	Gray raiding				
Weak state	Black raiding				
Institutional environment and features of the raiding action		*Criminal state*	*State crime*	*Corporate crime*	*Crime*
		Single-pyramid patronal system	Multi-pyramid patronal system		
		Monopolized	Oligarchic		Competitive
		Oligarch capture	Partial state capture		

The widespread phenomenon of black raiding assumes weak state power and a murky legal environment governing ownership. The transformation crisis of the early 90s stripped the broad masses of their meagre, but secure livings, while at the same time opening the field for the violent redistribution of newly privatized property.

The category of **gray raiding**—narrowing Thomas Firestone's general definition for corporate raiding down to this specific form—is defined as

> the seizure, or attempted seizure, of a business or a substantial part of its assets, through the corrupt reliance on a legal document, including, but not limited to, a court order, judicial decision, corpo-

rate resolution, corporate charter document, or state registration document. The execution of a corporate raid typically involves the following three stages: (1) the raider creates or corruptly obtains a legal document establishing faux legal title to some assets, usually shares or real property of a business; (2) the raider carries out a forcible takeover of the target property; and (3) the raider launders the seized property through a series of shell companies to an ostensible 'good faith purchaser' from whom it is essentially impossible to recover the property. . . . Each stage relies on abuse of the legal system.[46]

The typical initiators of gray raiding are no longer necessarily criminal groups, but may be business rivals or even members of the lower, local levels of organs of public authority. We can speak of a form of **state-facilitated corporate crime** in the first case, and of **corporate-facilitated state crime** in the latter.[47] The ideal terrain for gray raiding features a lack of strong state power, on the one hand, and the elimination of "wild-West style" criminality based on direct physical violence, on the other. But even in this phase, the free competitive mode of gray raiding gradually loses its predominance and gray raiding comes to be organized around competing patronal networks. At this point, it is not only the hostile exploitation of the existing legal environment that comes into play, but decrees tailored to individuals or specific companies also appear. This is the world of partial (local) state capture. Here the necessary professional expertise is provided—in a fashion similar to that provided by corruption brokers—by **raiding brokers**, "professional service providers, such as lawyers or bankers, who charge a fee or take a percentage of the ultimate gain in exchange for facilitating a raid."[48]

By **white raiding**—breaking with the usual application of the term—we refer to a form of corporate raiding by which property is expropriated by top authorities of the central state, typically at the command of and through coordination with the highest holder of executive power. In this case, instead of the legal environment being misused, it is adapted and tailored to individuals and single companies in a targeted manner. This sort of corporate raiding becomes dominant when a multi-pyramid patronal system is replaced by a single-pyramid patronal system and corporate raiding becomes a tool for subjugating oligarchs who had heretofore enjoyed relative autonomy and fought their battles among themselves. Here we can speak not of state capture, only of oligarch capture, which presumes the monopolization of political power by a patronal network. White raiding may be combined with gray raiding, in which case smooth cooperation is required between institutions for legislation (including the passage of decrees), on the one hand, and the tax authorities, secret services, prosecutor's office and police, on the other, all under the direction of the chief patron. The monopoly on power that is usually concentrated around the position of the president supplies the raw political force for replacing **oligarchic anarchy** with a form of criminal state, the **mafia state**. Such a switch took place in Russia starting in the year 2000 under Vladimir Putin and was attempted in Ukraine under the presidency of Viktor Yanukovych, when "according to one [Ukrainian] tax official, ministries have become weapons of the Presidential Administration against any business."[49]

The single-pyramid patronal system creates white raiding's "legal" room for maneuver—as described above—through legislation and decrees. On the one hand, a feature of the resulting regulations is that the laws, contrary to their publicly stated function (namely, that they apply impartially to everyone), have been tailored to individuals or companies. This can be done in either a positive or negative way. On the other hand, these laws set regulations (e.g., bankruptcy law, tax evasion law, various environmental protection and healthcare prescriptions) that make it possible for the dominant patronal network to drive the companies selected for *reiderstvo* into bankruptcy through politically selective law enforcement. This is how the "legal environment" serving the predatory character of the mafia state is brought into being.

Each post-communist regime has varied in traversing the spectrum from black raiding to white raiding, from spontaneously violent to centrally directed and "legalized" corporate raiding. **Russia** progressed through all three stages, ultimately (largely) monopolizing, centralizing and appropriating the means of expropriation by establishing a centrally directed form of corporate raiding that facilitates the accumulation of both power and wealth. Paradoxically, in accomplishing this centralization, it also created a certain form of property protection that is in some tension with the lower-level, guerilla actions characteristic of gray and black raiding. The preconditions for secure ownership in the mafia state are, first, loyalty to the chief patron, and, secondly, a situation whereby closer circles of the adopted political family do not feel like grabbing the property in question. However arbitrary the system may be, it creates more predictable security for private property than existed in the earlier period of oligarchic anarchy, which was characterized by a weak state. Where the size of the empire demands it, the chief patron may delegate the right of corporate raiding and corruption (excluding the realms of raw material extraction and strategic branches of industry) to regional governors in the adopted political family, where the national system is replicated on a smaller scale.

In **Ukraine**, the first two forms dominated, though corporate raiding directed from the presidential level became prominent when attempts were made by Leonid Kuchma and Viktor Yanukovych to establish single-pyramid systems. The consolidation of these efforts was blocked by the Orange Revolution and the Euromaidan Revolution. In fact, after the latter revolution, the vacuum left by the dissolution of the state and the emergence of civil war was filled at the regional level by temporarily granting positions of public authority to locally dominant oligarchs. In **Hungary**, by contrast, the black and gray versions of corporate raiding were never present due to the stability of its liberal political institutional system and the maturity of its legal institutions protecting private property. Skipping these first two "evolutionary" stages of raiding, centrally organized white raiding was introduced directly by the mafia state that Orbán established after 2010. Paradoxically, the situation is similar in the **former Soviet republics of Central Asia**, where the economy was privatized to a much smaller degree. There, it was not the institutional system of liberal democracy, but former communist rulers holding onto power at the highest level that secured a monopoly on corporate raiding for the chief patron.

Alongside the categories of structural and circular mobility that are widely used in sociology, we can introduce the concepts of 'structural' and 'circular' accumulation of private wealth and capital for post-communist regimes. By **'structural' accumulation of private wealth**, we mean that the basis of enrichment is the privatization of state assets that had long been under state ownership, resulting in a change in the proportions of state and private property on a national level. The extent of privatization (*prikhvatizatsiya*) partly circumscribes the potential circle of new owners, whereupon, when state power is weak (as observed earlier), bottom-up violent redistribution of property begins. If the extent of privatization has reached the limits of the possible, the field of centrally distributable property that could be privatized (*prikhvatizatsiya*, not accumulated through market competition) decreases, and so if the adopted political family wishes to remunerate new owners with property, then some existing family oligarchs (perhaps the disloyal, rival, or simply less powerful) have to be stripped of their wealth in order to extend the field of redistributable wealth. This is the essence of the **'circular' accumulation of private wealth**. Thus the reprivatization (*reprikhvatizatsiya*) of state assets, concessions, rental rights, etc.—in lieu of distributable state assets—follows the renationalization or centrally lead *reiderstvo* of private properties. But it does not result in a change in the proportion of state and private property on a national level.

VIII/3. Nationalization versus deprivatization, renationalization

Nationalization, as practiced in post-communist autocracies (meaning the expropriation of private property through the coercive instruments of public authority) is fundamentally different in function from both its practice under capitalism and from how it works under the communist command economy, which is based on state monopoly of property. Under capitalism, though non-economic objectives also appear among the motives of the regime, the operation of nationalized property nevertheless fits into the rationale of the market. In communist regimes, on the other hand, the whole of the economy operated in an irrevocable and homogeneous way under the ownership of the state, with politics dominating. In post-communist autocracies, however, renationalization simultaneously serves to increase the wealth of the adopted political family, to provide regulated remuneration for those built into its vassal chain of rule, and to keep society in check.

Table 17. The nature of nationalization, deprivatization, renationalization in three ideal-type political regimes

Liberal democracy	Post-communist autocracy	Communist regime
Property is taken into state ownership, but operated along the principles of competitive market	Property is taken under the control of the dominant patronal network and operated along the principles of relational market	Private property is abolished and nationalized property is operated along the principles of administrative market

All the same, it is perhaps more appropriate to speak of **renationalization**[50], **deprivatization** or **patrimonialization**[51] since a majority of the nationalizations concern the re-appropriation of property that had been privatized only a short while earlier. But it is not only the usual nationalizations of corporations that we can list among renationalizations or deprivatizations. This is not the only means of extending the influence of the adopted political family through the instruments of the state, as this can also occur through, for example, the extension of state control and influence over various ownership entitlements in ways amounting to institutionalized state blackmail. Taking this into account, let us look at the main types of renationalization—aiming at patrimonialization—practiced in post-communist autocracies.

- **Cold nationalization is the nationalization of certain market elements of the economic environment**: the state expropriates the market environs of a given economic sector without directly nationalizing the businesses involved in it. Techniques used for this include: using state authority to determine prices; instituting special taxes; regulating/restricting fields of activity through decrees; imposing stipulations affecting those who operate the businesses; forcing consumers to use certain suppliers or service providers.

    These measures—serving to bleed owners of businesses dry, to prepare for a permanent or "transit nationalization" (a transitional move aimed at future reprivatization, as discussed further below) of a business, to ensure the subordination of key players in a sector—personalize and impose a politically directed chain of command on market relations that otherwise, on the whole, involve impersonal connections and economic calculus. Cold nationalization does not necessarily turn into permanent nationalization or transit nationalization (as discussed in the following), but opens the way to many potential ways to extract resources from businesses. This phenomenon tends to accompany the process where by the adopted political family brings more economic positions into its orbit and wealth accumulates within the organized upperworld. As the remaining stock of privatizable state property is meager, the classic techniques of privatization do not apply any longer for the political family.

    Whereas among post-communist countries that later became EU member states market and economic prerogatives were tied naturally to the ownership of property, with some of these then becoming part of the state's domain through cold nationalization, heading further east these prerogatives were only partially tied to nascent private property, if at all. In these parts, therefore, the task at hand is not the renationalization of entitlements but, rather, keeping them in state ownership. (Such entitlements may include the centralized disposal of raw-material distribution capacity and logistics, or the phenomenon often called overregulation, which makes it possible for the public authorities to harass and blackmail entrepreneurs in many unjustifiable ways.)

- **Bandit nationalization, which means the nationalization of private assets** (e.g., private pension funds).
- **Market-acquiring nationalization is the nationalization of an economic activity or the right to it**: in this case, the state does not strip business owners of their property directly, but monopolizes the economic activity in question. This can take the forms listed below:
  - making the continuation of an activity **conditional on a concession** and redistributing these concessions;
  - stipulating that **only companies in state or municipal possession** are permitted to carry on certain activities (such as local public transport, water management, waste management, metal trade etc.);
  - making a given activity **the sole province of a newly established state company.**
- **Competency nationalization means a central appropriation of municipal responsibilities**, as a result of which a given economic activity or responsibility is diverted to a central state organization.
- **Transit nationalization is the taking of a private company into "temporary state care,"** when by means of this interim phase of nationalization private fortunes are forced into the ownership orbit of the adopted political family. The nationalization may be facilitated by prior actions of cold nationalization, forcing the owner to surrender and eventually leave the market. A state loan may be ensured to oil the reprivatization within the adopted political family. It is a kind of "reprivatization what was defined as 'repeated privatization': nationalization of the already privatized companies followed up by the alternative 'fair' privatization."[52]
- **Money-pump nationalization is the nationalization of the losses of an economic activity and the privatization of its profits.** This occurs primarily in the sphere of public utilities, where the central govern-

ment is simultaneously intent on getting rid of foreign ownership in the name of a populist nationalist ideology and decreasing the immediate burdens on the population in the name of a populist socialistic ideology. However, public utility providers that are taken into state ownership by these means will, on the one hand, reduce the quality of services provided in an effort to cut the costs of routine maintenance, and, on the other, pump into private coffers a significant part of the state budget support required to keep the system running. The latter is usually accomplished through supply subcontractors belonging to the adopted political family.

- **Ordinary renationalization** can be defined as the complete seizure of a formerly privatized company by the state for a longer-lasting period.
- **Deprivatization** is the expansion of state shareholding among privatized companies.[53] The essence of this policy lies in forcing state and private corporations in certain especially important strategic sectors (e.g., the raw material extraction industry, military industry, high tech manufacturing, etc.) into a single state holding company. This method serves the power and financial purposes of the adopted political family, without completely blocking the economic operation of the companies belonging to this sector. Thus this simultaneously serves a range of functions, from ensuring loyalty to the placement of cadres and rents, in a sustainable manner.

VIII/4. Corruption versus centralized and monopolized rent-seeking

Rather than seeking to describe the phenomenon of corruption in close detail, the focus of this study is still the mafia-like operation of post-communist autocracies characterized by the single-pyramid patronal system. In particular, the focus is on phase of political system evolution that goes beyond petty—occasional and individual—corruption and even beyond state capture, in which criminal or oligarchic groups and the lower or middle level state apparatus are involved. This is because the mafia states seen among post-communist autocracies that are dominated by single-pyramid patronal networks represent a new evolutionary plane of corruption. At this level, corruption is not eliminated, but appropriated through monopolization and operated centrally. Corrupt transactions are not initiated from below, the oligarchic sphere of the economy, but from the top, the world of the poligarchs. We are not talking about traditional bribes and kickback money, but protection money collected through state coercion. This ends the free enterprise of "corruption" in the market, with state-dictated coercion taking its place. Naturally this system does not limit itself merely to diverting current income. Rather, through a more comprehensive regime, over and above specific instances of income diversion, the system includes public administration offices with rent-seeking potential and the redistribution of state property.

For the mafia state, in fact, traditional corruption tends to interfere with the state authorities' operations. The mafia state thus has three options in dealing with traditional corruption:

- **Restrain** or try to eliminate it, since pillaging of income and property does not require the maintenance of a traditional corruption network. This procedure is more typical of post-communist regimes that have joined the European Union.
- Deliver it into the hands of the chief patron, who can then hand out these corruption opportunities to loyal subpatrons in the form of **concessions**. Those receiving the concessions can then, in turn, gather and monopolize the various channels of corruption on a local level under themselves.
- **Take over** the "autonomous," decentralized corrupt networks and centralizing their operation.

In the two latter cases, the chief patron and subpatrons may also establish new, alternative corruption networks that operate along the lines of traditional patterns. Furthermore, traditional organized crime groups (those trafficking in drugs, weapons, prostitution etc.) can be incorporated into the state criminal organization and may even gain a permanent and substantial role here. Meanwhile, the incorporated organized criminal groups may also provide other services to the chief patron, including maintaining order, intimidation or the liquidation of opposition figures.

The state, operated as a criminal organization, can secure privatized rents from three main sources:[54]

- **administrative rent** can mean, on the one hand, the delegation of members of the adopted political family to the growing number of positions overseen by the state, in which they are able to receive state allowances and corrupt concessions simultaneously, and, on the other hand, trade in state prerogatives for personal gain.

- **budgetary rent** refers to the tapping of budget resources for personal gain.
- **rents derived from extractive industries**, on account of their unusually lucrative nature, refers to rents that are monopolized at the level of the chief patron and are typically not delegated as concessions to the lower, or local levels.

The expression "rent-seeking" does not, however, allude to the peaceful or violent nature of the action. So long as it only concerns the legal provision of state positions and income, the **rent-seeking state** appears as a state engaged in expensive and inefficient policies. If one refers to the illegal yet nonviolent appropriation of income controlled by the state, the definition **kleptocratic state** applies. Where this includes property acquisition by blackmail and the appropriation of income or property partly or whole through coercion using state instruments (tax authorities, prosecution,

Table 4.18. Patterns of corruption in three ideal-type political regimes

Liberal democracy	Post-communist autocracy	Communist regime
competitive market corruption	relational market corruption	administrative market corruption
surplus corruption	n.a.	shortage corruption
sellers' corruption	n.a.	buyers' corruption
system destroying corruption	system constituting corruption	system lubricating corruption
corrupting individuals + firms + organized underworld	organized upperworld + organized underworld + corrupting individuals	corrupting individuals
kickback money + protection money	protection money + kickback money	kickback money
generally/normatively sanctioned	selectively preferred (*krysha*, "roof") or sanctioned	moderately tolerated

police, secret services), whether it formally be considered inclusion in state-owned property or channeling to the adapted political family, the term that seems most appropriate is **predatory state**. The post-communist mafia states naturally belong to this latter category.

VIII/5. Evidence versus *kompromat*

The mafia state, as mentioned earlier, monopolizes and centralizes both "legalized" and criminally organized forms of rent-seeking to the advantage of the adopted political family. It is in its utmost interest to secure the loyalty of those belonging to its patronal network. Meanwhile, it criminalizes its rivals and opponents, as well as eliminating them from the political and economic competition through the instruments of politically selective law-enforcement employed in the course of anti-corruption campaigns. In Western democracies, the anti-corruption struggle is not a tool for rival patronal networks to settle scores, and so the evidence of corruption will trigger the impartial operation of law enforcement authorities in an ideal-typical instance. In post-communist autocracies, to the contrary, almost everyone participates in the illegal mechanisms of wealth accumulation, and so their actions can be docu-

Table 4.19. Role of law and legality in three ideal-type political regimes

Liberal democracy	Post-communist autocracy	Communist regime
rule of law / citizen subordinated to law	rule by law / law subordinated to the adopted political family	lawlessness / law subordinated to the party
normative law enforcement	individually tailored / politically selective law enforcement	repressive law enforcement
impartial jurisdiction	politically selective jurisdiction	show trials
Evidence *crime committed: process launched automatically*	kompromat *crime committed: process launched on the basis of a political decision*	fabricated accusation *crime not committed: process launched on the basis of a political decision*

mented and compiled. Yet the purpose of these documents is not to start the administration of justice irrespective of the perpetrator. Rather, their purpose is to serve as a means of blackmail to enforce loyalty to the chief patron at the helm of the dominant patronal network. Such documentation is called *"kompromat"* in the Russian slang, referring to compromising documents that can be used to launch a criminal process after a political decision has been made to punish or remove an insubordinate actor.

Conclusion

This exercise has had two major aims. Initially, it has sought to demonstrate the inadequacy of existing concepts (including the very vocabulary we have at our disposal) to understand post-communist politics and economics. Existing concepts were originally developed to generally describe and analyze systems prominent in the developed West, and our continued dependence on these notions and terminology has seriously warped our understanding of post-communist systems, not to mention made it very hard to describe those features that we do understand. This situation has fostered a state of conceptual confusion that has greatly complicated the advance of research. The second major aim of this chapter has thus been to take a major step toward remedying this problem by developing a new conceptual "tool kit" for understanding and describing post-communist politics. In particular, it has proposed a set of categories for important actors, processes, and (often informal) institutions that are often mischaracterized or missed entirely by preexisting analytical frameworks. The hope is that these new categories, summarized for readers' convenience in the tables above, will lay an important foundation for a more productive research agenda on post-communist politics.

NOTES

[1] Jenő Szűcs, *Vázlat Európa három történeti régiójáról* [An outline of the three historical regions of Europe] (Budapest, Magvető Kiadó, 1983).
[2] Ibid., 8.
[3] Herbert Kitschelt, Zdenka Mansfeldova, Radoslaw Markowski, and Gábor Toka, *Post-Communist Party Systems: Competition, Representation and Inter-Party Competition* (Cambridge: Cambridge University Press, 1999).

4 Henry E. Hale, *Patronal Politics: Eurasian Regime Dynamics in Comparative Perspective* (Cambridge University Press, 2014), 59.
5 These analyses do not include those communist regimes of the East Asia (China, North Korea, Vietnam) in which the political monopoly of the communist party continues to this day.
6 Claus Offe, "Political Corruption: Conceptual and Political Issues," in *Building a Trustworthy State in Post-Socialist Transition*, ed. János Kornai and Susan Rose-Ackerman (Palgrave Macmillan, 2004), 78.
7 Hale, *Patronal Politics*.
8 Max Weber, *Economy and Society: An Outline of Interpretive Sociology*, translated by Ephraim Fischoff, Hans Gerth, et al., and edited by Guenther Roth and Claus Wittich (Berkeley: University of California Press, 1978), 233.
9 Claus Offe, "Political Corruption," 78–79.
10 See the chapter János Kornai, "The system paradigm revisited: Clarification and additions in the light of experiences in the post-socialist region," in this volume, 37–39.
11 For examples, see Iván Szelényi, "Weber's theory of domination and post-communist capitalisms," *Theory and Society* 45, no. 1 (2016): 1–24; Tamás Csillag and Iván Szelényi, "Drifting from Liberal Democracy: Neo-conservative Ideology of Managed Illiberal Democratic Capitalism in Post-communist Europe," *Intersections: East European Journal of Society and Politics* 1, no. 1 (2015): 18–48, https://doi.org/10.17356/ieejsp.v1i1.28; Oleksandr Fisun, "Rethinking Post-Soviet Politics from a Neopatrimonial Perspective," *Democratizatsiya: The Journal of Post-Soviet Democratization* (2012): 87–98, http://ssrn.com/abstract=2645304; Fisun, "The Future of Ukraine's Neopatrimonial Democracy," *PONARS Eurasia Policy Memo*, no. 394 (October 2015).
12 Hale, *Patronal Politics*, 9–10.
13 Hale, *Patronal Politics*; Bálint Magyar, *Post-Communist Mafia State: The Case of Hungary* (Budapest–New York: Central European University Press–Noran Libro, 2016).
14 Worldwide Governance Indicators, http://info.worldbank.org/governance/wgi/index.aspx#reports
15 Péter Szakonyi, ed. *A 100 leggazdagabb Magyar* [The hundred richest people in Hungary], published by Napi.hu, 2014; 2015; 2016.
16 See the study "The Institution of Power&Ownership" by Andrey Ryabov in this volume.
17 Olga Kryshtanovskaya and Stephen White, "Inside the Putin Court: A Research Note," *Eurpe-Asia Studies* 57, no. 7 (November 2005): 1066.
18 Ibid., 1066–1069.
19 Ibid.
20 For examples, see Saltanat Berdikeeva, "National Identity in Kyrgyzstan: the Case of Clan Politics," paper presented at the 11th Annual World Convention of the Association for the Study of Nationalities titled "Nationalism in the age of Globalization," (New York, Columbia University, March 23–25, 2006) http://www.aytmatov.org/metinler/national_identity_of_kyrgyzstan_-_the_case_of_clan_politics.pdf; Alisher Ilkhamov, "Stalled at the Doorstep Of Modern State-

hood: The Neopatrimonial Regime in Uzbekistan," in *Stable Outside, Fragile Inside?, Post-Soviet Statehood in Central Asia*, ed. Kavalski, Emilian (Farnham: Ashgate, 2010).

21 On the basis of an interview with Dr. Dosym A. Satpayev (director KRAG Assessment Group, Almaty, Kazakhstan).

22 Yuliy A. Nisnevich, "Political Corruption in Post-Communist Russia," National Research University Higher School of Economics Working Paper WP14/2013/08, Series WP14, Political Theory and Political Analysis, Moscow, 2013.

23 Hale, *Patronal Politics*, 95–118.

24 https://en.wikipedia.org/wiki/Political_party, accessed on September 19, 2018.

25 Hofmeister, Wilhelm, and Karsten Grabow. *Political parties: Functions and Organisation in Democratic Societies* (Singapore: Konrad Adenauer Stiftung, 2011), 16. http://www.kas.de/wf/doc/kas_7671-1442-2-30.pdf?120920114650

26 Hale, *Patronal Politics*, 66–76.

27 Ibid., 72.

28 Max Weber, *Die Politik als Beruf*, 1919.

29 Eric J. Hobsbawm, *Primitive Rebels: Studies in Archaic Forms of Social Movement in the 19th and 20th Centuries* (Manchester: Manchester University Press, 1959), 55.

30 Ibid., 40.

31 Janine R. Wedel, "Corruption and Organized Crime in Post-Communist States: New Ways of Manifesting Old Patterns," *Trends in Organized Crime* 7, no. 1 (Fall 2001): 33

32 David O. Friedrichs, *Trusted Criminals: White Collar Crime in Contemporary Society* (Belmont: Wadsworth Publishing, 2010).

33 David O. Friedrichs, "Transnational Crime and Global Criminology: Definitional, Typological, and Contextual Conundrums," *Social Justice* 34, no. 2 (2007): 9.

34 Friedrichs, *Trusted Criminals*, 132–158.

35 Friedrichs, "Transnational Crime and Global Criminology," 10.

36 Act CI of 2006 on the promulgation of the United Nations Conventions against transnational organized crime, as established in Palermo on 14 December 2000.

37 Weber, *Economy and Society*, 229.

38 Oleh Havrylyshyn, "The Formation and Role of Oligarchs," in *The Political Economy of Independent Ukraine: Slow Starts, False Starts, and a Last Chance?*, ed. Oleh Havrylyshyn (London: Palgrave Macmillan, 2017), 201–22.

39 Dávid Jancsics, "'A friend gave me a phone number'—Brokerage in low-level corruption," *International Journal of Law, Crime and Justice* 43, no. 1 (2014): 68–87, http://www.sciencedirect.com/science/article/pii/S1756061614000500

40 Katherine Stovel and Lynette Shaw, "Brokerage," *Annual Review of Sociology* 38, no. 1 (2012): 139–58.

41 See the chapter János Kornai, "The system paradigm revisited" in this volume, 31.

42 *The private sector's share in GDP*. Structural and institutional change indicators table of EBRD data until 2010. www.ebrd.com/downloads/research/economics/macrodata/sci.xls

43 Wedel, "Corruption and Organized Crime," 13.

44 Primary literature used: *Reyderstvo kak sotsial'no-ekonomicheskiy i politicheskiy fenomen sovremennoy Rossii. Otchet o kachestvennom sotsiologicheskom issledo-*

vanii. Issledovaniye *"Tsentra politicheskikh tekhnologiy" pod rukovodstvom Bunina* [Raiding as a socio-economic and political phenomenon of the modern Russia: A report on the qualitative sociological investigation. An investigation conducted by the Center of Political Technologies led by Bunin]. Moscow, May 2008. Accessed September 18, 2016. http://www.politcom.ru/tables/otchet.doc; http://www.compromat.ru/page_22765.htm; Thomas Firestone, "Armed Injustice: Abuse of the Law and Complex Crime in Post-Soviet Russia," *Denver Journal of International Law and Policy* 38, no. 4 (2010) 555–80; Philip Hanson, "Reiderstvo: Asset-Grabbing in Russia," Chatham House Russia and Eurasia PP, no. 3 (2014); Matthew A. Rojansky, "Corporate Raiding in Ukraine: Causes, Methods and Consequences," *Demokratizatsiya: The Journal of Post-Soviet Democratization* 22, no. 3 (2014): 411–43; Ilja Viktorov, "Corporate Raiding in Post-Soviet Russia," *Baltic Worlds*, no. 2 (2013), Published on balticworlds.com on 29 October 2013.

[45] Viktorov, "Corporate Raiding in Post-Soviet Russia."
[46] Firestone, "Armed Injustice," 563.
[47] Friedrichs, *Trusted Criminals*.
[48] Rojansky, "Corporate Raiding in Ukraine," 429.
[49] Ibid., 427.
[50] Lucy Chernykh, "Profit or Politics? Understanding Renationalizations in Russia," *Journal of Corporate Finance* 17 (2011): 1240 (referring to the Russian Interdepartmental Analytical Center, 2000).
[51] Sebastien Peyrouse, "The Kazakh Neopatrimonial Regime: Balancing Uncertainties among the 'Family,' Oligarchs and Technocrats," *Demokratizatsiya* 20, no. 4 (Fall 2012): 345.
[52] Chernykh, "Profit or politics?" 1240.
[53] Ibid.
[54] See Andrey Ryabov's chapter "The Institution of Power&Ownership" in this volume.

II.
ACTORS OF POWER

NIKOLAY PETROV

Putin's neo-nomenklatura system and its evolution

The current Russian state can be seen as a hybrid regime. This hybrid is not, however, one of authoritarian and democratic models, but rather of Stalin's nomenklatura system and of the mafia state. This latter term is analyzed in detail by Bálint Magyar, referring to the case of Viktor Orbán's Hungary, which has developed an increasingly similar state model to Putin's Russia.

Introduction: The restoration of the nomenklatura system—Putin's longest and most successful political project

Cementing the construction of the neo-nomenklatura system (NNS)[1] has been one of the most important political accomplishments after Moscow's annexation of Crimea, a period of radical transformation for the Russian regime. It is the NNS which determines the new political design of Putin's regime, based on the ruler's military leadership (the chief patron's personal monopoly of state coercion institutions and methods) rather than electoral legitimacy. The leader thus depends less on political elites and is largely able to bypass them, deriving his legitimacy directly from the citizenry instead. The NNS can therefore be categorized as both the result of the regime's changed political geometry, and, simultaneously, its base.

Restoring a functional system of capable management from a single center, and controlling personnel recruitment to this center, is perhaps the lengthiest and most strategic of Putin's projects, having been implemented step by step since he first came to power. The sharp confrontation with the West, starting from 2014, has helped to bring this project to a logical conclusion. It was in 2014–15 when Putin's NNS, in confrontation with the West and becoming increasingly closed, assumed its final shape. From this point of view, if there was no confrontation with Ukraine, one would have to be invented.

The aim of this paper is to outline the essence of the neo-nomenklatura system (NNS), the peculiarities of its formation and function, and its future prospects.

Neo-nomenklatura system formation

The classical nomenklatura[2] system (NS) was created by Stalin in the late 1920s and early 1930s, and subsequently existed in a state of inertia, propped up by the fear it inspired in the past. It had been aging and ailing for decades, but took on a new lease of life with Putin's ascension to power. It has since been modified to function under the new market conditions.

A stable institutionalized political system produces an elite that later helps the system to reproduce itself, while a poorly institutionalized personalized system substitutes the elite with a new nomenklatura,[3] serving as a form of unofficial institutionalization. The system's most important demands are unconditional loyalty from all of its members, which is ensured by their affiliation with a particular network or clan, and subordination to a higher authority.

Under Boris Yeltsin, himself a former nomenklatura member who initially held the reputation of a crusader against privileges, the NS deteriorated but was not fully dismantled. It was penetrated by some outsiders, but its behavioral norms and overall framework remained largely unchanged. The dissolution of the Communist Party and elimination of the party hierarchy stripped the system of its main structural element, its backbone. Opening borders and markets removed the barriers to transforming the NS into a system for the elites, a system where elites hold—and not merely use by virtue of their position—certain inalienable powers. The ascent to power of Vladimir Putin, a low-level nomenklatura member during the Soviet era, did not just see the restoration of the NS, but its active development with the addition of previously absent components. These were intended to ensure the closed nature of the system, and its control over every member, in the context of a state-regulated market and formally democratic institutions.

Accordingly, we can speak of three successive phases of NS development: its prime during Stalin's era, its stagnation and decay under Brezhnev, and finally its revival as a neo-nomenklatura system (NNS) created by Putin. During Putin's reign, some important mechanisms, such as the horizontal rotation of federal representatives in the regions, were restored, having previously degraded or disappeared. The strict hierarchy of nomenklatura levels has been restored on the base of the presidential vertical: Putin himself, his administrators and envoys to federal districts, and the chief federal inspectors in the regions.

The NNS, then, is not just a product of the incomplete decay of the NS, but is also its restored and modernized version. External conditions have changed: commercialization has allowed its members to convert power into property, and the system became open to the outside world. In the post-Soviet period, individual members of the "nomenklatura elite" have gained access to greater opportunities and face fewer risks, while the risks for the system itself have increased—its resources may be irreversibly privatized and transferred overseas. Being an organic part of an authoritarian regime, the NS is incompatible with freedom, elections and federalism. The strengthening of nomenklatura institutions occurred at the expense of democratic institutions.

Political institutions, in the course of their evolutionary development, were transforming internally, rather than being dismantled and replaced by new ones. In an authoritarian electoral system, they carry both decorative and constructive functions. Strengthening the former at the expense of the latter leads either to the appearance of new institutions which carry the same constructive function, or to the disappearance of the very function which is no longer fulfilled by the system. The latter can provoke accumulating problems with the potential for political crisis. The goal—immediate preservation of power—leads to short-term planning, and makes long-term political investment pointless. Only those institutions which provide immediate results survive. This is why the system lacks the reproductive capacity to invest in growth.

Putin's NNS: variations from Stalin's NS

The neo-nomenklatura system built up in recent years appears, to some extent, to be a replica of the Stalin-era system, but one which is adjusted to new quasi-market realities and short-termism. It has been constructed along old patterns, though with a different foundation—a Chekist rather than Communist organizational strategy. As such, it has sophisticated control techniques, but lacks mass personnel selection and training, is less formally institutionalized, and does not have a collective leadership. It is neither self-sustaining nor self-replicating, and appears to be disposable, not capable of surviving beyond the leader without engaging in large-scale transformation.

The absence of connecting horizontals in different level party committees, and the absence of two major competing verticals, are also basic differences between the neo-nomenklatura system and its nomenklatura predecessor. The presidential plenipotentiaries in federal districts, chief federal inspectors in the regions, and boards of federal representatives in the regions led by them, can all be seen as a replacement of sorts for the previous hierarchy of party committees. The NNS does not have horizontal, collective leadership-run bodies to provide coordination between different agencies and for large scale horizontal rotation. The competition between two powerful verticals—namely the Communist one and the Chekist one—which provided greater internal rigidity for the NS is also absent. With a certain degree of simplification, one may consider that under Yeltsin a weakened administrative vertical had taken over the party vertical function, while the Chekist vertical was reduced, though it retained its subordination to Moscow. Under Putin, the administrative and Chekist verticals were strengthened significantly and effectively merged, with the Chekist element playing a dominant role for the first time. There was no cleansing of the NNS until recently, which allowed the Stalinist NS to maintain its relative efficiency, despite the lack of public competition. Putin's NNS thus resembles Stalin's classic NS, while eschewing mass purges of personnel, the party committee horizontal, and the two competing central verticals that fortified the system. Another fundamental difference is the ability to convert power into property, which came to replace or weaken the network of special distribution facilities (that is, the system of *raspredeliteli*, designed to supply nomenklatura personnel with goods and services—

including food, imported clothes, books, and so on—which were not available to ordinary citizens).

The monetization of elite privileges radically changed the system, allowing the elites to accumulate resources for future use. This "hybrid" type of system only recently became viable. Since 2012, however, the elites are being forced to give up their foreign assets to Russian state jurisdiction through "elite nationalization," so-called "deoffshorization," and the increasing prohibition on owning foreign property and bank accounts. The elites' dependence on the regime is increasing, through the threat of possible probes by the Investigative Committee and the requirement to declare personal income. In addition, the regime resorts to "soft purges," destroying competing patronal networks and autonomous positions. Some notable victims of such "soft purges" include: Defense Minister Anatoly Serdyukov and his circle, Ministry of Internal Affairs (MVD) General Denis Sugrobov, along with half a dozen of his subordinates, and the prominent businessman Vladimir Yevtushenkov in 2014; governors Alexandr Khoroshavin and Vyacheslav Gayzer in 2015; and governor Nikita Belykh, Customs Service head Andrey Belyaninov and the Minister of Economic Development Alexey Ulyukayev in 2016.

The elimination of gubernatorial elections in 2004—despite the fact that the regime could have easily filtered out undesirable candidates by that point—is directly linked to creating the administrative tier of the nomenklatura model. Direct elections could not ensure system loyalty through controllability and guarantees inside the corporation. The current model of filtered selection is reminiscent of Communist-era practices, when the Central Committee "recommended" candidates for the first secretary of regional committees, and the regional committees themselves unanimously voted for the candidates with no opposition. The current model of pseudo-competitive elections is, however, somewhat more complicated, as it requires the candidate selected by Moscow to deliver the required election results in his region. In five years of this new "filtered election" system, 34 regional heads have been replaced—33 of whom were appointed by Putin, with only one winning an election against Putin's appointee. In the other 70 gubernatorial races, incumbents appointed by Putin celebrated victory.

While the NS acted as a substitute for normal democratic institutions, the NNS today is a substitute of a substitute. It replaces the key nomenklatura concept, according to which different party committees were responsible for appointing candidates to specific positions, with a more amorphous principle of making appointments which correspond to a certain administrative level. The personification of power and the adopted political family, in place of institutions, distorts the system's strict political geometry, making access to the leader more important than the actual position held. Without the leader, the whole system of cadres is slack, which again illustrates the major problem with the NNS: it is a single-use system, incapable of self-replication.

The functioning of the NNS involves a number of costs for which the regime has to compensate. The NNS blocks elite renewal and social promotion, forcing the regime to intensify purges and rotate executives. The nature of the NNS induces its members to monetize their status, but the uncertainty associated with property ownership prevents them from becoming the rightful owners and gaining independence from the system as a result. Instead, they live in constant fear of losing their holdings, amply illustrated by the fate of Andrey Borodin. Borodin headed the influential Bank of Moscow during the rule of the city's mayor, Yuriy Luzhkov, but had to flee the country following the mayor's fall from grace. The former mayor's spouse Yelena Baturina lost her company, Inteco, once a powerful and profitable business. In the so-called "Bashneft affair," there were two victims: Vladimir Yevtushenkov, known as "Luzhkov's oligarch," and the family of the former Bashkortostani leader, Murtaza Rakhimov. In a situation of property rights relativism, oligarchs like Vladimir Potanin and Oleg Deripaska claim that they are ready to surrender their companies to the state at any time.

Unlike its Soviet predecessor, the NNS functions openly, which creates numerous risks for its operation. Confrontation with the West solves this problem by cordoning off the nomenklatura with both external and internal fences: self-sanctions, such as the ban on so-called "siloviki"[4] and numerous state companies' workers traveling abroad to more than a hundred countries, lead to hindrances many times greater than the initial Western sanctions.

The NNS lacks the two core verticals which were present in its Soviet counterpart; moreover, there is a disconnect between government agencies, especially evident in the absence of party committees, which provided a horizontal link among all agency verticals. These factors lead to the corporatization of the system, which consists of relatively autonomous corporations linked only at the very top—separated patron-client chains tied to the chief patron. As such, the NNS requires constant personnel rotation and reshuffling to counteract corporate and regional autarky. In recent years, regions are treated as territorial divisions of the corporation, with governors being transplanted from one region to another. The cases of Nikolay Merkushkin, who was moved from the Republic of Mordovia to Samara Oblast, Viktor Tolokonsky (from Novosibirsk Oblast to Krasnoyarsk Krai), and Oleg Kozhemyako (from Koryak Autonomous Okrug to Amur Oblast, and subsequently to Sakhalin Oblast) are all illustrative of this process.

There is single major core vertical which matters in the NNS, namely the Chekist one. Although the term "militocracy"[5] is often applied to this system, it is misleading, not only due to the large number of KGB and FSB descendants within the system. Indeed, it is more about the functioning of the system, its internal rules and behavioral matrix. The structure prioritizes informal rules and practices over formal ones, and not just a weak rule-of-law, but the outright misuse of law.

Finishing the construction of the NNS, 2014–2016

As already mentioned, both the economic crisis and increasing confrontation with the West contributed to the strengthening of the NNS. The economic crisis has also led to the growing dependence of business on state budgetary money, in parallel with the mounting etatization of the economy.[6] First, in 2014, weak formal institutions like elections, judiciary, and local self-administration were further weakened. Then came the turn of informal institutions, and unwritten—though strictly observed—rules were increasingly jettisoned. The effects of this could be seen in numerous societal groups: business (for instance, the arrest of Viktor Yevtushenkov, and the confiscation of his Bashneft company); *siloviki* elites (including an investigation against one of the leading Ministry of Interior departments, accompanied by numerous arrests, the arrests of several regional police heads, and of top ranked officials in the Federal Service for Execution of Punishments); and regional elites (including the arrests of three governors and targeted purges in the Sakhalin and Komi regions affecting a small percentage of regional elites).

The new centralization, with its increased control over corporations or clans and isolated verticals, began in 2014, with the replacement of the leadership of agencies and state companies. This occurred in an extraordinary way—with sharp conflicts and criminal investigations, sometimes over the head of the government. Old rules, both formal and informal, no longer held, while new rules were not announced. On the one hand, this increased the dependence of elites on the Kremlin's hook, but on the other, it led to growing tension within elites and their increasing discontent.

The 2013–14 court reform resulted in the de facto subordination of the judiciary to the Kremlin. The Supreme Court of Arbitration was liquidated, the Supreme Court moved to Saint Petersburg, the Constitutional Court reformed, law enforcement gained new extrajudicial powers, and the system of simplified proceedings was widened, while jury trials narrowed. Several scandalous cases with evident political interference—including cases relating to Alexei Navalny, Ilya Farber, Mikhail Khodorkovsky, and the Constitutional Court decision on Crimea—contributed to undermining the authority of the judiciary and the rule-of-law. To this, one may also add a number of cases when courts were used to intimidate opponents and critics of the government: so-called "Basmanny justice,"[7] judicial tyranny, and disproportionately long sentences in the cases of Pussy Riot, the Greenpeace ship *Arctic Sunrise*, the activist Ildar Dadin and others.

At the end of 2015, it was jury trials that attracted the attention of the authorities. Vladimir Putin, summing up the year at a gathering of regional courts' heads in February 2016, spoke of the ongoing court reforms, and the positive effect from the merger of the Supreme Court and the Supreme Court of Arbitration. He also addressed the perceived weakness of jury trials, which considered only 490 cases and returned 84 not guilty verdicts.[8] The reorganization of jury trials was announced, leading to a wider spectrum of crimes to be considered, increasing the number of courts and decreasing the number of jury trials (a potential move to a Soviet-type "people's assessors" system), to begin in 2016.

As a result of the local self-administration reforms of 2014–15, the last remaining group of relatively autonomous actors—namely mayors, especially mayors of large regional centers—was effectively liquidated. The overwhelming majority of them are no longer directly elected by popular vote. Along with the weakening of elections as an institution, due to their intentional delegitimization by the government, deliberate reduction of competition, and suppression of observation, political parties and the party system were also weakening. The pressure placed on civil society increased, divided into "good"—socially oriented, assisting authorities—and "bad," where critics of the government were silenced, and civil society was transformed into an appendage of the state.

With regard to control over bureaucracy, the deoffshorization and nationalization of elites which began in 2012 has started to bear fruit, alongside the construction of an infrastructure of purges and control over the whole army of officials at all levels, with its center at the presidential staff. An anti-corruption "Cheka" has emerged, to control the state apparatus and deputies at all levels. It was announced at the Presidential Anti-Corruption Council in January 2016 that over 2,500 anti-corruption units are already in place.[9]

Deinstitutionalization: weakening democratic institutions and strengthening nomenklaturian ones

The weakening of institutions has continued on a practical level. It was accompanied by the widening of existing institutional proxies and the establishment of new ones, such as the All-Russian Peoples' Front, the new system of primaries for the United Russia party, different extraordinary management bodies and control formats. The negative results of judicial reform and of the additional powers granted to law enforcement, bypassing the courts, became even more evident.

The system of institutions—democratic, formal and informal—lies at the base of any political regime. The weakening and disappearance of some institutions and practices must be compensated by the emergence of new ones. The modern Russia, with its establishment and strengthening of quasi-Soviet institutions, is no exception. There are mass meetings in support of the government, with their basis in the so-called "putings" which began in early 2012.[10] The May 1 workers' demonstrations are now organized by the government, rather than the Communists, along with the revival of collective letters to support or oppose policies. The scheme of de facto appointment by the president spread recently to Crimea, in the Sevastopol and Northern Tyumen districts; here, one can see an analog of the Soviet-era election of regional Party secretaries by regional Party committees.

There are also direct borrowings from the Soviet past, like the restoration of the "Znaniye" (Knowledge) educational organization, or the new Russian Movement of Schoolchildren—an analog of the Soviet Pioneer organization. The problem is that "institutional re-Sovietization" of this type, where certain elements from the past are renewed or their functional analogs appear, can solve some isolated problems. However, it fails to make the political-managerial system any more stable. Indeed, it can have the opposite effect, due to a lack of unity and internal conflict between new and old institutions.

In his presidential address of December 2015, Putin cited frightening figures on the unfounded opening of criminal cases against entrepreneurs, and their arrests in order to gain control over their businesses.[11] In early 2016, the Working Group to Monitor and Analyze Law Enforcement Practice in Entrepreneurial Activity was established, consisting of the Presidential Administration leadership, law enforcement agencies and entrepreneurial unions. This establishment of yet another proxy institution coincided with yet another illegal arrest, this time of the businessman Dmitry Kamenshchik, accompanied by a new round of the confrontation between the Investigative Committee and the Prosecutor General.

In general, one can speak about the further simplification of the system and the shrinking autonomy of political actors: firstly, mayors, who became elements of the executive vertical chain of command, then politicians and public activists, who were either included into the government or marginalized. Systematic simplification was taking place at a time when the system was faced by more and more complex challenges. The very development of the system in the last two years, in conditions of extraordinary legitimacy, was moving in the opposite direction to that which was required.

Substitutionalization

As Putin's personal power regime subsists and strengthens, his Russia becomes a state of more and more developed institutional proxies. These proxies aim to functionally replace democratic institutions, while being at the same time absolutely dependent on the government, without any ability to act directly. Most of them are connected to the president personally and are not autonomous in nature, like mechanical prostheses.

Proxies or substitutes, intended to replace institutional mechanisms which function badly, are created ad hoc to fix concrete individual problems, and often have a single use character. This is why they are often referred to as "special" or "extraordinary": a special representative, special forces, commissioners and ombudsmen. The basic feature of political substitutes is an absence of independent powers or any mechanism of direct action. Being established predominantly by presidential decrees and governmental regulations, substitutes, unlike "living" institutes, are deprived of the capacity for self-development. However, once they are created, they have huge bureaucratic inertia. If they are reused for other issues, they require a manual overhaul from outside. Table 5.1 gives a list of these substitutions and proxies, which began to appear in 2014.

Table 5.1. Major substitutions and proxies, beginning in 2014

2014
- Ratings of governors' efficiency by the Foundation for Civil Society Development (FoRGO), connected to the Kremlin (January)
- A special qualification collegium and commission to examine judges (SKKS and SEKS), to select candidates for the unified Supreme Court (March)
- Public arrests of top-ranked police generals, including regional police heads, and of the Ministry of Interior leadership, under the pretense of their involvement in organized criminal groups (March–present)
- The extension of a special order of consideration of criminal case procedure for especially grave crimes
- The Ministry for Crimean Affairs (March 2014–July 2015) and Crimean Federal District (March 2014–July 2016)
- Ban on foreign travel for law enforcement officers (April)
- The beginning of municipal counter-reform, leading to subordination of local self-administration to regional authorities and the dismantling of directly elected mayoral positions (May)
- The Ministry of North Caucasus Affairs (May)
- Public councils in ministries and governmental departments, formed through the Civic Chamber and Russian Public Initiative
- Conferring functions of public control and identifying public preferences to the All-Russian People's Front
- Internet ombudsman (July)
- Eurasian Economic Union (October)
- Deprivatization of the large oil company "Bashneft," appropriated by force from its owners (October)
- Introduction of new taxes, given to companies owned by the children of "Putin's friends": for the use of road infrastructure (the "Platon"

system, Igor Rotenberg, November), and for capital improvements of the housing stock in Moscow (Igor Chaika, August 2015)
- Territories of Advanced Development (TOR) with preferential tax regimes and other special benefits for business (December)

2015

- All-Russian forum "State and Civil Society: Cooperation in the Name of Development" (January)
- "Anti-Maidan" movement including "Combat Brotherhood" representatives, the Council of Afghan Veterans, Cossacks, the "Night Wolves" and martial arts experts to counter the "fifth column" (January)
- Anti-crises headquarters in regions headed by governors (February)
- Completion of the municipal counter-reform transferring functions of a single municipal head to a formally hired, but de facto bureaucratically appointed, official (February)
- Public, on-camera arrests of governors (March)
- Federal Agency for Nationalities (March)
- The Unified Development Institution in the Housing Sector (May)
- Ban on "undesirable organizations" executing projects on Russian territory (May); the Federation Council initiative to compile a "patriotic stop-list" of foreign groups (July)
- All-Russian youth educational forum "Territory of Senses at Klyazma" (May)
- Federal Corporation for the Development of Small and Medium Enterprise, based on the Credit Guarantee Agency (June)
- Anti-corruption commissions in the regions (July)
- All-Russian public civic-patriotic movement "Russia's immortal regiment" (September)
- National youth organization Russian Movement of Schoolchildren (the new Pioneer movement) (October)
- All-Russian public-governmental educational movement "Knowledge" (December)
- Plenipotentiary presidential envoy to the Contact Group on Ukraine (December)

2016

- Project Office of the government (January)
- Full-scale primaries of the United Russia–All-Russia People's Front grouping (February)
- Working Group to Monitor and Analyze Law Enforcement Practice in Entrepreneurial Activity (February)
- The United Russia Center for Evaluation of the Efficiency of Federal Target Programs (March)
- Public council overseeing the Crimean bridge construction (March)
- National Guard Forces Command (April)
- The Center for Strategic Research, headed by Alexei Kudrin, to formulate a strategy for Russia's development after 2018 (April)
- Working Group of the Economic Council under the President of the Russian Federation group "Priorities of Structural Reforms and Sustainable Economic Growth" (May)
- Special email address for businessmen to write to the Prosecutor General (July)
- Presidential Council for Strategic Development and Priority Projects (June)
- Agency for Technological Development (July)
- Special presidential envoys on environmental issues and transportation, and on development of Russian-Ukrainian trade and economic ties (August)
- Dismissal from the state service of a number of high-ranked officials who violated presidential orders and ran for election to the Russian Academy of Sciences (November)
- Detention of the Minister of Economic Development Alexey Ulyukaev on corruption charges, and his removal from office due to "losing the trust of the president" (November)

2017

- Russian foundation for the development of information technology (January)
- Selection of candidates for governors' offices, based on an "ideal governor" profile and the model of regional demand (February)

- Coordination Committee for conducting tenders for granting of presidential grants, headed by the First Deputy Chief of Staff of the Presidential Administration, Sergey Kiriyenko
- Creation of the "Expert Institute for Social Research" (EISI), for liaison between experts and the presidential staff (March)
- Putings-2, a set of meetings "against terrorism" inspired by the authorities after anti-governmental protest action on March 26 and a terrorist attack in the St. Petersburg metro on April 3
- The special monitoring system and analysis of citizens' appeals to the government, municipalities, and other organizations fulfilling publicly important functions (April)
- Special presidential envoys to the World Congress of Finno-Ugric Peoples and on issues of humanitarian and economic cooperation with the Caspian states (September–October)
- Competition of managers and personnel reserve, "Leaders of Russia," based on the Academy of State Service (October)

In 2014–15 the trend of state-of-emergency-style management continued, with the following bodies being introduced: the special collegium of judges (2014); special presidential envoys (2015–17); the Internet ombudsman (2014); a special procedure for dealing with criminal cases (2014); anti-crises headquarters in the regions and anti-corruption commissions (2015); a special email address for businessmen to write to the Prosecutor General (2016); and the special monitoring system and analysis of citizens' appeals (2017).

These led to the primitivization of the entire management system, due to further centralization and tougher subordination, strengthening the state management vertical and embedding local self-administration into it. The creation of special bureaucratic bodies for problems which emerged along existing templates became another strand of this primitivization. Where problems arose, organizations of various forms had to be established, including: 1) a special ministry; 2) agencies and/or corporations; 3) working groups; or 4) a council, or at least an ombudsman's position. As a result, the following were founded: 1) Ministries for the Far East (2012), Crimea (2014–15), and the North Caucasus (2014); 2) the Credit Guarantee Agency (2014) and the Federal Corporation for the Development of Small and Medium Enterprise (2015), followed by agencies dealing with residential development (2015) and technological development (2016); 3) the Working Group to Monitor and Analyze Law Enforcement Practice in Entrepreneurial Activity (2016) and the Working Group "Priorities of Structural Reforms and Sustainable Economic Growth" (2016); 4) the Presidential Council on the Russian Language (2014), and the Presidential Council for Strategic Development and Priority Projects (2016).

Bureaucratic bodies are founded and dissolved regularly, with replacements often having the same responsibilities as their predecessors. For example, the Federal Agency for Nationalities, established in 2015, is the sixth reincarnation of this body in twenty years; its predecessor, the Ministry for Federation Affairs, Nationalities and Migration Policy, was dissolved in 2001. In 2014–16 alone, two ministries have been established and two ministries abolished, including one of the newly established ones;[12] one federal service has been established and four federal services abolished;[13] and the Supreme Court of Arbitration (1992–2014) has been liquidated.

A third approach from the Russian government is the creation of new means and bodies of internal control. These include: FoRGO[14] ratings of governors' efficiency (2014); public councils under ministries and agencies (2014); the transfer of public control functions to the All-Russia People's Front (2014); the Internet ombudsman (2014); anti-corruption commissions in the regions (2015); the Working Group to Monitor and Analyze Law Enforcement Practice in Entrepreneurial Activity (2016); the United Russia Center for Evaluation of the Efficiency of Federal Target Programs (2016); the public council overseeing the Crimean bridge construction (2016); and the special email address for businessmen to appeal to the Prosecutor General (2016).

At the same time, transparency is declining. As such, the state budget becomes more and more closed, with around one-fifth of the 2017 budget spending secret. Genuine external public control is declining as well, whether in local self-administration, elections, or public supervisory commissions to ensure compliance with human rights standards in prisons, in which jailors are now included. The pressure on the elite is growing: both directly, as seen in the ban on foreign travel (2014), and in an untargeted way, with the public arrests of top level federal and regional officials (2014–present), and the dismissal of state officials who were elected to the Academy of Sciences (2016).

Moscow's fourth approach involves the development of systemic substitutes in breadth and depth, adding new competencies to existing substitutes. The first of these was the All-Russian People's Front, established in

2011, which is used as a universal tool to provide for governmental interaction with citizens, public control and the identification of public preferences (2014), the organization of large scale primaries (2016) and so forth. The People's Front, which was initially considered to be a potential replacement for United Russia, became an integral part of the existing party system, developing into a versatile tool with interchangeable functions.

The Civic Chamber is another multifunctional substitute. It was established in 2005, partly as a body of broad public representation, to compensate for the weakening of the State Duma in this capacity, and partly as a ministry of civil society. It was growing in depth—adding 85 regional chambers, each with representatives at the federal chamber—and in width, along with the formation of public councils in ministries and agencies (2014), the identification of successful civic projects and the replication of their success (2015), and conducting public examination of draft laws. It is illustrative that the Civic Chamber secretary Alexander Brechalov is, at the same time, one of the co-chairmen of the People's Front.[15]

Substitutes which appear, first of all, as a reaction to the system's dysfunctionality are illustrative of the administration's important deficiencies. What are these deficiencies? Firstly, **low managerial efficiency and an inability to fix emerging managerial tasks and problems in a systemic way**. Here the ministries for Crimea, the Far East and North Caucasus should be mentioned, along with the Credit Guarantee Agency, the Federal Corporation for the Development of Small and Medium Enterprise, the Government's Project Office, the restoration of the Institute for Strategic Studies as a headquarters of reform strategy, and the Working Group "Priorities of Structural Reforms and Sustainable Economic Growth." Secondly, there is an **absence of effective external control**: control functions have been increasingly given to the People's Front, public councils formed by the Civic Chamber and Russian Public Initiative, the United Russia Center for Evaluation of the Efficiency of Federal Target Programs, and the public council overseeing the Crimean bridge construction. Thirdly, there is a lack of **development and support of innovation**, as demonstrated by the example of the Agency for Strategic Initiatives with its representative offices and projects. There are also numerous substitutes to compensate for the lack of competitive elections and independent local self-administration, such as ratings of governors' efficiency, the United Russia primaries, city-managers' models and composite councils of deputies in large cities.

The "inverse Midas effect" should be mentioned in this regard: it is due to an increasingly personalistic system that, from one side, working institutions are transforming into substitutes, and from the other side, any new institutional projects take the shape of substitutes. Political parties, both old and new, serve as good examples. There are also numerous examples from executive power, like development institutions, many of which according to Putin "have become a real dump for 'bad' debts."[16]

The lifespan of these substitutes is relatively short, and in most cases only the date of their foundation is known; later, the intensity of its activism can dissipate, or the substitute can be quietly laid to rest. A hierarchical system of personnel reserves can serve as a good example, which was actively developing since 2008 but later ran out of steam. The reason for this is fairly clear: the system resists against even limited institutionalization. Its real personnel reserve consists of the children of Putin's entourage in a broad sense, and the bodyguards who form his entourage in a narrow sense.

Substitutes flourished on such a scale that there are even cases of their subsequent dismantling, as in the case of the Ministry for Crimean Affairs, along with the Crimean Federal District and a special deputy-premier to supervise Crimea. Alternatively, substitutes could be replaced by other substitutes, like the example of the National Guard, which became a kind of third generation FSB, replacing the Federal Drug Control Service of Russia, which was called an "FSB-2." However, usually substitutes undergo conversion and adjustment to better fit their new tasks, like presidential plenipotentiary envoys to federal districts, the People's Front and the Civic Chamber.

Substitutionalization leads to an increasing bulkiness of the system and decreasing manageability, to the growing cost of state management, both direct and indirect, and the estrangement of both citizens and elites from decision making. It is the replacement of institutes with substitutes that provides for the strengthening of the regime's personalistic character, and increases the risk of managerial paralysis if Putin leaves power.

Cadres versus elite structure

It is the political mechanics of the regime, the model of Putin's elite composition and functioning, which has undergone the most serious changes in the last three years. There are four well-known pillars of Putin's elite design:

the "Kremlin towers," the "planet system," the "Politburo" and the "business-corporation." The "Kremlin towers," however, are no longer that solid; in the "planet system," the "orbiting" partners were replaced instead with loyal servants; the present day power arrangement more closely resembles a Tsar's court than a Politburo; and in the case of "business-corporation," the role of shareholders has diminished while that of managers has increased.

Almost a decade ago Alexei Makarkin, when analyzing elite development at the end of Putin's second term, considered the "atomized" character of the president's entourage as one of the most important peculiarities of the regime. Makarkin has counterposed the structure of Yeltsin's "family" group, whose positions were weakened by that time, to the atomized political elites model.[17] When the article was written, at the very eve of transition to the Putin–Medvedev "tandemocracy," Putin had undertaken a personnel maneuver that separated the political weight of the important figures in his entourage from material-organizational resources, most prominently power resources. Since that time, the most important figures named "atoms" by Makarkin could have either one resource or the other, but not both. Some of them retained their political weight but then lost material-organizational resources, like Nikolay Patrushev who became the Security Council secretary after serving as the director of the FSB. Others obtained organizational resources but lost their political weight, like Viktor Ivanov, who became the head of the anti-drugs committee, but lost his position as Putin's "grey cardinal."

Over the last decade, Putin's elite gained a greater structure, with separate groups becoming parts of larger corporations and acquiring their own pyramids-clients. Distinct clans of adopted families appeared. Nowadays, this development has somewhat reversed, with heavyweights having their own networks of allies and clients leaving, to be replaced by more atomized managers. Not only the personal composition of the elite changes as a result, but its entire configuration as well. At the same time, a forced generational shift is occurring within the elite organized by supreme power.

With the departure of longtime leaders—"feudal lords"[18] like Vladimir Kozhin, Vladimir Yakunin, Viktor Ivanov and Yevgeny Murov—the very concept of the state's composition changes. Centralization and instrumentalization of *siloviki* is taking place, where the power resource is cut off from politics, in order to ensure that appropriate bodies act on the direct orders of the Kremlin, not according to their own interests or those of their power corporation.

Putin's inner circle has shrunk. Although it still consists predominantly of his erstwhile St. Petersburg colleagues, the so-called "Pitertsy,"[19] those former partners who are no longer part of the system and lack real resources, whether financial-economic, administrative or political, have left. Putin started to clean the ranks, getting rid of those who switched from being assets to passive figures: his powerful superintendent Vladimir Kozhin, head of the Russian Railways Vladimir Yakunin (who commanded over an organization that was almost a state within a state), the former Kremlin chief personnel officer Viktor Ivanov, the power broker Yevgeny Murov, and the man who ultimately lost to Medvedev in the competition to succeed Putin, Sergey Ivanov. All of these strong men had a Chekist background. These former comrades-in-arms were replaced by young career managers, who were incapable of inheriting their responsibilities in full.

Putin's regime sometimes is called a "militocracy,"[20] although the term "Chekistocracy" is more appropriate to describe the Russian system of governance. In the decade and a half since Putin and his team came to power, they went beyond establishing the essential numerical superiority of the FSB and other secret services officers in positions of power. Appropriate elite codes and norms of behavior have also been formed during this time. Authorities' actions and decision making are entirely closed to scrutiny, in a special operations-type regime. The regime has opacity at its core, striving for control, and control over the controllers, rather than transparency; inspiring and maintaining conflicts in corporations' leadership and between corporations; reinforcing numerous verticals, alongside a lack of horizontal connections and trust. All these techniques have been borrowed from the secret services, becoming part of a "matrix," which is maintained and reproduced even without the physical presence of secret service members in government. Table 5.2 shows the levels of Putin's elite, along with their orbits of influence.

Putin's elite design is rapidly changing. The first orbit—of partners and comrades-in-arms—became much thinner, due to a kind of "Autumn of the Patriarchs" effect, often observed during Stalin's final years when he alienated his former closest comrades. Several figures left Putin's first orbit during the last few years, including Matthias Warnig, Vladimir Strzhalkovsky, and Vladimir Litvinenko, while no one replaced them in this group. One can notice that the two upper orbits are predominantly populated by representatives of business—either state-owned or closely con-

Table 5.2. The "planet system" of Putin's elites, as of January 2017

	Businessmen	Siloviki	Government members	Others
First layer	Yury Kovalchuk Sergey Chemezov Arkady Rotenberg	Sergey Shoygu	Dmitry Medvedev	
Second layer	Igor Sechin Alexei Miller Gennady Timchenko Alisher Usmanov Roman Abramovich	Viktor Zolotov		Sergey Sobyanin Alexei Kudrin Herman Gref Patriarch Kirill Andrey Fursenko Ramzan Kadyrov
Third layer	Nikolay Tokarev Andrey Kostin Petr Aven	Yevgeny Shkolov Alexander Bortnikov Yury Chaika Nikolay Patrushev Alexander Bastrykin Sergey Ivanov Sergey Naryshkin	Igor Shuvalov Dmitry Kozak Tatyana Golikova Sergey Lavrov Anton Siluanov	Vyacheslav Volodin Valentina Matviyenko Elvira Nabiullina

nected to the state—while *siloviki* and members of the Cabinet compose the third orbit of loyal servants.

Elite structure is not atomized and can be described by clientelistic-corporate networks or pyramids, which include three orbits. The networks cut across orbit lines; for instance, they connect Yury and Mikhail Kovalchuk with Sergey Shoygu and Andrey Fursenko, and Sergey Chemezov with Yevgeny Shkolov and Alisher Usmanov. A more detailed picture of the internal network structure and connections between representatives of the Putin elite is provided by the regularly updated work of Yevgeny Minchenko.[21]

The idea that *siloviki* influence has radically grown is true only to the extent that generals become more important and visible during wartime. However, this does not mean that generals are becoming actors; their role is rather instrumental. With the exception of one *siloviki* politician, Sergey Shoygu, the *siloviki* are either junior partners like Viktor Zolotov, or "loyal servants" like Yevgeny Shkolov, Nikolay Patrushev, Alexander Bortnikov and Yury Chaika. The reproduction of "Pitertsy" ended around a decade ago. It is now the Federal Protective Service (FSO) officers, and children of the elite, who form Putin's immediate communication circle. However, none of them, in spite of their rapid career growth, have managed to penetrate even into the third orbit: Boris Kovalchuk, Andrey Murov and Pavel Fradkov remain the closest to entering this circle. A *siloviki* background no longer plays any serious role, unlike at the stage of property redistribution, as it appeared to be more useful at the stage of redistribution of property than at the stage of its management.

The beginning of the third year of Putin's new regime has been marked by a reformatting of the whole system of law enforcement agencies, whose role increased significantly after the annexation of Crimea in 2014. In April 2016 the new power agency, the 340,000-strong National Guard, was formed from the Ministry of Internal Affairs (MVD) Internal Troops, special forces units and so-called "private security" groups (extra-departmental security). At the same time, the Federal Drug Control Service of Russia and the Federal Migration Service, which was growing in might, have been liquidated. In both cases, personnel were transferred to the MVD, whose power bloc was transferred in near-totality to the National Guard.

In May–June 2016, a near-total renewal of the FSO leadership took place. Prior to this, experts were discussing its expansion, including numerous appointments to the management office of the president and top positions in the MVD and the Ministry of Defense, as well as to governors' positions.[22] It was a colonel, Dmitry Kochnev, who replaced his former boss, three-star general Yevgeny Murov, as the FSO head. His former position at the head of the Presidential Security Service was filled by a former Putin adjutant, major general Alexei Rubezhnoi. A similar succession model—initial expansion and suppression of competitors, with subsequent total renewal of leadership—occurred at the key Economic Security Department of the FSB. Initially, in combination with the Internal Security Department, they crushed the Main Directorate for Economic Security and Combating Corruption at the MVD; later, their entire leadership was changed. These large-scale personnel shifts form a complex combination according to which a "cleansing" of certain agencies should be followed by the "cleansing of cleansers," in order to ensure no one gains additional benefits as a result. Such a process also happened to the FSB Internal Security department, to the Federal Protective Service, and to the Investigative Committee.

Finally, in August 2016 Sergey Ivanov left the second most important position in the country—the head of presidential staff—to switch to a modest presidential advisory position on ecology. He was considered to be one of the power bloc's major leaders, and continually occupied key positions at the very top, beginning by succeeding Putin as the Security Council secretary in 1999, and later taking the role of minister of defense, a vice-premier.

Thus, in less than six months several Chekist heavyweights, Viktor Ivanov, Konstantin Romodanovsky, Yevgeny Murov and Sergey Ivanov left the *siloviki* bloc. Only the Chekist Viktor Zolotov grew into a politically significant figure as a result of these perturbations. He began as Putin's bodyguard, later heading the Presidential Security Service, a division of the FSO, for many years, and has now become the head of a new large power agency. It is important to consider that all of these figures were succeeded not by their immediate subordinates from appropriate agencies, but by figures from the bottom of the hierarchy. Not only did these new appointees represent a new generation, they also emerged with a notably different level of authority, being not the leader's comrades-in-arms, but subordinates whose entire career was developing under Putin as leader.

The young guard

Meanwhile, the second generation of Putin's elites is now taking on active leadership positions. There are already two sons of Putin's first circle of elites who are regional governors. Andrey Turchak, the son of Putin's deputy at the St. Petersburg regional party branch, Anatoly Turchak, and one of Putin's martial arts partners, has led the Pskov Oblast since 2009; Andrey Vorobyov, the son of Yury Vorobyov, a long-time associate of the current Defense Minister Sergey Shoygu and now deputy chairman of the Federation Council, has served as Moscow Oblast governor since 2013.

"Children" of prior elites head a number of large corporations, including Inter RAO UES (led by Boris Kovalchuk[23] since 2009), Rosselkhozbank (led by Dmitry Patrushev[24] since 2010), the Federal Grid Company EES (led by Andrey Murov[25] since 2013), the Federal Agency for Fishery (led by Ilya Shestakov[26] since 2014), the Russian Export Center (led by Petr Fradkov[27] since 2015), the SOGAZ insurance group (led by Anton Ustinov[28] since 2016) and the Management Office of the President (whose deputy heads are Pavel Fradkov and Olga Sergun, the daughter of the former GRU military intelligence head, Igor Sergun). There are also other representatives of Putin's second generation elites who occupy top positions in state businesses or in close affiliation with them. The most popular companies in this regard are Gazprom and Gazprombank (Yury Shamalov, Sergey Ivanov Jr., Andrey Patrushev, Roman Rotenberg), Rosneft (Ivan Sechin, Andrey Patrushev), Russian Railways (Artem and Igor Chaika), and VTB Bank (Denis Bortnikov, Sergey Matviyenko, Dmitry Patrushev).

Serious positions in state management are occupied by the aforementioned Ilya Shestakov and Pavel Fradkov. It appears, however, that in the situation of dismantling the elite pyramids, their current achievements constitute a ceiling of sorts for these "princes," as Yevgeny Minchenko calls them.[29] They will not become "sovereign princes" as their fathers themselves are no longer "princes" due to the general centralization of the system, and the dismantling of the previous one which could be called a "federation of corporations."[30] Dynastic succession did not exist in Putin's Russia, and never will. At best, children may capitalize on the role and influence of their fathers, and when occupying top positions sometimes even serve as guarantors of their fathers' loyalty, in case of their demotion or resignation.

Regional level

At the regional level, shifts in the power configuration have been especially serious. Due to extensive replacements of governors since the ban on direct gubernatorial elections in 2004, governors became far less capable and influential. Today, there are almost no strong independent figures in the position. In most cases regional heads switched from being senior regional elite reps at the federal center to senior central representatives in a region. The situation did not change significantly after the formal restoration of direct gubernatorial elections in 2012. Indeed, of the seventy gubernatorial races since this restoration, Putin's nomination has lost only once, in the Irkutsk Oblast in 2015.

Today, the regional elite is not very consolidated, and is represented by two major groups of actors: regional players themselves and federal actors within a region. The former are well rooted, but often rather disunited. The latter, at the level of bosses, are typically non-local and very loyal to the center, though they are represented by several competing power verticals. Federal actors are led and coordinated by a regional FSB head and chief federal inspector, appointed by a presidential envoy to each federal district. Regional actors, in most cases, are fractured. The era of their total control by a regional head passed long ago; the political weight and independence of figures like regional assembly speakers and mayors of regional centers have also significantly decreased. Due to the serious pressure under which public politics functions, there is a lack of leadership among regional elites. As a result, today's situation is very different from that of the 1990s, allowing us to speak of the degradation of regional political elites.

The system of regional personnel rotation, when Putin came to power, was in place only in the FSB. Step by step, it has been reintroduced; initially for prosecution, then the MVD system, Investigative Committee and so forth. This took a long time, and it was only in 2013 that a law was adopted on the obligatory rotation of territorial leaders of federal executive bodies exercising control and supervisory functions. This law only began to function properly in 2016. With a certain degree of conditionality, it is possible to speak also about governors' rotation.

The spreading of the rotation system, and thus capture by the center of control over bosses of territorial bodies, had begun long before this law was adopted; indeed, it had spread little by little for more than a decade.

The first two key positions for which a struggle was fought were the MVD and the prosecution. In the MVD, where regional chiefs were de facto (and in republics, de jure) appointed by a regional leader, the system of "two-man rule" was initially introduced. Later, Moscow had to approve a candidate with a governor; today, it merely has to inform a governor. From the second half of the 2000s, the establishment of direct central subordination of regional branches has been reflected in their names; they are no longer Internal Affairs departments of a region, or Ministries of Internal Affairs of a republic, but merely departments of the federal Ministry of Internal Affairs for a region. This process ended with the 2010 MVD reform, when forty percent of all regional police chiefs were replaced.

The prosecution service plays a special role as a bridge between investigations and court trials. It is no coincidence, therefore, that prior to the establishment of the Investigative Committee, it was prosecutors who played the role of informal *siloviki* leaders. The center's aim to capture control over prosecutors was facilitated by the establishment of an intermediate level between the regions and the center: federal districts and plenipotentiary envoys administrations, created in 2000. The instantaneous campaign to "bring regional legislation in line with federal law" related directly to this. If this campaign promoted anything, it was the evaluation of regional prosecutors' loyalty to the center, followed by the replacement of those who were disloyal. The Investigative Committee only began active rotations in 2011, as when this body was initially established as a branch separate from the prosecution service in 2007, it was headed by local deputy regional prosecutors.

The chairmen of regional courts are considered to be the most conservative element, as many of them have occupied their offices for a decade or more. The same is true at the federal level, where the heads of both higher courts—the head of the Supreme Court, Vyacheslav Lebedev, and Valery Zorkin, the head of the Constitutional Court—have retained their positions for over two decades. Lebedev has been in his post since 1989, while Zorkin has been in his position since 1991, with a ten-year break from 1993–2003.

Although the system is able to oppose its lack of coordination by strengthening the horizontal level, politically it is faced by an "equity-efficiency" dilemma. An ideally adjusted system of rotation can provide the center with greater control, but at the expense of decreasing efficiency. Under these circumstances, the bureaucratic might of governors who are not very well rooted in their regions is defined by their connections with federal "families." The paradox here is that criminalization is growing in the absence of public political competition, under both strong and weak governors. In the first case it is growing from the top down; in the second, from the bottom up. Thus, if Putin's regime dismantled two-level delegative democracy during its early stages, now a relatively independent second level is completely disappearing. Besides Chechnya, where the personalistic regime of Ramzan Kadyrov is entirely separate, there are a few regions which remain relatively autonomous in a political sense. They are the Tatarstan, Kemerovo and Belgorod Oblasts. Interestingly, four of the five governors who were systemically purged from 2015–17 were locals relying on a rather consolidated regional elite, but at the same time they were not an organic part of any influential federal "family."

The system of rotation, which began in the cases of regional elites, including governors, has recently spread to the leadership of corporations at the center, where it began to work in full in 2014. Before this point, personnel replacements were of a sporadic and non-systemic character. Afterwards, they increased in scale and became connected to the cleansing of the leadership. In usual recent personnel replacements, predecessors led corporations for three to five years. However, in the case of the Federal Protective Service (FSO, 2016) it was sixteen years; at the Presidential Property Management Department (2014), fourteen years; at the VEB bank (2016), twelve years; at the Federal Migration Service (2016), eleven years; at Russian Railways (2015), ten years; and at the Federal Drug Control Service (2016), eight years.

There are both political-economic (the rent-redistributing character of economy) and institutional factors of mafia state formation in Russia. These include the absence of division of power, fusion of power and property, and a lack of formal institutions. To this, we should also add the genesis of the ruling elites. The core of today's Russian elite was formed in St. Petersburg, at that time called "Russia's criminal capital," and has a Chekist background, accustomed to living by their own special laws, beyond usual rules and norms. This "Pitertsy" criminal institutional design was replicated at a country-wide level when its members formed the federal elite.

If we are to consider the three-story state territorial composition of Russia, it is possible to speak of a mafia state at the top level. The lower, local level can be purely criminal, with towns and districts coming entirely under bandits' control. From time to time it comes to the surface, giving rise to major scandals like those in Kushchevskaya, Krasnodar Krai (2010),

Engels, Saratov Oblast (2010), Makhachkala, Dagestan (2013), Bratsk, Irkutsk Oblast (2011), and so on. Not only can these areas find themselves in a state of total lawlessness (known by the Russian term "bespredel"), often there are stationary bandits who provide order, like Makhachkala's long-time mayor Said Amirov, Engels' mayor Mikhail Lysenko, and Krasnoyarsk's "authoritative businessman" Anatoly Bykov.

Cadres, purges, and the spiral of repressions

If a stable institutionalized political system produces elites, and reproduces itself through these elites, it is the nomenklatura, as a form of non-public institutionalization, which substitutes for the elite in a personalistic system with weak institutions. It is the nomenklatura, understood as a hierarchical and depersonalized personnel system, in which the influence of a person is determined not by personality but by a position in the system, which is the order or "internal party" about which Stalin spoke. The most important requirement in the nomenklatura system is the absolute loyalty of all its members to the system, provided by both belonging to a network or clan, and by total dependence on the bosses above (the pyramid principle).

In conditions where a leader enjoys very high levels of popularity, there is no need for repression against ordinary citizens. Instead, they are used in intra-elite struggles as a way for elite groups to realize their interests, and as a threat to ensure control over elites and society. For the elites, the increasing use of a "stick" looks quite natural when there are fewer "carrots." The targeted repressions seen today are not excesses, but a system launched by, and sanctioned from, the very top. However, repressions introduced to provide for "highest state interests" are to be used in private corporate interests as well.

The repressions which have escalated since 2014 are directed primarily against the elites: civic, business, and managerial. They cannot be called mass repressions, although nor are they individual; an illustrative example is the Komi case, when around twenty people—almost the entire leadership of the republic—were announced to be an organized criminal community. A similar incident, the Sakhalin case, is slightly smaller-scale and less publicized. It should be noted that at the federal level, in the MVD headquarters, an "organized criminal group" was uncovered in 2014, when the GUEBiPK (Main Directorate for Economic Security and Countering Corruption) case investigation began with numerous detentions of officers and generals, phantasmagoric charges, and the mysterious suicide of one of the major suspects.

Along with the cleansings in Sakhalin and Komi, a whole range of top regional officials became defendants in criminal cases. In 2016, the governor of Kirov Oblast, Nikita Belykh, was arrested, along with thirteen deputy governors and four mayors of regional capitals. Arrests in 2017 swept up two governors, ten deputy governors or deputy chairmen of regional governments, and one mayor of a regional capital. The total number of top regional elites in the country is around eight to nine hundred people, resulting in approximately two per cent of them meeting their demise annually.

It is notable that large scale cases like "Bolotnaya," GUEBiPK, Sakhalin and Komi have been occurring non-stop over the past few years, turning into a lever applying constant pressure against targeted social or elite groups. In other words, repressions are used in order not to prevent something—elite splits, betrayal and so forth—but to regulate relations between elite groups. It is important that when doing this, the system constantly expands the scope of what is permitted, gradually inuring society, or at least dulling its reaction, toward the arbitrariness of the judicial process and law enforcement.

From 2012 onward, it is possible to speak of the acceleration of serious repression in Russia. The famous "Bolotnaya case," where more than thirty participants of the protest march on Bolotnaya square received sentences of up to four and a half years in prison, can be regarded as the starting point. In 2012, two hundred investigators were involved in this case, dispatched to Moscow from various regions around the country. Although the investigation was extended in August 2016 for another seven months, no further arrests were ultimately made, and all those convicted left prison by January 2018.

Why is it fair to talk of Russian repression "spiraling"? Simply put, repressions are used more frequently, more broadly, and involve new categories of targets, including business, civil society, the state apparatus and even the repressive bloc of the state apparatus. More and more often, arrests and prosecution are used as a form of control, as seen in the case of Anatoly Serdyukov and Oboronservis, the case of GUEBiPK, and the arrests of regional governors.

Why do repressions spiral? This can be predominantly attributed to intra-elite rivalry, which intensifies as potential rents shrink. As such, from one side the Kremlin has less carrots, and uses more sticks instead; from the other side, elites become "hungry," and can "eat" each other. New precedents are being created: the on-camera search of the apartment of Minister of Defense Anatoly Serdyukov's mistress, early in the morning in October 2012, resulting in the minister's resignation and a large-scale anti-corruption case against him and his closed circle in Oboronservis; the detentions of officers and generals in GUEBiPK; the arrest and demise of regional governors; and the connection of top ranked officials in the Investigative Committee to the criminal underworld.

There is also the political logic of exploiting populism and anti-establishment feelings, along with an increase in control over elites. The publicity of high-ranking officials' arrests since the cases of Serdyukov, Surkov, GUEBiPK and so forth serve as an illustration of this. It is interesting to note, however, that although from 2012 many high-level officials have found themselves in the firing line, including acting governors and federal ministers, none of them have ultimately ended up in prison—indeed, many have fled abroad, and usually investigations remain unresolved. The 2013–16 GUEBiPK case, and the more recent arrests and replacements at the Investigative Committee and the highest echelons of the FSB in 2016, demonstrate a new round of the repressive spiral: namely, repressions against those who have repressed. The system also moves from isolated repressions to local ones.

Ultimately, repressions can be seen as serving three main purposes:
a) tools to replace the top management of a corporation leadership;
b) levers to keep corporations under tough control (as in the cases of GUEBiPK, Minkult, Spetsstroy, Rusnano and RusHydro);
c) methods of intimidation and erosion of trust among elites.

The trends behind Putin's "staff revolution"

One way of tracking the evolution of the Russian political regime is by noting how various political actors are deprived of their role and excluded from the circle of active participants in the political process. At various times, this has applied to governors and regional political elites as a whole, independent media, the "Yeltsin oligarchs," and political parties. Today, it is a question of a systemic assault on the lawlessness of functionaries, including the security agencies.

In the personnel sphere, it was a bumper summer, though not so much in terms of replacements as of punishments—the consequence of replacements that took place a little while ago. The trial of Alexey Ulyukayev began, and sentences were announced for Alexander Reymer, the former head of the Federal Penal Service (FSIN), who received eight years in a penal colony, and for Denis Sugrobov, the former head of the GUEBiPK, who received twenty-two years in a high-security prison. The latter case involved what was termed an "organized criminal group," comprising about fifteen people. A trial is currently underway involving former Sakhalin governor Alexandr Khoroshavin and three functionaries from his team, who are also accused of creating an organized criminal group. Another investigation has been completed in a case involving former Komi Republic head Vyacheslav Gayzer and fifteen of his supposed accomplices, including Vladimir Torlopov, Gayzer's predecessor as head of the republic, who was arrested last year.

It should be noted that the case involving the GUEBiPK—a useful structure that exercises oversight over business and that still exists within the Interior Ministry system, albeit in a weakened form—is continuing to develop. Within the framework of this case there have been detentions of, for example, "billionaire" Dmitry Zakharchenko and his former boss Alexander Tishchenko, and also a whole series of regional administration officers, including those in the Moscow Oblast, Sverdlovsk Oblast and others.

The assault on bureaucracy

If the role of certain actors declines, that of others may grow, although as a rule this is not a zero-sum game. For many years, the bureaucracy was considered the beneficiary of the weakening of political actors. Consequentially, the concept of the omnipotence of functionaries arose, and the terms "sovereign bureaucracy" and "byurokratura" (bureaucratic dictatorship) came into circulation. It should be noted that over recent years, when the public have been asked to rank the segments of society that Vladimir Putin represents, the bureaucracy has been in third place, after the security agencies and tycoons. If civilian functionaries are combined with security-related ones, they account for as much as seventy per cent.

However, by mid-2012, the situation had already begun to change. At the very start of the current presidential term, immediately after the 2011–12 political protests, the screws were tightened both for the protesters and for the political and managerial elite, which the Kremlin believed had the potential to split and, following the Ukrainian example, "turn orange." Processes were launched whereby functionaries had to declare an array of financial information, including their income and family property holdings. Furthermore, mechanisms to begin the "deoffshorization" and "nationalization" of the elite, including bans on officials holding foreign assets and more detailed ownership reports, kicked in. This had nothing to do with oversight by the public, but it created a situation where all representatives of the elite found themselves on the hook. The line from this hook led to the Kremlin, particularly to the anti-corruption council, under the leadership of Sergey Ivanov, Yevgeny Shkolov and Oleg Plokhoi. In 2014, with the annexation of Crimea and the transition to sharp confrontation with the West, the elite found itself "bound by Crimea," and the existing internal barrier was compounded by an external one, represented by punitive measures such as sanctions.

Against this backdrop, a series of significant staff moves has taken place, starting in June 2012 with the dismissal of Federal Penitentiary Service head Alexander Reymer, who was later detained on fraud charges. A flurry of firings and rotations followed: Defense Minister Anatoly Serdyukov (November 2012); deputy head of the Federal Protective Service Viktor Zolotov (September 2013); Vladimir Kozhin, head of the Presidential Property Management Department (May 2014); Russian Railways head Vladimir Yakunin (August 2015); Federal Protective Service head Yevgeny Murov (June 2016); Viktor Ivanov, head of the Federal Service for Drug Control (June 2016); Federal Customs Service head Andrey Belyaninov (July 2016); and head of the Presidential Administration Sergey Ivanov (August 2016).

This is only to speak of figures from the president's inner circle. Further afield, similar incidents occurred with Yevgeny Dod from RusHydro (September 2015); Vladimir Dmitriev from Vnesheconombank (February 2016); Konstantin Romodanovsky from the Federal Migration Service (April 2016); Mikhail Fradkov from the Foreign Intelligence Service (October 2016); Sergey Naryshkin from the State Duma (October 2016); Vyacheslav Volodin from the Presidential Administration (October 2016); and Alexey Ulyukayev from the Ministry of Economic Development (November 2016).

It is clear from these cases that the situation reached a turning point in 2016, a year which accounted for two-thirds of the key dismissals in recent times. The following year produced more modest results, with the loss of Federal Bailiffs Service head Artur Parfenchikov (February 2017) and the Military Prosecutor General, Sergey Fridinsky (April 2017), as well as several heads of minor governmental agencies and state corporations.

In these examples, which constitute only the tip of the iceberg, the question of whether departures were voluntary, compelled or forced is not as important as the fact that they were prompted by external factors, and the bosses who replaced them were drawn from external bodies. For this reason, for example, the list does not include Rosatom, where Sergey Kiriyenko, who moved to the Presidential Administration, was replaced by Alexey Likhachev, his protégé and associate of many years.

We should endeavor to look at the overall picture of the last few years, which is in many ways unprecedented, and is sometimes described as a "staff revolution."[31] Certain experts regard the Kremlin's actions as purely reactive, a response to declining systemic effectiveness amid increasingly complex external challenges, but others see some sort of premeditated strategy behind them. How the future might look varies accordingly. What is taking place seems to be less a reactive personnel revolution, and more a large-scale personnel maneuver for some other revolution. Moreover, the current state of affairs seems to be a transitional one, certainly not a new equilibrium.

Tactics or strategy?
In order to answer this question, let us look first at four elements of the staffing problems facing the regime in 2012:

1. Protests and the possibility that, if the elites split, a segment of them could join those protests; perceived scheming by the West to split the elites;
2. The aging of the top echelon of the elite and the upcoming major generational change;
3. Strong corporate interests that could oppose more general ones;
4. The shrinking capacity for rent extraction and the need to redistribute flows/ownership during the regrouping of the elites.

It was in response to these problems that a personnel revolution project was launched which goes significantly beyond resolving purely personnel problems, and could be dubbed "Putin's perestroika." As was the case with the original Gorbachev version, Putin's perestroika means major changes in ideology, economics and politics, but in the opposite direction. It is not a single strategy implemented according to a particular plan, but a combination of steps, sometimes in different directions, which nevertheless amount to a common vector. As in the case of the first perestroika, Putin's perestroika implies the launch of mechanisms that could easily move beyond the control of their initiators.

Let us return, however, to the list of problems. Today they have all been resolved in one way or another. The personnel revolution of 2012–16 demonstrates that the Kremlin is capable of tackling the problems of the system, but cannot construct a system that would tackle them independently. The elite has been subjected to rejuvenation, but this has been carried out by means of personnel implantation, rather than nurturing from below. As a result, it has become a more reliable resource, but only for a limited time. The vertical chain of power, which aligns corporate interests with the common interest, has largely been restored, but in the form of a bayonet; as Napoleon said, a bayonet is comfortable to lean on, but not to sit on.

What general tendencies lie behind staff moves? Here I have identified four trends:

1. Centralization as decorporatization. Experts have noted the departure of a series of Putin's associates, which have taken place not with goodwill, but tough measures including compulsion and extortion. This toughness has become possible against a backdrop of raised confrontation with the West and the "nationalization" of the elites. Moreover, it is necessary in order to change not just the leading figures as individuals, but the entire top echelon of the corporation, to weaken corporate solidarity and the possibility of upholding corporate interests to the detriment of the interests of the system as a whole.
2. A clearer separation of functions between managers and shareholders in the top echelon of the elite. The "multiple post-holders" remaining at the very top are participants in a structure approaching the model of the Soviet Politburo, with responsibilities including defense (Sergey Shoygu), the military-industrial complex (Sergey Chemezov), the oil industry (Igor Sechin, Alexei Miller), and Moscow (Sergey Sobyanin).
3. The restructuring of the system, and its adjustment to suit new realities. This restructuring includes rearranging the numerous pyramids of the

past into one monocentric one. The general pattern is broken (at least for now) by Rosneft, whose head, Igor Sechin, appears to be the "last of the Mohicans": other grandees no longer aspire to the status of a "state within the state."
4. The transformation of repression into a systemic mechanism for personnel renewal and the maintenance of relative managerial effectiveness. The escalation in repression, including the repression of elites, has not yet met significant resistance from the latter; indeed, these processes are meeting far less opposition than might have been initially thought.

What comes next?

The neo-nomenklatura system in Russia today does not appear to be absolutely finished: it is not self-sufficient, is currently incapable of reproduction, and cannot provide for a long and stable existence. Its current configuration, with very weak institutions, both democratic and authoritarian, should be considered as transitional. In this current form, the system can be easily moved in any direction, but it remains hard to predict the direction of upcoming changes. Serious transformation of the NNS in the near future, including new institutionalization with concomitant strengthening of institutions—democratic or otherwise—appears inevitable. This could lead either to further restoration of the Soviet-style nomenklatura system, or to its wholescale dismantling.

If the system moves towards authoritarian mobilization, it requires more rigid affiliation of nomenklatura positions and appropriate appointments throughout the "presidential vertical," including the Presidential Administration, Presidential Envoys to federal districts and collegiums of federal agencies' representatives in the regions. It also needs an effective system of personnel selection and training to be constructed, which may incorporate existing elements like the All-Russia People's Front projects, youth summer camps, and the multi-level United Russia primaries. The existing imbalance between hypertrophied verticals and underdeveloped horizontals should be obviated. Furthermore, the system currently lacks a universal mechanism for returning property from private individuals back to the state. It will require an efficient system of monitoring—a kind of political *Gosplan*, which partially exists already, under the auspices of the

Civil Society Development Foundation (FoRGO). The entire construction of the NNS could be continued to its logical end, with individual repressions transformed into systemic ones, and horizontals to be properly developed in order to control the hierarchical levels which connect all verticals with each other.

In the case of authoritarian modernization, a strengthening of property rights and an independent judiciary is essential, which would lead to the weakening of the NNS. Electoral institutions should be reinforced and public political competition should be promoted; furthermore, federalism should be restored and developed, as well as local self-administration. Division of powers should take place, which may lead ultimately to the dismantling of Russian authoritarianism. In reality, this would require turning back the development of Russia's political system under Putin. This is effectively impossible without changing the leader.

Notes

[1] In Magyar's terms, a single-pyramid patronal system (SPPS) of the adopted political family.
[2] The term initially referred to a register of important power positions to be filled by a Communist party committee, from municipal level right up to the CPSU Central Committee.
[3] In this context, the nomenklatura is understood as a hierarchical personnel system in which the influence of a particular figure is mainly linked to his position, rather than personality.
[4] This term refers to politicians drawn from the security and/or military services, including members of the former KGB.
[5] See for example, Olga Kryshtanovskaya and Stephen White, "Putin's Militocracy," *Post-Soviet Affairs* 19, no. 4 (2003): 289–306; also David W. Rivera & Sharon Werning Rivera, "Is Russia a militocracy? Conceptual issues and extant findings regarding elite militarization," *Post-Soviet Affairs* 30, no. 1 (2014): 27–50, http://dx.doi.org/10.1080/1060586X.2013.819681.
[6] From 2006–2015, the share of the state in the Russian economy has grown from 35 to 70 per cent. See Sergey Medvedev, "Tanets chernykh lebedey," Radio Svoboda, last modified January 1, 2017, http://www.svoboda.org/a/28205895.html.
[7] This phrase takes the name of one of the district courts in central Moscow, which became well-known due to several prominent misuse of law cases, starting with the Khodorkovsky/Yukos case and ending with the Ildar Dadin case in 2015.
[8] Nikolai Sergeev, "Verkhovnyy sud dobilsya podderzhki sverkhu," Kommersant.ru, last modified Feb. 17, 2016, http://www.kommersant.ru/doc/2917918.

9 "Zasedaniye Soveta po protivodeystviyu korruptsii," Kremlin.ru, last modified January 26, 2016, http://www.kremlin.ru/events/president/news/51207.

10 This term, a portmanteau of "Putin" and "miting," the Russian term for a rally, came to represent these pro-Putin gatherings.

11 According to the president, there were almost 200,000 criminal cases initiated in 2014 dealing with economic crimes, with only 46,000 leading to a trial and 15,000 of them falling apart at that stage. Meanwhile, 80–83% of entrepreneurs who became objects of these cases lost their businesses—either partially or totally. "They were pressed, robbed and released," Putin lamented. See "Poslanie Prezidenta Federal'nomu Sobraniju," Kremlin.ru, last modified December 3, 2015, http://kremlin.ru/events/president/news/50864.

12 The Ministry of Crimean Affairs lasted only one year (2014–15). The Ministry of North Caucasus Affairs (founded 2014), and the Ministry of Regional Development (2012–14) also existed during this time.

13 The National Guard Forces Command was established (2016), while the Federal Tariffs Service (2004–15), the Federal Service for Fiscal and Budgetary Supervision (2004–16), the Federal Migration Service (2004–16), and the Federal Drug Control Service (2003–16) were merged or abolished.

14 The term refers to the Civil Society Development Foundation, a government-organized non-governmental organization (GONGO).

15 In April 2017, Brechalov was appointed the head of Udmurtia.

16 This was how Putin put it in his 2015 presidential address. See "Poslanie Prezidenta Federal'nomu Sobraniju," Kremlin.ru, last modified December 3, 2015, http://www.kremlin.ru/events/president/news/50864.

17 Alexei Makarkin, "Rossiyskiye elity i kremlevskiye 'atomy'," *Pro et Contra* 38, no. 4 (2007): 19–29. http://www.intelros.ru/pdf/pro_et_contra_38/makarkin-19-29.pdf, accessed December 12, 2016.

18 A "feudal lord" or "sovereign prince" is a head of state within the state. Under Yeltsin, this position was occupied by regional leaders, and under Putin, by heads of corporations. The prior weakening and destroying of corporations, and first of all of corporations' power, means their loss of autonomy and greater centralization.

19 Vladimir Putin himself came to Moscow in 1996, due to his network of fellow-countrymen connections, and when he became first the FSB director, and later the head of the state, he surrounded himself with trusted figures from the St. Petersburg mayoral office and the FSB.

20 Olga Kryshtanovskaya and Stephen White, "Putin's Militocracy," *Post-Soviet Affairs* 19, no. 4 (2003): 289–306. See also David W. Rivera & Sharon Werning Rivera, "Is Russia a militocracy? Conceptual issues and extant findings regarding elite militarization," *Post-Soviet Affairs* 30, no. 1 (2014): 27–50, http://dx.doi.org/10.1080/1060586X.2013.819681

21 See "Politburo 2.0: demontazh ili perezagruzka," Minchenko Consulting, November 2016, http://www.minchenko.ru/Politburo%202.0_2016%2007.11.pdf

22 See Yevgeny Minchenko, cited in Nikolay Petrov, "Postroenie silovikov," *Vedomosti*, last modified Jul. 25, 2016, http://www.vedomosti.ru/opinion/

articles/2016/07/25/650380-postroenie-silovikov; also Tatiana Stanovaya, "Korporatsiya 'silovikov': kadrovaya ekspansiya na fone vnutrennikh 'voyn'," Politcom.ru, last modified May 19, 2014, http://politcom.ru/17594.html.

23 The son of a leading figure in Putin's inner circle, Yury Kovalchuk, who heads the bank "Russia" (he is sometimes called Putin's "personal banker") and Russia's major private media holding, "National Media Group."

24 The son of Nikolay Patrushev, who succeeded Putin as the FSB director in 1999, and has been secretary of the Security Council since 2008.

25 The son of Yevgeny Murov, who headed the Federal Protective Service (FSO) from 2000–2016.

26 The son of Vasily Shestakov, Putin's classmate and judo partner, now a State Duma deputy.

27 The son of Mikhail Fradkov, Putin's trusted contact at the federal government when he was vice-mayor of St. Petersburg, later prime minister (2004–2007), and subsequently head of the Foreign Intelligence Service (2007–2016).

28 The nephew of Vladimir Ustinov, the Prosecutor General under Putin (2000–2006), now the plenipotentiary envoy to the Southern Federal District.

29 "Politburo 2.0: demontazh ili perezagruzka," Minchenko Consulting, November 2016, http://www.minchenko.ru/Politburo%202.0_2016%2007.11.pdf

30 Nikolay Petrov, "Ot federatsii korporatsiy k federatsii regionov," *Pro et Contra* 56, nos. 4–5 (2012): 101–18, http://carnegieendowment.org/files/ProEtContra_56_all.pdf

31 Nikolay Petrov, "Putinskaya perestroyka," *Vedomosti*, last modified August 22, 2017, https://www.vedomosti.ru/opinion/articles/2017/08/23/730610-putinskaya-perestroika

MIKHAIL MINAKOV

Republic of Clans:
The evolution of the Ukrainian political system

Today's Ukrainian political system is an interplay of public institutions hijacked by competing clans and patron-client networks specific to post-Soviet political cultures. In combination, these elements constitute a "clan state" with a specific cyclic development and dependency of formal institutions on informal patronal groups.

The development of post-Soviet Ukraine provides researchers with rich material for the study of patronalism and the clan state. The brave attempt to build liberal democracy and a market economy after the dissolution of the Soviet Union, alongside social disorientation in a period of huge socio-economic crises in the mid-1990s, has resulted in the construction of an oligarchic republic. In this republic, the clans became real actors of political and economic competition, and facets of the political system adapted to fit the needs and style of the major actors.

In this chapter, I will show the historical roots of the contemporary Ukrainian political system. I will focus on how clans and their informal structures have emerged as key political subjects of independent Ukraine. How did formal political institutions come to depend on the clans in Ukraine? To answer this question I will discuss the methods for a study of patronal (clan) states in section 1 of the chapter, analyze Soviet roots of the regional principle of the clans' formation in section 2, and show how the post-Soviet Ukrainian political system was constructed to support clans, to facilitate their development and to let some of them build mafia state power verticals in section 3.

The foundational hypothesis for this article is the assumption that the gap between formal and informal power institutions and practices is a core factor defining development of the Ukrainian political system. The Ukrainian political system reinforces poverty and limited access to decision making by the vast majority of the population, and makes its citizenry dependent on patron-client networks of wealth redistribution. As such, the core institutions of the Ukrainian political system are designed to facilitate competition and cooperation of clans.

1. A model to describe the post-Soviet Ukrainian state

In order to describe the development of the Ukrainian "clan state," I will use analytical models proposed by Henry E. Hale and Bálint Magyar.

In recent decades Henry Hale has developed a theory of post-Soviet (Eurasian) patronal politics.[1] He describes patronalism as a key feature of post-Soviet political structures and actions, with its own cyclic nature of development, with roots in both Soviet and pre-Soviet political culture. He defines patronal politics as one that "refers to politics in societies where individuals organize their political and economic pursuits primarily around the personalized exchange of concrete rewards and punishments through chains of actual acquaintance, and not primarily around abstract, impersonal principles such as ideological belief or categorizations like economic class that include many people one has not actually met in person. In this politics of individual reward and punishment, power goes to those who can mete these out, those who can position themselves as patrons with a large and dependent base of clients."[2] "In short," Hale writes, "highly patronalistic societies are those in which connections not only matter (as they do just about everywhere), but matter overwhelmingly. Such societies typically feature strong personal friendships and family ties, weak rule of law, pervasive corruption, low social capital, extensive patron-client relationships, widespread nepotism, and what sociologists would recognize as "patrimonial" or "neopatrimonial" forms of domination."[3]

In the proposed model, patronal networks organize themselves into pyramids that compete with one other to become a single pyramid.[4] The competition between these pyramids causes specific oscillations in the quality of democracy, or autocracy, in post-Soviet societies.[5] This model is very well applicable to events in the post-1991 history of independent Ukraine and its neighboring societies.

Hale's model pays close attention to the specificity of post-Soviet presidentialism and its compliance with a patronal political logic. In his study of democratic regress in post-Soviet Eurasia, he has rightly focused on a damage that "a combination of patronalism and presidentialism" does for democratic prospects of post-Soviet societies.[6] Furthermore, Hale's model takes into account the roots of post-Soviet patronalism. He specifically shows that post-Soviet political culture is embedded in forms of elite organization dating from both imperial and Soviet times.[7]

As I will demonstrate in sections 2 and 3, the proposed model is appropriate for analysis of the macropolitical structures and dynamics of contemporary Ukraine. It is also useful for comparing political systems of contemporary Eurasia. However, this model lacks an understanding of the internal dynamics of patronal networks, of their own "political culture." To analyze the micropolitics of post-Soviet patronal networks, I combine Hale's model with the model of "clan/mafia state" proposed by Bálint Magyar.

A scholar and politician, Bálint Magyar has proposed a model describing elites' behavior in post-communist countries. In his book *Post-Communist Mafia State*, Magyar focuses on the question of how post-communist society—with its political and economic peculiarities—practices the creation and reproduction of patronal networks in an interplay between a mafia underworld (mafia criminal groups) and mafia upper-world (mafia state).[8]

Magyar also proposes a dynamic picture of patronal politics as seen from within clans, or "adopted political family" organized "by means of mafia culture."[9] It shows the formation of a new elite organization, which "is built on a network of contacts grounded essentially in family relationships—as is the case in the mafia—or the *adopted family* sealed by businesses in common. New, and then further families link up to the organization along ties of kinship and loyalty, fitting into the highly hierarchic, pyramid-like order of subordination that has the head of the *adopted political family* at its summit."[10] When the adopted political families illegitimately consolidate power in their hands, a "mafia state" is established.

The major actor in the "mafia state" political system, a family-like clan, is described as a patronal network with specific features. Here, different networks of acquaintances are organized into (1) a single-pyramid adopted political family that (2) extends over formal institutions, (3) is based on patronal, not organizational loyalty, and (4) follows the cultural patterns of a patriarchal family or clan.[11]

Another important element of Magyar's model are the actors of the political-economic clan. In his description, this structure includes: (a) *poligarchs*, highly visible, core political personalities with invisible economic power, the patrons of a clan; (b) a circle of *oligarchs*, with visible economic power and invisible political power (which vary according to their history of adoption and closeness to the patron: inner circle, adopted, surrendered, autonomous and so on); (c) other circles including *stooges* (middlemen between the legitimate and illegitimate spheres for the public), *corruption brokers* (those bringing the partners of the corrupt transaction together), *security providers* and so forth.

Finally, unlike Hale who looks back to the patronalism of imperial times, Bálint Magyar ensures that the communist legacy is taken into account. Magyar shows how post-communist elites used the communist experience and the residual elements of communist political culture to recreate patronal politics. He emphasizes that "[t]he use of *post-communist* in the designation does not refer merely to a historical sequence, but rather to the fact that the conditions preceding the democratic big bang have a decisive role in the formation of the system. Namely that *it came about on the foundations of a communist dictatorship, as a product of the debris left by its decay.*"[12] In the case of Ukraine, the Soviet experience was instrumental in creating conditions that favored the development of regional clans, and a political system characterized as a "republic of clans."

In this combination of the two models, I see an opportunity to analyze and describe the ways the Ukrainian political system was created and has developed in the last 25 years. As I have demonstrated, the models of Magyar and Hale do not contradict each other. On the contrary, they make it possible to describe the post-communist and post-Soviet realities of Ukraine and its neighbors.

2. The Soviet legacy: Emergence and evolution of Ukrainian regional financial-political groups

Regional groups were at the core of political development and wealth distribution in Ukraine. After the fall of the Soviet Union, Ukrainian regional groups evolved by applying Soviet nomenklatura culture to the new realities of emerging political pluralism, privatization and the market economy. The Communist Party of the Soviet Union (CPSU) was a huge organization that functioned as a mechanism for the selection and promotion of leaders and active loyal citizens into positions of power. The party demanded the full loyalty of its members and local units to its central leadership; in return for loyalty, members of the nomenklatura were allowed to hold their status irrespective of their success as public managers. Under the new conditions after independence, these regional clans became a generic form of organization for the emerging power elites' in Ukraine.[13]

Among many other features of the Soviet nomenklatura, the principle of self-organization around regional party units turned out to be decisive.[14] The Soviet power elites developed as regional groups in a response to the prohibition of factions in the CPSU.

In early post-revolutionary times, the inner life of the party was energized by internal discussion between numerous factions: "leftists," "rightists," "left-rightists," "right-leftists," followers of Trotsky, Zinoviev, Bukharin, Sapronov, Smirnov and others. These factions were organized around alternative solutions for issues such as the constitution of the Soviet Union, the role of the Party in governance, the role of professional unions and, of course, control over key positions in the Party. In order to guarantee stable control over the Party and the Soviet governments in both the center and republics of the Union, the polylogue inside the CPSU had to be destroyed.

Iosif Dzhugashvili, more famously known by his *nom de guerre*, Stalin, managed to reorganize the Communist Party and monopolize control through the prohibition of the existing party factions. Richard Pipes has described how this prohibition allowed Dzhugashvili to prevail in the intra-party competition between 1921 and 1933.[15] Initially, decisive power was removed from the Party Congress and given to the Central Committee. Secondly, power shifted from the Central Committee to the Politburo. Thirdly, power was informally consolidated by three individual members of the Politburo: namely Zinoviev, Kamenev and Stalin. Finally, the fourth critical step constituted the actual prohibition of factions (or *oppositions*, as they were then called). This was the moment when Stalin completed his personal monopolization of power.

One of the many consequences of Stalin's "revolution from above" was a change in the principle of internal party competition: instead of groups being organized around ideological principles, the major competitors became regional groups. Old and young members of regional party units supported each other in their careers at all levels of Soviet power structures. These groups did not undermine the ideological monopoly of the party's "magistral line" (the policies approved by the General Secretary and the Politburo), instead channeling the energy of emerging leaders into controlled behavior for the benefit of the Party. The ideological blindness of these regional groups was especially visible in the case of the Southern regional group: Mikhail Suslov (a Stalinist and leading ideologist of the Brezhnev era) supported the career of his younger comrade Yuriy Andropov (a conservative reformist, later to become the chief of the KGB and General Secretary in 1982–84), who in turn supported Mikhail Gorbachev (a social-democratic reformist and General Secretary from 1985–91).

It is important to stress that the regional groups were informal units with blurred identities and limitations. Looking at the groups from the 1960s to 1980s (those from Leningrad, Pribaltika, the North, Eastern Siberia, Dnipropetrovs'k and so on), one can see that same nomenklatura representative could be a member of several groups. For instance, Andropov was supported simultaneously by the Southern group and the Northern group in his career. He belonged to the first group by origin, having been born in the Stavropol Province (*Stavropolskaya gubernia*), and to the second by virtue of his initial career in the Karelo-Finnish Soviet Socialist Republic (*Karelo-Finskaya SSR*). As this example shows, the belonging to a group was rather flexible and informal. However, this distance between formal party structures and informal units was very important for Soviet political culture, especially in the later, post-totalitarian Soviet periods.

In the Ukrainian context, the regional principle has become very strong in the post-WWII context. This power arrangement has its origins in the access to the huge funding provided by central government for industrial reconstruction projects in the Ukrainian Soviet Socialist Republic. As Paul R. Magocsi described, World War II left Soviet Ukraine a wasteland. There was a desperate depletion of the labor force, with 5.5 million Ukrainians killed, 3.9 million evacuated eastwards, and a further 2.2 million transferred to Germany as forced laborers. Moreover, 714 cities and towns, along with 28,000 villages, were totally or substantially destroyed, 16,150 enterprises were demolished, 833 mines were blown up, 872 state farms were destroyed, and a further 27,910 collective farms were shattered. Infrastructure too was devastated: all major roads, bridges, and electric power stations had to be rebuilt.[16] Ukraine had to be restored, and this restoration needed proper managers.

The Soviet government invested a great deal into economic reconstruction in the post-war period: according to the calculations of Mark Harrison, by 1948 the GPD per capita had reached the USSR's level in 1938.[17] The resources invested were not only financial; indeed, human resources were also imported wholesale to the Ukrainian SSR. These included all levels of Party, government and industrial hierarchy: from rank-and-file Party members, workers and miners to regional party leaders and "red directors."[18] As such, the newly appointed leaders of the local party, governmental and industrial agencies managed huge resources and had enormous power.

To manage the fourth Five-Year Plan (1946–50) in the Ukrainian SSR, a new management structure had to be created. Eric Duskin has rightly noted that the post-war recovery in the Soviet Union—unlike other major participants of WWII—was undertaken with the guidance of the same pre-war leaders.[19] Nevertheless, in all formerly occupied territories, and particularly in Ukraine, the regional leadership was deeply influenced by the consequences of Nazi occupation. The central and regional Ukrainian leadership was literally filtered; up until the final days of the USSR, citizens who lived under the Nazi occupation were regarded as suspicious. The continuity of the Soviet political regime in Ukraine, therefore, took place in the realm of public management, not through individuals. Some dislocated regional leaders returned to Kyiv, Kharkiv, Dnipropetrovs'k and Stalino/Donets'k. However, many new people were coming to start new lives as party, government and industrial managers in Ukraine. Moreover, both old and new cadres soon organized themselves into regional groups resembling those that existed before the war.

The funding from the Union center led to increased competition between re-emerging regional groups within the Ukrainian SSR. New and old party leaders predominantly gathered around the three biggest party units and industrial clusters in Kharkiv, Stalino/Donets'k and Dnipropetrovs'k.

Although Kharkiv lost its status as Ukrainian capital before the war, it remained one of the administrative, industrial, cultural and scientific centers of Soviet Ukraine. Post-war funding here was largely invested into scientific industry. The local party unit was also influential in the nearby Poltava and Sumy oblasts. From my interviews with several local party and Komsomol activists, I learned that the Kharkiv regional group cultivated close ties to culture and science; they also cherished the idea of belonging to the pre-Stalin Bolshevik tradition of party politics.[20] This group was also more concerned about "Ukrainian bourgeois nationalism," ideological issues, and supported what they called "equal opportunities for Ukrainian and Russian cultures" in the republic. It was critical for this group to differentiate itself from the Kyiv-based Central Committee and from the Donets'k regional group.

With the heavy inflow of financial and human resources, Stalino/Donets'k re-emerged as a heavy industrial and mining center. The local Party leadership was also influential on issues in the Voroshilovgrad/Luhans'k oblast, an important part of the *Donbas* cluster. Through interviews with former local Party officials, I observed that this group associated itself less with ideological issues and more with industry.[21] As one of the former oblast secretaries said to me, "Here, I always felt myself more of a manager and engineer than a Party boss." This vision of their connection to industry, and a special attachment to "simple miners and workers" seems to have been an important part of the Donets'k regional Party group's identity.

Here it is important to add some data from a conversation with two retired investigators of the Soviet economic police, the OBKhSS (Department Against Misappropriation of Socialist Property), in 2012. Both of the investigators began working in the Donets'k OBKhSS in 1971: one remained in Donets'k until his retirement in 1998, while the other finished his career in Kyiv's Ministry of Interior in 2004. Both described the Donets'k regional group as the most financially connected, both to the formal Soviet economy and its black market counterpart. Moreover, they also stated that it was quite easy for this group to survive the USSR's dissolution: they managed to sustain control of the Donbas region and maintain informal autonomy from Kyiv until 2003.

The Dnipropetrovs'k regional group was probably the most successful in terms of competition. Its representative, Leonid Brezhnev, became USSR General Secretary in 1964. From this point, this regional group provided cadres not only to organizations in Kyiv but also in Moscow. This group connected Party officials, local government bureaucrats, "red directors," Komsomol leaders, and the so-called "technical intelligentsia."[22] The influence of this group extended to the Zaporizhzhia and Kirovograd oblasts.

From my interviews with several retired local Party, industry and Komsomol employees, I found that—at least by the 1970s—this group had gained the ability to lead not only republican, but also all-Union organizations.[23] In these interviews, all three interlocutors stressed that they felt themselves in "competition for power and resources in the republic."

They additionally felt that the dominance of the Dnipropetrovs'k group was unquestionable during the rule of General Secretary Brezhnev and Ukraine's First Secretary Volodymyr Shcherbytsky, who held this position from 1972–89.

As I have previously stated, it is important to stress that these regional groups had very blurred and unstable identities during the Soviet period. All three of my interlocutors agreed that they felt a sense of belonging to the regional group only when they were leaving their oblast (for instance, at republican and all-Union congresses, or during business trips in other republics). In their everyday life and work, however, they instead identified themselves with Party or Komsomol activists and "Soviet men," rather than representatives of a regional group. When they were asked to analyze retrospectively how they began identifying themselves with a particular regional group, my interviewees referred to three decisive factors for becoming a member of the group: firstly, entry into the CPSU in a local Party unit; secondly, entry into one of the regional higher education institutions; and thirdly, the fact that they were born in the region. It appears that local Party units and educational centers created a feeling of regional identity in local nomenklatura circles by the end of the USSR's existence.

Based on my interviews, along with the scarce extant scholarly literature dedicated to local elites in the Soviet Union, I have been able to reconstruct the structure of a regional group in different periods.[24] By the end of the 1980s, it united leaders of three generations. The first generation was one of mixed origin, with the majority coming from other regions or republics of the Soviet Union after World War II. In the next two generations, the majority of members were born, and/or educated, in the region. These groups were organized during the Fourth Five-Year Plan, though their institutionalization took place when a new generation of leaders came to power within the same group (between 1950 and 1965). This institutionalization also coincided with the end of Stalin's rule, which provided regional groups with more predictability, safety and autonomy vis-à-vis the oversight of the center.

The core of the regional group (proto-poligarchs) consisted of the First Secretary of the Party unit, the head of the oblast's KGB division, the chief of police, and a handful of directors of key industrial units. These leaders were recognized based on their official positions. The second layer of leaders (proto-oligarchs) included other secretaries of the oblast Party unit, leaders of the Komsomol and professional unions (at oblast and city levels), heads of police agencies, oblast and city courts, high-ranking members of industrial and trade organizations (at oblast and city levels), heads of local educational institutions, and others. The third important layer, from which the Ukrainian independentist leadership emerged, included leading representatives of the intelligentsia (such as editors of the local press, leading journalists, some visible writers, poets and/or scholars), informal members of the shadow economy (for example, *tsekhoviky*, the underground entrepreneurs of the Soviet era whose activity was regarded to be criminal), alongside members of the cooperative movement, agricultural companies and so forth. The communication within and between these circles was mediated mostly by the Party and local government during their official and unofficial meetings. The importance of the latter was growing ever greater by the 1980s.

In this structure, the most stable positions were occupied by people from the second and third layers. They had more informal power and assets, and were rarely victims of unsuccessful competition with other regional groups. The cadres from the core of the group were more tightly controlled by Party and KGB structures, both republican and all-Union, and had a shorter life-cycle; their assets depended more on their post. Since their position was more vulnerable, they promoted group ethics that demanded not only loyalty to state and Party, but also personal loyalty to them in exchange for a stable income, career and safety. Moreover, the core group promoted a distinct regional group identity. With the change of figures at the core, the safety of the second and third layers usually remained intact.

The above description pertains to the micropolitics of regional groups. The macropolitical picture, on the other hand, can best be described as managed competition of the groups for leading positions in the Ukrainian Soviet Socialist Republic. Even though the Ukrainian SSR provided the Union structure with two General Secretaries (Nikita Khrushchev from 1956–64, followed by Leonid Brezhnev from 1964–82), the major aims of the Ukrainian regional groups' competition were for two positions: firstly, the First Secretary of the Central Committee of the Ukrainian Communist Party; and secondly, the Chairperson of the Council of Ministers of the Ukrainian SSR. Competition at the central Union level was much tougher, while in the Ukrainian SSR, the groups faced lesser risks if they lost the contest. This moderate competitive strategy created a system of balances in the Ukrainian republic: if the First Secretary was chosen from one group, the Chairperson of the Council of Ministers would usually come from another. As Table 6.1 shows, this balance was in place since the end of the 1950s, when regional groups became more or less institutionalized.

Table 6.1. Rulers of Soviet Ukraine since 1957

First Secretary of Central Committee of Ukrainian Communist Party, period of service	Regional group	Chairperson of the Council of Ministers of Ukrainian SSR, period of service	Regional group
Mykola Pidhornyi, 1957–63	Kharkiv	Volodymyr Shcherbytsky, 1961–63	Dnipropetrovs'k
Petro Shelest, 1963–72	Kharkiv	Ivan Kazanets', 1963–65 Volodymyr Shcherbytsky, 1965–72	Donets'k Dnipropetrovs'k
Volodymyr Shcherbytsky, 1972–89	Dnipropetrovs'k	Oleksandr Lyashko, 1972–87 Vitalii Masol, 1987–90	Donets'k Donets'k
Volodymyr Ivashko, 1989–90	Kharkiv	Vitalii Masol, 1987–90	Donets'k
Stanislav Hurenko, 1990–91	Donets'k	Vitold Fokin, 1990–92	Dnipropetrovs'k/Donets'k

From this table, we can see that political competition in the Ukrainian SSR occurred between three regional groups. These groups represented one of the sub-types of Soviet nomenklatura patronalism where socio-political equilibrium was reached at two levels, local and republican. At the local level, the regional group organized the political and economic activities of local elites primarily around the personalized exchange of concrete rewards, with downsides including the increasing loss of the Party's ideology by the 1980s. At the republican level, the regional groups were reaching equilibrium in a balanced hierarchy of First Secretaries and Chairmen of the Council of Ministers.

When the Soviet Union was dissolved and the central Politburo's oversight vanished, political competition in independent Ukraine continued to organize itself around the contest between regional groups.

3. Establishment of the political-economic clans' dominance in independent Ukraine

With the dissolution of the Soviet Union, Ukrainian elites found themselves in a situation where their Moscow based-supervisors—namely President Gorbachev, the Union government, the KGB, the CPSU Politburo and the Central Committee—had lost any control over them. Left alone, Ukrainian ruling groups in Kyiv were divided into two major blocs, namely national communists and national democrats.[25] The former were in power in 1990–92, and their strategy was to legitimize their power as rulers of the newly independent state. Their party, the Communist Party of Ukraine, was dissolved in September 1991, before even the referendum on independence (December 1, 1991) and the formal dissolution of the Soviet Union (December 25–26, 1991). However, some of the Communist party leaders, led by Leonid Kravchuk, managed to maintain their control over government. When he obtained the post of parliamentary speaker, Kravchuk abandoned the Party in August 1991. A number of other party bosses did likewise, exchanging Party positions for formal government or local administrations' posts.

The second group, the national democrats, was in "constructive opposition" to the communists: they were eager to cooperate with the national communists on the creation of an independent state, and stood opposed to attempts to recreate the Soviet Union under another name. Their leaders originated from both the dissident movement of the Soviet period, and from the reform communists of the perestroika period. They promoted the idea of Ukrainian independence and the construction of a nation-state, while resisting attempts to create strong post-Union links.

The consensus of these two groups around the idea of independence made it possible for Leonid Kravchuk to be elected as the first president of Ukraine in December 1991. However, Kravchuk did not manage to establish his own lasting rule. Although he managed to transfer from his

Party post to a government position in a timely fashion in 1991 (unlike his formal Party boss Stanislav Hurenko), he did not have the support of any regional group. Kravchuk instead ruled as a mediator between national communists and national democrats in Kyiv, among regional groups around Ukraine, and between Russia and the West. This mediation role was too limited to provide him with the ability to sustain his domination of Ukrainian politics.

As many other former Soviet republics, Ukraine was reinventing itself as a post-communist polity and a modern society in the 1990s. This post-Soviet society was essentially forced to make from scratch the fundamental institutions governing both private and public spheres, which had been absent in the Soviet Union until the era of perestoika. These inventions included political pluralism, new democratic procedures (parliamentarism, elections, local self-governance and so forth), a plurality of economic actors, a market economy, entrepreneurship, the rule of law and many others. Every invention of this period was simultaneously rooted in Soviet totalitarian and perestroika experiences, pre-Soviet traditions, Western political and economic models, and experimentation with new forms of political and economic life.

For the purposes of this study, it is sufficient to mention that the competition of many different political and economic forms of elites' self-organization in this hugely complex situation has led to the victory of relatively small, highly solidified regional elites' groups. These groups first managed to take control of major industries, later commandeering local governments, and then, finally, the central government. In the absence of a more or less stable order, the old patronal networks of Soviet regional groups have gained new life in a socially, politically and economically disorganized country with disoriented populations. Even though there were other forms of elites' organizations in Ukraine (including ideology-based parties), the principle of an informal personal union of leaders, all of whom had common experience of living and cooperating in their region, won out by the end of the 1990s.

The competitive advantage of regional patronal networks was based on four key elements:
- stable solidarity within the group, based on personal loyalty to the leadership hierarchy;
- the safety of its members and their businesses in an era of conflicts between criminal groups and power abuse by officials from Kyiv;

- their support in growing the assets and power of loyal members according to their position in the hierarchy of the group;
- informal ties that reduced the price of interactions between political and economic actors belonging to the same group.

However, the dominant regional political-economic clans' advantage was connected with their seamless transfer from the public to the private sphere in the emerging Ukrainian state. Emerging triumphant from the local conflicts between criminal groups, mass privatization, and entrepreneurial competition, the clans' leaders have been easily converting their new economic force into political power, initially in local administrations, and later in central government. This principle of indifference to the private-public divide was a legacy of Soviet regional groups which were deeply influential in the formation of the new Ukrainian republic. The so-called "systemic corruption" of Ukraine was an after-effect of the victory of regional clans as the major form of elites' self-organization in Ukraine. Moreover, the long-term post-Soviet devolution of democracy, as outlined by Henry Hale,[26] was another result of the same victory.

Historically, the victory of regional groups took place over a lengthy period between 1993 and 1999. In 1993, a political crisis, caused by the rivalry between President Kravchuk and Prime Minister Leonid Kuchma, led to early presidential elections and the appointment of Acting Prime-Minister Yukhym Zvyahilsky. This latter appointment was the first display of the increasing strength of the regional groups.

Zvyahilsky made his career as an engineer and a mine manager. In the Soviet period, he moved from the third layer of the regional group into the upper circle of the second group when he became a director of the largest Donbas mine, Zasyadko. When the Party monopoly was lifted, he and other "red directors" came to constitute the core of the regional clan. The transition of power went smoothly, former party bosses retired safely, and those representatives of the second and third layers who were successful in privatizing local industries or establishing personal control over formally state-owned enterprises established a new hierarchy. Zvyahilsky's career is illustrative of this change: he became a Ukrainian MP in 1990 and 1994, a head of Donets'k city council in 1992, vice prime minister and then acting prime minister in 1993.

Conversely, this moment did not yet confirm the triumph of the regional clans. Half a year later, in 1994, Zvyahilsky was fired, while Leonid

Kravchuk lost the presidential elections to Leonid Kuchma, a representative of Dnipropetrovs'k regional groups. It is important to note that during the presidential elections of 1994, candidates supported by parties adopting Western ideologies, along with perestroika-era political organizations, failed to advance beyond the first round: five candidates supported by the Socialist Party, and others affiliated to Rukh, the Republican Party, the Democratic Party and other perestroika-era groups all gained less than 15% of voters' support. In the second round of elections, Kuchma won with 52% of the vote.

However, it is also important to stress that in 1994, regional groups were not that united. From interviews with members of Kuchma's electoral team of 1994, it became clear that the winning candidate was supported only by part of the Dnipropetrovs'k regional group because of local rivalries. Kuchma also gained very limited support from the Donets'k and Kharkiv groups. Kuchma's victory was likely based on the votes of the Russophone population, who feared Kravchuk's alleged "fast Ukrainization."[27]

President Kuchma ruled Ukraine for two terms: from 1994–99, and 1999–2004. It was the presidential elections of 1999 that manifested the hegemony of the regional clans. During his first term, Kuchma once again played the role of dispatcher between different financial-political groups, as Kravchuk had. However, Kuchma and his team also promoted the institutionalization of an oligarchic republic. In June 1996, under pressure from Kuchma, the Verkhovna Rada approved a new Constitution with very strong powers for the president. By using constitutional powers, his informal role of dispatcher between emerging clans, and his own power interests, Kuchma used both legal and illegal means to be re-elected in 1999 and establish the so-called post-Soviet power vertical—in other words, a single-pyramid patronal system—in Ukraine.

The "power vertical" system was tested in the 1990s in Lukashenka's Belarus and Yeltsin's Russia. The post-Soviet power vertical was merging into a single top-down structure incorporating all nominally separate branches of power and institutions, as well as local institutions of self-government.[28]

The power vertical was an ideal environment for the development of clans in Ukraine and other post-Soviet countries. In such a structure, formal institutions (like the presidency, cabinet of ministers, parliament, local councils, and courts) function in accord with two parallel codes. Nominally, they were subject to the formal rule of law. In reality, the power institutions followed the informal rules of the vertical, the adopted political family. Formal rules could have been violated (though a law-abiding façade has always been maintained), while the real distribution of power and wealth was conducted according to a social contract consisting of informal, unwritten rules. Thus, the courts served as a tool to legitimize corporate raiding, not to provide justice for citizens.[29] The police tended to function both as a government-controlled racket and the provider of public security. The cabinet of ministers managed shadow financial flows in parallel with its formal role in the executive body.

To fulfill the major macropolitical role of the clans' coordination and peaceful coexistence, the Ukrainian political system needed to re-establish a CPSU-type pyramid with the Politburo and Central Committee at its summit. The Soviet legacy was reconstituted in the new political culture of Ukraine as a specific institution, known as the Presidential Administration (PA). This institution did not function as the Communist Party had within the nomenklatura, but as the decision making center of the adopted political family. In terms of strategic decision- and policy-making, the monitoring of the implementation of informal rules, as well as arbitrage in the clans' conflicts, the Presidential Administration was already functional by 1998. I have interviewed two employees who worked for Kuchma's PA from 1994–99, and both told me that they left their jobs because of a significant change in the style and functionality of the organization: from its foundation as a patronage service to the president in 1994–96, the PA's agenda had shifted to permanent arbitrage in semi-criminal conflicts among clans by 1997, providing cover for shadow political and economic deals, and collecting rent from the clans. Since both interviewees had experience of working in Soviet power institutions, they have compared the Presidential Administration of 1998–99 as a "perverted version" of the old Central Committee that made strategic decisions for formal and informal institutions, managed the clans' balance of interests, and promoted corruption at all levels in Ukraine.

Even though the power vertical is a common model for most post-Soviet political systems, there are country-related specificities. In Russia, for example, the functions of the Central Committee were transferred to the Presidential Administration based on the personal experience of old and new employees. While this transition was not smooth, it was largely completed thanks to the adoption of the new super-presidential constitution of 1993. Since then, major decisions on domestic, international, and local issues have been made in a largely systematic fashion by the PA.

Alexander Lukashenka's regime, which was established in 1996–97, put the Presidential Administration above all other institutions of the state. Yet Belarus lacked the necessary human capital to fulfill all of the Central Committee's functions. These limitations have forced Lukashenka to play a lead role in both strategic and tactical decision-making. The CPSU Central Committee employees were seemingly not involved in the creation of the Belarusian PA.

As in Belarus and Russia, the Ukrainian Presidential Administration had developed into the country's leading institution by 1998–99.[30] Ukraine's Presidential Administration was built in accordance with the Belarusian model, when Central Committee functionality was accepted without a transition of Soviet experience to PA officials. However, the Ukrainian PA has specifically focused on the facilitation of balance among different regional clans. The Presidential Administration's dual function, along with the weakness of the Cabinet of Ministers and the limited power of parliament, helped Ukraine's oligarchs develop a form of pluralistic authoritarianism, a multi-pyramid patronal network based on the balance of interests among several patronal networks.

This pluralistic authoritarianism was a highly contradictory political model. It demanded that the president be an impartial broker who balances the interests of key clans, yet also allowed him to function as the country's sole ruler. As such, the model has several built-in weaknesses that limit its lifespan. For example, it lacks institutional mechanisms that commit the president to impartiality: the clans' system of patronalism is applied by the president himself if/when he creates his own clan and tries to subdue the others. When such attempts arose from the presidency, the clans used formal means, such as parliamentary procedure, and informal means, such as the Maidan protests, to sack the dysfunctional president.

Pluralistic authoritarian systems were fully functional in Ukraine on two occasions: during the latter period of Kuchma's first presidency (1998–99, and during his second term in 1999–2004) and in the years of Viktor Yanukovych's presidency (2010–14). In both cases, they disintegrated almost immediately when the president attempted to promote himself to a Lukashenka-style position and ceased to be an impartial, honest broker of the system. Rivalries among key clans then reached a breaking point and toppled the newly formed power vertical.

The system of pluralist authoritarianism was based on the functioning of clans that developed between regional groups in the 1990s. Between

1993 and 2010 there were two major regional groups that gave birth to Ukrainian oligarchic clans: namely, the Dnipropetrovs'k and Donets'k groups.

The Dnipropetrovs'k group was the first to end up with control over Kyiv and Ukraine. Leonid Kuchma used his personal ties with Dnipropetrovs'k elites to find cadres for many positions in government. Simultaneously, the local leaders used their contacts with the president to promote their smaller groups' interests. As a result, there were several strong clans organized from within this regional network (see Table 6.2). Here are a selection of them:

Table 6.2. Clans of Dnipropetrovs'k regional group

Clan	Period of activity	Poligarch(s)	Controlled public posts/institutions
Kuchma—Pinchuk clan	1994 for Leonid Kuchma; 1998 for Victor Pinchuk; active until today	Leonid Kuchma, Victor Pinchuk	President (1994–2004), MP (1998–2006), parliamentary factions and MP groups, control over separate ministries and general prosecutor's office (1994–2005); low-profile clan since 2005, with control over separate MPs, deputy-ministers and vice-general prosecutors
Pavlo Lazarenko clan	1995–99	Pavlo Lazarenko, Yulia Tymoshenko	Governor of Dnipropetrovs'k (1992–1995), prime minister (1996–7), party and parliamentary faction "Hromada" (1997–9); arrested in USA in 1999, sentenced to 9 years' imprisonment
Privat Group	1992–present	Ihor Kolomoyskyi, Gennadii Bogoliubov	Governor of Dnipropetrovs'k (2014–15), separate MPs, parliamentary parties and factions (from 1998 to today), deputy heads of National Bank, managers and Board members of state-owned gas and oil companies

To study the Dnipropetrovs'k clans, I conducted 21 interviews with former and present members of these clans from 2007–16. Based on the data received from these interviews, as well as information from open sources,[31] I can conclude the following:

1. The Dnipropetrovs'k regional group is a common name for many big and small clan-like patronal organizations. They emerged in Dnipropetrovs'k and Kyiv in the mid-1990s, and were often competing against and attacking each other. To limit the damage from these conflicts, the groups asked President Kuchma to judge on their issues. Later this function was also used for clan conflicts from other regions.
2. The Dnipropetrovs'k clans have never been able to create a common political party to represent them at national level. Their conflicts in the city were transferred to Kyiv when the emigration of the group's leaders began. For example, competition between Ihor Kolomoyskyi and Viktor Pinchuk started back in 1994. The last grand conflict of the same persons and their corporations was settled by a London court in 2016.
3. The Dnipropetrovs'k clans shared an indifference to political ideologies and church issues. They supported equally Ukrainian Orthodox and Protestant churches, and Ukrainian Jewish communities. For example, the Privat Group and Viktor Pinchuk were supporting the Jewish community in Dnipropetrovs'k (or even presiding over it, as in the case of Gennadii Bogoliubov), but also local Orthodox communities. Lazarenko's clan was often cooperating with Baptist and other Protestant religious groups in Ukraine.
4. By the beginning of 2000, these clans from within have organized as adopted political families. In terms of the methodology described in section 1, these clans were informal groups incorporating individual political and economic leaders and their small groups into a clan loyal to one or two patrons. In the terminology used by interviewees, words like "papa" (father), "sam" (he/himself) or similar were respectfully added to the patrons' names, and were pronounced with some awe and respect, resembling the cultural patterns of the patriarchal family.

The major rival of the Dnipropetrovs'k clans, the Donets'k regional group, has also been a common name for several clans that became visible in Ukrainian national politics only in 2002–2003. The Donets'k regional group featured both "old" and "young" clans. The "old" clans were organized by members of the second layer of the Soviet-era group: Yukhym Zvyahilsky, Volodymyr Boyko, Volodymyr Rybak, and Victor Yanukovych. These figures held leading posts in local enterprises during the Soviet period. The most visible "new" clans were founded by Rinat Akhmetov and Borys Kolesnikov (for details see Table 6.3).

To study the Donets'k clans, I conducted 37 interviews with former and present members of these clans from 2009–2016. Based on the data received from these interviews, as well as information from open sources,[32] I can conclude the following:

1. The Donets'k regional group is a common name for many clan-like patronal organizations, both big and small, that were much more tightly connected than their Dnipropetrovs'k rivals. These clans emerged in Donets'k in the mid-1990s and coalesced around the figure of Viktor Yanukovych from 1997 onward.
2. In 2001, they (together with some minor clans from Crimea, Vinnytsia and other regions) established the Party of Regions. This party was successful at liaising between established clans and groups of local elites from southeastern Ukraine. Even though Viktor Yanukovych was rarely the formal head of the party, he was its informal leader up until his escape to Russia in February 2014.
3. The Donets'k clans shared an ideological framework, incorporating elements of neo-Soviet nostalgia, support for the Ukrainian Orthodox Church (Moscow Patriarchate), and support for Russophones. As a result, they were a gravitational core for Kharkiv, Crimea, Odesa and other regional groups.
4. By the late 1990s, these clans were already organized as adopted political families. This is reflected in the terminology used by interviewees, including words like "papa" (father, a respectful name for Viktor Yanukovych), "aktsioner" (shareholder, a respectful name for Rinat Akhmetov), and "stariki" (old guys, a respectful reference to old clans' masters). In some cases, criminal nicknames[33] were also used for leaders (for instance, "Parus" for Victor Yanukovych).

In addition to these two major regional agglomerates of clans, there were other smaller groups who organized the local elites of Kharkiv and Lviv oblasts, the city of Chernivtsi, Podillia (the region consisting of Vinnytsia and Khmelnytskyi oblasts), and other regions of Ukraine.

Table 6.3. Clans of Donets'k regional group

Clan	Period of activity	Poligarch(s)	Controlled public posts/institutions
"Old" clans	1991/2–present, in varying forms	Yukhym Zvyahilsky, Volodymyr Boiko, Volodymyr Rybak, Mykola Azarov and some others	Acting prime minister, vice prime ministers, governors, heads of Oblast Council/City Council, MPs, MP groups, separate ministers and deputy ministers, Party of Regions, Tax Administration, etc.
Yanukovych clan	2003–2014	Victor Yanukovych, Oleksandr Yanukovych (since 2010)	Governor of Donets'k (1997–2002), Head of Oblast Council (1999–2001), prime minister (2002–05, 2006–07), president (2010–14), Party of Regions and parliamentary factions (2003–14); most public institutions in 2010–14; in exile since February 2014
"New" clans	1995–present	Rinat Akhmetov (since 1995), Borys Kolesnikov (since 1998)	Governors and mayors of Donets'k (1996–2014), Party of Regions, Opposition Bloc, separate MPs, parliamentary factions (1998–present), deputy heads of National Bank and general prosecutor, separate ministers and state-owned companies
Smaller and newer clans: Kliuyev brothers, Yuriy Boiko's group, "Odesa" clan, Kharkiv groups, etc.	1996–present	Andriy Kliuyev (since 2000), Yuriy Boiko (since 2001), Sergii Kivalov (since 2002), Yevhen Kushnaryov (1996–2007), Mikhail Dobkin (2006–present)	Judiciary/separate courts, Central Electoral Commission, separate ministers and state-owned companies

These clans were also connected with organized crime. The formation of Ukrainian clans took place in the era of the post-Soviet "criminal revolution."[34] Some of the leaders of this "revolution" turned out to be among the poligarchs and oligarchs of the clans (among them the twice-convicted Victor Yanukovych, and Rinat Akhmetov, who is believed to have led criminal groups in Donets'k since 1995). Others remained at the level of security providers and chiefs of teams responsible for corporate raiding.[35] The criminal underworld was one of the most important sources of cadres for Ukrainian clans.

Structurally, these clans evolved tremendously: starting as fairly straightforward adopted family-like groups, they soon became sophisticated multi-layer organizations.

1. In the initial stage, the clans centered around the key patronal figure of the "poligarch" (or several partners/poligarchs), central figures demanding loyalty from all the members of a clan or a group of clans. They were surrounded by an inner circle of oligarchs, "adopted oligarchs" and "surrendered oligarchs" who controlled key plants, banks, and other economic assets. The next circle (of "stooges" and political partners) included leaders of dependent political parties, heads of executive, legislative and judiciary institutions and de jure state-owned enterprises, and managers of media holdings. A separate group of associates would be "security providers": criminal groups and dependent officers of the secret services and the police. This structure was strong enough to succeed during privatization, survive the criminal wars, and successfully conduct (or defend its interests from) corporate raiding attacks.
2. Around 2000–2002, the major clans started moving from shadow political and economic activity into a more public posture. Those economic assets that were legally owned by poligarchs and the inner oligarchic circle were incorporated; this process produced the largest Ukrainian corporation of 2000–2014. The same organizational process was occurring with political assets and client networks. Small parties were merging into larger, more durable organizations, such as the Party of Regions or Yulia Tymoshenko's Batkivshchyna. Client networks were managed by emerging private and corporate philanthropic foundations.[36]

The Orange Revolution of 2004 has halted the process of creating a unified authoritarian regime, sustained political pluralism, and reinforced the strength of the parliament with constitutional changes in 2004–2006, which created a divided executive branch. However, the Presidential Administration (which was renamed the Presidential Secretariat during the presidency of Yushchenko, though its functions remained the same) re-emerged in 2006–2007 as an important part of the political system. Strong presidential rule was re-established in 2010 by decision of the Constitutional Court, giving new impetus to the attempts of creating a single-pyramid system, a "mafia state."

In essence, between 1993 and 2014 Ukraine has gone through numerous attempts to transform a regime dominated by a multi-pyramid network system (patronal democracy) into a single-pyramid patronal system (mafia state). Two Maidan protests (the Orange Revolution of 2004 and the Euromaidan of 2013–14) provided the Ukrainian citizenry with chances to break the government's dependency on clans organized around one dominant patronal network. Both times the protests led to the establishment of a mixed parliamentary-presidential system, political and ideological pluralism, the decline of the prior presidential administration, and a reduced role for clans in public politics.

The protests' impact on the establishment of a mafia state can be seen from recent developments in Ukraine. Between December 2013 and March 2014, Yanukovych's attempt to stabilize a mafia state and its power vertical collapsed.

The first stimulus of the collapse was the police's heavy-handed response to youth protests in late November 2013, which encouraged mass demonstrations the following month. The Euromaidan protesters took over several administrative buildings in Kyiv and the surrounding regions, and by the end of December, the Yanukovych family had lost control of parts of Ukraine's territory.

The second decisive moment was on January 16, 2014, when a group of pro-Yanukovych MPs, who did not actually have a majority in the Rada at the time, voted for a package of dictatorial laws. The suddenness of their imposition in Ukraine radicalized the protest movement and led to the first deaths in the streets of Kyiv. Some clans from the ruling party turned on Yanukovych in the hope that they could benefit from any change in regime. Many officials abandoned their prior loyalty to the president, covertly switched sides, and sabotaged their patron's orders.

The third crack to the regime came on February 19–21, 2014, when clashes between police and protesters resulted in mass bloodshed. Viktor Yanukovych and his family fled Kyiv for Russia. By that time, most clans subordinated to the Yanukovych family were looking for opportunities to survive the revolution, while retaining their assets and power. As the clans knew from the post-Orange Revolution period, the new leaders would look for support for their emerging regime from all powerful individuals and groups. As such, by the end of the Euromaidan most influential clans distanced themselves from the Family and started looking for new possibilities, leaving the short-lived Yanukovych mafia state and its power vertical to fall.

With the power vertical shattered, bold steps were taken toward democratic renewal. The new leaders restored the constitution of 2004, which mandated a parliamentary-presidential system, and returned some of the political liberties that the Yanukovych regime had erased. However, the slow pace of reforms, the rise of both old and new clans, and the impact of the Donbas war often seemed to suggest the probability of new mafia state development, when a dominant patronal network tries to force its competitors into surrender.[37] Furthermore, there is a growing body of evidence suggesting that the Euromaidan and the Donbas war forced the clans to adapt and evolve into groups with a new structure.

It is important to stress that the Euromaidan events had a mixed impact on clans. On one hand, the Donets'k clans have lost their power. On the other hand, many other clans have attempted to increase their own wealth and power. For example, the Privat Group (a surviving remnant of the Dnipropetrovs'k group) has had tremendous success in 2014 and the beginning of 2015. One of its poligarchs, Ihor Kolomoyskyi, supported the revolutionary government in the fight against separatists in Donbas and Russian occupants in Crimea. In return for his loyalty, he was appointed governor of Dnipropetrovs'k. His clan's informal control stretched to Odesa, Kherson, Zaporizhzhia, Donets'k and Kirovograd oblasts. Furthermore, the Privat Group was creative in its evolution. To survive and prosper in post-Euromaidan Ukraine, the clan has developed new structures, including several volunteer battalions (which fought separatists but also provided military support to the clan's economic and political interests), several NGOs (supporting battalions with money and other resources), and several new extreme right political parties. However, the growth of this clan ceased due to conflict with President Poroshenko and his own emerging clan.

Today, Ukraine is a battleground in the struggle between clans and formal political institutions. The reforms of 2014–15 aimed to support the institutional development of the government, parliament, judiciary, local communities and political parties. In 2016, the danger of a return of the republic of clans emerged. Will Ukraine decisively break with the clan state? It is too early to come up with a definitive answer.

Conclusions

In spite of revolutionary attempts at democratic state building, contemporary Ukraine continues to function as a "republic of clans." As I demonstrated in sections 2 and 3, clans and their informal structures have emerged as key political subjects within independent Ukraine. The Ukrainian political and socio-economic system was constructed in such a way that it afforded clans an opportunity to develop their patronal networks and pyramids while controlling vast public and private industries, and yet limited possibilities for one clan monopoly. The balance of Ukrainian pluralist authoritarianism was guaranteed by the president and Presidential Administration, as well as by a partially free parliament. Even though each clan had its own authoritarian agenda, the political system of pluralist authoritarianism resulted in three distinctive characteristics, which I will list here.

Firstly, pluralist authoritarianism produced a decay in democratic standards, but with some considerable level of pluralism in media and politics. The oscillation of Ukraine's political development, about which Henry Hale wrote, has repeatedly centered upon equilibrium of the "clan state" stage, with short periods of freedom (within the framework of the "patronal state" before 1998, and in 2005–2008) and aborted attempts to erect a "mafia state" (2001–2004, 2012–13).

Secondly, the authoritarian rule of the mafia state has thus far been confined to short periods. In the moments of single-clan supremacy and attempts of "power vertical" establishment, the regime was usually making a huge number of critical mistakes, consolidating the dissatisfaction of clients-citizens and failing to fully subdue the clans. In both the cases of 2004 and 2013–14, the Ukrainian political system led to the establishment of a parliamentary-presidential rule that limited the power of the president and his clan-dispatching role for some time.

Thirdly, the "clan state" repeatedly re-emerged after authoritarian attempts and revolutionary protests. All major political institutions can effectively function only as agencies with formal façades and informal agendas. But because of the persistent survival of competing patronal networks, these revolutions—in spite of their democratic agenda—do not result in the birth of liberal democracy, but only of *patronal democracy.*

I have also shown that Soviet Ukrainian elites' experience was constitutive for the formation of regional clans and the construction of a post-Soviet political system. The role of CPSU leaders and the Central Committee was taken by presidents and the Presidential Administration, respectively. Up until 2013, the regional groups dominant in Soviet times remained the strongest among other clans' agglomerates. The destruction of Soviet state property and the Communist administrative system, the rapid impoverishment of the vast majority of the population, and the privatization of Soviet industry provided a politico-economic basis for the emergence of the republic of clans. Moreover, I did not find any proof of Henry Hale's hypothesis that patronal networks apply also to pre-Soviet political culture; this may be a Ukrainian specificity.

By merging Hale's "patronal networks" model and Magyar's "clan state" model, I was able to describe the evolution of clans in both macro- and micro-political contexts. The Ukrainian clans evolved from the Soviet nomenklatura's regional groups into smaller but more stable adopted political families, which with time developed more formal structures with political parties, corporations, media holdings and philanthropic foundations, and adapted to the socio-political changes after the Maidan.

I also presented some evidence that the ideological indifference of patronal networks, about which Henry Hale wrote, was present only in the case of the Dnipropetrovs'k clans. Donets'k clans, rather, were attached to a sort of nostalgic neo-Sovietism and clericalism. The same ideological markers are associated with the identities of smaller clans from Central and Western Ukraine. As such, the notable role of ideology in determining identity within patronal networks may need to be re-examined.

As the above facts and deliberations show, the Ukrainian political system is premised largely on the gap between formal and informal power institutions and practices. The distance between formal and informal power institutions can be neither minimal, as in states with strong rule of law and open access order, nor maximal, as in stages of the mafia state when this gap was so big that it destroyed the legitimacy of the regime. The republic of clans is designed to facilitate competition and cooperation of clans, while limiting access to resources for all alternative forms of elites' and counter-elites' organization.

NOTES

[1] Henry E. Hale, "Democracy or autocracy on the march? The colored revolutions as normal dynamics of patronal presidentialism," *Communist and Post-Communist Studies* 39, no. 3 (2006): 305–29; Hale, *Patronal Politics: Eurasian Regime Dynamics in Comparative Perspective* (Washington, DC: George Washington University, 2014); Hale, "25 Years after the USSR: What's Gone Wrong?" *Journal of Democracy* 27, no. 3 (2016): 24–35.

[2] Hale, *Patronal Politics*, 9–10.

[3] Hale, "25 Years after the USSR," 28.

[4] Hale, *Patronal Politics*, 10ff.

[5] Hale, "25 Years after the USSR."

[6] Ibid., 26.

[7] Ibid., 28–29.

[8] Bálint Magyar, *Post-Communist Mafia State: The Case of Hungary* (Budapest–New York: Central European University Press and Noran Libro, 2015.

[9] Ibid., 9.

[10] Ibid., 51.

[11] Ibid., 54ff.

[12] Ibid., 2015, 50.

[13] For more on the Soviet roots of Ukrainian elites, see Mikhail Minakov, *Development and Dystopia: Studies in Post-Soviet Ukraine and Eastern Europe* (Stuttgart: ibidem, 2018).

[14] For an in-depth analysis of Soviet nomenklatura, see Mervin Matthews, *Privilege in the Soviet Union: A Study of Elite Life-Styles under Communism* (New York: Routledge, 2011).

[15] Richard Pipes, *Russia under the Bolshevik Regime: 1919–1924* (Boxton: Vintage, 1995).

[16] Paul R. Magocsi, *A History of Ukraine* (Toronto: Toronto University Press, 2010), 684–85.

[17] Mark Harrison, "The Soviet Union after 1945: Economic Recovery and Political Repression," 2. Last modified April 14, 2010, https://www2.warwick.ac.uk/fac/soc/economics/staff/mharrison/public/pp2011postprint.pdf.

[18] David Filtzer, *Soviet Workers and Late Stalinism: Labour and Restoration of the Stalinist System after World War II* (Cambridge: Cambridge University Press, 2002), 28ff.

[19] Eric Duskin, *Stalinist Reconstruction and the Confirmation of a New Elite, 1945–1953* (London: Palgrave Macmillan, 2001), 3.

20 In 2009–11, I made interviews with three persons who worked at middle-level posts in Kharkiv oblast Communist Party office and two persons who worked at leading levels in Kharkiv city Komsomol office between 1968 and 1991.
21 In 2011–12, I made interviews with two persons who worked at high-level and two persons who worked at low-level posts in Donets'k oblast Communist Party office between 1961 and 1991.
22 A Soviet term for people working as chief constructors, senior engineers and professionals alike.
23 In 2008–2009, I made interviews with three persons who worked at high and middle-level posts in Dnipropetrovs'k Communist Party and Komsomol offices between 1975 and 1991.
24 For the role of local elites in Soviet Union, see Sue Bridger and Frances Pine, eds. *Surviving Post-Socialism: Local Strategies and Regional Responses in Eastern Europe and the former Soviet Union* (New York: Routledge, 1998); Kimitaka Matsuzato, "Local Elites under Transition: County and City Politics in Russia 1985–1996," *Europe-Asia Studies* 51, no. 8 (1999): 1367–1400; Matthews, *Privilege in the Soviet Union*; Peter Rutland, *The Politics of Economic Stagnation in The Soviet Union: The Role of Local Party Organs in Economic Management* (Cambridge: Cambridge University Press, 1993).
25 Georgii Kasianov, *Ukraina 1991–2007: Ocherki noveishei istorii* (Kyiv: Nash Chas, 2008).
26 Hale, "25 Years after the USSR."
27 For details, please see Alex Kireev, "Ukraine: Presidential Election 1994," *Electoral Geography 2.0*, accessed July 30, 2017, https://www.electoralgeography.com/new/en/countries/u/ukraine/ukraine-presidential-election-1994.html.
28 Andrew Monaghan, "The Vertikal: Power and Authority in Russia," *International Affairs* 88, no. 1 (2012): 1–16; Vladimir Gel'man and Sergei Ryzhenkov, "Local Regimes, Sub-national Governance and the 'Power Vertical' in Contemporary Russia," *Europe-Asia Studies* 63, no. 3 (2011): 449–65.
29 See Matthew Rojansky, "Corporate Raiding in Ukraine: Prevention, Defense, and Policy Reform," *Review of Central and East European Law* 39, nos. 3–4 (2014): 245–89.
30 See results of the Ukrainian experts' poll conducted by journalists of "Mirror Weekly" (Rating of influence, *Zerkalo nedeli*, October 7–14, 1999).
31 For more information on the Dnipropetrovs'k clans, see Viatcheslav Avioutskii, "The Consolidation of Ukrainian Business Clans," *Revue Internationale d'Intelligence Économique* 2 (2010): 119–41; Sławomir Matuszak, *The Oligarchic Democracy: The Influence of Business Groups on Ukrainian Politics* (Warsaw: Centre for Eastern Studies, 2012); Svitlana Konochuk and Viacheslav Pikhovshek, *Dnipropetrovska Simia – 2* [The Dniprpetrovs'k family] (Kyiv: Pravo, 1997).
32 For more information on the Donets'k clans, see Hans Van Zon, "Is the Donetsk Model Sustainable?" *Geographia Polonica* 78, no. 2 (2007): 70–82; Van Zon, "The Rise of Conglomerates in Ukraine: The Donetsk Case," in *Big Business and Economic Development*, ed. Alex E. Fernández Jilberto and Barbara Hogenboom (Basingstoke: Routledge, 2007), 378–97; Avioutskii, "The Consolidation of

Ukrainian"; Matuszak, *The Oligarchic Democracy*; Sergei Kuzin, *Donetskaia mafia: Antologia* [The Donets'k mafia: Antology] (Kyiv: Poligrafkniga, 2006).

33 Criminal nicknames are important part of specific post-Soviet political and business sub-cultures as they indicate certain level of importance of a person in the criminal hierarchy and his/her specific personal qualities. They are also often used in non-public conversations of politicians and businesspeople, as well as by the press when writing about the politicians in question.

34 For more on the post-Soviet criminal revolution, see Alexander Kupatadze, *Organized Crime, Political Transitions and State Formation in Post-Soviet Eurasia* (New York: Palgrave Macmillan, 2012).

35 Kuzin, *Donetskaia mafia*, 17ff; Kupatadze, *Organized Crime*, 90ff.

36 By 2006, over sixty poligarchs and oligarchs had their own registered philanthropic foundations. They all were visible participants of Victor Yushchenko's philanthropic initiatives, such as the restoration of Baturyn castle or the "Zihriy lyubovyu dytynu" programme ("Warm a child with love" program, aiming to support families with ten or more children).

37 The possibility of new construction of the mafia state is proved by facts discussed in Balázs Jarábik and Mikhail Minakov, "Ukrainian Hybrid State," Carnegie Endowment for International Peace, last modified April 22, 2016, http://carnegieendowment.org/2016/04/22/ukraine-s-hybrid-state-pub-63417; Sergii Leshchenko, "Poroshenko creates his own 'family' clan," *Kyiv Post*, July 24, 2016, http://www.kyivpost.com/article/opinion/op-ed/sergii-leshchenko-weve-returned-to-the-family-poroshenko-creates-his-clan-419429.html; Mikhail Minakov, "A Decisive Turn? Risks for Ukrainian Democracy after the Euromaidan," Carnegie Endowment for International Peace, last modified February 3, 2016, http://carnegieendowment.org/2016/02/03/decisive-turn-risks-for-ukrainian-democracy-after-euromaidan-pub-62641.

ULADZIMIR ROUDA

Is Belarus a Classic Post-Communist Mafia State?

Introduction: The political system under which Belarus lives

The Byelorussian SSR, during the era of communist rule, was characterized by the weakness of national communism. As such, the formation and development of the Republic of Belarus as an independent democratic state was extremely complex; nevertheless, the project was not entirely doomed. The country's favorable geographical position in Europe, its relatively developed industrial economy, its largely urbanized society and its unique history all assisted in its democratization. Ever since the emergence of statehood in the territory of Belarus and up to the end of the 18th century, the country belonged to the Western, rather than Eastern, tradition of Christianity. Numerous factors bear this out, including: the dominance of the Uniate Church in the Belarusian lands up to the 19th century; religious tolerance; separation of religious and secular authorities; the rule of law, established in the Statute of the Grand Duchy of Lithuania in 1588; the development of local self-government based on the Magdeburg Law; and the formation of representative government at the end of the 15th century, as well as the gentry democracy institutions in the Grand Duchy of Lithuania and the Polish-Lithuanian Commonwealth. The European legacy of Belarus' history did not fall into oblivion; indeed, it is reflected today in the system of values of the Belarusian citizens, as the data of various sociological studies collected by the American political scientist Magen Knuth attest. In particular, she questioned the attitude of respondents to the view that the "democratic system is not perfect, but still superior to all other forms of government," and analyzed the replies. Only 58.9% of Russian respondents shared this view, while it was supported by 80.8% of Belarusian citizens and 76.3% of Ukrainian ones. As a result, she makes the claim that "Russian political culture is less democratic than that of Belarus and Ukraine."[1]

Soviet traditions, despite their powerful effect, were not exclusive and in no case uncontested. According to the British scientists Stephen White and Ian McAllister, in their substantial comparative analysis of attitudes towards the political system among the citizens of Belarus, Ukraine, Russia and the countries of Central and Eastern Europe, the overwhelming majority of Belarusian citizens did not hold a pro-Soviet orientation. For the purposes of their study, they used the respondents' assessment of former (communist) political practices, the current political regime and its likely status in five years. In 2003, the researchers asked respondents to evaluate these parameters on a scale from minus 100 (the worst estimate) to plus 100 (the best estimate). The Soviet system scored lower in Belarus (65) than in Ukraine and Russia (75), contrary to the popular opinion of some researchers that the benefits of the communist system were implemented to the fullest in Soviet Belarus.[2]

All this means that after the collapse of the Soviet Union, the Republic of Belarus had two options: the first would take it back to Europe, with consequent democratization of the current political system and liberalization of the economy. The second carried the threat of losing its still fragile independence, immediately followed by dissolution into the vast Russian imperial world. Belarusian elites have played a decisive role in the ultimate path of the country's development.

Vyacheslav Kebich, who held office in 1990–94 as Chairman of the Council of Ministers, the highest public post, had a difficult and controversial attitude towards the state's sovereignty. Although he put his signature to the Belavezha Accords in Viskuli on December 8, 1991, which concluded the dissolution of the Soviet Union and founded the Commonwealth of Independent States (CIS), he focused mainly on the restoration of economic ties with the former Soviet republics, primarily Russia. The summer of 1993 saw a situation of severe economic crisis, caused by the withdrawal of the Russian ruble from circulation in the CIS countries. The premier saw Belarus' accession to the Russian ruble zone as the only solution to this crisis. This measure, a clear danger to the fledgling independence of the Belarusian state, has never been implemented, since Kebich lost the presidential election of 1994 to his main opponent—a former state farm director, Alyaksandr Lukashenka, who stood for election under openly social-populist slogans in a situation of complete *elite atomization*, when both the "party of power" and opposition experienced a deep rift from each other.

Belarus lagged considerably behind its neighboring countries in terms of economic reforms; its ruling elite was not ready for the transformation of power into property. Instead, much as in Soviet times, Belarusian officials were using state property for personal gain, bringing the problem of *ordinary corruption* to the fore. In an emergency situation, when public opinion polls revealed that "among the most important challenges faced by the country, the population placed the fight against corruption and the mafia first, followed by the fight against inflation and price increases, and finally—the restoration of order," an extremely active former head of the parliamentary anti-corruption commission easily claimed a victory over his rivals.[3]

Belarus' so-called *defective democracy*—to use the terminology of the political scientist Gerardo Munck[4]—was, to some extent, an achievement for Kebich. The presidential election of 1994 was held with minimal deviation from free and fair electoral standards, a fact recognized by all observation missions, including the OSCE. Unlike his main opponent in the first presidential election, Lukashenka after 1996 considered it unnecessary to acknowledge the opinion of the European observers. Since then, no electoral competition in Belarus has been recognized as free and fair. This fact alone gives reason to believe that the nature of the Belarusian political regime today is far from being democratic, even in a *defective* way.

The Belarusian president, who has ruled the country individually for the past twenty-three years, could not confine himself to hybrid models of political systems, combining elements of democracy and authoritarianism. Since the constitutional changes of 1996, Lukashenka set a course for the transformation of Belarus—using Max Weber's term—into a *sultanistic system*, similar to some in the post-Soviet states of Central Asia. He almost succeeded in the elections of 2010, when the majority of the opposition candidates ended up behind bars. After the release of the opposition leaders (the last of whom, Nikolai Statkevich, only emerged from prison in 2015), there was a minimal liberalization of the regime. This liberalization only affected human rights, failing entirely to address the nature of power, the degree of political pluralism, the role of ideology and the degree of political mobilization. The causes of Belarus' sultanistic transformation, and the characteristics of the country's political system, are described in detail elsewhere by the author of this text.[5]

The sultanistic character of the political regime prevents us from classifying Belarus as a "mainstream" mafia state. The most important feature of sultanism, in accordance with the renowned American political scientists Juan Linz and Alfred Stepan, is the "highly personalistic nature of power."[6] This feature is no different from one pertaining to a mafia state, namely that the power in it belongs to an adopted political family, in this case the family of Alyaksandr Lukashenka. However, his power is rooted deeply in the state bureaucracy, and is not interwoven to such a great extent with oligarchs. Lukashenka began to rule the state using autocratic methods earlier than the incumbent Russian President Vladimir Putin. He defeated Kebich by focusing on the problem of *ordinary corruption* in the minds of the Belarusian citizens. However, he immediately turned the fight against this evil into a force at the very top of the pyramid of power. In reality, Lukashenka's political family used the fight against corruption to remove all potential competitors from the political and economic arenas. Ultimately, it weakened the professional ethos of the bureaucracy, and led to a decrease in the competitiveness of senior officials, both in the center and at the local level. In the long term, this fight, which has acquired a different meaning, may lead to the complete disintegration of the ruling elite, resulting in the fall of the current regime.

Certainly, there are some specific features which distinguish Belarus from classic mafia states, and they deserve to be analyzed in detail in a separate section.

Internal and External Causes of the Transformation of the Republic of Belarus into a Post-Communist Autocracy

As is clear from the introduction, the system of values that guided Belarusian citizens in the mid-1990s was of a contradictory nature. This system of values opened up two paths for further development. On the one hand, the young country could follow the European path; to achieve this, liberal economic reforms and democratization of the political system were necessary. On the other hand, there was a looming threat of loss of statehood followed by complete incorporation into Russia. This alternative was backed by a number of politicians at the time. In the elections of 1994, the European way of development was most consistently defended by the Belarusian Popular Front (BPF) Party and its leader, Zianon Pazniak. Supporters of the former Speaker of the Parliament, Stanislav Shushkevich, took a similar stance. The Russian card was openly played by the former Prime Minister Vyacheslav Kebich. However, the elections in 1994 were won by the little-known populist politician Alyaksandr Lukashenka; the eminent Polish journalist Adam Michnik justly nicknamed him "not a Moscow puppet, but a Soviet one."[7]

The Soviet values in Belarus beat the European ones at that time, resulting in a major political regression. The victory of these values in Belarus had numerous internal reasons. Firstly, a clear anti-democratic trend had formed in the public consciousness by 1993, nourished by popular frustration in the Russian liberal reforms and their reformers. This trend had nothing to do with the objective difficulties of the initial stage of transition to a market economy, as was the case in the Russian or Ukrainian examples. In Belarus, the economic crisis resulted from inadequate reconstruction of the socialist model; however, ordinary people understood things differently. The Belarusian system was never democratic, but Pazniak and Shushkevich failed to explain this to their electorate. The simple fact that they belonged to the democratic camp made them unpopular, if not responsible, for the hardships that millions of ordinary people had to face. Slander against them on the part of the Kebich-controlled governmental media was yet another important factor.

Secondly, Belarus belonged to the countries of the so-called *late modernization*, where industrialization, urbanization and their associated benefits had arrived relatively recently—in the 1960s and 1970s under the Communists. As a result, Soviet values were still popular among a large part of the population. This fact, however, was not taken into account by the democratic forces in their election platforms. Therefore, we should agree with the American researcher Kathleen Mihalisko, who stated that "the same moral force that made [Zianon Pazniak] the bravest of regime opponents (and probably the most outrageous Belarusian of his day) also made him too strident and extreme for Belarusian tastes."[8] As for Shushkevich, in this writer's opinion, he lost the moral right to lead the democratic forces of Belarus in 1992, when, as Speaker of the Parliament, he refused to endorse the initiative of a referendum on the dissolution of the Supreme Council and an early election. More than half a million signatures were collected to support this initiative. All this led to an inevitable split of the democratic forces.

Thirdly, the Belarusian Popular Front (BPF)—the main opposition force—had underestimated the propagandistic significance of the political fight against corruption. It allowed Lukashenka, a little-known official, to take the lead in criticizing the Council of Ministers in a most sensitive matter. Thus, Lukashenka used an anti-corruption report as a formidable weapon in the fight against both the government and the opposition. The BPF report on power abuse in the structures of the presidential administration, delivered by Siarhiej Antonchyk, was behind schedule and only arrived in December 1994, after Lukashenka's accession to the top job. As such, it did not have the expected political effect. It is likely that a more timely delivery of this report could have prevented the rapid transformation of anti-communist and populist sentiment into anti-establishment and anti-democratic populism—the mental base of Lukashenka's power.

Thus, none of the internal causes of the Belarusian return to Soviet-type politics had an objectively natural character, nor was it an "adamant necessity, impossible to get around," as is the view of the Belarusian political analyst Valery Karbalevich.[9] Instead, its reasons were rather subjective and situational; they only occurred in a situation that had arisen by chance. External factors played a much more important role in Lukashenka's accession to power and its consolidation. On the one hand, there was a lack of interest in the problems of Belarus on the part of the United States and the countries now commonly known as the "founding states of the EU."[10] For them, Belarus was a new post-Soviet state, despite its European history until the end of the 18th century, its favorable geopolitical position, and, indeed, its nuclear potential. The democratic West was concerned only with the latter issue, and insisted on the withdrawal of missiles from the territory of the Republic of Belarus to the Russian Federation under Russian, British and American guarantees of its sovereignty and territorial integrity. Belarus, along with Ukraine and Kazakhstan, fulfilled these conditions. However, the recent annexation of the Crimean Peninsula by Russia, and the ongoing Russian aggression against Ukraine, indicates that Russian guarantees today are idle promises. Moreover, it is difficult to predict Russian behavior in the crisis, as far as the relations between Belarus and Russia go. In any case, in the mid-90s, the democratic West failed to suggest any alternative for Belarusian development.

The lack of Western influence on the Belarusian situation was immediately compensated by Russia. The Russian leadership was not frightened by the fact that Lukashenka tried to position himself as a Soviet leader. Moscow sought to expand its territory in the mid-90s, and therefore welcomed the idea of the Belarusian president to establish the so-called Union

State of the two countries as the first stage of the USSR's territorial restoration. Lukashenka expressed these ideas even before he was elected president of Belarus.[11]

The Russian leadership used the idea of integration to impose a joint defense agreement on Belarus, resulting in Russian military bases being positioned on Belarusian territory. In 1996, the two countries signed an agreement on the establishment of the Union State, which created a system of economic preferences for Belarus. According to the Belarusian political analyst Vitali Silitski:

> The total amount of Russian annual subsidies to the Belarusian economy in the period 1997–1998 can be estimated at 1.5–2 billion dollars. . . . The different transversal aspects of Belarusian and Russian integration turned it into a one-goal game, where the economic growth of Belarus was only possible at the cost of a Russian slowdown. On the one hand, the unreformed Belarusian economy was able to demonstrate a rapid growth due to the Russian sacrifice, with its large government borrowings, budget deficit, written-off debts and waiving of customs duties. On the other hand, while the Belarusian authorities actively subsidized its industry, the Russian enterprises, producing similar products, experienced a painful restructuring.[12]

The unprecedented Russian economic support resulted in the consolidation of the authoritarian regime in Belarus. In November 1996, Lukashenka held a constitutional referendum, allowing him to replace the presidential republic with a super-presidential one. This plebiscite made a mockery of legal norms and was recognized only by the Russian leadership, which shared the responsibility for the concentration of supreme power in the hands of Lukashenka's political family. An equally important target of Kremlin policy was the governance of Russia itself. The Belarusian president began to challenge the leadership potential of Boris Yeltsin. In the late 1990s, he undertook regular trips to the regions of Russia, seeking to create an impression of a more reliable leader of the Russian *polyarchy* than the ailing Russian president. Such attempts ceased only in 1999, when Vladimir Putin was appointed prime minister by Boris Yeltsin.

Putin's rise to power resulted in the rationalization of Russian-Belarusian economic relations. However, liberalization did not follow, since it was clear for the Russian leader that it would inevitably lead to the weakening of Russian influence on Belarus. Instead, he chose a strategy of slow but steady moves against his Belarusian partner, aimed at smothering Belarus within the friendly embrace of Russia. Realizing that Lukashenka would not turn towards the West (which may have saved Belarus from its fate), Putin tried to ensure the advantages of Russian amity in Belarus, fencing the country off from any economic resources other than Russian ones. The so-called Eurasian Economic Union was created to serve these purposes. Putin aimed at establishing in Belarus a strong local model of the Russian *polyarchy*—a model so dependent on Russia that it would leave no room even for an autonomous Belarusian *polyarchy* headed by Lukashenka. All in all, the special preferences enjoyed by Belarus cost Russian taxpayers at least 14 billion US dollars in 2007, a figure which continued to increase until 2015.[13]

However, the implementation of this plan was suspended in 2015–16, due to the deep crisis that hit the Russian economy, providing Lukashenka some opportunities to act independently. However, he failed to seize them: instead of strengthening relations with the EU countries and Ukraine, Lukashenka elected to court China and Pakistan. In this matter, the dependence of the Belarusian leader on the near-sultanistic Russian political regime is clearly manifested, and the head of the Belarusian political family appears unable to weaken it.

Ultimately, it was not the internal contradictions of the formation and development of the post-Soviet Belarusian state, but rather external factors that led to the domination of Lukashenka's political family in the mid-90s. The absence of Western democratic influence was used by the Russian leadership to create and gradually consolidate the sultanistic political regime, fully dependent on the Russian *polyarchy*.

Property Rights in the Mafia State of Belarus

It is initially important to consider that property relations in Belarus are very different from those in classic mafia states. As mentioned above, the absence of radical socio-economic reforms led to the collapse of Vyacheslav Kebich's government. When Alyaksandr Lukashenka came to power, he began implementation of a social-populist economic program, based on preserving state ownership of the means of production.

According to Stanislav Bogdankevich, a former Chairman of the National Bank of Belarus, "the Belarusian achievements have been ensured without any serious social upheaval, by the means of a return to the proven Soviet practice of centralized management as part of the pronounced social and economic policies [of social populism]. Unlike other countries with transition economies, the Belarusian government managed to retain direct control of about 75–80% of its economy."[14] According to Lukashenka's speech at the All-Belarusian People's Assembly in June 2016, "there are currently 1005 companies under the operational control of ministries and state corporate groups, comprising almost half of Belarusian net assets."[15] The European Bank for Reconstruction and Development estimated the number of privately owned Belarusian businesses at 25–30% in 2015, a very low figure for a European state. This shows that the structural changes were not of a fundamental nature, and a strong public sector remains the basis of the national economy. Therefore, due to the absence of large-scale privatization, there was no discernable evolution of a wide oligarchic social stratum which could later be surrendered to a single chief patron.

Despite the pessimistic forecasts of many Belarusian and European experts, Lukashenka has made some progress in implementing his program; the Belarusian economy has demonstrated positive trends since 1996. According to the World Bank, the growth of the Belarusian economy can be divided into two periods, 1996–2000 and 2001–2011. They differ significantly in their internal and external conditions, as well as their basic characteristics. In the period 1996–2004, the Belarusian GDP grew by 77.4%, an annual growth of 6.6%. In 2006, the GDP (in comparable prices) increased by 10%, and by a further 8.2% in 2007.[16] According to a World Bank report on the country:

> The Belarusian experience is somewhat at odds with the standard transition paradigm, and the relative stability of the Belarusian economy has even been called a "puzzle."[17] Belarus has now experienced nine years [now fourteen] of an unbroken growth record, and an impressive decline in poverty rates, supported by rapid growth in real wages and pensions and low unemployment rates. At the same time, growth has not been backed by sound and consistent macroeconomic policies, advanced structural and institutional reforms, and a thriving private sector. Despite some liberalization undertaken

in the course of reforms, the economy remains highly regulated and under predominant state control.[18]

As for the progress in structural reforms, the report's authors noted that:

> In general, Belarus is lagging behind most of the transition economies in various aspects of the transition. . . . Across nine broad reform areas [large-scale privatization; small-scale privatization; governance and enterprise restructuring; price liberalization; trade and foreign exchange system; competition policy; banking reform and interest rate liberalization; securities markets and non-bank financial institutions; infrastructure reform], most of the progress attained relates to price and trade liberalization. However, it is indicative that among all transition economies Belarus . . . remains the least advanced country in this area [Belarus, Turkmenistan and Uzbekistan have the lowest rating]. Small-scale privatization has yet to be completed, while large-scale privatization has been minimal . . . small private businesses and individual entrepreneurs in Belarus face one of the most hostile business environments among the European transition economies.[19]

Since no significant structural reforms followed, the country's leadership had to carry out an extremely ineffectual currency devaluation in 2011; by 2015–16, Belarus entered a period of systemic crisis. All notions of economic growth, therefore, have proven somewhat ephemeral. In the author's opinion, the Belarusian economic paradox ceased to exist in 2011. The late Belarusian opposition figure Viktor Ivashkevich summed up the economic situation in that year:

> On May 23, 2011, having let the Belarusian ruble collapse by 56%, Lukashenka took away more than half of people's monthly salaries in one fell swoop. Because of the devaluation, the average pension amount in dollar terms declined from 193 USD to 115 USD in May. Pensioners immediately became 40% poorer. Meanwhile, inflation in Belarus already reached 36.2% this year. But in reality, most essential goods experienced a twofold to fourfold price increase. In these conditions, even the government admits that prices would continue to rise. In early May, household deposits in national currency amounted

to 10.1 trillion rubles, or 3.3 billion dollars. However, due to the devaluation, the amount of deposits decreased to 2 billion dollars. This means that depositors immediately lost 1.3 billion dollars.[20]

By the end of 2011, salaries in Belarus were the second lowest among the CIS countries—only Kyrgyzstan had a lower average indicator. The devaluation of the Belarusian ruble inevitable reflected negatively on the president's credibility, as well as on his projected approval rating. Both figures fell to an unprecedentedly low level. According to a survey conducted by IISEPS in September 2011, 87.6% of Belarusians believed that the Belarusian economy was in crisis, the vast majority of the population (61.2%) indicated that the responsibility for the crisis lay with the president, and almost 70% believed the country was moving in the wrong direction.[21]

The difficult economic situation caused a collapse of confidence in Lukashenka. In September 2011, only 24.5% of Belarusians stated that they trusted the president; prior to the presidential elections in December 2010, the number was 55%. Only 20.5% said they would vote for him then, which was a record in itself: these indicators were even lower than in 2003, when his projected electoral rating fell "below the knee," in Lukashenka's own words.[22]

The author of this text wrote at the time that the regime of personal power could collapse in the near future "as a result of confidence and legitimacy challenges, as well as the lack of trust in basic institutions of power."[23] However, this did not happen for one important reason: Putin came to Lukashenka's rescue, in order to prevent the weakening of Russia's influence in such an important region of Eastern Europe. Putin came up with a plan to create the Eurasian Economic Union under Russian patronage, which was intended to guarantee the economic growth and political stability (that is, preservation of power in the hands of political families) of the signatory countries. The latter suited Lukashenka perfectly; as for the economic growth, he had to pay for it by refusing to cooperate with countries unfavorable to Putin's Russia. Lukashenka's loyalty allowed Belarus to escape the economic disaster of 2011 and ensured a trivial growth in GDP in 2012.

In 2013, the Belarusian focus on the Russian market played a very negative role in its economic development, since Russia faced a deep recession resulting from the fall of oil and gas prices on the world market. This fall had been predicted by foreign and independent Russian experts, such as Grigory Yavlinsky, who criticized Putin's model as the "economy of the pipe." However, such opinions were ignored by the head of the Belarusian political family. For Lukashenka, the strengthening of personal power had always been more important than any rational economic considerations. In 2014–16, Belarus was hit by two crises at once, both internal and external. The sanctions against Russia, imposed by the European Union after the Russian annexation of the Crimea and the undeclared war against Ukraine, caused significant damage to Russia's economy, and Belarus' in turn. At the same time, there was an internal structural crisis, similar to that which ruined the government of Kebich in 1994. It was only possible to overcome it by reorienting foreign economic relations, moving away from Russia as a protected market for Belarusian producers, and radical structural reforms.

Despite the acknowledgement of these requirements at the Belarusian National Assembly in June 2016, the process had not moved forward by the end of the year. This failure was not only the result of inertia in the Belarusian political family, represented by the leader's environment. The leader himself had fears about Vladimir Putin's opinion, who maintained important levers of influence on his authority.

Thus, the long existence in Belarus of a somewhat modernized state socialism should not be understood as the domination of social equity and social justice. State-owned property was beneficial only to one person—the head of the political family, who used it to establish full control over society, the media, non-governmental organizations and political parties, regardless of their orientation.

Non-Economic Features of the Mafia State in Belarus

The most important political feature of the mafia state of Belarus was its development of a non-party political system. Since the time of Kebich, no government has been formed on a party basis. As such, ever since the Republic of Belarus gained its independence, it has been widely recognized as a non-party system, in accordance with the criteria of the famous French sociologist Maurice Duverger.[24] The head of the political family chose not to follow Putin's lead, and did not create a so-called "party of power" in Belarus, despite encouragement and attempts from many influential members of his entourage.

The former Minister of Education Alyaksandr Radkov was the first to make such an attempt in 2007. Just prior to the upcoming parliamentary elections, he held a founding congress, establishing a potential party of power, *Belaya Rus*, which was to unite in its ranks all of Lukashenka's supporters. Then, a year before the elections for the House of Representatives in 2012, a similar initiative was put forward by the then-Speaker of the Upper House of Parliament, Anatoly Rubinov. However, both attempts failed. Lukashenka harshly criticized the initiators, stating that he would "find additional work for them, if they don't have any."[25] As such, *Belaya Rus* exists today not as a political party, but as a public association. Lukashenka criticized the political parties operating in the country at the Belarusian National Assembly in 2016.[26] It can be concluded that the current non-partisan status of Belarus is fully consistent with his strategic objectives. This raises an obvious question: why was Lukashenka so critical of the parties created to serve his interests?

There are two possible answers to this question. The first can be found in Lukashenka's speech given in 2008, dedicated to the formation of the party of power. Amongst other things, he stated that "his attitude towards all organizations and movements which 'help build lives' is positive: even if they are in opposition and critical to what the president and the authorities are doing, they tend to help."[27] Remarkably, the head of the political family places parties and authorities on opposing sides. The system of power, in his opinion, must not be partisan, and some parties (in opposition) are only meant to criticize the government. As a result, competition for power—the most important function of any political organization—is banned. In this issue, Belarus lags behind Russia and other mafia states. But the head of the political family adheres to this position, as is clear from the results of the last elections for the House of Representatives, when two representatives of opposition parties were appointed to criticize the government, not to fight it on equal terms. The fact that the leadership of some opposition organizations agreed with the choice of the president, attests to the political and moral degradation of the Belarusian opposition.

The second response was given by Lukashenka, when he established a vertical power structure, a replacement for the party of power in classic mafia states. While Russia in this respect has a dominant-party system, Belarus could be described as a non-party system. Two Presidential Decrees[28] led to the actual appointment of local heads of executive committees by leaders of higher executive committees.[29] Lukashenka does not need a presidential party even in the role of a "transmission belt"—he relies wholly on the state bureaucracy.

Lukashenka, therefore, has established an entirely vertical executive power, with himself in the leading role. He personally appointed the Chairman of Minsk City Executive Committee, as well as chairmen of executive committees in all regions of the country. Heads of the regions chose heads of district executive committees, who chose, in turn, the heads of local administrations. Additionally, the decree eliminated a number of lower-level councils. Executive committees became unaccountable to the local representative bodies elected by the citizens, violating Article 119 of the 1996 Constitution: "Heads of local executive and administrative bodies shall be appointed and dismissed by the President of the Republic of Belarus or in the manner prescribed by him while their position shall be approved by local Councils of Deputies."[30]

The power vertical is subordinated to the political head of the family and is a much more disciplined and efficient tool than any party of power in classic mafia states, since it endangers not only the official position of those involved, but also their freedom and even their life. Therefore, in the author's opinion, the creation of a Belarusian multiparty system, or even a dominant-party system of the Russian or the Hungarian type, is only possible after the collapse of the current political regime or the replacement of the head of the political family.

According to Steven Levitsky and Lucan Way, the weakness of a ruling party, and even more so its absence, creates difficulties for an authoritarian system.[31] This opinion, however, is only partially borne out by the Belarusian experience. Undoubtedly, the political situation negatively affects the development of political institutions, making them highly personalistic. The Belarusian example suggests that such a situation can persist for years, and even decades. However, the clear predominance of social populism over national populism as a method of power exercise is dangerous for the political family of Lukashenka. In this regard, Belarus also lags behind almost all other countries employing a similar strategy. All the attempts of the Belarusian ideologists to claim that the Republic of Belarus stands for the prevalent values in the Soviet Union, and therefore nationalism here is identical to sovietism, are unconvincing and somewhat ridiculous. Neither the flag of the Byelorussian Soviet Socialist Republic (BSSR), nor the Soviet emblem or the Soviet-era Independence Day (coinciding with the Day of Liberation of Minsk by the Red Army in 1944) are considered sacred by the intellectual elite.

One can fully grasp the initial reasons that prompted Lukashenka to replace Belarusian national symbols with the Soviet ones, and identify the history of Belarus with the history of the BSSR. They are associated with the low cultural level of Lukashenka the farm director, yet to become the head of state. However, it is impossible to understand why, after twenty-three years in power, his cultural level remained unchanged. After all, his power is now threatened by the above-described imbalance of populism. National populism works very well in times of crisis, as is evidenced by the experience of Russia, Hungary and many other countries with mafia state systems. Social populism in the current economic crisis, however, cannot bring anything but disappointment and frustration. Thus, if the head of the Belarusian political family does not find the strength to replace social populism with national populism, and if the crisis endures much longer, his power may soon be called into question.

"Law of Rule" in Place of "Rule of Law" in Contemporary Belarus

Today's Belarus abides by the Constitution of 1996, adopted in a referendum whose results were outrageously falsified, allowing us to speak of a "constitutional coup" by the head of state. According to the Fundamental Law, the institutions of a presidential-parliamentary republic, with a bicameral legislature, were formally introduced in Belarus. However, they are almost completely dependent on the head of the political family. Therefore, it seems more appropriate to speak of Belarus as a super-presidential republic, similar to those operating in Central Asia, with the concentration of all powers in the executive and the atrophy of the other two branches of government.

There exists in Belarus a *two-headed executive body*, characteristic of any democratic state, where presidential power is balanced by the powers conferred on the prime minister. In Belarus, however, the prime minister merely plays a role of an economic manager, subordinated to the president, rather than an independent politician. The president of Belarus is entirely responsible for determining the legislation of the country, depriving the deputies of the right to perform their primary legislative function. In the years following the referendum, only a handful of laws were drafted within the walls of the Parliament. In fact, it is the head of the political family who carries out *recruiting*: the selection and appointment of the leading cadres. He shares this responsibility with the Upper House of the Parliament, which he, either directly or indirectly, appoints. Additionally, the president enjoys the right to appoint and remove all major judges in the country, which makes the courts highly dependent on the head of state. A change in the jurisdiction of the Main Chamber of Parliament in 1996, making it accountable to the Presidential Administration, turned Lukashenka into an "all-controlling and unruly political actor."[32] The non-legal nature of the Belarusian Fundamental Law affected the functioning of both central and local power institutions.

The time that has passed since the constitutional coup was characterized not just by a "freezing of political institutions at the level of 1996," as the Russian expert Vladimir Gelman pointed out, but by the further curtailment of them to complete Lukashenka's personalization of power.[33] The Constitution, as well as the Government and the Parliament, all served one person—Alyaksandr Lukashenka, adapting to all his whims and oddities. For example, in 2004, another referendum was held to amend the Constitution of the Republic of Belarus. According to official results, 79.42% of participating voters agreed that the incumbent president had the right to run for presidency as many times as he wished.[34] The announcement of the results, perceived by many Belarusians as a crude falsification, provoked spontaneous protests in Minsk.

The Government of the Republic of Belarus, as well as the Parliament, are subordinate to such structures as the Presidential Administration and the Security Council, which gained constitutional recognition in the Fundamental Law of 1996. The Presidential Administration is the most important reservoir of cadres for central and local higher public administration units. Its numerous departments mirror the competencies of the ministries and departments of the Council of Ministers, defining their path of development, just as was done by the departments of the Central Committee of the Communist Party of Belarus in relation to the Soviet government. Additionally, the Presidential Administration ensures the "leading and guiding" function of the president in his interaction with the legislative and judicial branches. In particular, it is reflected in the development of all major bills within the walls of the Administration, and delivered to the deputies of the Parliament for rubber-stamp approval.[35]

Bureaucracy in central and local institutions is numerous, and contradictory principles were laid in its foundation from the very beginning. On the one hand, the political head of the family constructed a power vertical that influenced the entire state from top to bottom. On the other hand, Lukashenka did not abandon social populism—the most important legitimizing principle of the Belarusian political regime—even after his consolidation of power. The belief of ordinary people in the national character of the supreme power came at a price: namely, a series of public campaigns and scandals surrounding numerous corrupt officials. No official in Belarus, apart from the president, has ever received guarantees of security; this is negatively reflected in the integration of the ruling elite. Not only it does not own the means of production, as is the case in both Russia and Hungary, but it is also poorly protected from arbitrary action by the head of state. However, bureaucrats do not protest and generally support the authorities, as the Belarusian officials operate in an artificially destroyed competitive environment, just as in the Brezhnev era, characterized by the rapid degradation of the elites.

The autocracy's unlawful nature formed in Belarus earlier than in Russia and Hungary, and this has a deeply negative effect on political institutions, as well as the degree of integration of the bureaucracy and the elite in general. Unlike in Belarus, the autocracy in Russia and Hungary does not suffer from discrepancies brought about by the unlawful state or the president's unpredictable behavior, which only increases in times of crisis.

The Liquidation of Social Autonomy in Belarusian Society

The Belarusian authorities headed by Alyaksandr Lukashenka quickly began to eliminate the autonomy of Belarusian culture, which they perceived as a threat to the Russification policy that was given a new impetus—and the Kremlin's financial support—after a referendum, dedicated to the use of language and symbolism, held in 1995. The Belarusian language was pushed into a niche generally occupied by ethnic minorities in the least democratic countries of the world. However, it survived as the language of the Belarusian intellectual elite. Literary works are created in the Belarusian language, often superior in quality to the works of Russian authors.[36] The Independent Writers' Union has no state support, while the Belarusian education system obediently works on the assimilation of Belarusian society into Russian culture. In this regard, higher education is beyond competition—there are no universities teaching all subjects in the Belarusian language. Scientists in academic establishments have never had the autonomy enjoyed by their colleagues in Europe.

Domestic Belarusian media is controlled by the government; radio and television are completely monopolized by the state. The recently established company *Belsat*, broadcasting from Poland, is not yet able to compete with BT, ONT, STV or the Third Channel for a number of reasons. Firstly, it is more difficult for *Belsat* to respond to the latest news and events immediately, and it is impossible to protect their journalists and experts from detentions by the Belarusian police. Through conventional viewing means, *Belsat* is a pay-channel, and common Belarusians are not used to it (a cheap cable TV package is imposed on them by the Housing Maintenance Service). However, the service is broadcast on the Internet, and many people choose to watch it online, maintaining their anonymity and security. In this author's opinion, *Belsat* needs a quality advertising campaign to encourage online viewers. In 2010, the Internet influenced the political position of only 10% of voters. Though it is also subject to government control, it remains the most free medium in Belarus, with more than 4.8 million users in 2013. By March 2016, this figure rose to more than 5 million people.[37]

Non-governmental organizations suffer from retaliatory measures at the registration stage; the declarative principle is replaced by the permissive one. This led to a significant quantitative reduction of genuine NGOs, and a freezing of existing NGOs' growth. After the re-registration campaign held in 1999, the sector was only able to repair itself by 2009, when there were about 2500 authentic organizations, though they also experienced political pressure.[38] A measure of criminal responsibility for activities on behalf of unregistered organizations has been in place since 2006, suppressing the most engaged and talented activists. At the same time, the authorities have supported so-called government organized non-governmental organizations, or GONGOs, which seek to monopolize the representation of important societal sectors. Well-known examples are the Belarusian Republican Youth Union (BRSM) and the public association discussed above, *Belaya Rus*.

Political pluralism in Belarus has faced severe restrictions in the past twenty years. Belarusian political parties, deprived of the possibility to compete for parliamentary and local authority positions and mobilize their voters via the media, became isolated from society; today, most of them are not so different from political clubs and non-governmental organizations. The so-called "street politicians" were also isolated from parties and political organizations, as a result of draconian laws against initiators of unauthorized protests.

Elections in Belarus do not strengthen political parties, regardless of their ideology or political orientation—no matter whether they are "for" or "against" Lukashenka. Over the past twenty years Belarus has lived through nine elections, including five national parliamentary campaigns (in 2000, 2004, 2008, 2012 and 2016) and four presidential elections (in 2001, 2006, 2010 and 2015). All were officially won by figures from the president's list, or by Lukashenka himself. None of the elections were recognized free and fair by the OSCE observers, and Freedom House has consistently given Belarus its lowest possible scores for democratic freedom.[39] Meanwhile, the government set a course for further depoliticization and departization of the Belarusian parliament and the general public, releasing it from the influence of any political organizations whatsoever. The election campaigns, as well as outright fraud and falsification, helped the authorities attain these goals.

The last elections to the House of Representatives did not differ much from the previous campaigns. They resulted in the election of eight deputies from the Communist Party of Belarus, three members of the Patriotic Party and two opposition representatives (one from the United Civil Party of Belarus, and another from the social organization, "Belarusian Language Society"), resulting in a total of thirteen party-affiliated deputies.[40] In 2012, there were only five party members in the House of Representatives, a ridiculously small number for a European country. All this further confirms the ongoing struggle waged by the head of the political family against all political parties, the reasons for which are discussed above.

Thus, the elimination of the autonomy of important social institutions took place in Belarus, just as in other classic mafia states. This process led to the formation of the so-called "strong power," quite controversial in its nature. To begin with, there is a stark contradiction between Belarus' economically developed society and the most primitive political system in Europe based on personalistic dictatorship, or the total domination of the political family, in terms of the mafia state theory. The vulnerability of the Belarusian regime is manifested in the fact that essential modern political and social institutions have not developed here, and twenty years later, it remains the cultural "kolkhoz" in the geographical center of Europe.

Patron-Client Relations in Belarus

The development of patron-client relations in Belarus was influenced by the events of recent history. The BSSR was one of those Soviet formations, where industrialization and urbanization came relatively late, in the 1960s and 1970s. Until 1960, agriculture played a key role in the structure of the Belarusian economy.

The reasons for this economic policy lay in the desire of the Soviet Union to turn Belarus into a kind of analog of eastern Ukraine. Both regions were to cover the needs of up to a quarter of the entire military-industrial complex of the USSR. This fact also helps explain the rapid development of energy-intensive heavy industry in the country. The structure of the industrial sector was mainly represented by mechanical engineering and metal processing, the chemical industry, optics and electronics. Belarusian enterprises depended on the supply of raw materials and components. Little by little, Belarus became an assembly shop for the entire Soviet Union.

Industrialization was accompanied by rapid urbanization, with the urban population increasing significantly. Arriving in the city, former residents of Belarusian villages fell into a different cultural environment. Most of them were forced to adapt to the Russian language and culture, which was dominant throughout urban areas. The Belarusian language was pushed out to the periphery of cultural life, spoken mostly by villagers and citizens of small towns. At the same time, while its use was characteristic of intellectuals after the collapse of the Soviet Union, it became a symbol of opposition after Lukashenka's accession to power.

The processes of assimilation into Russian culture were difficult and controversial, despite the proximity of the two languages. The head of the political family himself speaks "trasianka"—a mixed form of Russian and Belarusian. Lukashenka may also be described as a first generation urban citizen, with a slightly different value system than the urban residents of other European countries. These first generation urban Belarusians are far more authoritarian, and committed to paternalism and patron-client ties and relationships. Unfortunately, the value orientation of the country's president coincided with the value orientations of the majority of the Belarusian population at the time he came to power. According to the Belarusian political analyst Anatoly Lysyuk:

> The Belarusian president's ambition to represent a father of a patriarchal family is apparent. The image of the father generally covers the entire state, including all citizens, even those who do not consider themselves akin. Consequently, the Father skillfully applies the concept of "people," careful not to refer to "social groups" or "classes." Generally, the image of the father is the personification of truth,

embodying the wisdom of previous generations, knowing all about the past, present and future. The imperious image of the father, protecting his children from all dangers, is bound to possess a heroic aura of victories over hordes of enemies. The Father of the nation is an image containing the image of the Patriot, having a salutary influence on the fate of the Fatherland, the Motherland and all the Belarusian people.[41]

In this author's opinion, the choice of authoritarian values by the Belarusian citizens in the mid-90s was some form of "rebellion" against late industrialization and urbanization. Later, however, people were not properly asked anymore, since every election failed to meet the basic democratic criteria. It was taken for granted that people shared the political values of the head of the political family, enjoying the privileges of his being their "bats'ka" ("father" in Belarusian).

However, the processes of industrial development and urban growth brought inevitable change. With every passing year, the percentage of second and third generation citizens (with a consequently different value system) increases. While there were no significant changes in attitudes, ideals and orientations of the political head of the family, we can imagine a quiet but constant change in value orientations of the majority of Belarusians, who no longer fit into the Procrustean bed of the ruling regime. This process is intensified in times of crisis, shedding light on the weaknesses of the regime.

As such, elements and ideological panels of patronalism have formed in Belarus, similar to those in classic mafia states. Nevertheless, their timeframes are limited, as they are constantly eroded by the processes of socio-economic development.

The Ideological Justification of a Mafia State in State Ideology

To strengthen the established system of power handover to future generations and increase the legitimacy of the regime, Lukashenka came up with the so-called "state ideology" in 2003. The regime of personal power in Belarus is not rigidly ideological, making it different from totalitarian regimes. At the same time, anti-Western and anti-democratic ideas are openly instilled in the public consciousness. Panslavism is widely promoted. The importance of Belarus is emphasized, the country portrayed as preventing the spread of pernicious liberal values and attitudes, while its president positions himself as the leader of the forces within the former Soviet Union who actively opposed the imperialist Western conspiracies against the fallen socialist state. The so-called state ideology presented by Alyaksandr Lukashenka in his speech at the permanent seminar of executives in March 2003 was no different.

The development of a state ideology allowed some political analysts and opposition politicians to talk about the totalitarian transformation of Lukashenka's political regime. In this author's opinion, such a transformation had a pronounced sultanistic character. Sultanistic leadership does not typically have a well-developed dominant ideology, but it can use the statements of leaders as a type of ideological basis, as "it has an extremely manipulative character and, more importantly, can hardly be perceived as something restraining the head of state, while it remains relevant as long as it is used by the leader."[42] Thus, a so-called "pseudo-ideology" is formed, which the developers of the Belarusian state ideology have come very close to building. It is superficial. The worldview is represented by an eclectic combination of some Marxist-Leninist, liberal and conservative positions. According to Lukashenka's report:

> Thus, the Marxist-Leninist, conservative and liberal ideology can all be attributed to us in different degrees, say, quantities. And in some sense, this is exactly the case. Some characteristics are more pronounced, others are less evident. . . . The Belarussian ideology shall focus on the traditional values of our civilization: the ability to work not only for profit, but for the good of society, the respect for collective values. . . . In fact, in the East Slavic world (given the fact that our territory was inhabited by other nations), we are the only country that openly promotes our loyalty to the traditional values of civilization. All this suggests that time, destiny, and circumstances served as a combination of factors for Belarusian advancement, perhaps, to a position of a great spiritual leader of the Eastern European civilization."[43]

In 2016, before his visit to China, the head of the political family considered it appropriate to recall his devotion to communist ideas. In his speech at the All-Belarusian People's Assembly, he said:

> We have to understand one thing: today we do not have the Communist Party, which was once bearing an enormous responsibility of education, including ideological education of our society, thus, today this burden is placed on us—the vertical power structure. Since we do not have appropriate, real parties at the moment—they have not been established yet—it is necessary to rely on what we have: our youth organizations and our veteran organizations, our Women's Union and our trade unions. We must use them to solve the problems once solved by the Communist Party, which was doing a lot for the country's development. Well, since there are none, it is necessary to replace them. Until a party market has formed, if I may say so, it is necessary to replace them with the existing organizations that stand up for the sovereignty and development of our country.[44]

It is clear from the practice of ideological work that this system of ideas and opinions in no way limits the current government. On the contrary, it serves to ensure the achievement of pragmatic goals set out by Lukashenka: to strengthen his personal control over the state apparatus, the education system and the media. Finally, official ideology is despised by "the leader's entourage, the citizens and the outside world," which, according to Linz and Stepan, is peculiar to sultanism. It is also one of the distinctive features of a mafia state, which relies heavily on state bureaucracy.

Conclusion

In conclusion, it is necessary to dwell on all the features bringing Belarus closer to an ideal model of a mafia state. The primary feature is disregard for the rule of law, affecting not just the society but the ruling elite as well. The country was ahead of other mafia states in eliminating the autonomy of the most important social institutions, from the Academy of Sciences to political parties. The head of the political family manipulated popular vestiges of paternalism that became the basis for the development of patronalism. Finally, the Belarusian state ideology was introduced, serving to perpetuate the power of Alyaksandr Lukashenka and ensure its continuity.

However, some features distinguish the Belarusian model from classic mafia states: the predominance of state ownership, the absence of a party of power, and the weak role of national populism, replaced by social populism. However, the above should not be understood as insurmountable obstacles for a Belarusian transformation into a classic mafia state. The head of the political family has learned to profit personally from state ownership, removing all of his dangerous economic and political rivals, including the Russian ones. He has a rich experience in using his own vertical, instead of the party of power, as a means of strengthening personal power. The most serious problem is a marked imbalance between social and national populism, with the predominance of the former. President Lukashenka refuses to make even minimal steps to solve it, for fear of an extremely negative Russian reaction—not least since Russia has invested a lot of money to support the current head of the political family. At the same time, Belarus is hardly doomed for a Russian-type polyarchy. Lukashenka fully understands all the weaknesses of this model, as well as the possible risks of losing personal power.

Most likely, a unique, rustic and provincial model of an underdeveloped mafia state will be established in Belarus. It is characterized by the following features:

- a great deal of property is state-owned, so the weight of oligarchs is somewhat less than in "classic" mafia states;
  - there is a far lower level of centrally led governmental corporate raiding—as a means of property redistribution—than in the genuine mafia states;
  - the power is much more bureaucratic, and tied more closely to formal bureaucratic positions than in Hungary or Russia, where the political actor is the adopted political family, with some members not even having any formal position;
  - the rewards for Lukashenka's clients are provided mainly in positions of state bureaucracy and state enterprises, and not necessarily in property;
  - the "grand corruption" therefore is more restricted than in Russia, the value of single instances of corruption is smaller, and the social differences are less pronounced, than in other post-communist regimes;
  - there is no dominant party acting as a "transmission belt" of the adopted political family; the unique character of the regime is that it is much more based on bureaucratic positions than in "classic" mafia states;
  - consequently, Belarus is closer to a bureaucratic, sultanistic autocracy than to a "classic" mafia state; but it has some features that resemble

it (for instance, an emerging dynastic element with the positions of Lukashenka's sons).

Notes

1. Magen Knuth, *Russia, Ukraine, and Belarus: A Comparative Study on Political Culture and Democratization Success* (Chicago: Midwest Political Science Association Conference, 2004), 24–27.
2. Steven White and Ian McAllister, "Patterns of Political Culture," in *Post-communist Belarus: In Search of Direction*, ed. Stephen White and Elena Korosteleva (London: Rowman & Littlefield, 2004), 21–22.
3. *Pervye prezidentskie vybory v Respublike Belarus: osnovnye itogi* [The first presidential elections in Belarus: basic results] (Minsk: NCSI "Vostok-Zapad," 1994), 50.
4. Gerardo Munck, *Measuring Democracy: A Bridge between Scholarship and Politics* (Baltimore: The Johns Hopkins University Press, 2009), 158.
5. Uladzimir Rouda, "Belarus: Transformation from Authoritarianism towards Sultanism," *Baltic Journal of Political Science* 2 (2012): 64–79.
6. Juan Linz and Alfred Stepan, *Problems of Democratic Transition and Consolidation: Southern Europe, South America and Post-Communist Europe* (Baltimore and London: The Johns Hopkins University Press, 1996), 45.
7. Quoted in Valery Karbalevich "Put' Lukashenko k vlasti" [Lukashenko's way to power], in *Belorussia i Rossia: Obshchestva i gosudarstva*, ed. Dimitry Furman (Moscow: Prava cheloveka, 1998), 246–51.
8. Kathleen J. Mihalisko, "Belarus: Retreat to Authoritarianism," in *Democratic Change and Authoritarian Reactions in Russia, Ukraine, Belarus and Moldova*, ed. Karen Dawisha and Bruce Parrott (Cambridge: Cambridge University Press, 1998), 240.
9. Karbalevich, "Put' Lukashenko k vlasti," 246–51.
10. The importance of the influence of democratic countries for general democratization was stressed by Steven Levitsky and Lucan Way. They also mentioned its absence in Belarus and other countries of the former Soviet Union, with the sole exception of the Baltic states. See Steven Levitsky and Lucan A. Way, *Competitive Authoritarianism: The Emergence and Dynamics of Hybrid Regimes in the Post-Cold War Era* (Cambridge: Cambridge University Press, 2010).
11. Lukashenka addressed these ideas again in his speech at the All-Belarusian People's Assembly on June 22, 2016. Alyaksandr Lukashenka, "Sila v dvizhenii!" [The force is in the movement!] in *Sovetskaja Belarus – Belarus' Segodnia*, No. 118, Jun. 23, 2016.
12. Vitali Silitski, "Ekanamichnaja palityka Lukashenki" [The economic policy of Lukashenka] in *Belaruska-rasijskaja integracyja Analitychnyja artykuly* (Minsk: Encyclopedics, 2002), 65.
13. "Vladimir Putin: podderzhka Rossiei belorusskoi ekonomiki, nachinaya s etogo goda, znachitel'no sokratitsya" [Vladimir Putin: Russia's support of the Belaru-

sian economy, starting from this year, will be significantly reduced], *Belaruskija Naviny*, Jan. 15, 2007, http://www.naviny.by/rubrics/politic/2007/01/15/ic_articles_112_149358.

14 Stanislav Bogdankevich, "Transformacija politicheskoj i ekonomicheskoj sistemy" [Transformation of political and economic system] in *Presidentskie vybory v Belarusi: ot ogranichennoj demokratii k neogranichennomu avtoritarizmu* [Presidential elections in Belarus: From restricted democracy to unlimited authoritarianism] (Novosibirsk: Vodolei, 2006), 28.

15 Lukashenka, "Sila v dvizhenii!"

16 Elena Novozhilova, "Skol'ko vesit belarusskaja ekonomika?" [How much does the Belarusian economy weigh?] *Belarusskie novosti*, Mar. 24, 2008, http://news.tut.by/economics/105797.html.

17 Stanley Fischer and Ratna Sahay, "The Transition Economies after Ten Years," IMF Working Papers, no. 00/30 (Washington, DC: IMF, 2000); Oleh Havrylyshyn and Thomas Wolf, "Growth in Transition Countries 1990-1998: The Main Lessons," paper prepared for the Conference "A Decade of Transition," IMF, February 1-3, 1999, Washington, DC.

18 World Bank, *Belarus: Window of Opportunity to Enhance Competitiveness and Sustain Economic Growth, A Country Economic Memorandum (CEM) for the Republic of Belarus*, vol. 1, Main Report. (Washington, DC.: World Bank, 2005), 8.

19 Ibid., 5.

20 "Viktor Ivashkevich: Narodniy skhod i Narodniy sud" [Viktor Ivashkevich: The People's Assembly and the People's Court], *Charter '97*, Jul. 29, 2011, http://charter97.org/ru/news/2011/7/29/41066/; also Gennady Fedynich, "Vlast' delaet vsio, chtoby narod pomog ey ujti" [Authorities do their best for people to make them go], *Belaruskij Partizan*, Sep. 17, 2011.

21 "Preface," *IIESPS News* 3, no. 61 (September 2011), http://www.iiseps.org/?p=2136&lang=en, accessed Jan. 7, 2018.

22 Oleg Manaev. "Hmuraja osen" [Cloudy autumn], *Narodnaja volia* 149-150, Sep. 30, 2011.

23 Uladzimir Rouda, *Palitychnaja sistema Respubliki Belarus'* [The political system of the Republic of Belarus], (Vilnius: EHU, 2011), 187-88.

24 Maurice Duverger, *Politicheskie patii* [Political parties] (Moscow: Academic Project, 2000). In 2008, the author of the above article was among the first Belarusian political analysts to come to a conclusion of a non-partisan nature of the Belarusian political system; see Vladimir Rovdo, *Sravnitel'naja Politologia* [Comparative Politics] (Vilnius: EHU, 2009), 327-32.

25 Rouda, *Palitychnaja sistema Respubliki Belarus'*, 245.

26 Lukashenka, "Sila v dvizhenii!"

27 "A. Lukashenka otvetil na voprosy predstavitelej belorusskih i rossijskih SMI" [A. Lukashenka replied to the questions of Belarusian and Russian Media representatives], *Prezident Respubliki Belarus'*, Apr. 26, 2008, http://president.gov.by/ru/news_ru/view/aleksandr-lukashenko-otvetil-na-voprosy-predstavitelej-belorusskix-i-rossijskix-smi-2817/.

28 Namely, Decree no. 476, "On the Approval of the Statement on the Chairman of the Regional and Minsk City Executive Committee," dated November 20, 1995, and Decree no. 519, "On Some Issues to Ensure the Activity of Local Councils of Deputies in the Republic of Belarus," dated December 26, 1995.
29 Mihail Smiahovich, "Stanaulenne i razvicce instytuta presidenckaj ulady" [Presidential power formation and development], in *Historyja Belaruskaj dziarzhaunasti*, 2nd ed. (Minsk: Belaruskaja navuka, 2012), 471–72.
30 *Stat'ja 119 Konstitucii Respubliki Belarus* [Article 119 of the Constitution of the Republic of Belarus] (Minsk: Nacionalnyj centr pravovoj informacii, 2007), 36.
31 Levitsky and Way, *Competitive Authoritarianism*, 59.
32 Rouda, *Palitychnaja Sistema Respubliki Belarus'*, 135.
33 Vladimir Gelman, "Iz ognia da v polymia. Dinamika postsovetskih rezhimov v sravnitelnoj perspective" [From the frying pan into the fire: Dynamics of post-Soviet regimes in comparison], *Polis* 2 (2007): 11. http://csis.org/images/stories/Russia%20and%20Eurasia/061207_ruseura_acgelman.pdf.
34 Yury Chavusau, "Manipuliacyi u infarmacyjnaj prastory i pagroza referendumu" [The manipulation of informational space and referendum threat], in *Palitychnaja gistoryja nezalezhnaj Belarusi* (Vilnius: Instytut belarusistyki, 2006), 466.
35 See the website of the Administration of the President of the Republic of Belarus, http://president.gov.by/en/administration_en/. See also the presidential decree no. 40, of February 13, 2017, "Ukaz Prezidenta Respubliki Belarus' ot 13 fevralia 2017 goda no. 40," http://www.pravo.by/document/?guid=12551&p0=P31700040&p1=1&p5=0; as well as the Article 84 of the Constitution of the Republic of Belarus.
36 For further information on the status of the Belarusian language in the country, see interviews with Svetlana Alexievich, the Russian-speaking Nobel Prize laureate in Literature in 2015: Svetlana Alexievich, "Slava Bogu shto liudzi hochuts gavaryts pa-belarusku" [Thank God people want to speak Belarusian], https://www.svaboda.org/a/25176047.html; "Alexievich: Lukashenku uzho dakladna nia vyrvacca" [Alexievich: Lukashenka won't get away]: https://www.svaboda.org/a/25334939.html.
37 Pavlyuk Bykovsky, "ByNet-2013: pervye itogi goda" [ByNet-2013: First results of the year], *Deutsche Welle*, Oct. 17, 2013, http://dw.de/p/1A1SK.
38 Viktor Chernov, "Tretij Sektor v Belarusi" [The third sector in Belarus], *Nashe mnenie* 4, Mar. 26, 2008.
39 Freedom House's evaluation of Belarus over the last ten years is available online: "Belarus: Country Profile," *Freedom House: Nations in Transit 2017*, https://freedomhouse.org/report/nations-transit/2017/belarus, accessed Jan. 8, 2018.
40 "Itogi parlamentskih vyborov" [Results of parliamentary elections], *Novosti ONT*, September 11, 2016.
41 Anatoly Lysiuk, "President i narod: specyfika politicheskoj kommunikacii" [The president and the people: Specific features of political communication], in *Predidentskie vybory v Belarusi: ot ogranichennoj demokratii k neogranichennomu avtoritarismu* [Presidential election in Belarus: From restricted democracy to unlimited authoritarianism] (Novosibirsk: Vodolei, 2006), 156–57.

[42] Linz and Stepan, *Problems of Democratic Transition*, 53.
[43] Alyaksandr Lukashenka, "O sostojanii ideologicheskoj raboty i merah po ee sovershenstvovaniju" [On the state of ideological work and means of its improvement], in *Materialy postojanno dejstvujushcego seminara rukovodiashchih rabotnikov* (Minsk: Akademia upravlenia pri presidente RB, 2003), 17–21.
[44] Lukashenka, "Sila v dvizhenii!"

LÁSZLÓ NÁNDOR MAGYARI

The Romanian Patronal System of Public Corruption

This study begins with a brief clarification and methodological introduction, then seeks to introduce and analyze, in two ways, what might be considered a unique type of public corruption, and its connections to the operational modes of "transitional democracy" in Romania. Two key questions must be addressed: what is the nature of the public corruption system in Romania, and how does it function? I will first summarize in an operational model the most important dimensions and connective mechanisms of the extensive, deeply embedded and organically permeating public corruption system which has captured or colonized the state (Part 1). Then, in the framework of a comparative study, I will outline the unique type that is the present system of Romanian democracy, classifying it in comparison with the single-pyramid post-communist mafia state as described by Bálint Magyar[1] and the concept of patronal politics developed by Henry E. Hale[2] with respect of the political systems that have developed in Hungary and other post-Soviet states (Part 2).

1. Sequential capturing of the state

1.1 Public corruption: definitions, concepts and methods

The appeal of the positivist and structuralist approaches dominant in Romanian political science and political sociology is that they allow for a smaller margin of error in analysis. Yet the price we pay for avoiding errors, for the certainty of the researcher's judgment—which ideally is supported statistically or with some measurement-based approach—is that he/she can only make *post festum* interpretations, thus limiting the predictive force and projective opportunities of the process. Furthermore, positivist macro-analysis characteristically struggles with a lack of data and information: there are hardly any well-founded, well-structured measurements that are methodologically sound. Those that do exist tend to deal with the perception of corruption and its spread—as for instance Transparency International's annual reports do—while traceable official statistics are partial and distorted. Recent such research projects which utilized questionnaires and interviews with people found guilty of corruption are interesting. Such an approach offers a viewpoint of the phenomenon "from the other side," showing how persons enter the networks of corruption, what motivates them and so forth. On the other hand, ethnographic or ethnological analyses of the corruption phenomenon on the micro level are too narrow—focusing mainly on corruption networks and acts in the lower regions of society—and, as prisoners of a concept narrowed to mutual gifting, they offer no path out, but merely describe the everyday culture of corruption.[3] I consider the analysis of actual speech (modes) on corruption important, but it is still insufficient to interpret the problem as a whole and impart predictive knowledge that can help combat corruption itself. For this reason, I follow the theoretical and methodological rules of political anthropology, structuring a mid-level but at the same time heuristic, theoretical, predictive and projective set of ideas. These offer a framework for the phenomenon of corruption, and at the same time make visible the expected results of acts, which today have become primarily media-negotiated.

A qualitative strategy becomes primarily important when and where new concepts need to be created or correlations—which actors, politics and the media hope to hide—need to be exposed. This is all the more important as the wide-scale efforts made to hide corrupt practices are an organic ingredient of corruption itself. An entire institutional apparatus strives to make corruption invisible when entanglements of power take on a structural character and a general structure of "shadow politics" develops. These networks may be initiated in legislatures and continue by using a wide array of regulations, institutions, and other means. They may establish an entire cover-up industry along with white-collar crime networks and a mechanism for making administrative corruption confidential. For this reason, *bottom-up* or *grounded* theory[4] research approaches (to which we will return below), which are utilized widely in political anthropology, can be much more informative in our case than the analysis of positivist/quantitative data and information. The study of corruption through fieldwork and case studies is difficult, given that researchers must abide by the deontological rules of research, the rights of studied subjects, and so on. On the other hand, such fieldwork can easily become "dangerous fieldwork," given that subjects are often underworld figures who, through their equally dangerous political contacts, operate widespread networks with a "far reach." For this reason, most research follows—as does this study—the approach of *multi-sited ethnography*,[5] which means tracking the studied events as they enter the realm of media and the Internet, where they become observable. This, however, is largely the field of qualitative media analysis,[6] which cannot examine phenomena in real time, but can offer only *post factum* secondary and indirect analysis. Romanian public corruption, given its spread and depth, only truly became visible (and hence researchable) when, given the work done by the DNA (*Direcția Națională Anticorupție*, National Anticorruption Directorate), a sufficiently large number of significantly meaningful cases became widely known. This was especially true after the DNA's prosecution documents, as well as the court opinions in cases of sentencing for corruption, began to become public, giving the phenomenon momentum in a real, legal sense as it became relevant and media-negotiated.

The essence of the political anthropology perspective is that "emphasis is put on the interweaving of the various dimensions of the political field and social life."[7] In our case, this means focusing on the direct environment of corruption phenomena, on how "informal roles and networks organized in formal institutions" develop.[8] This is all the more important as corruption is a "multiply mediated" phenomenon, which is why its investigation must target not only its contact with the state-political sphere and its institutions, but also the narrative areas concerning its daily functioning and, furthermore, the way it appears in the world of media discourses.[9] Against this backdrop, an anthropological approach to the problem involves the research of—and critical reflection on—issues such as "mental corruption" and the nature of the knowledge instrumental in it, the "analysis of symbolic power forms" related to corruption,[10] the effects and development of the anti-corruption industry, and even corrupt research methods.

The topic of my study is *public corruption*,[11] which goes beyond fields like administrative acts, the administrative institutional system and disloyal competition for economic advantages, as well as beyond taking advantage of strictly political power. Instead, it encompasses clientelistic relations as well as associated mentalities, pervading and characterizing the entirety of political culture.[12] In this sense, public corruption is not an individual act, a moral fault or leaning (which of course it is in other respects) or a simple form of crime. It is instead an institutionalized matrix embedded in wider political/power operations,[13] or, in other words, a social phenomenon. The culture of corruption in Romania is best described using the term *public corruption*, with its foundation in the reality of a "status society" and the mentality appropriate to it. In essence, laws are not equally applicable to all; rather, responding to social status pervades all of public life, informing the notion that "what is deserved should be given" based on social rank and "lifestyle." *Corruption* is not primarily driven or made attractive by material profit—this is a derivative, but not ignorable, product[14]—but instead primarily by higher rank, the socially accepted and legitimate goal of status raising, the currency of which is *influence*.[15] The functioning of public corruption is an obstacle to the development of democratization, mainly through the loss and deconstruction of public trust in public institutions.[16] That is to say, it is built and blooms on a lack of public trust, which is an inheritance from previous regimes in East-Central European states; a phenomenon which in Romania—as a result of the activities of the secret services (which in a number of respects continue the legacy of the communist-era *Securitate*)—is rather widespread. The most persistent visible heritage of the Ceaușescu dictatorship's "national communism" is the virtually complete and persistent deconstruction of public trust, the perpetuation of an atmosphere of distrust, and in certain cases—through the *Securitate*'s successor organizations—its fortification and spread to new phenomena and institutions, with general distrust becoming a "social paradigm," a breeding ground for public corruption.

The public corruption I analyze is, in reality, a *composite* phenomenon[17] and concept. The "matrix" that serves as its foundation becomes larger and more complicated as it connects elements of various natures, characters and structure with divergent mechanisms and dynamics. It should be stressed that this conceptual pluralism is part of the essence of public corruption, and within this the combination of various phenomena sees them mutually support or strengthen one another. Such interactions ultimately produce a very solid construction, with rather divergent (polyvalent) interpretations attracted and formed into a complex whole. This complexity and diversity is usually simplified by anti-corruption movements, defining them in accordance with their own fields of activity. This is why I deem it necessary to use a relatively new sociological and anthropological term. This analytical category is, further, able to lead research, to allow us to pose multilayered, heuristically valuable questions concerning the phenomenon.[18] The composite concept of Romanian public corruption refers to its changing geometric character, as such is more integrative than exclusionary, and tends to indicate a unique structure and dynamic, evolving process, as opposed to a closed and out-of-context linguistic-logical construction.

When analyzing the reality of the corruption that has appeared in Romanian public life, which has taken an increasingly central role while at the same time appearing obscure, and when trying to distinguish it from other social realities, it appears that the framework, theory and methodology designed by Erving Goffman in 1974 can be most effective. When developing his framework theory and methodology, Goffman used as a starting point the assumption that "definitions of a situation are build up in accordance with principles of organization which govern events—at least social ones—and our subjective involvement in them."[19] He uses the term "frame" to refer to these fundamental elements, to identify and interpret them as much as possible. What this term enables analysts, according to Goffman, is to identify those interpretive schemes which make it possible for both individuals and groups "to locate, perceive, identify, and label" events and the circumstances of their emergence—schemes that help people to grasp the meaning of things, organize experiences, and guide action.[20]

The risk of the framing theory or discursive analysis I follow is that it is imprecise in quantitative terms; however, this approach builds on what is available and accessible. I conduct secondary analysis, organizing, framing and criticizing those discourses and pieces of information and data that are created by the (mainly political) actors of public corruption, in conjunction, of course, with the actors of the media and the mass of acceptors/victims. On the other hand, I grant my approach greater heuristic and predictive power, given that I take into account a high number of manifestations that can serve to orient and show the well-masked order of corruption related developments. The advantage of this method is that it grants acts and behaviors based on deceptions and misunderstandings the same status and significance as corrupt acts and behaviors that are conscious and based on recognized interests. As such, it is capable of following the events of "real reality." Then, I calculate and base my projections and—in all likelihood—rationally founded forecasts on a certain level of stability and foresight in the behavior and attitudes of the actors. As such, I attempt to follow how public actors, commentators and media mediators on one hand, and public opinion, society and external consumers of the discourse on the other, frame events themselves, or how they express them in a discourse, and to which narratives they connect the existing world of corruption.

In the first part of my paper I will describe the operational modalities of Romanian public corruption, using the theory and concepts of political anthropology. I will primarily utilize media texts for my empirical base. In the second part I will examine the nature of the system in a comparative context. The methodological aspect of this descriptive and interpretive part includes a "typological analysis," in the framework of which I use existing studies and research results that supplement incomplete data and information through deductive methods. This process is assisted by the thought-provoking study of Rasma Karklins, who outlined a possible typology of post-communist corruption in the early 2000s.[21] She classified sixteen types of corrupt acts on three levels, with the weakest level being the bribery of civil servants in order to have them ignore certain rules or to expedite administrative processes. At the top level is media corruption, which, given its original function, ought to be a field for anti-corruption action, but which in its corrupt form[22] serves previous forms very effectively.[23]

In the second half of the study I strive to introduce and interpret both similarities and differences between Romanian and Hungarian public and political corruption in a comparative context. To do so, I first adopt the procedure used by Bálint Magyar in his examination of the post-communist mafia state, which he, borrowing a term coined by Stephen Hawking and Leonard Mlodinow, calls "model-dependent realism."[24] This is similar to the above-mentioned political anthropology concept of mental corruption, given that it refers to imagined "thought models" from the point of view of actors in social reality, which structure the reality of networks of corruption, and to which researchers must adjust their procedures. Then I attempt to utilize for Romania a theory from political science, namely that recommended by Henry E. Hale, the *theory of the real*, and its subsequent set of concepts along with the category of patronal politics.[25] This is done while continuing to use the comparative perspective of political anthropology. Hale's theory applies to the hybrid political systems in the post-Soviet region consisting of patronal politics, which are quasi-democratic and quasi-autocratic, or a "unique" brand of democracies. The *theory of the reality* demonstrates the need to examine experienceable, empirically existing and studied phenomena, behavior and process, or *political practice*, as the focus of study. However, the theory only gets as far as creating ideal types. The uniqueness of these—as Max Weber's methodological viewpoint would suggest—lies in overemphasizing certain characteristics of social phenomena to form "pure types," that is, sociological concepts.[26] These are then compared to the facts of empirical research, which are later corrected, supplemented, shaded, or kept when they are confirmed—that is, not falsified. Patronal political systems are in the end such ideal types of the post-Soviet region's "unique" democracies. They are "pure types" that, compared to the democracy scales of transitology research and theories, and the ideas surrounding Western democratic ideas and comparative models, are based on other—more empirical—foundations and the conceptual conclusions of the analysis of real processes.

1.2 The public sociology of the DNA (National Anticorruption Directorate)

The facts and mechanisms of public corruption are not directly accessible. The hiding of acts and mechanisms in corrupt transactions can require just as much effort as the corrupt acts themselves. Further, this all takes place in a black or grey zone, to which researchers rarely have access. For this reason, we first hear of corrupt affairs through the media, investigative reporters, analyses, news reports and so forth. A pivotal question arises at this point regarding the degree to which these texts in themselves are distorting, filtered and manipulative. We require serious critical procedures to reach the actual cases. The existence of media corruption has been proven at many levels, and we receive word of it primarily through the sphere of economic ties, but also through the world of political networks as well.[27] We later receive information via public prosecution documents and news about them, which have recently multiplied. However, on reading these documents, the cases still contain unclear areas. The phenomenon is accompanied throughout by the impression of unfinished business,[28] given that stories of corruption introduced when knowledge of temporary detention becomes public never have an unequivocal end game. Long court procedures, extended cases, ever changing charges,[29] sentencing remarks that are barely understandable without a legal background, and so on, cloud the vision of the observer and in certain cases the researcher. Essentially, the scripts of corruption cases and procedures become impossible to follow.

In some form, as something regularly experience, but more typically as a media-filtered reality, everyone in Romania has faced public corruption since the regime change. However, this experience somehow becomes "impersonal" when we ourselves become a part of the issue (for instance, when paying or accepting a kickback), and this anonymity is particularly true when it comes to representation: public corruption, for the major part of two decades, despite experiences and appearances, has been represented and operated in public awareness without naming (or having the ability to name) the corrupt.[30] Its deconstruction or *post festum* uncovering has been initiated in the last year by the acts of the National Anticorruption Directorate. The organization's investigations and reports are in and of themselves quite spectacular and it has initiated a high number of arrests, highly covered in the media, replete with handcuffs. It is not clear whether the DNA's actions truly uncover or eliminate the core of public corruption,[31] or whether only the tip of the iceberg has been revealed. But it is almost certain that in the wake of the activities of the DNA, the phenomenon and its scale and extent have gained a sociological dimension, also giving us our first news of the meaning, affected levels and depth of corruption. We do not know whether the DNA's visible efforts have led to the disruption or uncovering of centrally directed corruption networks. Thus far, the results of the struggle against corruption (which from many points of view are doubtful or have been questioned) have been modest,[32] but the system has been increasingly exposed:[33] the dimensions of corruption are revealed through publicly known cases. As such, reversed (*post facto*) analysis can help us become knowledgeable of and understand the phenomenon. The number of initiated prosecution and court proceedings regarding the corruption of politicians has increased year on year. Until October 2015, 237 politicians stood accused, compared to 2002 when only one was accused. This number is likely to be even higher for this year. Concerning the political affiliation of the accused in 2014, whether by design or not, it appears that all parties are affected by corruption and the prosecutor's work against it. Interestingly, the degree to which parties are affected is (essentially) correlated to their number of seats in parliament. Looking over the political backgrounds of those accused over the past twelve years, this proportionality distorts somewhat toward the Social Democratic Party (PSD). PSD politicians had the most prosecution procedures (255) directed against them, with the other two main parties (National Liberal Party, or PNL, with 122, and the Democratic Liberal Party, or PDL, with 158) and the Democratic Alliance of Hungarians in Romania (RMDSZ, 30 procedures) affected in accordance with their proportions. Based on these numbers, the DNA maintains that politically motivated procedures do not occur. However, the issue invites suspicion, given that the balanced proportions make it appear that each initiated case (or the timing thereof) is strictly thought through, and in this sense the prosecuting agency acts in a politically influenced manner.[34]

Today the DNA is the mediator of sociological recognition. This organization alone offers access to procedures and presents the dimensions,[35] operational modes,[36] and characteristic forms of public corruption. Below I will use publicly known DNA procedures to present the characteristics of the phenomenon. I will emphasize how, and the degree to which, Romanian public corruption diverges from the Hungarian "post-communist mafia state."

1.3 The state and the corrupt system

Above, when discussing how the Romanian state fell prey to networks of corruption, I stated that corruption had become a general phenomenon in all areas and all institutional frameworks. However, there remain territories unoccupied by corruption, while there also exists civil society (despite its weakness and low level of organization), and party and media pluralism, which favors transparency. To this point the "coercion-free communication field" had been more or less maintained and reproduced. As such, Romanian state and public corruption is an imperfect, inconsistent and heteronomous system (in essence, the corrupt system itself is inconsistent, and therefore corrupted!). The pervasiveness of corruption, which at times leads to the use of labels such as endemic, generic, structural or institutionalized corruption, does not, however, translate into a comprehensive system. That is to say, the state and system do not converge under the authority of a single center of power. There coexist—as I pointed out above—a number of power nodes that are on their own strewn by corruption; however, they do keep one another in check. Although the parties are ideology-free,[37] quite interoperable, and crossing the floor is common (some 25% of elected representatives and senators changed party or faction during their last mandate), the democratic election system formally fulfills its function, and political competition exists. Even more importantly, checks and balances are still in place: despite the presence of corrupt operations within the system, the separation and mutual control of powers is more or less working.[38]

Paradoxically, the structurally corrupt Romanian system is in all likelihood not as consistently corrupt as it seems, less centralized, and less managed from a single power center than is often assumed. Actual corruption and its culture take place in the present, and its history does not reach back in perpetuity to undefinable traditions and the world of historical legends, as is often suggested in historical-ethnological analyses. The rational, valid and practical interpretation of the phenomenon of corruption is complicated by consistently emphasizing all kinds of Romanian specificities, or by too often pointing at confused pre-histories. We exclude the possibility of cultural change when we point in the direction of cultural tradition too often, as if Romanians traditionally leaned toward attitudes and habits that favored timeless corruption.[39]

On the contrary, I hold that the phenomena responsible for the spread of the culture of corruption are, on the one hand, multiply mediated and countlessly manipulated public discourse, with daily discourses and interpretations arising from widespread and dominant discourses also playing a role. I maintain that for the majority of regular citizens, the belief in "reality show" reality is stronger than the acknowledgement of direct and brutal "existing" reality. Our zombified world[40] has become duplicated and incalculable, and we have stripped reality of its realism only to replace the original meaning and calculability of things with another media-framed and simulated form created in the background, behind the curtains. The tabloidization of reality, stripping reality of its original meaning—distancing ourselves from that which was in other times and places obvious—has not at all been a spontaneous social phenomenon, which would have occurred naturally, but rather emerged from the background, as a result of the struggle between various interests, taking place behind the scenes. At the same time, the widespread effort to hide corruption is also responsible. Public discourse infected by manipulation has become so widespread that it has created an unheard-of deeply rooted public mistrust, which presents manipulation and corruption as a perfect fate, or a cultural and/or national feature. But this is not inevitable. Over the years, the beneficiaries of the transformation of reality into a sequential simulation, namely the heads of corrupt networks, have been more or less visible. The tabloidization of the media, the classification of information, and the manipulation of reality all served to weave the political "*over*world" together with the criminal underworld and thus hiding the ruling presence of structural corruption at all levels and across institutions. The popular narratives on corruption that have become general (which emanate primarily from the media, namely the tabloidized media and its environment) can and do lead to public corruption appearing as the most visible and widespread mechanism of the state's "discursive construction."

Akhil Gupta's observations of Indian society appear relevant in this regard: "The discourse of corruption turns out to be a key arena through which the state, citizens, and other organizations and aggregations come to be imagined. Instead of treating corruption as a dysfunctional aspect of state organizations, I see it as a mechanism through which 'the state' itself is discursively constituted."[41] The raison d'être of the state, projected and presented through corruption, is evident throughout public culture, the media, and intellectual public discourse: it is the mainstream discourse regarding the state and its representation. Then there is the realm of everyday corruption with its own perceptual dimension. **All interactions with the state, power, bureaucracy, organizations of state violence, and even run of the mill service providers and so forth, are interactions with corruption.** All interactions with the state—not just in practice, but potentially and in the imagination—are interactions with corrupt officials, or an imagined version thereof. Furthermore, it is clear that dominant representations of the state in mass media, intellectual discourses and regular experience—interpreted both unsystematically and intuitively, according to local conditions, in accordance with common sense, or even from the specific point of view of the affected actors—are connected in the culture of corruption. Truncated and manipulated discourses originating in the media, as well as "cultural intimacy" and "structural nostalgia" formed on the border area of unsystematic regular experiences (which in their functioning constantly compare the "fallible" present with a lost, yet morally perfect past), provides the phenomenon with a strong consistency, and almost guarantees its permanent re-creation and derivation.[42]

In Romania, the culture of corruption—in its interpretation, that is, approached from its cultural and social reproduction functions—is a socialization factor built upon the daily experience of the representation of the state, corrupt institutions and offices, and the continuing, unceasing expansion of networks. This makes it practically impossible for anyone to stand up to it. **In Romania, the state and the perception and representation of corruption are interconnected**, while the majority of citizens face only the mediation of corruption and interact with the state. Moreover, the state itself is the embodiment of corruption. At the same time, the culture of corruption is also about moral tradition, and the tolerance or public indignation experienced in relation to various forms of corruption. If we view Heidenheimer's classification categories[43] as generally valid, according to which we distinguish black, gray or white "shades" of corruption and grade corrupt acts accordingly, then we can conclude that in Romania a more primitive, two-category system exists in practice. According to this, the state and the political scene are wholly in the corrupt category, in what could be termed as the "wiseguy [*smekker*] world," which also includes the members of the criminal underworld.[44] It must be noted that, for average people, the notion of "smekker" does not have a negative connotation and does not necessarily imply corruption. I lean toward using it as a metaphor that expresses a simplified, dichotomous interpretation of the world. It is clear to me that the division is connected to corruption (among other things). Victims, the shiftless and average people are placed in the "loser" (*frájer*) category, where they may be joined in exceptional cases by exposed politicians, officials, or those members of the underworld who have been caught; but essentially, the category is composed of the plebeians who put up with those in power. The term can be used in a pejorative sense, but also as a way to express a sense of being at the mercy of others, disappointment, victimization and so forth.

1.4 Institutional corruption as a form of knowledge

The entirety of Romanian society is blanketed by what Alina Mungiu-Pippidi calls, following the steps of Max Weber, a collectivist and hierarchized society that is "based on the organizational mode called *particularism*. It runs directly counter to *universalism,* the norm and practice of individualistic societies, where equal treatment applies to everyone regardless of the group to which one belongs." As Mungiu-Pippidi notes, in a society based on particularism, particularly a "status society" such as Romania, the treatment of individuals "depends on their status or position in society, and people do not even expect to be treated fairly by the state."[45] The key unit of currency in this case is not money, but influence, through which one can acquire privileges and power positions, both being essential assets in the operations of a society based on particularism and status. In a society characterized by "competing particularisms" corruption seeps through everything and becomes a unique mode of institutional or official operations: in essence, corruption becomes the rule, rather than the exception. If this indeed applies to Romanian society and the operation of state institutions, its implications extend not only to the modes of moderating corruption, or the content of the policy of corruption, but also to the recruitment procedures selecting the cadres of officialdom, the public servant attitudes preferred by the institutional establishment, and the knowledge required of those preparing to enter the system. It can generally be stated that in central Romanian official apparatuses, and especially in their local equivalents, scientifically based expert knowledge has a fairly small role. In contrast, a kind of experiential knowledge, pertaining to modes of finding legal and procedural loopholes (whether creatively or intuitively) is highly valued. Necessary conditions for careers in officialdom include trustworthiness and skill in finding loopholes, uncovering resources that can be monopolized, and operating such monopolies. The **"neo-traditional" management** utilized in the public sphere is founded on **"translation mechanisms"** which, despite uniform regulations, allow the preferential treatment of clients with varying statuses, all the while ensuring that the system operates without obstacles and formally delivers on its tasks. The key criteria of official suitability and promotion hold that actors must have precise knowledge of all those translation procedures in all situations and affairs that open up loopholes within uniform regulations; an official must be aware of others who can be bribed, be they above—which often has more importance—horizontally equal, or beneath them. But through their activity, and in each phase of it, they must be clear on which statuses are accompanied by preferential treatment, and how each client should be handled in accordance with their status, position in the hierarchy, level of influence and so forth. Experiential knowledge, which must be acquired by members of the official apparatus for success and prestige,[46] concerns knowledge of the institutional structure of corruption and its operational mechanisms. In these cases, **corruption is transformed into a kind of unique knowledge**, without which offices could not function.

When I claim that corruption in its administrative mode is a kind of *knowledge form*, I mean so (also) in a Foucauldian sense.[47] The (background) knowledge (*savoir*) functioning in Romanian administration directly concerns informal corrupt power relations, hidden in plain sight, that go around, or rewrite, the institutional hierarchy. This is a kind of knowledge that conditions; that is, it shows not only the opportunities to utilize knowledge, but its boundaries as well. In the end, this knowledge concerns "what can be done, and what cannot," beyond given regulations and operational modes. Corruption as a form of knowledge is very creative in the sense that it opens almost unbelievable horizons, and at times "solves problems" that can barely be comprehended using common sense. One example may be found in the highway construction issue in Romania (a country with very few highways), where some employees of the state highway building firm (at least a half dozen persons) rank highly on the list of the richest Romanians.[48] The acquisition of this knowledge in fact begins at the very start of recruitment procedures, and such skills are tested for among young officials. It is not rare for offices to appear as direct or indirect goods. On the one hand, positions of influence are distributed according to ties of family, clientelism, friendship, relationship status, business partner status, and so on, in a virtual market, in the second public sphere (through "making a phone call" or other net interventions). On the other hand, there are examples of official and even elected functions being bought with cash.

2. The multi-pyramid patronal system, made in Romania

2.1 Hierarchies and actors of power

Top-down constructed pyramidal power and corruption networks, starting from the mafia state to those systems consisting of several pyramids—which only partially or occasionally overlap—raise a number of questions. Firstly, where are the tops of these pyramids located in the social/political field? Directly derived from this question, we may ask many others: which figures are found at the top; who rules in the key locations of the pyramids? Furthermore, it is worth asking why a single-pyramid system—that is, a mafia state type of system—did not develop in Romania. What factors in law making, institutional/administrative ordering, and the modes of practicing power obstructed such a development?

In our case, reliable and seemingly credible data lies in the text of not only media reports, but of DNA reports and court opinions as well. These mostly provide an opportunity to record the formal pyramidal system. From an informal perspective, we have considerably less relevant information, and as such, in the following sections I will essentially review formal positions and roles.

2.1.1 The peaks of the pyramids and their dynamic positioning

2.1.1.1 Presidents vs. Prime Ministers

The Romanian political field, and by extension the dispersion of public corruption, has been characterized for at least the last decade[49] by a fundamental cleavage, whereby a gap exists between, and is deepened by, continuous and intensive competition between the president(s) and the prime minister(s), or between governments. The legal and political foundations of this gap are provided by the confusing arrangement of powers regulated and established in the constitution. This holds that **Romania is a semi-presidential or hybrid state** with divided executive power, the institutional expression of which is the large and heterogeneously empowered Supreme Council of National Defense (CSAT).[50]

It is a system within which the division of power between the highest public power institutions is not clear, and for this reason the personality, character and moral habits of the president or prime minister define the relationship between the two positions. Experience and the materials of the anti-corruption prosecutor show that when the relationship between the president and the head of government is poor and characterized by competition and conflict, corruption networks and clientelistic systems will organize around the very strong power poles of these two highest public offices. Heads of government have never truly crossed over into the president's sphere of power, while the latter have consistently attempted to "expose" governments or accuse them of corruption. However, **both parties have tended to create their own oligarchs (moguls)** and taken them under their wing. Political corruption networks have operated and become more or less public (and visible) as a function of mutual exposures or blackmails in a dynamic of "war among palaces."[51] When, however, the president and head of government are from the same political family—that is, when the prime minister supports the presidential system—then the presidential patronage positioned itself not only above the secret services and the prosecutor/courts, the organizations of state violence, but made the government subservient as well. In these instances, there was a good chance that a centrally led mafia state similar to that in Hungary or the post-Soviet region would develop. In such a framework, the president would become a "godfather" and gather excessive powers that would lead to an "illiberal democracy."[52] What prevented this from happening was ultimately not the ambitions or character of the president, but the public outcry arising from the 2009 economic crisis and subsequent unpopular cutbacks—that is, in the end it was the will of the voters, alongside the public acts of civil society and the existing political constellation, that forestalled the emergence of a Romanian version of the mafia state.

2.1.1.2 Party patronage system

The party system in Romania is not founded according to ideological classification, nor the organization of parties according to various political philosophies, but instead through party patronage systems constructed within parties. It is important to stress that the party patronage system, as described by Petr Kopecký and Gerardo Scherlis,[53] demarcates the power of parties to place their own people in state administration and other influential institutions. In the Romanian case, this extends to directorships or board positions in state companies, supervisory boards of banks and other offices, leadership posts in media and cultural institutions, and so on.[54]

The single organizing principle that essentially divides the party political field is whether a given party is in government or in opposition, which fundamentally influences the functioning of the patronage system. The internal power pyramids of parliamentary parties, the heads of which are party presidents and those at the top of the internal party hierarchy (in accordance with organizational rules), are granted administrative functions when in government. The party president often fills the post of prime minister as well, and as such, the party leaders fulfil both elected and nominated administrative functions downward at every level: every party has an expansive clientele whose members are rewarded with administrative and other posts. When, however, the party is in opposition, it is the role of those who remain in administrative positions or who are elected into the party hierarchy that become more important, creating an impression of a kind of unspoken agreement between parties regarding the maintenance of the alternation system. In this sense, the corruption pyramids are organized around parties, and the number of potential or existing corruption pyramids with changing dynamics is equal to the number of parliamentary parties at a given time. The horizontal organization of the political scene is characterized by power competition for attainable functions, and for this reason, parties practice a kind of control over one another, establishing an **alternating system of corruption networks**. Characteristically, the highest number of accused or proven corrupt persons are from the most entrenched party, namely that which has been in power most since the regime change, the PSD (Social Democratic Party). Chief among these is the once popular former Prime Minister Adrian Năstase, and the recently accused former Prime Minister Victor Ponta.

2.1.1.3 Vertical power distributions
Large patronal systems and power pyramids are composed of smaller ones at regional or local levels, which remain organized according to similar principles. Vertical party and administrative institutional hybrids are established and operate both in the center and the countryside. This is the system of "local fiefdoms" (*baronni locali*), which are constructed primarily around local elected leaders, county council presidents and mayors, and the leaders of local institutions. On the other hand, the institutions of prefects constitute a formidable rival, constructing their own power centers in the sphere of local representatives of central power and influential company directors, serving as a kind of brake on local administration. The pyramid system, which is constructed vertically and consists of relatively autonomous units, results in a situation in which (at least formally) there are no obvious subservient-superior relations within the strict system of party and administrative hierarchies: the relations between the center of the hierarchy and regional or local actors are not completely asymmetric. Moreover, it is possible that the entangled web of local political and economic interests can lead to the construction of cores or pyramid tops stronger than those of the parallel segment within the power center of a given party. Such power inversions are possible when given parties or coalitions become opposition actors, and when the influence of locals—or that of local potentates or oligarchs (moguls)—can grow above the level of the center. In the wake of the expansion of vertical and communication schemes of Romanian party political corruption networks—and in accordance with the clientele model—money, business, income, tailor-made privileges, as well as (imagined or real) "protection" flow downward. Flowing upward are illegally organized kickback money as well as political support and loyalty measured in votes.[55] Functioning as a model, the *system* benefits the upper, central power level: however, it is not fully asymmetrical, as the horizontal alternating system of parties is accompanied by the operation of corruption's similar horizontal, yet simultaneously vertical, alternating system. The analysis of the vertical redistribution of political corruption in Romania reveals a truly interesting characteristic, whereby local "cells" are relatively independent. They are not fully at the mercy of the center (as in the Hun-

garian mafia state case, with its decision-making organ, its chief patron's court cabinet and its godfather, who stands above all), but instead enjoy a degree of autonomy. When a given party or power group representing a clientele enters "opposition," an inversion often takes place, and **for a time, the local fiefdoms command** the center. The Romanian patron-client system is visibly flexible and malleable in a vertical sense as well: the up-down poles invert from time to time,[56] and local oligarchs gain an advantage over party leadership or expropriate the center's themes and decision making. In the vertical dimension, we find actors who gain significant regional and local power vis-à-vis the center, who profit from the country's hesitant decentralization, such as county council presidents ("*baroni locali*," or local princes[57]), the mayors of important cities (county seats and municipalities),[58] as well as district representatives and senators, or bureaucrats appointed in the central and local apparatus. At the lower levels, these actors either construct (or commission the construction of) their own regional or local corrupt networks, or they diversify and fritter away the corrupt system, which can hardly be seen as unified to begin with.[59] These actors not only take steps—often quite successfully—against the center, with the goal of defending their own corrupt interests or unreasonably advantageous redistribution conditions: they also compete with one another, defending their territorial interests from other similar demands, and as such dividing the corruption market, serving as a good example of **"free market corruption."** At other times, however, they cooperate within certain issue areas, on interest-defense acts within parties, or in background interest-defense procedures.

2.1.1.4 Horizontal arrangements

Last but not least, there exist operational horizontal party and party-ruled administrative units which compete with one another, and whose efforts to build up hierarchical orders are essentially based territorially, on local pyramids of political power and economic interests. This is an interesting development, as relations between regions or between local parties can be significantly different than those characteristically found between party centers.[60] Should strong alliances form between parties that otherwise compete, or should a given party rule the entire political life of a certain area for an extended time (for instance, there are counties where the Social Democratic Party has been in power essentially since the regime change) then the given county or city, in all likelihood, will be led by a power center that operates in a mafia manner and is directed by a local oligarch (the best example of such is the poverty-stricken Vaslui county). Such local alliances then become capable of applying pressure on the development of central party relations, or opposing alliance-building or cooperation commands from the center, and, last but not least, revealing corruption affairs to blackmail the higher levels in the hierarchy.

2.1.2 Obstacles to the development of a single-pyramid patronal system

Militant and often manipulative anti-corruption campaigns in the political and public field frequently utilize moral arguments, and emphasize the presentation of plans based on such arguments to rein in corruption. However, the phenomenon's sociological dimension does not operate at a moral level at all. Far more significant is the unique political and administrative order, or the unique structuring of the field of public life. It is the legal and organizational background of institutions—including the divided executive power between the president and the prime minister, party pluralism and related competitive patronal networks, the formally democratic and proportional election system, the structure of administration, the system of checks and balances, civil society organizations and so forth—that obstructs the development of a single-center, mafia state-like, corruption system. In the following sections I present these structural, sociological and institutional components.

2.1.2.1 The semi-presidential system—divided executive power

Paradoxically, the constitutional inconsistency that makes it impossible to clarify the hierarchical relationship between the president and the government, or which lays down a semi-presidential system as the foundation of state administration (and which despite several attempts has not been changed through constitutional amendment), has had the perverse effect of obstructing the development of a single-pyramid corruption political center, or at least has not allowed the maintenance of one. In the system that has emerged, the president stands foremost above the CSAT and the most influential secret services (SRI, SIE), and uses his nomination powers to practice predominantly indirect, but sometimes direct and at other times only potential, control over the General Prosecutor and the highest levels of the courts. The prime minister has power over both central (government) and county administration (prefectures), supervisory authorities, and partially or wholly state-owned companies ("de-concentrated" units). The Office of the President and the government, given the regulations governing them and their situation and modes of operation, are not immune to becoming hubs of corruption networks. However, they are structurally competing with one another, and for this reason a single-pyramid power system cannot develop. They are the peaks of the two highest pyramids or patronal networks: should they use their power to construct and operate corruption networks and patron-client systems, then they have *a priori* modeled a power system with two pyramids.

2.1.2.2 Proportional election system
The development of a general single-center style of public corruption and the "mafiazation" of corrupt networks, which is to say, the monopolization of the national level, have been obstructed—until now effectively—not only by the semi-presidential system, but also by the political consequences of the proportional election system. Together with other regulations, this resulted in a situation where, since the change of regime, all Romanian electoral winners have been more or less compelled to form coalition governments.[61] Until the 2012 elections no government has enjoyed a two-thirds majority, enabling them to draft a new constitution (the government in power from 2012 to 2016 was established through a coalition, which quickly dissolved). For this reason, the chains of corruption close to the government (or governments) have never been able to embed themselves or solidify their power. Most often, it seemed that despite valiant anti-corruption rhetoric, which parties emphasized during their campaigns, the political class did not work to dissolve the system but instead—at almost all levels, from drafting laws and attacking crime-fighting organizations to filling clientele positions—**fought a fierce struggle against anti-corruption**. Members of parliament and senators quite often sought office to gain immunity from investigation and prosecution-court procedures,[62] and promises of protection also explained a large portion of the regular transfers of membership across parliamentary factions.

Political parties, especially when in opposition, often take up the mantle of fighting corruption and place it prominently in their policy platforms. However, these program points and militant anti-corruption promises are quickly forgotten, especially when taking on a governance role. At the same time, those parties and media outlets closely associated with parties dedicate themselves to exposing their "opponents" night and day, in accordance with the government-opposition dynamic. Party elites especially make use of television news channels to supposedly "uncover" the corruption of their opponents, usually using questionable sources or manipulated, distorted information. This leads to the establishment of a unique and silent balance within which the party-based division of corruption develops in accordance with election results. However, the balance has also meant that none of the power centers has had the opportunity to rule over the entire field and establish a power monopoly.

2.1.2.3 Checks and balances, the existence of liberal democracy

There is no doubt that numerous attempts have been made to destroy the separation of powers and mutual control in Romania—especially by the strongest power nodes, namely the president and the government. However, it is also clear that such efforts have consistently failed, and the formal roles of relatively independent legislative, executive and judicial branches, along with the independent media institutions—especially due to pressure from the EU and the USA—have not been successfully dismantled. The institutions, and especially the actors, of all branches of power are the subject of intense debates and multi-sided criticism. However, despite all revelations and corrupt operations, the system still formally exists. Moreover, the role of control is undamaged in the sense that no single-pyramid power system, which would publicly overstep the institutional bounds of checks and balances, has been able to take form. As such, even though the scale of corruption within systems is rather wide, the relations that have formed between them have created mutual control.

In other words, in its current situation Romania is walking the path of formally liberal democracy, despite several politicians having stated their aim to dismantle liberal democracy (especially through influencing media and dissolving its independence). There is no publicly stated goal of changing this system, as has happened elsewhere in the post-Soviet region, or explicitly in Hungary.

2.1.2.4 Actions by civil society and media, and the rule of the anti-corruption industry

An important characteristic of Romanian civil society and its operational NGOs is that they are not so much products of local society, nor deeply embedded in Romanian political life, but are instead intrinsically bound to global civil society and its institutional forms present in Romania. The local branch of Transparency International has become quite influential in the anti-corruption struggle, but Freedom House, the World Bank, the Expert Forum and Active Watch are also all highly functional.[63] These organizations are all part of the international anti-corruption industry and respond to the "corruption paradigm" which developed in the 1990s to address the challenges of the post-Cold War period and assist the integration of post-communist states into the global order.[64] For this reason, the definitions and anti-corruption procedures they use aim at this general goal. The global anti-corruption paradigm aims at aspects of global integration and attempts to spread developed procedures over an entire region. In contrast, a uniquely Romanian civil society trend has also become visible, one rooted much more deeply in local society than those mentioned above, established and led by the foremost Romanian expert on the issue, Alina Mungiu-Pippidi. As a result of the emergence of "Romania Curata" (RC) and its excellent media presence, the operation of its own website[65] and its generally successful PR, the organization effectively assists "real" anti-corruption activities, those reflecting local conditions, through indigenous awareness of how they function. At the same time, the organization and its staff introduce anti-corruption topics, prepare reports and so forth in other media channels, establishing an entire hub of anti-corruption media. This presence, through its consistency, and through, of course, cooperation with other present organizations, often emerges more effectively than all other active civil society movements in the field of political corruption, and scores at least partial victories in uncovering and beating back corruption.

The vertical and horizontal interconnections that characterize public corruption networks in Romania discussed above are often revealed by RC, which reports its hidden sides and points the attention of public opinion to the alternating system of operation mechanisms of corruption in various areas. Further uncovered is the existence of multi-centered pyramid power constructions in the background, along with their undesirable activities in practically every area.

Civil society organizations, with their weak backgrounds, are surprisingly capable of causing government crises and forcing the resignation of leading officials, including the prime minister, through their street demonstrations and movements. The President of the Republic referred to them and consultations with them during the establishment of the new technocratic government.[66]

2.2 Summary and further considerations

The general comparative framework of my analysis is "model-dependent realism" as outlined by Bálint Magyar, which, projected onto the post-communist mafia state in Hungary (and some other post-Soviet states, most notably Russia), provides a vital conceptual framework.[67] The post-communist mafia state model uses as a starting point the idea that the "system" and the "state," through certain unique conditions, become synonymous—with the most important factors being the history of their origin, the discretional operation of power (through a kind of continued de facto single-party system, or a two-thirds majority in Hungary's case), the existence of a single power center, the pyramid-like construction of power (in a top-down direction), the complete conquest of official institutions, and so on. That is to say that the Orbán (Fidesz-KDNP) system has conquered every corner of the state: the basis of the system is state capture, upon which mafia-like operations and networks are then constructed. According to this model, the capture of the state and its imprisonment serve the goal of constructing the mafia state or the "system," bringing into existence a new kind of state. The building of "illiberal democracy" at the same time fortifies the existence of the mafia state. In this equation, political entrepreneurship transforms into economic entrepreneurship, while elsewhere—such as the Romanian example—the various key economic actors (oligarchs or "moguls" with loose party affiliations) acquire disproportionally high political power and reach a level, at least in certain areas, where they capture the institutions of the state. There is a high degree of consciousness, consistency and planning in the Hungarian mafia state described by Bálint Magyar and his colleagues, which are characteristics impossible to find in the Romanian corrupt state. Entropy in regulations and institutional operation procedures is much higher in Romania, and the dissolution of the state is clear in many areas, while deregulation processes can be found in almost all sub-systems. Quite often there is no consistency in how the state works, or indeed paralyzes, in administration or in the execution of rules—a role in this is played not only by the alternating political system, but also by the fact that a number of laws and regulations were, thanks to "pressure from the West," simply transplanted into the Romanian system of regulations, but without execution systems, rules or apparatuses created alongside them. The 25 years of reprivatization-restitution regulations, still unsolved, serve as a good example.[68] It would be unwise to assume that behind the areas of land, forest or property restitution, there lies some consistent will and plan that reaches across mandates. It was not the political power sphere that established a dominant mafia state in these areas; instead, competing "mafias" conquered this area,[69] but naturally with various kinds of political and power assistance.

I analyze the phenomenon of public corruption—in accordance with the comparativism expressed in anthropology, or at times merely undeveloped comparativism—in a comparative manner. That is to say, I examine the degree to which the schemes and procedures, areas and modes, intensity, embeddedness, evolution and sidetracks, actors and victims, and loot redistribution networks of Romanian public corruption match the patterns of post-communist mafia states. And given that my hypothesis holds that the systematic nature of Romanian corruption, regarding its public law, social, political and even cultural and social consequences, appears not to match the given model, alongside homologies and typologies I place my emphasis on structural divergences between Hungarian and numerous other post-Soviet states and Romanian public corruption. The utilized analytic concept of public corruption is similar to the one used in modelling the post-communist mafia state, in the sense that it sees the primary criteria as not the economic-financial scale of corruption, nor its real and/or perceived extent, but the severity of its political consequences, its hollowing effect on democracy, or its support for introducing an autocratic system. The Hungarian model, as exemplified by the Hungarian prime minister's public defense of the illiberal state and illiberal democracy, is a different scheme, given that no political actors in Romania have publicly made similar programmatic claims.

The idealized model of Western liberal democracies—as a basis for comparison used in contrast to transition theories—claims that the **patronal system** is a characteristic of political power in the states of the post-Soviet region, which is not only a political science term, but a sociological term as well. Patronalism concerns that social balance in which "the economic efforts of individuals are organized around personal transactions and concrete rewards, and not primarily around abstract, impersonal principles like ideological convictions or categorizations, which many people internalize," and which create social balance.[70] This idea is very similar to that expressed by Alina Mungiu-Pippidi concerning the Romanian corruption system.[71] Society is a "status society" in which regular people do not even expect the state to deal with citizens in a general way, with equal treatment and a system of regulations that holds for all. Instead they expect individuals to be treated, served, favored, or in contrast disfavored, according to their social position by the administration representing power and/or the state. The relative balance created as such is threatened not by the fact and operation of corruption; instead, the threat lies in situations in which the conduct of those in power, such as public officers, diverges from the informal set of societal customs, rules, and social expectations. In this sense the Romanian political field is typically a **patronal system**, but as noted above, it functions through **a multi-pyramid patronal system with not one but several centers**. The balance of corrupt institutions constructed on preferential procedures and promoting personal prerogatives is created by those working in public administration, and, moreover, is a result of their personal procedures. When I characterized corruption as a unique type of (predominantly) experiential knowledge, I was inferring that, through its use, bureaucrats working in the administration would be able (or not) to establish, manage, legitimate, but most importantly recreate balanced situations appropriate to their status. This mode of procedures and operations is unique to public corruption defined as a composite phenomenon, despite the fact that at the social level it is accepted that trust in power and bureaucratic institutions is rather low.[72] The personal activity of politicians and bureaucrats, like the balance-creating skills that contradict the general goals of institutions, appreciate enormously: people do not believe in institutions, but again and again believe corrupt and manipulative politicians, whom they regularly re-elect.

Political-public corruption in Hungary, manifest in the post-communist mafia state, does not (regularly) connect to petty corruption or the everyday world of the culture of corruption, but instead remains in the "political overworld" of the clientele elite, which is initiated and accepted by members of the family as a type of political inclusion. In this sense, **Hungarian society is at its roots is less of a patronal system than Romanian society** (or the other post-Soviet societies). The Hungarian mafia state does not build upon an existing patron-client system, but for the most part creates one itself. In the political overworld, however, corruption, the mafia state, the development of the new ownership stratum, the stuffing of national oligarchs, and so on, become political programs, or even the direct *raison d'être* of the state. As such, the prime minister and the government (with all its offices, including the no-longer independent National Bank), the Parliament it controls, as well as the central prosecutor's office and other state functions, become parts of the closed overworld. Its components and beneficiaries, or later—and increasingly frequently—its victims, are the class of poligarchs and oligarchs, who cooperate with the government and together co-opt the bureaucrats who carry out corruption affairs, becoming the actors of organizational corruption,[73] who are paid but not initiated into the inner secrets of the corruption machinery.

From here, the corrupt overworld integrates the elite of the post-communist mafia state into another network system, namely the godfather overworld, while for the other parts of society the generally known "subject world," where small-scale corruption is sought out and punished, remains in place, although another set of rules holds for the initiated. It is a hybrid system, in which regular life adheres to regular rules regarding crime (including white-collar crime) and corruption, and the combined fight against them. But the mafia overworld is removed from the sphere of regular rules, from crime fighting and judicial procedures, or its activities are "made legal" or papered over through amendments to laws, whether in advance or after the fact. The Hungarian post-communist mafia state's "family," or patron-client system, has a cover-up ideology that aims at delivering a "calling," and creating a new "national" oligarchy: this, ultimately, is what supposed to justify its privileges. The legitimacy of Orbán's corrupt system, or its very explanation, is expressed most clearly by one of the government's main ideologues, András Lánczi, when he states: "There is a system that we may criticize as being corrupt, but I state that this is the execution of a political vision," or when he considers that "corruption is acceptable if it serves a clientele change according to political will."[74]

In contrast, Romanian public corruption is organically connected to traditional forms, to the manifestations of the social culture of everyday corruption. The political enclaves it engenders, including the circles of those protected by it, are much more mosaic-like, layered and more dynamic than the more centralized Hungarian system, and reach across both party affiliations and ideologies. At the same time, for the aforementioned reasons, it is incapable of becoming a single-centered, single-pyramid power system. This cannot be explained by any deep commitment to moral values, nor by a lack of political will. Instead, this is a result of the unique structure of both the Romanian political/power field and of society, which prevented the formation of a single party-type "presidential party," one that could ultimately dominate parliament, the political field, and, essentially, party coalitions. The party patronage system gave competing parties an interest in exposing one another when one side believes that the other tries to gain an unfair share in the informal, secret but tacit redistribution of corruption loot. Conflicts between the center and the countryside (counties, large cities), and the unique interweaving of interests within regions color the vertical dynamic of political competition; relations are for the most part not asymmetric, and from time to time are (potentially) inverted, when the region controls the center. Horizontal political competition (and within the framework of such, among other things, ethnic-based politics) creates territorial inclusion, within which corruption interests are homogenized, or unique competition is created at the borders of the regions.

Romanian corruption networks—at least according to proclaimed principles—have no central, regional or local defenders. All actors proclaim anti-corruption policies, but in practice, in their own territories and with their own tools, they remain the maintainers, re-creators, beneficiaries and even the victims of the corrupt system. This, however, distinguishes the Romanian corruption model from that experienced in today's Hungary.

The typological analysis within a more concrete comparative procedure results in one key observation. In Romania, public corruption is widespread, and the criteria of state capture have been fulfilled in numerous areas, including the area of customs and border control, for which reason the country has not been accepted into the Schengen zone.[75] Nevertheless, it does not fulfill the conditions for a single-pyramid, post-communist mafia state. This is because on the one hand, it contains a minimum of expressed mutualities in lawlessness, while on the other it is not directed from a center. Staying with our example, businesspeople benefit from corruption in the customs field, as by paying kickbacks they avoid paying more expensive customs tariffs. The generalized kickback system is not fully formed, given that transporters can decide to pay the full tariff, even if this results in greater expenses, time, and waiting in line. Then, the unit of exchange in public corruption is not kickback money, but instead the potential to profiteer vis-à-vis the state, the utilization of monopolies tied to status, or the purchase and acquisition of preferential treatment. The universal currency is "influence," which exists and is expressed in a hierarchical system: for instance, in the case of customs officers and border guards, this hierarchy is manifest first in the cost of acquiring the office, then in the distribution of attained bribes, but also in the manner through which officers apply charges to clients according to their status.

Beyond the accessible "loot" of customs agents and border patrol stands the prerogative of every regime in accordance with the alternating party system, which uses loot as a resource for its own parties and clients. This same procedure exists in other offices as well, and when changes occur in political power, then the circle of beneficiaries changes as well, along with the redistribution system. As such, in the end, the loot-acquiring elite—including officials, political actors, local kingpins, businesspeople— profits from a more general corruption. The latest studies and accusations of the DNA have had a "politically balanced" nature, with a homogeneous distribution to match various party affiliations,[76] showing that risk too is distributed, that not everything is under the sphere of one "godfather," and the members of no one political camp are singled out for exposure or "getting away with it."

Above, I mentioned that as a result of the proportional election system, not only did an all-powerful two-thirds majority never develop in Romania over the past 25 years, but moreover, the dissolution of the separation of powers and the system of checks and balances never entered the political agenda (although something like this was suggested when ex-President Băsescu and his team were suspended in 2012). Further, as a result of the semi-presidential system, the head of state and the head of government controlled the activities of corrupt groups developed around one or the other power pole. At the same time, an unequivocal hierarchy did not develop between the center and the regions or important municipal leaders, all the less so as changes in parliamentary power relations could upset the established status quo. In reality, public corruption is not divided among two classes embedded in two hierarchies—namely the godfather and his adopted family, the organized overworld, the patrons of the corrupt system and so forth, against all the others, who stand outside the system and find themselves at the mercy of superiors and vassals. Instead, it is comprised of the horizontal competition between teams within various statuses, or the conflict for the acquisition of status (bribes, personal obligations, and so on, all means which can lead to the acquisition of influence, or favorable status, for those who aim to enter the corrupt system). The Romanian corruption field is complex and composed of multiple levels. It is built upon the complicated division of corruption hierarchies, and has several centers. At the same time, the system contains a high level of entropy, given that influence, which everyone dreams of attaining, is in itself malleable. Often the "poetics of corruption" depend only on impressions and misunderstandings. The real use (and abuse) of merely imagined power-influence is not at all a rare phenomenon. The system has an allegorical, symbolic feature that in the case of the post-communist mafia state is much more raw, unequivocal and brutal, given that it is based on generalized intimidation and fear. In the case of competing corrupt subsystems, however, intimidation is not universal. One influence-holder, oligarch or mogul can be turned against another, and the competition between them—at least in principle—can have two outcomes: most everyone strives to seek out an oligarch (a patron, mogul or higher contact) for themselves, but the market of influence is quite open and dynamic.

The control of the Romanian multi-centered corruption system, or the attempt to decrease the side-effects of corruption, grants a different set of roles to challengers than is the case for those standing up to Orbán's post-communist mafia state. In the latter, the state and the system become unified—one of the key aims of the Fidesz-KDNP coalition, which, often enjoying the advantage offered by its two-thirds majority, is investing all its efforts in attaining this goal, admittedly quite successfully, with hardly any opposition—while in the Romanian system, the development of anti-corruption policies pose a different challenge, given the relative lack of structure, lower degree of centralization, and larger entropy factor in Romania, all within the framework of an alternating political power situation.

The Hungarian mafia state is a unique phenomenon in the region; it is "system specific" and made visible principally by the proclaimed "Eastern opening," which does not at all apply to Romania. The only states that belong in a similar category to Hungary are a significant portion of post-Soviet states, along with certain dictatorships in Asia (as we know from Orbán's speech in Tusnád in the summer of 2014).[77] The model of Romanian public corruption is better grouped with other states in the region; primarily Bulgaria, but also states further to the west, such as Slovakia, with its system of corruption that is similar in type, if not in scale. As outlined above, public corruption in Romania largely matches the "global corruption paradigm." However, it also has a number of different characteristics that are typical of post-communist states. A review of regional characteristics not only points our attention to the need to modify the global corruption model, but also buries the notion of the universal globalized version.[78] The model is typically South-East European, even though it is a pervasive phenomenon that has entwined every bracket of society, and as such, diverges from the newly constructed Orbán regime, the model of the Hungarian mafia state.[79] Part of the essence of the issue is that the Hungarian state mafia is almost monophonic, "speaking the language of the System of National Cooperation," which is in reality the voice of Viktor Orbán. The Romanian system is, however, polyphonic, with no uniform voice. This is true despite the fact that the right-wing elite of the Hungarian minority in Romania views, and projects as nationalism, all voices heard in the Romanian political field. In contrast to the Hungarian ethno-nationalist, Christian right-wing discourses, Romanian nationalism nowadays tends toward an indirect type of "laissez-faire" nationalism, with particularly powerless parliamentary representation never approaching positions of power.[80]

Should the Hungarian mafia state appear destructible, exclusively, through a "regime change"—at least in theory—the Romanian corruption system appears tough and more difficult to topple, even though it is less imposing. Modifying the system of Romanian corruption primarily requires **a cultural change**,[81] which is a slower and more all-encompassing process. Mungiu-Pippidi (whose attempt to characterize societies in regards to their social-political system, based upon universalism and particularism and mixing the public and private spheres or mixing their borders, I happily accept) names the phenomenon an "anti-particularism revolution," which is more than an alternating political system, but not a real regime change, nor a literal social-political revolution. It is possible that the initiated processes will provide an opening for such deep-reaching political changes, which can show that no one is above the law, and can popularize a kind of universalism whereby "everyone is equal in the eyes of the law." However, it is also clear that the rolling back and control of corruption cannot be executed through legal procedures alone. Mungiu-Pippidi has dedicated an entire book to proving that those states which come up with complex, and at the same time positive, harmonized answers are the ones that succeed in fighting back against corruption, and they mostly aimed at forms characteristic of their own countries, with adequate means, not following anti-corruption policies forced upon them from outside. Successful anti-corruption policies concurrently aim to reduce popular dependence on the vulnerable public administration, economic openness, reducing overarching bureaucracy, eliminating the informal economy, simplifying legal regulations, making the entire budget transparent and accountable, putting an end to all types of monopolies, and establishing stringent supervision through the media and civil society. In contrast, in today's Romania we see only the efforts of crime-fighting organizations, which in themselves stand no chance at controlling corruption, and further weaken the credibility of procedures through poorly communicated statements via media corruption.

Notes

1. See, Bálint Magyar, *Post-Communist Mafia State: The Case of Hungary* (Budapest–New York: Central European University Press and Noran Libro, 2016) and Bálint Magyar and Júlia Vásárhelyi, eds., *Twenty-Five Sides of a Post-Communist Mafia State* (Budapest–New York: Central European University Press and Noran Libro, 2017).
2. Henry E. Hale, *Patronal Politics: Eurasian Politics Dynamics in Comparative Perspective* (New York: Cambridge University Press, 2015).
3. Filippo M. Zerilli, "Jucînd (cu) mita, imagini etnografice ale corupției în România," in *Cercetarea antropologica în România: Perspective istorice si etnografice*, ed., Filippo Zerilli and Giovanni Pizza (Cluj-Napoca: Editura Clusium, 2004); A. Zoltán Bíró, "Mindennapi ellenfelünk, a rend: Esettanulmány a korrupció társadalmi hátteréről," in *Írások a korrupcióról*, ed. Csaba Gombár (Budapest: Helikon-Korridor, 1998).
4. Barney G. Glaser and Anselm L. Strauss, *The Discovery of Grounded Theory: Strategies for Qualitative Research* (New Brunswick, NJ: Aldine Transaction, 1967).
5. George E. Marcus, "Ethnography in/of the World System: The Emergence of Multi-Sited Ethnography," *Annual Review of Anthropology* 24 (1995): 95–117.
6. David L. Altheide, *Qualitative Media Analysis* (New York: Sage Publications, 1996).
7. Marc Abeles, *Az állam antropológiája* (Budapest: Századvég Kiadó, 2007), 12.
8. Violetta Zentai, ed. *Politikai antropológia* (Budapest: Osiris Kiadó, 1997), 13.
9. Akhil Gupta, "Narrating the State of Corruption," in *Corruption: Anthropological Perspectives*, ed. Dieter Haller and Chris Shore (London: Pluto Press, 2005).
10. Abner Cohen, "Political Anthropology: The Analysis of the Symbolism of Power Relations," *Man* 4, no. 2 (June 1969): 215–35.
11. The concept goes beyond the expression "'grand' corruption" as used by Susan Rose-Ackerman, which implies a focus not on "minor" payoffs, kickback and bribery exchange events, but on corruption appearing at the governmental-power level that reaches decision-making, legislative work and governmental activity—at all levels—that infects and "rots" the institutions of democracy, producing and reinforcing the culture of corruption. Susan Rose-Ackerman, "Democracy and 'grand' corruption," *International Social Science Journal* 48, no. 149 (1996): 365–80.
12. LaPalombara, Joseph, "Structural and Institutional Aspects of Corruption," *Social Research* 61 (1994): 325–50; András Sajó, "A jogállam és az ő megrontása," *Beszélő* 3, nos. 7–8 (1998): 39–56, http://beszelo.c3.hu/cikkek/a-jogallam-es-az-o-megrontasa, accessed Sep. 27, 2017.

13 Gerhard Anders and Monique Nuijten, "Corruption and the Secret Law: An Introduction," in *Corruption and the Secret of Law: A Legal Anthropological Perspective*, ed. Monique Nuijten and Gerhard Anders (New York: Ashgate, 2007), 1–25
14 Over the past 25 years the Romanian party and election system have been characterized by regulations of party and campaign financing that do not provide space for accountability and transparency. One of the consequences of this is that "corruption done for loyalty and party faith" has become a widespread phenomenon. This is so much the case that those who are "slick" in the interest of parties can feel they are protected in corruption cases carried out in the interest of the party and not necessarily for private profiteering reasons. The salaries for (especially young) public servants (which for beginner doctors, teachers or clerks is near the minimum wage, a mere 250 Euro per month, in spite of recent rises) have brought to the fore "corruption committed for organizational interests." Sajó, "A jogállam és az ő megrontása." The regulations for campaign financing only became stricter and more transparent beginning with the elections of 2016.
15 Alina Mungiu-Pippidi, "Corruption: Diagnosis and Treatment," *Journal of Democracy* 17, no. 3 (2006): 86–100.
16 Rose-Ackerman, "Democracy and 'grand' corruption"; Rasma Karklins, "Typology of Post-Communist Corruption," *Problems of Post-Communism* 49, no. 4 (July/August 2002): 22–32.
17 I use the term in the same sense as for composite materials, implying that complexity increases as things of various structures, characteristics, natures and dynamics are connected, while the combination of various things mutually support or fortify one another. The dictionary claims the following about composite materials: "Composite materials, or composites for short, are complex materials that are built on the material combination at macro, micro or nano levels of two or more differently structured materials."
18 Steven Sampson, "Integrity Warriors: Global Morality and the Anti-Corruption Movement in the Balkans," in *Corruption: Anthropological Perspectives*, edited by Dieter Haller and Chris Shore (London: Pluto Press, 2005), 103–31.
19 Erving Goffman, *Frame Analysis: An Essay on the Organization of Experience* (Boston: Northeastern University Press, 1986), 10–11. First published in 1974.
20 Ibid., 21
21 Karklins, "Typology of Post-Communist Corruption."
22 Mara Mendes effectively characterized the modes and dangers of media corruption in her analysis of early 2013, which was published on the Transparency International website. See Mara Mendes, "Overview of corruption in the media in developing countries," *Transparency International* 368 (2013), http://www.u4.no/publications/overview-of-corruption-in-the-media-in-developing-countries/. Of the areas she lists, the most relevant to the Romanian media world is that which holds that it is mostly due to the ownership background of the largest media trusts that corruption arises, given that owners are oligarchs (or using the term of former President Băsescu, "media moguls") who use their extraordinary media influence in the interests of acquiring economic advantages (for instance, through blackmail) and political manipulation. Many among them were accused

or sentenced to prison (Sorin Ovidiu Vântu of Realitatea TV, Dan Diaconescu of OTV, Dan Voiculescu of Antena TV, and Adrian Sârbu of ProTV).

23 Mendes, "Overview of corruption in the media."
24 Magyar, *Post-Communist Mafia State*, 1. For the original concept, see Stephen Hawking and Leonard Mlodinow, *The Grand Design* (New York: Bantam Books, 2010), 42.
25 Hale, *Patronal Politics*, 6.
26 Max Weber, *Economy and Society: An Outline of Interpretive Sociology*, ed. Guenther Roth and Claus Wittich (Berkeley: University of California Press, 1978).
27 A media corruption phenomenon, one which in all likelihood is widespread, was brought to the public's attention—for a mere three days, as usual—by the "case" of the PR director of the Democratic Alliance of Hungarians in Romania, who was fictitiously employed at the state radio for an extraordinarily high salary. This is a good example of not only corruption in public media but of the party patronage system as well (see Nándor László Magyari, "Alvilági klánok tagjaival táncoló," http://systemcritic.blogspot.ro/2014/06/alvilagi-klanok-tagjaival-tancolo.html) in which the party "rewards" clients with high paying but fictitious state jobs. The case going public (after which there were no consequences, beyond a resignation) offers insight into the corrupt system in state media, and as such, it is unlikely to be an isolated incident (see Nándor László Magyari, "Médiakorrupció," http://systemcritic.blogspot.ro/2015/04/mediakorrupcio.html). It should be noted that after the scandal, the party once again placed its PR person in a high media authority position for a year.
28 The biggest catch, or at least initiated procedure, launched by the DNA was the so-called Microsoft licensing corruption scandal, in which several former ministers, presidential advisors, oligarchs, local "little kings" and former tennis stars were accused (see "Microsoft-ügy: öt volt miniszter esetében indulhat meg az eljárás," http://itthon.transindex.ro/?hir=37522). The procedure, by modifying preliminary arrest to house arrest—apparently—came off the agenda. It is interesting that the prosecution likely counted on the testimonies of the co-accused against one another, but the case was typical in the sense that who among those involved reported the crime is unknown, as is the true direction of the procedure. The most well-known accused are Elena Udrea and her ex-husband, Dorin Cocos, who were both ex-president Băsescu's "people." They both played the role of "stooges" in the affair, all the vectors of which point to the ex-president and his party, but the investigation has not continued, and uncertainty surrounding the case implies a cover up.
29 Often interrogations and preliminary detentions and accusations are based on dossiers with rather weak evidence (often based on phone taps or the confessions of suspected co-criminals). The former Prime Minister Viktor Ponta is subject to just such an old and weakly founded case. In other instances, the prosecutor's leaks indicate more crimes and bigger damage than is entailed in the case at hand. This raises the suspicion of political influence, as evidenced in the procedure against Róbert Ráduly, the former mayor of Miercurea Ciuc.
30 For a decade this has been a central topic, not only in political battles but in public discourse as well. Only in the last year or year and a half—following the public

actions of the DNA—has it taken on a form and visage, with those charged with corruption named, at least on the television screen.

[31] The DNA image appearing in the media brings up mainly affairs indicating partiality, politically motivated cases and procedures, and instances when cases were covered up or inexplicably dragged out or delayed. It is difficult to pass judgment on this issue, and the same holds for the question of whether the prosecutor is truly independent—and being familiar with this institutional system independence would be a rather remarkable or standalone situation (see the case of the attorney dealing with organized crime (DIICOT) where the director was an accused in several corruption cases: Biro Attila, "Şefa DIICOT, Alina Bica, reținută de DNA într-un dosar de corupție cu un prejudiciu de 62 milioane euro," http://www.gandul.info/stiri/sefa-diicot-alina-bica-retinuta-de-dna-intr-un-dosarde-coruptie-cu-un-prejudiciu-de-62-milioane-euro-13608109)—or based on available information and data the question is unanswerable. In any case, it is not only political actors (often the accused themselves) but analysts too who assume that the DNA is itself part of the corrupt system, and subject to its political influence, pressure, and expectations.

[32] Nándor László Magyari, "A magyar polip természete," *Beszélő*, last modified Nov. 19, 2013, http://beszelo.c3.hu/onlinecikk/a-magyar-polip-termeszete; idem, "A közéleti korrupció román modellje," in *Magyar polip: A posztkommunista maffiaállam 3*, ed. Bálint Magyar and Júlia Vásárhelyi (Budapest: Noran Libro Kiadó, 2015), 521–47.

[33] In an interview, Laura Codruta Kövesi, the leading prosecutor of the DNA, reported on the numerical "results" of the institution she leads, and stated that the institution had examined 7000 cases since 2002, with more researched every year. In 2014 decisions were passed in more than 1100 corruption cases, and in 2015 this number reached 1500 (See "Hétezer ügy: Egy erős ember Sepsiszentgyörgyről," https://mno.hu/hetvegimagazin/hetezer-ugy-1282361).

[34] Peter H. Frank and Roxana-Maria Gaina, "Political Corruption in Romania: The DNA Database," last modified Nov. 27, 2014, http://www.peterhfrank.com/political-corruption-in-romania-the-dna-database/.

[35] I emphasize that I do not wish to pass judgment on the corruption cases currently under trial (I am not competent to do so from a legal perspective), and I view indictments and court opinions, i.e., legal texts and discourses, as sociological statements of fact or as "data," or information that assists in analysis and interpretation, independent of legal content or verification of their "truth-untruth" content. If I infer judgment in cases, then I am conveying "public judgment" or the dominant opinion that emerges in political and media discourse.

[36] The indictments of entrepreneurs "close to those in power," ex-ministers, county council presidents and mayors of large cities who ended up in preliminary detainment or accused indicate that in most (or all?) large-scale public procurement procedures, successful applicants mandatorily paid an "obulus" of varying proportions to private accounts or party coffers. The largest such uncovered economic-political corruption affair was the Microsoft case (which was significant enough to merit its own Wikipedia page), in the framework of which large scale cheating and money laundering took place through purchasing software. For several years,

through the Ministry of Education, most all members of the government were continuously involved. The key accused are an ex-minister, Elena Udrea, and her husband Dorin Cocos, both of whom were under Băsescu's wing, and whom we can view with increasing certainty as the ex-president's primary stooges.

37 The two key parties, which tend to exchange one another in government, are not what they claim to be. The PSD is deeply integrated (Iliescu remains the party's honorary president) and built on the power of local power brokers. It is everything but not a social democratic party, as its policies are neoliberal and pro-*nouveau riche*, inconsistent, and serve the interests of small groups. Further, the members of the recently dissolved USL (Social and Liberal Union) party coalition follow strongly heterodox policies. The "New PNL" ("New" National Liberal Party) is controversial and not at all liberal, but is a populist/popular partly confused over its political philosophy. The third force is the ethnically organized Democratic Alliance of Hungarians in Romania (RMDSZ in Hungarian, DAHR in English), which does not accept any ideology but which ethnicizes politics. Ideology-free parties are marked by, on one hand, a move toward people's party features, attempting to address all, while on the other hand they are typically loot-acquiring parties, wholly characterized by "party patronage" based on distributing available public life functions and taking advantage of such. See Petr Kopecký and Gerardo Scherlis, "Party Patronage in Contemporary Europe," *European Review* 16, no. 3 (2008): 355–71.

38 Justice organizations are formally independent, although there are a number of corrupt prosecutors and judges (many have stood accused, or have been found guilty of corruption, including, among others, the chief prosecutor of the anti-organized crime prosecutor's office [DIICOT], Alina Bica); the constitutional court is relatively independent, although the actions of the author of the "supplementary document" concerning Băsescu's suspension is being investigated. But what is unique is that the Euro-Atlantic allies, in their own way, are making themselves heard in politics concerning corruption. The embassies of foreign countries (the USA first among them) are taken seriously by most all Romanian governments, and their monitions are accepted. As such, these serve as a kind of balance, or a way of preventing assumed "slippages."

39 Filippo M. Zerilli, "Corruption, Property, Restitution and Romanianness," in *Corruption: Anthropological Perspectives*, ed. Dieter Haller and Chris Shore (London: Pluto Press, 2005).

40 Achille Mbembe, *On the Postcolony* (Berkeley: University of California Press, 2001).

41 Akhil Gupta, "Blurred Boundaries: The Discourse of Corruption, the Culture of Politics, and the Imagined State,." *American Ethnologist* 22, no. 2 (1995): 376.

42 Michael Herzfeld, *Cultural intimacy: Social Poetics in the Nation-State* (Routledge, New York, 1997).

43 Arnold J. Heidenheimer and Michael Johnston, eds., *Political Corruption: Concepts and Contexts* (New Brunswick, NJ: Transaction Publishers, 2002).

44 This expression originated in the Roma underworld and "manele" music, before entering the areas of journalism and ultimately everyday discourse. For the best analysis of the term, based on a study of a "ghetto" in Bucharest, see (Pulay 2012).

45 Mungiu-Pippidi, "Corruption," 88.
46 Mihály Szívós, "Tudományos, tapasztalati és szakértői tudás, valamint a szakpolitika és tudásgazdálkodás viszonya Kelet-Közép-Európában," in *Tudás és politika. A közpolitika-alkotás gyakorlata*, ed. Eszter Berényi, Gábor Erőss, and Eszter Neumann (Budapest: L'Harmattan, 2013), 23–61.
47 Michel Foucault, "A 'kormányozhatóság'," in *A fantasztikus könyvtár: Válogatott tanulmányok, interjúk és előadások* (Budapest: Pallas Stúdió-Attraktor Kft., 1998), 106–23.
48 The personal worth of the director, who wasn't building any roads, is estimated at three hundred million Euro (http://www.digi24.ro/Stiri/Digi24/Actualitate/Stiri/Alin+Goga+director+suspendat+CNADNR+receptie+lucrari). The situation of the director of the state railway company, which went bankrupt, is similar. He is in prison, after having been extradited from Florida following a long legal procedure (http://www.dcnews.ro/mihai-necolaiciuc-condamnat-la-10-anide-inchisoare-pentru-devalizarea-cfr_476904.html/). While paying kickbacks to corrupt networks can help one move up on the waiting list for organ transplants, often seemingly simple, and in all senses legal, affairs cannot be managed when the mood or especially the interests of the "boss" do not allow for it.
49 The period of the Iliescu presidency was marked by antagonism between the president and the government, the most extreme case being the conflict with Prime Minister Petre Roman. In its aftermath, President Iliescu was a participant in, and initiator of, the forceful toppling of the government and the firing of the prime minister. This became even more evident during the so-called Băsescu era, given that the "playful president" principle he announced had a goal of spreading the power of the president at all cost (in a similar manner to Viktor Orbán) in the interest of rising above the power of the prime minister and the government. The new president, Johannis Klaus, is in many ways following in these footsteps.
50 The CSAT (Consiliul Suprem de Aparare a Tarii) functions under the auspices of the President's Office, fundamentally aiming at harmonizing security policy interventions. It is led by the President of the Republic, while its deputy leader is the prime minister. But thanks to confusion in constitutional regulation at its foundations, it is one of the most public forums of the entangled executive powers of the president and prime minister. The ex-president—for all intents and purposes—used the operations of the authority to spread his own power, and introduced topics in the Council which were an attempt to force his own political ambitions on the government (education, health care reform, media regulation, etc.). At a given moment he tried to pass the reigning in of the media by presenting the media as a "factor equaling a security risk" in the framework of a strategy for national security.
51 Former Prime Minister Adrian Năstase was found guilty in two corruption cases, and has finished serving his sentence for the first (http://www.mediafax.ro/social/adrian-nastase-condamnat-definitiv-la-4-ani-de-inchisoare-cu-executare-in-dosarul-zambaccian-dana-nastase-3-ani-cu-suspendare-11855245). During his mandate, ex-president Băsescu was twice suspended by Parliament while accused of corruption and abuse of power—most recently in 2012, when, in the

framework of a referendum, nearly 8.5 million voters voted against him, yet he managed to retain his office through a great deal of legal and statistical manipulation. At the same time, there were nearly eighty investigations into him: for a few of these, the DNA and the Attorney General have submitted official indictments.

52 The former president of Romania was entirely incapable of managing political differences through compromise. Following his election, he almost immediately turned against his fellow party member Călin Popescu-Tăriceanu, who became prime minister. The "war among palaces" continued through the entire liberal mandate, with each side alternately gaining a foothold over the other. When Băsescu's nominee Emil Boc became prime minister (despite being voted against by Parliament on several occasions), it was for all intents and purposes the president who dominated the government. This situation remained in place during the short governance of Mihai Răzvan Ungureanu. The president was so entrenched in power that he himself announced the draconian cutbacks of May 2010, when the salaries of public servants were slashed by 25%. The conflict between the president and prime minister resumed after the election victory of the PSD-PNL (USL, the Social-Liberal Union) in 2012, under the leadership of Prime Minister Victor Ponta, and continued after the PNL left the coalition.

53 Kopecký and Scherlis, "Party Patronage in Contemporary Europe."

54 This is not to be confused with the category of patronal politics formulated by Henry E. Hale and used below, which concerns not party organization, but the system personalizing the entire political field to "ensure balance." Hale, *Patronal Politics*.

55 Abeles, *Az állam antropológiája*, 116–21.

56 The phenomenon is national, and is characteristic foremost of the Social Democratic Party, the current leader of which is Liviu Dragnea, a "local kingpin" who has been sentenced for corruption. The county council presidents of Bacau and Constanta also attained such overextended power, as did the mayors of Oradea, Craiova and Brașov. I will illustrate this again through the case of the Hungarian political field in Romania, where the political weight, decision-influencing and interest-defense capabilities of the county council presidents of Harghita and Kovasna, along with the mayors of the two urban centers of the "Szekler counties" (of whom Harghita council president Csaba Borboly and Miercurea Ciuc mayor Róbert Ráduly have come into the crosshairs of the anti-corruption prosecutor's office) grows significantly when the Democratic Alliance of Hungarians in Romania (DAHR) is in opposition. Their separate politics often is a source of confusion in the alliance, and brings to the fore the hidden antagonism between the Szekler lands and the rest of Transylvania (see http://systemcritic.blogspot.ro/2012/12/az-utolso-pecset-es-budos-nagy-pofonok.html), while they succeeded in turning the DAHR into an ally of the Hungarian government and making the autonomy of the Szekler lands a central topic.

57 Characteristically, of the forty-two elected county council presidents, more than half today have been accused of or sentenced for corruption, with their cases being in various phases. It is no coincidence that many of them stood for re-election and succeeded in winning new mandates, given that party presidents cannot carry out their interests vis-à-vis the county council presidents.

58 Like the county council presidents, among the mayors of county centers, procedures have been initiated, or guilt has been established, against 24 of them. The most well-known of these are: Sorin Oprescu, Bucharest's independent mayor; Marean Vanghelie and Andrei Chiliman, district mayors; Radu Mazăre, the resigned mayor of Constanța; Gheorghe Nichita, the socialist mayor of Iași; Sorin Apostu, the former mayor of Cluj Napoca, who is currently serving time in prison; and George Scripcaru, the mayor of Brașov, just to mention the most important figures. The majority of accused mayors—including the mayor of Baia Mare, who was in pre-trial detention—won new mandates in elections and are now in office or awaiting their swearing in (see https://www.scribd.com/doc/289567033/Inițiativa-Romania-listă-politicieni-penali).

59 During election campaigns, when parties corralled together, or when in party finance local and central threads converged, local and central funds were often collected jointly. The former prime minister and social democrat leader Adrian Năstase was found guilty in a party finance affair, and is the highest-ranking politician to be indicted yet.

60 A well-known and oft-criticized phenomenon is the "secret alliance" between right and left parties in Cluj Napoca, a kind of agreement not to attack one another, which overrides conflicts that occur in the center. Such ad hoc Romanian party alliances also function in Târgu Mureș, more or less on an ethnic basis, where there has been a long-standing effort to block the election of a Hungarian mayor. Another such phenomenon, one that restructures political relations and county and municipal political fields, is found in the behavior of the DAHR, which, following this year's municipal elections, formed alliances with right-wing Romanian parties in some places and left-wing Romanian parties in others, thus establishing majorities in county or municipal councils, accessing functions and so forth.

61 Over the past 25 years, government coalitions in Romania have never been stable, with their construction often changing, parties leaving and re-entering, and offering one another extra-governmental support in parliament, both formally and informally. In terms of public corruption, however, coalitions have been stabilizing factors, with the distribution of loot, until recently, flowing unobstructed: the coalition partners distribute the "profit" of corruption in accordance with their political-election result weight, and as such every political formation (with perhaps the significant exception of the Greater Romania Party, which has never been in a governing position) has been a beneficiary of the corrupt system.

62 The issue of parliamentary immunity has sparked heated debates. During the run-up to the 2014 presidential election, the cutting back or liquidation of said immunity was one of the key points of Klaus Iohannis' governance platform. Immunity has, however, remained in place, and it is often capable of serving as a political obstacle to the actions of prosecutors and courts vis-à-vis certain politicians. It would be difficult to list those parliamentary representatives, senators and ministers whose immunity the prosecution unsuccessfully asked to have suspended. Parliament voted in favor of investigations or even pre-trial detention of many of them (trustworthy statistics hold that of all representa-

tives and senators, almost thirty percent have ultimately been involved in such corruption cases). There are at least three infamous Hungarian-Romanian examples of the obstruction of court procedures. One concerns former senator Gergely Olosz, who quite clearly stood for election in the hope of winning immunity. He has since been found guilty of corruption in the first instance (further, his case has been dragging on for no apparent reason at the level of appeal). Another instance is the case of Attila Markó, whose "fellows in fate" have tried to obstruct his case's investigation and his arrest. He finally "fled" to Hungary to escape the accusations of corruption the ANRP likely has against him (which are not to be confused with the case of the Mikó trial). The most public attempt to hide corruption, protect the accused and obstruct the work of the prosecutor in parliament was the case of representative László Borbély and senator Varujan Vosganian. The DNA twice tried to suspend their parliamentary immunities, but to no avail.

63 For the latter two, see www.expertforum.ro, and www.activewatch.ro.
64 Alena Ledeneva, "Corruption in Postcommunist Societies in Europe: A Re-examination," *Perspectives on European Politics and Societies* 10, no. 1 (April 2009): 69–86.
65 See http://www.romaniacurata.ro.
66 It is difficult to decide whether the failure of the social-democrat led by Victor Ponta was a result of real civil society pressure or whether, in accordance with the goals of state president Klaus Iohannis, the movements of civil society were a cover for removing the government. The street demonstrations were sparked by a nightclub fire in the summer of 2015, in which 73 people died. In response, Iohannis consulted with a number of NGOs, and appointed a new technocratic government (see http://www.euractiv.ro/politic-intern/consultari-politice-la-cotroceni-pentru-desemnarea-noului-premier-2367).
67 Magyar, *Post-Communist Mafia State;* Magyar and Vásárhelyi, *Twenty-Five Sides*.
68 In rural areas, the biggest problem is the legal disorder of lands—especially formerly private held forest areas—and the gaps in land registries; indeed, in some areas there is no land registry at all. In urban areas, the process is characterized by property restitutions marked by delays and lawsuits that drag on for years, making corruption and non-transparency possible.
69 The legal basis for corruption concerning restitution is provided by the opportunity to purchase contested concession rights, under which skillful oligarchs use contracts to buy the contested concession rights of "rightful claimants" and turning ten-fold or even hundred-fold profits, after counter-suing for properties, forests and land plots—Filippo M. Zerilli examines such a case. See Zerilli, "Corruption, Property, Restitution." The regulation of (re-)privatization procedures, which usually are a stark contrast to economic rationality, not only lack the inclusion of "institutional guarantees to prevent (or hinder) corruption," but directly create regulations that promote or facilitate corruption. See András Sajó, "A vesztegethető államtól a zsaroló államig," *Mozgó Világ* 27, no. 7 (July 2001): 3–16.

Ever since the leader of the prosecution against organized crime and terrorism (Alina Bica) was arrested and accused of corruption during her term as president of the Restitution Authority (ANRP), new light has been shed on an entire corrupt network, which operated unobstructed for decades (see http://www.revista22.ro/articol.php?id=51162 and http://www.revista22.ro/mafiaretrocedarilor-anrp-cum-s-au-imbogatit-samsarii-si-evaluatorii-pe-spatele-ugetuluide-stat-si-a-proprietarilor-cit-de-sus-ajung-conexiunile-politice-50813.html). Attila Markó, a former Hungarian Romanian representative who was a member of the presidency of the ANRP, has been a suspect in restitution affairs corruption on multiple counts in the view of the DNA. Markó escaped responsibility by fleeing to Hungary (see http://itthon.transindex.ro/?hir=39547 and http://www.maszol.ro/index.php/belfold/52098-masodszor-is-birosag-ele-allitottak-tavolleteben-marko-attilat).

[70] Hale, *Patronal Politics*, 9–10.
[71] Mungiu-Pippidi, "Corruption."
[72] Recently trust in public institutions has been on a continuous decline, according to public opinion survey data (see http://www.inscop.ro/aprilie-2016-increderea-in-institutii/), but at the same time the popularity of the DNA has grown. According to a recent study (available at http://adevarul.ro/news/politica/sodnaj-csci-dna-duce-mai-topurile-popularitate-1_55646ea2cfbe376e359d14d7/index.html) it has an approval rating of 63%, which is higher than that of the president (55%).
[73] Jávor István, and Dávid Jancsics, "The Role of Power in Organizational Corruption: An Empirical Study," *Administration & Society* 48, no. 5 (2016): 527–58. First published in 2013.
[74] András Lánczi, "Lehet maffiaállamozni, de akkor ki fog nyílni a privatizációs doboz is," *HVG*, May 13, 2016, http://hvg.hu/gazdasag/20160513_Lehet_maffiaallamozni_de_akkor_ki_fog_nyilni_a_privatizacios_doboz_is.
[75] Remus Anghel, Gyula Kozák, and Nándor László Magyari, *Romania and its borders with non-EU countries* (Cluj: Desire, 2007).
[76] Frank and Gaina, "Political Corruption in Romania."
[77] Such countries mentioned by Orbán in a positive light include Turkey, Azerbaijan and the Philippines.
[78] Ledeneva, "Corruption in Postcommunist Societies."
[79] Relative to the perception of average citizens, the Romanian corruption system did not construct fear-inspiring communications, and when an attempt to do so took place through the Băsescu regime, the result was spectacular failure on more than one occasion. His fall was caused by counter-mafias on the one hand and the resistance of civil society on the other. A kind of counter-balance was built and society-crippling ethno-national and exclusionary discourses failed to monopolize or even penetrate society, unlike in Hungary.
[80] The DAHR, which represents Hungarians in Romania, has been a coalition partner with every mainstream Romanian political formation, and in these instances it reeled in its nationalist discourse, but began to stress it once again upon entering the opposition. The Romanian Hungarian alliance, facing this, has been "pragmatic" in government and "autonomist" in opposition. In any case, all corruption accusations against Romanian Hungarian politicians are politically communicated as expressions of Romanian nationalism.

81 I have already referred to the culture of corruption concerning its function as a socializing agent, which can pass on a matrix or cultural "meme" that makes corrupt behavior a cultural feature. But here it is worth noting that corruption management and the "fight against it" have also become part of this culture, knowledge and attitudes, in which the positions of accountability and equality under the law are very weak, and in which the detection of corrupt acts, etc., is missing.

III.
TECHNIQUES AND TOOLS

ZOLTÁN SZ. BÍRÓ

The Russian Party System

> "Whatever party we establish... it always becomes a CPSU."
>
> *Viktor Chernomyrdin*

1. The first steps of moving to a multi-party system

The first multi-party elections in independent Russia to meet the most fundamental standards of liberal democracy were held in December 1993. These elections were not only contested by multiple parties—there were four such elections in Russia at the beginning of the 20th century—but were also secret, equal, direct and general. This was the first time in Russian history that elections meeting all these conditions were held. But this is not the only reason the 1993 elections should be seen as extraordinary. The elections were held a mere two months after the Russian political class that had stood behind Boris Yeltsin—both at the time of the attempted coup against Mikhail Gorbachev in the summer of 1991 and during the collapse of the Soviet Union—split into two factions, which entered an intense period of conflict with one another, marked by street battles and bombardment of the parliament. The head of state thought the solution to the political conflict lay in violently disciplining the parliamentary majority that had turned on him and his government. As a result, both the final drafting of the Constitution offered to the Russian people in a referendum, and the passing of the new electoral law, took place in the new political environment which began with the storming of the Supreme Soviet—which fulfilled the parliamentary role—in October. That is to say, the conditions and rules for executing the "founding elections" of 1993 were not passed as a result of negotiations between various political forces, but instead drafted by the winner of the conflict of that autumn.[1]

There is no doubt that the character of the party system is defined primarily by the type of electoral system—although numerous other factors, such as historical traditions, are also at play.[2] This is even more the case when, following a sharp political turn, a new party system must be developed: in such situations, the goal is to "break with tradition" to create something that had not existed previously. This is what took place in Russia after the collapse of the Soviet Union. The antecedents to this, however, reach back to the late Soviet period and the years of Gorbachev's *perestroika*. The development of an electoral system that met the expectations of a competitive democracy had begun in the fall of 1991. It was at this time that the *Supreme Soviet* of the Russian Soviet Federative Socialist Republic, which at that point was still a member state of the Soviet Union, passed new regulations on electing local political leaders. A year later, the act that regulated the election of the *Congress of People's Deputies*, which held sessions twice a year, was also modified. Work on the legal form of elections, however, only began in earnest in early 1993. It was at this point that a working group, charged with the task of drafting a new election act, was established under the supervision of the *Constitutional Affairs Committee* of the parliament inherited from the Soviet era. The first draft of the act was completed in May of that year. However, a number of issues remained unresolved at the time: for instance, whether the members of the lower chamber of the bicameral legislature should be elected via a majority system, or one that combined majority and proportional elements. Ultimately, Yeltsin made the decision on October 1, 1993, when he published his decree on elections,[3] some key points of which were amended in early November.[4] This decree established that the elections would take place under a mixed system. The German and Hungarian systems served as models for the writers of the legislation, with the key difference being that the Russian elections would be executed in a single round, with the system not containing any compensation mechanism for the distribution of mandates. According to Yeltsin's decree, half of the mandates in the 450-strong State Duma were to be selected via a proportional system using party lists, while the remaining 225 mandates would be contested in single-member districts based on majority principles. Commitment to the mixed system was almost certainly influenced by the notion that proportional elections would help strengthen emerging political parties,[5] while the majority model could limit the parliamentary gains of authoritarian parties.[6] This mixed system remained in force until 2005, when a new election law was passed under President Putin.[7]

Another important characteristic of the 1993 electoral system was that the right to nominate candidates was put in the hands of so-called voters' associations and various voters' groups. This was in contrast to the Soviet period, when workplace collectives were the only and the exclusive holders of these rights. This was an important step in dismantling the Soviet-style parliamentary system, given that earlier the basic organizations of the Communist Party functioned in workplaces. In the new system, the parties were organized on territorial principles, and executed their political activities as such.

The new act on the franchise unified the method of selecting candidates: from this point on this was done exclusively through collecting signatures. The exclusive majority principle that had been in place to that point was erased: it was only kept for individual district candidates. At the same time, the requirement to reach an absolute majority to win the mandate in individual districts was cancelled; from this point on, a relative majority was sufficient to win individual representative mandates. The Gorbachev-era stipulation that multiple candidates must run in each district was fortified; elections that did not meet this condition were declared null and void. Decisions were made on necessary guarantees to ensure election committees operated in a non-biased manner and on ensuring that all candidates had equal access to the mass media tools of the state. The new electoral law also regulated campaign finance. Last but not least, the forms of the ballots themselves were changed. According to the new rules, the will of the voter would not be expressed by crossing out the rejected candidate's name—as was done during the "elections" of the Soviet era—but instead by marking the supported candidate. In the interest of limiting electoral abuse, the ballot contained an "against all" (*protiv vsekh*) box as well.[8] This move created the opportunity to express dissatisfaction with the full political "offering," while simultaneously ensuring that protest votes were not expressed through blank ballots that could be easily manipulated after the vote.

All in all, a framework of election norms developed in the fall of 1993, one which was truly capable of moving the country from the "elections without choice" system of the Soviet era to the world of "free and fair elections." At the same time, the establishment of a legal framework was a necessary but insufficient condition for reaching this goal. The free and fair execution of the elections scheduled for the end of 1993 was not only overshadowed by the conflicts splitting the political class and mutual distrust, but also by the lack of democratic experience and fear of the irreversibility of the democratic political transition. It is likely that these factors led Yeltsin and his group to delay authorizing the participation of the Communists—who were the most serious opponents of reform—in the Duma elections to the last minute. Characteristically, it was not the courts but one of the key actors in the political conflict, namely President Yeltsin himself, who finally authorized the Communists, under Gennady Zyuganov's leadership, to participate.[9]

Independent Russia's first multi-party election was also extraordinary given that elections in December 1993—exceptionally, the elections for both the upper and lower chambers were taking place at the same time—were electing representatives to bodies that did not exist, neither de jure nor de facto. This was because both the lower house, the State Duma, and the upper house, the Federation Council of Russia, would be established by the new Constitution, which was subject to a referendum occurring at the same time as the elections. It was therefore possible that—should the new Constitution fail to pass in the referendum—representatives would be elected to institutions that did not exist. It appeared that this possibility was not taken seriously by the authorities organizing and carrying out the elections. They were concerned, however, about whether the new "political design" would stand the test of time, and thus they decided that in the first round, mandates for the newly established institutions would only be half their normal duration. As such, before the elections they established that the first cycle of parliament would be two years instead of four. This was by no means the only political safeguard. Yeltsin's group did not want to make mistakes, and for this reason they did not structure and summarize the arriving election results on the computers of an independent institution—such as the Central Election Committee—but instead did so on the computer of one of the KGB's Conference of Chiefs, which happened to be functioning independently at the time. The inclusion of a secret service agency charged with protecting the government's news circulation, known as FAPSI (*Federal'noye Agenstvo Pravitel'stvennoy Svyazi i Informatsii pri Prezidenta RF*, or Federal Agency of Government Communications and Information), in a delicate phase of the voting process, could not have eased voter concerns about the fairness or transparency of the elections.

Thirteen parties contested the first multi-party competitive elections. Among them, according to official statistics, eight managed to surpass the five percent threshold necessary to acquire mandates through party lists. According to calculations by Alexander A. Sobyanin and Vladislav G. Sukhovolsky, two parties—the *Party of Russian Unity and Accord* (PRES) as well as the *Democratic Party of Russia* (DPR)—were given significant political "assistance." The former—in contrast to the official result of 6.73 percent—only acquired 3.41 percent of the votes, while the latter—in contrast to the announced 5.52 percent—only received 2.8 percent of votes.[10] The likely reason interference from the executive power was necessary was that without these two parties, there would not have been a majority of factions in the lower chamber to support reform policies. As such, those in the president's circle thought it better to "adjust" the results a little. Taking into account the severe social costs of Yegor Gaidar's economic "shock therapy," it would have been surprising to see pro-reform parties attain a majority without this type of "adjustment." Reforms resulted in a sudden explosion in inflation, with its annual level reaching 2600 percent in 1992. This—among other factors—resulted in the sudden devaluation of the population's savings accrued during the Soviet period, with the level of consumption and its structure falling back to early 1970s levels.

At the same time, it was surprising that a rather low number of voters chose the "against all" option on the ballot. The proportion of those who did so—according to official results—was under four percent. The most likely explanation for this was that those dissatisfied with the political situation voted for either the so-called *Liberal Democratic Party of Russia* (LDPR), led by the shrill nationalist leader Vladimir V. Zhirinovsky, or for the Communists and their allies, the Agrarian Party.[11]

The first free elections held in December 1993 showed, at least, that the electoral system was functional. Despite some interventions in vote counting, all in all the system proved capable of providing democratic legitimacy to those in power. Luckily for Yeltsin and his political allies, there were no influential players who had an interest in maintaining Russian instability, neither within nor outside the country. Given that no such players arose, no one was particularly critical of the fairness of the elections. The representatives of parties with mandates in the lower chamber felt that the elections placed them in positions they deserved, which took precedence over any other concerns. Moreover, they likely suspected that their presence in parliament was the only guarantee that they would not end up on the political garbage heap, at least not as long as they had solid mandates. The first free elections had shown how risky it was for parties to be excluded from the most important field in new Russian politics, the parliament. There were of course some parties that grieved for their election failures by questioning the legitimacy of the vote. Their efforts were, however, unfruitful; so much so that within a short span of time they drifted to the Russian political periphery, from where there was no return.

Indeed, there is only one example of a political party failing to win seats in parliament and then successfully returning, namely the liberals, who frequently changed the name of their party. During the first free elections, under the name *Russia's Choice* and with strong support from the executive branch, they came second in party list results with 15.51 percent. Adding to this the mandates they won in individual districts, they formed the largest party faction with 64 seats, alongside the Zhirinovsky-led Liberal Democratic Party of Russia, which, despite its name, was neither liberal nor democratic.[12] However, in the next election held two years later, Russia's Choice were unable to cross the five percent threshold. They did manage to win in nine individual districts,[13] and as such, were present in the lower chamber, but were unable to form a party faction. In 1999, however, using a new name—*Union of Rightist Forces*—they succeeded in winning list-based mandates (8.52 percent) primarily because the executive deemed their presence in parliament important. In total they won 29 seats, and as such were able to form the fourth-largest party faction.[14] However, it later turned out that their return was in vain: they were unable to win list-based mandates in the next four elections. The most likely reason they failed in 1995 was they were viewed as the shock therapy-executing president's key Duma support group, and the electorate punished them accordingly. With their exception, however, no party has ever succeeded in returning to parliament after losing all their seats.

The liberals led by Yegor Gaidar, as a result of the 1993 election returns—and despite the executive branch's efforts to support them with all available means—did not enter a position of dominance. Their faction was the largest in the chamber, but its members made up less than one-seventh of all Duma members. Even in conjunction with their political allies, they barely controlled one-third of the lower chamber mandates. The first Duma, as such, was remarkably divided; no party was in a position to rule the house.

However, two very different parties capable of forming factions after the next six parliamentary elections were already visible. The first was the successor party to the Soviet state party, namely the *Communist Party of the Russian Federation* (CPRF); by contrast, the second, the LDPR, was the key challenger to the first. It formed in the late Soviet period, and it has long been suspected that the secret service of the period, the Committee for State Security (KGB), was present at its founding. It was likely established with the goal of manipulating and "tying down" the emerging opposition during the transformation to a pluralist system. The LDPR, led by Zhirinovsky, was able to adapt to the circumstances of the new Russia. The party's case was unusual: it was effectively "cobbled together" by the executive of another state, yet it remained loyal to its role as a **quasi-opposition party** even after the state structure of the Soviet Union collapsed. The party continues to play this role—set out for it in the early nineties—to this day; the only difference is that it no longer serves the Soviet Union's communist leadership, but the autocratic Putin system instead. It can be most precisely defined as a party created by the executive, which was inherited by those currently in power.

In contrast, the Communist Party led by Zyuganov is a typical case of a "domesticated party," though this was not always the case; rather, the party was domesticated step by step. As the successor to the Communist Party of the Soviet Union (CPSU), in the nineties it became a hub of opposition to political and economic reform. It presented itself as a party that, once in power, would turn back the tide of history. However, given it never entered a position of power, its aspirations remained unfulfilled. In 1993, the party only won 42 mandates, forming the third-largest faction in the Duma.[15] Two years later, however, it won 157 seats, meaning it constituted the largest faction in the lower house.[16] They were almost three times as large as the second biggest faction, the *Our Home – Russia* party, whose faction contained 55 members,[17] and which the executive supported with all means possible. But for the Communists, winning the largest faction was nevertheless in vain, as it was not big enough to rule the legislature. To do so would have required a coalition with another parliamentary faction, and none of the other factions was willing to do so; they were only prepared to conduct case by case cooperation. In theory, the communists could have allied with independents, and did make an attempt to do so, but this too was unsuccessful. Nevertheless, at this point the Communists' political influence was at its peak. From this point on, their results consistently declined from election to election. By the early 2000s this led to a scenario whereby the party largely abandoned its actual oppositional stance and only mimicked an opposition to those in power. Formally they remained an opposition group, but in issues important to the executive, they began to overwhelmingly vote with the parties in power. To reward their loyalty, they were not squeezed out of parliament, unlike the western liberals. They continue to sit in the Duma as a "loyal opposition," doing nothing to cause concern for the president and his circle.

Another unique aspect of the 1993 election was that the executive branch, which at the time was still supporting liberal reforms and intended to execute them, was still doing all it could to ensure that the parliament contained liberal parties that would force the issue of approaching the West. For this reason—and because public opinion was still amenable to the prospect of Western-type development—two liberal parties entered the lower chamber. Yegor Gaidar's party, Russia's Choice, which was a liberal group in the Western sense, accompanied by the social-liberal *Yabloko* party, which was able to form a faction of its own, winning 7.86 percent of the list vote. This would be the only time in the history of Russia's lower house that a liberal party formed the largest faction. Besides Gaidar's group, the social-liberals also managed to form a relatively large faction, winning 27 seats. They formed the lower chamber's fifth largest faction.[18]

During the first free elections, it appeared that small parties had a good chance of successfully winning parliamentary mandates. In 1993, eight parties managed to enter the lower chamber, a number which has not been reached since. In fact, by 1995 the number quickly halved to four, and ultimately stabilized at a low level. While their number temporarily grew to six in 1999, over later elections only four parties managed to reach the electoral threshold, which has raised from five to seven percent since 2003. As a result of the last four elections—held in 2003, 2007, 2011 and 2016—the lower chamber has been operating with much the same composition; indeed, during this time only one change took place. The *Rodina* bloc,[19] which was the fourth-largest party in the Duma after the 2003 elections, was replaced by the *A Just Russia* party at the next election.[20] What is interesting about the "switch" is that it took place despite the fact that both parties were essentially "creations" of the executive branch. Rodina was established with the goal of attracting "patriotic" voters away from the Communist Party, while A Just Russia was created as a left-of-center alternative to the governmental party *United Russia*, which covered the center-right, in a two-party system envisioned for the future. When the goal was to win over nationalist voters—because the biggest perceived threat was the renewed fortification of the Communist Party, which appealed to nationalist sentiment—the Kremlin established a nationalist party. When, however, the communist successor party no longer posed a serious threat—because Putin had succeeded in limiting its influence during his second term as president—the president and his apparatus could return to the old dream of the executive branch: the development of a party structure that resembled the two-party system in the United States. Although the two parties were established with different goals in mind, they were nevertheless similar in the sense that they were both artificially "created from above." It is clear—despite numerous political and economic difficulties—that the executive power successfully managed to construct a fairly stable party system in Russia in a relatively short period of time. The key role in this process was played not by society, but instead by the executive branch, including the presidential administration.

In important post-Soviet states like Ukraine, the political transition—including the shift to a multi-party system—unfolded much more slowly than in Russia. The first multi-party elections were held later than in Russia, and all mandates were won in individual districts. The party affiliations of candidates were, of course, public knowledge, but the lack of a proportional element made the elections somewhat reminiscent of Soviet-era ballots. Fourteen parties won mandates in the 1994 Ukrainian election, but only six of them won more than five seats. The largest party faction in the *Rada* was that of the Ukrainian Communists (85 seats), but they did not constitute the largest group in the single-chamber Ukrainian parliament; this honor belonged to independents, who gained 168 seats in total. The second-largest party group after the Communists, with 20 mandates, was that of the People's Movement of Ukraine (*Rukh*), which was popular in the western half of the country, and emphasized and represented Ukrainian traditions. The *Socialist Party of Ukraine* formed a 14-person faction, while the *Peasant Party of Ukraine* won 18 representative seats.[21] Both the electoral system, and the composition of the elected parliament, signaled that Ukraine was still in an early phase of political transition, lagging far behind Russia at that point.

2. Attempts to stabilize the party system

The next election in the Yeltsin era was held in December 1995, as previously agreed. The executive branch was able to better prepare for these elections, having gained a little experience. Their experience showed that the desired election result must not be generated during the actual vote counting (the "output" point), as occurred during the 1993 elections, but during the election campaign itself (the "input" point); in short, political advantage must be cemented during the campaign stage. It was difficult to meet this expectation in the mid-1990s for several reasons, not least the pliable nature of the party system. Many factors played a role in this malleability, perhaps most importantly the ease with which parties could be established and registered. Another factor, however, was the ambition of the executive branch to mold a new political system. This was the period in which the plan to develop an American-styled two-party system first appeared in the president's circle, with the intention—according to its architects—of stabilizing the Russian party system.

In mid-1995, efforts were launched to create two parties—one covering the center-left, another the center-right—or voting blocs that, as creations of the presidential power, would be "convenient" partners in power games. The execution of this ambitious plan, however, was blocked by several unanticipated obstacles. The establishment of a center-left voting party or bloc was especially difficult. For this reason, the Kremlin was only able to complete the creation of its parties immediately before the elections. On the one hand, it constructed the party Our Home – Russia to represent the center-right, and on the other, it created the *Ivan Rybkin Bloc* to represent the center-left. The executive branch did all it could to help its political creations easily overcome obstacles, in order that they not just simply enter the lower chamber of parliament, but also form comfortable—and hopefully absolute—majorities. The mobilization of so-called "administrative resources" was facilitated by the fact that Our Home – Russia was headed by the prime minister, Victor Chernomyrdin, while the other bloc was led by Ivan Rybkin, who was about to complete his first mandate as Speaker in the State Duma. Despite this, the project was an abysmal failure. Chernomyrdin's party managed to surpass the five percent threshold, but its results were much weaker than expected, winning just over ten percent of list votes, to which it added a further ten mandates from individual districts. As such, the newly established party had a faction of only 45 members.[22] At the same time, the Rybkin-led election bloc's results were even weaker. They did not win any mandates on the party list, given they garnered only one percent support in the proportional system. As they won three individual districts, they were at least represented in the lower chamber, albeit without a faction of their own.[23]

The 1995 election showed not only how difficult it was for the executive branch, with its weak economic and social policy results, to establish parties and make them successful. It also demonstrated the value of limiting the number of parties contesting the elections, which was deemed too high. A record number of parties and election blocs contested the elections, but of the 43 groups participating, only four managed to surpass the five percent threshold. This also meant that 49.5 percent of party list votes—as opposed to the 12.9 percent in 1993—were effectively "lost"; this was the proportion of votes garnered by the 39 parties and election blocs that did not manage to enter the Duma.[24] Since almost half the voters—at least party list voters—were not able to see their parties represented, the legitimacy of the election itself was questioned. The Rybkin bloc submitted the issue to the Constitutional Court, but their submission was rejected. Yet not only was the high proportion of "lost" votes a problem, but also the fact that the electoral system redistributed these "lost" votes to parties that had surpassed the five percent threshold and gained parliamentary factions, initiating a kind of multiplier effect.

The system functioned such that the list winner was granted considerably more representative seats than the proportion of votes it achieved. As such, whoever won the list was a big winner when mandates were being handed out, while those who were less successful hardly saw any increase in their number of seats. Characteristically, the Communist Party, which was supported by 22.3 percent of voters, ultimately won 44 percent of the seats available through the proportional part of the system, almost doubling its results. This was also the case with the weakest party managing to cross the threshold, the Grigory Yavlinsky-led Yabloko, that also managed to form a faction. However, the number of extra mandates "gifted" to the latter party was much smaller than that granted to the Communists. The CPRF—thanks to the multiplier effect—accessed 43 extra seats, Yabloko gained only 15. It must be noted that a distortion of results of this scale can only take place when a very high number of parties contest the election, the majority of which do not manage to overcome the threshold. This type of situation did not occur in later elections; in the late 1990s, the registration of parties became stricter, as did the authorization required for their participation in elections.

Thanks to these new restrictions, the proportion of "lost" party list votes in the next elections held in 1999 was only 18.6 percent.[25] At the next election this number grew somewhat, but still remained under 30 percent.

At the 2007 and 2011 elections, by which point mandates could only be won through the party list, the proportion of "lost" votes was under 10 percent on both occasions.[26] As such, it appears that the attempts to eradicate this problem were successful.

The State Duma elected in 1995 posed the most problems for the executive branch, given that the Communists constituted its largest faction. But despite controlling the largest group, the Communists only constituted a relative majority. Working together with independent representatives, they had the ability to form absolute majorities on occasion. However, in Russian politics even an absolute majority in the Duma is insufficient to block the head of state from having the last word. No law can enter into force without the approval of the president, and the presidential veto can only be dismissed by a supermajority of both the lower and upper chambers. No such supermajority ever formed during the Yeltsin years, nor during the Putin or Medvedev years; the legislature did not pose any risk to the presidential power. Opposition factions could cause minor "inconveniences" by forcing the executive branch into dialogue, but they were never capable of any further action.

Before the third Duma elections held in December 1999—even more so than at the end of 1995—there was serious concern that parties loyal to the Kremlin would not gain more than one-third of the mandates; this fear was not unfounded. Furthermore, the next presidential election was approaching, which would see Yeltsin complete his second term and leave office. The search for an appropriate successor was a heavy burden on the late Yeltsin system, which had only just managed to survive partial state bankruptcy. It was against this backdrop that the president's party *Unity*, which was established mere months before the election and which mobilized regional elites and bureaucrats, was able to win 23.3 percent of party list votes, coming in a close second to the Communists.[27] This election also saw the two Western-styled parties, Gaidar's Union of Rightist Forces and Yavlinsky's Yabloko, enter the lower chamber. This result led to not only relief for Yeltsin and his circles, but outright satisfaction; indeed, the election result played an important role in convincing the elderly and increasingly incapable head of state that his early retirement would not be politically risky. It would later emerge that what the Yeltsin group saw as the primary political threat—namely an alliance between the Communists led by Zyuganov and *Fatherland – All Russia*, led by Yuriy Luzhkov and former Prime Minister Yevgeny Primakov—would not come to be. Moreover, after some time it became apparent that Fatherland – All Russia could be convinced to ally with the Kremlin, given that its base, like that of Yeltsin's Unity, consisted of the bureaucracy that operated the state apparatus. And when this indeed happened, with the two parties merging into a new "party of power" named United Russia, the result was something that had been absent throughout the Yeltsin period: a power constellation within the Duma that provided the executive with a comfortable majority within the legislative branch.[28]

In the meantime, in March 1998, the second multi-party elections were held in Ukraine. These elections were conducted using a mixed system, with half the mandates won through party lists, while the other half were contested in individual districts. Unlike the previous elections, winning a district mandate no longer required an absolute majority. In 1994, this condition led to several districts requiring not only a second, but a third and in some areas even a fourth round of voting. In the new system a relative majority was sufficient to win a district mandate, while winning seats in the proportional system required a party to win at least four percent of the list vote. Of the 30 parties contesting the election, eight managed to pass this threshold, three of which gained under five percent shares of the vote. The largest faction was once again formed by the Communists, with 112 seats. They were followed by *Rukh* (46 seats) and the electoral bloc led by the Socialists (34 seats). The People's Democratic Party and Greens each had relatively large factions (27 and 19 members respectively).[29] The Rada's party composition was still tightly connected to Ukraine's Soviet past, and at the time, there was no indication yet that the country's party preferences would split the country in two geographically. Groups espousing nationalist views had appeared, but they were not yet strong enough to become leading forces in Ukraine. The Communists were popular throughout the country, not only in its eastern half. This was clearly related to the fact that, at this point, Ukrainian politics had not yet uncovered what would become the leading issue of the 2000s, namely the strategic dilemma over whether the country should look to the West or the East.

3. The Putin era: interventions aimed at protecting stability

The unexpected first-round election of Vladimir Putin as president, having quickly emerged from political anonymity, is clearly connected to the social-psychological shift that took place in the wake of terrorist attacks in the fall of 1999, which the executive blamed on Chechens. This psychological state contributed not only to Putin's surprisingly easy electoral win, but also to the wide social acceptance of his policies of the time. The new president, elected in March 2000, felt his primary task was to gradually reacquire the public powers that had been "appropriated" during his predecessor's terms. This meant bringing regional and ownership elites into line, alongside a near-parallel restructuring of the party system and electoral rules. In the latter area Putin was patient, moving forward step by step.

The first incident worthy of attention took place in April 2002, when presidential posts of parliamentary committees were redistributed.[30] The background to this was that the Duma elected in 1999 had the Communists forming the largest party faction, but one not large enough to form an absolute majority, even when supplemented by independent representatives. At the time of the elections, the parties in second and third place behind the Communists—namely Unity and Fatherland – All Russia—were still rivals. As such, the Communists were able to make use of their relative majority when it came to distributing committee posts. However, it soon became apparent that the second and third place parties were capable of cooperating in a surprisingly effective manner. It also became clear that these parties, recruited from the *chinovnik*, could support Putin's stabilization objectives, while simultaneously benefitting from the increasing sympathy the population had toward Putin. These conditions allowed for the unification of the two parties, creating in December 2001 a new "party of power," which, under the name United Russia, would finally be able to obtain a supermajority at the 2003 and 2007 elections. Following the merger, the new organization would form the largest faction in the Duma with 139 seats, while also enjoying—as an important parliamentary support structure for the reformer Putin—the support of the liberal parties, namely the Union of Rightist Forces (29 seats) and Yabloko (20 seats). This new parliamentary composition—alongside the support of a few amenable independent representatives—was sufficient to place the redistribution of committee presidential posts on the agenda for 2002. As a result, the Communists, who had held nine committee president posts to that point, were forced to hand over seven to the "party of power" and the liberal factions cooperating with it. At the time, everyone—the liberal factions included—acknowledged this as how things ought to be.

In the meantime, revisions to the existing party law began. The need to do so was justified, as it was necessary to reduce the large number of parties contesting elections. In December 1999, over a hundred parties could theoretically have participated in the elections. Even discounting those which would only have been members of electoral alliances, the number of parties and election blocs would still have reached twenty-six. This number appeared unmanageably high, and served as an obstacle to the formation of a stable party system. The first step towards correcting this came with a new act, passed in July 2001, that made the registration of parties more difficult at several points.[31] For example, it set as a condition that organizations requesting registration have at least ten thousand members throughout the country, with branches in at least half the counties and republics in the Russian Federation. These revisions ensured that only 44 of the 199 previously registered parties were able to re-register.[32] But even among these registered parties, many were unable to stand in the next elections because the electoral act demanded parties and election blocs collect at least 225,000 support signatures, with signatures coming from at least 70 "elements" of the federation. Only 23 parties and election alliances met these criteria. In the fifth Duma elections of December 2003, only four parties managed to surpass the five percent threshold to gain seats. This was mostly due to the inequalities in the conditions for election campaigns.

The 2003 campaign perfected all the presidential branch's earlier techniques to influence the elections. The executive power again did all it could to support its favored parties. This support entailed the mobilization of "administrative resources" and unequal access to politically valuable media. Furthermore, conspicuous differences appeared in the financing of parties and in the selective use of the judiciary. Nonetheless, the election did differ from earlier plebiscites in one important aspect: the 2003 election was the first in modern Russian history in which the Kremlin did not have a serious challenger. For the first time, those in power had the potential to create equal and fair competition conditions for election contestants without any serious political risk. The political achievement of Putin's first presidential mandate—impressive economic growth and the re-establishment of political stability—would be more than adequate for the Kremlin-supported party (or parties) to win.

However, this is not what happened. Putin and his circle felt that total victory, with little regard to the methods used, was more important than electoral fairness. Their political pettiness, however, had unexpected consequences. A portion of the political elite—disgusted at the circumstances under which the December elections were conducted, which led to OSCE observers claiming for the first time that the Russian elections were *free, but not fair*[33]—kept its distance from the presidential election slated for the following March. Characteristically, Putin's reelection was a plebiscite in which the president had no serious challengers, because no one among the great "survivors" of Russian politics decided to participate. This was the first and last time that neither the Communists' Zyuganov nor the LDPR's Zhirinovsky decided to run. The social-liberal Grigory Yavlinsky also declined to run a campaign, even though he won more support than Zhirinovsky in both 1996 and 2000. This situation—when every challenger to the incumbent president was, without exception, a political novice—came close to making the presidential election a joke, even though Putin's political achievements to that point could have served as a guarantee of risk-free victory in fair elections. But Putin and his circle did not choose that path. Their choice was clearly influenced by the elite power transformations induced by the Yukos affair. This affair led several important politicians, who had been close to Yeltsin, to resign from their posts, including the exceptionally influential leader of the presidential administration, Aleksandr Voloshin, and the prime minister during Putin's first presidential mandate, Mikhail Kasyanov. These changes of personnel in the apparatus created an opening for future President Dmitry Medvedev, who replaced Voloshin, to take his first leading position in the political sphere.

Political pettiness, however, appeared in other areas as well. The distribution of parliamentary committee president posts in the new Duma—where two-thirds of the seats were held by United Russia, partly through "buying off" a number of independent representatives—was even more obviously one-sided than before. As a result, all 29 committee president seats were given to the "party of power."[34] Even this was not enough for the ruling establishment, as the majority of deputy presidential positions were also gobbled up by the increasingly insatiable party. Even the traditions that had developed for the formation of the Council of the State Duma (House Committee) were broken. Previously, the council that defined the operation and agenda of the lower chamber was composed of the Duma's speaker and the leaders of factions. Now, in possession of a two-thirds majority, Putin's party decided that there was no room in the council for faction leaders, but that the speaker and deputy speakers should be accommodated. As such, of the nine elected members of the Duma Council, six were representatives of the "party of power." This distribution of lower chamber offices clearly served as security for the representatives of *United*

Russia, who saw it as a guarantee against unpleasant surprises. Indeed, one of the leaders of the "party of power" had already stated that the Duma was not an arena in which debates should take place.[35] If the Duma was not a forum for debates, then it was not worth interfering with the distribution of parliamentary offices.

The results of the 2003 elections determined the composition of the lower chamber for several electoral cycles. From this point on, only four parties or election blocs were regularly able to surpass the threshold, and the question of which should receive the status of "party of power" received a clear answer. This was the first election in which United Russia ran in this role and won. Moreover, it did not only win, it achieved a mandate large enough to be able to amend the constitution single-handedly. This was not initially attributable to direct election results, but instead to the fact that as clear victor, it was able to convince nearly one hundred independent representatives, or those that were not able to form factions, to join its ranks.

The direct election results in and of themselves were not strong enough to provide the party an absolute majority. They were only three seats short of doing so, and seventy-eight short of forming a constitution-amending supermajority, but the party would ultimately form the constitution-amending majority it wanted. Besides the dominant United Russia, a faction was also established by the Communists, although it was less than half the size of its faction in the previous parliament (52 seats, compared to its previous 113 seats). It was at this point that the domestication of the Communist faction, and the party standing behind it, was accelerated. Zhirinovsky's LDPR succeeded in increasing its number of seats from four years prior, growing from seventeen to thirty-six. Its role, however, remained unchanged. As an "artificial party" inherited from the Soviet era, it continued to serve the executive branch. One other "artificial party" managed to enter parliament, albeit for only a brief period. The Rodina bloc, meaning "motherland" in English, entered the Duma as a creation of the Kremlin. Its role was to further split the nationalist vote, much of which went to the Communists. To help it fulfill this role, it was provided with significant financial, informational and other forms of support, which helped it achieve nine percent support on the party list portion of the election. Thanks to victories in eight individual districts, their number of seats—37 in total—surpassed the number held by the ultra-nationalist LDPR by one. The Duma was once again populated by four parties, but differed from its 1995 predecessor due to the fact that it contained no liberal parties: neither

Yabloko (4.3 percent) nor the Union of Rightist Forces (3.9 percent) passed the threshold. Despite their failure in the proportional system, both parties managed to win a handful of individual districts; this, however, was not enough to form factions.

Azerbaijan serves as an example of a country where the local "party of power" became quickly dominant, much like United Russia. The *New Azerbaijan Party*, which served as President Heydar Aliyev's parliamentary support, won an absolute majority in the elections of November 2000. Five years later, supporting his son Ilham Aliyev, the party came up a few seats short of an absolute majority, but managed to achieve this at the 2010 and 2015 elections.[36] Although the party has not yet gained a constitution-amending supermajority, its dominant position has gone unchallenged by any opposition parties. The simple reason for this is that the second largest group in parliament, after the executive-supporting faction, is that of independents. For a long time now, the factions of other parliamentary parties have comprised only a handful of representatives who—even if they were to unite—pose no threat to the regime.

A similar situation developed in Armenia. Here too a "party of power," named the *Republican Party*, supporting the president, emerged relatively early, in the mid-1990s. It began as part of a party alliance, whose composition shifted numerous times, but has been an independent party since 2003. This party first achieved an absolute majority in 2012,[37] but since has had to be satisfied with having the largest faction in parliament. Since all the other parties to enter parliament have been considerably smaller, however, this has posed no obstacle to their remaining the dominant party. Much like a number of other post-Soviet states, the party enjoying the support of the executive branch has never faced a serious challenger in parliament.

In Russia, the first time such a "protected" situation for the "party of power" could be established was in 2003. But after having carried out the parliamentary, then the presidential elections successfully, the Putin system—as indicated above—faced an unexpected challenge. It had to find a way to motivate a high enough number of constituents to vote, despite the fact that the outcome of the elections was not in any doubt. In these circumstances the reworking of both the party and election acts was undertaken again. One of the modifications removed the requirement for a necessary level of participation to declare elections valid; this was not, however, the only rule to be reworked. The mixed system used in parliamentary elections was redrafted: from 2007 onward, mandates could only be won through party lists[38] (at least until 2011, because the mixed system was reintroduced for the 2016 elections), and individual district seats were eliminated. At the same time, the threshold for forming a parliamentary faction was raised from five to seven percent.

The transformation of the act on parties and elections made it theoretically possible for the executive branch to guarantee fair campaign conditions for all candidates. The last revision of the act on parties and elections in 2004 created a legal environment in which interference in the electoral campaign, or in the counting of votes, became entirely unnecessary, because the victory of the "party of power" could be guaranteed without manipulation. With these changes, the entirety of political processes came so much under the control of the Kremlin that the results of the elections would not have been significantly influenced by greater fairness in the campaign itself. In these conditions, the election results were decided not weeks before the election, but much earlier. This was thanks to the new norms and rules introduced by Moscow in 2004, in a manner highly dismissive of the recommendations made by the OSCE in the same year.[39] Indeed, Russia took only one of the several dozen recommendations made concerning electoral processes seriously, namely the removal of the "against all" box on the voting ballot. It is not entirely clear why this provision concerned the OSCE; after all, the "against all" box was not simply an exotic exception of the Russian election system, but an important guarantee element, providing a difficult-to-manipulate means to express general disapproval of the political class. It is interesting to ponder why the Russian rulers found this European recommendation noteworthy, while discarding all the rest.

The 2004 OSCE recommendations contained several pieces of noteworthy advice. The document's general political message encouraged Moscow to further fortify its party system. It recommended greater ease in establishing parties that could effectively represent regional and minority group interests and provide them with operational support, further advising that the financial burdens facing all parties contesting elections be reduced. The Russian legislature did the opposite. The amendment to the party act which came into force in early 2006 made the establishment and registration of parties considerably more difficult. Registration was made contingent on having at least 50,000 members, and furthermore, the territorial distribution of these members was strictly regulated.[40] This meant that without "administrative support" from the executive branch, it was practically impossible to establish a new party; moreover, the operation of existing parties could easily become precarious. As a result of the new rules indicated above, the number of parties capable of running in the elections was cut in half. While 26 parties and party alliances competed in 1999, and 23 competed in 2003, only 11 were able to participate in 2007, thanks to the new act on parties. In 2011 this number was even lower, with a mere seven parties able to make it to the starting line. The restrictions not only served the goal of limiting the number of parties within a reasonable frame, but also helped to conserve the party structure developed in 2003, along with its internal proportions.

In light of the European observers' earlier experiences, it was recommended that the provision demanding parties pay for freely provided television and radio advertising space after the fact—should the party not get at least two percent of the total votes—be revoked. Moscow not only failed to cancel this provision, they actually raised its threshold to three percent. As such, following the elections in 2007, all but four parties had to pay significant sums after the fact. Furthermore, they also lost the deposits they had to pay to the Central Election Commission to avoid having to collect signatures supporting their participation; these deposits amounted to 60 million rubles per party, which at the time was the equivalent of 2–2.2 million USD. Parties like Yavlinsky's Yabloko generally chose to pay the deposit because, based on earlier experiences, they knew it was easy for the ruling party to claim the signatures they amassed were fake. The true goal of the deposit and the post facto payment of advertisement fees was to allow the Kremlin to disqualify parties it did not like with more than just political means; in some cases, these costs could easily drive parties into bankruptcy. Furthermore, another novelty of the 2007 parliamentary and 2008 presidential elections was that summarized data on invalid votes was no longer made public; even this indirect form of dissidence was denied recognition by the state.

The intensive lawmaking activity in Russia concerning party operations and electoral practice in the latter half of the 2000s justifiably leaves the impression that, unlike the consolidated democracies of the West—where the competitive conditions for elections are changed very rarely, and the expected result is typically difficult to predict—in Russia elections were held in a constantly changing legal environment, while the expected result could be foretold with greater precision. The practices of this era were legitimized primarily by appealing to the importance of political stability, and as such were accepted by the majority of the political community. As such, we can ascertain that Putin's "stability cult" had truly scorched the Russian public sphere by the middle of the decade. This situation would hold until the sixth Duma elections of December 2011, which brought about an unexpected shift.

In the meantime, noteworthy political restructuring had begun in Ukraine. The 2002 parliamentary elections were held under the same conditions as those which occurred four years prior. This time, however, the Communists did not win; instead the former president of the central bank, and then head of government, led his own electoral alliance to victory. The pro-Western *Viktor Yushchenko Bloc* won 112 seats, compared to the 65 won by the Communists. Also establishing a large faction was the *For United Ukraine!* bloc—led by Volodymyr Lytvyn, who served in various influential offices under Leonid Kuchma—which gained 101 seats. This was also the point when the Yulia Tymoshenko Bloc appeared on the scene, gaining 22 seats.[41] The Ukrainian situation continued to be significantly different to that in Russia; the primary difference was that, unlike in Russia, the executive branch still did not play an important role in the development of parliamentary power relations. As a result, there was no development of a dominant "party of power," meaning political competition remained open and meaningful.

The next parliamentary elections were held in 2006, two years after the Orange Revolution, by now employing an exclusively proportional (list) system. By this point the election results came to reflect the country's east-west split, much as the 2004 presidential election had previously. In eastern counties, the winner was Viktor Yanukovych's *Party of Regions* (186 seats), which sought closer ties with Russia, while in western counties the winners were the pro-Western *Yulia Tymoshenko Bloc* (129 seats) and the *Our Ukraine Bloc* (81 seats), which supported President Yushchenko.[42] The results clearly signaled that a "party of power" had not emerged in Ukraine, to the extent that the highest number of seats was won by the party of the president's main political rival. It was clear that the executive branch did not assemble its own party and start supporting it with various means, either because it was not strong enough or it did not feel the need to do so.

The early elections of 2007 produced almost the same situation. The highest number of seats, 175 in total, was once again won by the Party of Regions party alliance led by Yanukovych. Second place once again went to the Yulia Tymoshenko Bloc, which significantly increased its number of seats to 156. The third-largest faction was formed by the Our Ukraine Bloc, with 72 seats.[43] Yet again, a "party of power" did not emerge. Further, the reason why the Communist Party, which had been strong throughout the 1990s, lost much of its popularity was not because of the machinations of the executive branch, but instead because the party was not able to renew itself and present issues worthy of attention to the electorate. The party supporting the president was once again unable to take a step forward, but as the third-largest faction it was able to maintain its parliamentary position. No one considered this a failure, or a situation that needed to be remedied using the force of presidential power.

4. Fissures in the system of "sovereign democracy"

The unexpected results of the 2011 Duma elections[44]—beyond the tactical mistakes made by Putin and the "party of power"—are likely attributable to the joint effects of two essential and enduring processes. On the one hand, the political system that had operated efficiently until then began to wear down, while on the other, Russian society began a new period of restructuring. The former was visible in the crisis of the Putin-Medvedev "tandem," the wearing out of their personal "brand" and the exhaustion of the ruling power's political rhetoric and communications strength. Finally, but no less importantly, the party system that had been constructed and maintained by the executive branch, and the political manipulation it conducted through the party system, began to lose its efficacy.

This process was accelerated by the announcement of the public role reversal planned by Putin and Medvedev, which essentially brought to an end the "tandem" they had been operating up to that point.[45] Following this announcement, the formal and informal power roles that had previously been separated were once again fused in the person of Putin. Meanwhile Medvedev, through accepting this new distribution of roles, lost most of his supporters in the blink of an eye, and as such became incapable of addressing social groups with an interest in modernization. Perhaps even more important than these factors, however, is that the naked arrogance by which the role switch was announced and implemented was a slap in the face to the Russian political community, which to that point had tended to acknowledge, or at least accept, Putin's political results.

The dissolution of the power center's political rhetoric and communications strength was best illustrated by Putin and his circle's bemusement when they initially tried to interpret the behavior of those demonstrating against the manipulation of election results. The Kremlin was only capable of understanding the protests in large cities following the elections of late 2011 by using the analogy of a "color revolution." This interpretive scheme was also massively utilized at the end of the presidential election campaign. There is no question that the analogy was, to a degree, realistic. The success of the so-called "color revolutions," however, required the concurrent fulfillment of at least four conditions. First, the holder of power had to falsify election results. Second, the opposition had to be capable of credibly presenting the fact of falsification and convincing a large portion of the political community of the truth of their claim. Third, election fraud had to have a meaningful effect on the results. Fourth, a portion of the political elite had to desert the ruling class, and cross over to stand with the protesters. If only one of these conditions was not met, the demonstrations could be long-lasting, but would in the end likely be ineffective. At the 2011 elections, three of these four conditions appeared to have been met, but the fracturing of unity in the power center did not emerge. There were no deserters. Of course the power center denied that it had interfered with results, and instead shifted emphasis elsewhere—to supposed external intervention, external command of events, and to subversive actions by the West.[46] Alternatively, the power center could have faced the facts provided by mathematical models, and the public database of the Central Election Commission, that showed the fact and scale of election result falsification—and the scale was shocking. Across the country, United Russia's support was artificially inflated by around 17–18 percent; the scale of "distortion" may have been even higher in Moscow.[47]

On top of this, another important sign of crisis seemed to be that the artificially created and maintained Russian party system—which reflected the needs of the executive branch—and the political manipulation it conveyed saw its earlier effectiveness continuously decrease. Each party that entered the lower chamber, with the exception of the now domesticated Communists, was now a so-called "artificial party," established as part of the executive branch's political plan and with its active cooperation, following clear power politics goals as opposed to expressing and conveying the interests of different social groups. Unquestionably, one such group was the Zhirinovsky-led LDPR, which moved from being an "artificial party" that had broken free of its chains into a purely "domesticated" party.

Somewhat more complicated was the situation of A Just Russia, whose results had exceeded expectations. Originally, this party too was a typical "artificial party." It was created by the Kremlin prior to the 2007 Duma elections as a center-left counterpart to the center-right "party of power," United Russia. It played the role of left-wing supporter of the Russian president in a trustworthy manner for years. In the 2011 elections, however, a portion of the party leadership tried to break free of this role and to position the party as an independent social-democratic organization. It ultimately turned out that those who were loyal to the Kremlin—that is, those who saw dependence on the Kremlin as more useful and important than political independence—were stronger.

Among the parties that gained entry in parliament was, of course, the primary beneficiary of Kremlin interference, United Russia. The current form of this typical "artificial organization," which in a short time came to be the "dominant" party in the system, was established in 2001, when—as mentioned above—it was created through the merger of two parties of similar character. The unified "party of power" viewed the parliamentary support of the head of state as its key function. To do so successfully, it required nothing more than control over more than half of the seats in parliament, but in a worst-case scenario, it was sufficient for forces loyal to the president to control a little more than one-third of the lower chamber mandates. The only time anything more than a comfortable majority was necessary was when the executive wished to amend the constitution, or in the case of an extraordinary political situation, like that produced by the "tandemocracy." In the latter situation it was not the president, Dmitry Medvedev, who required such a strong majority, but the then-Prime Minister Vladimir Putin instead, who saw the constitution-amending supermajority as the guarantee that his political stunt double would not suddenly dismiss him. This was because the prevailing president only ever faced one political risk: a supermajority of parliamentary forces standing against him. Such a situation could cripple the presidential powers, including the power of veto. As pointed out earlier, however, Putin never faced a situation similar to that of Yeltsin; indeed, in both 2003 and 2007 the forces in the Duma lining up behind Putin had a constitution-amending supermajority. To attain this supermajority, however, equal and fair campaign conditions had to be sacrificed in 2003, while the act on parties and elections had to be radically amended in 2007. After these steps were taken, it appeared Putin and his circle could settle into their power positions, because given the altered competitive conditions, they would not have to face serious challengers. This applied to both the presidential and parliamentary elections.

The system worked perfectly until the 2007 Duma and 2008 presidential elections. This is illustrated by the fact that the execution of the "tandemocracy" system went off without a hitch, with the election of Dmitry Medvedev as president. This took place in a situation where the Russian economy was growing at 7–8 percent annually, and a portion of the "income" gleaned from this growth could be redistributed to Russian society. As such, it would have been justified to think that tight control over political processes would remain for the long term, and there would consequently be no need to falsify election results. The 2011 parliamentary elections, however, showed this assumption to be false. The Kremlin was visibly late to "wake up" and take control of the situation, and was thus forced to employ methods it had not utilized in some time, at least not on a mass scale. However, in the era of smartphones and global connectivity, it is more difficult to hide election fraud, especially its more haphazard forms. Voters are more inclined to believe what they see over oral reports and election board minutes—and there was plenty to see. On the night of the elections, a series of shocking cases were shared on the internet: from the organized transportation of voters, who voted several times in several places, to dozens of cases of submitted fake ballots. Furthermore, there were some more extravagant cases of forgery, such as when the captain of a local police station decided that voting must continue, despite the fact that ballot boxes were mysteriously full even before the polls officially opened. Of course, we would be justified in noting that it is as easy to produce fake pictures and videos as fake texts and reports; that is, the strength of recordings posted on the Russian web as evidence *in itself* is inadequate. This is why the power center tried to label the videos as "fakes filmed in advance in studios,"[48] to quote Vladimir Churov, the president of the Central Election Commission, although he did not provide evidence to substantiate this claim, and has not done so to this day. The potential credibility of the recordings is increased not only by their very high number, but also the fact that a significant portion of eyewitness accounts by voters, as well as those mathematical analyses that appeared a few days after the election, not only presented the fact of intervention, but its massive scale as well.[49]

The Kremlin's unpreparedness and hasty responses were even more surprising because the erosion of support for the "party of power," United Russia, had been noted by public opinion pollsters long before the elections.

A continuous loss of popularity was notable at the beginning of the year, and the September 24th announcement of Putin's return to the presidential post fortified this process. Further, the announcement was tactically a mistake. Its timing made it possible for groups opposed to Putin—which sensed society's quickly emerging rejection of him—to "prepare" for the elections on December 4. Furthermore, unlike the parliamentary elections of 2003 and 2007, the 2011 elections were not being held in a country on the rise, with increasing self-confidence. Russia had been badly affected by the 2008–2009 global crisis and its consequences. The dramatic drop in performance reached its worst point in summer 2009; following this, by 2010, the Russian economy had returned to growth. But this growth—which from a European point of view was admirable—hardly exceeded four percent for the two years before the election; about half the rate of growth experienced before the crisis. Although Putin and his group did all they could to avoid cutting social expenditures, the growth of real incomes could not retain the dynamism it had prior to the crisis. Real incomes did indeed increase in 2010, but in the following year, for the first time since 1999, they stagnated. This was in sharp contrast to the average annual growth of real income between 2000 and 2008, which reached a rate of ten percent per year.

This all suggested that the main challenge to the Putin power circle would be neither the three "opposition" parties that entered parliament, nor those groups that demanded that the December elections be held again, this time fairly, along with the democratization of the political system. A far more formidable "antagonist" than the organized opposition, both within and outside parliament, was Putin's own campaign promises. Furthermore, at the end of 2011 and beginning of 2012, Russia had not just endured a small political crisis, but had to face the fact that the rate of economic growth was declining. This all happened when the price of a barrel of oil was still well over 100 USD and domestic consumption was on the rise; moreover, the crisis in Ukraine and the consequent Western sanctions against Russia were still a long way away. Putin thus began his third term as president in a situation in which he had to put down the wave of demonstrations concerning the elections—an emerging revolt from the urban middle class—and on the other hand had to respond to the continuously declining performance of the economy. If these "uncomfortable events" had not emerged, it is likely that Moscow's policy toward Ukraine would have developed differently. But in the circumstances, the Kremlin did not dare take on another failure—letting Ukraine leave its sphere of influence—and instead launched an "active operation" employing numerous tools to boldly interfere in the domestic affairs of its neighbor to the west. The annexation of the Crimean Peninsula not only caused an explosion of nationalist sentiment, but also an unexpected result whereby a segment of the middle class that had been protesting against Putin now returned to the president's fold. From the spring of 2014, Russian domestic politics were increasingly ruled by false triumphalism, warmongering and long-forgotten anti-Western rhetoric. In this emotional environment, the Kremlin continued its campaign against civic organizations launched in summer 2012, and persisted in marginalizing those parties it viewed as a threat. Of the two liberal parties that previously fell out of the lower chamber of parliament, one—the Union of Rightist Forces—had dissolved before the 2011 elections. However, the other, Yabloko, continued to operate, though its election results were regularly so poor that it had posed no threat to the power center for some time. The Union of Rightist Forces' decline was terminal; in 2003 the party finished one percent short of the five percent parliamentary threshold of the time, while four years later it was six percent short of reaching the threshold, which had in the meantime been increased to seven percent. Following the failure of 2007, the party dissolved itself. This decision was ostensibly taken by the party membership, but it would be more accurate to state that the liberal organization was liquidated. As such, the Union of Rightist Forces ought to be labeled a "liquidated party," or a group whose operation was made impossible by the power center, thereby forcing the organization to disband. It was replaced by one of the Kremlin's new projects under the name *Right Cause*, headed by billionaire Mikhail Prokhorov, and it was an abject failure. At the 2011 election, it managed to win only 0.6 percent of the votes.[50] The liberal portion of Russian society had no trust in this new "artificial party." Liberal voters yearned for a party that represented their beliefs, but not one that the Kremlin created for them.

The other liberal party, Yabloko, almost made it into parliament in 2003, missing the threshold by only 0.7 percent. At the next elections, when the mixed system was replaced by the pure proportional system and the threshold rose to seven percent, its support was barely more than 1.5 percent. This is not surprising, given that the party's candidates were given no opportunity to promote themselves in politically valuable media, and had no means to seek significant financial backers—all the more so as the Kremlin made sure to block the party's access to any financial resources. Despite this, it was able to improve its results in 2011 to 3.5 percent, though this was not enough to gain seats in parliament.[51] The social-liberal Yabloko, given that it was not an "artificial party" and could not be domesticated, became a "marginalized party." Again and again it participated in elections, but it had no hope of gaining entry into the lower chamber.

After the Kremlin had completed the development of its circle of "artificial parties"—like the Liberal Democratic Party of Russia or A Just Russia—and "domesticated parties"—like the Communist Party of the Russian Federation—these parties were prepared to accept their subjugation to the "party of power," and even more so to the executive branch. To have complete control over political processes, the executive power now only needed to break civic organizations. The first round of doing so took place shortly after the Orange Revolution of 2004 in Ukraine; the second began in the summer of 2012. The weakening or dismantling of potential political opponents and groups capable of limiting the power center, the continuation of wartime psychosis, and the repeated use of fraudulent electoral practices in the 2016 Duma election was so effective that the "party of power" succeeded in winning over three-quarters of seats. Of the 450 available seats, United Russia won 343.[52] The elections were once again held using a mixed system. The three remaining parties, which lacked independent political will, split just over 100 mandates among themselves. They did not have the capacity to limit the executive power. However, they had no intentions of doing so anyway; nor did the now-dominant United Russia. For the role of these parties was no longer to serve as checks on political power. They were now transmitters: that is, conveyors and servants of the will of the executive.

Nevertheless, this impressive result was misleading in several aspects. Foremost, this result was attained by the "party of power" in an election with an unprecedentedly low turnout. The rate of participation was seven percent below the lowest official turnout in the past twenty years, failing to reach 48 percent. What was even more illustrative was the fact that in the country's two great metropolises—Moscow and St. Petersburg—only one-third of those with the right to vote felt motivated enough to do so.[53] Given that the executive power did not want another controversial election result, it did not interfere with the results in the two large cities, and instead acknowledged them. The cost of this is reflected in the following statement: the support of barely 15 percent of the 110 million Russian citizens with the right to vote was sufficient to raise the United Russia party to control of more than three-quarters of lower chamber seats.[54]

For a long time—since at least 2003—the Russian party system has been such that, within the framework of the act on parties and elections, those in power cannot be removed. Shortly after shifting to a multi-party form, the party system and its operation was reorganized in such a way that it was defined by the dominance of one party, created and strongly supported by the executive branch. The key role of the dominant party is to endorse the will of the executive branch in the legislature, while maintaining the façade of democratic discourse. Both the party system and the dominant party, United Russia, continue to carry out this "mission."

In contrast, no one in Ukraine has been able, to this day, to create a similar situation. Until 2012, no party supporting the president had ever been able to win the elections. Although in the 2012 elections the Party of Regions—which stood behind Viktor Yanukovych, the winner of the 2010 presidential elections—managed to gain 186 seats and become the strongest faction in the Rada, this win still secured only a relative majority.[55] Of the five parties that entered parliament, three were in opposition to the Party of Regions. Only the 32-strong Communists were willing to cooperate with the president's party, but even this was not enough to form an absolute majority.

The October parliamentary elections taking place after the transfer of power in 2014 brought about the same situation as in 2012. Once again, the president's party emerged victorious, albeit this time with a different president. The head of state was elected in May, and he was able to develop a party alliance with which he won almost one-third of the mandates. The *Petro Poroshenko bloc*—along with its allies in parliament—had control of over half the representative seats.[56] Despite this, this is not a situation in which the head of state controls a constitution-amending supermajority; no such situation has ever unfolded in independent Ukraine. Many factors are at play here. Firstly, Ukraine's east-west political division, which already existed in the 1990s, only became definitive in the early 2000s. The fortification of territorial divisions became a serious obstacle to the executive branch's efforts to organize a dominant party that could spread its influence throughout Ukraine. Secondly, a scenario like that which occurred in Russia could not unfold because, as a result of territorial division, no hierarchically organized patron-client network developed. In its place, competing networks emerged. Thirdly, a Russia-type system did not emerge because in Ukraine the constitutional status of presidential power is always changing; it is weak when the political system takes on the presidential-parliamentary model, and is strong when the presidential system is reestablished. By contrast, the constitutional situation of the president in Russia has remained unchanged since the ratification of the 1993 Constitution.

Given that "Ukraine is not Russia," to this point not one party has managed to cement its dominance and rise above the rest.[57] This situation forces the party with the largest parliamentary faction to engage in dialogue with the other parties, something that has long been absent from Russian politics. At the same time, the Russian system differs not only from that of Ukraine, but also from those of Central Asia as well, especially the Turkmen system, which until 2008 functioned as not only a de facto, but also a de jure one-party system. The 2008 election was the first in which the local successors to the Communist Party, the *Democratic Party*, could potentially face competitors for the first time. This did not occur then, but ensued in the next elections, five years later. This, however, did not change the fact that the local legislature, under the strict control of the successor party, does nothing more than carry out the will of the president. Conversely, the party system in Uzbekistan followed a different path. In the fall of 1991, the new *People's Democratic Party of Uzbekistan,* was established, replacing the local Communist Party. The last leader of the Uzbek Communists, Islam Karimov, who by that point was serving as head of state, was elected president of the party. He was not present at the founding convention, but this did not seem to bother anyone. The People's Democratic Party won the two elections held in the 1990s, but during the 2000s another party, the *Liberal Democratic Party of Uzbekistan*, repeatedly won. This, however, did nothing to change the style of governance from the autocratic head of state, who died in 2016. The legislature was so subservient to the executive branch that the president had the "luxury" of not needing his own party to have the largest parliamentary faction. What was also needed, though, was the Liberal Democratic Party's lack of ambition to provide any genuine opposition. Indeed, this lack of ambition was so extreme that in 2007, the Liberal Democratic Party themselves nominated Karimov for yet another mandate as president.

The "Russian model," however, is different; democratic façades still play an important role. This is why parliamentary and presidential elections are still held from time to time in Russia as a way of granting "the opposition" and "opposition candidates" serious roles. These, however, are merely simulated roles, because for some time now there has been no risk of even an "opposition" party created by the executive branch itself gaining power. This intention is merely imitated, because such parties are aware that this was why they were created in the first place.

Notes

1. Vladimir Ya. Gel'man and V. P. Yelezarov, "'Uchreditel'nyye vybory' v kontekste rossiyskoy transformatsii," in *Pervyy elektoral'nyy tsikl v Rossii (1993-1996 gg.)*, edited by V. Gel'man, G. Golosov, and Ye. Meleshkina, M. (Moscow: Izdatel'stvo "Ves' Mir", 2000), 26.
2. A.V. Kynev and A. Ye. Lyubarev, *Partii i vybory v sovremennoy Rossii: evolyutsiya i devolyutsiya* (Moscow: Novoye literaturnoye obozreniye, 2011), 102.
3. Ukaz Prezidenta RF ot 1 oktyabrya 1993 g. No. 1557, "Polozheniye o vyborakh deputatov Gosudarstvennoy Dumy v 1993 godu," http://pravo.gov.ru/proxy/ips/?doc_itself=&nd=102027052&page=1&rdk=1#I0, accessed Dec. 30, 2017.
4. Ukaz Prezidenta RF ot 6 noyabrya 1993 g. No. 1846, "Ob utochnenii Polozheniya o vyborakh deputatov Gosudarstvennoy Dumy v 1993 godu i Polozheniya o vyborakh deputatov Soveta Federatsii federal'nogo Sobraniya RF v 1993 godu," docs.cntd.ru/document/9022956, accessed Dec. 30, 2017.
5. Kynev and Lyubarev, *Partii i vybory*, 108.
6. Ibid., 117.
7. Federal'nyy zakon ot 18 maya 2005 g. No. 51-FZ, "O vyborakh deputatov Gosudarstvennoy Dumy Federal'nogo Sobraniya Rossiyskoy Federatsii," http://www.consultant.ru/document/cons_doc_LAW_53536/, accessed Dec. 30, 2017.
8. This this legal institution, codified by Art. 35 of the 1993 law was erased in new electoral law passed in 2005. See ibid.
9. Vladimir Gel'man, *Iz ognya do v polymya: Rossiyskaya politika posle SSSR* (St. Petersburg: BHV-Peterburg, 2013), 51.
10. Alexander A. Sobyanin and Vladislav G. Sukhovol'skiy, *Demokratiya, ogranichennaya fal'sifikatsiyami: Vybory i referendumy v Rossii v 1991-1993 gg.* (Moscow: Intu-Press, 1995), 77.
11. The Agrarian Party was established in 1993 with the express purpose of replacing the Communists, in the event that the latter were barred from standing in the elections.
12. *Rezul'taty vyborov deputatov Gosudarstvennoy Dumy po obshchefederal'nomu okrugu 12 dekabrya 1993 goda*, http://www.cikrf.ru/banners/vib_arhiv/gosduma/1993/1993_itogi_FS_obshefed_okrug.html, accessed Dec. 27, 2017. For more on Zhirinovsky and the LDPR, see, for instance, Andreas Umland, "Zhirinovskii as a Fascist: Palingenetic Ultra-Nationalism and the Emergence of the Liberal-Democratic Party of Russia in 1992–93," *Forum für osteuropäische Ideen- und Zeitgeschichte* 14 (2010): 189–215.
13. *Rezul'taty vyborov v Dumu sozyva 17 dekabrya 1995*, http://www.politika.su/fs/gd2rezv.html, accessed Dec. 27, 2017.
14. *Protokol Tsentral'noy izbiratel'noy komissii RF o raspredelenii deputatskikh mandatov mezhdu ibiratel'nymi ob"yedineniyami, izbiratel'nymi blokami i o rezul'tatakh vyborov po federal'nomu izbiratel'nomu okrugu*, http://cikrf.ru/banners/vib_arhiv/gosduma/1999/index.html, accessed Dec. 27, 2017.

15 *Rezul'taty vyborov deputatov Gosudarstvennoy Dumy po obshchefederal'nomu okrugu 12 dekabrya 1993 goda,* http://www.cikrf.ru/banners/vib_arhiv/gosduma/1993/1993_itogi_FS_obshefed_okrug.html, accessed Dec. 28, 2017.
16 *Rezul'taty vyborov v Dumu sozyva 17 dekabrya 1995,* http://www.politika.su/fs/gd2rezv.html, accessed Dec. 28, 2017.
17 Ibid.
18 *Rezul'taty vyborov deputatov Gosudarstvennoy Dumy po obshchefederal'nomu okrugu 12 dekabrya 1993 goda,* http://www.cikrf.ru/banners/vib_arhiv/gosduma/1993/1993_itogi_FS_obshefed_okrug.html, accessed Dec. 28, 2017.
19 *Itogi golosovaniya po federal'nomu okrugu 3 dekabrya 2003 goda,* http://gd2003.cikrf.ru/, accessed Dec. 28, 2017.
20 For the results of the 2007 Duma elections see: http://www.vybory.izbirkom.ru/region/region/izbirkom?action=show&root=1&tvd=100100021960186&vrn=100100021960181&region=0&global=1&sub_region=0&prver=0&pronetvd=null&vibid=100100021960186&type=233, accessed Dec. 28, 2017.
21 "Istoriya ukrainskogo parlamentarizma," RIA Novosti Ukraina, last modified Oct. 24, 2014, http://rian.com.ua/analytics/20141024/358680489.html.
22 *Rezul'taty vyborov v Dumu sozyva 17 dekabrya 1995,* http://www.politika.su/fs/gd2rezv.html, accessed Dec. 28, 2017.
23 Ibid.
24 Ibid.
25 *Protokol Tsentral'noy izbiratel'noy komissii RF o raspredelenii deputatskikh mandatov mezhdu ibiratel'nymi ob"yedineniyami, izbiratel'nymi blokami i o rezul'tatakh vyborov po federal'nomu izbiratel'nomu okrogu,* http://cikrf.ru/banners/vib_arhiv/gosduma/1999/index.html, accessed Dec. 28, 2017.
26 Regarding the final results of the 2007 elections see: *Vybory, referendumy i inye formy pryamogo volez'yavleniya,* http://www.vybory.izbirkom.ru/region/region/izbirkom?action=show&root=1&tvd=100100021960186&vrn=100100021960181&region=0&global=1&sub_region=0&prver=0&pronetvd=null&vibid=100100021960186&type=233, accessed Dec. 28, 2017. For the 2011 results see: *Rezultaty vyborov,* http://www.cikrf.ru/banners/duma_2011/itogi/result.html, accessed Dec. 28, 2017.
27 *Protokol Tsentral'noy izbiratel'noy komissii RF o raspredelenii deputatskikh mandatov mezhdu ibiratel'nymi ob"yedineniyami, izbiratel'nymi blokami i o rezul'tatakh vyborov po federal'nomu izbiratel'nomu okrogu,* http://cikrf.ru/banners/vib_arhiv/gosduma/1999/index.html, accessed Dec. 28, 2017.
28 See Gel'man, Vl.: "Evolyutsiya elektoral'noy politiki v Rossii: na puti k nedemokraticheskoy konsolidatsii?" in *Tretiy elektoral'nyy tsikl v Rossii 2003-2004 gody* (St. Petersburg: Yevropeyskiy universitet v Sankt-Peterburge, 2007), 30–31.
29 The elections results can be seen at: http://www.cvk.gov.ua/pls/vd2002/webproc0v?kodvib=1&rejim=0, accessed Dec. 28, 2017.
30 "U dumskikh kommunistov otobrali sem' komitetov," https://lenta.ru/news/2002/04/03/duma/, accessed Dec. 30, 2017.
31 Federal'nyy zakon ot 11 iyulya 2001 g. No. 95-FZ, "O politicheskikh partiyakh," http://duma.consultant.ru/page.aspx?688150.

[32] Kynev and Lyubarev, *Partii i vybory*, 616.
[33] *Vybory v Gosudarstvennuyu Dumu (7 dekabrya 2003 g.) Otchet Missii OBSE/ BDIPCH po nablyudeniyu za vyboramy (27 yanvarya 2004 g.)*, http://www.osce.org/ru/odihr/elections/russia/21482?download=true, accessed Dec. 31, 2017. See also OBSE: rezul'taty dumskikh vyborov "chrezvychayno ikazheny," https://www.gazeta.ru/2003/12/08/na1070883420.shtml, accessed Dec. 31, 2017.
[34] "'Yedinaya Rossiya' vozglavit vse komitety Gosdumy," *Vesti.ru*, http://www.vesti.ru/doc.html?id=40159&tid=19251, accessed Dec. 31, 2017.
[35] "Tekst stenogrammy zasedaniya Gosudarstvennoy Dumy, zasedaniye ot 29.12.2003.," in *Gosudarstvennaya Duma. Stenogramma zasedaniy (Byulleten')*, No. 1 (715) part 1, 4–31.
[36] Regarding the parliamentary election results in Azerbaijan, see "Milli Məclisə seçkilər," Azərbaycan Respublikası Mərkəzi Seçki Komsissiyası, http://www.msk.gov.az/az/elections/milli-meclise-seckiler/, accessed Jan. 3, 2018.
[37] Regarding the parliamentary election results in Armenia, see Republic of Armenia Central Election Commission, http://www.elections.am/electionsview/, accessed Jan. 3, 2018.
[38] M. V. Ivanova, "Reforma izbiratel'noy sistemy i regional'noye izmereniye vyborov v Gosudarstvennuyu Dumu 2007 g.," *Politicheskaya Nauka* 1 (2012): 94–109.
[39] *Vybory v Gosudarstvennuyu Dumu (7 dekabrya 2003 g.) Otchet Missii OBSE/ BDIPCH po nablyudeniyu za vyboramy (27 yanvarya 2004 g.)*, http://www.osce.org/ru/odihr/elections/russia/21482?download=true, accessed Dec. 29, 2017.
[40] Kynev and Lyubarev, *Partii i vybory*, 140.
[41] For the results of the 2002 Ukrainian parliamentary elections, see Vybory narodnikh deputativ Ukraini, http://www.cvk.gov.ua/pls/vd2002/WEBPROC0V, accessed Jan. 4, 2017.
[42] For the results of the 2006 Ukrainian parliamentary elections, see Central'na Viborcha Komisija Ukraini, http://www.cvk.gov.ua/pls/vnd2006/w6p001, accessed Jan. 4, 2017.
[43] For the results of the 2007 Ukrainian parliamentary elections, see Central'na Viborcha Komisija Ukraini, http://www.cvk.gov.ua/pls/vnd2007/w6p001, accessed Jan. 4, 2017.
[44] For the official results of the 2011 Duma elections see *Vybory, referendumy i inye formy pryamogo volez'yavleniya*, http://www.vybory.izbirkom.ru/region/region/izbirkom?action=show&root=1&tvd=100100028713304&vrn=100100028713299&region=0&global=1&sub_region=0&prver=0&pronetvd=null&vibid=100100028713304&type=233, accessed Jan. 4, 2017.
[45] *Putin podtverdil namereniye ballotirovat'sya v prezidenty*, Grani.ru, Sep. 24, 2011, http://graniru.org/Politics/Russia/Election/m.191694.html, accessed Jan. 5, 2018.
[46] The following volume is a detailed and convincing account of the experiences of election observers concerning cheating: I. Berlyand and M. Stupakova, eds., *Razgnevannyye nablyudateli: Falsifikatsii parlamentskiye vybory gpazami ochevidtsev* (Moscow: Novoye literaturnoye obozreniye, 2012).

47 See Sergey Shpilkin, "Statistika issledovala vybory," Gazeta.ru, Dec. 10, 2011, https://www.gazeta.ru/science/2011/12/10_a_3922390.shtml, accessed Jan. 5, 2018.
48 "Churov: 'Kino' o narusheniyakh na vyborakh snimali v 'fal'shivikh izbirkomakh'," Gazeta.ru, Jul. 12, 2011, https://www.gazeta.ru/news/lastnews/2011/12/07/n_2125762.shtml, accessed Jan. 5, 2018.
49 See "O chem mozhet skazat' elektoral'naya statistika," Polit.ru, http://polit.ru/article/2012/01/12/elections/, accessed Jan. 5, 2018; Sergey Shpilkin, "Statistika issledovala vybory," Gazeta.ru, https://www.gazeta.ru/science/2011/12/10_a_3922390.shtml, accessed Jan. 5, 2018; Yan Rachinskiy, "O churodeystve i fal'shebstve," Polit.ru, http://polit.ru/article/2011/12/23/raczynski_vybory/, accessed Jan. 5, 2018.
50 For the official results of the 2011 Duma elections see *Vybory, referendumy i inye formy pryamogo volez'yavleniya*, http://www.vybory.izbirkom.ru/region/region/izbirkom?action=show&root=1&tvd=100100028713304&vrn=100100028713299&region=0&global=1&sub_region=0&prver=0&pronetvd=null&vibid=100100028713304&type=233, accessed Jan. 5, 2018.
51 Ibid.
52 Tatiana Zamakhina, "TSIK utverdil itogi vyborov v Gosdumu vecherom 22 sentyabrya," Rossiyskaya Gazeta, https://rg.ru/2016/09/22/cik-utverdit-itogi-vyborov-v-gosdumu-vecherom-22-sentiabria.html, accessed Jan. 5, 2018.
53 Elizaveta Surnacheva, "Na vyborakh v Moskve i Peterburge zafiksirovali rekordno nizkuyu yavku," RBK, http://www.rbc.ru/politics/18/09/2016/57debade9a79472dc621d336, accessed Jan. 5, 2018.
54 Although officially United Russia received 28.5 million votes, the credibility of this numbers is questioned by a number of experts, including Sergey Shpilkin, who estimates that the real number of votes cast was around 16.5 million, that is, only 15 percent of registered voters. See Baydakova, A., "Real'no 'Yedinuyu Rossiyu' podderzhali 15 % izbirateley," *Novaya Gazeta*, September 20, 2016, https://www.novayagazeta.ru/articles/2016/09/20/69897-realno-edinuyu-rossiyu-podderzhali-15-izbirateley, accessed April 26, 2018.
55 For the results of the 2012 Ukrainian parliamentary elections see: *Centralna Vyborcha Komisija*, http://www.cvk.gov.ua/vnd_2012/, accessed Jan. 5, 2018.
56 For the results of the 2014 snap Rada elections, see *Centralna Vyborcha Komisija*, http://www.cvk.gov.ua/vnd_2014/, accessed Jan. 5, 2018.
57 Phrase is taken from the title of Leonid Kuchma's book *Ukraina – ne Rossiya* (Moscow: Vremia, 2003).

Andrei Kazakevich

The Belarusian non-party political system: Government, trust and institutions, 1990–2015

Introduction

Belarus is not a typical political system in many aspects, particularly when compared to other Eastern European nations. There are a number of opposing systemic arrangements that serve to highlight these differences: authoritarian populism versus oligarchy;[1] competitive versus uncompetitive authoritarianism;[2] and authoritarianism versus sultanism.[3] However, the special nature of the Belarusian system has not only a metaphorical dimension, but an institutional one as well.

Since 2008, there have been significant changes in the structure of the Belarusian national economy due to the impact of world economic crises, and a major role played by private enterprise, particularly in the services, trade, and IT areas. However, **the government maintains its dominant position in the key areas of the economy**, and remains the country's major employer. Public and political debates on the chances for large-scale economic reforms continue apace, having grown stronger after a dramatic economic decline in 2011, and became even more intense by the end of 2014, when the new wave of crises started. However, neither privatization programs[4] nor bankruptcy procedures of the large state-owned companies have been implemented so far, while the government dominates in most areas of economic activity.

Another peculiar characteristic of Belarus was the choice of **the Soviet identity as the basis for nation building.** Intellectuals, both domestically and abroad, have repeatedly debated this phenomenon. They stressed the antagonism existing between the "Soviet" and "national" concept of the nation, where the former was officially embraced by the government, and the latter was perceived as an oppositional idea.[5] After 2008,[6] this concept was significantly modified and many elements of the "national" vision of history were gradually introduced into the official realm, including the improved treatment of the Belarusian language, previously subordinate to Russian in the public sphere. Nevertheless, the Soviet element continues to dominate.

Belarus also stands out among the former Soviet republics due to the significant and often definitive **Russian influence** in its economy, foreign policy, and media landscape. Russia takes about 50% of Belarus's turnover of foreign trade in goods.[7] This is a record not only for the post-Soviet region, but the entire world. Indeed, for a long time Belarusian foreign policy strictly followed that of Russia: Belarus supported all of Russia's integrationist initiatives, and it is a Collective Security Treaty Organization (CSTO) member and a co-founder of the "Union State" of Belarus and Russia.[8] After 2008–2010, there were attempts to modify the country's foreign policy course. These attempts increased after 2014: when the Russo-Ukrainian conflict erupted, Belarus tried to counterbalance Russian influence by normalizing its relations with the European Union and the United States and enhancing its relations with developing nations (such as Iran and Venezuela), while significant economic and investment expectations were placed on China. However, Russia remains its main trade partner, while also dominating Belarusian foreign policy both in terms of quantity (number of visits, treaties and so forth) and quality.

Another peculiar characteristic of the Belarusian political system is the overwhelmingly dominant position of **executive bodies** in almost every area of society, while in neighboring countries political parties, NGOs, media, and business tend to play significant supplementary roles. Bureaucracy and the executive branch enjoy near-total domination in Belarusian politics. The only key group of influence outside of the executive vertical of power is the close circle of the president. Business influence is quite limited, while the impact of political parties and NGOs is close to zero. As a result, Belarus has developed a non-party political system, with few similarities to any current political system in Eastern Europe.

The list of peculiar characteristics is still not complete, but what is even more important is that these unique features do not exist in isolation: common institutions and rationale link them with each other. In this article, we are going to focus only on one highlighted peculiar property: the non-partisan political system. We are going to answer the questions of why such a system has been developed, what makes it peculiar, what has secured its stability, and how it works.

In other words, the purpose of this paper is to research the main reasons and conditions for putting the non-partisan system in place, as well as to demonstrate how authority is distributed within the system, and how functions usually performed by political parties are implemented. We will try to grasp the institutional conditions for the creation of such a system as well as the mechanisms, which serve to make political parties irrelevant while securing political sustainability in Belarus.

Indeed, the non-party system is unusual in the contemporary world. It would suffice to point out that it has no parallel in the post-Soviet region, though it does exist in a handful of nations where political parties are banned by law. These are mostly Persian Gulf monarchies: the UAE, Kuwait, and Oman. There are also countries where political parties are officially allowed, but were either never created or do not play any significant role. These are mostly tiny island nations, such as Nauru and Tuvalu. In recent political history, there are many examples of political parties' activities being suspended, such as in Uganda from 1985 to 2005, Burma, Thailand and so on. As such, Belarus is the largest nation in terms of population to have a non-party political system without any *force majeure* justification. All other post-Soviet republics, including authoritarian ones, feature political parties as an integral part of their political system.

Officially, there are fifteen political parties in Belarus, along with four organizing committees or political movements (such as *Movement for Freedom* and *Tell the Truth*), but none of the political organizations are integrated into political decision-making processes.

I. The current party system: some contributing factors

Formally, Belarus has a multiparty system. The Constitution ensures the right to create a political party, and this provision is regulated by law.[9] Political parties began to register in 1991, and the peak of parties' activities was during the parliamentary elections of 1995, when candidates running on party lists received 53% of the available seats. Parliamentary groups were built on a party basis, and political parties became active and crucial participants in political processes. Immediately after the constitutional crisis of 1996, the influence of political parties began to decline, while President Alexander Lukashenka consolidated his authority, resulting in the restoration of the non-partisan system.

By the end of the 1990s, there were up to 40 political parties in Belarus. Currently, the existing fifteen organizations represent practically the entire ideological gamut. However, the process of new party creation is severely limited. As such, a number of non-registered parties exist, some of which position themselves as social movements or campaigns.

Since the end of 1996, when the authoritarian regime began its consolidation, political parties were clearly divided into two camps: pro-government (and, by extension, pro-president) and opposition, though neither the former nor the latter have a chance to make any meaningful difference in domestic politics. The opposition parties are not represented in either the legislative or executive branches of power.[10] Some of the loyal parties have insignificant representation in the parliament and local councils without having any real say in political matters or any influence on executive bodies. There were a few cases when parties' representatives (pro-government Communist Party of Belarus) were appointed to bureaucratic positions without having any significant impact on the political essence of the state. There were several attempts to create a ruling party, the most significant of which is "Belaya Rus." The executive agencies, which are the foundation of the political system, are non-partisan on both national and regional levels. Any party membership would be detrimental rather than beneficial for a political career.

Despite the apparent vulnerabilities and lack of consistency, the system has its own institutional foundation and rationale for choosing to address political issues in post-Soviet Belarus as it does. The system was a product of the conjunction of various circumstances: post-Soviet heritage, conflict of interests, instability of political processes, and some incidental events became the basis for the emergence, consolidation, and preservation of the system to the present day.

We believe that the emergence of the non-partisan system in Belarus occurred due to an intertwining of several factors: the crisis and vertiginous collapse of the Soviet *nomenklatura* (the ruling class in the USSR), the pursuit of "direct rule," the confrontation between the president and the other political institutions (political parties, parliament, and *nomenklatura*), and the continuing government control of the economy. The low level of mutual trust among the participants of the political process, as well as the fact that the new president lacked any experience as a political organizer, also contributed to this outcome.

By no means did the aforementioned factors preordain the exclusion of political parties from politics (particularly if the presence of the authoritarian leader is taken into account), but they have significantly limited the choice of political development and nipped political pluralism, as well as politics-oriented groupings, in the bud. In our analysis below, we will attempt to take a closer look at the fundamental reasons for the creation of such a system, to describe its existing mechanisms, the factors which secure its preservation, and debates regarding the evolution of the system.

II. The crisis and collapse of the Belarusian Soviet *nomenklatura*, 1990–1994

In former Soviet republics, the evolution of the *nomenklatura* developed under different circumstances. In some cases, local branches of the Communist Party of the Soviet Union (CPSU) were modified into new ruling parties (as in many of the Central Asian states). In the cases of Latvia, Lithuania, and Georgia, former communists created new left-wing political parties. However, in Russia, Ukraine, and Belarus, the communist parties identified themselves as direct successors of the CPSU, using its ideology to be rebuilt by mid- and low-level party functionaries. In other words, the Soviet *nomenklatura* either created a ruling party (sometimes after a period of political instability) or a new political force, which was successfully integrated into the democratic political process.

Belarus was an exemplary exception, which significantly defined the further political development of the nation. The Belarusian Soviet *nomenklatura* failed to build sustainable political structures, though in 1991 it managed to preserve political power without much effort, or any significant competition from rival political forces. Given the ease with which the Belarusian Soviet *nomenklatura* managed to preserve political power during the upheaval of 1990–1991, its political weakness looks particularly bizarre. At any rate, there were institutional reasons for its frailty, chiefly the structural crisis brought by generational change with new political groups moving to the top of the party ladder.

The Belarusian *nomenklatura* took shape after World War II, when three men dominated Belarusian politics: Pyotr Masherov (Piotr Masherau),

Kiril Mazurov (Kiryl Mazurau), and Tikhon Kiselyov (Tikhan Kisialyou). All three came to power in the 1950s and quit before the mid-1980s. Their demise brought a cadre instability, a leadership crisis, and a lack of political skills and experience on the part of the new leadership, which resulted in the political weakness of the two governments led by Vyachaslau Kebich from 1990 to 1994.

With the three chief leaders abandoning the scene, there were significant structural changes among the political elites in the early 1980s. By the mid-1950s, the major political force in the Belarusian (Byelorussian) Soviet Socialist Republic (BSSR) was the so-called "partisans" (WWII resistance fighters). However, the so-called "industrialists" group (Minsk City Industrial Group, MCIG) gradually drove them out by the mid-1980s.[11] This change was stipulated for a number of reasons, including demographic ones. Internal contradictions were not fierce and the conflict between the two groups could not be deemed as open. The new political force was closely linked to the Soviet Union Central Government/CPSU apparatus by origin, mentality, as well as professionally, and was poorly prepared for independence. Moreover, the period when the MCIG came to power overlapped with a general political crisis in the USSR, which created even greater problems for the consolidation of the new elites.

At the beginning of the 1990s, the Belarusian *nomenklatura* was completely unprepared to build a new independent state. Its lack of preparedness manifested itself most in the *nomenklatura*'s inability to set up a new sustainable political framework after the CPSU was disbanded. Throughout the entire period of Kebich's government (1990–1994), it had no support, neither from the "ruling party," nor from a party coalition. By its very nature, it was a technocratic government. The parliamentary group "Belarus," created to support the government, remained an amorphous group with no definite political or party character.

The careers of key BSSR Communist Party leaders further illuminates how weak the Belarusian Soviet *nomenklatura* was. In many other Soviet republics, former Communist Party leaders took an active role in political development, assuming the presidency of all the Central Asian republics (with the exception of Kyrgyzstan), Azerbaijan, Georgia, Moldova and Lithuania. However, top leadership figures within the Belarusian Communist Party (like A. Malafeyeu and A. Kamay) failed to continue their political careers.

After the failed coup d'état attempt in August 1991, the CPSU ban, and the collapse of the USSR, the Belarusian *nomenklatura* preserved its positions in top government positions, but was unable to create a new political framework. Chairman of the Council of Ministers Kebich did not dare to embark on the path of building a new political framework, which would take the shape of a political party; instead, he opted to reinforce the power of the bureaucracy. The bureaucratic leadership assumed the role of the *nomenklatura,* and the new status quo remained frozen until 1995, when parliamentary elections finally took place.

This time period (1991–1994) is when the first version of a non-partisan political system was established. It was created without any plan, as a byproduct of the CPSU framework collapse, when governmental bureaucrats filled the administrative void. The executive branch bureaucracy, and the politically unstructured Supreme Soviet, had the bulk of power concentrated in their hands. With the absence of political will, only the bureaucratic rules and regulations could minimize political risks, and eventually political parties came to be perceived as a destabilizing factor, rather than a consolidating one. As a result, the non-partisan bureaucracy was counterbalanced by a mostly non-partisan parliament and equally non-partisan local councils, while political parties had no influence in the main power centers.

Kebich's loss in the 1994 presidential elections, and the rise to power of "anti-politician" Alexander Lukashenka, threw a monkey wrench in the system of power continuity. The Soviet *nomenklatura*'s fragmentation augmented. With no political framework supporting it, it yielded the stage easily and ceased to exist as an independent political force. When the authoritarian regime began to take shape after the 1996 debacle, the *nomenklatura* was still an important but subordinate player in the new power coalition, and for a variety of reasons (including the advancing age of its members) it was gradually dislodged from the political sphere by the mid-2000s.

III. The crisis of trust in political institutions, 1994–1996

The crisis of trust in political institutions was the second key factor for the emergence and preservation of the non-partisan system: at the beginning of the 1990s, many lost confidence in the new political institutions and politics in general. Many people believed that the way out of the economic and political crisis was through getting rid of "politics." Political parties were new institutions, which were not perceived by the majority of voters as useful or competent bodies. They were not associated with real authority, but were seen as a tool of political struggles for power—whether in parliament or on the streets.

The majority could not grasp the idea of what political parties were for. Though a certain number of voters did support political parties for ideological reasons, the majority were focused on figures who were outside of "politics."[12] The political and economic crisis increasingly nudged this majority to embrace apolitical positions, as politics were perceived as a source of problems, instability, conflict, and corruption.

In these circumstances, political parties could prove advantageous in parliamentary electoral campaigns, since they could secure support from certain social groups and a strong position in some electoral districts. A political party was also a handy tool to mobilize supporters for street protests or an electoral campaign. However, in a presidential campaign, a political party was more of a liability for reaching out to the "man on the street." In the 1994 presidential campaign, candidates who used political parties as their support base failed to gain any noticeable advantage, and even lost votes.

President Lukashenka won in the summer of 1994, thanks to the "electoral revolution," when he received 43% of the vote in the first round and 80% in the second. Lukashenka positioned himself as an apolitical or even anti-political figure, keeping a distance not only from authorities, but from other political groupings as well. He took great pains to present himself as a "man of the people," an independent figure who was not involved in political games and intrigue. Any coalition with existing political parties, or the creation of his own party, would harm his image of an anti-corruption crusader who was opposed to political chaos. Therefore, the non-partisan strategy choice at the first stage of Lukashenka's presidency was quite logical. Moreover, it helped to secure the continuity of the political system which emerged after the collapse of the CPSU in 1991.

IV. The impotence of political institutions

The crisis of the Soviet *nomenklatura*, and the crisis of trust in politics and political institutions, was combined with the general weakness of the structure of political parties, which lagged significantly behind their counterparts in neighboring countries in terms of development. The entire party system, as it emerged in 1991–1994, was extremely amorphous.

Political movements in Belarus, unlike in other western republics of the USSR, had not acquired a mass scale, and people's organized political activity was significantly lower. The country's first relatively free elections in 1990 had a completely different outcome: only about 30 of the new legislators (out of a total of 360) were representatives of the organized opposition. More than 90% of the new legislators were CPSU members, and no less than two thirds were *nomenklatura* members. After the collapse and ban of the CPSU, the parliament (which played the central role in national political life in 1990–1994) became strikingly non-partisan. When the opposition Belarusian Popular Front (BNF) suggested early parliamentary elections in 1992, the majority of legislators declined this initiative, and the non-partisan nature of the parliament was preserved until the next elections in 1995.

As a result, in the early 1990s political parties had very limited electoral and organizational resources and were not very useful to the new administration. Lukashenka felt no need to enter into any sustainable political agreement with political parties, since they would have been weak partners. They essentially had no positive record of activity, and their loyalty was questionable. As such, the new administration was looking for a non-partisan alternative for structuring power.

In addition, no major political entities in Belarus fully supported the new president, preferring to keep their distance and adopt a critical approach toward him. This trend was reinforced during the 1995 electoral campaign to the parliament, since the new president was trying to postpone these elections, and appealing to the nation to ignore them. The 1995 elections were conducted under a majoritarian electoral system, which did not require the involvement of well-structured political parties, and politicians were predominantly focused on their constituencies.

V. The crisis of trust and build-up of the authoritarian system after the 1996 constitutional crisis

The key political developments of the first years of Lukashenka's presidency included the parliamentary elections in 1995, the large-scale protests in spring 1996, a conflict with the parliament, and the constitutional crisis and referendum in the fall of 1996. These developments could be boiled down to a confrontation between the president and the assorted political parties with their wide range of ideologies.

The political parties were the main winners in the 1995 elections (54% of legislators represented political parties). However, the president, in spite of his popularity, managed to secure victory from only a third of his supporters (the Zhoda parliamentary group), showing the limits of his political capacities. The electoral results indicated a potential for building a classic multi-party system: though the share of political parties' representatives in parliament was smaller than that in most of the neighboring countries, they still comprised more than half of all the legislators. The parties became a crucial tool for consolidating MPs; all MPs' groups were created along the party lines. When non-partisan deputies joined them, 80% of the legislators were linked, to a greater or lesser extent, to political parties. The parties were the dominant force in defining the parliament's policies and leadership.

Meanwhile, the political parties which failed to make it to the parliament, especially the BNF, became the main mobilization force for street protests in spring 1996. Eventually, during the 1996 constitutional crisis, the political parties became Lukashenka's main opponent. They shaped the consolidated position of the parliament in confrontation with the president, when the latter tried to amend the constitution and expand the authority of his office.

The outcome of the 1996 constitutional crisis was the defeat of political parties and victory for the president who acquired unlimited authority to transform the political system into a new model. After winning the referendum, the president secured sufficient power to fully control the political system. The parliament was disbanded, and the president appointed the new one (the House of Representatives) from loyal MPs. This new environment made political coalitions irrelevant, and any forms of organization along partisan lines were perceived as a risk to stability, regardless of their political stance.

The events of this period revealed a mutual distrust in the political system and the significant risk of disloyalty. When many of Lukashenka's former "friends" and allies switched to the opposition, he treated this as treason. Communists and agrarians in the parliament, who were ideologically very close to the president and were previously eager to cooperate with him, became his main opponents when the 1996 constitutional crisis erupted.

Throughout the entire period of unstable democracy (1990–1996), the parliament was essentially seen as a source of instability and risk to the executive branch. This was typical of the period between 1991 and 1994, as many Belarusian politicians contemporaneously noted. It is noteworthy to consider that Lukashenka himself made it to the country's highest office thanks to the parliamentary podium. Even more strikingly, this instability and risk manifested in the 1994–1996 confrontation between the president and the parliament, during which time the parliament acted as the main restraint on the president, and eventually became an outright threat to Lukashenka.

Once the parliamentary factor was essentially removed from the system, the executive branch saw no purpose in developing political parties and organizations, and had additional incentive to move to a non-partisan system, even though a significant number of deputies in the first House of Representatives (1996–2000) were party members. Political parties' activities ceased, no parliamentary groups were created, and the entire political activity of the parliament was frozen. The president's policy was essentially aimed at removing parties from the political arena, and this policy was not only applied to opposition parties.

The "anti-political" strategy became dominant. The executive branch officially distanced itself from politics, political squabbles and conflicts while focusing on management issues. This was reflected in both the government's rhetoric and in various analytical papers.

VI. Current guidelines for the non-partisan system

With the absence of political parties, a key question arises: which bodies step in to perform their functions? As a rule, political science identifies the following functions of political parties: interest aggregation, articulation of interests, political socialization (recruitment), redistribution of political power, segmentation of the electorate, and raising political awareness among the population, including encouraging its participation in politics. Of course, this definition is far from being complete, and does not reflect the whole gamut of political party functions, which can vary significantly depending on the region or historic period. However, we are going to use the selected set of functions as the basis for our analysis, since in general these are sufficient to illuminate particular features of the current Belarusian political system.

Interest aggregation. Like many other authoritarian regimes, Belarus has certain limitations on public interest aggregation, since it is implied by default that the government knows the needs of both the entire nation and specific social groups. The Belarusian model encourages neither group consolidation nor, by extension, group interest aggregation.

With the absence of political parties, the main channels for interest aggregation are national and local executive bodies. The representative bodies (parliament and local councils) play a diminished role, and interest articulation there is unstructured since these bodies do not have institutionalized political groups.[13] Additional roles are played by government-organized non-governmental organizations (GONGOs) and trade unions.

It is also worth mentioning that interest aggregation and articulation has only a semi-public nature, and seldom turns into a subject of wide public discussion. Debates on interest aggregation take place within government agencies, special interagency committees, or representative bodies. However, the public has practically no access to the findings or conclusions of most of these debates.

Until recently, it made no practical sense to employ public campaigns for the purposes of interest aggregation and articulation. A much more efficient approach would imply the usage of government channels and GONGOs.

Redistribution of political power. The issue of substantial political change cannot be raised, and in fact, there has been virtually no competition as far as elections go. However, the system has existed for more than twenty years, a the certain redistribution of political power became inevitable. At the national level, and to a great extent at the regional level, the president plays a key role, and the outcome of redistribution depends mostly on the result of behind-the-scenes power struggles within the executive branch for influence on the head of state and other officials. These processes are neither public nor transparent. Representative bodies, GONGOs, and the business community are largely excluded from these processes.

Political recruitment. In most political systems, political parties play a strong role in political socialization and bringing new people into the political environment. In Belarus, today's political elites come mostly from the executive bodies. Extensive work experience at government agencies is most often a good reason for promotion. Another good reason for being recruited is work experience in state-owned enterprises. In other words, recruitment is mostly a bureaucratic process.

Initially, in order to get top political positions, personal acquaintances of the president would play an important role. Another important recruiting source was the former Soviet *nomenklatura*; currently, however, this source has been exhausted, predominantly for demographic reasons. GONGOs, most notably the Belarusian Republican Youth Union (BRSM), are additional recruitment sources. Though the role of business has begun to grow in recent years, it remains insignificant.

It is most certainly the president who makes the key decisions. The executive bodies and agencies (which coordinate their activities with the Presidential Administration, security agencies, and regional elites) play a crucial role at lower levels. Sometimes a choice might be determined by personal skill and merit. Loyalty is also a critical characteristic.

The interested groups are clearly structured along regional or agency lines. It is hard to say whether there might be other groupings based on other criteria: ideology, foreign policy and so forth. Such groupings tend to be structured around individuals and bureaucratic agencies, rather than political views.

Raising political awareness and encouraging participation in politics. In general, the government is not interested in raising political awareness and encouraging popular political participation. This is a striking difference between Belarus and many mobilizing authoritarian systems, like that of Hugo Chávez's Venezuela. It is likely that the government perceives active popular political engagement as a risk to stability, with the potential to lead to mass collective action and other forms of dissidence and advocacy.

Under the current circumstances, a rise in active political engagement would likely have an adverse and undesirable impact. In practical terms, the only kind of event which requires the involvement of vast masses of people is an election, though the government has no issue with high electoral activity. Traditionally, a significant amount of the population goes to polling booths anyway; moreover, there is the so-called administrative mobilization (government employees, students, school teachers and so on) encouraging citizens to vote. As a result, political parties are not required for addressing this issue.

Structuring the electorate. Unlike democratic political systems, where the political process incentivizes structuring political groups, Belarus' government policies have always been directed toward restraining, not stimulating, collective political activity. Political amorphousness is considered to be more amenable to political stability. In post-communist Russia, the division of political space between "liberals," "leftists," "patriots" and so on, who were assigned political roles, was crucial for political processes. This is not the case in Belarus, where the political system was based on a vertical framework of bureaucracy, while a manifestation of collective political activity was explicitly perceived as a destabilizing factor, regardless of the political orientation and position of a given political group. The rules of the political game were quite simple, and were based on the dichotomous opposition between presidential supporters and presidential adversaries. Outside of the bureaucratic framework, supporters are not organized.

However, starting in 1996, there were debates over moving to a more sophisticated political order, and while some attempts to implement these projects were made (particularly during the 2000 parliamentary elections), so far these initiatives have been extremely limited.

VII. The idea to create a ruling party post-2006

Debates about building a multi-party system have continued since 1996, and they became particularly popular during the period between the third presidential elections of 2006 and the parliamentary elections of 2008. Supporters of political reform argued that a mechanism for transition of power would be required in the case of Lukashenka's absence. Given that the Belarusian system is centered around one person, a potential mechanism of transition is important.

The idea behind creating a political party (or several parties) was the purpose of subordinating bureaucracy and subjecting it to more political control. However, putting bureaucracy under any kind of control is quite a challenge, and in some situations the replacement of bureaucracy is essentially impossible. Therefore, the primary motivator was to ensure the stability of the political system, and reduce risks in the eventuality of leadership change. Additional factors, which have never been definitive, include liberalization and improvement of relations with the West. The sustainability of this process would imply a display of political pluralism and some elements of democracy.

The major pro and con arguments. The creation of a ruling party would require a drastic reconstruction of the political picture with unpredictable consequences. Evidently, it would cause a redistribution of power in favor of a parallel political hierarchy, at the expense of the bureaucracy. This process would bring certain opportunities to some groups within the system (particularly those without a sturdy position in the executive bodies, or those about to start climbing up the hierarchy) as well as risks of disruption and change to the existing rules of the political order. Obviously, the executive branch hierarchy and officials who had reached the apex of their careers would lose out in such a transformation.

Given the lack of trust among various groups within the system, it might generate new conflicts and destroy the existing balance of power. Therefore, a key argument for the preservation of the existing system is that it proved to be very efficient for the last twenty years in overcoming external and domestic issues and minimizing risks. In other words, the challenge would be not the loss of partial power per se, for which the bureaucracy would be somewhat prepared, but the danger of instability. Stability was always considered to be a vital part of the system.

Another key argument against the changes is that the current political elites lack any experience of party-building. Since 1996, the political parties have not been involved in the national decision-making process, and a "ruling party" would be a completely new phenomenon, totally unfamiliar to the vast majority of bureaucrats and politicians.

The most crucial factor is the resistance of the bureaucracy. Regardless of how it was pursued, the creation of a parallel political framework would lead to a redistribution of power. In certain areas and regions "party" and bureaucracy framework might overlap, while in others there is a danger of competition between "the ruling party" and bureaucracy, which would make many bureaucrats unhappy.

The salient feature of all the political parties and quasi-party organizations created in Belarus after 2006 was **reversibility**. This is why all the decisions regarding the construction of a party framework were of piecemeal nature, and were often stonewalled or canceled. All the steps taken so far essentially have no constitutional foundation and can be easily revoked. This is a key factor in *Belaya Rus'* framework and political foundation; if it is dissolved, the system would continue without a hitch. The same is true of other pro-government parties.

Conclusion

In the Belarusian non-partisan system, the central political role is assigned to the executive bodies. The process of recruiting new political elites, aggregation and articulation of interests, mobilization and so forth are mainly implemented through government channels.

The establishment and sustainable development of the non-partisan system in Belarus happened due to an intertwining of several causes: the crisis and collapse of the Soviet *nomenklatura*, a relatively low level of popular mobilization in the late 1980s and early 1990s, confrontation between the President and the rest of the political institutions (political parties, parliament, and *nomenklatura*), a low level of mutual trust in politics, as well as Lukashenka's lack of experience as a political organizer when he first attained power in 1994.

Due to the concentration of political power within bureaucratic institutions, the non-partisan political system appears to be sustainable in Belarus and all attempts to create either a ruling party or multiparty system thus far have failed.

Notes

[1] Kimitaka Matsuzato, "A Populist Island in an Ocean of Clan Politics: The Lukashenka Regime as an Exception among CIS Countries," *Europe-Asia Studies* 56, no. 2 (2004): 235–61.

[2] Steven Levitsky and Lucan A. Way, "Elections without Democracy: The Rise of Competitive Authoritarianism," *Journal of Democracy* 13, no. 2 (2002): 51–65.

[3] Uladzimir Rouda, "Belarus: Transformation from Authoritarianism towards Sultanism," *Baltic Journal of Political Science* 1 (2012): 62–76; Steven M. Eke and Taras Kuzio, "Sultanism in Eastern Europe: The Socio-political Roots of Authoritarian Populism in Belarus," *Europe–Asia Studies* 52, no. 3 (2000): 523–47.

[4] For more details see Dzmitry Isajonak and Tatsiana Čyžova, "Evolution of Production Facilities' Privatisation Model in Belarus from 1990 to 2013: Background, Concepts, Results," *Belarusian Political Science Review* 3 (2014–15): 33–57.

[5] See Imke Hansen, "The Space of the Belarusian Political Discourse and Its Visual and Performative Elements," in *The Geopolitical Place of Belarus in Europe and the World*, ed. Valer Bulhakau (Warsaw: Elipsa, 2006), 121–33; Alexandra Goujon, "Natsionalizm i identichnost' v Belorussii" [Nationalism and Identity in Belarus], *Franko-rossiyskiy nauchnyy al'manakh*, no. 1 (2010), http://www.centre-fr.net/IMG/pdf/Almanach1GoujonRU.pdf; Anna Brzozowska, "Symbols, Myths, and Metaphors: the Discursive Battle Over the 'True' Belarusian Narrative," *Slovo* 15, no. 1 (Spring 2003): 49–58; Natalia Leshchenko, "A fine instrument: two nation-building strategies in post-Soviet Belarus," *Nations and Nationalism* 10, no. 3 (2004): 333–52. For more details see Andrei Kazakevich, "Concepts (Ideas) of the Belarusian Nation since Gaining Independence (1990–2009)," *Belarusian Political Science Review* 1 (2011): 50.

[6] When the first so-called political "liberalization" began.

7   51% in 2016, see *Foreign Trade of the Republic of Belarus: Statistical yearbook, 2017*, 47–48, accessed Dec. 17, 2017, http://www.belstat.gov.by/ofitsialnaya-statistika/makroekonomika-i-okruzhayushchaya-sreda/vneshnyaya-torgovlya_2/ofitsialnye-publikatsii_12/index_8009/ (in both Russian and English).
8   The CSTO arose from the ashes of the Soviet Union, in an attempt to provide mutual defence assistance, predominantly under Russian auspices. It currently comprises six members (Russia, Belarus, Armenia, Kazakhstan, Kyrgyzstan and Tajikistan).
9   See Article 5 of the Constitution of the Republic of Belarus of 1994 (with changes and additions adopted at the republican referenda of November 24, 1996 and of October 17, 2004). Available online at http://www.wipo.int/edocs/lexdocs/laws/en/by/by016en.pdf, accessed Dec. 13, 2017; "O politicheskikh partiyakh" [Law on Political Parties], *The National Legal Internet Portal of the Republic of Belarus*, accessed December 17, 2017, http://pravo.by/document/?guid=3871&p0=v19403266.
10 In 2016, following the last parliamentary elections, one representative of an opposition party became an MP, the first such case since 2000.
11 Michael E. Urban, *An Algebra of Soviet Power: Elite Circulation in the Belorussian Republic 1966–86* (Cambridge: Cambridge University Press, 1989), 116–35.
12 The so-called "economic persons" or experienced managers were in high demand at this time.
13 Andrei Kazakevich, "Bielaruski parlamient epochi niezaliežnasci: evaliucyja deputackaha korpusu, 1990–2010" [Belarusian parliament of the independence period: Evolution of the body of deputies, 1990–2010], *Palityčnaja sfiera* 15, no. 2 (2010): 60. Available online at http://journal.palityka.org/wp-content/uploads/2015/04/15-2010_02_Parliament.pdf.

MIKLÓS HARASZTI

Illiberal State Censorship: A Must-have Accessory for Any Mafia State

The observation that any sustainable, entrenched political system will impact media governance is both a commonplace and an understatement. In fact, media regimes have, since Gutenberg, been practically appendixes to the political systems, largely determined by the latter, with the obvious exceptions of short adjustment periods.

We tend to forget this truism in the post-Cold War period, when communication technologies have gone global, and a majority of nations have officially embraced elective democracy and private ownership of the media. Since the great wave of post-1989 democratizations, scholars and journalists alike have largely relied upon a generic assumption of the media's relative autonomy in a democracy, a notion originating from the American context.

The media however, are not autonomous in and of themselves. Despite the nominally large club of democratic nations, with practically all of them declaring freedom of expression to be one of their constitutive principles, only liberal democracies allow for what could be described as media pluralism and autonomy.[1]

The gap between the claimed media freedom and the sorry reality of state control in an ever growing number of new democracies has since the late eighties been bridged by the "drawn-out development" theory of transitology, which supposes a kind of educational hold-up. But the "childhood disorder" theorem is obviously inadequate to describe the characteristic capture of the media by the state and its oligarchs, occurring even in such EU member states as Hungary and Poland, for example. The methods of state censorship and propaganda are largely similar in numerous post-Soviet, post-colonial, post-dictatorial, post-conflict democracies on all continents, and lately even in post-Arab Spring democracies.

Very few of these governments could be described as "sliding back" to old authoritarianism. They are democratic liberal capitalist turned illiberal states, usurping all venues of the state's political and market influence. They preserve a scenery of nominally competitive elections and multi-owned private media, but only to utilize them to perpetuate the rule of a political clan, aptly described by Bálint Magyar as a politically organized mafia family, regardless if it is kin- or allegiance-based.

However, even when illiberal state capture evolves into a mafia-like control scheme, with the core purpose of enriching the leader's family and clan, that usurpation can be sustained only through continued electoral victories. For multiple reasons, among them national, international, economic, and political, the ruling clans in the post-Cold War illiberal regimes must also be legitimized in elections or referenda. Hence having a meticulous censorship and propaganda machine at their disposal is inevitable. Even though illiberal systems are clearly neither remnants nor remakes of the old ones, they must rely on a media mechanism that is nearly as capable of suppressing informed choice, pluralistic information, and thereby chances of change as the overt censorships of earlier non-elective dictatorships.

And it is for the same reason, the necessity of an electoral legitimation, that the propaganda themes that fill the illiberals' mixed state-private media machine are not the rigid ideological doctrines of the past, but ever-changing variations of opportunistic populism, designed to maximize electoral gains. Its elements are nationalism; majoritarian anti-pluralism; the promise of stable governance as opposed to chaotic and volatile liberal democracy; conspiracy theories about foreign influence and local quislings; and, invariably, ready-made, enhanced and weaponized xenophobic and ethnic prejudices.

What follows is an outline of the typical restrictions on freedom of the press in illiberal democracies, which are applied in service of electoral gains in tandem with their populist propaganda.

Illiberal media governance: quasi-democratic state censorship

In the 1990s, I served as head of the media freedom watchdog arm of the 56-nation Organization for Security and Cooperation in Europe (OSCE). When confronted with the many limitations on media freedoms in post-1989 democracies—including self-censorship and general acquiescence to political elites—the prevailing habit of media freedom watchdogs was to rebuke those policies on a case-by-case basis, as "violations" of democratic standards. The violators then received an education concerning how to correctly achieve the supposedly shared and desired standards, in hopes that this would provide a learning curve.

However, what I had to face at OSCE went far beyond concepts of anomalies and delayed adaptation. Rather a transition from democracy than towards it, the 2000s brought the global resurrection of methodical state censorship—albeit, in a democratic disguise.

After the collapse of colonialism and European communism, as dozens of new democracies sprung up, it seemed that the wide-ranging state censorship that can become part of a nation's political culture and be sustained over generations was a thing of the past.

What is widely acknowledged, at least in academic scholarship, under different names by different authors, is that many of the new elective democracies in post-Soviet, post-communist, post-colonial, post-dictatorial, and post-conflict countries have turned illiberal, or even outright authoritarian, at a rapidly growing pace.

Hungary's Viktor Orbán proudly calls his regime illiberal democracy,[2] turning Fareed Zakaria's oxymoron into his credo.[3] Others label them as hybrid, managed, majoritarian, and populist democracies, or new, elective, or competitive authoritarianisms.[4] The inevitable, constitutive greed at the base of all of these formations has led authors to call them mafia states: criminal seizure of the economy from above, so to say, by politicians via the electorally captured and then streamlined state, as opposed to good old bottom-up state capture by mafia conglomerates.[5] Bill Clinton simply calls the leaders of mafia states "those guys" who are lured by the Russian and Chinese models, and use authoritarian capitalism to "stay forever and make money."[6]

What remains understudied, even in political science so far, with a few notable exceptions,[7] is one of the most fundamental features of all these regimes, namely that they curtail media freedoms as systematically and efficiently as old state censorships had before them. The blueprint is there from Russia to Turkey, from Singapore to Azerbaijan. You can see the same principles at work on all continents, from Kazakhstan to Venezuela, to Uganda, and to the Philippines.

They do not generally outlaw free speech (with the exception of the few remaining ideological tyrannies, such as China or Iran) so they may still be registered as democracies. Nevertheless, the first liberty that is taken away in all post-Cold War illiberal democracies is the local version of the First Amendment. Take as an example the media regulatory overhauls in the EU member states of Hungary (Media Law Package 2010) and Poland (Public Broadcasting 2015) which preceded all other illiberal designs.

I toy with the name "quasi-democratic state censorship" in order to pinpoint the type of media control which is globally taking root as a mainstay of illiberal and neo-authoritarian governance. I also like to call it State Censorship 3.0, because it is modernity's third broad, globally spread model of government-installed censorship. The first was the "prior restraint" censorship methods witnessed in the pre-broadcasting, mostly-print era, which was then followed by the "state ownership" communications systems of the totalitarian 20th century.

Quasi-democratic, illiberal state censorship is backed by parliament-set rules that are majority-passed, quasi-constitutional, quasi-market-friendly, and may even pay lip service to values stipulated by international human rights commitments. The new censorship regimes grew especially methodical in response to civil uprisings against the illiberal capture of democracy, the famous "color revolutions." We already see the features of "Censorship 3.0" emerge in the Middle East, in the wake of transitions sparked by the "Arab Spring."

The new censorship regimes do not prescribe the perimeters of individual expression as much as old censorships did. Rather, they are cleverly devised to stifle diversity and limit media independence, especially in broadcasting, and increasingly in the realm of online media. Of course, they, too, set purposeful limits to expression understood as actual speech content, and in often brutal ways. But primarily they operate via government-imposed structural hurdles—including administrative, licensing, ownership, advertising, and punitive regulations. The entire subsequently restrictive environment is set up in a "quasi-rule of law" manner (that is, perverted into "rule by law"). Huge amounts of taxpayer money may be poured into state media, but the main ploy is to coerce privately-owned media into assisting the government in reducing diversity and guiding the flow of information. In the last ten years, oppressive media governance regimes have actually copied each other's illiberal patterns much more than they have any Western blueprints.

The four media rights suppressed by illiberal regimes

Let us then very briefly look at some of the typical ways which illiberal regimes employ and combine to maintain state censorship of media. As one can see, they are superimposed simultaneously onto democracy's four basic media freedoms. These liberties were first identified by Article 19 of the Universal Declaration of Human Rights.

> *Everyone has the right to freedom of opinion and expression; this right includes freedom to hold opinions without interference and to seek, receive and impart information and ideas through any media and regardless of frontiers.*[8]

- The right to freedom of opinion, to speak out. Let us call this the "the right to speak";
- Freedom of information, or "the right to know";
- The right to free online communication, or "the right to connect";
- And the liberty of pluralism or diversity, which in fact is one's "right to choose."

(The right to connect and to choose are seemingly new liberties, but in fact they were already contained in the last seven words of Article 19: "through any media and regardless of frontiers.")

Illiberal curtailments of the right to choose

I hold choice to be the most important right in question, and the main target of the illiberals. Pluralism of the media is the final product of freedom of actual expression, and at the same time its ultimate sustainer.

Unlike some Western media development strategies, illiberals acknowledge the centrality and power of broadcasting, especially of television, in safeguarding or threatening democracy. Electoral majorities, even in old democracies, are still predominantly shaped by broadcasting, despite the growing penetration of on-demand aggregators and social media.[9] The editorially organized evening news that enter family living rooms, or the hourly news of FM radio stations, widely listened to while cleaning, shopping, or on the road, are still the main shapers of the party-political public opinion. Therefore, illiberals bent on curtailing freedom of the press first limit or block pluralism in broadcasting.

Covering up what is otherwise effectively robbery of diversity, is the fact that various forms of entertainment remain in use. What disappears is not the variety of media genres but their politically and editorially multi-centered character.

Invariably, illiberals invade—legally and then via appointments—media licensing and broadcast regulatory bodies. In liberal democracies, these bodies have to be structured in such a way as to represent pluralism, just as their vocation is to adjudicate licenses in a way that assists the maximum diversity of the media scene even when scarcity of resources, such as radio frequencies, makes the task difficult.

In an illiberal setting, direct government appointment of members of the regulatory bodies, obviously based on the interests of the ruling clan, is followed by arbitrary, politicized, and corrupt decision-making—regardless of whether the independence of the body is imitated, as in the case of Russia's *Roskomnadzor* or Hungary's *Media Council*, or is a straightforward part of the administration, as is Kazakhstan's *Ministerstvo Informatsii i Kommunikatsii*. They will license and de-license to maintain control over the information flow even when, on the face of it, they comply with the principle of ownership pluralism by splitting the media between several hands. Special regulations to squeeze diversity are also constantly being fabricated. Examples include Azerbaijan's and many other states' ban on foreign ownership of local FM licenses, or Radio Liberty Russian Service's forced migration to the Internet.

Illiberal governments act this way out of bitter experience. "Color revolutions," which were attempts at re-democratization—or at least re-pluralization—of the political system, have all occurred where at least one independent broadcasting channel existed and could therefore be used by a budding civil society. These were *B92* in Serbia, *Rustavi 2* in Georgia, *Channel 5* in Ukraine, and *Channel 35* in Kyrgyzstan. Vladimir Putin's counter-color-revolution since 2005 has additionally focused on closing down all venues of global assistance to media, providing a model for illiberal and neo-authoritarian regimes around the globe.

Illiberal regimes retain the post-totalitarian achievement of privately owned broadcasting, something audiences have valued highly ever since democratization. But their broadcasting governance is a faux version of the Western dual broadcasting system.

The Western dual system is based on ownership types which are strictly tied to the type of pluralism achievable within a property form. Liberal democracy does not tolerate state ownership in media; public broadcasting is of course taxpayer-paid, but it has systems in place to ensure internal pluralism. The role of the multitude of privately owned channels is to provide external pluralism nationwide, especially since the emergence of digital distribution of broadcasting signals ended scarcity in available platforms, and made regulatory care for internally pluralistic licensing obsolete.

Not so the broadcasting outlets under the new state censorship: they, too, have both taxpayer-paid and privately-owned channels, but their duality is based on their relation to government propaganda. Regardless of ownership, a channel is either providing political information, in which case it has to toe the official line, and become in fact part of the propaganda machinery, or provides entertainment only or mostly, supporting thereby the de-politicizing, neutralizing effort of the regime.

As Walker and Orttung pointed out, direct state ownership of broadcasting, something that cannot coexist with liberal democracy's revolving-stage politics, is of course still the safest property type from the point of view of the illiberal political establishment.[10]

But family and oligarchic ownership is as good as that. Several specifically illiberal TV genres, such as the anti-opposition and anti-civil society "hate hours" as well as pseudo-investigative smear campaigns, are usually retained for privately owned channels, disguised as infotainment.

There exist many other tools to fortify the government's voice and debilitate independent media:
- Fake de-monopolization with the help of a lack of ownership transparency
- Guided licensing through the lack of independence of the regulatory body
- Renationalization with the aim of reprivatization to cronies
- State subsidies, content grants for subservient media
- State guidance of advertising revenue
- Administrative discrimination to hinder start-up activities & market entry

A textbook example of anti-pluralistic yet legalistic media governance could be the three-layered Belarusian media registration system which is widely copied:
1. A discretionary authorization process for any outlet disguised as registration, thus asking in fact for a governmental permission, even for internet-hosted media, instead of mere notification of the state register as it is habitual in rule-of-law settings;
2. Kafkaesque rules of registration, with built in arbitrariness, where registration becomes practically impossible;
3. And de jure criminalization of all unregistered media activities, triggered into de facto criminal procedures whenever the authorities see it tactically fit.

Censorship against undesirable views

This is a question of the limits imposed on actual speech, or freedom of opinion—in fact, on what can be uttered in public. The West, spoiled by a lack of most of the other types of media limitations, is fixated on this issue. Western advocacy in illiberal settings is often based on various reformulations of the First Amendment of the US constitution, overwhelmingly targeting jurisprudence on gag laws, and thus ignoring the more structural problems impeding the genuine pluralism of views.

Illiberal state censorship systems disguise their suppression of critical speech by imitating democracy's habit of protecting human rights—in this case, rights other than the right to free speech, to be sure. They criminalize defamation, libel, and insult—and do it by playing off personality and privacy rights against critical expression. When they choose to use civil defamation law instead of criminal, or fines instead of incarceration, their laws and practice ignore ceilings or proportionality, and their fines are annihilating and discriminative.

One universal illiberal pretext for curbing free speech is the claim that the state is combatting hate speech. Illiberals are also great in forging new speech crimes such as "extremism" or "defamation of religions."[11] All illiberal regimes have instituted different bans on debating the official version of local history. Turkish president Recep Tayyip Erdoğan has long been the champion of such tactics, no different to those of Daniel Ortega of Nicaragua, or Alyaksandr Lukashenka of Belarus.

A classic example is the Russian Dozhd TV case.[12] In 2014, it was squeezed off the nationwide cables and thus limited to internet-based access, exploiting the uproar caused by one of its programs asking the audience whether or not they believed that Stalin's order to defend Leningrad to the last bullet and at any price was indeed necessary. The real reason for this sanction, however, was Dozhd TV's straightforward coverage of Russia's aggression in Ukraine.

Censorship against unwelcome facts

Illiberals methodically restrict the right to know, or the freedom of information, reversing liberal democracies' Copernican revolution in fact-finding, where the citizenry has become the default "owner" of information handled by the state, and state classification is allowed only as a justified exception.

At stake is the media's watchdog and investigative capacity, especially regarding corruption and human rights abuses. But the actual goal is, again, not the total silencing of corruption or abuse stories. Just as in the case of nominally allowing for dissenting opinion in marginalized media, illiberals strive to eliminate from the nationwide television screens all journalistic investigations of government corruption or the mafia-like capture of the economy by the ruling political elite and its oligarchs. Embarrassing facts will be exiled to the fragile, dying print press and to insular social media outlets.

As always in illiberal systems, part of the tools are administrative, like
- Arbitrary classification
- Denial of access to government data
- Lack of legal remedy in case of denied access to data of public interest.

Suppression of investigative journalism also extends to punitive measures.
- They criminalize the disclosure of classified information
- But they also criminalize the non-disclosure of confidential journalistic sources
- Instead of shield laws that protect journalists' right to fact-finding, they create a myriad of custom-designed gag laws.

Censorship by violence and even murder is most prevalent in the case of investigative journalists. The way the state practically facilitates these censorship acts are

- by employing constant anti-media rhetoric against independent-minded outlets;
- by conspicuous impunity of violence. In illiberal settings, law enforcement refuses to handle anti-journalism motivations as crimes against democracy's basic order; they are treated as ordinary crimes, thus making it practically impossible to find the masterminds, even if the actual perpetrators are apprehended.[13]

One of the most telling situations is when countries like Russia have surprisingly no "breach of secrecy" type of trials at all, despite their draconian secrecy restrictions. The reason, obviously, is that violence against journalists has sufficiently frightened investigative journalists away from using leaks.

A fast-spreading fashionable tool is to forge bogus criminal charges against unruly investigative journalists. Typical tricks include lodging false allegations such as
- drug abuse
- hooliganism
- tax fraud
- embezzlement charges

Censorship online, or the suppression of the right to connect

Unquestionably, the new internet-based media represent (already? or still?) relatively diverse sources of information. But a barrage of new illiberal policies strives to domesticate online media. Domestication is meant literally here, as an essential objective of new state censorship is to reinstate territorial control over online media content and access. (Those boundaries, we once believed, that had been melted away by the global Internet).

True, quasi-democratic censorship systems do not go as far as China or Iran in carving out national intranets. Their solution is to make the limitations arbitrary, selective, and politicized. Good old fear tactics do the job.
- The bloggers, commentators, online fact-finders, the users of circumvention or anonymization technologies know very well that the system keeps an eye on them; they are targeted by surveillance, filtering, blocking, and bogus criminalization.

- Censorship can be outsourced to the internet service provider companies (ISPs), and paid social media trolls.

The counter-revolution of territorial control over online content can also rely on administrative tricks, such as
- Lack of ISP pluralism (which is easy, as providing internet to users is a licensed business—they only have to copy the ways broadcast licensing is tampered with).
- State registration procedures for website hosts, web-based media ventures, and even bloggers.
- Prescribed physical territoriality inside the country for servers, websites, web hosts, and even bloggers.
- Harsh third-party responsibility rules, with obligation for web hosts to remove user-posted content upon warning from a number of authorities without waiting for judicial decisions.

Internationally, the illiberal powers of the world unite efforts to place the Internet itself under intergovernmental control, where the new governance mechanism would obviously endorse national control. They hope to replace Internet Corporation for Assigned Names and Numbers (ICANN) as the global regulator with the International Telecommunications Union (ITU) of the United Nations, a government-delegated body—and thus get rid of the self-governing model, which they claim represent in fact US control, disguised under the multi-stakeholder approach of the ICANN.

What illiberal state censorship is good for

The novelty of fast-spreading illiberal state censorship lies in its multifaceted exploitation of the loopholes in democracy's protection of media pluralism and autonomy. Liberalism's classical rules for power sharing and governmental restraint are ultimately unable to secure constitutional liberalism; at best they are post-election correctional tools, and at worst they can even facilitate the electoral success of anti-liberal forces. They prove to be feeble against well-organized groups which conspire to turn popularity grabs into power grabs precisely via electioneering. Unlike old dictatorships, illiberal regimes perpetuate their power not by eliminating multiparty elections but by eliminating the obstacles to their successful electioneering.

Of course, eliminating the public's access to tools of informed choice, severing media pluralism, restricting freedom of opinion, and suppressing fact-finding are not goals in themselves but necessary measures to clear the way for an unopposed inundation of the electorate with their own messages. Just as in the past, censorship's Siamese twin is propaganda, even if the message is not a set ideology but an ever-changing assemblage of popular ingenuities. In brief, the immediate goal of illiberal state censorship is far beyond the dissemination of fake news—it is the creation of a fake media.

Here is a summary of the media policies of our era's illiberal to kleptocratic regimes. These policies combine to enable the electoral perpetuation of their capture of democracy:

- The hardware is quasi-democratic and quasi-market-compatible state censorship over media freedoms, especially over media pluralism.
- This hardware is then wired for the software: the populist propaganda messages, which typically enhance and weaponize nationalism, xenophobia, and other kinds of prejudice.

Obviously, no censorship and propaganda could result in the perpetuation of electoral success if parliamentary gains would not be utilized to change all other bits and pieces of democracy as well. In order to enter the new electoral cycle on fortified grounds, illiberals have to streamline the electoral laws, hollow parliament's control function, degrade opposition parties into stooges of imitated parliamentarism, abolish the independence of justice, dominate oversight bodies, smash autonomies in all walks of life, capture the economy, enrich the rulers' family and clan from state resources, and raise a new class of politically engaged oligarchs.

At the moment of writing, State Censorship 3.0 is the globally winning media governance regime, a basis as universal for the illiberal development as communicational dictatorship used to be for global communism. The clones of the Soviet Union had been quite different from East Germany to Mongolia economically or culturally, but their media governance was invariantly built on strictly observed state ownership of all media and the state employment of all media workers. One can detect the basically identical illiberal usurpation of media freedoms in Viktor Orbán's Hungary after his fourth electoral win, in Vladimir Putin's Russia, or Recep Tayyip Erdoğan's Turkey after their own countless victories. They may have arrived in different ways from an originally liberal design of democracy to illiberal and kleptocratic and finally mafia states, however they all managed to instill an all-embracing self-censorship in journalism, and a general stupor towards populist propaganda in the electorate. The way they achieved this was practically identical: they manipulated the laws and the institutions that protected free speech; mercilessly purged independent broadcasting of any clout; poured tax-payer money on fake media, state or private; exiled pluralism of the media into the online domain, while fragmenting the critical public opinion into self-entertaining, narcissistic communities—and kept winning elections.

NOTES

[1] Some disagree: Noam Chomsky and perhaps surprisingly, Donald Trump, see even the American media as systematically rigged to serve certain political interests, although they are poles apart on what these influences may be.

[2] "Prime Minister Viktor Orbán's Speech at the 25th Bálványos Summer Free University and Student Camp," 26 July 2014, Tusnádfürdő (Băile Tuşnad), Romania, *Website of the Hungarian Government*, posted on July 30, 2014, http://www.kormany.hu/en/the-prime-minister/the-prime-minister-s-speeches/prime-minister-viktor-orban-s-speech-at-the-25th-balvanyos-summer-free-university-and-student-camp.

[3] Fareed Zakaria, "The Rise of Illiberal Democracy," *Foreign Affairs* 76, no. 6 (November–December, 1997): 22–43.

[4] Steven Levitsky and Lucan A. Way, *Competitive Authoritarianism: Hybrid Regimes after the Cold War* (New York: Cambridge University Press, 2010).

[5] Bálint Magyar, *Post-Communist Mafia State: The Case of Hungary* (Budapest–New York: Central European University Press and Noran Libro, 2016); Bálint Magyar and Julia Vásárhelyi, eds., *Twenty-Five Sides of a Post-Communist Mafia State* (Budapest–New York: Central European University Press and Noran Libro, 2017).

[6] Extended interview with Bill Clinton, *The Daily Show with Jon Stewart*, September 18, 2014.

[7] Jonathan Becker, "Lessons from Russia: A Neo-Authoritarian Media System," *European Journal of Communication* 19, no. 2 (June 2004): 139–63; Robert Orttung and Christopher Walker, "Authoritarian regimes retool their media-control strategy," *Washington Post*, January 11, 2014; Sergei Guriev and Daniel Treisman, "How Modern Dictators Survive: Cooptation, Censorship, Propaganda, and Repression," CEPR Discussion Paper No. DP10454 (2015), https://ssrn.com/abstract=2572452.

[8] UN General Assembly, "Universal Declaration of Human Rights," 217 (III) A (Paris, 1948), http://www.un.org/en/universal-declaration-human-rights/.

[9] Mérték Médiaelemző Műhely, "A politikai tájékozódás forrásai Magyarországon 2016," last modified on November 25, 2016, http://mertek.eu/2016/11/25/politikai-tajekozodas-forrasai-magyarorszagon/.

10. Christopher Walker and Robert W. Orttung, "Breaking the News: The Role of State-Run Media," *Journal of Democracy* 25, no. 1 (January 2014): 71–85.
11. Volha Siakhovich, "Belarus' counter-extremism laws used to restrict free expression," *Index on Censorship*, December 8, 2015, https://www.indexoncensorship.org/2015/12/belarus-counter-extremism-laws-used-to-restrict-free-expression/; Miklós Haraszti, "In God's Name," *Index on Censorship* 38, no. 2 (2009): 108–15, DOI: 10.1080/03064220902976266.
12. Andrew Roth, "Independent News Station, Feeling Kremlin's Wrath, Asks 'Why?'" *New York Times*, February 9, 2014, https://www.nytimes.com/2014/02/10/world/europe/independent-news-station-feeling-kremlins-wrath-asks-why.html.
13. "The inability of authorities to protect Russian journalists must be tackled at highest level, says OSCE media freedom representative," OSCE, February 19, 2009, https://www.osce.org/fom/50623.

Dumitru Minzarari

Disarming Public Protests in Russia: Transforming Public Goods into Private Goods

The puzzle

The series of popular protests in Moscow and other Russian cities, triggered by widespread disagreement with the December 4, 2011 Russian Duma election results, were described by many observers as the largest protest rallies in Russia since the early 1990s. The highly attended demonstrations in Moscow, known as the Bolotnaya protests, were believed to have brought together as many as 150,000 protesters.[1] For a few years after 2011, these protests were held annually, involving tens of thousands in Moscow, and hundreds more in the regions. However, in contrast to other post-communist countries where citizens challenged election results—such as Georgia, Ukraine, or Moldova, among others—the Russian protests did not force the incumbent government into concessions.

This raises an important question about the Russian government's ability to effectively contain mass protests. What makes it more resilient to popular protest and large public discontent, in comparison to other authoritarian governments? More generally, what makes some authoritarian states more successful than others in neutralizing public protests, either through force or waiting them out? A potential answer is that the protest movements do not have sufficiently high support among the population to be able to pressure the government into pursuing democratic reform. It is therefore worth asking, given the many similar conditions in authoritarian regimes, why anti-authoritarian protest movements manage to attract more popular support in some countries than in others. While these questions may seem somewhat disconnected to the reader, they target a single causal mechanism, which this analysis intends to illustrate.

One influential argument highlights the ability of authoritarian governments to use coercive mechanisms that create high costs for potential protesters, thus discouraging their participation.[2] This ability and readiness of governments to impose oppressive costs may not necessarily take violent forms. For instance, in order to defuse the social tensions within an authoritarian society, those who express displeasure with official policy may be afforded the opportunity to emigrate. Officials may also use elaborate means in addressing the protests tactically, using targeted arrests of opposition leaders to defuse and control the gatherings.

These coercion mechanisms, as observers and researchers acknowledged, had been consolidated in post-Soviet Russia following the term of the first Russian president, Boris Yeltsin.[3] At the beginning of the Yeltsin administration the population at large had mixed perceptions of freedom; by the end of his term, these perceptions transitioned into despair. It can be argued that two mutually reinforcing factors considerably contributed to the population's limited acceptance of a coercive governmental approach, used since the start of President Vladimir Putin's administration. It was nationwide despair with the draconian, Yeltsin-approved economic reforms that left swathes of the population in severe poverty, fostering deep grievances. This feeling intensified against the backdrop of the post-Soviet privatization that created, in stark contrast to the general poverty in Russia, a very rich class of oligarchs.[4] In fact, this logic is very consistent with some psychological approaches to human decision-making. They suggest that an individual's "time horizon" decreases along with an increasing pessimism about their life conditions, pushing the individual to accept instant solutions that fix immediate problems.[5] The population, thus, was more likely to accept coercive measures against the oligarchs or dissidents, perceiving them as attempts to repair the economic situation or avoid social turmoil.

Under these conditions, it became easier for the new Russian authorities under President Putin to exert tighter control over the economic and political life of the country. Henry E. Hale argued that a political framework of patronalism consolidated in Russia, in which a system of awards and punishments were exchanged among networks of personal acquaintances, rather than among formal institutions such as political parties.[6] These personal acquaintances mattered to a great extent, and typically involved member of the former Soviet security apparatus "family."[7] Bálint Magyar refers to such a political framework as constituting a "mafia state."[8]

This consolidation of state control during the first term of President Putin generated a greater coercive capability for Russia's ruling elites. One of the most well-known selective coercion cases is that of the rebel oligarch Mikhail Khodorkovsky, who was jailed on charges of fraud and tax evasion. However, some other powerful Russian oligarchs were also persecuted, such as Vladimir Gusinsky and Boris Berezovsky, whom the Russian authorities also perceived to have interfered in politics. These persecutions actually had the effect of increasing President Putin's ratings in the polls.[9] The oligarchs, with their independence from the authorities, operated as an additional state institution, often pushing for initiatives resisted by the Russian government. As Richard Sakwa noted, Putin's administration's efforts to limit the oligarchs' penetration of state led to the "liquidation of the oligarchs as a class."[10]

This selective and sporadic demonstration of the state's resolve to apply its coercive tools has likely allowed the Russian authorities to improve their ability to deter political dissent. However, this alone cannot explain the puzzle of our analysis. This leads us to another influential argument in the literature on protests, referring to the co-optation of the middle class by authoritarian governments, a mechanism that decreased the pressure for democratization.[11] Co-optation is implemented through an incentive-building approach. The targets of co-optation are either offered attractive deals not to obstruct the authorities, or are faced with potential losses if they nevertheless decide to challenge the regime. Co-optation can occasionally be confused with selective coercion by misinterpreting the target. In the case above, the jail charge was a coercive measure against Khodorkovsky, but a deterring element in the wider strategy of co-opting the protesting popular masses, including the middle class.

This is arguably an optimal behavioral strategy when authorities perceive the risk of popular protests as being high. They cannot ignore the protests, as this may be perceived as weakness or hesitation. However, given that coercion is a costly measure, the authorities did not employ it by repressing the protesting popular masses to a significant degree. Instead, the authorities in Russia detained a few of the protesters, who were accused of assaulting the police during the rallies.[12] A number of them received substantial prison sentences, ranging from about two to over four years. Some of the most extensively covered cases were of the Left Front's Sergei

Udaltsov and Leonid Razvozzhayev, who were accused of instigating and organizing violent public disorder.[13] By doing this, the authorities set a red line not to be crossed, signaled that they would not tolerate physical attacks against police, and separated some of the most active opposition leaders from their supporters. While the authorities targeted individuals, the main audience of these costly signals (using a game theory term) was still the larger part of the protesters—namely, Russia's growing middle class. The selective coercion against some protest leaders, as well as the oligarchs who were perceived to be playing their own game, pursuing actions incongruent with governmental policies, aimed to marginalize both groups.

The implied logic is that, having noticed that in some countries the middle class supported and joined the protests, or even took leadership over them, an authoritarian government would start co-opting its own growing middle class. The intention of this co-optation, as will be elaborated further in the text, was to prevent the protest movements from becoming stronger and more threatening to the governing elites.

In the perception of Russian political elites and government-affiliated experts, the most illustrative examples in terms of dangerous anti-governmental protests were those in Georgia, Kyrgyzstan and Ukraine, but also Yugoslavia and the "Arab Spring"-related events. In particular, considerable attention was paid to the post-Soviet area protests that led to regime change in these countries, consequently triggering among the Russian political establishment the paranoia of "color revolutions."[14] They claimed that the "color revolutions" were instigated by the United States, and that similar protests were planned in Russia.[15] Therefore, it becomes clear that the Russian authorities see the threat of mass protest as very high, linking such mass movements to concrete cases of the forceful replacement of incumbent governments and even civil conflict. It is, then, even more important for researchers to understand the dynamics of popular protest in Russia, as this allows us a better grasp of the conditions under which the authorities may switch from a co-optation strategy towards a coercive one and vice versa.

The effects of modernization

In order to address the puzzle of this analysis, I would like to logically connect the literature on state response to public unrest with the building block of modernization theory. This is useful because it offers valuable insights into the costs and incentives of the protesters, as well as those of the government that is being challenged. Given that the interaction between the protesters and the government is of a strategic nature—the actions of the two actors are interdependent[16]—without a complete grasp of the key driving costs and incentives of the actors, we are not able to understand the protest dynamics accurately. Modernization theory literature is expected to fill this gap.

The literature on authoritarian states often portrays them as existing in a potentially reversible transition, inhabiting a position on a linear scale between totalitarianism and democracy.[17] It assumes that given a set of favorable conditions, authoritarian states can transition to democracy by slowly consolidating formal and informal democratic institutions that would be able to better restrain political elites, making them more accountable to the people.[18] One of these factors is believed to be economic development.

The notion that economic development is a key precursor for democratization has been an essential element of the modernization theory.[19] Even critics of this idea[20] have convincingly shown that development is an essential ingredient for a democracy to consolidate and prevent regression back into autocracy. In fact, according to their findings, a democratic regime is almost certain to survive in those countries that have a per capita income above $4,000, though this is not the case for lower levels of welfare.[21]

Russian GDP per capita increased from $4,109 in 2004 to $11,700 in 2008. In 2012 this figure reached $14,037, according to World Bank data. If we adhere to either modernization theory or its critics, who nevertheless accept the role of economic development in encouraging democratic political development in authoritarian states, then Russia does look like an outlier. In fact, to many observers this might look like a failure of modernization theory. However, we could be facing a case that only requires a more precise elaboration of the conditions under which the theory is valid. As such, it is necessary to ask if it is possible that we might be dealing with an additional obstacle, inhibiting the ability of economic development to effectively trigger democratic development in Russia.

Social scientists tended to explore citizens' response to a government through the voice-exit framework.[22] Through voice, citizens participate in the building and adaptation of policy-making, and when the cost of voice is too high, the citizens will exit. This implies some specific responses by the government, which can either oppress the protesters or co-opt them. Depending on the goal and the approach of the analyst, one may see these two possibilities as opposing ends of a spectrum, with its practical application between the two extremes of co-optation and oppression. In this paper, I am going to ignore the cases of overt, violent oppression on the part of authoritarian governments.

The reason is that the specific country I am investigating, the Russian Federation, has been exploiting the cover of democratic mechanisms to address public discontent. Overt oppression can be very costly, as it diminishes the base of potential support for a regime, affects economic development, and undermines the regime's legitimacy both at home and abroad. Moreover, from an empirical point of view, it has been used more frequently by totalitarian governments. It is not surprising then, as some analysts have astutely explained, that many authoritarian states display attributes of democratic political life, including regular elections, democratic constitutions, and limited political space for opposition and civil society.[23] The literature refers to such approaches as "façade democracies,"[24] or "smart authoritarians."[25]

Given the significant effort and material investments that some authoritarian governments, including that of Russia, make to build up their democratic façade, this would suggest it has a specific rational purpose. Considering the domestic political realm is more important for a political leader than the international realm, the target audience of the democratic façade policies would primarily be the domestic public.

The claim that violent oppression may be a prohibitively costly strategy for the Russian Federation seems to be confirmed empirically. Ever since the 1993 constitutional crisis in Russia, when army units were used by President Boris Yeltsin to quell the parliamentary opposition,[26] the Russian authorities have never used armed violence against protesters. Although the Russian government used military force against armed insurrection in its southern regions, it never used such force against manifestations of popular discontent.[27] In fact, Russian authorities used targeted coercive actions against selected powerful individuals, such as disobedient oligarchs, in order to deter the less powerful popular masses. The logic is simple: if the authorities punished such a powerful person for their dissent, they can easily punish an ordinary citizen. Following this, I will mostly be exploring in this text the co-optation strategy a government can use against popular rallies.

The co-optation argument, while opening up an opportunity to attract a larger base of popular support, also brings its own specific costs. For instance, it may require non-sunk cost resources, in contrast to what the oppression strategy tends to generate. It has nevertheless been very popular among researchers in explaining governmental responses to potential public discontent. However, the co-optation argument in the literature, though attractive for a number of reasons, has an important weak analytic spot.

The different strains of the literature exploring co-optation logic, such as the redistribution explanation, do not manage to explain in a consistently logical fashion the origin of the resources required for co-optation. This seems to be a key requirement for any internally valid theory. The resources that any government has are finite. This means that in order to redistribute resources, the government would need to take them from a currently funded project, which could have far-reaching effects throughout the political arena.

It appears, then, that the theoretical explanation of redistribution or any other co-optation argument fails to clarify the empirical mechanisms of redistribution, which is of key importance to these theories. As we will see from the exploration of the selectorate theory[28] further in the text, redistributing goods in an economy meant to co-opt protesters may actually alienate the current support base of the authoritarian regime, since it will upset the status quo balance of resource distribution. That impact can be quite dramatic, especially for the subset of political interactions this paper examines—namely, popular discontent. We need a valid theoretical foundation to explain the source of the redistributed resources, given their finite nature.

In authoritarian countries, most available resources are used as private goods to buy the support of a small but powerful winning coalition—a group allowing the ruling elite to stay in power.[29] Reducing the share of private goods distributed to the winning coalition allows the support of a larger group to be bought, but at the expense of decreased loyalty from the current winning coalition. This rationale offers, then, a starting point for weakening the redistribution argument. Its logic would suggest that due to limited resources, an authoritarian government should not have sufficient resources to buy the loyalty of potential protesters. The protesters took to the streets in the first place because they were unhappy with the authorities' mechanism of goods distribution in society.

If the authoritarian ruler wants to extend and increase the provision of public goods, this will have to be done at the partial expanse of the private goods delivered to the winning coalition. The winning coalition already receives the minimal level of private goods to keep them loyal, as a rational leader would have no reason to provide an excessive level of private goods.

Therefore, goods redistribution is a very risky policy, since it may diminish existing support for the political leader, to the point that they could be ousted from power.

The selectorate theory, which develops the relationship between coalition size and the relative choice distribution between public and private goods, claims that welfare distribution per selector increases as the size of the winning coalition becomes larger, manifesting in a J-shape.[30] In fact, this is only a snapshot of the welfare level and its distribution in different regimes. This theory says little about the dynamics driving this process: how exactly authoritarian states with smaller winning coalitions and lower welfare per capita are transforming into democratic regimes with a large winning coalition and higher welfare per capita. The current analysis is aiming to fill in this gap as well.

So how is it possible for an authoritarian government to co-opt a part of its dissatisfied population, in order to prevent it from joining protest movements to the level that it begins to threaten the regime? The Bolotnaya protests described at the beginning of this piece were not social but political, and they predominantly attracted a majority of its participants from the Russian middle class, as modernization theory claims should happen. A poll conducted by the influential Russian public opinion research center WCIOM suggests that the Bolotnaya protests have been gradually attracting young and middle-aged protesters who feel secure financially and have self-expression[31] values at the top of their preference ranking (78%).[32]

What I refer to above as the "middle class," a rather contested term among social scientists, is used as a relative concept.[33] Given the context of modernization and economic development in which this concept is used, I am defining the term "middle class" with an emphasis on the middle class consumer.[34] It should be noted that this categorization—the middle class as a group of citizens that are secure financially by being able to provide for both their survival needs and leisure—is often an implicit assumption in the modernization theory literature, which is not always obvious. The financial security condition is critical: particularly in authoritarian countries, financial security means these citizens do not depend on the government to receive their income. Instead, they rely on a relatively free market where they are competitive economic agents. Alternatively, especially in democratic regimes, they rely on the rule of law, specifically the safeguarding of private property rights. Therefore, my operationalization of the middle class concept is not dependent on that group adopting "modern" values.

Not depending on the government for income allows these consumers to voice dissent against the authorities on any day-to-day issue they value. As already alluded to, in democratic countries even governmental employees are protected from employer pressure, due to the effective enforcement of the rule of law that conforms to the principles of universal human rights. The evidence from Russia is consistent with this logic, where governmental staff or employees of government-controlled companies are less likely to join public protests.[35] The rationale behind this idea reflects very well a burgeoning current of social research that departs from fixed definitions, oriented at the United States or other developed countries. Instead, they evaluate the middle class in a specific country by considering the official poverty line.[36] Alternatively, it is assessed by taking into account the existence of a steady and well-paying job by local standards, which allows investment into health, for instance.[37] Why is this important? Investing in healthcare is a matter of choice in economic thinking. It reveals the existence of sufficient savings, which can also be invested into leisure, as captured in my explanation of the concept, making these two descriptions conceptually similar through an emphasis on their ability to accumulate surpluses of income.

Thus, it is often the case that the middle class in developing countries is considered to represent the segment of the population that consumes between $2 and $10 a day, at purchasing power parity exchange rate. This corresponds with William Easterly's representation of the middle class, who assigns this label to citizens located between the twentieth and eightieth percentile of the consumption distribution.[38] This categorization finds significant empirical support too; for instance, Banerjee and Duflo found in their study of thirteen developing countries that many individuals within the $2–$10 consumption range fall even above the eightieth percentile.[39] Finally, the notion of middle class that I employ in this analysis also reflects the vulnerability to poverty measure, which captures well the essential condition of not being financially dependent on the government.[40]

A theoretical framework for conflict dynamics

In contrast to the cases that became large-scale protests, or achieved their wider goals, there are far more failed attempts to organize mass protests in authoritarian countries, and protests that did not reach their objectives. We are less aware of those instances when "the dog did not bark," or the cases when protest movements failed. In analytic literature on conflict, this phenomenon is often referred to as the selection bias problem, and is a major source of analytic error.[41] For a better understanding of the arguments advanced by this analysis, it would be helpful to have a succinct illustration of some key ideas of protest process dynamics.

There is a cumulative body of research on popular protest dynamics that allows us to single out important factors which determine protest emergence and its scale. Economic deterioration does not seem to be one of them, for instance, although it can act as a catalyst under certain conditions. The economic austerity argument reflects the grievance-based theory of popular discontent. It is contained in Ted Gurr's concept of relative deprivation, and indicates that strong social discontent emerges following a perceived discrepancy between people's expectations about the benefits they believe they deserve, and society's ability to provide these benefits.[42] However, relative deprivation needs to be activated through the behavior of elites who place it in a frame of reference, making it a politically relevant notion.[43] This is why the marginalization of protest leaders or dissident elites can be an effective strategy to prevent further protest mobilization. Furthermore, there is vast empirical evidence to suggest that many societies are highly resilient to economic deprivation, and in fact it takes extreme scarcity of essential goods for the people to consider challenging the authorities. This is one reason why international economic sanctions against totalitarian or authoritarian states are often ineffective. Even though such sanctions put pressure on the population, this rarely leads people to relieve themselves of the ramifications of sanctions by rebelling against, or trying to overthrow, the regimes in question.

One explanation refers to the calculation a potential protester would have to make between the costs of protesting and the costs of accepting the status quo. As an alternative strategy, public discontent is a risky and costly action in a "transition" society, where protesters can be persecuted, imprisoned, and sanctioned economically. A person would choose to protest only when believing that they have a high chance of success, or when the involved costs (including the risk of losing everything) are lower than those generated by the status quo conditions that they face.

A second significant obstacle to successful protests is the so-called collective action problem.[44] When an individual believes that other citizens will go to protest and bear its costs, this person is incentivized not to protest. They would be able to enjoy the potential positive results of the protests while not paying the costs of participating, which also include the costs related to any potential protest failure.

However, the larger the number of protesters is, the more costly it is for any political regime to persecute them. Larger numbers of protesters also make it less likely that violence will be employed against the crowd. As such, the collective action problem leads to a significant decrease in probability that any protest will grow sufficiently large to deter a government from violently dispersing it. Similarly, if the dynamic of the protest keeps it small and, more importantly, constant in size, this decreases the probability that more people will join.

In fact, influential research supports the above observation. Mark Granovetter suggested a threshold explanation to describe the growth of protests, considering individuals with heterogeneous preferences.[45] This means that citizen A would join the protest if x people were crowded on the square, citizen B would only join if the number of the protesters was x+1, and so on, until a citizen Z would be attracted to participate if the number of protesters was no less than x+n. According to this model, more radical citizens would join a protest when a handful of protesters gathered, but a moderate citizen would only choose to join if the crowd grew sufficiently large.

This indicates the importance of radical protesters for protest initiation. However, they are not sufficient for triggering large-scale unrest, since they need the moderates who join the modestly-sized crowd, and then the more reticent members of society who would only be attracted when the protest grows even further. Different people have various thresholds for filling in the ranks of the protesters, and these thresholds are distributed across different values according to the size of the crowd. A protest is thus expected to grow very large, according to Granovetter, when it manages to attract people of gradually differing levels of dissatisfaction with the status quo. As will become clear in the next section, this can be done more effectively through specific information signaling.

Public protests thus either increase gradually or stagnate. Their critical mass consists of the moderates, not of the radicals, and the chance of a protest growing large in scale increases with its ability to attract moderates. Protests attended only by radicals are rarely successful, and only then if the regime is hesitant to use its violent resources to protect itself. This approach has proved quite robust across time and geography. Timur Kuran, for instance, explored its logic and used a "tipping point" concept in his attempt to explain the mass uprisings in East-Central Europe in 1989–1990.[46]

The previously described dynamics of protests, involving a threshold, had also revealed a mechanism of signaling information. The size of the protesting crowds reveals information to other potential protesters about the expected cost of the protests, thus allowing them to decide whether or not to join. In fact, Susanne Lohmann claimed, while describing the 1989–1991 demonstrations in East Germany, which led to the collapse of its communist regime, that the protests generated informational cascades sending signals both to the protesters and the regime.[47] The size of the protest, besides informing potential sympathizers on the costs of participation, had also signaled to the regime the potential costs of cracking down on protesters.

This still leaves one essential question unanswered. How are these information signals sent, and more specifically, what are the effective channels to achieve their transmission? Social network research has offered a number of vital insights into this issue.[48] An insightful condition, suggested by network-based research, is that the probability of conflict propagation is higher when different network clusters become strongly connected. This can happen, for instance, when two protest movements unite in advancing a common goal.

A second important condition is that the percolation of both friendship and conflict feelings is dependent upon the density and timing of agents' connection. The timing condition resonates with the theoretical arguments and the empirical findings of Sidney Tarrow, who promoted the theory of political opportunity as the underlying factor explaining social unrest.[49] However, political opportunity can also be viewed as a point in time and space where information exchange is at its optimal efficiency. It is easy to confound the factor of opportunity with the structural dynamics of information exchange if one does not pay close attention to the role of information. Not least because human beings are more sensitive to observable events than to such abstract ideas as the flow of information. To avoid this potential bias, the analyst must ask two questions. Firstly, why does this particular timing offer the best political opportunity? Secondly, what is there in common among the range of protests that are singled out as reflecting cases of optimal political opportunity for social unrest?

In her treatment of the public protests in the GDR, Lohmann reveals that the Leipzig mass demonstrations in the fall of 1989 were, to a large extent, fuelled by the many attendees of the religious services at the Nicolai

Church and other churches around the city center. After the services, the churchgoers would come streaming out of these churches and would then cross the central town square, the hub of the protests. Lohmann also cites a poll of thirteen hundred residents of Leipzig conducted after the protests, which found that most of the participants were more likely than non-participants to be members of social groups.[50] These two important empirical details offer further support to the two key conditions of network-based information dissemination, presented earlier in this section.

What are the significant lessons that a conflict analyst can derive from these protest dynamics traits? First of all, the examined research suggests that societies with a smaller number of veto players[51] are less prone to successful mobilization of large-scale protests. The logic behind this claim is that given fewer veto players, the informational infrastructure built by these powerful actors through the network of their supporters and sympathizers, in order to advance their own agenda, is lacking. As such, every individual outside of the network of a veto player, which in an authoritarian society is a member of the ruling elite, is less connected in an information sense. From a network perspective, the citizens outside of this network are either separate nodes, or are at best connected only to small local networks.

In societies with a higher number of veto players, there are more informational connections in place, allowing for the transfer of information with a higher efficiency and speed. In modern times, this function may be partially fulfilled by personal communication devices, mass media and the Internet. When these are controlled by a central authority, political protesters have a diminished capacity for relevant information dissemination. Besides, it is only inside an already established network that they are particularly effective. These conditions allow for a higher probability that larger protests will emerge, as it is easier to mobilize people, an essential activity for protest organization. However, this story does not totally exclude protests in authoritarian societies. Civil unrest on a smaller scale, which is thus not very threatening to the regime, can be organized based on small local networks. Following this logic, then, protests may have a larger scale in urban areas, due to a better informational interconnectivity for any potential participants.

Moreover, social groups connected through high-stakes economic and social activities, including trade unions, sermon-attending religious groups, and civic initiatives (environmental, anti-war, anti-globalism, animal rights activists, and so forth) have the potential to generate larger scale protests due to their strong informational networks. As argued by Anthony Oberschall, individuals who are better integrated in various collective groups are considerably more likely to be involved in popular unrest, in comparison to individuals who are socially isolated or uprooted.[52] In support of this idea, Doug McAdam posed that interpersonal contacts and personal networks, which he labels "micromobilization context," are very important for recruitment to high-risk activism, which public protests represent in authoritarian societies.[53]

However, as underlined earlier, these micromobilization contexts usually lead to smaller scale protests attempting to defend narrow group interests, typically of social rather than political nature. As such, they are not very threatening to the regime, as long as they are well contained and cannot connect with other clusters of protesters, failing to increase their informational reach. For example, across China there are multiple small-scale social protests conducted on a daily basis, many of which are not even addressed by the authorities.[54]

Small-scale social protests are more likely to occur in authoritarian regimes, because the participants consider them low-cost, and perceive them as a mechanism to communicate with the authorities about their social needs. In less authoritarian societies, larger protests and demonstrations are generally perceived to have a low cost, which makes them more frequent tools of political signaling to the authorities. Unless the opportunity cost of protest is reduced, citizens are less likely to gather in large numbers to defend their interests.

This is why it is common to observe in authoritarian societies that citizens facing social and economic deprivation are coming up with improvised local solutions, and are increasingly using kinship connections to address their daily problems. This is especially the case in Central Asian countries, where the population uses unconventional forms of political participation, which strengthen local and regional political connections. In fact, the risk of these citizens mobilizing for protest is higher when the authorities interfere with their local solutions, which seldom occurs in practice. Finally, it is worth considering Gordon Tullock, who argued that genuine popular uprisings are quite rare, and that the most dangerous challengers to autocrats come either from their own ruling coalition, or from local disenfranchised elites within the opposition.[55] In states where non-ruling political elites have been either co-opted or discouraged to protest, the chance of dangerous protests against authorities is brought to a minimum.

An analysis of Russian protests

My main claim is that the Russian government has managed to artificially increase the level of its available de facto private goods, which allows it to co-opt larger numbers of the growing middle class. But how is this possible? The selectorate theory suggests that in order to increase the number of beneficiaries, the bundle of public and private goods offered by the government should be modified in its structure. This results in increasing the level of public goods and decreasing the level of private goods. However, the largest protests in post-Soviet Russia occurred when the level of public goods funding in Russia was already at its peak. In fact, after the protests, the Russian government decided to decrease the funding of social programs it supported from the state budget.[56] I am going to argue that in order to extend its pool of available private goods, the Russian government transformed goods, which in the West are traditionally public, into de facto private ones. It has done this by using informal institutions to restrain access to some traditional public goods, making them more scarce as resources, and distributing them selectively.

Before going further into this argument, it is necessary to clarify the private-public goods transformation claim that this analysis is advancing. In political science literature, the concept of public and private goods came from economics, where it developed theoretically. Public goods are thought to exhibit two key properties. One is that the consumption of a good by one person should not reduce the quantity that is available for others to consume (non-rivalry). The second property is that all potential consumers have unrestricted access to the good, and an effort to exclude non-payers from consuming the good is extremely expensive (non-excludability). The economics literature has come to the conclusion that pure public goods are hard to find in a market as even the clearest example of a public good, national defense, can be apparently limited by a controlling body.[57] There are disagreements as to whether some global commons, such as international waters or the ozone layer, reflect pure public goods properties, but since my analysis operates at the national level, I shall ignore them.[58]

Based on this, I conclude that what are traditionally considered public goods in a democratic country may well materialize as private goods in an authoritarian country. One reason for this transformation is the fact that limiting public goods in a democratic state may be extremely costly, although not unfeasible. A democratic regime that attempted to restrict access to freedom of public assembly, for instance, would likely be harshly penalized by its voters, to the point of losing office. As such, this restriction is highly unlikely in a democratic state. However, the cost matrix for an authoritarian government would be different, as plenty of empirical evidence seems to suggest.

I have identified a number of traditionally public goods that the Russian government has been making efforts to explore as private goods. These include access to jobs, fair legal process, and entrepreneurial activity, among others. This list is not exhaustive, but the purpose of this paper is to explore the autocratic process of generating additional private goods, while keeping the overall distribution of private and public goods to the selectorate constant.

Access to jobs, which is one of my candidate cases, reflects the income levels of Russian citizens. The rate of government-supported jobs in the Russian economy was estimated at around 24.5% in 2013,[59] while in 2014 some estimates put this figure at over 30%.[60] According to a World Bank 2013 report, during 2008–2010 the average total share of employment in the public sector was higher than in other developed and many developing countries. Compared to developed countries, Russia had an above average rate of employment in public administration, defense, and education.[61] Moreover, these jobs offered salaries at levels which were frequently competitive in comparison to other sectors of the economy.

However, this is not the whole story. The Russian government has also control over many private companies, especially those with the highest capitalization on the market: mining industry, energy, transportation, communications, finance, and so forth. This allows the government to be able to control access to jobs in the private sector. By 2006, the Russian government controlled around 30% of Russian private companies' capital.[62] Furthermore, available statistics do not always accurately estimate the number of state-supported jobs in the security sector, given that they are routinely classified (including police, military and emergency services positions). It is, therefore, highly likely that over 50% of jobs in the Russian economy are dependent directly on the Russian government. Moreover, because private business in Russia is highly vulnerable to governmental pressure (sanitary inspections, accusations of tax evasion, licensing, access to credits, and so on) their employees can also be discouraged from attending anti-governmental public protests, making the job market even more vulnerable to credible governmental influence. In fact, through this dependency, the Russian government has created a de facto patron-client relationship with a segment of the country's middle class. Using Bálint Magyar's terminology, it has managed to "domesticate" the citizens that are wage-dependent on the government.[63]

Another candidate for public-private goods transformation is the access to a fair legal process. In terms of the selectorate theory, the legal system favors members of the winning coalition. If one is outside of the winning coalition, any chances of obtaining an honest legal ruling are very low. Those chances practically disappear to zero if the opposition member is in court against a governmental agency or a member of the winning coalition. Support for the anti-governmental protest movements can also prove disadvantageous. Governmental agencies are quite good at this type of monitoring, given the transparency of this process in Russia. Even big private companies which choose to challenge the government are not secure. The companies operating in Russia, either foreign or domestic, are very much susceptible and vulnerable to the highly effective pressure from the state.

One illustrative example is the case of VKontakte, one of the biggest Russian social networks. It has been seriously pressured by the government through asset acquisition and manipulation of the legal process. The company's CEO, Pavel Durov, was forced to leave Russia and was removed from the company's management positions. The reason for this, as reported in the media, was that Durov publicly refused to give the FSB, the Russian equivalent of the FBI, contact details for the network's Ukrainian Maidan group members.[64]

Based on these considerations, I claim that the Russian government is exploring two major economic goods which remain public in the West, transforming them as they effectively appear in the material world, into private goods. In relation to the individual citizen, these include free access to jobs, both in the public and private sectors. In targeting businesses, the authorities limit their right to unrestricted entrepreneurial activity. For this purpose, it uses formal and informal institutions, including the justice system, thus manipulating the public good nature of justice.

But why is the Russian government able to undertake that transformation without incurring prohibitively large costs, as a democratic regime would? To answer this question, we need to understand the potential protesters-government strategic interaction. This should identify the most optimal responses by both actors, given a set of preferences and perceptions that these actors might have. To examine that strategic interaction I intend, informally, to use the principles of decision theory and game theory.

Consider three actors: a protest movement, a potential protester who has to decide whether or not to join the movement, and an authoritarian government. The government would like to keep the protest movement weak, with little support from the majority of the selectorate. However, the government represents an authoritarian regime, which has a smaller winning coalition than a democracy. It also has finite resources, which it has distributed as both private goods to the winning coalition, and partly as public goods to the rest of the selectorate. When the protest movement is active, this suggests that the public goods the selectorate receive are not enough to keep them from protesting. Parts of the selectorate are likely to begin actively supporting the protest movement, which is in opposition to the government. By increasing the size of the protest, the government is increasingly at risk of being ousted.

As such, the government would be interested in preventing more selectorate members from joining the protest movement. The redistribution literature suggests that the government co-opts the potential supporters of the protest movement. However, as pointed out in detail earlier in the text, the government does not have unassigned resources. It is risky to redistribute private goods, used to buy the loyalty of its minimal winning coalition, into public goods that aim to keep the selectors outside of its winning coalition from joining the protest movement. It could trigger a decrease in loyalty from the members of the winning coalition, thus making the government vulnerable to replacement by the protest movement.

The government, then, can either ignore the risk of potential protesters joining the existing protest movement, or can take action. If allowed to continue unrestricted, the protest movement becomes powerful and begins to put pressure on the members of the government's winning coalition, creating high risks for them and their businesses' security. Workers may strike or attack public order organizations, forcing the government to consider violent oppression, as has happened in other post-Soviet countries. Violent oppression is extremely costly for any authoritarian government that utilizes a democratic façade to boost its legitimacy, both at home and abroad.

Envisaging this in advance, the government is not going to ignore potential protesters joining the opposition movement, unless it has no cost-effective option. It also cannot offer more public goods, due to the scarcity of its resources. However, it can selectively restrict access to some public goods, which are at the top of potential protesters' preferences. One of these top preferences in an authoritarian state is physical survival, and ability to care for family and loved ones. This is determined by reduced economic development and lower income per capita in comparison to a democratic state.

It seems we need to offer more clarification on why a potential protester could be so significantly affected by governmental limitation of their access to what used to be public goods. Modernization theory, for instance, would imply that one reason why authoritarian governments survive is because survival values are prevalent in a large part of the population. In democratic states, self-expression values are much more dominant, and the population of these states is more secure and eager to challenge a government.

All this would imply that the preferences ranking of the selectorate depends on the type of regime. This follows some psychological scholarship; for instance, Abraham Maslow's hierarchy of needs seems to offer a good theoretical framework, suggesting that individuals would tend to achieve their needs in a specific order.[65] Initially, they would target the establishment of their basic living needs; only after fulfilling these requirements would they consider self-expression needs (for instance, individual liberties). This allows us to fill in another analytic gap, explaining why in democratic states the middle class is not afraid of challenging the government, while in authoritarian regimes it may be. In the latter case, they may be credibly deprived of some basic needs, which is higher on their preference ranking list than individual liberties.

Access to jobs is a very effective pressure point. The authoritarian government does not need to do this on a massive scale; instead, it can identify high-profile potential protesters and target them exclusively, restricting their access to important public goods. Through this action, the authoritarian government sends credible and costly signals to its population, emphasizing both its ability to use such incentives and its resolve.

Examining data and ideas on modernization, and considering the empirical data referred to earlier in the text, it can be suggested that there is a potential equilibrium for the middle class to choose the strategy of not challenging the government. Any potential protester, including members of the middle class who have not yet joined the protest movement, must choose between becoming a part of the protest movement, or continuing to explore the lack of interference from the government. The potential protester would choose the action that offers the highest expected payoff, in the parlance of game theory.

That is, the potential protester will choose a strategy that brings more of the benefits and goods that are at the top of her preference ranking. If the protester opposes the government, she risks losing access to jobs, and faces additional costs such as unequal legal treatment. Alternatively, in a best case scenario, should the government ultimately be overturned, the protester would expect benefits from the current opposition, which would then take its place.

Given the conditions of the economy, any potential protester must understand that the overall level of resources available to a new government, after overthrowing the old one, would not be higher. It actually is highly likely to be lower, considering that overthrowing the government would generate some general costs for the economy. Moreover, the potential protester does not know for sure (as is often the case in authoritarian states) that, after coming to power, the current opposition is actually going to redistribute the goods in the economy. A protester would hope that the authorities would reduce the amount of private goods in favor of increasing the level of public goods. As a result, protests become a risky prospect, and most potential protesters, unsure of the consequences, would choose not to join the opposition rallies.

Authoritarian states with a growing middle class can use informal institutions to credibly threaten the newly acquired welfare and wellbeing of that middle class. Officially, this is illegal, but unofficially it is a practice put in place through informal institutions. To some extent, this works like a second-layer winning coalition. If you challenge the government, you are denied access to these goods (employment, due process, entrepreneurial activity), while those who support the government are given access to them.

However, in order for an authoritarian government to be capable of enacting this public-private goods transformation mechanism, it requires considerable influence on the national economy, including both its public and private sectors. As such, we would expect authoritarian states with greater economic jurisdiction to better control and prevent the influence of the opposition. It also would be able to better explore the democratic façade, since it has efficient leverage on selectors outside its winning coalition. In fact, as I believe I have emphasized, such authoritarian governments tend to have a larger winning coalition, at levels comparable to those of democratic regimes. They can maintain this coalition at lower costs, in comparison with democratic states. Finally, this allows authoritarian leaders to remain in power longer, based on their ability to maintain large winning coalitions. What I am essentially offering is an additional mechanism that explains how economic development may contribute to the development of democratic political institutions, or to their manipulation, in authoritarian states.

Therefore, in order for an authoritarian regime to transition towards higher democratic development, it requires more than a specific level of economic development. The GDP per capita level that the Russian Federation has shown for almost a decade would suggest its ascent into the camp of democratic states, but this did not occur. This analysis suggests that authoritarian states, with significant presence in and control over the economic sector, are able to prevent any moves towards democratic development. They are able to maintain control over political power by diminishing the support of selectors outside their winning coalition for the opposition. These regimes create credible risks of economic deprivation, making the selectors vulnerable and dependent upon the regime.

Conclusion

The high level of governmental penetration of the economy seems to operate as a supporting element for the survival of authoritarian regimes. The more diminished the government's control of the economy, the more independent the private sector is, thus ensuring citizens are freer from the authorities' potential pressure. Being economically independent, they face lower costs of protesting against the government. Therefore, the role of the middle class in advancing democratic development continues to be significant, but becomes conditional on their financial independence from the government. The larger the share of the public sector-employed workforce, the more unlikely for the middle class to be independent. This suggests that we can increase the explanatory power of economic development in the modernization of states, and their transition from autocracies to democracies.

In addition to contributing to the literature on modernization and on the transition from authoritarianism to democratic regimes, this analysis makes a few other important points. It describes the strategic conditions under which protests are more likely to generate higher public support, and thus more seriously threaten authoritarian regimes. Such conditions may lead to an increase in concessions made by authoritarian rulers to protesters, if the government does not have a high level of control over the economy. It also explains that increasing a regime's control over the economy is a rational move of the authoritarian government, if it wishes to cement its grip on power. Empirically, it suggests that the Russian government is unlikely to decrease its presence in the private economic sector anytime soon, even though it understands that its presence makes these sectors less profitable.

The paper also points out the need to review how we theorize economic goods, and the extent to which our theoretical models about these goods affect our understanding of empirical observations. As technology advances, this allows us a greater ability to affect the non-rivalry and non-excludable character of what we label as public goods; clean air is one example used in the text. National defense seems to be the next candidate, as non-state actors increasingly challenge the ability of governments to physically control portions of their territories, and thus provide defense to their inhabitants. The authoritarian nature of a government allows it to transform public goods into private through deliberate policy choices, which is hardly possible for a democratic government. This allows authoritarians to increase the pool of resources under their control and exert more influence on their populations.

This paper also suggests new insights for other authoritarian regimes that maintain control over the private economic sector, such as China. It reveals to us strategic incentives of these governments that were not considered earlier in the literature. These actions were poorly understood, with analysts and academics claiming Russia and China are making an enduring mistake, and that their current regime structure will become unsustainable before long. However, if we consider the consequences that the liberalization of such large states might bring—including losing parts of their territories—it is possible that under the existing specific conditions, this is optimal, rational behavior on the part of the Russian and Chinese governments.

Russia, and to a lesser extent China, are multinational states, which puts pressure on the central governments in terms of preserving their territorial integrity. Research on domestic conflicts and revolutions show convincingly how high the risk of territorial separatism is when social and economic conditions in a country deteriorate. More research is required to understand the relationship between intentionally maintaining authoritarian regimes in large multinational countries and the risk of separatism that the leaders perceive. It may be a considerable incentive for the leaders, then, to sacrifice improved economic development and democratization in an attempt to preserve the country's territorial integrity. If this is the case, and that incentive structure plays a role in Russia's continuous control of the economy, then international organizations could help Russia by devising mechanisms that would reduce the risk of territorial secession. Such mechanisms should increase the probability that the Russian government will be willing to decrease its control over the economy, thereby encouraging both active economic development and, by extension, democratization.

Notes

[1] Sergey Goryashko, "Pyat' let Bolotnoy: kak vlast' otreagirovala na protesty" [Five years of Bolotnaya: How authorities responded to protests], *Russian BBC Service*, December 10, 2016, http://www.bbc.com/russian/features-38266529, accessed December 25, 2016. Also, see Novye Izvestiya, "Kak zhe nas mnogo..." [There are many of us], December 26, 2011, http://www.newizv.ru/politics/2011-12-26/156953-kak-zhe-nas-mnogo.html, accessed December 25, 2016.

[2] Susanne Lohmann, "The Dynamics of Informational Cascades: The Monday Demonstrations in Leipzig, East Germany, 1989–91," *World Politics* 47, no. 1 (October 1994): 42–101.

[3] Lilia Shevtsova, *Russia—Lost in Transition: The Yeltsin and Putin Legacies* (Washington, DC: Carnegie Endowment for International Peace, 2007); Pierre Hassner, "Russia's Transition to Autocracy," *Journal of Democracy* 19, no. 2 (April 2008): 5–15.

[4] Padma Desai, "Russian Retrospectives on Reforms from Yeltsin to Putin," *Journal of Economic Perspectives* 19, no. 1 (Winter 2005): 96–97.

[5] Vladimir Shlapentokh, "The Short Time Horizon in the Russian Mind," *Communist and Post-Communist Studies* 38, no. 1 (March 2005): 1–24.

[6] Henry E. Hale, "25 Years after the USSR: What's Gone Wrong?" *Journal of Democracy* 27, no. 3 (July 2016): 29.

[7] Daniel Treisman refers to these former members of Soviet security agencies as "silovarchs," a portmanteau of *siloviki* (active members of the military and security services) and oligarchs. See Daniel Treisman, "Putin's Silovarchs," *Orbis* 51, no. 1 (Winter 2007): 141–53.

[8] Bálint Magyar, *Post-Communist Mafia State: The Case of Hungary* (Budapest: Central European University Press, 2016).

9. Marshall I. Goldman, "Putin and the Oligarchs," *Foreign Affairs* 83, no. 6 (November–December 2004): 33–44.
10. Richard Sakwa, "Putin and the Oligarchs," *New Political Economy* 13, no. 2 (June 2008): 185–91.
11. Beibei Tang and Jonathan Unger, "The Socioeconomic Status, Co-Optation and Political Conservatism of the Educated Middle Class: A Case Study of University Teachers," in *Middle-class China*, ed. Minghong Chen and David S. G. Goodman (London: Edward Elgar Publishing, 2013), 90–109.
12. "'Bolotnoye delo' blizitsya k finalu" [The 'Bolotnaya' case is coming to an end], *NTV.ru*, February 5, 2014, http://www.ntv.ru/novosti/838304/, accessed December 22, 2016.
13. "Udaltsov i Razvozzhayev poluchili po 4.5 goda kolonii" [Udaltsov and Razvozzhayev were each sentenced to 4.5 years of jail], *NTV.ru*, July 24, 2014, http://www.ntv.ru/novosti/1156496/, accessed December 22, 2016.
14. The Russian government-funded news agency RIA Novosti presents a comprehensive list – "'Tsventye revolyutsii' na postsovetskom prostranstve. Spravka" ["Coloured revolutions" in the post-Soviet area. Reference], *RIA Novosti*, November 30, 2011, https://ria.ru/spravka/20111130/502208028.html, accessed December 20, 2016.
15. Sergey Kara-Murza, S. Telegin, A. Alexandrov, and M. Murashkin, *Eksport revolyutsii: Yushchenko, Saakashvili...* (Moscow: Algoritm, 2005); Andrei Viktorovich Manoylo, "Tsventnye revolyutsii i tehnologii demontazha politicheskih rezhimov," *Mirovaya Politika* 1 (2015): 1–19.
16. For a more detailed explanation of strategic interactions please see Steve Tadelis, *Game Theory: An Introduction* (Princeton, NJ: Princeton University Press, 2013), 3–11.
17. Thomas Carothers, "The End of the Transition Paradigm," *Journal of Democracy* 13, no. 1 (January 2002): 5–21.
18. Anna Grzymala-Busse, "The Discreet Charm of Formal Institutions: Postcommunist Party Competition and State Oversight," *Comparative Political Studies* 39, no. 10 (December 2006): 1–30.
19. Ronald Inglehart and Christian Welzel, *Modernization, Cultural Change, and Democracy* (New York: Cambridge University Press, 2005); David Epstein, Robert Bates, Jack Goldstone, Ida Kristensen, and Sharyn O'Halloran, "Democratic Transitions," *American Journal of Political Science* 50, no. 3 (2006): 551–69.
20. Adam Przeworski, Michael E. Alvarez, José Antonio Cheibub, and Fernando Limongi, *Democracy and Development: Political Institutions and Well-Being in the World, 1950–1990* (Cambridge: Cambridge University Press, 2000).
21. Przeworski et al, *Democracy and Development*, 273. Przeworski and his co-authors reached this conclusion through statistical analysis. "Almost certain" indicates that among a certain number of cases, the great majority corresponded to this conclusion. Given the inherent uncertainties of such analysis (due to multiple variables affecting social processes), this assertion is a probabilistic one, which some research paradigms believe to be more useful for policymakers. Nevertheless, the statement indicates that if a country *was democratic*, and the *average* per capita income was high, it will almost always stay democratic, should that

income level decrease while remaining above $4000. Should it drop beneath this figure, the risk of losing democracy is very high.
22 Albert O. Hirschman, *Exit, Voice and Loyalty: Responses to Decline in Firms, Organizations and States* (Cambridge, MA: Harvard University Press, 1970).
23 Carothers, "The End of the Transition Paradigm"; Andrew Wilson, *Virtual Politics: Faking Democracy in the Post-Soviet World* (New Haven: Yale University Press, 2005); Ivan Krastev, "Democracy's 'Doubles'," *Journal of Democracy* 17, no. 2 (April 2006): 52–62.
24 Robert Dahl, *On Democracy* (New Haven: Yale University Press, 1998).
25 Nicu Popescu, "Russia's Soft Power Ambitions," *CEPS Policy Brief* 115 (October 2006).
26 Daniel Sneider, "Yeltsin Prevails, Military Crushes Parliament Forces," *The Christian Science Monitor*, October 5, 1993, http://www.csmonitor.com/1993/1005/05012.html, accessed December 20, 2016.
27 I do not qualify the selective detention of a few individual protesters by police, and their consequent charging with administrative or penal offenses, as a coercive response. Punishing a very small number in order to deter the masses would fall under the co-optation scheme, as authorities need to send credible signals to the protesters, revealing the regime's resolve and the price of confrontation for the protesters.
28 The concept of "selectorate" is developed by Bruce Bueno de Mesquita and his co-authors and captures all persons who have a say in choosing a leader—in democratic countries these are all registered voters. See Bruce Bueno de Mesquita, Alastair Smith, Randolph M. Silverson, and James D. Morrow, *The Logic of Political Survival* (Cambridge: MIT Press, 2005), 41.
29 Ibid., 51.
30 Ibid., 130.
31 I use the term "self-expression values," as defined by Ronald Inglehart and Wayne E. Baker, to reflect the factors of trust, tolerance, and political activism, which emerge only when people feel secure—as a rule this happens, according to these two authors, in post-industrial societies. These values are in contrast to survival values. Ronald Inglehart and Wayne E. Baker, "Modernization, Cultural Change and the Persistence of Cultural Values," *American Sociological Review* 65, no. 1 (February 2000): 25–26.
32 RBK Daily, "WCIOM: Protestnoye dvizhenie sostoit iz molodyh, tvorcheskih i nebednyh," June 27, 2012, http://www.rbcdaily.ru/society/562949984195380, accessed July 20, 2016.
33 A good attempt to disambiguate the concept of middle class, which responds well to critics that take the US middle class as the standard, is "Who's in the middle? It's a matter of definition," *Economist*, February 12, 2009, http://www.economist.com/node/13063338, accessed December 18, 2016.
34 Seymour Martin Lipset, "Some Social Requisites of Democracy: Economic Development and Political Legitimacy," *American Political Science Review* 53, no. 1 (March 1959): 69–105; Barrington Moore, *Social Origins of Dictatorship and Democracy* (New York: Beacon Press, 1966).

35 Nikolay Petrov, "Is Russian Society Waking Up?" *PONARS Eurasia Policy Memo* 213 (Sept. 2012): 4.
36 Joseph G. Eisenhauer, "An Economic Definition of the Middle Class," *Forum for Social Economics* 37, no. 2 (August 2008): 101–113.
37 Banerjee, Abhijit V., and Esther Duflo, "What is Middle Class about the Middle Classes around the World?" *The Journal of Economic Perspectives* 22, no. 2 (Spring 2008): 3–28.
38 William Easterly, "The Middle Class Consensus and Economic Development," *Journal of Economic Growth* 6, no. 4 (December 2001): 317–35.
39 Banerjee and Duflo, "What is Middle Class," 6.
40 Luis Lopez-Calva and Eduardo Ortiz-Juarez, "A Vulnerability Approach to the Definition of the Middle Class," *Journal of Economic Inequality* 12, no. 1 (March 2014): 23–47.
41 Robert Jervis, "War and Misperception," *Journal of Interdisciplinary History* 18, no. 4 (Spring 1988): 675–700; James Morrow, "Capabilities, Un-certainty, and Resolve: A Limited Information Model of Crisis," *American Journal of Political Science* 33, no. 4 (November 1989): 941–72; Jack Levy, "Political Psychology and Foreign Policy," in *Oxford Handbook of Political Psychology*, ed. Leonie Huddy, David O. Sears, and Jack S. Levy (New York: Oxford University Press, 2003), 253–84.
42 Ted Robert Gurr, *Why Men Rebel* (Princeton, NJ: Princeton University Press, 1970).
43 Max Kaase and Alan Marsh, "Political Action: A Theoretical Perspective," in *Political Action: Mass Participation in Five Western Democracies*, ed. Samuel H. Barnes, Max Kaase et al. (Beverly Hills, CA: Sage Publications, 1979), 27–56.
44 Mancur Olson, *The Logic of Collective Action* (Cambridge, MA: Harvard University Press, 1965).
45 Mark Granovetter, "Threshold Models of Collective Behaviour," *American Journal of Sociology* 83, no. 6 (May 1978): 1420–43.
46 Timur Kuran, "Now out of Never: The Element of Surprise in the East European Revolution of 1989," *World Politics* 44, no. 1 (October 1991): 7–48.
47 Lohmann, "The Dynamics of Informational Cascades."
48 Maksim Tsvetovat and Mark Rouleau, "Conflict Cascades and Self-Organized Criticality in Dynamic Networks," *Artificial Societies* 3, no. 1 (2008): 5–15.
49 Sidney Tarrow, "States and Opportunities: The Political Structuring of Social Movements," in *Comparative Perspectives on Social Movements: Political Opportunities, Mobilizing Structures, and Cultural Framings*, ed. Doug McAdam, John D. McCarthy, and Mayer N. Zald (Cambridge: Cambridge University Press, 1996), 41–61.
50 Lohmann, "The Dynamics of Informational Cascades," 67–69.
51 A veto player is an individual or collective actor who has to agree for the (legislative) status quo to change. For more details, see George Tsebelis, *Veto Players: How Political Institutions Work* (Princeton, NJ: Princeton University Press, 2002).
52 Anthony Oberschall, *Social Conflict and Social Movements* (Englewood Cliffs, NJ: Prentice-Hall, 1973).
53 Doug McAdam, "Micromobilization Contexts and Recruitment to Activism," in *International Social Movement Research, Vol. 1*, ed. Bert Klandermans, Hanspeter Kriesi, and Sidney Tarrow (Greenwich, CT: JAI Press, 1988).

54 Brendon Hong, "China's Hidden Protests," *The Daily Beast*, January 5, 2016, http://www.thedailybeast.com/articles/2016/01/05/china-s-hidden-protests.html, accessed December 22, 2017.
55 Gordon Tullock, *The Social Dilemma: Of Autocracy, Revolution, Coup d'Etat, and War* (Indianapolis, IN: Liberty Fund, 2005).
56 Dimitri Bulin, "Novyi bjudzhet Rossii: bolee voennyi, menee sotsial'nyi" [New Russian Budget: More Military, Less Social], *BBC Russian Service*, October 25, 2013, http://www.bbc.co.uk/russian/russia/2013/10/131025_russia_budget_2014.shtml, accessed August 18, 2016.
57 Richard Cornes and Todd Sandler, *The Theory of Externalities, Public Goods, and Club Goods* (Cambridge: Cambridge University Press, 1996), 4.
58 Inge Kaul, *Global Public Goods: International Cooperation in the 21st Century* (New York: Oxford University Press, 1999). Economists may point out that what I refer to as public goods are in fact club goods. However, as Kaul and Ronald Mendoza rightly suggest, "the properties of goods do not always correspond to this standard definition. The main reason is that society can modify the (non)rivalry and (non)excludability of a good's benefits. Goods often become private or public as a result of deliberate policy choices." Inge Kaul and Ronald U. Mendoza, "Advancing the Concept of Public Goods," in *Providing Global Public Goods: Managing Globalization*, ed. Inge Kaul, Pedro Conceição, Katell Le Goulven, and Ronald U. Mendoza (Oxford: Oxford University Press, 2003), 80. For instance, clean air was long presented as a classical public good. However, in the modern era of heavy pollution and advanced technological developments, which allow for the purification and storage of clean air, this is already becoming a tradable commodity.
59 World Bank, "Structural Challenges to Growth Become Binding," *Russia Economic Report* 30 (Sep. 2013), 11, http://www.worldbank.org/content/dam/Worldbank/document/rer-30-eng.pdf, accessed August 15, 2016.
60 "Issledovaniye RBK: Skol'ko v Rossii chinovnikov i mnogo li oni zarabatyvayut," [How many public employees are in Russia and how much do they earn?], *RBK.ru*, October 10, 2014, http://www.rbc.ru/economics/15/10/2014/543cfe56cbb20f8c4e0b98f2, accessed December 15, 2016.
61 According to the same World Bank report, Russia had a lower, on average, rate of employment in the public sector based on examination of the health and social services sectors.
62 "V Rossii gosudarstvo stalo glavnym sobstvennikom," *Polit.ru*, February 13, 2006, http://polit.ru/news/2006/02/13/ecomgos/, accessed August 10, 2016.
63 Magyar, *Post-Communist Mafia State*, 139.
64 Anastasia Golitsyna, "Durov doshutilsya," *Vedomosti.ru*, April 22, 2014, http://www.vedomosti.ru/companies/news/25653911/durov-doshutilsya?full#cut, accessed August 22, 2016.
65 Abraham Maslow, "A Theory of Human Motivation," *Psychological Review* 50, no. 4 (1943): 370–96.

IV.
WEALTH AND OWNERSHIP

Andrey Ryabov

The Institution of Power&Ownership in the Former USSR:
Origin, Diversity of Forms, and Influence on Transformation Processes

The institution of power&ownership *(vlast'-sobstvennost')* became an object of intense scholarly interest in Russia in the 2000's, particularly among experts in the social sciences and economists. The notion however, had already been on the scholarly agenda during the decline of the Soviet era.[1] Back then, the concept was used to describe a phenomenon characteristic of the specific development of pre-industrial Asian societies. By the beginning of the 21st century, it became apparent however that the institution of power&ownership is by no means a historical artifact but rather part of a new reality, an institution that has become an important factor in the contemporary socio-economic and political life of a country and in the process of complex intersystem transformation.

The advent of power&ownership in the context of post-Soviet development largely came as a surprise for the political class as well as the academic community who were of the conviction that after the disintegration of the Soviet Union, Russia—along with the other newly independent states—would develop along liberal democratic lines. However, these countries have taken a different developmental path. Scholarly publications and social and political essays usually associate this path with a halted, unfinished transformation. In this line of thinking, the transitional situation of post-Communist society is "between democracy and dictatorship,"[2] with "hybrid" political regimes emerging instead of liberal democracies.[3]

Yet, it was the specifics of intersystem transformation in Russia, as well as partly in other post-Soviet states, that drew researchers' attention to a whole stratum of economic, social, and political problems related to the all-important role that the institution of power&ownership plays in the shaping and consolidation of a new social order.

In the post-Soviet Russian case, this institution has been defined by a number of distinctive features. These were perhaps most clearly presented in Igor Berezhnoy and Vyacheslav Volchik's work as the following: "1. The granting of ownership rights for certain property is only possible with active participation of the state as the main agent of distribution (or redistribution); 2. Any property might be expropriated at any time if the authorities (at any level) become interested in its redistribution; 3. State or other authorities collect rent (either explicitly or implicitly) from the property within the framework of power&ownership."[4] Authors like Berezhnoy and Volchik have stressed that power&ownership is based on full or partial monopolization by the state (or rather by the groups that control it), of whole sectors of the economy, or even the whole national economy itself.[5] Such authors argue that the institution of power&ownership was inherent in the majority of civilizations in the Ancient World and during the Middle Ages. It was most fully developed, however, in places with the existence of, "on the one hand, significant and stable income from any kind of rent and, on the other hand, opportunities, based on fears, for the super-exploitation of a nominally free population."[6] It is therefore not accidental that in many Eastern countries, the institution has survived up to the modern era.

In Russia, power&ownership has demonstrated amazing vitality, having played a huge role in the country's history since the 15th century. It was conditioned by the fact that the Russian Kingdom (*Moskovskoe Tsarstvo*), which had its roots in the Moscow Princedom, had assimilated the statehood and political traditions of the Mongol invaders. This included important features of the "nomadic state" of the Golden Horde, where, as in many countries of the East, all land was considered the property of the sovereign, the khan. As American historian Richard Pipes has noted, the Russian state arose from the domain of the Tsar ("votchina," or ancestral lands).[7] The Tsar's monopoly on land, like in oriental societies, was what constituted the economic basis of the authoritative autocratic state and its dominating role in national economy until the collapse of the monarchy in 1917. At the same time, however, traditions of private property ownership did simultaneously exist. As such, the Russian economy was heterogeneous to a limited extent due to its combination of the imported institutions of Eastern despotism and the institution of private property from Europe.[8]

Thus, before the Socialist era there existed in Russia a powerful tradition related to the institution of power&ownership. Following the Bolshevik take-over in 1917, the institution gradually turned into the backbone of a new socialist social and political order. The Soviet project, from the very outset, sought to transfer the means of production into state ownership as the basis of the economic foundation of a new order, as well as to give full control of the state to the Communist Party which identified itself as the new state. Such ideas emerged under the influence of an important process characteristic of the world capitalist economy of the late 19th and early 20th centuries. Namely the formation of, and subsequent monopolization of, state-monopoly capitalism based on the merger of the power of state and economic forces of private capitalist industrial and financial monopolies, which became especially conspicuous during World War I. The architect of the Soviet state, Vladimir Lenin, regarded this phase as one of transition towards socialism. In 1917, he wrote, "socialism is none other than state capitalist monopoly turned to the good of the people and therefore ceased to be capitalist monopoly."[9] The Bolshevik leaders were captivated by the prospect of concentrating power and property in the hands of the government, which in turn, according to the Bolshevik idea, was supposed to distribute public goods fairly among all the members of society and rule the country in a way that was in the best interest of the working class. It was this system that gained its mature and comprehensive form during the 1930's. It spread all over the country including the former colonial possessions of the Russian empire, which by then had obtained the status of "union republics" within the USSR.

The backbone of the system was the unrestricted power of the Communist Party, which had created a new ruling class, the nomenklatura, which united in their ranks a privileged bureaucratic strata involved at different levels in the processes of leadership and control of the country. The criteria that distinguished nomenklatura members from the rest of the officialdom, as well as the rules and procedures for their recruitment, were established and strictly controlled by the Communist Party. The political economic nature of the Soviet ruling class was very accurately described by Mikhail Voslensky, who wrote, that "The most important thing in the nomenklatura is power. Not property but power."[10] It was precisely unrestricted and unchecked power in a country where almost all property was in fact transferred to the state that enabled the nomenklatura to be in full command of that property. That is, in the institution of power&ownership, power has always been primary, while ownership, a derivative of the former, a secondary category. It was the consequently established functional hierarchy of political leadership and control of material production that predetermined the structural features of the nomenklatura. In fact, the real owner of property was the Communist Party apparatus who took supreme political responsibility for its usage and carried out monitoring functions. Its managers were general directors of the enterprises and other economic leaders (the so called "economic nomenklatura"), who were charged with overseeing the ways in which property was used and disposed of.

Economic reforms between 1987–91 toward a less centralized grip on the economy, designed to ensure higher efficiency and give enterprises further power over their own resources, opened a path for a real transfer of ownership from the Party nomenklatura to industrial managers. It was the starting point of the disintegration of the Soviet power&ownership system,[11] which led to swift privatization by the nomenklatura of former state property. This disintegration and consequent changes were of great significance for the future, not only for Russia, but also for the rest of the newly independent states that emerged from the ruins of the former "union republics" of the Soviet Union. As it eventually turned out, the Soviet system's influence on their further development was greater than many could have predicted.

Reasons Behind the Survival of the Institution of Power&Ownership's in the Post-Soviet Period

What the history of the Moscow Kingdom, Russian Empire, and the Soviet Union shows is that while the institution of power&ownership demonstrated "its relative efficiency during periods of social development characterized by mobilization and instability, of wars and territorial expansions,"[12] its efficiency during eras of peaceful development proved invariably inferior to that of systems based on private property and political and economic competition. By the end of the 1980's it became obvious that the Soviet system was losing economic, social, and technological competition to contemporary Western capitalism. At the beginning of the era of market reforms, economic transformation in the USSR. was everywhere accompanied by the destruction of the centralized management system and the creation of a new competitive environment. It would seem that the collapse of the system based on the Communist Party's monopoly of power as well as the desire of the peoples of the former USSR. for democratic societies and open market economies would leave the institution of power&ownership with little chance of survival.

Yet after a while it became clear that in the majority of the post-Soviet states the institution of power&ownership not only survived, but actually once again became the backbone of a new social and political order.[13] The key question is therefore how to explain the institution's vitality and adaptability to dramatic changes in socio-political conditions.

The majority of contemporary authors attribute the survival of power&ownership to the leading role the former Soviet nomenklatura played in the transition from the Soviet system to a new social order. It is worth noting that the possibility of a "bourgeois regeneration" of the nomenklatura, who after having accumulated certain amount of resources would grow tired of social restrictions imposed upon them by the Socialist regime and would try to replace it with capitalism, had been predicted by one of the leaders of the world communist movement of the 1920-30's, Leon Trotsky.[14]

Two key elements were crucial in assuring the preservation of the nomenklatura's role during the transition from socialism to the open market: firstly, the retention of control over economic resources, primarily over the enormous amount of state property; and secondly, the possession, of economic and social management skills that other social strata did not have. The latter was especially important during the early periods of the new independent states, when the economy Russia had inherited from the USSR. was bordering on collapse. One important factor that helped preserve the domination of the nomenklatura in the transition process was the fact that there was no demand even by private business for "good institutions," at least not during the initial period of transformation. There were numerous reasons for that, but primarily it was economic chaos that reigned at that time and the lack of any generally accepted rules. By the beginning of systemic economic and political changes, there were no groups, to use Mancur Olson's terminology, with "all-encompassing interests" in the former Soviet Union[15] which "would be in a position to act as institutional innovators for structures capable of changing the trajectory of institutional development enclosed around the institution of power&ownership."[16] Moreover, the fragmentation of Soviet economics promoted "a tendency, either forced or voluntary, for the debris of socialist statehood to join a larger community, to act 'under one roof.'"[17] That led to the domination in the new independent economies of large-scale interest groups or clans who acted solely in their own interest. Consequently, the actualization of a democratic future in Russia with equal opportunities for all was gradually pushed off to a symbolic level of politics, becoming a mere political slogan meant to placate the public.

Relying as they were on the advantages of the "founder effect"[18] the nomenklatura began to build a new economic and political order based on their own conceptions.

Now those conceptions were very different from what dominated post-Soviet countries' public opinion of the time, which saw a desirable future in the form of democracy and open market economy. Members of the nomenklatura were oriented toward the preservation of social and political hierarchy and monopolism, distrustful of any political and civil activity that was not authorized from above. They proceeded from the perception of government power as the main driving force of any social changes, including the formation of market. Such conceptions by the nomenklatura of a "correctly working economy" rather corresponded with "clannish capitalism, a decentralized system in which the state remains potentially able to interfere in any economic processes."[19] Thus the emerging system became a successor to the former "administrative market" which was widely expanded late in the life of the USSR. and in whose framework the institution of power&ownership had played a key role. In its fight against emerging elements of private capitalism that institution won a quick victory.

A new, post-communist social and political order in which market and political pluralism might co-exist with rigid hierarchy and monopolism was being created in different post-Soviet states at different paces. These regimes were crucially determined by the relative balance of forces between the nomenklatura and the mass democratic and national-democratic movements in the process of transition from the Soviet system to a market one. In the republics of Central Asia, with the exception of Kyrgyzstan, the role of mass democratic forces was insignificant, and in Turkmenistan it was next to none. This is why the domination of the former nomenklatura in the politics and economies of these states ever since their declaration of independence has been absolute. That was the main purpose of establishing stable authoritarian regimes in these countries with no political pluralism and domination of state economy in Tajikistan, Turkmenistan, and Uzbekistan.

Even in Belarus, where the proportion of urban and better-educated populations is high compared to the republics of Central Asia, the national-democratic movement has proved weak. This may be explained by the fact that at the time of the Soviet Union's disintegration the majority of Belarus' population showed no interest in creating an independent state. The reason for that is that the Belarusian economy within the USSR, despite its lack of natural resources, had functioned as an "assembly plant," and therefore a potential severing of industrial relations with other republics threatened a dramatic decline in the standard of living, which by Soviet standards had been relatively high. Besides, the process of shaping a national identity was rather slow and had not as yet led to the formation of a powerful demand for creating an independent Belarusian state.

Conversely, in the three republics of the South Caucasus—Azerbaijan, Armenia, and Georgia—it was mass national-democratic movements that initially came to power. In Moldova, too, the national-democrats gained strong positions in power structures. The nomenklatura in all these countries were under considerable pressure by civil and democratic forces, even though the latter had a strong nationalistic orientation. However, economic hardships during the early years of independence promoted the return of the former nomenklatura, because the democratic movement, even though it did come to power, had no managerial experience and was therefore unable to overcome hardships by means of an efficient policy of reform. The nomenklatura managed to capitalize on people's fatigue from the destructive changes wrought upon them and used that fatigue to sell promises of stabilization.

In Georgia, alone among these republics, the political positions of the nomenklatura by the time of independence were so undermined by anti-communist actions that for a number of years they were unable to play any significant role in political life. However, in a country exhausted by two bloody cross-ethnic conflicts (Georgian-Ossetian and Georgian-Abkhazian), the only alternative to the national-democrats was organized crime, which encouraged a gradual revival of the remnants of the nomenklatura's political influence, although only for a short period of time. As a result of the "Rose Revolution" in the Fall of 2003, national-democratic forces came back to power and forced the nomenklatura out of the political arena once and for all. This is why the institution of power&ownership in that country has largely been destroyed. This is despite the fact that ever since 2012, when billionaire Bidzina Ivanishvili became the de facto leader of the country, attempts were made to restore the institution partially—though these were not comprehensive and failed to affect the economy as a whole.

The uniqueness of Georgia's experience of "de-nomenklaturization" was determined not only by strong dissident traditions of the Soviet period but also by the specific educational features of its cultural elite which later formed the core of the national-democratic movement. During the USSR years, the Georgian higher education system had been largely oriented towards ethnic traditions, while during the post-Soviet period new elites preferred to study in the West. [20]

In the two largest states of the post-Soviet space, Russia and Ukraine, the nomenklatura restored their positions in politics and economics relatively quickly. In Russia, in the process of market reforms that caused considerable hardships for the majority of its population and their strong discontent, the nomenklatura had managed by 1994 to wrest the initiative from the democratic movement and gradually to marginalize it as a political actor. In Ukraine, the relative balance of forces between the nomenklatura and the democratic movement was at the beginning more or less equal, but by the mid-90's the former Soviet ruling class gradually restored itself to power.

Therefore, in the vast majority of the post-Soviet states, grass-roots movements have proved unable to assert themselves as major effectors of social and political change. The reason for that is the fact that during the late years of the Soviet Union, consumer society had already been formed while civil society remained extremely weak. During seventy years of totalitarian rule people had largely lost the abilities and skills required for self-organization and for building horizontal social networks. That is why society all over the former USSR proved unprepared for a prolonged and tenacious struggle for their rights.[21] Having comprehended, after the collapse of the Soviet Union, the impossibility of satisfying their consumer needs, which just a short time ago, on the tide of the revolution of expectations, seemed to them quite attainable, large numbers of people began to prefer individual social strategies of adaptation to new conditions of life. This was conducive to a sharp decline in populations' civil and political activities. It was growing social passivity that created an environment favorable to the restoration of the nomenklatura's influence.

Forms of Existence and Clannish Capitalism

The institution of power&ownership was not established in all post-Soviet countries simultaneously. In the states of Central Asia, it planted itself in key positions within the economy virtually the moment independence was declared. The same applies to Belarus and Azerbaijan. Elsewhere, the restoration of the institution of power&ownership under new conditions was only finalized after the nomenklatura regained domination in political life. Thus, according to Rustem Nureyev and Anton Runov, in Russia, the institutionalization of power&ownership in its new post-Soviet guise took place in 1996–2000.[22]

It should be noted that the institution gained leading roles both in those countries where the state retained key positions in the economy (Azerbaijan, Belarus, Tajikistan, Turkmenistan, and Uzbekistan) and in those whose economies were nominally dominated by private property (Armenia, Kazakhstan, Kyrgyzstan, Moldova, Russia, and Ukraine). In this connection it is perhaps possible to talk about two general forms of power&ownership in the post-Soviet region.

In countries with dominant state economies the leading role is initially played by the officialdom—the most powerful bureaucratic clans. It is the officials who define which spheres are open to business as well as the limits to entrepreneurial activity; they also make decisions concerning rights of ownership and access to property. Because of that, the officials themselves get involved in business, both legally through leading positions in state enterprises and illegally, capitalizing on their family connections, using fictitious companies and persons or extorting rent from state-owned and private enterprises for granting them business permits.

In the countries with nominally private economies the institution of power&ownership has a more complex structure. Large private capitalist enterprises have emerged there mainly in the process of nomenklatura-oriented privatizations that were administered from above through the distribution of assets among people and companies close to the authorities, which was exactly what led to the formation of financial and industrial "oligarchies." These oligarchies, aiming for more control of former state property, commissions for state-funded projects, and looking to enjoy all kinds of privileges they could, wanted to established exclusive relationships with government authorities. Major entrepreneurs tried to get "political benefits and privileges, access to state budgets and state property, and, very often, immunity from prosecution"[23] in exchange for making "political investments" into officials and politicians. Yet even in this political framework, authorities remained not only fortunate objects of investment by, and a prize for, competing "oligarchies," but also key actors on whom these oligarchs' well-being and prosperity depended. The authorities here, like in countries with state economies, were in a position to decide who should be given property, who should be granted privileges in conducting business activities, and whose property should be taken away. In this context it is perhaps difficult to dispute Vyacheslav Volchik, who declares that it was precisely the institution of power&ownership within the framework of the post-Soviet economic order that led to the formation of "oligarchies."[24] Naturally, the power setup and its functioning methods here were different from those in the countries where state ownership dominated. Those differences will be analyzed later.

As far as the legal forms of the institution of power&ownership are concerned, they too were notable for great diversity, including both companies with different forms of property and various kinds of cooperation between government institutions and enterprises (administrative control, financial support, credit subsidies, exclusive access to resources, etc.).

In the aftermath of the establishment of new economic and social orders in post-Soviet countries, coalitions have been formed that were interested in strengthening the institution of power&ownership. Commenting on the membership of such a coalition in Russia, Nureyev and Runov mention the new nomenklatura at national and local levels of government; owners and managers of export-oriented enterprises; law enforcement and military agencies; and the top of organized crime.[25] It might be assuredly stated that such breakdowns also apply to other post-Soviet states.

The domination of power&ownership penetrated the entire economies of those countries, including their "white," "gray," and "shadow" spheres. The post-Soviet economic realities in this respect differ from, for example, Latin American countries, where the clannish economies connected to the governments are propped up from below by a powerful and informal market sector.[26] In the new independent states that emerged on the territory of the former USSR an environment came into being which impedes such dynamics and thus prevents the demand for "good institutions" from emerging.

As regards the main parameters of the institution of power&ownership in the post-Soviet period, it must be noted that the political authorities, just as during the socialist era, have acted as the backbone around which the institution is constructed. But unlike the previous era, when the then ruling communist parties tried to integrate different industrial and regional interests into broader strategies of national development, during the post-Soviet time the prevalence of power&ownership has brought about the total domination of specific group interests in politics. This has led to consolidation of clannish ("nepotism," "crony") capitalism in the new independent countries of the region. It is no accident therefore that the most recent rating of "crony capitalist" countries by the Economist magazine placed the two biggest post-Soviet states in the top 5—Russia (the 1st place) and Ukraine (the 5th).[27]

INFLUENCE ON POLITICS

The influence of the institution of power&ownership on political processes in post-Soviet countries has not as yet been sufficiently studied. In one of the few studies on this subject, A. Melville, D. Stukal, and M. Mironyuk state that the intertwining of power and ownership in those countries has enabled firmly established elites to supplement the economic rent that they derive thanks to the new economic order, with political rent.[28] This, the authors assert, helps the elites and their authoritarian leader to preserve the existing political system and to block any demand for "good institutions." From this standpoint, therefore, power&ownership acts as an instrument of preserving the status quo in society, leaving political and economic power in the hands of the ruling strata. In my opinion, however, it is precisely this institution that is the fundamental principle of the post-Soviet political order and the primary cause of authoritarianism (or the tendency towards it) in post-Soviet political regimes as well as of the static nature of the new independent countries' political systems that have no internal impetus to change. Nevertheless, there is something in the above-mentioned authors' reasoning that can undoubtedly be seconded, and that is their thesis that the institution of power&ownership creates prerequisites for the turning of rent into one of the most powerful instruments of the new elites' domination. Yet the role of power&ownership in the structuring of the post-Soviet social order is not limited to that. Its existence also creates a politico-economic basis for the emergence and strengthening of rent-based capitalism in post-Soviet countries. This is a model in which the ruling elites aspire neither to their countries' social and economic development nor to any growth in creating surplus values, but to the deriving of maximum rent. Besides, it seems reasonable to subdivide rent itself not into political and economic types as is done in the above-mentioned article by the three authors but rather into administrative rent, which enables the elite groups to exercise exclusive control over state institutions for the extraction of profit, and budget rent, which enables them to extract profit by way of allocating funds from the state budget. Moreover, in four post-Soviet states (Azerbaijan, Kazakhstan, Russia, and Turkmenistan) the main foundation of the political domination and economic well-being of the ruling elite lies in their control over natural resources and deriving rent from them; in this particular case, the rent on the extraction of hydrocarbon raw materials—oil and gas. As the experience of other countries has shown, economic models based on the export of raw materials in addition to a lack of strong democratic traditions usually lead to the formation of authoritarian regimes. This fully applies to the four above-mentioned post-Soviet states.

The possession of power enables one to control sources of rent. The essence of political struggle among competing clans and groups boils down to ongoing redistribution of rent. It is not competition among different "projects of the future" as it is in the democratic model, where political process is linear and the future itself, open. Instead, it is a chain of repeating and repetitive developments, while essentially nothing significant changes in the society itself. Political platforms and ideologies vying for votes merely play the roles of markers that distinguish the supporters of one interest group fighting for control over sources of rent with the supporters of another interest group. In the sphere of politics, therefore, one of the consequences of the domination of rent-based capitalism is the cyclical character of the political process, which creates no favorable conditions for social changes. In its structure it typologically resembles political processes of the Middle Ages rather than modern times.

In authoritarian regimes, competition for control over the sources of rent unfolds in the nonpublic sphere (in circles close to the ruler). Under such conditions, elections, which are a mere hoax with predictable results, serve only to demonstrate the "democratic legitimacy" of authoritarian regimes. In the regimes that resemble, using Robert Dahl's terminology, "competing oligarchies"[29] elections are the key factor in determining who is going to control sources of rent from now on. However, shifts in power are possible in such countries, such as by exploiting mass protests (the most illustrative example is Kyrgyzstan in 2005 and 2010) that usually spring up as a reaction to falsified elections. In such cases, the discontent of powerful interest groups who feel that their "victory was stolen" by the authorities unite with mass public protests against the falsification of election results. As a result of such actions power can shift to the opposition and the shift gets legitimized by means of extraordinary elections (Georgia in 2004, Kyrgyzstan in 2005 and 2010). Another scenario involves cases in which authorities under pressure from an opposition movement are compelled to consent to an extraordinary election, lose it and become the opposition themselves (Ukraine in 2004, Moldova in 2009).

The domination of power&ownership means the concentration of all resources in the hands of closed elite groups. Even if the ruling elite is not consolidated but divided into several groups that compete with each other in public politics, a system based on power&ownership by its very nature narrows space for competition and marginalizes autonomous political actors. Ultimately, the government strives to become the only actor. Using their monopoly on resources, authorities create barriers preventing players they consider undesirable from entering the political market.

Judging by the the experience of post-Soviet countries, the institution of power&ownership is compatible with both authoritarian political regimes and "competing oligarchies," sometimes identified as democracies in publications on the region.[30] In authoritarian regimes power&ownership is either controlled by one or more groups (clans) of the ruling nomenklatura (Armenia, Russia); is of a family and dynastic character (Azerbaijan, Tajikistan); or else gets built around the strong figure of an authoritarian leader (Kazakhstan, Turkmenistan, Uzbekistan). In each case a rigidly hierarchical and centralized system of control over power&ownership is established. The authoritarian political regime in Belarus resembles those of the latter group. Unlike the regimes in Central Asia whose sole creator was the former Soviet nomenklatura, the rise of the authoritarian regime in Belarus was a result of a political compromise. Its authoritarianism, which bears a notable populist tinge, asserted itself owing to an informal agreement between the nomenklatura, which was wary of the idea of market reforms, and large segments of the population that were nostalgic about the Soviet period and therefore accepted the mobilization model of state capitalism as a form of social state.[31]

In all above-mentioned authoritarian regimes, the top groups that control the authorities are trying with varying degrees of success to position themselves as a mouthpiece of the entire ruling stratum. It is worth noting that authoritarianism in the post-Soviet space may also exist in realms other than state-dominated economies. In such cases the country's leader (president) plays the role of the head of a bureaucratic corporation which carries out the functions of disposal and control of state property. As demonstrated by the history of such countries as Armenia (starting approximately from the late 1990's, when Robert Kocharian was elected president), Kazakhstan, and Russia (from the late 1990's–early 2000's), authoritarian regimes are quite compatible with economic systems where private property dominates. In such cases the authoritarian leader carries out the function of a supreme arbitrator who plays the crucial role in deciding to whom property is to go to, under what conditions, how it is to be used, etc. The chain of command which he heads is not involved in direct control of major companies but has an extensive arsenal of means for influencing them. The president and his administration also aggressively involve private corporations in sponsoring all kinds of political projects initiated or supported by the authorities. In return major business persons are granted all kinds of benefits and privileges, including custom-made schemes of taxpaying.

Real opposition in the countries with authoritarian regimes either does not exist (Belarus, Turkmenistan, Uzbekistan) or is marginalized (Azerbaijan, Kazakhstan, Russia, Tajikistan). The only exception is Armenia, whose opposition, although it has so far had no chances to come to power, exerts considerable influence on the country's politics by constraining the ruling Republican Party who are forced to take it into consideration. Because of the opposition's weakness the governing regimes in those countries as a rule never experience any difficulties in redistribution of property, using to that end both formal (legal, administrative) and informal (nonpublic pressure) tools. It is also worth noting that as far as constitutional and judicial aspects are concerned, all the authoritarian regimes in the post-Soviet domain are either presidential or presidential-parliamentary republics. The only exception again is Armenia, which decided in a national referendum in December of 2015 to transition to a parliamentary republic.

In the regimes of "competing oligarchies" rivaling elite groups try, either through civil means (through elections) or through the use of force (mass protest actions), to win power in order to convert property to their own use. Now the very nature of power&ownership, which, as has already been pointed out, inevitably brings about authoritarian trends in politics, makes possible recurring attempts by different groups and their leaders to establish authoritarian regimes in their countries. This was the case in Ukraine during the second presidential term of Leonid Kuchma (1999–2004) and during the rule of Viktor Yanukovych (2010–2014). The same trend was evident even in a more rigid form in Kyrgyzstan under Presidents Askar Akayev (during his second and third terms 1995–2005) and Kurmanbek Bakiyev (2005–2010). In Georgia, the trend of establishing authoritarian regimes was evident during the later years of Eduard Shevardnadze's (1999–2003) and Mikheil Saakashvili's (2008–2012) terms. Nor did Moldova avoid steps at authoritarian evolution of its political regime during the absolute rule of the Party of Communists (2001–2009). But every time the efforts to bring about authoritarianism in the countries listed above were faced with objective restraints imposed by the specific national features of their politics. These features include the lack of consolidation among national elites; the lack of groups or clans able to subordinate and bend to their will the other groups; profound regional differences inherent in these countries; and competition among all kinds of identities while nationwide identities have not yet been established. It is also worth noting that all the states in that group have gradually moved from a presidential and presidential-parliamentary system to parliamentary-presidential and parliamentary systems, which offer more or less equally strong and influential elite groups official "platforms" for the coordination of interests and open competition. At the same time, competition among the top circles in "competitive oligarchies" does not give those countries opportunities to move towards full-fledged democracy because, of the presence of power&ownership, which gives rise to "bad institutions" as mentioned above in addition to the prevalence of informal relations and corruption.[32]

"Bad" institutions are not only those that are "inefficient" or work poorly but are also unstable, typically suffering from frequent changes. Such instability is caused by the utilitarian interests of the ruling groups and their intentions to adjust as best they can the institutions in order to solve various tasks which, more often than not, are subject to severe time constraints. Where demand for quality and stable institutions is lacking there prevails an instrumental approach to institutional changes which serve the short- and medium-term interests of the ruling groups that try to use them for securing their grip on power. Thus, in post-Soviet Russia there have been three reforms of the Council of the Federation, the upper house of the federal parliament (1995, 2001, and 2012), and two substantial changes in the electoral system. In Ukraine there have been two constitutional reforms that considerably changed its state system (2004 and 2010). In 2014, after the victory of the "Euromaidan" movement and the ousting of President Yanukovych a new process of constitutional change began in that country. Moldova has experienced four constitutional reforms (1994, 2000, 2009, and 2016). Frequent institutional changes never promote consolidation of statehood but hinder the process of structuring the political domain, which makes it easier for the ruling elites to preserve their domination of politics. The weakness of political institutions in the post-Soviet countries with authoritarian governments is largely balanced by the presence (in most of them) of a personified regime, in which stability of the state crucially relies on personal power and charisma of the national leader. Yet such regimes, even those that have achieved a high level of stability, are at the same time markedly vulnerable to challenges that come forth in the process of power transfer from one leader to another. This makes the ruling strata wary of prospects of change of power and results in support for the existing regime for as long as possible, even if its policies lead to the aggravation of pre-existing societal problems. Opportunities for urgent and timely reforms therefore substantially shrink.

"Bad" institutions promote widening of the sphere of informal political relations, of informal politics. This undermines the role of law as the universal regulator of social relations, which is instead replaced with informal rules and agreements and administrative arbitrariness. Yet another implication of the predominance of "bad" institutions is "the key role of clientelistic and patrimonial relations in the structuring of politico-economic process."[33] Clientelism not only plays the role of a backbone pivot around which power relations get built but also subordinates the state bodies' activities to various special interest groups. Where power&ownership dominates, the chief aim of those groups is seizure of bureaucratic resources that might be used for making lucrative decisions and promoting self-serving business interests. Groups that lose access to bureaucratic resources often also lose stability and break down unless they have family connections or can rely on regional networks, which are to various degrees present in the political practices of all post-Soviet states. Clientelism in aggregate with power&ownership means that access to various resources, privileges, and property is attained only by "serving" the relevant interest group. A severance of such "service" inevitably leads to the loss of such access. The clientelistic and patrimonial character of power relations prompts many an analyst in different countries to compare them typologically to feudal or neo-feudal relations. Even though this viewpoint appears questionable, the way it stresses the conditional nature of power&ownership relations in post-Soviet countries is significant, as this characteristic objectively impedes the formation of groups with all-inclusive interests.

The undivided unity of power&ownership together with the important role that informal relations play in economics give rise in the post-Soviet states to enormous amounts of corruption, which outgrows the administrative framework and assumes a systemic character. It enables, on the one hand, the new nomenklatura to penetrate deeply into business and, on the other hand, for big capital to seize the state machinery. It is often not even the official status of an entity that determines its ability to become an actor in political relations and economic activities, but participation in corrupt relations.

The most important implication of systemic corruption for the politics of post-Soviet countries is the fact that corruption is the critical factor in causing stagnation and in orienting their societies and institutions of power toward the preservation of the status quo. The problem is that in the context of systemic corruption any project aimed at changing the existing political and social order, be it a new attempt toward market and democratic reforms or toward the restoration of the old Soviet regime, gets inevitably blocked or perverted by the groups that are the beneficiaries of corruption. Thus, liberal reforms in an economy result, for the majority of the population, in an increase to the cost of living, a loss of social benefits, and an increase of fiscal burden. Meanwhile, the rest of the economic system's elements, which should be subject to reform, remain the same—monopolism, nepotism, retention of property in the hands of inefficient owners, etc.

In the political aspect, systemic corruption blocks the creation of an independent justice system so that civil and social rights of the citizenry remain unprotected, which impedes the country's democratic development. A vivid example of this is Ukraine at the beginning of the 21st century. After the revolutionary ousting of the semi-authoritarian corrupt regime in 2005 and again in 2014, that country seemed to have been creating real possibilities for a "democratic breakthrough." There were genuine preconditions for this outcome: a real multiplicity of parties, an influential and government-independent mass media, opportunities for really competitive elections with unpredictable results, and high civil activity and organization of the citizenry. And yet, both times the breakthrough failed because corruption in political and business circles, closely connected as they were with power&ownership, prevented such a development. Economic and political reforms aimed at the creation of an open market economy and of a political system principled on the rule of law are still blocked by the ruling stratum which, despite its internal difficulties and conflicts, is still interested in preserving the existing social order. It is apparently not by chance that in March 2016, the influential American newspaper *New York Times* compared Ukraine to a "bog of corruption."[34]

There is only one case within the post-Soviet domain of a relatively successful fight against systemic corruption. And that was the case of a country where the positions of power&ownership were indeed undermined and, as far as education was concerned, the new elites were oriented towards the West. It is Georgia. This is why it was there that the justice system, the police and the system of state services were reformed, albeit largely by authoritarian methods. The personnel of those offices were to a significant degree replaced by people not tainted by a Soviet past. However, the question still remains as to whether or not the "Georgian experiment" in struggle against systemic corruption would be possible to repeat in other post-Soviet states.

At the same time, it may be assumed with confidence that should the government circles in any of the post-Soviet states design, not market and democratic reforms, but a rebirth of Soviet socialism, they would fail to achieve that goal, too. The interests of the groups involved in corruption have become accustomed to the benefits imparted by their positions in the relations of power&ownership and would become an unsurpassable obstacle to any actualization of such a project.

Conclusion

The domination of power&ownership in the political and economic domains of the newly independent states that emerged in the aftermath of the disintegration of the Soviet Union hinders their further development. This institution brings forth strong authoritarian trends in the politics of the post-Soviet countries and narrows political competition. The undivided unity of power&ownership has largely predetermined the formation in these countries of rent-based capitalism with an inherently cyclical domestic political process and domination by special interest groups. This has created a specific environment which lacks quality institutions and in whose politics informal and clientelistic and patrimonial relations flourish and systemic corruption reigns. One specific feature of such systems is the extreme difficulty of forming within them social and political agents of modernization and development; given that those systems and their ruling elites are themselves interested in preserving the status quo. The majority of the population, on the other hand, are passive either due to the lack of skills of civil self-organization or the lack resources to affect change in the existing social and political order.

The preservation in the post-Soviet context of the institution of power&ownership, which has its roots in the socialist era or, in the case of Russia, even earlier, and the lack in the new independent states of any dynamics of positive political and socio-economic changes together reflect the most important feature of their intersystem transformation. It appears that the bulk of these countries are as yet not in the process of democratic development but got stuck somewhere in the middle of the disintegration of the former system. Three states (Moldova, Georgia and Ukraine) took only the first steps on the pathway of democratization. And whatever prospects there are of further development of all post-Soviet countries and their advancement towards democracy and the free market, these are dependent upon the necessity of severing power from ownership and overcoming the dominance of power&ownership.

Notes

[1] L. S. Vasiliev, "Fenomenon vlasti-sobstvennosti. K probleme tipologii dokapitalisticheskih structur" [The phenomenon of Power&Ownership: On the problem of typology of precapitalist structures] in *Tipy obshchestvennyh otnosheniy na Vostoke v Srednie veka* [Types of social relations in the Mediaeval East] (Moscow: Izdatel'stvo "Nauka," 1982), 60–99.

[2] Michael McFaul, Nikolai Petrov, and Andrey Ryabov, *Between Democracy and Dictatorship: Russian Post-Communist Political Reform* (Washington D.C. Carnegie Endowment for International Peace, 2004).

[3] L. F. Shevtsova, *Rezhim Borisa Yeltsina* [Boris Yeltsin and his regime] (Moscow: Moskovskiy Tsentr Karnegi, 1999).

[4] I. V. Berezhnoy and V. V. Volchik, *Issledovaniye ekonomicheskoy evolyutsii instituta vlasti-sobstvennosti* [A study of economic evolution of the institution of Power&Ownership] (Moscow: YUNITI-DANA: Zakon i pravo, 2008), 116.

5 R. M. Nureyev, *Politicheskaya Ekonomiya. Dokapitalisticheskie sposoby proizvodstva. Osnovnye zakonomernosti razvitiia*, [Political Economy: Pre-capitalist Modes of Production; The Main Patterns of Development] (Moscow: Izdatel'stvo MGU, 1991), 54–55.

6 N. M. Pliskevich, "'Vlast-sobstvennost' v sovremennoi Rossii: proiskhozhdenie i perspektivy mutatsii" ["Power&Ownership" in contemporary Russia: Origins and perspectives of mutation], *Mir Rossii* 15, no. 3 (2006): 66.

7 R. Paips [Richard Pipes], *Rossiya pri starom rezhime* [Russia under the Old Regime (1974)], translated from English by V. Kozlovskii (Moscow: "Nezavisimaya gazeta," 1993), 75.

8 R. M. Nureyev and Yu. V. Latov, *Ekonomicheskaya istoriya Rossii (opyt institutsional'nogo analiza)* [Economic history of Russia (experience of institutional analysis)] (Moscow: Izdatel'stvo "Knorus," 2009), 59–60.

9 V. I. Lenin, "Grozyashchaya katastrofa i kak s ney borotsya" [The imminent catastrophe and how to fight it], in *Polnoe sobranie sochinenii*, 5th ed. (Moscow 1958–65), 34:192.

10 M. Voslensky, *Nomenklatura: Gospodstvuyuschii klass Sovetskogo Soyuza* [The nomenklatura: The Soviet ruling class] (Moscow: Zakharov, 2005), 115.

11 Pliskevich, "'Vlast-sobstvennost' v sovremennoi Rossii," 93.

12 V. V. Volchik, "Evolyutsiya rossiyskogo instituta vlasti-sobstvennosti" [Evolution of the Russian institution of Power&Ownership], *Politicheskaya kontseptologiya: zhurnal mezhdistsiplinarnyh issledovaniy*, no. 1 (2009): 164.

13 We do not deal in the present text with the Baltic states because due to the policy dedicated to market and democratic reforms they have integrated themselves into Euro-Atlantic structures—NATO and the European Union. The organization and functioning of these countries' political domains, activities of their economic and political institutions, and their politics in general are formulated and controlled in accordance with principles, regulations and procedures which apply to the EU and NATO.

14 Leon Trotsky, *Predannaya revolyutsiya* [The revolution betrayed] (Moscow: NII kultury, 1991), 210.

15 Mancur Olson, *Vozvyshenie i upadok narodov: Ekonomicheskiy rost, stagflyatsiya, sotsialnyy skleroz* [The rise and decline of nations: Economic growth, stagflation and social rigidities (1982)], translated from English by V. Busygin (Moscow: Novoe Izdatel'stvo, 2013).

16 Berezhnoy and Volchik, *Issledovaniye ekonomicheskoy evolyutsii*, 140.

17 I. Prostakov, "Korporativizm kak ideal i realnost" [Corporatism as ideal and reality], *Svobodnaya mysl*, no. 2 (1992): 61.

18 Volchik, "Evolyutsiya rossiyskogo instituta vlasti-sobstvennosti," 172.

19 A. Libman, "Politicheskaya logika formirovaniya ekonomicheskih institutov v Rossii" [Political logic of the formation of economic institutions in Russia], in *Puti rossiyskogo postkommunizma* [Pathways of Russian post-Communism], ed. Maria Lipman and Andrey Ryabov (Moscow: Izdatelstvo R. Elinina, 2007), 133.

20 N. Mosaki, "Obrazovatelnyy bekgraund vlastnoy elity Gruzii i rossiysko-gruzinskie otnosheniya" [Educational background of Georgian ruling elite and Russia-

Georgia relations], *Mirovaya ekonomika i mezhdunarodnye otnosheniya*, no. 9 (2015): 93–104.

21 A. Ryabov, "Demokratizatsiya i modernizatsiya v kontekste transformatsiy post-sovetskih stran" [Democracy and modernization in the context of the transformation of post-Soviet states], in *Demokratizatsiya i modernizatsiya: k diskussii o vyzovah XXI veka* [Democracy versus modernization: A dilemma for Russia and for the world], ed. V. Inozemtsev and P. Dutkewich (Moscow: Izdatel'stvo "Evropa," 2010), 186

22 Rustem M. Nureyev and Anton B. Runov, "Rossiya: neizbezhna li deprivatizatsiya? (Fenomen vlasti-sobstvennosti v istoricheskoy perspektive)" [Russia: is deprivatization Inevitable? The phenomenon of Power&Ownership in historical perspective], *Voprosy ekonomiki*, no. 6 (2002): 10–31.

23 B. Tsyrlya and V. Chobanu, *Oligarhicheskaya Moldova* [The oligarchic Moldova] (Kishineu, 2013), 346.

24 Volchik, V. V., "Povedencheskaya ekonomika i sovremennye tendentsii evolyutsii instituta sobstvennosti" [Behavioral economics and contemporary trends in the evolution of the institution of ownership], *Terra Economicus* 8, no. 2 (2010): 76.

25 Nureyev and Runov, "Rossiya: neizbezhna li deprivatizatsiya," 26.

26 Libman, "Politicheskaya logika formirovaniya," 145–46.

27 "Comparing crony capitalism around the World," *Economist*, May 5, 2016, http://www.economist.com/blogs/graphicdetail/2016/05daily-chart-2.

28 A. Yu. Melville, D. K. Stukal, and M. G. Mironyuk, "'Tsar gory' ili pochemu v postkommunisticheskih avtokratiyah plohie instituty" ["The King of the Hill," or, why institutions in post-communist autocracies are bad"], *Polis*, no. 2 (2013): 138.

29 Robert Dahl, *Poliarchy: Participation and Opposition* (New Haven, London, Yale University Press: 1971), 7.

30 Moldova, Georgia, and Ukraine have adopted political systems in which power gets changed on a regular basis due to competitive elections whose results are unpredictable and where there is government-independent mass media. Yet the further development of those countries towards full-fledged democracy is hampered by persistent systemic corruption (in Moldova and Ukraine) and the lack of a justice system independent of executive power. That is why their political systems hold an intermediate position between authoritarianisms and democracies. American political scientist Thomas Carothers described such systems as "feckless pluralism" in Thomas Carothers, "The End of the Transition Paradigm," *Journal of Democracy* 13, no. 1 (2002): 10–11.

31 K. Rudiy, "Gosudarstvennyy kapitalizm v Belarusi" [State capitalism in Belarus], *Mirovaya ekonomika i mezhdunarodnye otnosheniya*, no. 4 (2016): 77.

32 V. Tambovtsev, *Ekonomicheskaya teoriya neformalnyh institutov* [Economic theory of informal institutions] (Moscow: PG-press, 2014).

33 A. Fisun, "Postsovetskie neopatrimonialnye rezhimy genezis osobennosti tipologiya" [Post-Soviet neo-patrimonial regimes: Genesis, specifics, typology], *Otechestvennye zapiski*, no. 6 (39) (2007): 17.

34 "Ukraine's Unyielding Corruption," *New York Times*, April 1, 2016, A 24.

ILJA VIKTOROV

Russia's Network State and *Reiderstvo* Practices:
The Roots to Weak Property Rights Protection after the post-Communist Transition

Post-Soviet corporate raiding: Introduction

Hostile takeovers and company captures have been an everyday reality of the Russian post-Soviet economy. This phenomenon is called *reiderstvo* in Russian, a term which is derived from the English word "raiding." A typical hostile takeover is based on the manipulation of weak legal institutions and the use of extralegal practices with the active involvement of courts, private and state security services, and corrupt government officials. Any entrepreneur in the country is a potential victim of groups that organize "raids" against both large and small companies. According to some estimates, about 60,000 cases of *reiderstvo* took place in Russia each year during the 2000s, and only a fraction of these cases led to legal prosecution.[1] This is telling, even though any kind of quantitative evidence on *reiderstvo* is problematic due to the sensitivity of the issue for influential political and business insiders.[2]

Corporate raiding in Russia has its historic roots in the initial process of the privatization of state-owned assets in the 1990s, when the first hostile takeovers were characterized by a high degree of criminal violence. Since that period, however, the methods of raiders have grown much more sophisticated and elaborate. Highly educated lawyers, advocates, accountants, judges, investigators, court enforcement officers, and journalists—rather than common criminals—have been typical participants of a raiding group. A raiding network is created by a particular group which coordinates a raiding attack, provides financial support to all participants, and finally appears as the main beneficiary of a hostile takeover (see Figure

14.1). The spread of *reiderstvo* entails profoundly negative consequences for Russia. It undermines the development of a market economy and the stability of its formal institutions, makes property rights insecure, and leads to failed investments and capital flight from the country.[3] The presence of *reiderstvo* practices is central to the question of what went wrong with Russian post-Soviet economic reform and why market capitalism, with well-performing formal institutions, like private property, failed to be established in Russia.

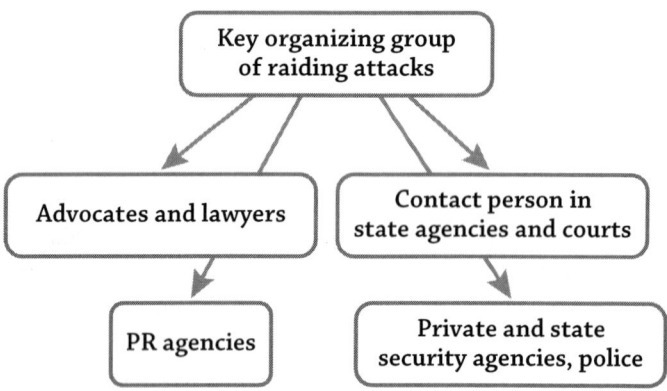

Figure 14.1. Corporate raiding (reiderstvo)

The problem is well known and broadly debated in Russia, from regional media and NGOs to the top of the Russian business community and bureaucracy.[4] On several occasions, the negative impact of *reiderstvo* on business in Russia was officially acknowledged and condemned by President Vladimir Putin and Prime Minister Dmitry Medvedev. Even Russian mass culture has reacted to the escalation of *reiderstvo*, with popular detective novels and films devoted to this topic.[5] *Reiderstvo* is not unique to Russia, and is equally common across the post-Soviet space. In Ukraine and Kazakhstan, the Russian term *reiderstvo* is applied in public discourse to similar corporate raiding practices.[6] This fact is an essential one, since it demonstrates that *reiderstvo* originated in particular policies of economic reform and privatization chosen by the majority of post-Soviet states in the early 1990s. However, as I will discuss below in the text, corporate raiding as it evolved in Russia since the early 2000s differs substantially from what can be observed in Ukraine. Fundamentally, this depends on the type of informal power networks that appear as the main organizers of raiding attacks on companies. The relationship between the character of the Russian post-Soviet network state and the prevailing *reiderstvo* practices in the country is the primary concern of this paper.

Though the definition of *reiderstvo* is etymologically derived from the English word "raiding," there is no English equivalent that would provide an adequate translation. Both "corporate raiding" and "hostile takeover" are not defined precisely enough to grasp the complexity of the phenomenon. I will therefore use the Russian term *reiderstvo* alongside the more conventional term "corporate raiding" throughout the text.

The evolution of *reiderstvo* and privatization: historical background

Reiderstvo practices have been deeply rooted in the process of Russian privatization. The initial nomenklatura privatization during and after the collapse of the Soviet system in the late 1980s and early 1990s is relatively well documented.[7] State managers of Soviet enterprises, so called "red directors," started to channel financial flows into newly created legal entities, often under the umbrella of emerging "cooperatives," which simply meant stripping enterprises of their assets. The quasi-legal character of transformation of state-owned enterprises into privately controlled companies appeared at this early stage of privatization already.

Yet the key to understanding the shaky grounds upon which private property is legitimized in Russia is the mass privatization of 1992–94. The political task of the neoliberal reformers recruited by President Yeltsin into his government in autumn 1991 was to carry out a quick and irreversible transition of formerly state-owned property into private hands. The reformers opted for tradable vouchers distributed to each Russian citizen as the main means of privatization, even though in reality this process employed a broader variety of schemes, auctions, and exemptions from general policies.[8] The initial effect was a transition of former state enterprises to insiders making a limited number of stakeholders into shareholders. The distribution of shares depended on the amount of vouchers each stakeholder could mobilize, not on a stakeholder's actual substantive interest within the company. According to David M. Woodruff, who compared the outcome of the privatization process in Russia and Poland, this had disastrous consequences for Russia in terms of the weak legitimacy of private property and the predatory character of its corporate governance alike. Because allocation of property rights in Russia excluded negotiations between the enterprises' stakeholders, the latter appeared as competitors in a zero-sum game: winners took all, as a rule securing control over companies very cheaply, making other stakeholders losers and outsiders. Furthermore, privatization had a fragmenting effect since formerly integrated productive chains were deliberatively split into a number of new joint-stock companies for privatization purposes. Lucrative entities were selectively privatized in favor of entrusted insiders while other, less valuable, subdivisions remained state-controlled or were handed over to less influential players. All these factors combined created a source of fierce conflict between former stakeholders over property rights. The legal fact of privatization alone, without the creation of supporting mechanisms to embed it into the social context of the law, was unable to provide a strong legitimacy to the institution of private property.[9]

The next stage of privatization was the distribution of the largest companies through a loans-for-shares scheme in 1995–96. The privatization of a number of lucrative giant companies in extractive industries in favor of a selected group of insiders, who would be later commonly called "oligarchs," was controversial from the standpoint of property rights legalization. Nor did it meet the basic requirements of an elite consensus regarding such a fundamental redistribution of assets as a considerable part of bureaucratic and business insiders were left outside this process.[10] One of the main participants of the 1990s loans-for-shares scheme, the oligarch Boris Berezovsky, later admitted (and rationalized) this form of privatization in an interview to Israeli documentary filmmaker Alexander Gentelev:

> I think that the degree of corruption in Russia corresponds completely to the degree of its transformation. It is neither more nor less than it should be. I do not think that officials in Israel have the same opportunity to redistribute wealth worth of tens and hundreds millions, or billions. [Compared to Russia], there is simply no available wealth of such size that is not already owned by someone. [In Russia], an official had an opportunity to decide just by his signature that you will own that [asset] while another person will own another [asset].[11]

It did not help that some of those oligarchs who secured control over this property at that stage of privatization turned out to be rather responsible managers. In the case of the *Yukos* oil company or *Norilsk Nickel*, for example, new owners restructured ineffective management practices and saved the industries from collapse of the early 1990s.[12] The subsequent fall of *Yukos* in 2003–2004 and arrest of Mikhail Khodorkovsky, the head of the *Menatep* business network (which acquired control over the company by such a loan-for-shares scheme in 1995), is telling. The Russian public never supported Khodorkovsky and remained largely indifferent to his fate, even though opinion polls demonstrated public awareness that the real reasons behind the state attack on *Yukos* were political, not legal ones.[13]

Privatization coincided with the collapse of the Russian state apparatus that followed the dissolution of the Soviet Union in 1991. In particular, President Yeltsin's efforts to secure personal political power against old power interest groups inside the Russian bureaucracy led to a weakening of state law enforcement agencies and security services, *inter alia* represented by the former KGB. These agencies were split into rival organizations, and a considerable part of its staff were fired. This paralyzed state capacity to combat growing criminality amid a severe economic crisis and ongoing privatization. In the middle of the 1990s, the spread of violent crime went hand in hand with the first wave of ownership redistribution throughout Russia. A considerable part of the male population was involved in that wave of criminal redistribution. Considering the extent of the violence and killing, that initial wave of "black raiding" was comparable in some respects to a civil war, and affected most of Russia's industrially developed regions.

The main stages of *reiderstvo* and its development throughout the period of post-Soviet transformation can be reconstructed as follows. Initial mass privatization evolved quickly into the first wave of ownership redistribution with a broad criminal presence in the middle of 1990s.[14] Above all, the primary concern of criminals was to take control over cash flows with a short-term perspective rather than to secure long-term ownership over former state enterprises. To what extent were criminal circles used in this violent stage of corporate raiding by other actors, such as former party officials or future oligarchs, and to what extent did the criminals appear as an independent force? Both practices actually happened, and a wide geographical variation between regions was evident. In the 1990s, the term *reiderstvo* was not in broad use.[15] The term "black raiding" (*chernoe reiderstvo*) denotes mainly violent criminal methods in company takeovers. However, it seems to be a later construction, invented in the 2000s to be applied retrospectively to the reality of the 1990s. Starting from the late 1990s, the presence of criminality in business environments decreased substantially.[16] Yet the traumatic experience of the 1990s produced a long-standing effect on Russian corporate culture, leading to the violation and manipulation of legal norms and the judiciary, including subsequent *reiderstvo* practices.

The next stage of *reiderstvo* was connected with the use of bankruptcy law as a specific takeover instrument between 1998 and 2002.[17] Vadim Volkov connects this wave of ownership redistribution to central authorities' attempts to strengthen control over the executive branch of state power in Russia's regions, particularly after the accession of Vladimir Putin to presidential power in 2000. When criminal groups of the 1990s disappeared from the scene, their niche as providers of security and guarantors of economic transactions was taken over by special police, the FSB (the Federal Security Service, the main successor of the former KGB), and other law enforcement agencies. At the same time, Volkov points out that these networks of state representatives were mobilized by private business groups. The latter were still the main organizers of enterprise takeovers between 1998 and 2002. Unlike the black raiding of the 1990s, this stage of *reiderstvo* was characterized by manipulative quasi-legal practices using the loopholes and illegal grounds of the 1990s privatization.

The decade after Putin's accession to power in 2000 witnessed a culmination of *reiderstvo* practices: hostile takeovers acquired a much greater degree of variety and sophistication. No "improvements" in the bankruptcy legislation proved effective: hostile takeovers only increased and intensified even though the bankruptcy procedure ceased to be used as a primary means of seizing property. The *reiderstvo* practices affected all levels of economic activity in Russia, from the largest oligarch groups—the *Yukos* case being the most famous example—down to small and medium-sized enterprises. It was during this time that the term *reiderstvo* found broad acceptance in Russian popular media discourse and in everyday language. This wave of what could be called "gray" corporate raiding started in Moscow in the early 2000s,[18] and then spread to the rest of Russia. Compared to the mainly criminal "black raiding" of the 1990s, legal and quasi-legal procedures of corporate raiding were employed in the 2000s.[19] A typical case of *reiderstvo* in this period would not be a result of the spectacular violent storming of industrial locations by groups of private enforcement agencies of unclear origin. Instead, a hostile takeover would be mandated by court decision through a corrupt judge based on falsified documentation, and enforced by official police forces, all in accordance with official judicial procedure. A judgment on a corporate property transition might be based on records of shares falsified by a real or fake registrar. It might also be based on non-payment of a real or invented bank loan by the victim, the owner of a company under attack. The entire process of a hostile takeover could now take place in public, with broad coverage in the media, controlled and mobilized by the raiding group. Only the best professionals in each particular sphere are involved in a carefully planned and successful raiding attack.

Reiderstvo and its victims

Small and medium-size enterprises have also been victims of raiders. Not only the economic activity of these firms themselves but also the commercial properties they own attract raiders. Agricultural lands are also widely targeted in *reiderstvo* practices, especially in the Moscow region. Public organizations with limited budget financing, such as schools, universities, hospitals, museums, and theatres, can also fall prey to raiding groups. This is because such institutions may be physically located in attractive properties inherited from the Soviet past. Using connections with corrupt decision-makers in public administration, raiders may organize the takeover of such properties by closing a public institution and then transferring its premises to a specially created private firm. In the largest Russian cities, particularly in Moscow, even private persons can become targets of raids as the value of their housing may be high enough to make "apartment raiding" (*kvartirnoe reiderstvo*) profitable. The same quasi-legal practices employed in company takeovers are used in "apartment raiding," though on a smaller scale. This is an additional reason why "corporate raiding" is not an adequate translation of the word *reiderstvo* in English. Post-Soviet *reiderstvo* practices are not exclusively confined to the sphere of corporate abuse, but can affect any economic agent or private person who possesses property of substantial market value.

A raiding attack may lead to different outcomes for an entrepreneur who becomes a target of *reiderstvo*. Usually, resistance is deemed to be futile since each raiding group has connections with corrupt officials in police, state security, and investigative agencies which either support or act as the real organizers of a company capture.[20] In rare cases, the victim can repel an attack by using the same quasi-legal methods and contacts among corrupt officials and judges. In other cases, the owner of a company may achieve a compromise by selling the company at a discounted price, well below its real market value. Although hardly any comprehensive statistics on *reiderstvo* practices are available, this seems to be the most common outcome. Alternatively, a businessman may be imprisoned during the prosecution process. Such a businessman may ultimately be freed, or even win an appeal in a higher court. Nevertheless, the owner's absence from the business provides an opportunity for a provisional administration to strip the company of all its assets. This provisional administration would naturally be a part of the raiding group.[21]

The organization of a hostile takeover as shown in Figure 14.1 is actually an oversimplification, since a greater variety of actors can participate in the process. For example, ecological organizations in the form of "independent" NGOs may appear as a blackmail tool in launching a raid against a particular industrial enterprise. Fire-prevention and tax-collecting authorities as well as sanitary services and private banks may contribute to the process of a hostile takeover. To make the issue more complicated, raiding can be based on real corporate practice abuses committed by entrepreneurs who are selected as victims of corporate raiding.[22] This was the case during one of the most famous *reiderstvo* cases, the hostile takeover of the company *Evroset* in 2008. The kidnapping of a mid-level *Evroset* manager, arranged by the company's top managers in 2003 after the mid-level manager had stolen from the company, was used as a pretext to start a lawsuit against *Evroset*'s owner. The owner was finally forced to sell his business to persons affiliated with the raiding group at a discount price and later emigrated to the UK. The unclear origins of ownership rights emanating from the shadow privatization of the 1990s also provides a rich source of pretexts to organize *reiderstvo* attacks against Russian businessmen.

The difference between the "predator" and the "victim" can be diffuse. In 2012, I conducted an interview with an individual who had previously been involved in *reiderstvo* attacks. The interviewee temporarily lost his job in the financial sector after the 1998 crisis. To escape unemployment, the respondent had participated in a raiding operation against an aluminum plant owner in Siberia in 2000. That particular company capture was organized by a famous oligarch with close connections to the former president Yeltsin's family. The victim was a criminal leader who had taken control of the plant during the 1990s privatization. Numerous details of the operation, which became highly profitable for the oligarch, emerged during the course of the interview.[23] More importantly, *reiderstvo* as a practice appeared as a very complex issue rather than as a simple corruption practice. It was actually the criminal leader, not the oligarch, who enjoyed popular support in the region during this *reiderstvo* case. The oligarch was perceived as an outsider coming to the region to grab property. Although the former owner was briefly arrested and finally lost control of the plant, he continued his political career and still serves as a member of the regional legislative assembly. The outcome of this *reiderstvo* case is quite common, if not banal, in post-Soviet Russia; similar examples can be found in other regions. Those criminal leaders who survived the 1990s strive today to distance themselves from their dark past to assume the image of respectable businessmen with legal economic activities. At any rate, it was apparent that the criminal leader, who had allegedly committed a long list of crimes in the 1990s, was inappropriate as the owner of an industrial giant with thousands of employees. From the point of view of corporate governance, the outcome of this particular *reiderstvo* case hardly made matters worse for the company concerned. Today, the same oligarch continues to control the plant, which has been one of the main assets in his holdings.

Reiderstvo and *siloviki*

Why did *reiderstvo*, in the shape of quasi-legal company take-overs, become so widespread in Russia in the 2000s? The reconfiguration of informal power groups that controlled Russian politics and business after 2000, in particular the strengthening of Putin's *siloviki* at the cost of alternative elite networks, framed these developments. The term *siloviki*, literally translated as "people of force," is used in Russia to define representatives from the security and military services, including former service personnel occupying positions of power in political and administrative authorities as well as in big business. At the level of the federal bureaucracy, *siloviki* are represented by a number of more or less coherent informal power networks inside the Russian ruling elite that steer the country in competition with so called "liberals." The latter refers to a number of groups, from high-rank Western-friendly reformers responsible for the transformation of the Russian planned economy in the 1990s, to a number of oligarchs who emerged after privatization.[24] The co-existence of both large elite fractions was present under Yeltsin's presidency already, but *siloviki* groups affiliated with the new president gained supremacy after 2000. Putin's success as a political leader depends much on his capacity to counterbalance the interests of the most influential "siloviki" and "liberals."

A hypothesis concerning the causes and persistence of corporate raiding was put forward by two analysts from the journal *Expert*, Alexandr Privalov and Alexandr Volkov.[25] They claimed that the main raiding groups were organized and controlled by high officials from the regional branches of the FSB who are the real beneficiaries of the largest hostile takeovers after 2000. This explains why only a fraction of all raiding cases were investigated by prosecutors and just a handful of raiders were sentenced in courts.[26] Later academic studies on *reiderstvo* confirmed this thesis. In particular, Vadim Volkov discusses the commercial activities of *siloviki* as the main reason behind *reiderstvo*. Following the re-emergence of the state monopoly on violence after 2000, the problem of criminality's capture of businesses had been to a large degree resolved. What happened instead, however, was not an installation of the rule of law, but the use of the judiciary, state apparatus and state monopoly on violence by *siloviki* networks for personal enrichment. *Siloviki* were successfully able to monetize their administrative resources by either capturing successful private businesses or taking a share of cash flows originating in these businesses. As a rule, such activities remained well-hidden from the broad public as the real beneficiaries of takeovers among *siloviki* were never publicly disclosed. The *Tri kita* ("Three Whales") affair, which involved illegal smuggling and scheming by a number of furnishing companies under control of *siloviki* networks, became one of the few cases to receive publicity. It culminated in resignations of a number of high-rank *siloviki* officials in 2007, revealing the scale and pattern of commercial activities employed by officials from a number of the Russian security services.[27]

Most remarkably, the head of a powerful law enforcement agency, the Federal Drug Control Service of Russia, and a close affiliate to Vladimir Putin, Viktor Cherkesov, made a public statement attempting to conceptualize *siloviki*'s commercial activities. He published an article "The Warriors Should Not Become Tradesmen" in one of Russia's popular business newspapers. Cherkesov's subordinates were directly affected by the *Tri kita* affair, some of them being arrested for presumed crimes. The *Tri kita* affair, labelled in Russian media as a "war between security services," originated in a rivalry between the Federal Drug Control Service and the FSB. It took place in a very specific political context of uncertainty when a future successor to Vladimir Putin would be appointed as Putin's candidate to run the 2008 presidential elections. Cherkesov claimed that the *Chekist* corporation[28] was the only force in the society that, starting from Putin's presidency in 2000, saved the country from a systemic collapse of the late 1990s by restoring governability to the political system. However, according to Cherkesov, instead of combating corruption and performing as guards guaranteeing the stability of the state, the *Chekists* became increasingly involved in business activities. His main message was a warning to *siloviki*, accusing them of greed and neglect of their professional duty to safeguard state interests.[29] The article barely helped his career; rumor had it that President Putin personally disapproved of Cherkesov's analytical exercises. He was removed from his position in 2008 and ended up by becoming a parliamentary member of the Communist Party's fraction in the State Duma, a sort of a political disgrace for a former high-rank associate to the president.

Reiderstvo and informal power networks

Whatever cases of *reiderstvo* are approached, both at a federal level including the largest corporations, or small and medium-sized companies in Russian regions, informal networks that organize and provide support to raiding attacks emerge as the main collective players in the field. Introduced in 2011, the analytical concept of the Russian network state—centered on informal power networks in Russian business and politics—offers new insights to our understanding of post-Soviet corporate raiding.[30] Although the concept does not deal with the phenomenon of *reiderstvo* specifically, it shows how power networks merged with new business elites to use property relations and wealth to consolidate their position. The network state concept's main point is that informal groups, or networks, infiltrate formal authorities at all levels, in effect merging with the Russian post-Soviet state, to maintain full control over key decisions and to proliferate in the most lucrative industries and branches of the economy. Basing on this concept, the informal power network is approached as a means of interpersonal interaction that shares "similar interests, allegiances and identification."[31] The activities of the elite network members, who always hold high-ranking positions within the bureaucratic hierarchy, are twofold. On the one hand, these networks considerably weaken the state's policy-making capacity; decision making is thus deeply embedded in informal interactions, instead of following formal rules and procedures. On the other hand, the existence of networks and their ability to rent seek depend on the Russian state's survival, making parts of the Russian state apparatus functional. Therefore, the merge of informal power networks with the Russian state enables selective policy implementation whenever interests of the state, society and informal power networks may coincide. At the same time, the very nature of such a merge makes it impossible for the state apparatus to perform its functions through well-functioning formal institutions.[32]

While the presence of informal power networks is common to all societies, the role these play in countries such as Russia is different compared to societies based on the supremacy of universal formal rules over particularistic interests. In the latter case, informal power networks exploit existing formal rules and institutions for their own gain without disrupting formal laws and procedures, which continue to endure after the dissolution of a particular informal network. An independent judiciary or electoral democracy representing commonly respected rules of the game, constitutes one of the main achievements of societal systems with stable institutional orders. These institutions are also used as a means of conflict resolution between elite power networks.[33] By contrast, in developing and transitional societies such as Russia, informal power networks are of greater importance than formal institutions. The latter can be redesigned, altered and manipulated in the interests of a particular informal power group. As soon as the influence of such a group diminishes, or the network itself disappears from the political and business scene because of the fall or resignation of its patron, the relative importance of a formal institution or authority it supports may decrease dramatically.[34] This is one of the reasons why business activities have not been de facto separated from the realm of politics in most of the post-Soviet countries. The institution of private property will remain fundamentally weak as long as such a merger between business and politics will endure.

Set against this background, we can better explain the evolution of *reiderstvo* in Russia, and compare it to similar practices in Ukraine. The Ukrainian cases of corporate raiding, described by Markus and Rojansky,[35] resemble much of what happened in Russia between 1998 and 2002. At that time, raiding networks were initiated and controlled by oligarchic groups in pursuit of the redistribution of newly privatized assets and companies. Representatives of state law enforcement authorities still played a subordinate role. What took place in Russia since then, and what has never happened in Ukraine, was a consolidation of the state and presidential power, followed in parallel by the rise of informal power networks connected to *siloviki*. The latter monopolized political and economic power at the expense of old oligarchic groups, and started to expropriate assets for their own interest, relying, among others, on *reiderstvo* methods. Knowing the informal rules of the game in today's Russia means understanding which interests of a particular *siloviki* network should not be disturbed while "doing business" in the country. In Ukraine, *reiderstvo* practices include a broad variety of raiding networks that organize and benefit from company takeovers, reflecting a more chaotic and fragile balance of power between Ukrainian political and business elites than in the Russian case. Two political upheavals in 2004 and 2014 entailed large-scale asset redistributions, which has had devastating implications for Ukrainian economic development.

High-profile company takeovers: what is *reiderstvo*, and what is not?

Using the concept of the network state, we also acquire a better analytical tool to approach seemingly accidental *reiderstvo* cases that affected the largest Russian companies. As a rule, such cases can be characterized by the involvement of representatives of the highest ranks of political and business elites. We can also separate real *reiderstvo* cases from property takeovers that have been a side-effect of conflicts within Russia's political elite.[36] *Reiderstvo* is always about the mobilization of an informal power network's resources that aims to grab the assets from other interest groups or owners. Political clashes, by contrast, may involve redistribution of economic assets as a byproduct of such conflicts. Such expropriations cannot be identified as *reiderstvo* because those are more related to control over political power rather than dependent on the kleptocratic interests of a particular informal power network. This is the main reason why I would not characterize the *Yukos* affair and the extermination of the Khodorkovsky business group as a *reiderstvo* case. The *Yukos* affair did include a number of components that would make it an example of carefully planned corporate raiding. One was its culmination in a takeover of *Yukos's* main assets by a fake company, *Baikalfinansgrup*, and the subsequent transfer of those assets to the state-controlled company *Rosneft*. However, the *Yukos* affair was primarily a matter of Russian high politics. Khodorkovsky attempted to challenge the political power of Vladimir Putin by taking control over a number of political institutions and breaking the informal unwritten rules of the game which were set up between the oligarchs and Putin when the latter came to presidential power in 2000.[37] Still, by adopting some basic *reiderstvo* practices, the *Yukos* case certainly revealed the main trend of ownership redistribution which affected Russian business during Putin's first two terms as president.[38]

Similarly, the state takeover of one of the largest Russian banks, the Bank of Moscow, officially owned by the City of Moscow, and the subsequent prosecution of its top management in 2010–2011 cannot be considered as a *reiderstvo* case either. When the Moscow group lost its political power after the resignation in 2010 of its main patron, the mayor of Moscow Yuriy Luzhkov, most of its businesses, including its main affiliated bank, Bank of Moscow, were expropriated in favor of other informal power networks. The Bank of Moscow was taken over by a state-controlled bank, VTB, in turn controlled by Putin's power network. Yet the primary intention of this move was a political one, not the redistribution of assets as such. In other words, the takeover of the Bank of Moscow made sense as a part of a broader political upheaval, while the matter of the assets presumably controlled by the bank was of secondary importance. Andrey Borodin, the former president and minority shareholder of the Bank of Moscow, characterized the takeover of "his" bank as *reiderstvo*.[39] His failure to explain why a takeover of a state-owned bank by another state-owned bank, VTB, should represent a corporate raiding case, demonstrates a vague distinction between what is state- and what is privately-owned in Russia. Likewise, the political reason of the takeover explains why the Russian court arrested Borodin *in absentia* while the state prosecutors did their best to put Borodin on the Interpol Red Notice list—making his voluntary return to Russia unlikely. This did not prevent Borodin from receiving political asylum in the UK and enjoying a millionaire lifestyle in London.[40]

In contrast, a recent state takeover of the oil company *Bashneft* provides plenty of empirical facts to qualify it as a typical high-profile *reiderstvo* case, albeit with a relatively favorable outcome for its main victim, the Russian billionaire Vladimir Yevtushenkov. The company *Bashneft* was created out of the old Soviet oil refineries in one of the Russian regions, the Republic of Bashkortostan. It was later privatized under very questionable circumstances in 2002–2003.[41] Its first "private" owner was Ural Rakhimov, son of the Republic's then President Murtaza Rakhimov. However, the Rakhimov power network was incapable of keeping ownership control over *Bashneft* because of its relative weakness vis-à-vis Moscow-based power interests. This was one of the main reasons behind the decision to invite Yevtushenkov, the owner of the *Sistema* business group and a deeply integrated insider within Russian political elite circles, as a minority shareholder of *Bashneft* in 2005. Yevtushenkov was fully aware of the problematic character of the company's privatization. However, he opted to undertake this risky move since he was eager to expand his business empire by entering the highly lucrative and at the same time, highly closed, Russian oil market famous for its opaque business practices. In 2009, *Sistema* acquired finally a full ownership control over *Bashneft* and its related companies. This acquisition as well as *Bashneft*'s subsequent win of a tender over the exploitation of two large oil fields in Western Siberia became possible thanks to Yevtushenkov's connections within the highest ranks of the Russian bureaucracy. In particular, his ties to the emerging power network affiliated with then President Dmitry Medvedev was decisive for a *Bashneft* takeover. Starting from 2009, high-rank ministers among the "liberal" fraction of the Russian elite revitalized the idea of privatizing state-owned corporations and companies.[42] Yevtushenkov's acquisition of *Bashneft* could be viewed as one of the first steps towards a new wave of privatization, although very few would agree to characterize him as a "liberal."

The return of Vladimir Putin as president in 2012 changed the balance of interests. While Dmitry Medvedev was appointed Russia's prime minister and remained as an important player in Putin's team, some members of his emerging power and business network suffered severely from this move. Large-scale privatization plans were gradually postponed or abandoned under endless deliberations. Yevtushenkov's agreements were not endorsed any more. In 2014, he was formally accused of the illegal acquisition of *Bashneft*'s previously state-owned stock of shares and was put under house arrest for three months. In October 2014, the Russian court decided on the renationalization of *Bashneft*, and Yevtushenkov's *Sistema* did not make an appeal to a higher court, thus accepting the state takeover of the oil company. Apparently, Yevtushenkov made an informal agreement with those who were behind this attack on *Bashneft* and *Sistema*, which immediately resulted in freedom from arrest. He was also able to receive some financial compensation for the loss of his company. In January 2016, all formal charges against Yevtushenkov were finally dropped. He was able to keep his old business empire, *Sistema*, and remained as an important player of the Russian business elite, even though he ultimately lost about half of his assets. In a public interview, Yevtushenkov confessed that he made certain conclusions after the affair, was still ready to shake hands with everybody involved in the events, and that he completely understood "all rules of the game."[43]

The lack of a political struggle in the *Bashneft* case and Yevtushenkov final readiness to understand and follow the informal rules of the game helped him to survive this raiding attack. These factors also prevented him from sharing the fate of Mikhail Khodorkovsky, who challenged supreme power in Russia, and Andrey Borodin, a member of a rival political power network that lost its influence. Meanwhile, the fact of the renationalization of *Bashneft* in 2014 should by no means seen as a sign of the Russian state's increased dirigisme in economic policy or return to a planned economy and active industrial policy. In February 2016, the Russian government made a decision to privatize again the company, with inevitable clashes between powerful business groups over this attractive asset following. The main actor that intended to "privatize" the recently renationalized *Bashneft* was the state-owned company *Rosneft* run by Igor Sechin, one of the front figures among *siloviki* and a close affiliate of the president. During 2016, the public witnessed a further development in this spectacular story. Unpredictably, on the night of November 15, at the *Rosneft* headquarters, the minister for economic development, Alexey Ulyukayev, was arrested. Ulyukayev, one of the most famous Russian "liberal" ministers who advocated for a new round of privatization, initially opposed a takeover of *Bashneft* by *Rosneft*. Later, his ministry made a dramatic turn and approved the takeover deal. According to the Investigative Committee of Russia, whose representatives arrested Ulyukayev, the latter came in person to the *Rosneft* headquarters to collect a 2 million-dollar bribe for this approval. Later, the Russian media reported that this presumed bribe was in reality a common "fee," a sort of informal transaction cost that economic ministries collected from Russian companies for approval of similar takeover deals. The media also stated that Sechin was present in person that night when 2 million dollars were passed into Ulyukayev's hands, while representatives of the state law enforcement agencies waited for Ulyukayev outside to detain him with cases loaded with cash. During his arrest, Ulyukayev attempted to make a phone call to his presumable powerful patron, but the mobile network was blocked.[44]

The *Bashneft* and *Rosneft* dealings, which leaked to the public, are reminiscent of a detective story. However, the *Bashneft* case reveals much more than just clashes between specific officials, business people and the informal power networks that protect all of them. Such unexpected moves towards privatization/nationalization/reprivatization/renationalization of companies demonstrates the relative nature of the formal ownership status of a particular company. Whether it is private or state-owned is less important; the relative power resources of an informal power network that controls the asset is of greater significance. This control can be achieved either through private ownership of a company or by appointment of entrusted managers to run a formally state-owned company and its cash flows.

Conclusions

What does the persistence of *reiderstvo* practices tell about the Russian state and the quality of its institutions, law enforcement agencies, and business environment? Following the collapse of the Soviet Union in 1991, Russia experienced a stalemate of its state governability.[45] In parallel, President Yeltsin's attempts to reform a planned economy towards a capitalism based on strong private property rights turned out to be unsuccessful. Such a deep transformation would never come without a price. However, as David Woodruff's comparative study of privatization in Russia and Poland demonstrated, Russian mass privatization created a much greater gap between the newly imposed formal property rights and the social context those rights were embedded into. The illegal corporate raiding that followed should be viewed against the background of the twin political and economic crisis of the 1990s. Among other things, this crisis resulted in a failed privatization reform. The lack of political will to negotiate reasonable conditions for the establishment of strong property rights was not coincidental. The collapse of the Russian state governability brought about the primacy of informal power networks and their group interests over formal institutions, rules and procedures. The subsequent evolution of illegal corporate raiding, with the strong presence of *siloviki* networks, was closely connected to how the governability stalemate was resolved after Putin's accession to power in 2000. The *siloviki* networks affiliated with the Putin administration consolidated the state apparatus and suppressed the criminal networks of the 1990s. However, the price the society paid for the restoration of this governability was also high; private business fell victim to raiding networks, now under the control of *siloviki* representatives.

There are two contrasting views on how *reiderstvo* of the 2000s should be viewed within the long historical perspective of Russian post-Communist transformation. Jordan Gans-Morse advocates a thesis that the *reiderstvo* of the 2000s, with its focus on the manipulation of formal rules and judiciary, can be viewed as a positive change compared to the disorder and lawlessness of the 1990s. Seen objectively, illegal corporate raiding is a negative phenomenon. Yet when it comes to the issue of conflict resolution in business, including the redistribution of property rights, transitioning from the violent control of informal criminal leaders to courtrooms controlled by corrupt judges and law enforcement officials still represents, argues Gans-Morse, an institutional improvement. Such a transition has a potential spillover effect in the future: economic agents learn to use judicial procedures for conflict resolution that finally will contribute to the full installation of the rule of law.[46] Andrei Yakovlev, on the other hand, forwards the opposite thesis. He claims that the diversity of economic actors in the 1990s permitted a situation of competition, not least in terms of the existence of low barriers of entrance for new actors into the market. This diversity could survive in spite of the presence of a highly criminalized environment, which meant that a sort of economic transformation in the country was still possible. Following this view, the predatory activities of *siloviki* after 2003 had a more negative impact on development since *siloviki* suppressed business activity, bringing about economic stagnation in Russia after the 2008 global financial crisis.[47]

These two conclusions are probably not as contradictory as they might seem to be. The future of property rights protection in Russia will heavily depend on the subsequent evolution of the Russian network state. The institutional stalemate connected to the spreading of *reiderstvo* practices in the 2000s would be probably hard to escape. In the 1990s, the degree of the Russian state's dissolution was high in terms of the loss of its monopoly on violence in favor of criminal and other private networks. In this sense, "gray" *reiderstvo* can be viewed as an inevitable outcome of the state consolidation in the 2000s. *Siloviki* networks compensated the state's inability to exercise its monopoly on violence in the 1990s, at the same time requiring their share of the cake. Russian elites may come to a new consensus concerning the institutionalization of procedures for conflict resolution between informal power networks. In this case, a more solid basis for power networks' long-term control over economic assets will emerge leading to a system of stronger property rights protection. An ongoing transition of economic assets from the older generation that gained from the privatization of the 1990s and the redistribution of assets in the 2000s is of crucial importance. If such a compromise between elite power networks fails, new waves of property redistribution will affect the country, putting Russia into an institutional deadlock of poor economic performance.

Notes

[1] Alexandr Privalov and Alexandr Volkov, "Rassuzhdenie o reiderstve po metode barona Kiuv'e" [Discourse on *reiderstvo* using the method of baron Cuvier], *Expert*, no. 18 (2007): 59.

[2] Michael Rochlitz, "Corporate Raiding and the Role of the State in Russia," *Post-Soviet Affairs* 30, nos. 2–3 (2014): 91; for comparison, Alena Ledeneva refers to 70,000 raids a year, see Alena Ledeneva, *Can Russia Modernise? Sistema, Power Networks and Informal Governance* (Cambridge: Cambridge University Press, 2013), 19.

[3] Andrei Yakovlev, Anton Sobolev, and Anton Kazun, "Means of Production versus Means of Coercion: Can Russian Business Limit the Violence of a Predatory State?" *Post-Soviet Affairs* 30, nos. 2–3 (2014): 187.

[4] Richard Sakwa, "Systemic Stalemate: Reiderstvo and the Dual State," in *The Political Economy of Russia*, ed. Nail Robinson (Lanham: Rowman & Littlefield Publishers, 2013), 73; Rochlitz, "Corporate Raiding and the Role of the State in Russia," 90.

[5] The most popular case of such crime literature is the novel *Raider*, written by the Russian celebrity lawyer Pavel Astakhov. The book was followed by a film version which was widely screened in Russian cinemas, and broadcast on TV in 2010. The first violent stage of *reiderstvo* was reflected in the earlier film *Magnetic Storms*, directed by the famous Russian filmmaker Vadim Abdrashitov in 2003. The film was inspired by real events that took place in industrial "monotowns," or company towns, in the Urals during the 1990s. At that time, a part of the male population participated in violence during the ownership redistribution of plants, usually in exchange for some form of payment. These workers supported competing groups vying to take control over the plants that were the main employers in such company towns. While the film did demonstrate rather high artistic qualities compared to crime thrillers such *Raider*, it remains relatively unknown to a broader Russian audience.

6. For Ukraine, see Matthew A. Rojansky, "Corporate Raiding in Ukraine: Causes, Methods and Consequences," *Demokratizatsiya* 22, no. 3 (2014), and Stanislav Markus, *Property, Predation, and Protection: Piranha Capitalism in Russia and Ukraine* (Cambridge: Cambridge University Press, 2015). For Kazakhstan and Central Asia see Barbara Junisbai, "Improbable but Potentially Pivotal Oppositions: Privatization, Capitalists, and Political Contestation in the Post-Soviet Autocracies," *Perspectives on Politics* 10, no. 4 (2012).
7. Steven Solnick, *Stealing the State: Control and Collapse in Soviet Institutions* (Cambridge, MA: Harvard University Press, 1998).
8. Alexandr Bim, "Ownership and Control of Russian Enterprises and Strategies of Shareholders," *Communist Economies and Economic Transformation* 8, no. 4 (1996).
9. David M. Woodruff., "Property Rights in Context: Privatization's Legacy for Corporate Legality in Poland and Russia," *Studies in Comparative International Development* 38, no. 4 (2004): 82–108.
10. Andrew Barnes, *Owning Russia: The Struggle over Factories, Farms, and Power* (Ithaca: Cornell University Press, 2006), 110–16. A descriptive account of the loans-for shares scheme see in David E. Hoffman, *The Oligarchs: Wealth and Power in the New Russia* (New York: Public Affairs, 2002), 296–324.
11. Interview with Boris Berezovsky, in Alexander Gentelev, *The Oligarchs* [documentary film] (Canada-Israel, 2004).
12. For *Yukos*, see Sarah Dixon, *Organizational Transformation in the Russian Oil Industry* (Cheltenham: Edward Elgar, 2008), 53–85. For *Norilsk Nickel*, see Yuko Adachi, *Building Big Business in Russia: The Impact of Informal Corporate Governance Practices* (London: Routledge, 2010), 88–113.
13. Richard Sakwa, *Putin and the Oligarch: The Khodorkovsky-Yukos Affair* (London: I.B. Tauris, 2014), 105.
14. Federico Varese, *The Russian Mafia: Private Protection in a New Market Economy* (Oxford: Oxford University Press, 2001), and Vadim Volkov, *Violent Entrepreneurs: The Use of Force in the Making of Russian Capitalism* (Ithaca: Cornell University Press, 2002).
15. Michael Rochlitz' statistical study on how *reiderstvo* has been debated in Russian newspapers demonstrates that before 2000 the definition had not been in use in the media. Instead, the definition of "property redistribution" was common and was used alongside definitions of "organized crime" and "corruption." See Rochlitz, "Corporate Raiding and the Role of the State in Russia," 94.
16. In Russian regions, corporate raiders who employed outright criminal methods for asset redistribution continued their activities well into the 2000s. For example, the infamous "raider of the Urals" Pavel Fedulev, who terrorized the business community of the industrial Sverdlovsk region, was arrested in Yekaterinburg as late as in 2006. He was later convicted to 23 years in prison for his crimes. See Aleksei Ivanov, *Yoburg: Gorod Khrabrykh. Sdelano v devyanostykh* (Moscow: AST, 2014), 494–500.
17. See Vadim Volkov, "Hostile Enterprise Takeovers: Russia's Economy in 1998–2002," *Review of Central and East European Law* 29, no. 4 (2004); and Adachi, *Building Big Business in Russia*, 22–24.

18 On how the Russian State Investigative Committee defines "black," "gray," and "white" *reiderstvo*, see the interview with a senior inspector of the Committee: Expert-TV, "Reiderstvo v Rossii: Intervju s Georgiem Smirnovym, starshym inspektorom Sledstvennogo komiteta Rossiiskoi Federatsii" [*Reiderstvo* in Russia: Interview with Georgii Smirnov, the Chief Inspector at the Russian State Investigative Committee], June 21, 2012, accessed on August 13, 2016, http://www.youtube.com/watch?v=NB1LGADanpU. See also Sakwa, "Systemic Stalemate," 73.

19 Jordan Gans-Morse, "Threats to Property Rights in Russia: From Private Coercion to State Aggression," *Post-Soviet Affairs* 28, no. 3 (2012).

20 Expert-TV, "Problema reiderstva v Rossii: Intervju s Yanoi Yakovlevoi, predsedatelem nekommercheskogo partnerstva 'Biznes-Solidarnost'" [The problem of *reiderstvo* in Russia: Interview with Yana Yakovleva, the Chair of the Non-Commercial Partnership *Business Solidarity*], October 10, 2011, accessed on August 12, 2016, http://www.youtube.com/watch?v=5za-HkWG4Tc.

21 See, for example, the interview with the Russian lawyer Alexandr Rappoport in which he briefly describes typical raiding practices and how they evolved during the 2000s: Alexandr Rappoport, "Reiderstvo v Rossii" [*Reiderstvo* in Russia], September 20, 2009, accessed on September 4, 2018, http://www.youtube.com/watch?v=8hdIH3k6ed4.

22 Yakovlev, Sobolev, and Kazun, "Mean of Production versus Means of Coercion," 187.

23 Interview with a middle-level employee at a Moscow-based investment bank, interviewed on January 26, 2012.

24 Susanne A. Wengle, *Post-Soviet Power: State-led Development and Russia's Marketization* (Cambridge: Cambridge University Press, 2015), 81–85.

25 *Expert* is one of the leading Russian business magazines. It is traditionally oriented towards professional audience in business, state apparatus and academy. Like the majority of non-academic political and economic magazines in Russia, it may contain biased materials ordered and paid by influential actors.

26 Privalov and Volkov, "Rassuzhdenie o reiderstve po metode barona Kyuv'e."

27 Vadim Volkov, *Silovoe predprinimatel'stvo, XXI vek: Ekonomiko-sotsiologicheskii analiz* [The violent entrepreneurship, 21st century: Economic and sociological analysis] (St. Petersburg: Izdatel'stvo Evropeiskogo universiteta 2012), 310–41. See also Olga Kryshtanovskaya and Stephen White, "The Formation of Russia's Network Directorate," in *Russia as a Network State: What Works in Russia when State Institutions Do Not?* ed. Vadim Kononenko and Arkady Moshes (Cambridge: Palgrave Macmillan, 2011), 24–34.

28 The word "Chekist" has been commonly used in Russia to refer to security services officers, in particular, those from the former KGB and its main post-Soviet Russian successor, the FSB. The definition derives from the Russian acronym CheKa, or the Emergency Committee, the first incarnation of the Soviet state security services existed between 1917 and 1922.

29 Viktor Cherkesov, "Nel'zya dopustit', chtoby voiny prevratilis' v torgovtsev" [The warriors should not become tradesmen], *Kommersant*, October 9, 2007, accessed on July 31, 2016, http://kommersant.ru/doc/812840. Cherkesov used a metaphor

of "the *Chekist* hook" to describe the mechanism that, according to him, saved the country in the early 2000s from falling into a state of total chaos and disarray.

30. Vadim Kononenko and Arkady Moshes, eds., *Russia as a Network State: What Works in Russia when State Institutions Do Not?* (Cambridge: Palgrave Macmillan, 2011). Anton Steen applied initially the definition of the network state with regard to studies of political elites in Russia, but his understanding of the network state had a narrower focus and differed from Kononenko's and Moshes' conceptualization. See Anton Steen, *Political Elites and the New Russia: The Power Basis of Yeltsin's and Putin's Regimes* (London: Routledge Curzon, 2003).

31. Vadim Kononenko, "Introduction," in Kononenko and Moshes, *Russia as a Network State*, 6.

32. Kononenko, "Introduction," 10.

33. See more on this in Douglass C. North, John Joseph Wallis, and Barry R. Weingast, *Violence and Social Orders: A Conceptual Framework for Interpreting Recorded Human History* (Cambridge: Cambridge University Press, 2009).

34. See more about this in Ilja Viktorov, "The State, Informal Networks, and Financial Market Regulation in Post-Soviet Russia, 1990–2008," *The Soviet and Post-Soviet Review* 42, no. 1 (2015): 5–38.

35. Rojansky, "Corporate Raiding in Ukraine"; Markus, *Property, Predation, and Protection*.

36. Here, I would rather disagree with Jordan Gans-Morse who classifies high-profile property redistributions originating in political clashes within the Russian elites as *reiderstvo* cases. See Gans-Morse, "Threats to Property Rights in Russia," 278–79. Likewise, my view of the *Yukos* case differs from the conclusions made by Richard Sakwa. The latter admits himself in the account of the *Yukos* case that the primary reason of attack on Khodorkovsky was concerns about power, while property redistribution was a consequence, not the reason of the attack. See Sakwa, "Systemic Stalemate," 78.

37. In 2000, directly after Putin's election, the presidential power and the Russian big business achieved an "informal contract" about recognition of the results of privatization in exchange for oligarchs' non-participation in politics. This informal contract was never endorsed in public by the president, only some oligarchs themselves talked about this "compromise" on several occasions. As it commonly happens with informal agreements, it remains unclear whether President Putin himself ever made a clear statement of this kind to any of the tycoons. About the relations between Putin and the Russian big business in the early 2000s see William Tompson, "Putin and the 'Oligarchs': A Two-Sided Commitment Problem," in *Leading Russia: Putin in Perspective. Essays in Honour of Archie Brown*, ed. Alex Pravda (Oxford: Oxford University Press, 2005), 179–202. The famous "shashlik" meeting between Putin and a number of selected oligarchs, presumably held at Putin's summer house outside Moscow in May 2000, was probably the occasion when this compromise was discussed, see Olga Kryshtanoskaya, *Anatomiya rossiiskoi elity* (Moscow: Zacharov, 2005), 359–60.

38. Richard Sakwa, *The Quality of Freedom: Khodorkovsky, Putin and the Yukos Affair* (Oxford: Oxford University Press, 2009).

39 Anton Belitskii, "Saga o Banke Moskvy: Konets glavy" [A saga about Bank of Moscow: The end of the chapter], April 12, 2011, accessed on August 4, 2016, http://ria.ru/inquest/20110412/363799279.html.
40 Interpol lifted this decision in May 2016, despite the objections from the Russian state prosecutors.
41 The descriptive accounts of the story of *Bashneft* and the Yevtushenkov case can be found in Irina Mokrousova and Yelena Hodyakova, "Prem'ernaya postanovka: Pochemu i u kogo zabrali kompaniyu *Bashneft*," *Forbes Russia*, no. 1 (2015): 66–74, and in Natalya Raibman, "Zakryto ugolovnoye delo Vladimira Yevtushenkova" [Vladimir Yevtushenkov's proceeding has been closed], *Vedomosti*, January 14, 2016.
42 See more on Medvedev's privatization plans and the struggle between different factions within the Russian government in Konstantin Gaaze, "Chuzhie zdes' ne hodyat: Igor' Shuvalov i privatizatsiya, kotoroi ne bylo" [Outsiders are not welcome here: Igor' Shuvalov and privatization that never took place], accessed on June 26, 2017, https://snob.ru/profile/30325/blog/112191.
43 "Vladimir Yevtushenkov's – RBC: 'Ya vse pravyla igry ponimayu'" [Vladimir Yevtushenkov to RBC: I understand all rules of the game], accessed on August 5, 2016, http://www.rbc.ru/interview/business/23/06/2015/55888d7b9a794720b762f924.
44 Konstantin Gaaze, "'Nel'zya trogat' Sechina': tikhii perevorot vo imya gromkikh peremen?" ["Do not touch Sechin": A quiet coup d'état in favor for large changes?], accessed on June 26, 2017, http://carnegie.ru/commentary/66142
45 For the governability concept, and how it differs from governance, see Jan Kooiman, "Exploring the Concept of Governability," *Journal of Comparative Policy Analysis: Research and Practice* 10, no. 2 (2008): 171–90.
46 Gans-Morse, "Threats to Property Rights in Russia," 287.
47 Andrei Yakovlev, "Russian Modernization: Between the Need for New Players and the Fear of Losing Control of Rent Sources," *Journal of Eurasian Studies*, no. 5 (2014): 15. This view is shared by the majority of Russian market practitioners whom I interviewed concerning the *reiderstvo* practices. One of my informants noticed regarding the difference of the business climate in Russia between the 1990s and the period after 2000: "This may sound strange but I have a much better experience from the so called hard times of the 1990s ["likhie devyanostye"] compared to the current time. Because you could arrange almost everything even with bandits, on mutually understandable conditions. Generally, people kept their word and fulfilled their obligations" (Interview with a regional investment banker, Yekaterinburg, interviewed on July 9, 2013).

BÁLINT MAGYAR

From Free Market Corruption Risk to the Certainty of a State-Run Criminal Organization
(using Hungary as an example)

Studies that examine post-communist regimes and define their characteristics primarily place an emphasis on describing the political system and its ideological determinants. The occurrence of corruption and its manifestations generally appear only as the unpleasant side-effects of imperfect systems. But if we model a distinction between the evolutionary phases of (1) petty corruption based on free competition, (2) state capture through oligarchs and the organized underworld, and, finally, (3) mafia state governance operated as a criminal organization, then we inevitably revise the popular definition that corruption is nothing more than the (mis)use of entrusted/public power/office for private gain. According to its descriptive function, it becomes a decisive element based on its occurrence in the regime. Movement toward this wider, system-defining direction is occurring not only in the world of academia, but also in political bodies such as the Council of Europe, which advanced a motion ("Corruption as a governance regime"[1]) that shows great development in the analysis and evaluation of the nature of corruption.

Let us distinguish between three levels of corruption:
    The first level is the simplest, the so-called day-to-day corruption, which is characterized by scattered, sporadic, face-to-face direct corrupt transactions, involving the players in the economy and public authority.
    The second level is when corruption vertically reaches even the higher layers of governance and rather than manifesting in only occasional trans-

actions, show signs of a regular nature. Players' cooperation becomes more complex not only on the side of corruption supply, but also on the side of corruption demand, given that the corruption partners on the side of the economy are in many cases oligarchs or criminals in the organized underworld. (We need to distinguish between the two above-mentioned groups: while criminal organizations carry out illegal "economic" activities supported by illegitimate access, oligarchs on the contrary usually conduct lawful economic activities, but mostly with illegitimate access.)

This level is known today as the realm of state capture. We can only speak about this phenomenon when certain segments of public authority are captured and not the governmental structure in its entirety. At this level, political competition may still continue. The transfer of political power is still possible under constitutional circumstances, and the oligarchs still maintain their relative autonomy, as they are not infinitely tied to certain political actors. Both sides can enter and leave the corruption transactions relatively freely. Organizational criminology refers to this level as state crime, which can take the form of corporate-facilitated state crime or state-facilitated corporate crime, depending on who the dominant or initiating actor is.

In the case of the **third** level, it is not appropriate to talk simply about state crime, as the phenomenon that we see already is rather a criminal state. It is no longer the oligarchs nor the organized underworld who capture the state, but a political enterprise—the organized upperworld—that captures the economy, including the oligarchs themselves. This is what we can witness **in some post-communist countries**. This evolutionary stage is possible when two conditions are met. Firstly, the monopolization of power by one political actor, accompanied by the systematic surrendering of the institutions of checks and balances. The second condition is the lack, or practical non-existence, of private property during the regime changes and widespread public distrust as privatization happened in these countries.

The emerging post-communist criminal states, where the governance bears the features of a criminal organization, can be described as post-communist mafia states. This is nothing other than the privatized form of a parasite state. In this case, the central bodies of the state itself operate in concert as a criminal organization, as the organized upperworld.

The Hungarian Post-Communist Mafia State

Let us briefly summarize the **basic features of the corrupt criminal state, namely the mafia state**[2]:

1. **The concentration of political power and the accumulation of wealth by the adopted political family occur in unison.** Public benefit becomes subordinated to private interests, not occasionally but permanently, and in a manner that influences political decision-making in a fundamentally determinant, systematic way.
2. **The alternation and systematic replacement of the political elite take place in parallel with that of the economic elite,** and these changes are not driven by the instruments of democracy or the market economy.
3. With the legalized instruments of the state monopoly on coercion, **the mafia state coercively extracts private fortunes**—sometimes indirectly through **different forms of nationalization**—to serve its own interests, and redistributes them amongst clients of the adopted political family.
4. The corruption of the organized criminal upperworld is neither a matter of incidental—even sporadic—back-door dealing, nor an occasional irregularity or deviance, but a centrally-directed and rationally-transacted plunder, a centrally-executed collection of protection money. For in the organized criminal upper world, **the mechanisms for the concentration of power and the accumulation of the wealth of the political family cannot be operated in disjoined systems**. But while the traditional mafia reaches its objectives through blackmail, intimidation and open violence, the spheres of influence in the mafia state can be shaped by the quasi-lawful instruments of coercion deployed by public authorities.
5. Let us specify the **key players** in this type of corrupt criminal state:
   - The **poligarch** is someone who uses legitimate political power to secure illegitimate economic wealth—while his or her political power is visible, the poligarch's economic power remains hidden. The poligarch manages his or her family business in the form of a political venture.
   - The **oligarch** is someone who, from more or less legitimate economic wealth, builds political power for himself—in this case his or her eco-

nomic power is visible, while his or her political power, if it exists at all, remains hidden.
- The **stooge** is someone who has no real power, neither in politics nor in the economic sphere, but bridges the gap between the real nature of power and its required legitimacy. So he or she formally serves as a middleman between the legitimate and illegitimate spheres for the public.
- The **corruption broker** brings the partners of the corrupt transaction(s) together in the role of mediator or expert lawyer. When the monopoly of political power is created, the criminal state surrenders the corruption brokers to the adopted political family and subjects them to strict order of dependency.
- The **family security guard** and the **secret services**.

6. **Decisions are taken outside the competence of formalized and legitimate bodies** of democratic institutions, and are brought into the topmost, tightly-knit **informal network of the adopted political family**.
7. Formalized and legal procedures give way to material and arbitrary actions. The head of the executive power does not govern, but illegitimately disposes of the country as if he (or she) owned it. State institutions, including the parliament, the government, the tax offices and the prosecutor's office do no more than rubberstamp and attend to the bookkeeping. They become the institutions of politically-selective law enforcement. The **"law of rule"** substitutes for the **"rule of law."** Proper jurisdiction is replaced by the arbitrary practice of justice. Legislation is no longer the field of lawful, normative regulations that are valid for all and brought to bear upon all equally, but where laws are tailored to fit the needs of those in power. **Equality before the law has been replaced by inequality after the law.**
8. In place of legally-protected autonomous positions, a **patron-client chain of vassal relationships** comes into being. This results in the elimination of the grounds of individual autonomy and forces livelihoods into a system of hierarchical dependency.
9. This new form of vassal dependency should not be called feudal or patrimonial, because **the material nature of power and its formal legitimacy do not converge**. The gap between them is bridged by state coercion and hypocrisy, using quasi-democratic procedures by restricting civil rights and the freedom of the press, and by manipulating electoral democracy. It is neither a liberal democracy nor a dictatorship.

10. **The mafia state is not ideology driven.** Rather, it builds on various ideological templates that suit its political agenda. While inconsistent in terms of public policy expertise, emotionally it remains consistent. This is also its strength: it resists a rational critique. The coherence of its values is ensured by the **cultural model of the dominance of the head of the patriarchal family.**

The need for big data analysis

Due to the lack of available data on the occurrence of corruption, researchers attempt to show it either by discussing institutional mechanisms, through case studies, or through the perception of corruption as measured in public opinion polling of businesses and the general public. Yet despite the utility of a model composed of a mosaic of case studies and legal analyses, there is still a need for a method that could verify the existence of a mafia state type of corruption through a large sample of individual corrupt transactions. Such ambition, however, also faces some limitations. First of all, the essential characteristic of decisions made in the informal power structure (the adopted political family) is that they are created in a non-public and non-documented way. Secondly, due to the small number of key decisions taken at the highest level, it is difficult to create a statistically appreciable database of such occurrences. Thirdly, broader procurement activities that are subordinate to these decisions are also not normally available in databases that can be examined for research purposes.

Moreover, the changes and manipulation of public procurement law after 2010 in accordance with the needs of centrally-managed corruption has also narrowed the scope of public spending not affected by politically motivated, discretionary decisions. A logical corollary of the established mafia state system is that for public procurements: the limit of public funds that can be spent without requiring a tender has been raised; the bidding period has been reduced; and cost makes up only 50 percent of the award criteria, while the rest is awarded by the politically-instructed assessment committee based on so-called qualitative, i.e. subjective, criteria.

All of this has increased the opportunity for manually-controlled government orders and clientele building in public administration and large state distribution systems. Another dimension of this phenomenon is that after 2010 low and mid-level officials are no longer "freely authorized" to engage in corruption. Municipal institutions and authorizations have undergone state centralization and become subject to political monitoring from higher-ups to such an extent that the freedom of such low-level corruption has been appropriated from them, and the right to exercise it granted instead to the central authority. It can ironically be stated that within such single-pyramid patronal networks, the former communist command economy regime has been replaced by a type of command corruption regime. Of course, it is also possible that these powers are occasionally delegated to subpatronal networks as a type of corrupt concession.

For major investments, however, the government has nearly unlimited power to officially designate an investment of economically-strategic importance, or prioritize it for national security reasons. These priority projects are exempted from regular public procurement procedures. Not to speak of the fact that from 2016 the government has given itself the direct authority to approve tenders exceeding 300 million forints.

Yet research led by István János Tóth of the **Corruption Research Center Budapest (CRCB)**[3] offers a unique opportunity within the post-communist region by attempting to detect signs of grand corruption, or the corrupt activity of a criminal organization operated by the central government, through a database that analyzes over 120,000 public procurement procedures between 2009 and 2015. Employing the tools of economics and political economics, a systemic difference between *state capture* and a *criminal state* can be detected in the periods of both pre- and post-2010. In addition, the use of big data analysis also provides an empirical base for a description and interpretation that satisfies the academic requirements of research and analysis in a way that helps the examination of the phenomenon go beyond the theoretical scope of Weberian model construction.

The drastic increase of **corruption risk** after 2010, though it could be assumed to be the result of a systemic, qualitative change in public procurements, could in theory also be explained simply by the extent of common corruption or state capture, both centrally directed and unorganized.

However, the change in the proportion of **non-advertised invitations to tender** appears to be disproved by individual offenders, which is to say, the theory of a *corruption service provider* that is not centrally directed. CRBC data shows that while less than one-fifth of all invitations to tender were unadvertised in 2009, this had become more than three-fifths by 2015. Such a dramatic increase in the rate of unadvertised tenders would necessitate decisions from the mid-level of the public administration apparatus

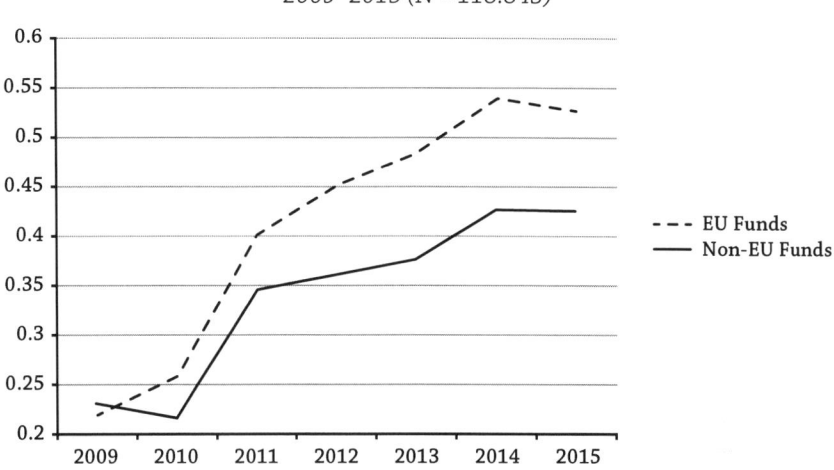

Figure 15.1. Corruption risk in public procurements, 2009–2015 (N = 118.843)

Explanation: The value of the corruption risk indicator is 0 if there was some type of strong competition during the public procurement process and it was preceded by a notice, and 1 if the public procurement occurred without a notice and without competition. A value of 0.5 was assigned if only one factor—either competition or a notice—was missing.
Source: CRCB, "Versenyerősség és korrupciós kockázatok: A magyar közbeszerzések statisztikai elemzése, 2009–2015; Adatok és leíró statisztikák" (February 2016), 36, 47.

at a minimum. At the very least, this can be understood as an evolutionary phase of *state capture*, since the bulk of non-advertised public procurements presume the existence of smoothly-operating channels of corruption.

From the economic side, an examination of overpriced public tender bids suggests a difference between the oligarch-directed *state capture* and the mafia state-directed *grand corruption* in relation to advertised and non-advertised public procurements. Indeed, the decision as to whether it should be advertised or non-advertised, or whether open, negotiated, or restricted tenders should be specified for EU or state funds, are decisions made at the government level. If the government finds that certain types of public procurements result in a large number of overpricing and partial deals, then it theoretically possesses all the necessary means to be able to steer tenders towards the direction of an open and advertised application process. Considering that the submission deadlines can be unrealistically short even for advertised tenders, it can be concluded that some mechanism allows the eventual winners to receive regular information required for the tender submission before its notice is posted. This could even be called **tender shorting**. And this is before a discussion of invitations to tender and technicalities that are tailor-made to an individual or company.[4] The technicalities are in fact nothing more than **tender personalization**, when the technical requirements of the tender outline the specifics of a bid that has already been selected to win. This is not a series of isolated incidents, but a wide-scale practice approved from the top.

However, this phenomenon might still fit into the *state capture* concept, as the collusion of the tender writer and assessor on the one side and the applicant on the other are sufficient. Yet the out-of-control overpricing demonstrated in Figure 15.4, which has raised the rate of overpriced bids by 140–320 percent for the bulk of these cases, cannot be explained through the concept of partial *state capture*.

The prices for public procurement contracts show a much stronger level of distortion in 2015 than at any time prior. This process distorts the bids so far from normal market prices that it cannot be explained simply

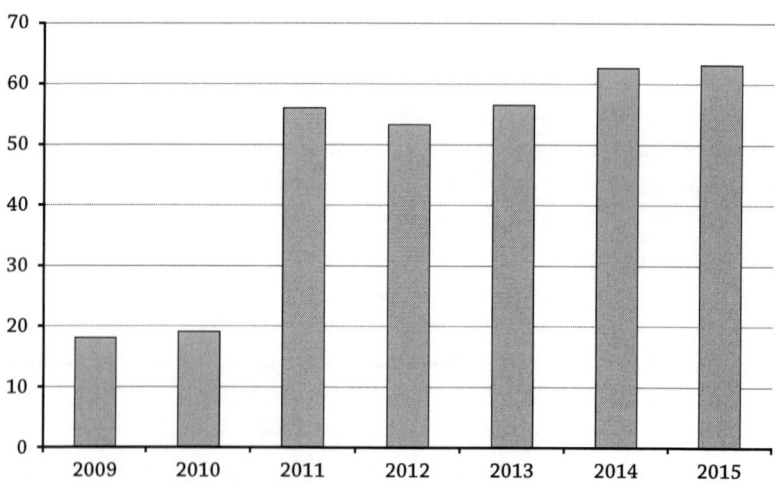

Figure 15.2. Proportion of public procurements without advertised tenders as a percentage of all public procurements, 2009–2015 (N = 121.849)

Source: CRCB, "Versenyerősség és korrupciós kockázatok," 31; Erdélyi Péter, "Közbeszerzésenként lopják el Magyarországot," *444.hu*, last modified March 9, 2016, http://444.hu/2016/03/09/kozbeszerzesenkent-lopjak-el-magyarorszagot.

Figure 15.3. Price distortion of Hungarian public procurements for each type, 2009–2015 (N = 124.693)

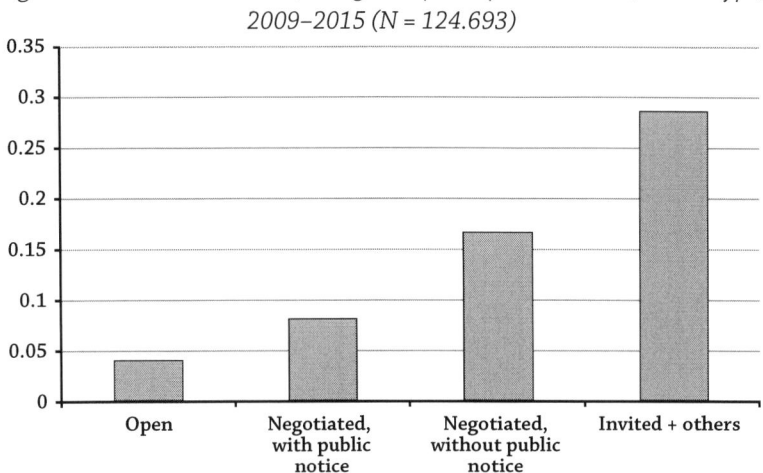

Note: Cramer's V values appear in the diagram. (Cramér's V is a measure of association between two nominal variables, giving a value between 0 and +1.)
Source: CRCB, "Versenyerősség és korrupciós kockázatok," 56

Figure 15.4. Price distortions for Hungarian public procurements, 2009–2015 (N = 123,224)

Explanation: The mean squared error (MSE) of contract prices of Hungarian Public Procurements from the theoretical (Benford's) distribution by year, first digits, 2009–2015, N = 123,224.
Source: CRCB, "Versenyerősség és korrupciós kockázatok," 53.

by a quantitative improvement or just the extent of corruption. Its scale likewise cannot be explained by an increase in the role of inherently more corrupt product markets within all public tenders. The increase in corruption is thus not the result of a spontaneous process. Therefore, it is worth taking a more detailed look at what this figure tells us.

The process of carrying out various public policy objectives through public tenders can be broken down into the following stages:
1. strategic public policy objectives (defining the problem, creating the program);
2. project planning;
3. invitation to tender;
4. tender assessment;
5. appeal lodged at the public procurement commission;
6. appeal lodged at court;
7. government review institutions that can impose legal consequences (Government Control Office, State Audit Office, Public Prosecutor).

Within the conditions of a democracy, these stages are separated from each other not only in terms of their content but also in regards to the persons representing and executing them. Although the first four stages concern the different layers and areas of the government, in a civilized setting the separation provides transparency, as well as enforcing normative procedures and fair competition within the government and from the review bodies that are independent from it.

- If these bodies operate separately from each other while the public tender is being managed, then the dominant terrain for corrupt transactions is the tender assessment (4th) stage. This is where the client of a corrupt transaction (the applicant) and the provider of a corrupt transaction (the assessor) meet each other. The offer is voluntary, and the value of the service is paid through a kickback. In such a case, it is closer to free market corruption, as the expected tender winner is not a person or company that has been pre-selected from above, and there is some competition regarding the amount of the kickback as well. The kickback or extra income paid by the client is sometimes included in the overpriced bid. Yet the other applicants competing for the tender can underbid the price that has been agreed-upon by the actors in the corrupt transaction, which **sets a scale** for it. The assessor, however, cannot accept a sky-high bid during the corrupt transaction—to each side's mutual benefit—since the losers, or those disqualified from bidding for any variety of reasons, can appeal the decision and win a ruling from the public procurement commission or in court. That is, assuming that these are independent bodies. Thus the scale of overpricing is regulated and kept in check in a market-based way by limits that are created as a result of such appeals against arbitrary deals.

- **Overpricing can increase** if the collusion, for example, is not only between the applicant and the assessor, but also with the tender writer, and by manipulating the deadline and technicalities, as previously mentioned. This is a case of partial state capture that can hinder the operation of the independent review bodies, since the very way the tenders are written can "legally eliminate" a significant portion of the competitors. But this form of corruption, although it may facilitate tenders in which a desired bidder will win the tender, cannot result in a significant increase in overpricing, as the review bodies may still reinstate applicants who have been illegitimately pushed out back into the competition.
- **Out-of-control overpricing**, however, can only occur under certain conditions. A centralized guiding hand and resolve monitors and coordinates the stages of tailoring the project planning, invitation to tender, and assessment to a specific person/company. It also ensures that those eliminated from the tender are unable to win an appeal, while also guaranteeing that the inspection and law enforcement agencies are unable to levy sanctions on the writers and assessors of the tender because of their biased decisions. This also means that the managing and supervising public authorities go beyond actively coordinating the activity of the actors in public administration referred to in the stages 1–7 above in a way that guarantees the private use of the funds gained through the tenders. They simultaneously also eliminate the free market type of corruption: after all, it is not the assessor, but the review and managing agencies in their totality that award the winner of the tender. The assessor is no longer bought off, but rewarded by being able to retain his or her status.

What facilitates out-of-control overpricing is either that the activity itself is difficult to standardize (e.g., for IT procurement), or, in case the commission is more prone to standardization (e.g., the construction industry), though the post-tender increase of funds, due to "unforeseen problems" or "additional tasks." (Naturally, in this system of centrally-directed collusion, selected winners are not disqualified from later tenders when they are unable, even by chance, to estimate correctly in advance the extent of work to be done.)

This type and size of rent-seeking is only possible with a centrally-controlled, state-run criminal organization, namely the operation of a mafia state. Thus the **scale of overpricing** can serve as an **indicator of the functioning of the mafia state**, one that helps through quantitative methods to distinguish this regime from other, more ordinary, corrupted regimes. For the former, it is an essential element that defines the system, while for the latter it is only an unpleasant side effect.

The operation of a state-run criminal organization is also exemplified by the "mafia war" between Viktor Orbán and Lajos Simicska, the head oligarch who used to be part of the inner circle of the adopted political family. With a two-thirds Parliamentary majority won again in 2014 for Orbán-led Fidesz, chief patron Viktor Orbán decided to terminate Simicska's monopolistic role in economic affairs within the adopted political family. Although the refashioning of the network of oligarchs connected to the chief patron began in 2014, the conflict broke into public view in February 2015. It caused a dramatic roll-back of companies linked to Simicska, the

Figure 15.5. Number of public tenders awarded to Lajos Simicska (S), and to István Garancsi, Lőrinc Mészáros and István Tiborcz (G+M+T) combined, 2013–2015

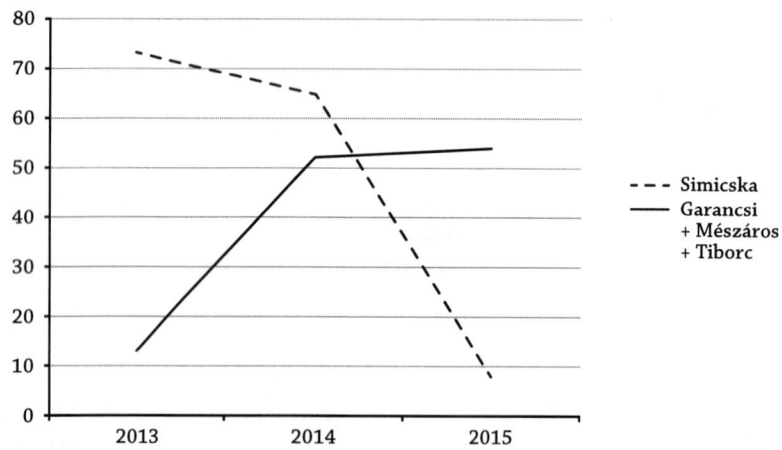

Based on data provided in CRCB, "Versenyerősség és korrupciós kockázatok," 75.

main winner of public tenders up to that point. Their replacements were primarily front men and non-autonomous oligarchs: István Garancsi is a friend of Prime Minister Orbán and the "appointed" owner of his favorite soccer team; Lőrinc Mészáros, a gas fitter from the prime minister's hometown who has become an omnivorous "entrepreneur"; and István Tiborcz, Orbán's son-in-law. Their surge into greater power could only have been more spectacular if the alternative media portfolio that has replaced Lajos Simicska's media empire also belonged to them and not to other newfound front men/oligarchs of the prime minister.

These indicators speak to how **free market corruption risk** is replaced by the **certainty of a state-run criminal organization** managed from above.

The perception of corruption and the problems with international comparative indicators

Various international comparative indices that measure of corruption worldwide show a similar difference between regions in terms of the contamination of corruption. Historical traditions and contemporary practices visibly overlap each other. The vast majority of such surveys are based on the experiences of businesses competing on the market, as it would be very difficult to make a consistent comparison of detectable corrupt practices in all countries through any other dimension. Yet while data obtained this way provides a suggestive picture of the degree of corruption, they do not offer a reliable picture regarding the prevalence of the various types of corruption, particularly that which is characteristic to a mafia state.

These data sets still offer partial insight into the extent of corrupt transactions that are initiated by economic actors, possibly under coercion, and whether these grow into the partial state capture stage on a systemic basis. But they do not provide a picture of the situation when the initiator of a corrupt transaction is neither the company, nor low or mid-level actors in public authorities with the potential to extort, but the criminal state itself. In a mafia state dominated by such a single-pyramid patronal network, it is politically-controlled enterprises, rather than the oligarchs, who hold the state captive, and then collect tax and protection money from economic actors and the public authority that they have designated. This situation may persist for countries such as Hungary, which are placed in

Table 15.1. The World Bank control of corruption (the ability of a state to curtail corruption) percentile ranking (Country rank among all countries of the world: 0=lowest; 100=highest)

Post-Communist Countries		1996	2004	2009	2014
EU-member Post-Communist Countries (not formerly part of the Soviet Union)	Croatia	24	61	57	62
	Czech Republic	77	69	67	65
	Hungary	74	76	68	61
	Poland	73	59	70	71
	Slovakia	66	69	65	60
	Slovenia	87	83	81	75
	Bulgaria	26	58	51	49
	Romania	49	49	51	53
EU-member Post-Communist Countries (former Soviet Republics)	Estonia	58	81	78	88
	Latvia	24	60	62	66
	Lithuania	58	65	61	69
Non EU-member Post-Communist Countries (not formerly part of the SU)	Albania	12	27	38	36
	Bosnia and Herzegovina	42	47	44	49
	Macedonia, FYR	17	38	57	59
	Montenegro		33	55	57
	Serbia	15	40	48	52
Former Soviet Republics in Europe	Belarus	20	17	29	48
	Moldova	51	15	28	21
	Russia	16	25	11	20
	Ukraine	13	18	16	15
Former Soviet Republics in the Caucasus	Armenia	36	29	33	40
	Azerbaijan	6	11	10	18
	Georgia	5	29	52	75

Post-Communist Countries		1996	2004	2009	2014
Former Soviet Republics in Central Asia	Kazakhstan	9	11	21	26
	Kyrgyzstan	36	13	6	12
	Tajikistan	5	10	10	14
	Turkmenistan	36	5	2	9
	Uzbekistan	12	12	7	11

Source: http://info.worldbank.org/governance/wgi/index.aspx#reports

the mid-range in terms of their corruption indicators, as well as for countries such as Russia or the post-communist nations of Central Asia, who are placed at the bottom of such indicators.

Along with the end of the shortage economy in Hungary following the change of regime in 1989, common corruption typical of the "third economy" became less prominent and also decreased in matters of public administration. The terrain for corruption was mostly concentrated in areas regarding decisions on privatization, state procurement and the disbursement of EU funds. It was here that centralizing the decentralized system of corrupt transactions and expropriation through a politically-controlled enterprise witnessed a significant change after 2010. It is no longer the economic actors who bid against each other in corrupt transactions, but the new political elite, the adopted political family, that designates in advance on different levels those who are positioned to win government and EU tenders. The lower level of the apparatus is paid with a position and not with a "corrupt concession right."

In Russia, in contrast, the private market sector continues to be heavily dominated by means that allow the state to intervene and guide, providing the possibility for it to collect restrictive, corrupt financial benefits. The centralized power structure there distributes regional powers for the collection of corrupt funds to its own clients, where the actors in temporary positions of public authority have an interest in maintaining and maximizing the channels of corruption. In Russia, such position offers access not to property but sources of revenue, a portion of which then flows back to the center through various channels. The chief patron situated at the top of the single-pyramid patronal network, however, takes complete sectors out of the system of regional redistribution and places them under the control of subpatrons that belong to his inner circles.

In the post-Soviet mafia states of Central Asia, the system of outsourcing corrupt channels is even more common. A hybridization of this system with the favor network of traditional clan and family structures adds a further flavor to this version of state-managed corruption.

Although questions in the latest Transparency International survey on business in Hungary follow the paradigm of common corruption and partial state capture, the data nevertheless indirectly suggests systemic corruption that is centrally organized by the state.

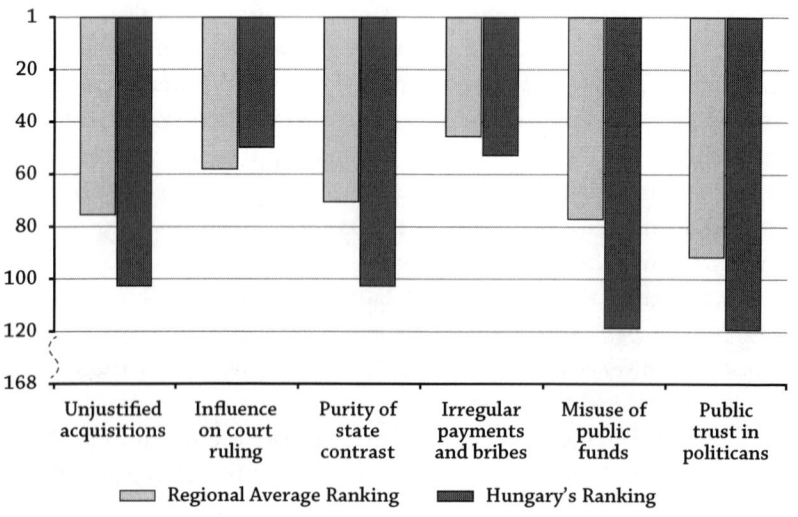

Figure 15.6. Ranking according to selected institutional competitiveness indicators in a world ranking of 168 countries (2015)

Region: Poland, Czech Republic, Slovakia, Slovenia, Estonia, Latvia, Lithuania, Hungary

Explanation: Transparency International's Berlin headquarters (Secretariat) generates the Corruption Perception Index (CPI) from 12 evaluation and assessment reports by 11 organizations. It measures public sector corruption in each country based on its contamination in public institutions, the economy, and society through interviews with experts and business people. In 2015, relevant data was made available for 168 countries, and Hungary was examined on the basis of nine different sub-indices. Source: Transparency International Hungary

In their analysis, it is not by accident that the concept **party state capture**, referring to a politically centralized and monopolized system of corruption, appears instead of **partial state capture**. Just as the classic mafia does not tolerate competition in its sphere of interest, the mafia state likewise wants to eliminate the free market actors in a corrupt competition. This can cause everyday petty corruption to recede and a number of measures to appear. Such is the case with cash registers now connected online to the Hungarian tax authorities, which is intended to supplant channels of corruption that operate without central authorization. The term party state capture, while an important step forward in understanding the operation of this criminal state, still perpetuates a common misunderstanding. Namely, it suggests that the acting subject was a political party formally in possession of power and not the informal power network, which can be defined according to its sociological nature as the adopted political family that dominates the mafia state.

The diagram above rather shows that the extent of petty corruption as typified by "irregular payments and bribes" conforms to the regional average, and the "influence on court rulings" score is even below that. However, interestingly, the perception of a state of affairs describing centralized and largely quasi-legalized corruption, such as "unjustified acquisitions," the "purity of state contracts," or "misuse of public funds," indicates that Hungary far surpasses the regional average.

Public perception of system-wide corruption in Hungary

The real question is how well the citizens of a country are able to perceive the difference between various evolutionary levels of corruption. This question is all the more valid given that the more a functioning autocratic regime takes advantage of centrally-organized corruption in the context of a single-pyramid patronal network, the less opportunity there is to conduct public opinion polling directly on this issue in that country. For such reasons, a nationwide representative surveys in Hungary by the **Medián Public Opinion Research Institute** in June 2016 and December 2017 are particularly valuable.[5]

The survey in question breaks with the paradigm of simply polling public opinion on corruption in general, its extensiveness, or even its development over time. Naturally, the standard question regarding the extent to which the public views corruption as a serious social problem also had to be measured. As the data clearly shows, after the abysmal state of health care, the public considers corruption to be as worrisome a problem as the economic situation, unemployment, or the refugee issue, which is the current focus of an anti-foreigner campaign by the government. It is revealing, but still within the framework of a quantitative description, that two-thirds of the respondents considered government-related financial abuses as typical of the system to either a large or a very large extent. What is more surprising is that even 25 percent of pro-government voters believe that financial abuses are characteristic of the current Fidesz government to a large extent, while 12 percent of them believe this to a very large extent.

This by itself, however, still does not inform us as to how the public assesses the relationship of the government itself to corruption. But the perception of politically-selective law enforcement is indicated by the fact that while only 17 percent of the respondents assert that the government "consistently takes action against corruption in all forms," a further 56 percent are of the belief that it "only takes action against corruption that it is not party to." In addition, 23 percent of those believe that "the government does not fight corruption at all." Even 11 percent of voters who support the ruling party think that the government does not do anything at all to stop corruption, and 47 percent of this group, detecting the government's partiality, believe that it only takes action against corruption that it is not party to.

The high proportion of responses suggesting politically-selective law enforcement poses the question as to whether the current nature of corruption in Hungary can fundamentally be classified as *petty corruption* or *grand corruption*. 60 percent of respondents stated that corruption is "more of a top-down, centralized, and systematically-organized activity," while only 31 percent view it as "more ad hoc private actions by dishonest public officials." Even 38 percent of Fidesz supporters view corruption in Hungary as a top-down, centrally-organized activity.

The question legitimately arises here as to whether or not the radical opinion of these respondents is reflected in the description of corrupt transactions or in its description in the linguistic categories that are used. The survey also allowed respondents to choose two categories from among a list of descriptive labels. It is understandable that the most general expression, **corruption**, was chosen for the first or second place in 56 percent of all cases, but its specific form of **bribery**, which could be described as a bottom-up corrupt transaction, was only picked by 15 percent of the respondents.

Figure 15.7. Is "petty corruption" or "grand corruption" more dominant in Hungary? (percentage of respondents, broken down by party affiliation)

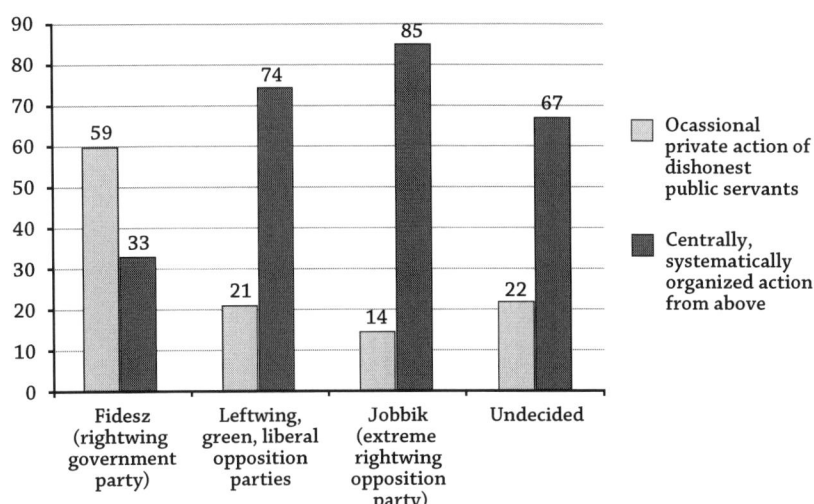

Source: Medián Public Opinion and Market Research Institute, December 2017

This was also the case with **theft**, a relatively neutral and technical term, that was also only chosen by 17 percent. And only 25 percent chose "**mutyi**," a common designation used in the Hungarian media to describe occasional small-scale corrupt transactions that do not presuppose a patron-client system. 41 percent of the respondents now talk of **collusion with family members**, while a total of 42 percent of respondents considered the phrases **state-run criminal organization** and **mafia methods** as adequate categories for characterizing corruption in Hungary.

Among the categories that characterize the government's financial abuses, it is worth highlighting those that originate from the top and are more related to grand corruption, such as the state-run criminal organization, mafia methods, and collusion with family members. For the latter case, news reports on the enrichment of the political elite are critical to creating awareness within the general public. The appearance of collusion with family members, clan identification, and dynastic elements is a part of a process that occurs when policy-making is removed from the world of formal institutions (the party, government, Parliament), and is moved to the informal world of the adopted political family, ruled by the chief patron.

Figure 15.8. Proportion of those who chose categories related to grand corruption to describe corruption (percentage of respondents, broken down by party affiliation)

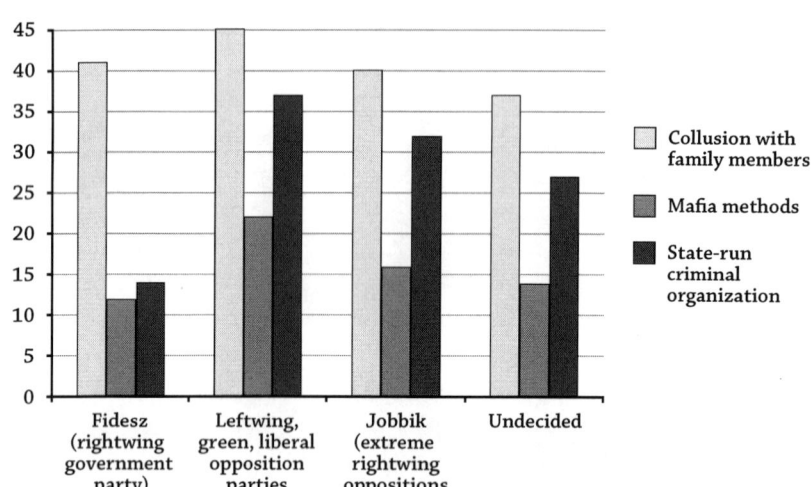

Source: Medián Public Opinion and Market Research Institute, June 2016

If we mention collusion with family members, then the question is how the public judges the financial situation of the chief patron, Prime Minister Viktor Orbán. Although Orbán declared in response to an opposition parliamentary member in April 2016 that "I have been a Member of Parliament since 1990, have never been a wealthy man, am not now, and will never be one,"[6] the citizens of Hungary believe differently: only 4 percent of them think that Viktor Orbán belongs to the middle class in terms of his financial situation, while 45 percent classify him as wealthy and 49 percent put him right among the wealthiest people in Hungary. Even 27 percent of Fidesz supporters also think that the prime minister—in contrast to his own assertion—is one of the wealthiest people in the country.

At the same time, if there is no trace of it in either Orbán's official career history or his declaration of assets as a politician, the question of where they think this wealth has come from cannot be avoided. Now we arrive at one of the key categories of the operation of the state-run criminal organization and mafia state: the front men, the function of which is to bridge the gap between one's legal and one's actual financial situation.

During the same parliamentary session in which he denied being a wealthy man, Orbán responded to the question of whether Lőrinc Mészáros was his front man by saying, "I have never had and will never have any type of front man."[7] But the survey respondents viewed this differently. The statement "accusations repeatedly heard nowadays and even in Parliament, that certain businessmen who have achieved outstanding success, such as István Garancsi, Lőrinc Mészáros and Andy Vajna,[8] are front men for Viktor Orbán, i.e. a substantial portion of their huge business profits is actually passed on to the Prime Minister," was thought of as conceivable by 47 percent of respondents, and very probable by 31 percent of them. Only 15 percent of respondents ruled out this possibility. But what is truly surprising is that 10 percent of the Fidesz faithful feel that it is very probable, and 51 percent of them think it is conceivable, that the prime minister is enriching himself from money relayed through his front men. After all, it is not possible to justify only through his official salary how he is widely perceived to be one of the wealthiest persons in the country.

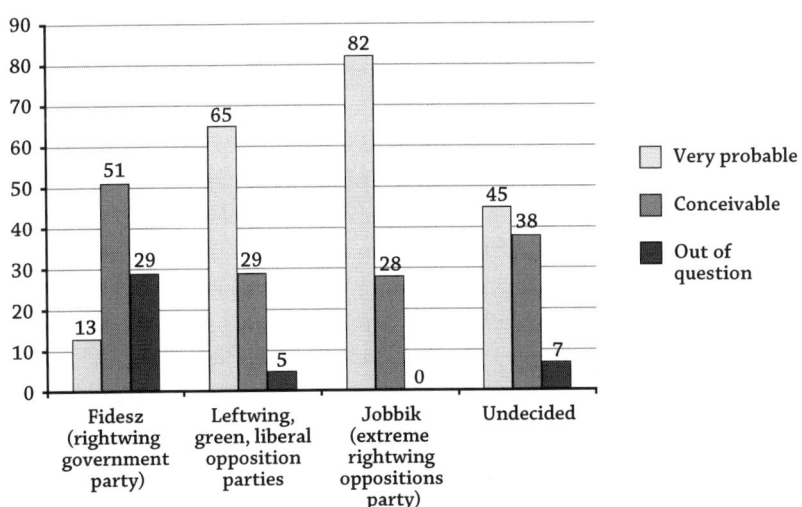

Figure 15.9. To what extent do voters in each party consider it likely that the Prime Minister is enriching himself through front men? (percentage)

The question asked: "In your opinion, is it likely that István Garancsi, Lőrinc Mészáros or Andy Vajna are the front men or stooges of Viktor Orbán, and significant part of their huge business profit is channeled to the prime minister?"
Source: Medián Public Opinion and Market Research Institute, December 2017.

The public opinion poll also explored how much of an effect the perception of the nature of corruption had on judging the political system as a whole. To assess this, of course, key changes made by **Fidesz, which achieved in 2010 a constitutional parliamentary majority through a disproportionate electoral system** must be taken into account. As a sole political actor following the elections, the party rewrote the constitution, made members of the adopted political family leaders in public authority institutions that are designed to maintain checks and balances, restricted the privately-owned media, appropriated the state-run media for itself, eliminated individual and institutional autonomy, and forced a significant portion of the citizenry into patron-client relationships. In a tripartite political space, where Fidesz' right-wing opposition is the far-right Jobbik party and its left-wing opposition is made up of largely discredited left-wing and miniscule green parties, Fidesz has been able to maintain its position as the largest, centrist party. In this regard, responses to the question of what term best describes the current Hungarian political system are particularly noteworthy. Fidesz' official self-designation, the **System of National Cooperation**, was chosen by 9 percent of respondents, with the term **civic democracy** selected by 18 percent. Proceeding from these towards more negative and critical designations, mentioned first could be **illiberal democracy**, a phrase chosen by 8 percent of respondents that simultaneously carries meanings both vindicating and criticizing the regime in Hungary. After all, the prime minister himself declared in the summer of 2015 that "the new state we are building in Hungary is an illiberal state, not a liberal one. It does not renounce fundamental values of liberalism like freedom, . . . but it does not make this ideology a central part of organizing the state, and applies its own divergent, national approach."[9] However, the critical liberal and left-wing intelligentsia uses it in a critical sense connected to the expression's Western interpretation. Among designations critical of the regime that are more comprehensible to the wider public, 17 percent of respondents chose **autocratic regime**, while 15 picked **mafia state**, and 20 percent **dictatorship**. Some of the left-wing and liberal intelligentsia, totaling only 3 percent of all respondents, showed a preference for the definition **fascistoid regime**, referring to the system's supposedly ideology-driven nature.

In the diagram above, it is striking that—if we discount those who were unable or unwilling to provide an answer—there is a similarly-structured distribution in the categories used to judge the regime by both the

Figure 15.10: Characterization of the present Hungarian political system by voters in each party (percentage)

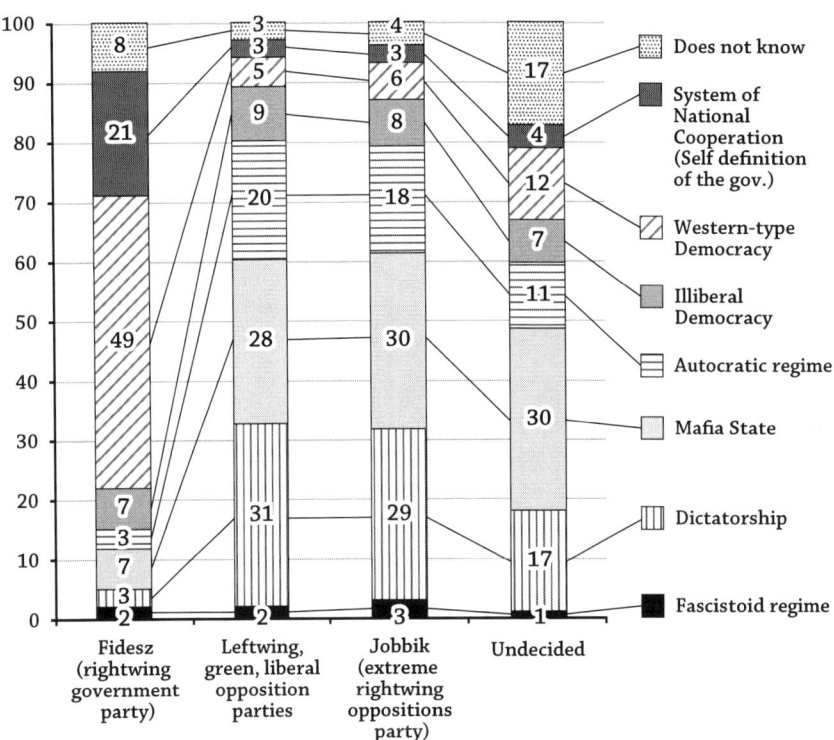

Source: Medián Public Opinion and Market Research Institute, December 2017

left and right-wing opposition to the central space dominated by Fidesz, and also by those with no party preference. Among the three categories most critical of the regime, the strong showing of the mafia state designation in addition to dictatorship and autocratic regime indicates that a significant share of society considers the state-run criminal organization and mafia state elements of grand corruption as integral factors in the system, rather than merely an unpleasant accompaniment to it. The terms dictatorship and autocratic regime directly refer, of course, to the restrictions on civil rights and to the elimination of societal autonomy and separate branches of power.

It is also not irrelevant that close to one-fourth of Fidesz voters characterized their own party's rule with categories that were the most radically critical of the regime. In the absence of an alternative, moderate center-right political force, they either got jammed in amongst Fidesz supporters or expanded the mass of those who were undecided. For them, choosing the far-right Jobbik is obviously not an option, but they have no path towards the left-wing opposition either, as their reservations against the features of the mafia state obviously do not result in the shedding of their moderate, right-wing conservative identity.

Regime criticism through the "fascist" approach, which is given relatively large weight by the government-critical intelligentsia and media, does not gain traction among those who are undecided, but neither with supporters of the left-wing parties. The government's policies of employing ideological panels that are racist, anti-Semitic, xenophobic and homophobic with a pragmatic expediency to increase its voter base are not ideologically driven. This "fascism," which stems from an ideology-driven, regime-critical paradigm, is a position that is unfollowable for the general public, and it puts representatives of such views into an ideological and political quarantine. While the general public considers them the "real" representatives of the left wing, it also, among other reasons, is a way of limiting the left-wing political parties from expanding.

A separate point of interest in the survey is that when broken down according to gender, age, level of education, and level of income, it does not show any significant difference when compared to the indicators taken together. It is only when broken down according to type of settlement is

Table 15.2. Support for particular corruption-related statements according to type of settlement (in percentage)

Proportion of those who believe:	Budapest	City/Town	Village
corruption in Hungary is more of an activity that is top-down, centralized, and systematically organized	50%	60%	55%
the present political system in Hungary can be characterized as a mafia state	11%	24%	19%

Source: Medián Public Opinion and Research Center Institute, December 2017

it clear that a significantly higher proportion of the population in provincial cities, compared to the population both in Budapest and in rural areas, shares the interpretation of corruption as a centrally-controlled mafia state. This may also be due to the fact that Hungarian cities range between 10,000 and 200,000 inhabitants. On the one hand, this is sufficiently large enough for centralized and state-monopolized corruption to manifest itself in specific localities in manifold ways. On the other hand, a settlement of this size is small enough for everyday instances of personal interconnectedness and family networks to remain in plain sight, without a level of remoteness or impersonality that would cloud perception. This is despite the fact that provincial cities in Hungary have a much narrower choice of government-critical media compared to Budapest.

Overall, it can be stated that the view of the current Hungarian political system as a functioning criminal organization, a view held by a broad swath of the Hungarian public, might be more insightful than that held by the majority of its academic community, political analysts, or even its opposition parties.

Notes

[1] "Corruption as a governance regime: a barrier to institutional efficiency and progress; Motion for a resolution," tabled by Ms. Chiora Taktakishvili and other members of the Assembly, Doc. 13551, June 25, 2014.

[2] Bálint Magyar, *Post-Communist Mafia State: The Case of Hungary* (Budapest: CEU Press-Noran Libro, 2016).

[3] Corruption Research Center Budapest, "Competitive Intensity and Corruption Risks: Statistical Analysis of Hungarian Public Procurement, 2009–2015; Data and Descriptive Statistics," March 3, 2016 / May 18, 2016, http://www.crcb.eu/?p=943. Following figures and data is from the Hungarian-language version of the report, "Versenyerősség és korrupciós kockázatok: A magyar közbeszerzések statisztikai elemzése, 2009–2015; Adatok és leíró statisztikák" (February 2016), http://www.crcb.eu/wp-content/uploads/2016/03/hpp_2016_crcb_report_2016_hu_160303_.pdf.

[4] Dávid Jancsics and István Jávor, "The Corrupted Industry and the 'Wagon-Wheel Effect': A Cross-Country Exploration of the Effect of Government Corruption on Public Service Effectiveness," *Administration & Society* 48, no. 5 (2016): 559–79.

[5] Endre Hann, Medián Public Opinion Research Institute, Budapest, June 2016 and December 2017.

[6] "Orbán egyszerű választ adott: Nincs strómanom," *HírTV*, April 11, 2016, http://hirtv.hu/ahirtvhirei/orban-egyszeru-valaszt-adott-nincs-stromanom-1337079.

7 Ibid.
8 István Garancsi is a newfound favorite oligarch of Viktor Orbán, and gas fitter Lőrinc Mészáros is his industrialist village neighbor. Figure 15.5 shows the public tenders that have been won by the two of them plus the prime minister's son-in-law. Andy Vajna is the beneficiary of a monopoly on the casino industry that came about through parliamentary legislation and government policy. All three of them have been listed as among the richest Hungarians in recent years.
9 Viktor Orbán, "A munkaalapú állam korszaka következik: Orbán Viktor beszéde a XXV. Bálványosi Nyári Szabadegyetem és Diáktáborban 2014. július 26. Tusnádfürdő (Băile Tuşnad)," http://www.kormany.hu/hu/a-miniszterelnok/beszedek-publikaciok-interjuk/a-munkaalapu-allam-korszaka-kovetkezik, last modified on July 28, 2014. For the English version of the speech (in a slightly different translation), see "Prime Minister Viktor Orbán's Speech at the 25th Bálványos Summer Free University and Student Camp," http://www.kormany.hu/en/the-prime-minister/the-prime-minister-s-speeches/prime-minister-viktor-orban-s-speech-at-the-25th-balvanyos-summer-free-university-and-student-camp, last modified on July 30, 2014.

V.
CONTRASTS AND CONNECTIONS

Alexei Pikulik

Belarus, Russia, and Ukraine as Post-Soviet Rent-Seeking Regimes

Introduction

If Leo Tolstoy were a student of post-socialism, he could certainly have applied what became known as the "Anna Karenina principle" to the post-socialist countries: namely, that "happy families are all alike; every unhappy family is unhappy in its own way." A few short years after the events of 1989 and 1991, socialist convergence had been replaced by post-socialist divergence. Today, hardly any other region of the world can boast such a striking variety of political and economic institutional domains. Between liberal democracies with regulated capitalisms at one pole, and fully-fledged autocracies with neo-planned economies at the other, there lies a wide variety of political and economic regimes. Indeed, the new wave of democratization (whether third or fourth) left the shore of the post-Soviet space inhabited with new animals of different species.

Aside from the trio of Baltic states that joined the Soviet Union later, all of the USSR's successor countries (making up the Former Soviet Union, or FSU), which were brutally communized, mis-developed, and homogenized throughout their existence, became immediately trapped in a turbulent grey zone of partial regimes after gaining their independence in 1991. Their paths could be characterized as pendulum-like swings between the bad and the terrible. The rise of non-democratic regimes in most of the post-Soviet Republics dramatically changed the scholarly agenda. Unreserved optimism for a glorious, democratic and capitalist future in the region at the beginning of the 1990s was soon replaced by bitter pessimism. If in 1996 the world community was surprised by the political choices of Europe's "last dictator" Alyaksandr Lukashenka in Belarus, seven years later the relatively timid and meek re-democratizations of Georgia, Ukraine and Kyrgyzstan were for some time hailed as breathtaking events and labelled democratic revolutions.

The wave of "capitalismization" of the region proved to be shallow as well. According to the economic freedom index provided by the Heritage Foundation in 2006, only three of twelve post-Soviet republics had "moderately free" economies, while seven were categorized as "mostly unfree," and two were labelled "repressed."[1] Moreover, in considering post-Soviet divergence as the predominant feature of post-socialism, and focusing on the comparison of somewhat successful cases of economic transformation (Georgia, Ukraine, Moldova) with unsuccessful cases (Belarus, Uzbekistan, Turkmenistan, and recently Russia), **scholars generally overlooked their strong convergence**. Specifically, this convergence manifested itself in the predominance of poor institutions, state capture, cronyism, and flourishing corruption. So, is converging divergence the outcome of their transitions? In other words, why, despite the divergent designs of the political and economic institutions across these cases, did all these countries converge in the absence of a liberal state capable of upholding political, civic and property rights through the rule of law?

Out of all the cases belonging to this "natural post-communist experiment," this article sets forth a theoretical framework that contributes to the understanding of the cases of Belarus, Ukraine and Russia. It argues that the key to explaining this converging divergence lies in the parameters of their state re-making. Central to this is the refined rentier state argument, in which the primary focus is placed on the structure of extraction and mode of ownership of economic rents present in the post-Soviet economies—that is, what this article terms "comparative rent-seeking regimes." The choice of these three cases is determined by a combination of empirical and theoretical concerns.

Firstly, the three cases denote a serious variation on a dependent variable (political and economic developments) across the entire post-communist universe. Belarus arrived at the combination of autocratic regime and a state-controlled economy having initially conducted something of an institutional detour. It experienced only one qualitative change in its political dimension, during 1995–96, and it never managed to decisively move away from its state socialist mixed economy (a term borrowed from Ota Šik, referring to economies dominated by the state with limited market mechanisms in some sectors). Nevertheless, in quantitative terms, the country experienced a stark reversal of reforms in conjunction with its autocratic relapse. Ukraine experienced one qualitative change in its political dimension, making some progress toward democratization after the Orange Revolution of 2004. In the economic sphere, it was slow to move away from central planning, and retained a state socialist mixed economy for four years; after this period, it became de facto stuck in another low-level equilibrium trap, with a distorted market economy in the post-liberalization years. Their initial developments are marked with a significant similarity: namely, that both flirted with reforms rather than actively pursuing them. Yet unlike Belarus, which began to take a different path in 1995, Ukraine made significant progress in its reforms after 1996.

Finally, Russia experienced parallel democratization and capitalismization that lead to a captured state, weak institutions and competitive oligarchy under Yeltsin. From there, it moved to a form of kleptocratic state capitalism and political autocracy by 2004. All in all, Russia left both Belarus and Ukraine far behind and rushed towards a market economy and democracy, getting stuck along the way in a partial reform equilibrium (partial democracy and partial liberalization). Belarus and Ukraine progressed hand in hand until 1995, when Belarus abandoned its fellow traveler and moved toward autocracy, de-liberalizing its economy. Ukraine continued, and very soon joined Russia in a partial reform trap.

After seven years of pendulum-like swings between democracy and autocracy, the two countries exited this trap in different directions. Russia followed the autocratic path of Belarus, yet without significant de-liberalization. Ukraine went in the opposite direction towards greater democracy, while simultaneously preserving its level of economic liberalization.

Secondly, notwithstanding some idiosyncrasies discussed later in the research, these three cases were the most similar out of all twelve post-Soviet republics as far as their starting conditions were concerned (levels of socio-economic modernization, levels of economic distortion, communist legacies, and anti-communist mobilization). In other words, it is not an exaggeration to label them as the most similarly designed systems, due to shared crucial similarities, which decisively eliminate numerous competing theories accounting for diverse outcomes later on.[2]

Thirdly, Belarus, Russia and Ukraine all constitute cases of undetermined transitions. They were neither blessed to board the ship of successful development together with the Central and Eastern European countries, nor doomed to be deadlocked in an autocratic socialist past like some other post-Soviet republics. Any outcome seemed plausible, and the pendulum could swing in any direction.

Defining the explanandum

A non-teleological study which underlines the nonlinear and underdetermined nature of political and economic change should be liberated (as much as it is possible) from the passive voice of "not-yet" democracy/capitalism. The Herculean task of focusing on what these regimes really are, instead of conceptualizing on the negative, requires new sets of concepts. Nevertheless, the goal of this article is very modest. On the one hand, it builds upon the theoretical framework proposed by Henry E. Hale and Bálint Magyar.[3] As such, it fuses two institutional domains, the political and the economic, into what will be termed a "rent-seeking regime." In all such regimes, both the liberal state, and the accompanying rule of law, are missing; the state is instead transformed into an apparatus that solves two problems simultaneously. On the one hand, it is the vehicle that generates and extracts rents both internally (in the Russian case, through energy exports) and externally (for Belarus and Ukraine, through their asymmetrical contractual relations with Russia). In the Belarusian case, however, a capable autocratic state could be maintained, given that the external rents were mostly spent on regime perpetuation through a vast and generous "social contract."[4] Unlike Belarus, in Russia and Ukraine the state mutated into a channel for rent extraction by competing domestic oligarchic groups. On the other hand, the state is used by its incumbents as a vehicle for regime maintenance and preservation of power, and thus ultimately the distribution of rents and the creation of uneven property rights.

The three examples comprising the focus of this study therefore present a case of divergent convergence. One example is the multi-pyramid system of Ukraine's rent-seeking regime, in which competition between "business-administrative groups"[5] over access to the extraction of rents through the state led to a systemic economic crisis caused by economic looting and the overappropriation of the sources of rent. In other words, it was an instance of "overfishing," or the dissipation of rent due to counterproductive fighting (as described by Gordon Tullock).[6] Paradoxically, this mode of rent-seeking in Ukraine—where rents are privately owned by competing groups—served as a panacea against autocratic backsliding; none of the clans was strong enough to monopolize power and the winner could not "take it all." In turn, it created great demand for the arrival of an arbiter, whose role would be to uphold the balance between the groups and control their rent-seeking appetites.

The second example, Belarus, is a case of a rentier state in which the incumbent president served as the chief extractor of rents from Russia (up to 22 percent of GDP in 2007). Notoriously, no competition over rents was permitted between private groups: the rents were external and state-owned, and the incumbent appointed his own figures (whom many believe to be cronies) to manage rents. Unlike in other cases, however, external rents were returned to the economy via redistribution, high levels of social welfare, and the maintenance of state-owned enterprises (up to 70 percent of Belarus' GDP is generated in the state sector).

Russia's pathway, the third case in our analysis, could be traced through two stages. In the initial stage under Boris Yeltsin, it could be characterized as a multi-pyramid rent-seeking regime, in which the state was fully hijacked by private interests (much like the Ukrainian case). Latterly, under Vladimir Putin, the rent-seeking regime evolved, encompassing the liberalization of the state from private interests, followed by their recapture within the framework of kleptocratic state capitalism.

Uneven distribution of property rights and post-Soviet rent-seeking regimes

The absence of the liberal state in the post-liberalization economies, with its concomitant rule of law and public regulation, is usually substituted with a complex system of asymmetrical distribution of property rights across the market, thereby allowing the conversion of public losses to private benefits for certain state and non-state actors. Unequally supplying property rights implies their uneven or unequal distribution, so that some receive more than others. Public goods are converted into private ones, favoring a tiny minority at the expense of overall welfare. The asymmetrical distribution of property rights by the state is associated either with the incumbents' propensity to directly self-enrich by predating on private property, or indirectly through the uneven distribution of property rights in favor of a few selected firms that exploit asymmetries of power and information to make unnatural profits and share them with state incumbents.[7] The former variant is usually associated with Evans' predation thesis,[8] while the latter depicts a typical case of "state capture."[9] Both extreme instances were well described by László Bruszt, who stated that while the main dilemma in the pre-liberalization stage was how to free the market from the state, the primary problem of the post-liberalization stage was how to liberate the state from the influence of the most influential market actors.[10]

The end goals of the preferential creation of rents and the uneven distribution of property rights are numerous. At the simplest level, the goal may be mere self-enrichment of the incumbent or some selected cronies. More complex goals may include the accumulation of extra-budgetary funds for incumbents that can be utilized for political purposes, including organizing their re-election and buying loyalty within the political-business cycle.

Both politics and economics have been absent from earlier versions of state capture literature. Such literature did a good job of explaining the upward mechanisms through which firms privatize public regulation to create unnatural profits by distorting the rules of the game. However, it failed to explain how political incumbents retain their public offices by having to please other constituencies who are interested in economic growth, and whose interests are threatened by the state captors. To tackle this problem, Amr Ismail Adly proposed the concept of "politically embedded cronyism" as the downward explanatory schema, central to which are incumbents permitting the uneven distribution of property rights in favor of politically-selected firms as a tactic to retain their political power beyond self-enrichment.[11] According to Adly, the state can involve itself passively through insufficient regulation, allowing powerful private actors to exploit asymmetries of power and information to generate unnatural profits and share them with state incumbents (for instance, though monopoly, collusion, insider trading, or lack of protection for minority shareholders and other stakeholders). Alternatively, the state can take an active role through shaping the rules that organize economic activities in a way that creates or reinforces asymmetries of power (for instance, by conferring monopoly rights, or allocating import quotas, public contracts and access to subsidies, tax exemptions and public bank credit).

Economically speaking, predation and capture leads to "overfishing," (exhaustion of economic resources through rent-seeking) since the captors/cronies practicing rent-seeking critically damage the profit-seeking economic sectors by deterring new entrants, halting investment and causing economic breakdown due to asset stripping and capital flight. Since the emphasis has hitherto been placed on incumbents using the state as a public actor to pursue their own particularistic interests, they must find a balance between the appetites of their cronies to capitalize on public welfare, and the constituencies whose political support depends upon the delivery of public welfare.

Having linked political and economic considerations in the post-liberalization instances of unequal supply of property rights, it is time to shift our focus to central parameters of Russia, Belarus and Ukraine's political economies—namely economic rents. The theory of rents is built on several layers. Firstly, there was the influential piece by Mahdavy in which he set forth a new concept of the "rentier state,"[12] a state that receives substantial rents from foreign individuals, concerns or governments, thus allowing it to subsist on externally generated rents, rather than from the surplus production of the population.[13] Following the work of Adam Smith, rents can be defined as profits reaped by those who did not sow.

The second layer is the popular petrostate variation of the theory, which brought the so-called "Dutch disease" economic effect, previously present in the oil-exporting countries, into politics, leading to the assumption that oil hinders democracy.[14] A group of scholars suggested that the commodity-structure of the economy has a determining impact on both political and economic developments.[15] Autocratic regimes and distorted economies with an uneven distribution of property rights are the usual outcomes in those resource-abundant economies which predominantly generate rents from raw-commodity exports (typically oil). Rents are believed to hinder democracy through the following mechanisms: firstly, uneven concentration of power, where those controlling rent extraction and distribution can afford costly coercive and co-optive tools; secondly, economic statism, weak institutionalization and corruption; and thirdly, an absence of accountability, in which economic development is not provided by the surplus of the society, the state can spend without taxing, and in turn citizens do not demand representation when they are not taxed.

The third factor was the assumption that the effects of oil revenues may not be unique, but rather similar to other externally generated revenues such as foreign aid, since the chief mechanism linking unearned revenues with regime types is the "no representation without taxation" argument of fiscal sociology.

Finally, there were those[16] who held that non-taxed government revenues (including foreign aid, borrowing from abroad, profits of state-owned companies and so on) have regime-stabilizing properties: since the state is capable of spending without taxing its citizens, it can pursue all manner of interests unconstrained, and secure its continuing survival through the redistribution of those rents throughout society. Since the most common non-taxed profits come from oil, this argument also encompasses the issue of rents through revenue mechanisms.

The framework which I am proposing here is fully concomitant with the latter interpretation of the rentier state theory. It borrows Mahdavy's original definition of a "rentier state" and treats rents as non-taxed revenues as far as the budget is concerned: that is to say, not as the surplus of the productive sector, but rather easy money obtained via various mechanisms both externally and internally.[17] I identify three key characteristics of uneven distribution of property rights in the cases under investigation: first, timing of rents; second, ownership of rents; and third, costs/stability of rents. Before explaining this in greater detail, some empirical observations must be made to justify the choice to make rents the central focus of this study, and also with a view to making the subsequent discussion more comprehensible for readers unfamiliar with the context.

Where do rents come from?

Both Belarus and Ukraine were mostly embedded in the Comecon zone and, therefore, heavily dependent on Russia for imports (mainly energy) and exports of finished goods. The asynchronous and non-coordinated transformation of the interdependent Comecon zone economies in the early 1990s opened up large rent-seeking opportunities for various private and public actors.

The economic disintegration of the Comecon zone lagged behind its political disintegration. The death of the USSR as a unified political entity in 1991 did not have an immediate impact on the integrated Soviet economy in which all of the post-Soviet republics had individual functional specializations. After 1991, Russia continuously served as a donor for various post-Soviet republics which could gain significant rents by remaining in the common currency zone with Russia. Moscow released currency to its neighbors' non-reformed economies and thus bore the inflationary burden for them, supplying them with negative interest credits, fueling them with subsidies and, most importantly, providing them with energy resources at significantly below market prices. Both state and non-state actors in some post-Soviet countries could establish beneficial linkages to Russia to their own advantage, and at Russian expense. Consequently, interstate rent-seeking opened up the possibility for various state and non-state actors in post-Soviet republics to convert external public losses into internal private benefits. Thus, Russian leverage and linkage could mutate the relations between donor and receiver. These rents had numerous origins, including: arbitrage opportunities contained in interstate trade and customs agreements; administratively stimulated demand for exports; foreign aid; negative interest credits; price imbalances; smuggling; barter agreements; and most importantly, discounted energy imports.

Belarus and Ukraine are the two transit countries through which Russia delivered energy (both oil and gas) to Europe. Their geographical location allowed both countries significant leverage over Russia, and the ability to extract significant rents. However, unlike resource-abundant economies in which rents are internal due to the abundance of oil and gas, here we deal with countries which must engage in interactions with rent-donors in order to obtain rent flows. Although seeking external rents might occur purely by chance, using a chaotic external environment to create various "rent havens" is a rather deliberative strategy. In a way, rents can be obtained via various asymmetrical contractual relations with external rent-providers, and may even be seen as an exchange. The provider supplies the rent flows to the receiver, and in turn obtains certain concessions. Those concessions could be numerous, potentially including political and ideological favors. Theoretically, this entails turning a rather static "non-taxed revenue" argument into a dynamic one, since the rentier states often have a capacity to seek, maximize and manipulate costs, and stabilize or institutionalize rent flows by creating certain linkages to rent-providers. One illustration of this was the proposal during the 1993 Massandra summit to write off Ukraine's gas debts to Russia, in exchange for the lease of the Sevastopol port and the sale of the Black Sea fleet to Russia. Another illustration is the purchase of Belarusian willingness to participate in integration projects with Russia (the Union State of Russia and Belarus, the Customs Union, and so forth) with generous energy grants.

All in all, the central pillars of my framework are the timing, ownership and stability of rents. The first of these is the "timing of external rents" hypothesis. This concerns the impact of external rents on political/economic developments, depending on the contexts (political and economic) in which the rents appeared. Simply put, it assumes that the timing of rents and reform sequences matter, and that external rents might have different impacts depending on the various stages of transformation. Secondly, I consider the "ownership/distribution of external rents" hypothesis. This assumes that external rents will have divergent impacts on political and economic developments, depending on whether their chief owners are state elements or competing private groups. These owners may include public or state actors, including incumbents and governments; various private actors; or alliances of business and administrative actors. Thirdly, the "costs of external rents" hypothesis mainly applies to the instances where the rents are external. The stability of the incumbent's expectations over the continuation of the external rent-flows hypothesis establishes a link between the reliance on rents and the political cost of external rent-seeking.

While the first hypothesis has a direct impact on the direction of institutional change in both political and economic domains, the second influences the stability and forms of institutional equilibriums. For those countries in which state incumbents/governments are the chief receivers/owners of rents, the political cost of rent-seeking (hereafter, costs of rents) and the perceived stability of rent flows (hereafter, stability of rents) are highly relevant. Conversely, in those countries where private actors own external rent flows, the design of political and economic institutions depends on the survival strategy of the incumbent, their management of cronies, and the infighting between the rent-seeking groups.

Below I will deal with these three considerations, sketch out the hypotheses and provide them with necessary justification.

Timing, ownership and cost/stability of rents

In the context of the hybrid political regime/state socialist mixed economy, the absence or reduction of cheap and stable external rents is likely to lead to economic liberalization and political democratization. Herein, there is a straightforward causal link: the loss or reduction of external rents entails economic crisis, and in turn incumbents have to implement welfare-improving reforms, in spite of their will or political beliefs. Conversely, in the context of the hybrid political regime/state socialist mixed economy, the perpetuation or expansion of cheap and stable external rent flows is likely to deter economic reforms and reinforce autocratic tendencies.

As was argued above, rents are believed to have stabilizing properties: according to this hypothesis, democracies endure by lowering taxation on the elites, while autocracies endure by redistributing and spending more on their societies.[18] Terry L. Karl argued that the effects of emerging rents depend upon the prior regime type: the more consolidated a democracy is when rents emerge, the less damaging the impact of discovering resources, such as oil, will be.[19] Extending this argument to the post-Soviet republics during periods of political and economic transition, timing of rent-expansion and rent-reduction may significantly impact the countries' pathways. The expansion of rents before any significant economic liberalization—before property was transferred into private hands—could serve as an alternative to politically dangerous liberal market reforms. Herein, the institutional circumstances, under which the rents kick in, largely determines the ownership of rents.

In the context of the state socialist mixed economy/hybrid political regime, **state ownership** of cheap and stable external rent flows is likely to dwarf political democratization and halt (or revert) economic reforms. Politically, democratization is likely to be dwarfed by the leverage of the incumbents who control rents (retaining state paternalism, coercion and consent). Economically, rents could be seen as anesthesia or a "survival kit" for the preservation of quasi-socialist economic institutions. Incumbents can use the rents to finance the inefficiencies of a wasteful economic structure, and secure their power positions through retaining high social spending, full employment, and state paternalism. This situation has the potential to develop into a rather stable equilibrium, and it explains well the path taken by Belarus.

Alternatively, in the context of the state socialist mixed economy/hybrid political regime, **private ownership** over external rent flows is likely to increase political competitiveness, deter autocratic backsliding, and entail partial reform. This equilibrium is rather unstable for two reasons. Firstly, competing rent-seekers are not pressed for side payments and care less about constituencies and public welfare; as such, there is the potential for popular dissent to topple the regime. Secondly, it is likely to result in a crisis of "overfishing" due to a lack of coordination.

The expansion of external rents when significant progress is made in destatization may lead to diverse outcomes. When socialist paternalism is replaced by unregulated market economies (as with Ukraine, which moved to a distorted market economy in 1996, and Russia some years earlier), the temporary "owners of the state," the incumbents and their cronies, become the owners of the external rents. Since the hybrid regime assumes low accountability, and the external rents unfold in the midst of a distorted market economy (due to predation, state capture or cronyism), the owners of rents are more often than not deaf—or even immune—to any electoral pressures for side payments. In this scenario, external rent flows may be fully appropriated by these grey oligarchic networks. Thus, the expansion of rents, when the state is captured by the "early winners," will likely not lead to a reverse of the reforms (that is, a return of sorts to socialism), but rather to the preservation of state captivity. Here, the impact of external rents will rather depend on a specific mode of interaction between the incumbents and their cronies, in the form of politically extended or restrained cronyism.[20] Likewise, the emergence of external rents in privately controlled sectors will likely increase the state's incentives to establish control over them, and this temptation will in all probability be acted upon by the state. Alternatively, when the ownership of rents remains under the control of feuding private groups, and the volume of rents possessed by each of the groups remains even, full-blown autocracy is unlikely, since the "winner takes all" situation is less likely than a "war of all against all." Overall, we can conclude that in this scenario, external rent-seeking may become extremely competitive.

Having described the potential linkages between the timing of rent expansion and political and economic change (via the variable "ownership/redistribution" of rents), it is important to consider what can induce potential changes in those countries where external rents are fully owned by the government, and have expanded before significant economic reforms were made. Under these premises, the first two interlinked variables come to the fore.

The first variable is the perceived costs of external rent-seeking ("costs of rent") and the second is the stability of the incumbent's expectation over the continuity of rent flows ("stability of rents").

Costs/stability of rents

Considerations regarding the costs of rent and stability of rents may be applied to cases in which the incumbents are the main owners of rents and are constrained by political accountability (whether this is an extended electoral accountability, or merely accountability to the groups of backers on whom the incumbent's political survival depends). In the context of a state socialist mixed economy/hybrid political regime, potentially high political costs (either real or perceived) of seeking rents from external actors (induced by either the excessive demands of external actors to be exchanged for rents, or the strong influence of groups whose interests are dwarfed by any external actors' demands) may minimize the incumbent's reliance on external rents and entail economic reform. Alternatively, in the context of a state socialist mixed economy/hybrid political regime, the high political costs (either perceived or real) of seeking rents from external actors may encourage the incumbent to pass the ownership of external rents to private actors, who are not bound by the issue of political survival and may thus disregard the costs.

Given that rent flows may emerge out of certain asymmetrical interstate contracts (both formal and informal) in which streams of rents are "purchased" with certain concessions, the incumbents are bound by the scope of issues which they can freely trade with the rent-provider without critically boosting the risk of being forced from office.

Political liability may spring from both the expansion of external rent-providers, and from the potential mobilization of domestic groups whose integral interests are betrayed and whose own resources are traded for external rent flows. The former may refer to a partial loss of independence and sovereignty, which results in a reduction in the scope of decision-making power for the incumbent. The latter refers to counter-pressures from groups with an anti-rent donor identity and conflicting interests. Therefore, the "cost of rent flows" represents the incumbent's *ex ante* calculations of the risk/reward ratio of external rent-seeking. The incumbents in this mode of interaction often have the capacity to alter the political cost of rent-seeking, either by playing off certain political and economic groups against each other within a country, or employing various forms of bargaining with the rent-provider in order to reduce the cost of external rents.

Apart from calculating the cost/profit/risk matrix, the second important factor is the incumbent's *ex ante* calculations of the stability of rents, in that any termination of rent flows will likely shatter the redistributing foundations of regime stability, and hence increase the risk of the incumbent's exit from office.[21] The incumbent should be rationally interested in stabilizing rent flows (institutionalizing them to make the flows more systematic and guaranteed) and reducing any risk of rent flow cessation. Rent flows risk management may include certain scenarios stretching from market-upholding measures[22] targeted at productive private sector growth (within certain politically appropriate limits) to creating linkages with other potential external rent-donors—such as the EU in the Ukrainian instance, or Venezuela in the Belarusian case.

Having interpreted Russian linkage and leverage through the prism of rents, we are left to consider Western leverage and linkage, along with the quality of political competition (which incorporates, for instance, nationalist movements and inter-elite feuds). When the quality of political competition is high, all competing actors have roughly equal resources and are likely to reach institutional compromises, resulting in a democratic stalemate. The appearance of the first independent variables—cheap and stable rents available for the government—is likely to decrease the quality of political competition and hinder democratization and market reform. However, the opposite may also be true: the presence of lively political competition (especially when nationalism is strong) may increase the political costs of external rent-seeking for the incumbent, and thus amplify the effects of the external rents.

Second, we may expect that cheap and stable external rents will diminish the impact of Western leverage and linkage, for the incumbents will have diminished market and political incentives to make credible commitments to the West. Alternatively, the presence of expensive and unstable external rents increases the role of Western leverage and linkage, which in turn promotes democratization and liberalization through the improved quality of political competition.

Having hypothesized the factors which might determine any departure from the institutional equilibrium of a hybrid political regime/state socialist mixed economy in the direction of further economic and political reforms, I have argued that the divergence between the cases might be rooted in the properties of external rent flows (including timing, ownership, redistribution, costs and stability). Table 16.1 consolidates the argument and links these variables to the empirical cases of the Russian, Ukrainian and Belarusian pathways.

Table 16.1. Rents in Russia, Ukraine, and Belarus

	Russia	Ukraine	Belarus
source of rents	domestic	domestic + external	external
timing of rents	after marketization	before marketization	before marketization
ownership of rents	centralized state pyramid	competing pyramids	centralized state pyramid
cost of rents	low	low	low
distribution of rents	self-enrichment	self-enrichment	welfare/social contract

Conclusion

As was mentioned in the beginning, the creation of a framework to explain the converging divergence between the pathways of Belarus, Russia and Ukraine was the main ambition of this chapter. As such, demonstrating the application of the framework to these three cases is a task for another article that would trace the processes in stages, and show the interplay of rents and the uneven distribution of property rights with particular political and economic outcomes.

This article makes a few theoretical contributions. First, it fuses political and economic institutions and sees their convergence in the dominance of uneven supply of property rights. As such, it treats Belarus, Ukraine and Russia as three instances of post-Soviet rent-seeking regimes. Second, it argues that various parameters of rent-seeking, such as timing, ownership, costs and stability of rents, have key value in determining the divergence of those regimes. Last but not least, it makes a step toward rethinking post-Soviet transitions in a non-teleological way, and may pave the way to further research on the region.

Notes

1. Marc A. Miles, Kim R. Holmes and Mary Anastasia O'Grady, *2006 Index of Economic Freedom* (Washington, DC: The Heritage Foundation, 2006).
2. Belarus and Ukraine were incorporated into the USSR in the 1920s; both were devastated by WWII, then modernized, urbanized, industrialized and Russified. Completely inexperienced with markets, democracy and the practices of modern independent statehood, both societies suffered from some forms of amnesia: they held insufficient knowledge of who they were, where they had come from and in which direction they were going. All three countries in this study scored very closely on certain structural indicators at the beginning of the 1990s: i) level of socioeconomic modernisation and level of human development; ii) level of socioeconomic inequality; iii) GDP per capita; iv) level of economic distortions; and v) percentage of urban population. Nonetheless, these three departed from each other dramatically in other ways.
3. See Bálint Magyar's chapter "Towards a terminology for post-communist regimes" in this volume.
4. Kiryl Haiduk, Elena Rakova, Vital Silitski, eds., *Social Contracts in Contemporary Belarus* (St. Petersburg: Nevsky Prostor, 2009).
5. Margarita M. Balmaceda, "Explaining the Management of Energy Dependency in Ukraine: Possibilities and Limits of a Domestic-Centered Perspective" (working paper no. 79, Mannheimer Zentrum für Europäische Sozialforschung, Mannheim, 2004).
6. Gordon Tullock, "Efficient rent-seeking," in *Toward a Theory of the Rent-Seeking Society*, ed. J. Buchanan, R. Tollison, and G. Tullock (College Station, TX: Texas A&M University Press, 1980), 3–15.
7. Amr Ismail Adly, "Politically-Embedded Cronyism: The Case of Post-Liberalization Egypt," *Business and Politics* 11, no. 4 (2009): 1–26. doi:10.2202/1469-3569.1268.
8. Peter Evans, *Embedded Autonomy: States and Industrial Transformation* (Princeton, NJ: Princeton University Press, 1995).
9. Joel S. Hellman "Winners Take All: The Politics of Partial Reform in Postcommunist Transitions," *World Politics* 50, no. 2 (1998): 203–34.
10. László Bruszt, "Market Making as State Making: Constitutions and Economic Development in Post-communist Eastern Europe," *Constitutional Political Economy* 13, no. 1 (2002): 53–72.
11. Adly, "Politically-Embedded Cronyism."
12. Hossein Mahdavy, "The Patterns and Problems of Economic Development in Rentier States: The Case of Iran," in *Studies in the Economic History of the Middle East*, ed. M.A. Cook (London, Oxford University Press, 1970), 428–67.
13. Terry L. Karl, "Understanding the Resource Curse," in *Covering Oil: A Reporter's Guide to Energy and Development*, ed. Svetlana Tsalik and Anya Schiffrin (New York: Open Society Institute, 2005), 21–26.
14. Michael L. Ross, "Does Oil Hinder Democracy?" *World Politics* 53, no. 3 (2001): 325–61.

[15] Hazem Beblawi, and Giacomo Luciani, eds., *The Rentier State* (London: Croom Helm, 1987); Karl, "Understanding the Resource Curse"; Pauline J. Luong, and Erika S. Weinthal, "Rethinking the Resource Curse: Ownership Structure, Institutional Capacity, and Domestic Constraints," *Annual Review of Political Science* 9 (2006): 241–63; Kevin M. Morrison, "Oil, Nontax Revenue, and the Redistributional Foundations of Regime Stability," *International Organization* 63, no. 1 (2009): 107–38; Ross, "Does Oil Hinder Democracy?"
[16] Daron Acemoglu and James A. Robinson, *Economic Origins of Dictatorship and Democracy* (Cambridge, UK: Cambridge University Press, 2006).
[17] Mahdavy, "The Patterns and Problems."
[18] Morrison, "Oil, Nontax Revenue."
[19] Karl, "Understanding the Resource Curse."
[20] Adly, "Politically-Embedded Cronyism."
[21] Morrison, "Oil, Nontax Revenue."
[22] Bruszt, "Market Making as State Making."

SARAH CHAYES

The Structure of Corruption:
A Systemic Analysis[*]

Introduction

Recent events have made corruption and its consequences difficult to ignore. In just the past few years, like a global rerun of the Arab Spring, mass protests have broken out in Brazil, Guatemala, Honduras, Hungary, Iraq, Lebanon, Malaysia, Moldova, Romania, South Korea and South Africa, among other countries, ultimately toppling a half dozen heads of government and threatening others. And those were hardly the most virulent demonstrations of corruption's destabilizing effects. It has fueled populist politics, including the election of Donald J. Trump as the 45th president of the United States; and its role in the rise of the self-proclaimed Islamic State or of the gangs that terrorize Central American neighborhoods is increasingly clear.

The issue has crept into mainstream focus in the West. In the wake of the 2014 Ukraine crisis, for example, the U.S. House of Representatives approved language authorizing the imposition of sanctions on officials "responsible for, or complicit in, or responsible for ordering . . . acts of significant corruption in the Russian Federation." Among the corrupt practices the original bill enumerated were "the expropriation of private or public assets for personal gain, corruption related to government contracts or the

---

[*] This chapter is a revised version of the text originally published as Sarah Chayes, *The Structure of Corruption: A Systemic Analysis Using Eurasian Cases* (Washington, DC: Carnegie Endowment for International Peace, Publications Department: June 2016). Courtesy of Carnegie Endowment for International Peace.

extraction of natural resources, bribery, or the facilitation or transfer of the proceeds of corruption to foreign jurisdictions."[1]

That's a fair list of the principal activities that make up corruption in this early twenty-first century. But corruption as it is currently manifested across much of the globe is not just a collection of disjointed practices indulged in by some—or even many—officials. In a striking number of countries, corruption represents the adaptive behavior of sophisticated structures. These structures have deliberately bent or crippled key elements of state function in order to capture important revenue streams, ensure impunity for network members, and provide opportunities to secure and flaunt the gains—in a world in which the accumulation and display of wealth has increasingly become the chief marker of social value and success.

The networks that perpetrate such whole or partial state capture frequently coalesce around a central kernel of kinship. They cross international boundaries and vertical echelons, and weave together public-sector (and state-owned-enterprise) and ostensibly private-sector actors with outright criminals, sometimes including violent religious extremists. But because the elaborate and purposeful nature of such structures has not drawn equally sophisticated study by those who would address the problem, remedial efforts often fail to make much impact.

Improved analysis could help guide more effective anticorruption initiatives. It must be informed by an intimate, on-the-ground understanding of the personnel and practices of the local kleptocratic networks and their international interlocutors, with attention to a calendar of internal and external events that might provide opportunities for—or thwart—initiatives.

To assist such analysis, a common framework of questions and a way of organizing the resulting information could help shape inquiry, improve legibility, and facilitate cross-country analysis, comparison, and action. Azerbaijan, Kyrgyzstan, and Moldova, alongside examples from elsewhere, model such a framework in the following pages, illustrating its key elements, typical country-specific divergences, and some knotty problems encountered during research, which would require further elaboration for a comprehensive examination of these or other countries.

These focus countries were deliberately selected to reflect different degrees of evident authoritarianism and different relationships with the European Union (EU) and other Western partners. The information provided here is derived from the practical experience of civil society groups on the ground (representatives of which met for a three-day workshop in September 2015 to launch this effort) together with more traditional research methods. A noticeable tightening of repression in Kyrgyzstan—including against some of the participants—made it the most difficult to depict in up-to-date detail. In any case, a definitive analysis would require more granular, on-the-ground research employing a variety of investigative techniques. These countries' role here is largely illustrative.

The Analytical Framework

Devising effective anticorruption approaches to countries like these requires digging beneath the narratives of their unique and divergent histories to find underlying structures. Tailored remedies require an understanding of the way each kleptocratic network has harnessed elements of state function to its own purposes and has exploited its circumstances and those willing to enable its activities. To gain such an understanding, it is helpful to apply a common set of questions to each situation, and depict the results as clearly as possible.

Any such depiction will, of course, represent a compromise: between clarity and detail, multidimensional realities and two-dimensional representations, well-founded suspicions and hard proof. Visually, the infographics that follow (see Gallery) may suggest separation between the sectors of what are in fact deeply interpenetrated networks. Some compromises had to be made in the interests of visual clarity. The shape chosen, reminiscent of a chemical molecule, is meant to imply that the three main elements form an inextricable whole, whose properties derive from its interconnected structure. Educated guesses will sometimes have to stand in for firm pronouncements about what are constantly shifting, but remarkably resilient structures. Nevertheless, the following provides a basic, if inevitably incomplete, entry point.

If corruption is seen as the deliberate practice of one or more networks of interrelated individuals that are at least somewhat organized, then the network structures and modes of operation should be ascertained and depicted in as much detail as possible, through answers to the questions below.

1. Does a single network dominate?

In the case of Azerbaijan, given regime continuity reaching back before the collapse of the Soviet Union, the answer seems to be yes. Still, some separation does exist between the networks controlled by the families of Ilham Aliyev and of his wife, Mehriban, born into the powerful Pashayev family.[2] President Aliyev must manage the competition. In the Azerbaijan infographic, therefore, the blue circle representing government elements of the network is labeled with the names of both of the leading families, to reflect the divided authority. (See Figure A.1.)

Moldova seems to present an entirely different picture. It is by far the most democratic of the three countries examined here. As of 2014, Moldova has been bound to the European Union by an association agreement. Civil society activists have taken over neighborhoods in the capital without serious fallout.

And yet, Moldova's kleptocratic network appears to be almost as unitary as Azerbaijan's. According to local and international experts, the separation that once existed between the larger and more powerful group controlled by Vladimir Plahotniuc, whose business empire covers banking, oil, and high-end real estate, and the smaller one structured around former prime minister Vladimir Filat had largely collapsed by 2016.

Unlike the situation in many other highly corrupt countries, Moldova's network is not dominated by a chief of state. Plahotniuc holds no government office, but from outside official institutions has managed to stack government structures with either his cronies or individuals too weak to threaten his operations. Perhaps reacting to—but reinforcing—this reality, international interlocutors sometimes seem to treat him as a stand-in for the government.[3]

The Moldova infographic illustrates this specificity by displaying the network leader's name not in the blue government circle, but in the green circle, which represents private-sector network elements. (Figure C.1)

> *1.1. How dependent is the network's functioning on the person of the chief of state? Or instead, is there a significant cadre of network members who could re-combine and retain their grip on the economy and key aspects of political function if the network is decapitated?*

This is an important question in the context of many dramatic anti-corruption transitions that have failed to generate systemic change. The identities, contexts, and inclinations of likely successors to the current ruling networks merit exploration in as much detail as possible. For, as recent events in Egypt, Guatemala, Tunisia, and Ukraine demonstrate, even networks that seem clearly to be dominated by a single individual display a remarkable ability to rebound after he and his family members disappear from the scene. The mechanisms by which that resilience is achieved should be carefully examined.[4]

In the case of Moldova, the identity of the chief of state is nearly irrelevant to the network's functioning. President Nicolae Timofti has complained of Plahotniuc's aggressive interference in political affairs.[5] Moldova's degree of formal democracy may not, therefore, be as important a factor shaping its real political economy as it appears.

In Azerbaijan, the person of President Aliyev is clearly central to the functioning of the current network.

1.2. How important is kinship to the network structures?

Family ties (principally relatives of Aliyev on the one hand, and his wife, born Pashayeva, on the other)[6] are key to dominance within Azerbaijan's allied network. The complex web of companies the Panamanian law firm Mossack Fonseca established for the Aliyevs was remarkable for the degree to which the entities were layered and fractured. The couple's children and other young or more distant relatives were built in as subsidiary beneficiaries of the fortune being amassed by the joint network.[7]

1.3. To what extent does competition exist within the dominant network?

Competition is a fact of life in this kind of system, animated as it is largely by self-interest. Even in Azerbaijan, evidence of rivalries can be discerned. They are far more pronounced in Kyrgyzstan. Both outside of President Atambayev's circle and even within it, considerable rivalries pit players against each other. This sometimes kaleidoscopic friction is greatest across the country's north-south ethnic and political divides, where conflict erupted in 2010.

Such identity-based cleavages often exacerbate the tendency for kleptocratic governance to fuel outright violence, as has been the case in Iraq and Syria. Canny network chiefs, like Syria's Bashar al-Assad or the Karzais in Afghanistan, often take pains to federate the top layer of their networks across these ethnic or sectarian cleavages, so as to co-opt at least some part of out-group elites. But perhaps because today's information technology and social media facilitate the organization of leaderless movements in which elite direction is no longer requisite, such efforts have in neither case succeeded in maintaining peace or restoring it once violence has broken out.

2. Where one network does not dominate, do relatively evenly matched networks peacefully coexist?

Pakistan is one of the rare example of such a set-up. There, military and civilian kleptocratic networks essentially divide up the cake, while criticizing each other publicly. Kyrgyzstan is the only country examined here that might be seen to fit this model, though competition or taking turns perhaps more accurately characterizes the relations among networks, rather than shared spoils or coexistence.

2.1. In the case of multiple networks, how contentious is their rivalry?

In Egypt, the 2011 revolution brought down an up-and-coming private-sector crony-capitalist network woven around then-President Hosni Mubarak's son Gamal in favor of an older military network. The latter, under the leadership of President Abdel Fattah el-Sisi, now dominates. A less intense degree of rivalry pits Thailand's economic elites against a military network empowered in a 2014 coup. In more chaotic countries, such as Somalia, the kleptocratic competition itself may be a main cause of chronic conflict. The obvious competition between the Moldovan networks of "the Two Vlads" has been largely conducted via leaks and judicial proceedings; in Kyrgyzstan, such competition arguably helped fuel the violence of 2010.

3. What elements of state function have been deliberately bent or distorted by the networks with the aim of extracting resources and/or ensuring compliance?

Corruption is still largely understood as the work of separate individuals, and as parasitic on government function—as a cancer or corrosion eating away at government institutions. In reality, in dozens of countries on almost every continent, corruption has become the central principle structuring governments. Ministries or government agencies become a set of instruments in the hands of the kleptocratic networks, harnessed for the purpose of sustaining and maximizing their personal revenues and assuring their impunity. (For the Moldovan example, see Figure C.2.)

Given the importance of impunity to the kleptocratic bargain that typically connects subordinate officials to their superiors—some proportion of the cash corruptly amassed in exchange for freedom from repercussions—the judicial branch is almost always at least partially captured.

Tax authorities frequently serve coercive purposes alongside their usual revenue-generation duties. In Tunisia, when Zine el-Abidine Ben Ali was president, even the Ministry of Agriculture or the local water department might play a role, as, for example, when network insiders sought to obtain high-quality dates for export at below-market prices.[8] There, as in Moldova, a compliant central bank allowed for network looting of private financial institutions.[9]

In resource-rich countries, oil ministries, or ministries of energy or mining, are almost always placed under direct network control. In Kyrgyzstan, hydroelectricity and the Ministry of Energy and Industry play a poorer but similar role to that of oil, the State Oil Company of the Azerbaijan Republic (SOCAR), and the Ministry of Energy in Azerbaijan.

Note that this question overlaps to some degree with another below on identifying which revenue streams are captured. In some cases, a judgment call will be required to determine to which category an agency or branch of government should be assigned. Kyrgyzstan's Ministry of Finance, for example, can be understood both as a repurposed element of state function that serves to ensure docility, and as the provider of revenue for the personal benefit of the network, through manipulation of customs enforcement.

According to several interviewees, the Moldovan Ministry of Economy fulfills a similar dual function, not only by way of differential tax and customs enforcement but also by requiring national utility companies to pass electricity or telecom services by way of network-affiliated intermediaries, which skim off some proportion of the rates being paid.[10] In the case of electricity, those rates rose by about one-third over just a few months at the end of 2015 and the beginning of 2016.[11]

Anticorruption agencies or economic crime investigations units are often cynically aimed against the opponents of a corrupt regime. The effect is not just to intimidate potential reformers but also to confuse the broader population (and sometimes international donors). Many Central and Eastern European civil society activists have decried the hijacking of the anticorruption narrative—and coercive tools—by kleptocratic networks.

Moldova's National Anticorruption Center is believed to keep files on various government officials and is criticized for preferentially targeting those who buck the Plahotniuc line. The Economic Crime Unit of the National Inspectorate of Investigations plays a similar role, with senior officers ensuring impunity by tampering with evidence.[12] According to civil society participants in this mapping exercise, the Special Operations Department collects information on potential Plahotniuc rivals and is sometimes deployed in ways designed to intimidate.

3.1. What instruments of coercion or violence do the networks rely upon to enforce discipline, both on network members and on the population at large, especially activists or media?
The Moldovan example leads directly to this sub-question on the use of physical force. From a security perspective for local activists—but also for international providers of military assistance, or training or capacity building for local police—it is critical to answer this question with precision. Careful intelligence collection and analysis should be devoted to understanding the real connections between informal armed groups operating in civilian clothes and official security structures.

It is important to remember, however, that sometimes the mere threat of violence or job-loss is sufficient to intimidate network members or the population at large.

3.2. What elements of state function have been deliberately crippled, allowed to languish or else cannibalized for the revenue streams they provide?

Here, overlap with the revenue-streams question below may be especially significant, as some branches of government may be disabled as a by-product of the theft of their budgets, rather than deliberately to advance a separate strategic objective. There is no reason not to double-list some branches or agencies of government to assist in forming a nuanced understanding. Egregious examples include the kleptocratic pillaging of the Iraqi and Nigerian militaries in 2014, which made them incapable of countering the Islamic State and Boko Haram, respectively.

4. How vertically integrated are the kleptocratic networks?

Too often, corruption is considered piecemeal, and so-called petty corruption, perpetrated against ordinary people by low-level civil servants, is dismissed as insignificant or "part of the culture," or is explained away by low salaries. In fact, in almost every case of severe and structured corruption, strong vertical connectivity is integral to the system. (For examples, see Figures A.2 and C.2.)

Typically, this integration takes the form of payments by subordinate echelons to their superiors either of a percentage of the bribes or kickbacks they extort (in money or in kind) or of a lump sum up front to obtain the government positions they hold—in effect, the purchase of office—or both.[13] In impoverished Afghanistan, by way of comparison, extorted bribes are estimated to total well more than $2 billion per year.[14] The usual recompense for such payments up the line and other forms of obedience is protection from any repercussions for corrupt and other criminal practices. In this context, civil servants' salaries may be kept low deliberately, so as to prime the pump that powers the upward flow of cash.

In Azerbaijan, this familiar vertical integration features a remarkable element. Civil society activists report that bribes (or spurious fines) collected at street level are sent upward as usual, but then are pooled centrally and shared back downward with street-level officials as bonuses, known as "envelope salaries."[15] While the practice has reportedly diminished amid the precipitous drop in oil prices, such informal top-ups are a critical income support for the significant numbers of (underpaid) government workers, who represent more than half of the active population, according to official statistics.[16] Such a system reinforces personal dependency on superiors. By the same token, a sudden, sharp drop-off in the downward distribution of benefits like these could give rise to aggrieved reactions on the part of an important segment of the population.

To illustrate the vertically integrated nature of these systems, these infographics include small circles to represent subordinate government echelons.

5. How horizontally integrated are the networks?

Political leaders, diplomats, legal and development practitioners, and investors often place private- and public-sector actors in separate conceptual categories, with criminals—not to mention terrorists—in an entirely different bag. Any overlaps are usually treated as abnormalities.

Reinforcing these distinctions, outsiders interacting with each sector usually belong to separate structures themselves. While international law enforcement may be poring over the identities of and interconnections among illicit actors, businesses normally try to avoid those individuals. Within partner governments, commerce ministries or trade representatives spearhead relations with the private sector, while diplomats and military officers interact with their counterparts, and development agencies may focus on local civil society organizations.

Even the far savvier activists or members of the population inside corrupt countries may unconsciously presume the groups are more distinct than they really are. Unpaid employees of a short-lived mining company in Azerbaijan petitioned multiple government agencies for help finding their employer and securing their back pay, ranging from the Ministry of Ecology and Natural Resources to the office of the president himself, to no avail. The Panama Papers revealed that the owners of the delinquent company were none other than the daughters of President Ilham Aliyev himself.[17]

To correctly understand the operations of today's kleptocratic networks, therefore, it is critical to see them as integrated, if sometimes loosely structured, entities that fully straddle all sectors of ostensibly licit as well as clearly illicit activities.

Figure A.1.

Infographic. The Structure of Kleptocracy in Azerbaijan

This diagram, especially its central elements, is meant to depict a fully interpenetrated network. The apparent separation visible here represents a compromise to ease understanding.

AZERBAIJAN

Azerbaijan presents a fairly clear example of a single dominant network, with some separation between the networks controlled by the families of President Ilham Aliyev and his wife, Mehriban Pashayeva Aliyeva. Aliyev must manage and occasionally discipline competition, however, as in the October 2015 purge of the Ministry of State Security. This network is vertically integrated in a remarkable way: observers describe what they call a bribe-pooling system, whereby bribes and spurious fines extorted at street level are sent upward and pooled centrally, and then a portion is redistributed back down in the form of so-called envelope salaries. The networks are also horizontally integrated, especially into massive holding companies that are composed of subsidiaries in a variety of lucrative economic sectors.

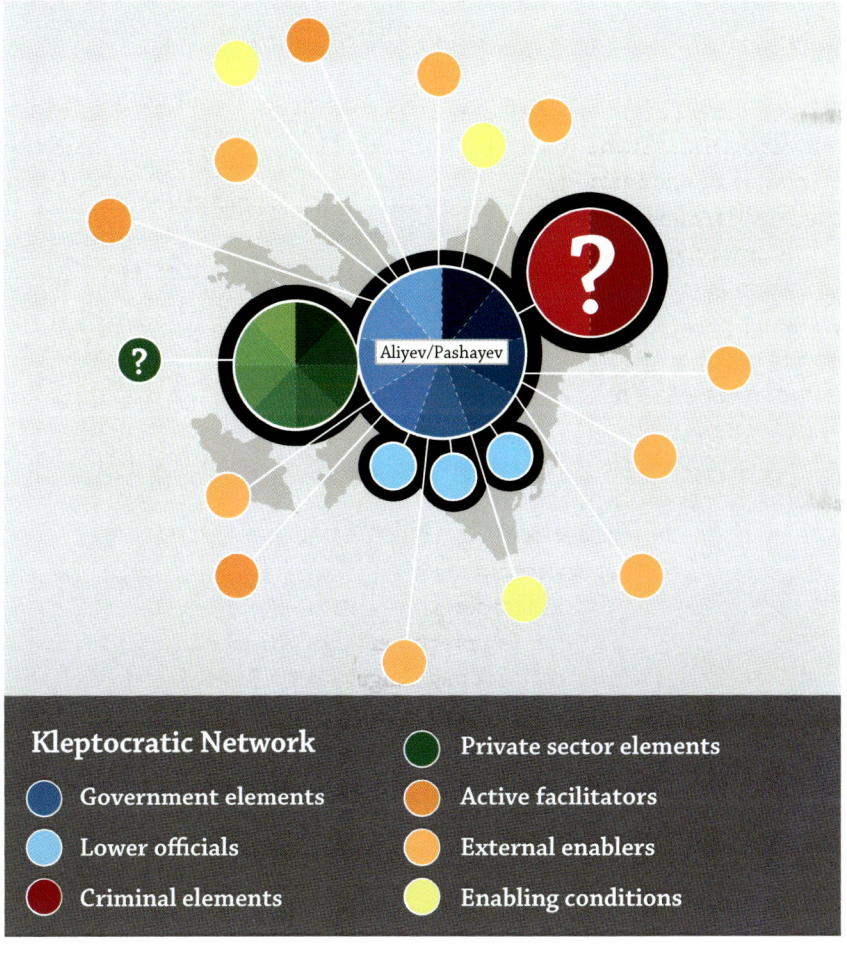

Kleptocratic Network
- Government elements
- Lower officials
- Criminal elements
- Private sector elements
- Active facilitators
- External enablers
- Enabling conditions

Figure A.2.

The Structure of Kleptocracy in Azerbaijan: Government Elements

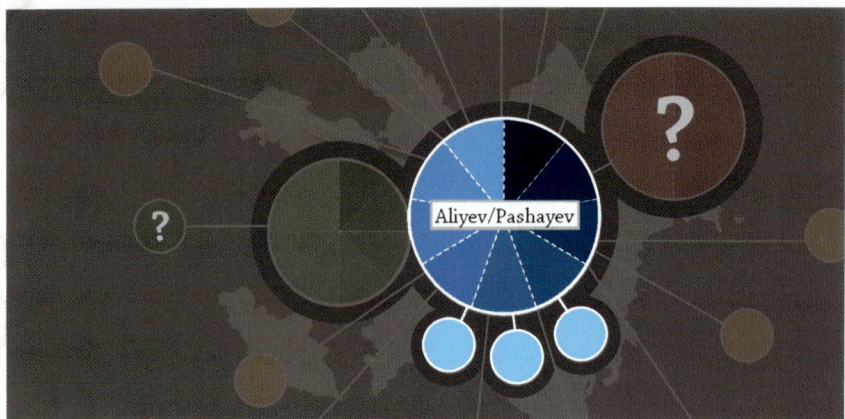

The elements of state function that are key to Aliyev/Pashayev network operations include most of the main ministries, especially:

▶ **Ministry of Energy**
In particular the State Oil Company of the Azerbaijan Republic (SOCAR), the national oil company.

▶ **Ministry of Internal Affairs**
Controls the police. In particular, the specialized unit on organized crime and the Special State Protection Service.

▶ **State Security Service**
One of the two reconstituted intelligence agencies that were left after the December 2015 dissolution of the Ministry of National Security.

▶ **Judicial Branch**
Including the prosecutor general. Widely seen to provide justice for sale, reducing sentences or fines and "disappearing" evidence for payment. Also relied upon by the Aliyev network to discipline dissidents or recalcitrant or independent-minded network members.

▶ **Ministry of Taxes**
Presses tax-evasion charges. The minister, Fazil Mammadov, also plays a role in structures controlling at least one of the Aliyev's conglomerates, Ata Holding.

▶ **Customs Committee**
A cabinet-level office, seen to protect Aliyev/Pashayev-linked monopolies.

▶ **Army**
Some close Aliyev/Pashayev associates hold high positions. Even the threat of force becomes a powerful coercive tool.

▶ **Ministry of Emergency Situations**
Charged with protecting the population from natural and man-made disasters. Oversees security installations and mining and oil facilities, as well as construction licensing. Disposes of significant infrastructure contracts. Ties to Customs Committee.

▶ **Central Election Commission**
Believed to execute various forms of electoral fraud, such as carousel voting, and to ensure participation by civil servants, including teachers.

Figure A.3.

The Structure of Kleptocracy in Azerbaijan: Private Sector Elements

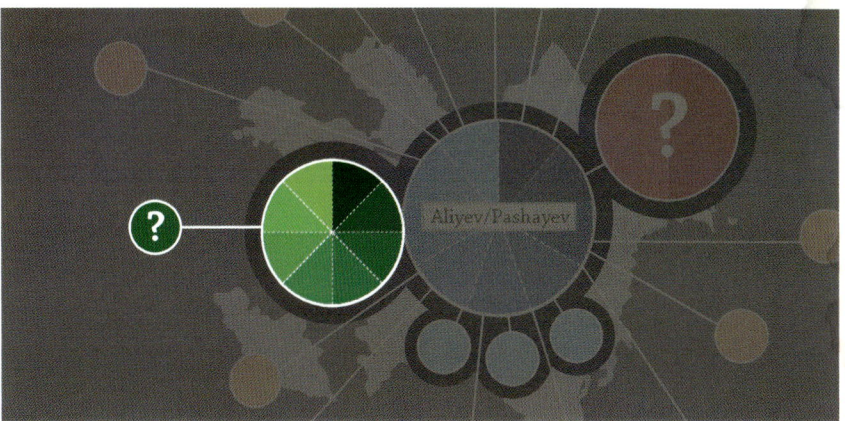

The main private sector network elements include:

▸ **Banks***
Such as Ata Bank, Kapital Bank, Pasha Bank, and Silk Way Bank.

▸ **Construction***
DIA Holding, Pasha Construction (part of Pasha Holding), and Silk Way Construc-tion, for example. Offshore companies such as Arbor Investments, LaBelleza Holdings, the Harvard Management Ltd., and the DDLAR Group controlled by children of the Aliyevs or other senior officials have also won major construction bids.

▸ **Oil and gas supply chain**
Including contractors for such state-owned companies as SOCAR and Azerenergy—often overlapping with construction companies listed above.

▸ **Mining**

▸ **Telecommunications**
Especially Azerfon.

▸ **Tourism and hospitality**
Such as AtaTravel and Excelsior Hotel Baku, also part of Ata Holding.

▸ **Charity**
Especially the Heydar Aliyev Foundation.

▸ **Food processing**
Via Azersun Holding, for example, controlled by Aliyev confidants Hassan and Abdolbari Goozal.

● **Turkish business interests?**

*Note: These large holding companies often include several subsidiaries, extending into different sectors of the economy. Construction and banking are particularly tightly interwoven.

Figure A.4.

The Structure of Kleptocracy in Azerbaijan: Criminal Elements

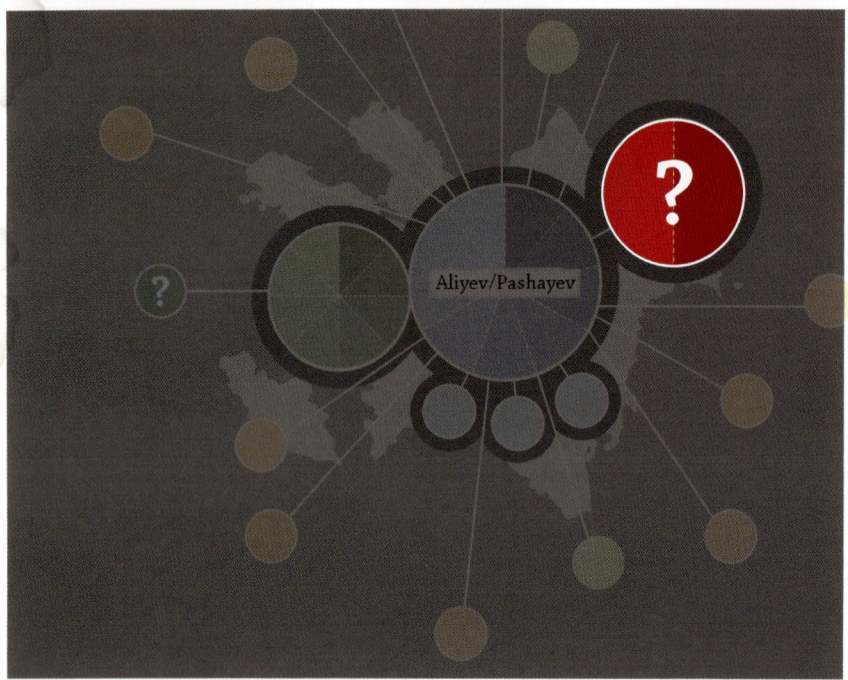

While no documentary evidence has been found proving links between the Aliyev/Pashayev network and drug or human trafficking, interviews with law enforcement personnel indicate collusion. The networks' control of other lucrative activities is suggestive.

▶ **Drugs?**   ▶ **Human Trafficking**

Figure A.5.

The Structure of Kleptocracy in Azerbaijan: Active Facilitators

Some significant external facilitators are:

- **Law firms and business registry services**
  Provided by specialized firms such as Malaysia-based Naziq & Partners, or Portcullis in Singapore, or London-based Child & Child.

- **Offshore banks**
  The key locations where corrupt Azerbaijani officials keep their money include Britain (London and the British Overseas Territories), the Czech Republic, Dubai, Malta, Switzerland, Turkey, and the United States.

- **Shell company domiciling**
  Some Aliyev-linked companies have been reported to be domiciled in the British Virgin Islands, Dubai, and Singapore.

Figure A.6.

The Structure of Kleptocracy in Azerbaijan: External Enablers

The main external enablers are:

- **International oil and gas industry**
  Given the role played by the oil revenues in enriching members of the Aliyev/Pashayev networks, this industry serves as an important enabler, wittingly or not. Key companies invested in Azerbaijan include BP, Chevron, ExxonMobil, Türkiye Petrolleri AO, and Japan's Inpex and Itochu. France's Total is expanding activities in the gas sector. Contractors such as KBR that do business with SOCAR can be included in this category.

- **European organizations**
  These organizations, including the Council of Europe, have bolstered Azerbaijan's image through high-visibility events such as the European Games and Eurovision Song Contest, held in Baku in 2015 and 2012, respectively.
  The construction projects associated with these events were largely captured by network-linked businesses.

- **Washington lobbyists**
  Azerbaijan has been a high spender among foreign countries lobbying in Washington, but the main lobbyist, Anar Mammadov, son of powerful Transport Minister Ziya Mammadov, curtailed his U.S. operation in 2015. Azerbaijan's embassy or other entities such as SOCAR USA have retained the Podesta Group, Roberti Global, Bob Lawrence & Associates, and others. The Azerbaijan America Alliance has also been active and works closely with the Congressional Azerbaijan Caucus. As is the case with European officials, U.S. officials are often wooed with generous trips, or offers of caviar.

- **International construction companies**
  Notably UK businesses.

- **Western real estate agents**
  Corrupt Azerbaijani officials buy property in Britain, Switzerland, and Turkey, among other countries.

- **Russia**
  Azerbaijan's chief weapons supplier (Israel also cooperates with Azerbaijan on defense and intelligence).

- **Turkey**
  Plays a significant enabling role, most visibly in its partnership in the Baku-Tbilisi-Ceyhan oil pipeline and the agreement for a new trans-Anatolian pipeline. This infrastructure is meant to secure Azerbaijan's position as a non-Russian supplier of gas to Europe, while Turkish companies executing pipeline-related projects are believed to be paying kickbacks to the Ministry of Emergency Situations among others, and might be considered external network members.

Figure A.6.

- **Georgia**
  To the extent that Georgia has made it somewhat more difficult for Azerbaijanis—especially activists—to travel back and forth or stay safely in Georgia, it is enabling Azerbaijani corrupt practices.

Figure A.7.

The Structure of Kleptocracy in Azerbaijan: Enabling Condition

The main enabling conditions are:

- **European desire for non-Russian sources of energy.**

- **Simmering conflict with Armenia over Nagorno-Karabakh.**
  Opportunity to distract the population and increase restrictions on civil liberties.

- **Access to statutory salaries of civil servants**
  Can be tapped in times of a budget shortfall.

Figure A.8.

The Structure of Kleptocracy in Azerbaijan: Revenue Streams

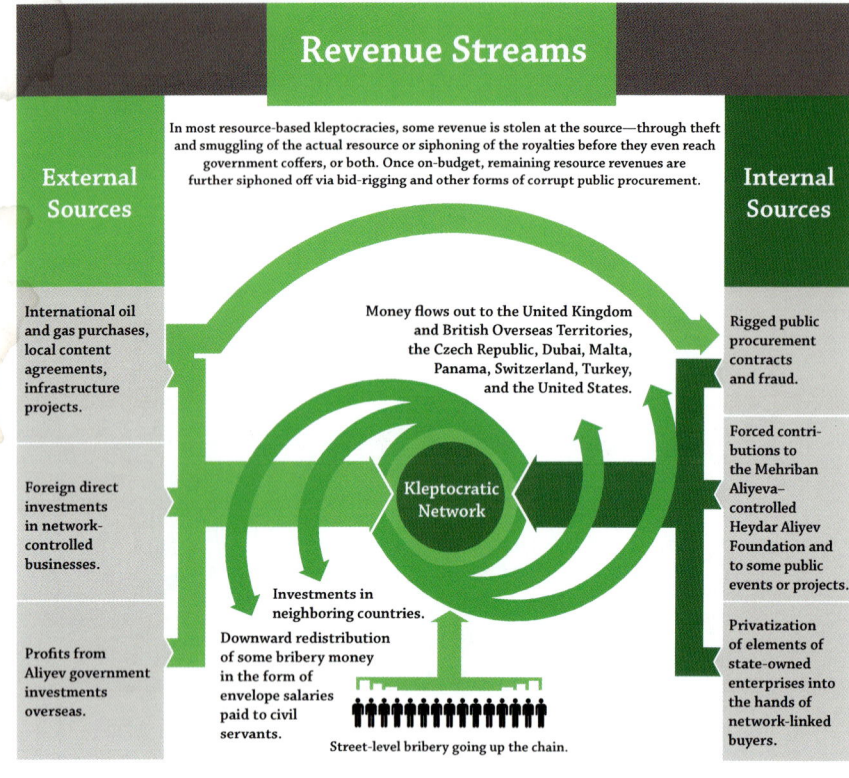

Figure B.1.

Infographic. The Structure of Kleptocracy in Kyrgyzstan

This diagram, especially its central elements, is meant to depict a fully interpenetrated network. The apparent separation visible here represents a compromise to ease understanding.

KYRGYZSTAN

A new constitution enacted on the heels of an anticorruption revolution in 2010 has increased the degree of competition among rival corrupt networks in Kyrgyzstan. Both outside President Almazbek Atambayev's circle and even within it, considerable rivalry pits members against each other. The friction is greater across the country's north-south ethnic and political divides. Elections in 2017 may mark an important transition, since, according to the constitution, Atambayev may not run for a second term. Competing networks are likely to seek to replace him. The current ruling network displays vertical integration, with a portion of street-level bribes paid up the line in return for impunity guaranteed by a notoriously corrupt judicial sector.

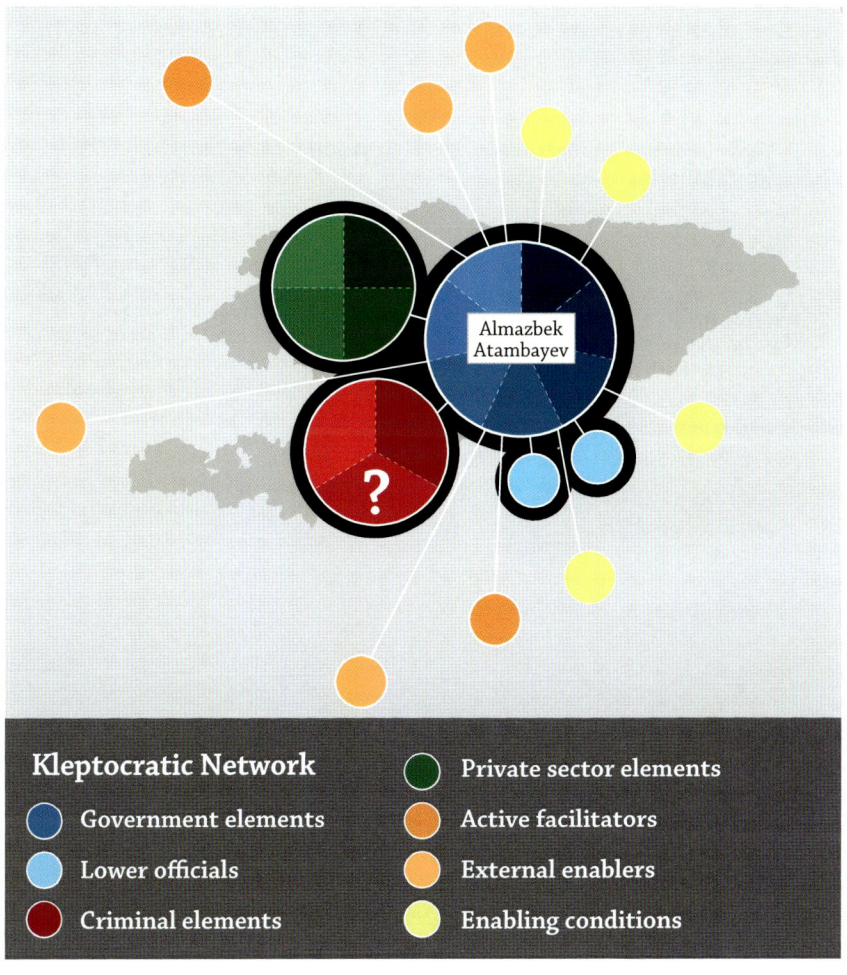

Figure B.2.

The Structure of Kleptocracy in Kyrgyzstan: Government Elements

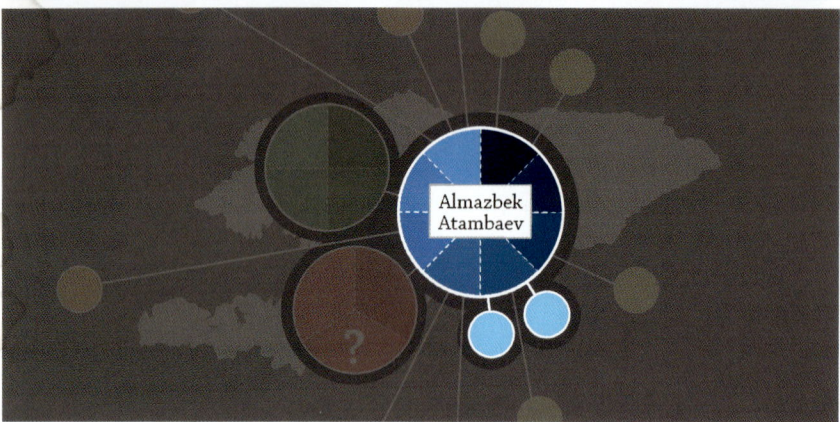

The elements of state function that are key to network operations include:

▶ **Ministry of Finance**

▶ **Ministry of Economic Development and Trade**
Especially for purposes of customs enforcement and non-enforcement.

▶ **Ministry of Interior**
With a variety of specialized branches, including a rapid-reaction unit known as Spetsial'nyi Otriad Bistrogo Reagirovaniia, or SOBR. For intimidation purposes.

▶ **Ministry of State Security**
Including its National Security Service.

▶ **Judicial branch**
Including the constitutional court and state prosecution.

▶ **Ministry of Energy and Industry**
Especially with regard to exporting hydropower, rate-padding, and establishing connections to the grid for businesses as well as residential customers.

▶ **Parliament**
Insufficiently checks the operations of the kleptocratic network, especially given the rule permitting parliamentarians to designate colleagues to vote in their place in case of absence from the chamber. A number of parliamentarians may be using political office to get into the corruption business on their own.

▶ **Local officials**
Including municipal land bureaus accused of illegally expropriating land via falsified documents. The practices of the Land Redistribution Fund, which controls some 25 percent of arable agricultural land, are contested.

Figure B.3.

The Structure of Kleptocracy in Kyrgyzstan: Private Sector Elements

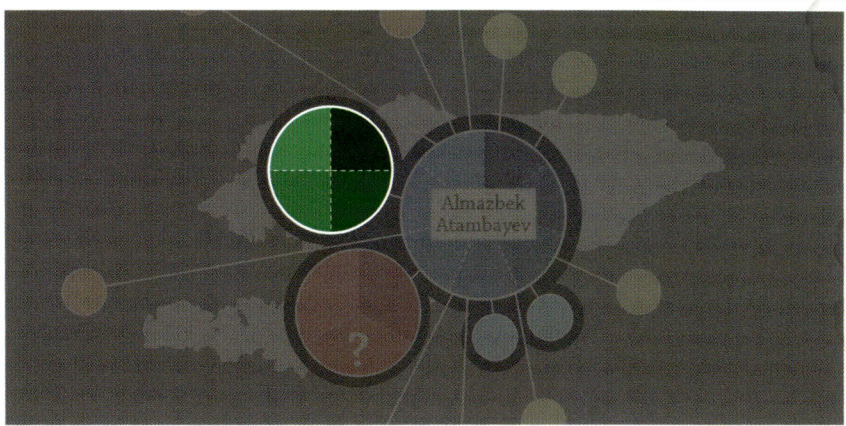

The main private sector network elements include:

▶ **Construction industry**
Companies under network control are believed to provide kickbacks and to benefit from sweetheart deals for buildings and infrastructure projects (including power generation and transmission) funded largely by external development partners. Often building materials are observed to be shoddy and the resulting structures left empty.

▶ **Mining and associated enterprises**
Gold represents some 10 percent of GDP, but output fell dramatically in early 2016.

▶ **Electricity generation and supply companies**
The various joint stock companies (JSCs) that manage electricity generation and distribution are almost entirely state-owned. The board of directors of Electric Power Plants, the electricity generation JSC, for example, includes a member of the Bishkek City Council among other officials; the chairman was a close confidant of Askar Akayev when he was president. The sector is infamous for corruption.

▶ **Consumer goods import-export and retailers**
Until Kyrgyzstan's 2015 accession to the Russian-sponsored Eurasian Economic Union (EEU), the re-export business, exploiting a tariff differential on Chinese imports between Kyrgyzstan and Kazakhstan, was highly profitable. The full impact of joining the EEU is not yet clear.

Figure B.4.

The Structure of Kleptocracy in Kyrgyzstan: Criminal Elements

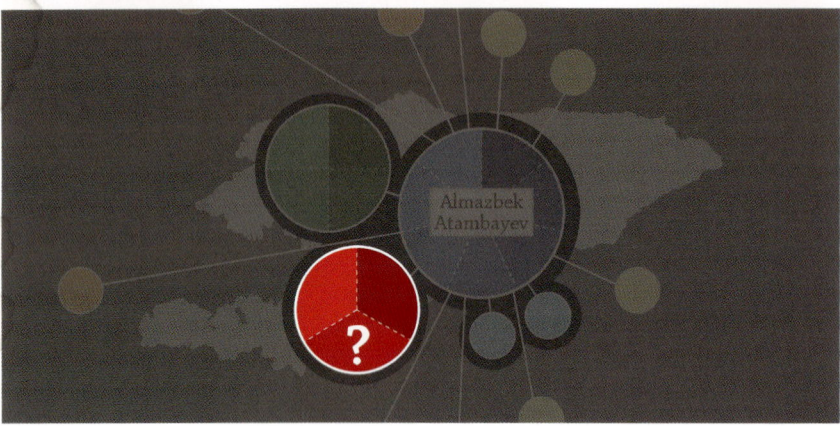

Criminal sector integration into kleptocratic networks is quite clear in Kyrgyzstan, though adherence to the Russian-sponsored EEU has disrupted smuggling patterns.

▶ **Narcotics traffickers**
Kyrgyzstan represents a significant transshipment zone for Afghan opiates, among other drugs, especially traveling toward Russia and China. According to some estimates, around 20 percent of Afghan opium production is trafficked through Kyrgyzstan. Atambayev's predeces-sor, Kurmanbek Bakiyev, deliberately disabled the nation's Drug Control Agency.

▶ **"Thugs?"**
These informal instruments of force and intimidation may have stronger ties to criminal groups than government officials, but they seem to be at the disposal of the integrated networks. Journalists and civil society activists report stepped-up harass-ment by such difficult-to-identify operatives in 2016.

▶ **Consumer goods smugglers**
These actors are key to networks' ability to exploit tariff differentials or evade customs altogether for consumer goods sold in Kyrgyzstan or re-exported. But this activity has been disrupted by Kyrgyzstan's 2015 adherence to the EEU, reducing customs barriers at its borders.

Figure B.5.

The Structure of Kleptocracy in Kyrgyzstan: Active Facilitators

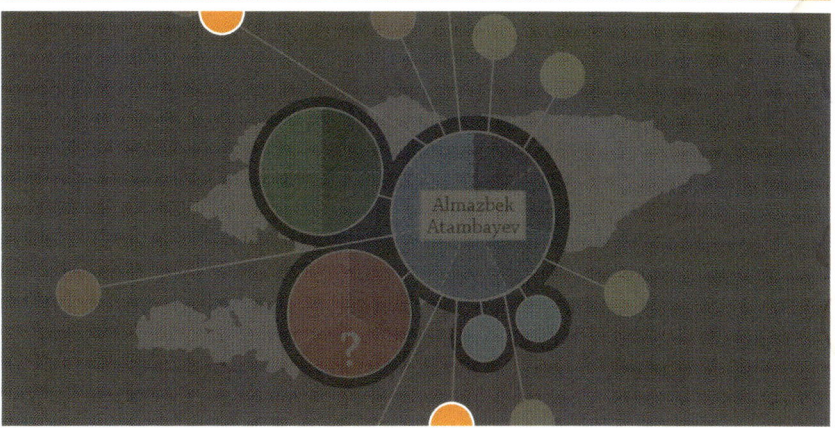

Some significant external facilitators are:

- **Latvian banks**
  These banks have been found to play an intermediate role in placing corrupt Kyrgyz assets offshore.

- **Shell company domiciling services**
  Providers, such as the Belize-based International Corporate Services Limited, are also located in the UK and Ireland.

Figure B.6.

The Structure of Kleptocracy in Kyrgyzstan: External Enablers

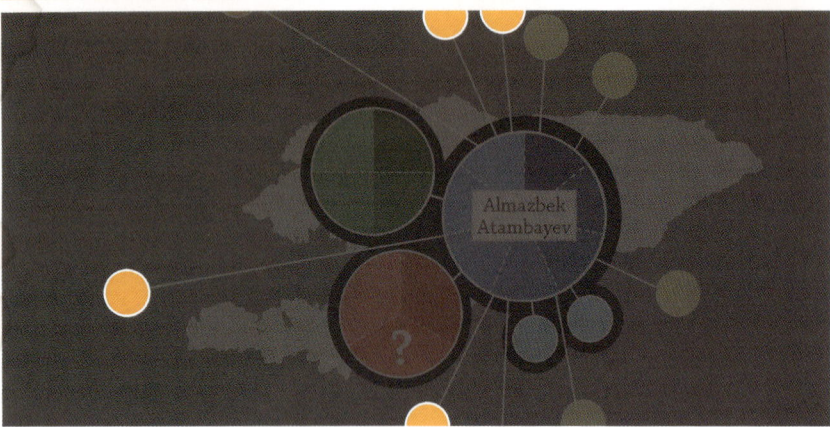

The main external enablers are:

- **The Russian government**
Moscow has provided a number of long-term loans, and has invested in Kyrgyz infrastructure projects. Significant entanglement with Kyrgyz networks is reported.

- **Infrastructure loans**
Major infrastructure projects represent a revenue stream for Kyrgyz networks when network-affiliated businesses capture the contracts or—as in the case of hydroelectrici-ty—the benefits of the project. So the provision of grants or even loans without detailed conditions and reinforced oversight may constitute an enabler. Loans provided by multistakeholder funds managed by financial professionals lacking a development lens or practice are particularly vulnerable.

- **Overseas security and development assistance and loans from development banks**
Support is currently provided by EU institutions, Germany, Japan, Switzerland, Turkey, and the United States, among others. Even in cases where development assistance is spent on such humanitarian priorities as health or electoral reform, it may bolster regime prestige.

- **Luxury real estate agents**

Figure B.7.

The Structure of Kleptocracy in Kyrgyzstan: Enabling Conditions

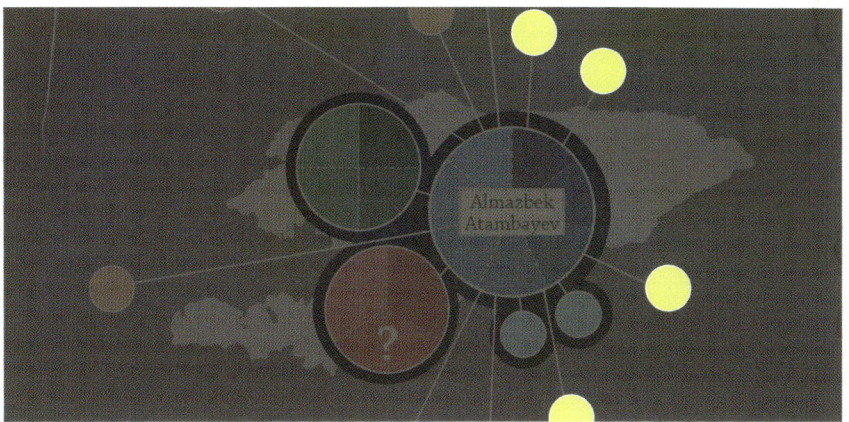

Some of the conditions that Kyrgyz networks may exploit are:

- **Remittances**
  Mostly from Kyrgyz working in Russia; estimated at up to 30 percent of GDP.

- **Porous border with Tajikistan**
  Eases narcotics trafficking.

- **Strategic location**
  Allowed the Kyrgyz government to bid up the competition between the United States and Russia for use of the Manas air base, especially during the height of the war in Afghanistan. No longer significant.

- **Image as Central Asia's lone parlia-mentary democracy**
  May reduce donors' selectivity and oversight in providing grants, loans, and assistance.

Figure B.8.

The Structure of Kleptocracy in Kyrgyzstan: Revenue Streams

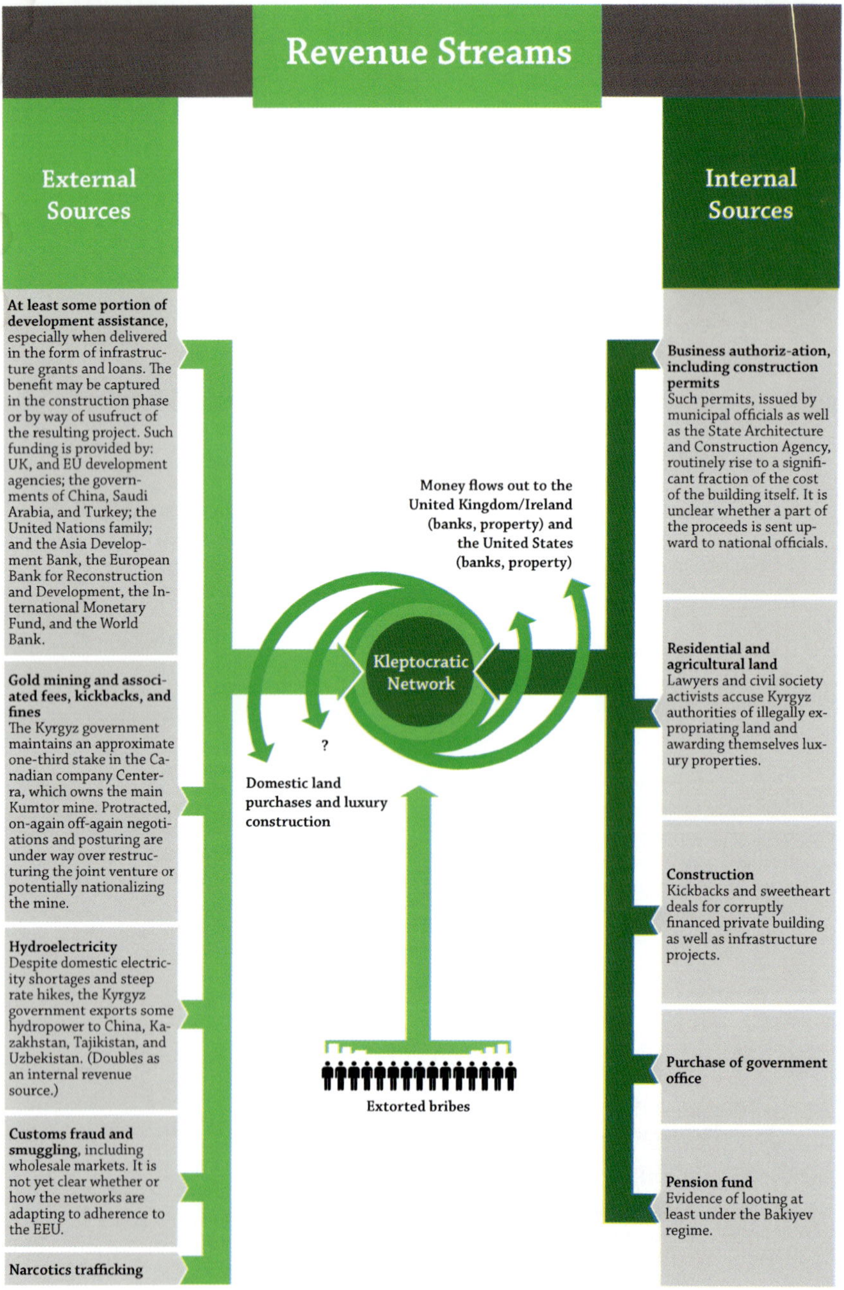

Revenue Streams

External Sources

At least some portion of development assistance, especially when delivered in the form of infrastructure grants and loans. The benefit may be captured in the construction phase or by way of usufruct of the resulting project. Such funding is provided by: UK, and EU development agencies; the governments of China, Saudi Arabia, and Turkey; the United Nations family; and the Asia Development Bank, the European Bank for Reconstruction and Development, the International Monetary Fund, and the World Bank.

Gold mining and associated fees, kickbacks, and fines
The Kyrgyz government maintains an approximate one-third stake in the Canadian company Centerra, which owns the main Kumtor mine. Protracted, on-again off-again negotiations and posturing are under way over restructuring the joint venture or potentially nationalizing the mine.

Hydroelectricity
Despite domestic electricity shortages and steep rate hikes, the Kyrgyz government exports some hydropower to China, Kazakhstan, Tajikistan, and Uzbekistan. (Doubles as an internal revenue source.)

Customs fraud and smuggling, including wholesale markets. It is not yet clear whether or how the networks are adapting to adherence to the EEU.

Narcotics trafficking

Money flows out to the United Kingdom/Ireland (banks, property) and the United States (banks, property)

Kleptocratic Network

?

Domestic land purchases and luxury construction

Extorted bribes

Internal Sources

Business authorization, including construction permits
Such permits, issued by municipal officials as well as the State Architecture and Construction Agency, routinely rise to a significant fraction of the cost of the building itself. It is unclear whether a part of the proceeds is sent upward to national officials.

Residential and agricultural land
Lawyers and civil society activists accuse Kyrgyz authorities of illegally expropriating land and awarding themselves luxury properties.

Construction
Kickbacks and sweetheart deals for corruptly financed private building as well as infrastructure projects.

Purchase of government office

Pension fund
Evidence of looting at least under the Bakiyev regime.

Figure C.1.

Infographic. The Structure of Kleptocracy in Moldova

This diagram, especially its central elements, is meant to depict a fully interpenetrated network. The apparent separation visible here represents a compromise to ease understanding.

MOLDOVA

Moldova's network is controlled not from within its government, but from the private sector, by business magnate Vladimir Plahotniuc. The leak in May 2015 of a central-bank-commissioned report detailing the suspicious transfer of some $1 billion—fully 12 percent of GDP—from the country's top three private banks sparked massive anticorruption demonstrations. It was also seen as a move by the Plahotniuc network to disable its lone competitor, the network around former prime minister Vladimir Filat, who was implicated in the report. It was a Plahotniuc confidant, Speaker of the Parliament Andrian Candu, who leaked it. The network is vertically integrated in the usual fashion, with bribe money paid to justice sector professionals, teachers, and doctors traveling up the line in return for protection from legal repercussions or the impact of institutional reforms. Both the Plahotniuc and Filat networks are nominally pro-European, so some degree of popular pro-Russian sentiment may reflect indignation at the corruption that even negotiations aimed at charting a path toward European integration have failed to reduce, rather than purely cultural affinities.

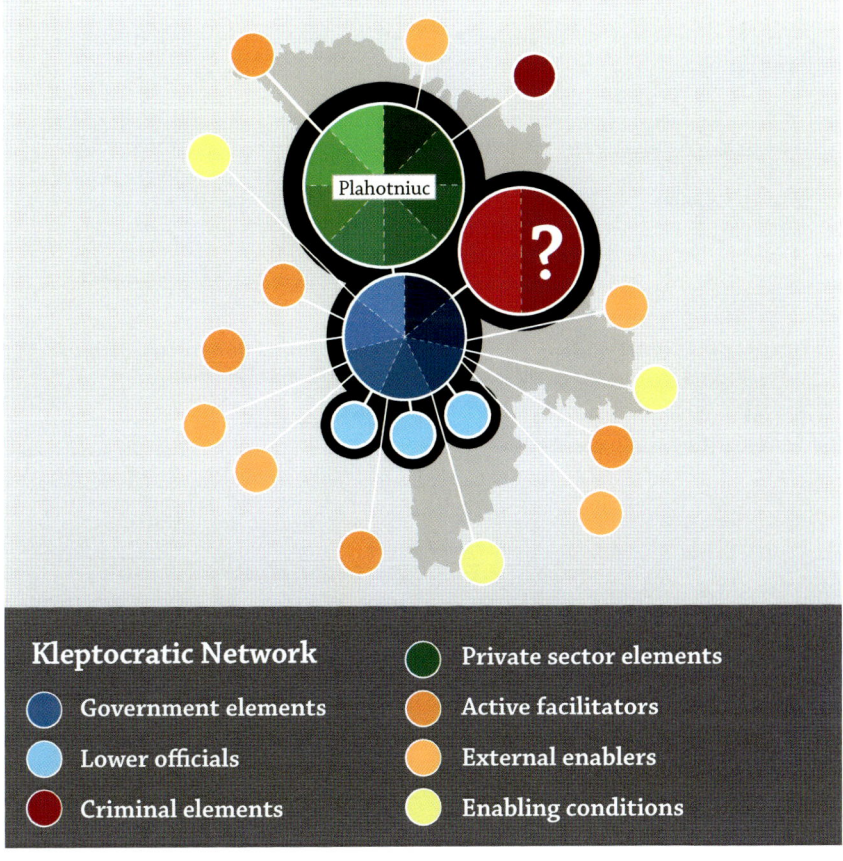

Figure C.2.

The Structure of Kleptocracy in Moldova: Government Elements

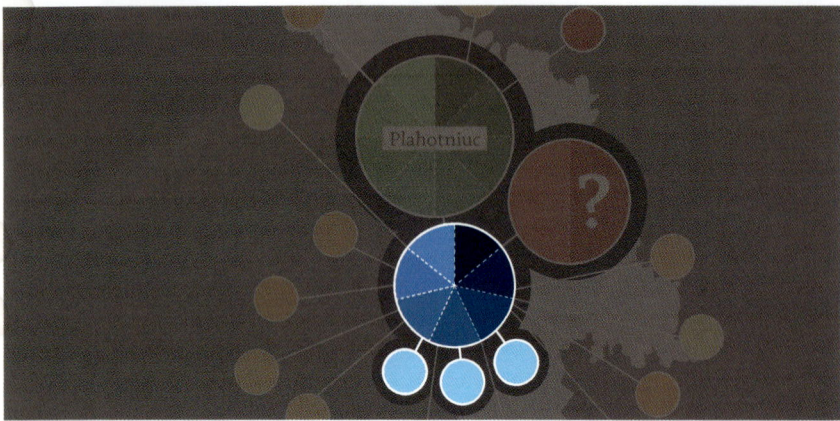

The elements of state function that are key to network operations include:

▶ **Judicial branch**
Prosecutors as well as judges. Justice sector personnel ensure impunity for corrupt customs officials or criminal bank executives by destroying or abandoning evidence, enforce fraudulent debt claims as part of money-laundering schemes, and block attempted institutional reforms. A number of judges have resigned or are under investigation, but whether these changes will be adequate to reform the system is an open question.

▶ **National Anticorruption Center**
This nominally independent agency keeps files on various government officials and is seen to preferentially target those who buck the Plahotniuc line.

▶ **National Investigation Inspectorate**
Especially the Economic Crime Unit and Special Operations Department, believed to tamper with evidence and collect informa-tion on potential rivals.

▶ **Ministry of Economy**
Agencies under its jurisdiction use customs and tax audits to discipline, handicap, or punish competing business- es. According to several interviewees, the Ministry of Economy has required national utility companies to route electricity or telecom services by way of network-affiliated intermediaries, which skim some portion of rates paid. (Electricity rates rose by about one-third over just a few months at the end of 2015.)

▶ **Ministry of Information Technology and Communications**

▶ **Central Bank**
Non-enforcement of banking regulations by the central bank has also been critical to Moldova's ability to provide money-laundering services.

▶ **Central Electoral Commission**
Plahotniuc's control of the autonomous Central Electoral Commission, whose chairman is a member of his inner circle, allows the network to influence elections via vote-buying and the disqualification of candidates. As a result of these levers and direct emoluments or intimidation, the parliament is largely under network control.

Figure C.3.

The Structure of Kleptocracy in Moldova: Private Sector Elements

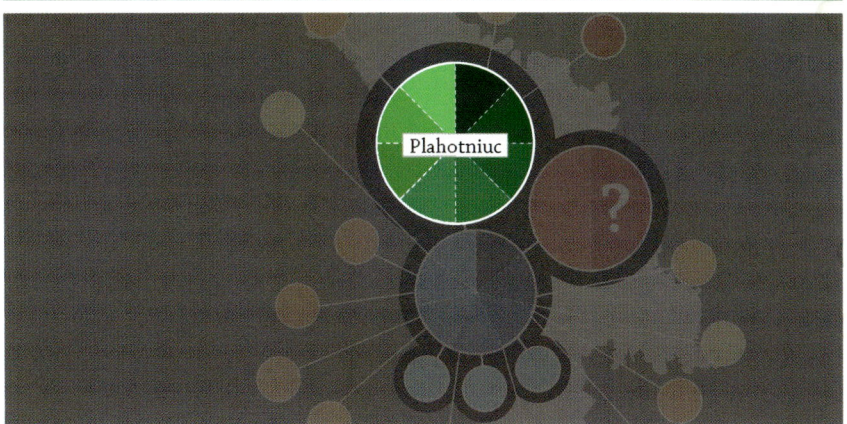

The main private sector network elements include:

- **Banks**
  Owners of Moldovan banks have used a variety of layered and opaque corporate structures and proxy owners, so it is difficult to determine who they actually are, or who is profiting from the money-laundering services that have been provided to Russian clients, or on whose behalf $1 billion was siphoned out of the three main banks.

- **Construction contractors**
  Contract fraud is suspected, especially regarding public buildings such as schools and hospitals, as well as roads. Moldova does not have the type of megaprojects that are evident in Azerbaijan.

- **Consumer goods importers**

- **Bakeries and butchers**

- **Media**
  Prime, Canal 2, Canal 3, and Publika, among others.

- **Hospitality and travel**
  Nobil Luxury Boutique Hotel and Codru Hotel, among others.

- **Real estate**

- **Public utilities intermediaries**

Figure C.4.

The Structure of Kleptocracy in Moldova: Criminal Elements

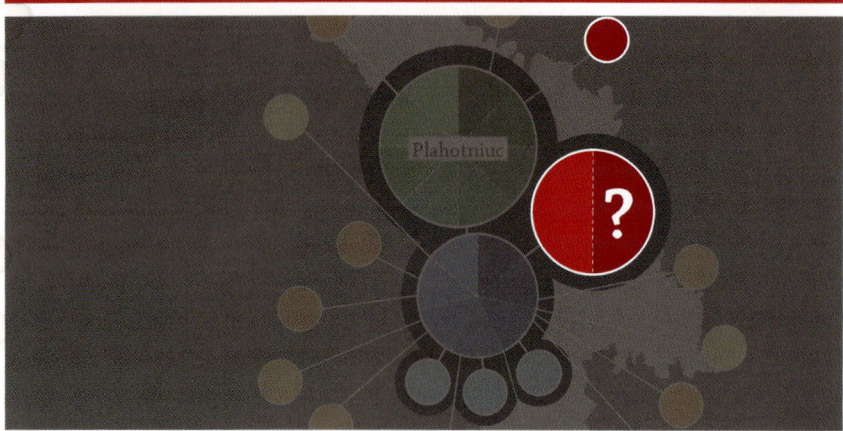

As elsewhere in this region, criminal actors are intertwined with kleptocratic networks.

▶ **Sex trafficking?**
Moldova has been famous for sex trafficking since at least the turn of the millennium. At that time, women entrapped in Moldova were trafficked across the still-chaotic Balkans, leaving for Italy in rubber dinghies. From Italy they were dispatched across Europe, ending up, for example, in Lyon, France, where they competed with regulated prostitutes. This trade continues, with other routes leading through Turkey to the Middle East. No evidence of concrete links to the Plahotniuc network has been publicly uncovered.

▶ **Smuggling**
Especially foodstuffs, alcohol, and cigarettes.

● **Russian corruption and organized crime networks**
These foreign networks have relied heavily on Moldovan banks for money-laundering services.

Figure C.5.

The Structure of Kleptocracy in Moldova: Active Facilitators

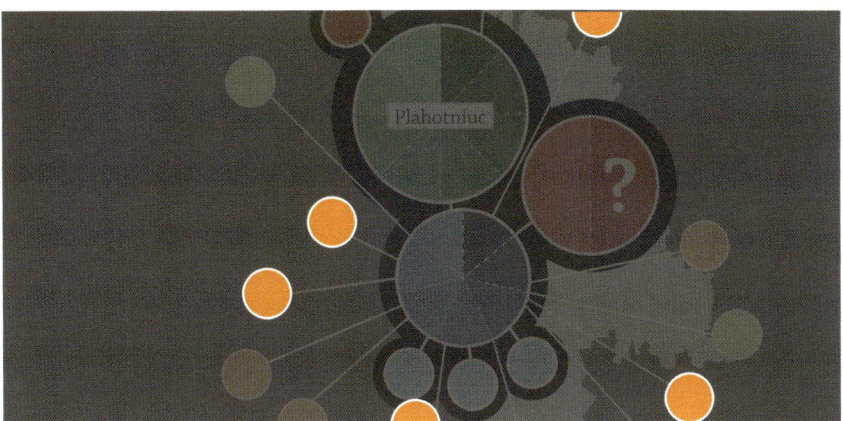

The main external facilitators are:

- **Shell company domiciling services**
  Providers have been identified in Belize; Cyprus; Hong Kong; the Netherlands; New Zealand; South Africa; the United Kingdom, including Scotland and the British Overseas Territories, and the U.S. state of Delaware.

- **Ukrainian smuggling rings**

- **Local branches of some international auditors**
  They have signed off on clean bills of health for banks providing illegal loans.

- **Russian banks**
  They provide fictitious deposits to disguise Moldovan banks' disappearing capital.

- **Moldovan citizens**
  Some Moldovans have allowed their names to be used as "owners" of shell companies in Russia that guaranteed fictitious loans between other paper companies. Payments by these Moldovan-owned "guarantors" to the supposed creditor when the supposed borrower "defaults" is the mechanism by which money has been laundered. In fact no loan would ever have been made. The fiction was concocted to provide an apparently legitimate paper trail explaining the transfer of funds.

Figure C.6.

The Structure of Kleptocracy in Moldova: External Enablers

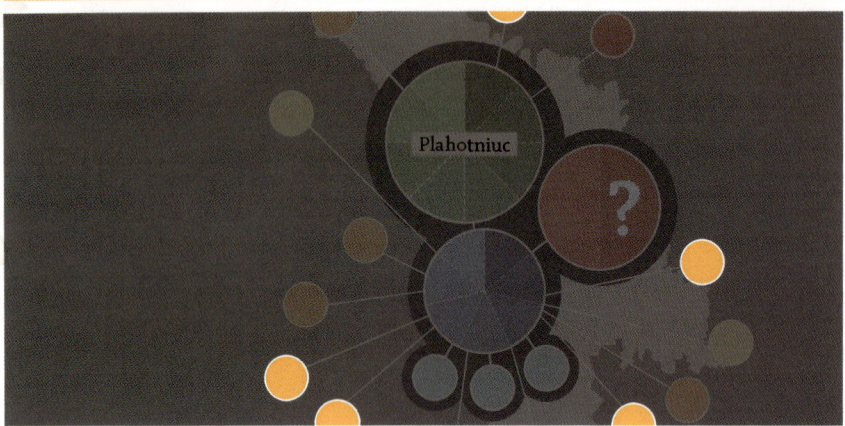

The main external enablers are:

- **Latvian banks**
  These banks are the first ports of call for money freshly laundered in Moldova.

- **U.S. foreign assistance**
  Donor funds from Europe and international financial institutions have been significant until quite recently. But most international donors and lenders are now freezing their programs with Moldova. The International Monetary Fund (IMF) has provided no new loans since 2013, and has made it clear that the current state of the political economy precludes negotiations for the moment. While the U.S. Millennium Challenge Corporation compact has not been renewed due to corruption concerns, the U.S. State Department included $41 million in civilian and military assistance in its fiscal year 2017 budget request. Activists see this U.S. support as moral reinforcement for the Plahotniuc network.

- **Russian gas**
  Gazprom owns a 51 percent stake in Moldovagaz.

- **Romanian foreign assistance**
  Despite pressure from other lenders, the Romanian government approved a $177 million loan in May 2016, though no funds have been disbursed as of mid-2016.

- **Romanian elite stature-enhancing interactions and business deals**

Figure C.7.

The Structure of Kleptocracy in Moldova: Enabling Conditions

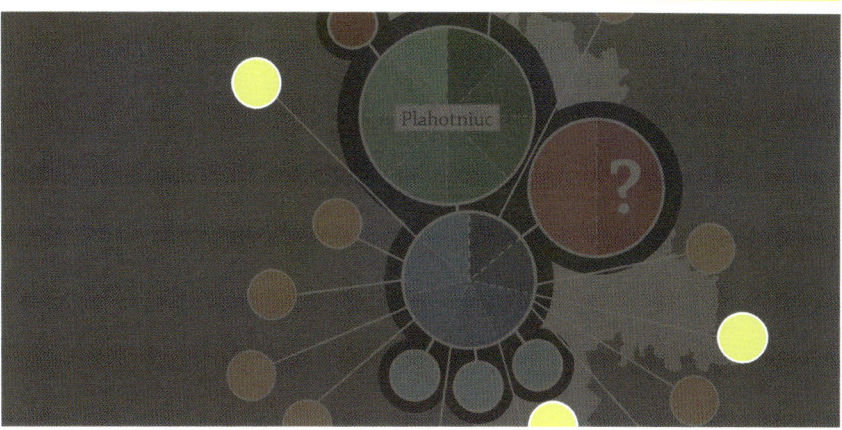

The main enabling conditions are:

- **EU-Russian tensions**
  This geostrategic context has played an enabling role for the nominally pro-EU Plahotniuc network. Ironically, the United States has remained more sensitive to this geopolitical alignment than the EU, which has suspended its financial support.

- **Frozen Transnistrian conflict**
  The unresolved claims and counterclaims to this piece of territory have left it in a degree of administrative limbo that facilitates cross-border smuggling from Ukraine.

- **Remittances**
  Most of the guest workers sending money back to families in Moldova are employed in Russia. The flow is estimated to total approximately one-quarter of Moldova's GDP. This cushion is vulnerable to Russia's economic contraction.

Figure C.8.

The Structure of Kleptocracy in Moldova: Revenue Streams

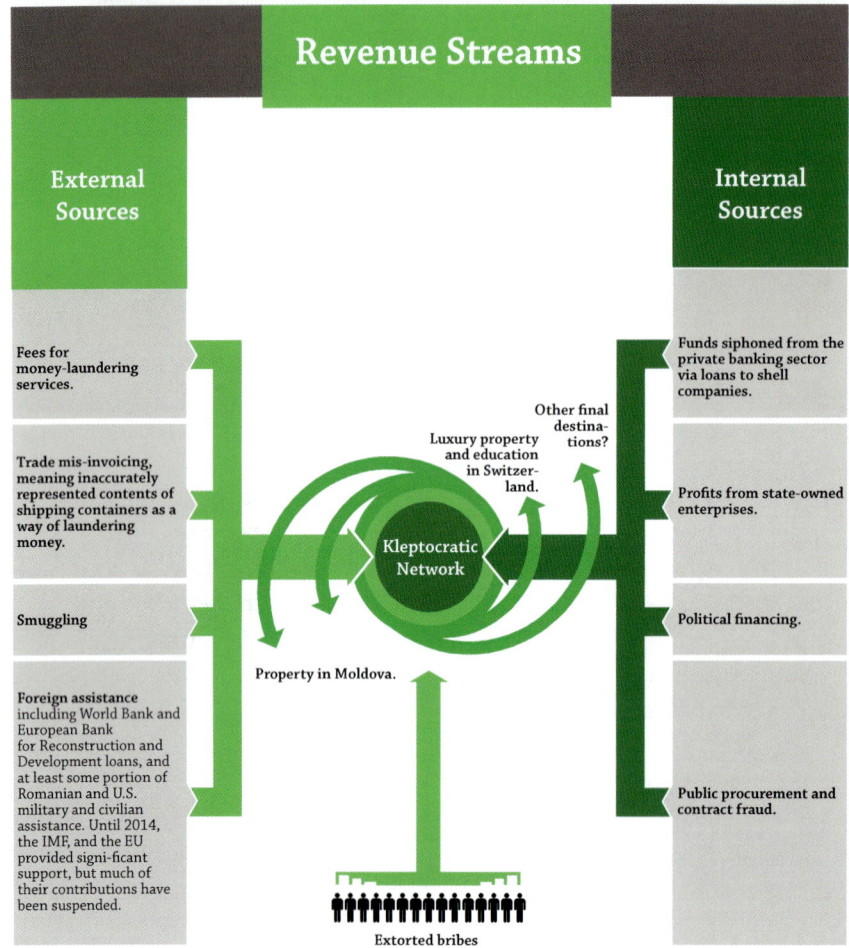

Ideally, the representation of such a structure would not be a flat picture, but a three-dimensional model, displaying the complete interpenetration among the sectors, especially as individuals move from position to position across ostensible boundaries. According to information revealed in the Panama Papers, for example, Azerbaijan's minister of taxes also maintained a controlling stake in a private-sector conglomerate whose principal beneficiaries are members of the Aliyev family,[18] so he's effectively double-hatted, occupying a position in the blue government circle and the green private-sector circle simultaneously. The role of U.S. President Trump's children, as heads of his business empire and policy advisors, may prove to be comparable. The infographics developed here treat each sector separately for the purposes of visual clarity. (See Figures A.1, B.1 and C.1.)

This type of integration is easiest to prove for Azerbaijan, where members of the Aliyev and Pashayev families and other high-ranking government officials hardly try to hide their ownership stakes, not just in gold-mining concerns, but in these massive conglomerates whose subsidiaries work in almost all sectors of lucrative economic activity.[19] DIA and Ata Holdings are notable examples, as is the Aliyev-controlled Silk Way Group, which includes banks and hotels as well as construction firms.[20] According to the Organized Crime and Corruption Reporting Project, the Aliyev/Pashayev clan owns no fewer than eleven banks.[21]

In the case of Moldova, the ownership structures of presumed private-sector network elements are more opaque. Numerous shell companies belonging to other companies with no physical existence, for example, were listed as owners of the banks that ran an industrial-scale money-laundering operation for years on behalf of Russian organized crime. A 2015 Kroll audit found that some of the same establishments had proffered the various loans totaling the $1 billion at the heart of the 2015 scandal to other, presumably separate, UK-based shell companies.[22]

More obvious network-affiliated businesses in Moldova include importers, especially of metals, foodstuffs (including flour), and consumer goods; public works contractors; bakeries; hotels; and media organizations.[23] In many formerly socialist countries, state-owned enterprises make up an intermediate group between the public and private sectors. In Moldova, telecommunications and the national railway might also be included in this category.

5.1. Does the horizontal integration include ostensibly charitable institutions?

With the rise since the 1980s in gifts by public agencies and private philanthropists alike to nonprofit organizations carrying out humanitarian or development projects, kleptocratic networks in many countries have sought to capture this important and often poorly supervised revenue stream. So commonly do government officials in Nigeria set up their own nonprofits, for example, that locals have dubbed them GONGOs, or government-organized nongovernmental organizations.[24]

In Ben Ali's Tunisia, civil servants were required to make "donations" to an ostensibly charitable solidarity fund called 20/20, whose activities were as opaque as its accounts.[25] In early March 2013, Gulnara Karimova, the daughter of Uzbekistan's president, held a gala fundraising event in support of her supposed charity, the Fund Forum of Culture and Arts in Uzbekistan. Western officials, representatives of aid agencies, and NGOs were invited, and their presence was generously televised.[26] This organization, or others like it, were frequently used to collect extorted payments from local and international businesses.[27]

The most obvious example of this element of private-sector networks in the three cases examined here is Azerbaijan's Heydar Aliyev Foundation, whose president is Mehriban Aliyeva.[28] In Kyrgyzstan, too, local officials have founded "NGOs" to make extra money, according to several interlocutors.

5.2. Does horizontal integration extend to outright criminals?

The interaction between corruption and organized crime is most frequently described, particularly by specialists who focus on the criminal dimension, as one of facilitation. The main characters in the drama from this perspective are the organized criminals, against whom significant institutional resources and capabilities are invested. Corrupt officials appear in supporting roles: the vicious cop, or the customs agent who looks away in exchange for a bribe.

The true picture in most systemically corrupt countries is different. The two sectors are wired together in a relatively equal symbiosis, with key individuals often playing substantial roles in both sectors.

In Afghanistan in the 2000s, the Karzai network and the locally competing southern network of Gul Agha Sherzai indubitably included opium trafficking and processing elements.[29] During the same period, Kyrgyzstan also exhibited almost overt kleptocratic penetration of the narcotics industry, as do several Latin American countries today. Consumer goods smuggling typically provides an important revenue stream for kleptocratic networks, whose street-level customs officials often let ordinary people skirt tariffs for a bribe, while ushering network-connected smugglers across the border with a wave of the hand.[30] Moldova—whose banking sector is clearly intertwined with Russian organized crime networks—has long been known as a point of origin for sex workers trafficked to Europe and the Middle East.[31] (Figure B.4.)

5.3. Does the network incorporate terrorists or other violent insurgents?
Such a question may seem even more counterintuitive than the last two, especially in the case of governments that are valued allies in counterterrorism operations, such as Ethiopia's or Algeria's. But international military assistance can prove to be so important in reinforcing a regime that some network members choose to cultivate at least a degree of insurgent activity in order to keep the money and visually intimidating support flowing. Or they may find uses for violent insurgents as "informal instruments of force," as discussed above.

6. Do the networks extend across national boundaries?

For simplicity's sake, kleptocratic networks are discussed here on a country-by-country basis. But they should really be understood as fully transnational organizations.

The national border between former President Viktor Yanukovych's network in Ukraine, for example, and the more powerful Russian networks with which it was entwined can hardly be said to have existed. Members of the new U.S. ruling coalition, including President Trump and his family and some close advisers, and Senate Majority Leader Mitch McConnell were nodes in that network. In Moldova, too, the banking sector might be seen as a fully integrated element of Russian criminal networks, at least until early 2014. Kyrgyz drug trafficking networks clearly cross borders, and are especially implanted in Russia. Ties are reportedly just as strong between the governmental leadership in those two countries. It would be interesting, finally, to explore the personal relationships among the executives of the principal energy and construction giants in Azerbaijan and Turkey, or those between top Moldovan network members and their Romanian counterparts.[32]

Perhaps a more sensitive question would be the degree to which political leaders or businesses headquartered in developed countries might be considered full-blown members of foreign kleptocratic networks, rather than just enablers. Decades of research on French political and economic penetration of that country's former colonies in Africa, including the diverse activities of government-protected oil giant Total, have birthed the epithet Françafrique to describe the phenomenon.[33]

Given the well-known state of Azerbaijan's political economy, a determination whether certain British oil companies and construction firms, or such U.S. equivalents as KBR or the Trump Organization, are functioning as members of the Aliyev/Pashayev network would depend on the nature of the personal interactions among those holding leadership positions on each side.

The infographics here (see Gallery) try at least to hint at this internationalism, through the orientation of the main structure diagrams and their placement athwart national boundaries. In a few cases of clear interpenetration with another country's networks, a small circle of the appropriate color is situated outside the focus country. Still, future work on this topic should better clarify and depict the transnational nature of such networks.

7. What are the key enablers for the kleptocratic networks, especially outside the country?

Distinguishing between different enabling functions will often require arbitrary judgement calls. (For the Moldavian example, see Figures C.5, C.6 and C.7.) On one end of the scale, an individual or business that provides tailored services to members of a single kleptocratic network might almost be considered a full network member. If, however, the entity is a business that provides such services to all comers, with no particular preference for, or entanglement with, a specific kleptocratic network, it might better be considered an active facilitator than a network member. The Panamanian law firm Mossack Fonseca would fit this latter designation. So would lobbying firms, such as Fabiani and Company, working to improve the images of several different kleptocratic governments in Washington or other Western capitals.[34] Examination should be devoted to providers of other services, such as air transport or logistics, contract negotiations, and forged documents.

The larger group of enablers—those whose contribution to consolidating or financing a kleptocracy may be unwitting—include the major multinationals doing business in captured sectors of economic activity. Increasingly, network-controlled state-owned enterprises, such as Azerbaijan's SOCAR, are requiring international investors to enter into joint ventures or use specific vendors. The international partner may find itself wired into the network willy-nilly.[35] Given current difficulties in determining the identities of those truly benefiting from offshore corporations and their transactions, Western banks or real estate agents that take money without carefully examining the ownership structure of the shell companies investing it might also be considered enablers, rather than active facilitators.

As well-intentioned as they may be, overseas development assistance and loans or grants from international financial institutions also constitute important enablers, especially when they support infrastructure projects that are contracted out to network-affiliated businesses. In these cases, some of the money they provide may simultaneously be serving as a revenue stream for the network. Similarly, pushing development bank loans into captured economic sectors often serves to reinforce kleptocratic structures, further victimizing populations the funding is ostensibly trying to help. Interviews with half a dozen officials in such institutions have exposed a high degree of explicitly stated "trust" in borrowers, despite clear indications of corruption or unfair capture of public and economic institutions.

Unless donors or lending institutions obtain evidence of (or require) significant reforms to the sector, or build in reinforced monitoring and evaluation and citizen oversight mechanisms, such investments must be understood in and of themselves as enabling kleptocratic practices. Even in cases where the money they provide may not constitute a significant revenue stream benefiting network members. The realization of the projects' overt objectives, such as expanding the population's access to a stable electricity supply, should be balanced against the uses to which that electricity is actually put (supply for other extractive industries, sale to neighboring countries potentially affording separate opportunities for capture of the cash generated) and the nonmaterial enabling impacts of these projects.

Often, incidentally, such international development support is provided via a combining or layering process reminiscent of that used by the beneficiaries of offshore shell companies or of the packaging of debt before the U.S. financial crisis. It becomes difficult to discern what funding comes from which institutions, and the capacity to perform independent oversight is often disabled. The Central American Bank for Economic Integration, which funds some contested infrastructure projects in that region, is partially capitalized by the governments of Spain and Taiwan, as well as by the United States Agency for International Development, the Millennium Challenge Corporation, and the Japan International Cooperation Agency.[36] It in turn has invested in specialized funds, such as the Central American Mezzanine Infrastructure Fund. In such cases, only general investment guidelines are provided to the fund managers, such as the poverty level of the countries to be invested in. Development banks do not examine the details of individual projects in which their money is invested.[37]

Alert to the potential enabling impact of overseas development assistance in Moldova, the EU, which provided approximately $623 million from 2007 through 2013,[38] froze its support in 2015 and is requiring significant reforms before "envisag[ing]" a resumption.[39] But Romania granted an undisclosed sum in emergency assistance in early 2016,[40] and approved a $177 million loan in May 2016 (though under international pressure, officials decided to delay disbursement of the first tranche until further conditions have been met).[41] Some see the ongoing high-level political involvement in Moldovan affairs by Romanian Prime Minister Dacian Cioloș as enabling the practices of the Plahotniuc network.

The other outlier with respect to Moldova is the United States. The Department of State has provided some $30 million in a combination of military and civilian assistance in 2016, and has increased that sum to $41 million in its request for the 2017 fiscal year.[42]

Unless assistance to a country like this is carefully channeled to independent journalists or civil society organizations struggling for reform, or to the rare government officials or agencies whose independence can be verified, almost all such aid must be considered an enabler, or a revenue stream. Careful study of specific programming—for which information is often not readily available—would be required to make these distinctions. Often, priorities for such assistance are negotiated with the government itself, making such specific tailoring or oversight mechanisms difficult to include.

International NGOs, including those focused on civil society, sometimes fall into the enabling trap. Their desire to be present in a country and to make small gains, as they often claim to do, may blind them to their entanglement with the kleptocracy, or the degree to which their presence, on balance, may provide a whitewashing effect that outweighs the good they do.[43]

Such unintended image laundering is one of the less concrete forms enabling can take. The prestige (as well as the revenue-generation opportunities) afforded by Azerbaijan's presidency of the Council of Europe is an egregious example.[44] Vladimir Plahotniuc's May 2016 visit to Washington, where he met senior officials, was seized upon by the Moldovan media. Private establishments, such as universities and research institutes also provide image-laundering services.[45]

Least intense on the scale of factors contributing to the health of kleptocratic systems are what might be termed enabling conditions. They include geopolitical contexts such as the frozen conflicts over Transnistria and Nagorno-Karabakh, which facilitate Moldovan smuggling and provide opportunities for Aliyev to distract the Azerbaijani population, respectively. Moldova's East-West cultural divide, which resembles Ukraine's, may be contributing to Washington's relatively tolerant attitude toward the nominally pro-Western Plahotniuc. Such conditions must be taken into consideration by policymakers, since the imperatives are real, and they will be called upon to make trade-offs.

Ideally, this type of rigorous analysis of the structure and functioning of a kleptocratic network should also include a parallel mapping of the networks—or, more likely, the isolated individuals—who are truly dedicated to more honest and responsive government and an economy providing more broadly accessible opportunities.

If the prime aim of the kleptocractic networks they are up against is personal enrichment, then it is also critical to understand the financial flows irrigating them in as much detail as possible.

8. What are the most important revenue streams the networks concentrate their efforts on capturing?

The sources of funds directly captured by the networks may overlap with, but will rarely be identical to, the main underpinnings of the country's economy. Extorted bribes should not be neglected in the calculations:

surveys in Afghanistan demonstrate that total yearly sums can be very significant even in poor countries.[46] As discussed above, some portion of foreign assistance, loans from international financial institutions (IFIs), or EU subsidies may constitute an important revenue stream.

Increased law enforcement focus on financial flows in the wake of the September 11, 2001 terrorist attacks, as well as more recent tightening of money-laundering protections, has prompted many corrupt officials to take pains to disguise their transfers of illicit wealth. Often money is moved in cash.[47] Needless to say, the upshot is excruciatingly difficult research.

One of the conceptual difficulties in mapping these revenue streams is the distinction between the initial origin of the funds, such as an IFI loan or international purchases of oil or gas, and the means by which the money is actually captured and transferred to network members, such as public-works contracts. As at other stages in this analysis, a degree of overlap is inevitable, and judgment calls will be necessary.

8.1. What are the illicit funds used for?

Are they invested in local property? Real estate overseas? Businesses, which in turn are incorporated into the network? Is the money deposited in off-shore bank accounts? Is it spent on lavish consumption? How much is directed back downward within the country, either as payments for the loyalty of network members who lack their own direct access to revenue streams or to finance electoral campaigns (often including vote-rigging or vote-buying)?

> Real estate purchases are one of the most common uses for the excess cash kleptocratic practices generate. When such purchases are made in luxury cities and neighborhoods, such as Hampstead or Hyde Park in London, or the Time Warner Center in New York, the purchases double as stature enhancement or image laundering for the corrupt buyer—indeed that's the point.[48]

Ideally, a more developed version of Figure A.8 would indicate at least an order of magnitude of the amounts of money generated by these various revenue streams. The clandestine—and sometimes hard to define—nature of corrupt practices makes such a task difficult.

Answers to the lifestyle questions above may in turn provide insight on a topic particularly relevant to would-be reformers, both inside and outside the country: the key vulnerabilities that potentially weaken the networks or render them more brittle than they might seem. These vulnerabilities are often tied to the aspirations of network members, their habits, or internal contradictions in the structures' cultures, practices, or personnel. Ascertaining just what these vulnerabilities might be often requires the imaginative powers of a devilish mind.

Much current knowledge about systems like these comes as detailed understanding of a disconnected splinter of the overall picture. Civil society organizations may know about the bribes that have to be paid to get an electricity meter installed, for example. Investigating a case under her country's antibribery legislation, an international prosecutor may have worked her way back from an offending company to the three foreign officials who were paid off. Aid agencies may do corruption risk assessments to reduce the likelihood that their programs will be subject to fraud or waste.

But, though the laws of many countries are defining it in ever-narrower terms, corruption cannot be reduced to bribery alone. It frequently constitutes a robust and sophisticated operating principle shaping most aspects of a government's structure and practices. Accurately fleshing out the pictures developed in these pages would require painstaking and wide-ranging research, making use of unpublished information that is not readily accessible. Such an effort might be dangerous for locals, or politically uncomfortable for partner governments. But given the significance and all-pervasive repercussions of corruption, it's hard to imagine a serious planning process taking place without this type of an understanding. To go into such a context blind to these realities would seem almost irresponsible.

Notes

[1] Ukraine Support Act, H.R. 4278, 113th Cong. (2013–2014), https://www.congress.gov/bill/113th-congress/house-bill/4278/text#toc-HA80E8C7FC-92747619C043AC34DC7E8A4, accessed on May 19, 2018.

[2] See for instance, Michael Weiss, "How Azerbaijan Is Like 'The Godfather,'" *Atlantic*, July 11, 2013, accessed June 15, 2016, http://www.theatlantic.com/international/archive/2013/07/how-azerbaijan-is-like-em-the-godfather-em/277717/; and for a somewhat dated but detailed study, see Farid Guliyev, "Political Elites in Azerbaijan," in *Challenges of the Caspian Resource Boom: Domestic Elites and Policymaking*, ed. Andreas Heinrich and Heiko Pleines (London: Palgrave Macmillan, 2012), 117–30.

3 "Representatives of Atlantic Council Welcome Government's Determination to Make Necessary Changes in Moldova," *IPN*, May 3, 2016, accessed June 15, 2016, http://www.ipn.md/en/politica/76333.

4 For innovative thinking on resilient networks, see "Stimson Lectures: Anne-Marie Slaughter, 'Network Strategies for Resilience, Action, and Scale,'" YouTube video, posted by "Yale University," November 24, 2015, accessed June 17, 2016, https://www.youtube.com/watch?v=UGj8dQJHZjs.

5 "Political Crisis Boosts Moldova's Pro-Russians but Corruption Real Threat," *Voice of America*, February 4, 2016, accessed February 4, 2016, http://www.voanews.com/content/political-crisis-boosts-moldova-pro-russians-but-corruption-real-threat/3176566.html.

6 Daisy Sindelar, "The Political Rise of Azerbaijan's First Lady," *Radio Free Europe/Radio Liberty*, June 13, 2013, accessed June 15, 2016, http://www.rferl.org/content/azerbaijan-rise-aliyeva/25016294.html.

7 Conversation with Miranda Patrucic, April 27, 2016.

8 Sarah Chayes, *Thieves of State: Why Corruption Threatens Global Security* (New York: Norton, 2015), 97.

9 See Beatrice Hiboux, *La force de l'obeissance: economie politique de la repression en Tunisie* [The power of obedience: The political economy of repression in Tunisia] (Paris: Editions la Découverte, 2006).

10 See, for instance, Natalya Melnik, "Skhemy radi: Moldova prodolzhit zakupat' elektroenergiyu cherez firmu-prokladku" [For a scheme: Moldova will continue buying energy through a company-mediator], *NewsMaker*, March 3, 2016, accessed June 15, 2016, http://newsmaker.md/rus/novosti/shemy-radi-moldova-prodolzhit-zakupat-elektroenergiyu-cherez-firmu-prokladku-22946.

11 For analysis of the planned increase, see "District Heating and Electricity Tariff and Affordability Analysis," World Bank, October 2015, http://pubdocs.worldbank.org/pubdocs/publicdoc/2015/11/9631446482837463/Moldova-Tariff-and-Afordability-Study-2015-10-26-FINAL.pdf; for coverage of the actual increase, which took place in November, see for instance, Eurasianet, "Unrest in Moldova After Shady Energy Deals," *Oilprice.com*, February 4, 2016, accessed June 15, 2016, http://oilprice.com/Latest-Energy-News/World-News/Unrest-In-Moldova-After-Shady-Energy-Deals.html.

12 For examples, see Paul Radu, Mihai Munteanu, and Iggy Ostanin, "Grand Theft Moldova," Organized Crime and Corruption Reporting Project (OCCRP), July 24, 2015, accessed June 16, 2016, https://www.occrp.org/en/investigations/4203-grand-theft-moldova; or Andrew Higgins, "Moldova, Hunting for Missing Millions, Finds Only Ash," *New York Times*, June 4, 2015, accessed June 16, 2016, http://www.nytimes.com/2015/06/05/world/europe/moldova-bank-theft.html?_r=0.

13 I watched the collection of these payments of a cut of bribes at Afghan customs in Kabul in 2005, and have been told of a similar system in interviews in Tunisia, Uzbekistan, and Nigeria. See Chayes, "Vertically Integrated Criminal Syndicates," chap. 5 in *Thieves of State*; especially pages 58–64 for a discussion of the system, as well as page 112 for Uzbekistan. For corroboration on purchase of office in Afghan-

istan, see Mohammad Razaq Isaqzedah and Antonio Giustozzi, "A Call for Government Determination Fighting Corruption in Afghanistan," *Integrity Watch Afghanistan*, May 24, 2015, http://integritywatch.co/wp-content/uploads/2014/12/moi_senior_appointments_and_corruption_english.pdf, 29–30.

[14] See for instance "Corruption in Afghanistan: Recent Patterns and Trends," *UNODC*, December 2012, http://www.unodc.org/documents/frontpage/Corruption_in_Afghanistan_FINAL.pdf; and "Key Findings – NCS 2014," Integrity Watch Afghanistan, May 28, 2014, http://integritywatch.co/key-findings-ncs-2014/.

[15] For a hint of how the system might be formalized, see Shahin Abbasov, "Azerbaijan Swimming in a Sea of Bribes, Despite an Anti-Corruption Tide," *Azeri Report*, June 15, 2016, http://azerireport.com/index.php?option=com_content&task=view&id=3584.

[16] Figures from "Number of Persons Engaged in Economy and Salaries," State Statistical Committee of the Republic of Azerbaijan, February 16, 2016, accessed June 17, 2016, http://www.stat.gov.az/news/?id=3117. Note these statistics systematically underestimate agricultural and grey-market activities.

[17] Miranda Patrucic et al., "Aliyevs' Secret Mining Empire," Panama Papers, *OCCRP*, April 4, 2016, accessed June 15, 2016, https://www.occrp.org/en/panamapapers/aliyev-mining-empire/.

[18] Juliette Garside et al., "London Law Firm Helped Azerbaijan's First Family Set Up Secret Offshore Firm," *Guardian*, April 5, 2016, accessed June 15, 2016, http://www.theguardian.com/news/2016/apr/05/panama-papers-london-law-firm-helped-azerbaijan-first-family-set-up-secret-offshore-firm.

[19] Stefan Candea, "Offshore Companies Provide Link Between Corporate Mogul and Azerbaijan's President," *International Consortium of Investigative Journalists*, April 3, 2013, accessed June 15, 2016, https://www.icij.org/offshore/offshore-companies-provide-link-between-corporate-mogul-and-azerbaijans-president; see also DIA Holding's website, http://www.diaholding.com/default.asp?LanguageID=2.

[20] Khadija Ismayilova, "Aliyevs Own Some of the Best Hotels in Baku," *OCCRP*, June 28, 2015, accessed June 15, 2016, https://www.occrp.org/en/corruptistan/azerbaijan/2015/06/28/aliyevs-own-some-of-the-best-hotels-in-baku.html.

[21] Oral communication, April 27, 2016; and see "Azerbaijani First Family Big on Banking," *OCCRP*, June 11, 2015, accessed June 16, 2016, https://www.occrp.org/en/corruptistan/azerbaijan/2015/06/11/azerbaijani-first-family-big-on-banking.html.

[22] Kroll, "Project Tenor – Scoping Phase: Final Report" (unpublished report prepared for the National Bank of Moldova, April 2, 2015), accessed June 16, 2016, http://candu.md/files/doc/Kroll_Project%20Tenor_Candu_02.04.15.pdf. For the wide press coverage, see, for instance, Tim Whewell, "The Great Moldovan Bank Robbery," *BBC News*, June 18, 2015, accessed June 15, 2016, http://www.bbc.com/news/magazine-33166383; for a less spectacular but similar system in Zine el-Abedine Ben Ali's Tunisia, see Hiboux, *La Force de l'Obeissance* [The power of obedience].

23 Mariana Rață, "Banii, Franzeluța," *Jurnal De Chișinău*, November 2, 2010, accessed June 15, 2016, http://www.jc.md/banii-„franzeluta"-pleaca-in-offshore-uri/.

24 Numerous personal conversations in Nigeria, during repeated visits between 2013 and 2015; and see Daniel Jordan Smith, *A Culture of Corruption: Everyday Deception and Popular Discontent in Nigeria* (Princeton: Princeton University Press, 2007), 97–107.

25 Discussion of the structure of Ben Ali's kleptocratic network with economics and business professors and graduate students at Manouba University, December 2014.

26 I was present in Tashkent working on a project implemented by the Slovenian NGO Regional Dialogue, whose director was insistent that I attend, but I declined.

27 Chayes, *Thieves of State*, 108.

28 See Roxana Jipa, Victor Ilie, and Daniel Bojin, "Building on a Shaky Foundation," *OCCRP*, December 4, 2015, accessed June 15, 2016, https://www.occrp.org/en/corruptistan/azerbaijan/2015/12/04/building-on-a-shaky-foundation.html.

29 Personal knowledge based on extensive interviews of Afghans and international law enforcement officials, as well as review of classified and unclassified U.S. government documents.

30 See, for an Uzbek example, Chayes, *Thieves of State*, 110.

31 See for instance Kelsey Hoie Ferrell, "History of Sex Trafficking in Moldova," *End Slavery Now*, February 9, 2016, accessed June 15, 2016, http://www.endslaverynow.org/blog/articles/history-of-sex-trafficking-in-moldova. Also my 2000 unpublished research conducted primarily in Vlore, Albania; Bari, Italy; and Lyon, France. At the time, French prostitutes were on strike against the influx of underage, trafficked sex workers, primarily from Moldova.

32 Recent reporting by the Organized Crime and Corruption Reporting Project indicates Romanian enabling—via at least two Moldovan nationals—of the Aliyev network in Azerbaijan, suggesting a triangular relationship. See Jipa et. al., "Building on a Shaky Foundation."

33 For a simplified overview, see for instance L'Obs, "La Françafrique, Mode D'emploi" [Françafrique, a user's guide], *Le Nouvel Observateur*, September 17, 2011, accessed June 15, 2016, http://tempsreel.nouvelobs.com/monde/20110915.OBS0438/la-francafrique-mode-d-emploi.html.

34 "Azerbaijan America Alliance," *Open Secrets*, accessed June 15, 2016, http://www.opensecrets.org/lobby/clientsum.php?id=D000064546.

35 Email communication with a former Western oil industry official who requested anonymity, June 13, 2016.

36 "Central American Bank for Economic Integration," Devex International Development, accessed June 16, 2016, https://www.devex.com/organizations/central-american-bank-for-economic-integration-44109.

37 Interview with the CEO of a development bank almost wholly owned by a European government, which has investments across most of Central and South America, Africa, and Asia, June 6, 2016.

[38] "European Commission's Support to the Republic of Moldova," press release, European Commission, June 25, 2014, accessed June 15, 2016, http://europa.eu/rapid/press-release_MEMO-14-355_en.htm.

[39] "Council Conclusions on the Republic of Moldova," press release, European Commission, February 15, 2016, accessed June 15, 2016, http://www.consilium.europa.eu/en/press/press-releases/2016/02/15-fac-moldova-conclusions/. The IMF has disbursed no money to Moldova since 2012: "Past IMF Disbursements and Repayments for All Members from 1984 to May 31, 2016," International Monetary Fund, accessed June 15, 2016, https://www.imf.org/external/np/fin/tad/extrans1.aspx?memberKey1=672; and has made it clear that conditions are not even ripe for renewing negotiations. Many countries routinely tie their bilateral aid packages to the existence of an IMF program, as the EU is doing in this case, so this suspension has implications beyond its own dollar amount.

[40] See for instance "Prima Parte Din Ajutorul Umanitar Oferit De România a Ajuns în țară; Au Fost Donate 203 Tone De Zahăr // FOTOREPORTAJ," Jurnal.md, March 10, 2016, accessed June 15, 2016, http://jurnal.md/ro/social/2016/3/10/prima-parte-din-ajutorul-umanitar-oferit-de-romania-a-ajuns-in-tara-au-fost-donate-203-tone-de-zahar-fotoreportaj/.

[41] AGERPRES, "ForMin Comanescu: Reforms in Moldova, Necessary for 150-Million-Euro Loan Granting," Romania's Permanent Delegation to NATO, accessed June 15, 2016, https://nato.mae.ro/en/romania-news/6474.

[42] U.S. Department of State, "Congressional Budget Justification: Department of State, Foreign Operations, and Related Programs," February 9, 2016, accessed June 16, 2016, http://www.state.gov/documents/organization/252179.pdf; for spending in the recent past, see, "Foreign Operations Assistance: Moldova," Fact Sheet, Bureau of European and Eurasian Affairs, U.S. Department of State, accessed June 16, 2016, http://www.state.gov/p/eur/rls/fs/2015/255712.htm.

[43] Extensive literature exists on the unintended consequences of international development assistance. While the word corruption is not always used, the substance of the phenomenon is depicted in lurid detail. See for example, Michael Maran, *The Road to Hell* (New York: Free Press, 1997); or Linda Polman, *Crisis Caravan: What's Wrong With Humanitarian Aid* (New York: Henry Holt and Company, 2010).

[44] For a withering commentary, see Gerald Knaus, "Europe and Azerbaijan: The End of Shame," *Journal of Democracy* 26, no. 3 (July 2015): 5–18, http://www.journalofdemocracy.org/sites/default/files/Knaus-26-3.pdf.

[45] All three celebrated former Nigerian finance minister Ngozi Okongo-Iweala (who has consistently whitewashed the epically corrupt administration of Goodluck Jonathan, in which she served) in 2015, and the Atlantic Council hosted Vladimir Plahotniuc during his 2016 Washington visit.

[46] See "Corruption in Afghanistan," UNODC; or bribery surveys by Integrity Watch Afghanistan.

[47] A U.S. intelligence official told me that millions of dollars in cash left Nigeria after the 2015 defeat of incumbent president Goodluck Jonathan. And the VIP

lounge at Kabul International Airport was infamous for years for being the site of massive unexamined cash exports, especially to Dubai.

48 Transparency International UK, "Corruption on Your Doorstep: How Corrupt Capital Is Used to Buy Property in the UK," *Transparency International*, March 2015, accessed June 15, 2016, http://www.transparency.org.uk/publications/corruption-on-your-doorstep/.

KÁLMÁN MIZSEI

The new East European patronal states and the rule-of-law*

Introduction

Both Ukraine and Moldova have recently celebrated the twenty-seventh anniversary of their existence as independent states. These countries were essentially born accidentally, as the result of the implosion of the Soviet Union and of the fact that the leaders of the USSR's key republics decided that the only way to eliminate the bankrupt Soviet power was to constitute the former republics as new independent states within their existing borders. Anything else would have opened a Pandora's box and triggered an unforeseeable chain of conflicts. The wisdom of this choice is evident in the fact that the former Soviet space did not produce another Yugoslavia, even if the process of dissolution was by no means conflict-free. However, the new states were born without any independent state tradition. Moreover, their national identities were highly disputed, both by neighboring states and even by much of the local population. These countries were also somewhat distant from major markets and the liberal political order. During the period of liberation from the Soviet yoke, their elites were very isolated from what in the West one would call modern political and economic thought. The combination of all these factors, and of the fact that indepen-

---

* I would like to recognize the research grant from the Open Society Foundation in 2016 when I wrote the bulk of this paper. I would also to thank Bálint Magyar, Nino Gogoladze and Vladimir Dubrovskiy for their valuable comments to an earlier draft of the paper. I also would like to thank Michael Cragg and József Litkei for excellent editing of the text.

dence came without the support of a deep, long-standing social movement, rendered the "transition" much thornier than that of the Central European or Baltic countries, which—at least until the economic crisis of 2008—showed a rapid convergence towards Western Europe.

The political scientist Henry Hale has argued that both Ukraine and Moldova have evolved along the same path as all post-Soviet states, aside from the Baltic states. He calls this ideal type towards which all these states converge the "patronal state."[1] There are signs that even more post-communist European states may fall (back) under this category. However, much is still to be established about the genesis and variations of such states, about external influences and, particularly, stability versus the propensity for fundamental systemic change. The stability of the patronal state in countries whose societies and leaderships show the most determination to join "Europe" or the "West" is also in question, as Ukraine has experienced two formidable revolutions, the second explicitly in the name of European values. Moldova also has experienced a major political crisis because of the apparent state capture by an unelected oligarch and a third, Georgia, has created an opportunity to gradually move away from a patronal state regime. Georgia's reform experience teaches us that major change within the system, and perhaps ultimately out of this system altogether, is possible. This chapter, while describing some important features of the two patronal regimes, tries to add evidence and analysis to the above questions.

The genesis of the system in the 1990s

The implosion of the Soviet empire initially brought democratic changes in almost the whole post-Soviet area and in post-socialist East-Central Europe. There were differences in the shape and quality of democracies from the beginning, but what is much more striking for the first period are the differences in the quality of economic reforms. Poland, Hungary, Czechoslovakia and the Baltic states experienced strong early reform pushes. This reform typically involved rapid consolidation of the macroeconomic situation, creating a two-tier banking system with some basic banking supervision emerging, opening opportunities for small private businesses, along with massive trade and price liberalization. The speed of privatizing communist-era factories was uneven. This reform push has had significant impact on the shaping of the new socio-political system, but it was less accentuated, or entirely absent, in most of the former Soviet Union. Generally, in Central and Eastern Europe this early radical reform push reduced the space for rent-seeking substantially when compared with much of the former Soviet Union, and particularly Russia and Ukraine. Reforms based on a free-market ideology caused highly competitive situations. This was not universal, but fairly widespread. There was room for corrupt lending and bribery during privatization—such as Hungary experienced in the early 1990s—but there was also a clear and fairly immediate answer to this in the form of highly technical reforms, like enabling objective assessments of the banks' balance sheets.

As a result, foreign direct investment began to pour in, and became crucial in shaping the socio-political system of the East-Central European countries. Its impact was manifold. Firstly, foreign owners were typically firm advocates of the rule-of-law, as this was the only way they could compete successfully on the local market. Secondly, the quick arrival of foreign owners saved some of the industrial culture and jobs that had been built by the forced industrialization of the socialist era and that was subsequently wiped out so spectacularly in countries without such investment: essentially everywhere in the former Soviet Union, except for the Baltic states.

In Ukraine, Moldova, and Georgia, these initial reforms either failed to occur, or were not at all comprehensive. As an illustration of the different environments, the economist Vladimir Dubrovskiy reminds us that during the post-communist period in Ukraine, an absurd tax system with rates of 90 percent marginal personal income tax and 52 percent payroll tax prevailed.[2] Such a tax system legitimized and very strongly incentivized keeping economic activities underground, and quickly gave rise to an emerging criminal state. Since nobody could even consider paying such exorbitant taxes, political strength derived from blackmail; specifically, who blackmails whom with the threat of criminal charges over tax avoidance.[3] The regulatory system inherited from the Soviet Union was full of the features that appear absurd to the outside observer, but which were highly functional against a cultural background where the most important thing was to get into a position to blackmail, and thus extract revenues, from others. Anyone who wished to become a businessman in countries with these traditions needed to be ready for strongly illegal activities—with all their concomitant blackmail. The only survivors were those who possessed or acquired such tools, and were ready to use them as more or less standard operating procedure.

There was illegal and outright criminal activity everywhere in the post-socialist space, but where reforms took hold early, they radically narrowed the room for such organizational evolution. However, as Taras Kuzio shows, in the early years of the Ukrainian transition criminal activities, racketeering, "insurance" payments, and local monopolies ensured by sheer force, including murder, were rampant. Such phenomena concentrated particularly in the East (Donbass), Crimea and Odessa.[4] Organized crime in the late Soviet period was already extremely developed, in direct opposition to the picture painted by Soviet propaganda. Cooperation between the officialdom, particularly enterprise directors, and the criminal underworld was rich and well developed.[5]

The extreme shortage economy experienced by Poland in the 1980s gave rise to a very elaborate shadow economy, closely linked to the authorities. The hard currency PEWEX shops were in state hands, but their price policy on vodka closely determined the shadow market price of the dollar on the Polish illegal foreign exchange market.[6] The official state airline, LOT, catered its passenger routes to the needs of the smugglers. As this shows, one major difference between Poland and Ukraine was the way in which communist rule was abandoned. As well as an extensive shadow economy, Poland had a similarly extensive movement to overcome Soviet socialism, with a strong national and Catholic character. These factors helped successive semi-democratic, and then fully democratic, governments to pursue radical market reforms; such developments did not occur either in Ukraine or in Moldova. The Solidarity movement, when it first took power, had a dedicated reformist team that took over economic governance. Leszek Balcerowicz and his entire team were absolutely beyond any corrupt intentions—they were indeed a dedicated reformist vanguard, coopting the best brains of Poles from the West, as well as the American Jeffrey Sachs and his team.

When comparing the ideology and the surrounding advisors of Balcerowicz with either Leonid Kravchuk or Leonid Kuchma and their circles, the difference could not be starker. Balcerowicz came to power stating that he would not "reinvent the wheel," whereas Kravchuk's advisors in particular spoke often of "local specificities."[7] A combination of a very strong national movement with a value-based, European agenda and a very dedicated, non-corruptible governmental cadre allowed Poland to quickly engage in radical reform. In Ukraine, on the other hand, despite the theoretical possibility of following the experiences of Poland (a neighbor of similar size), ultimately a different set of conditions prevailed that precipitated a tragic postponement of the reforms. The national movement could not have won on its own in Ukraine, as Andrew Wilson[8] as well as Kuzio and Wilson[9] have shown. In the era of Soviet disintegration, the reformers could only win by entering into coalition with communist elements who had staked their careers on change. This entailed major compromises. The inability of the national, reformist Rukh movement in Ukraine to win without some communist support had major consequences for the evolution of Ukraine's social system in the crucially important first post-communist years.[10] In Poland and the Baltics, the nationalist leaders' choices tended towards radical pro-market reform. In Ukraine, a combination of pro-third way and pro-communist advisors combined with emerging underworld-influenced policies.

Of Ukraine's three regional criminal traditions, that of the Donbass has exerted major influence on shaping independent Ukraine. Already in 1993, the miners' strikes there were not spontaneous workers' actions, but rather an organized rebellion against neglecting the interests of the East—or, more specifically, those of the emerging criminal elites in the region. Kuchma, a great tactician, coopted this dissatisfaction for his own presidential bid. It had elements of protest over a declining economy, belief that reintegration with Russia would eliminate the pain of transition, and a fear of losing the cultural identity associated with the use of the Russian language, all of which were exploited by the emerging "Donetsk clan." [11] For the "red director" Kuchma, using criminal elements was never taboo. In the Soviet environment, using them was an everyday practice of enterprise bosses, and Kuchma continued this. Privatization meant nothing more than theft by the regime's "favorites," and the sale of export licenses incorporated large kickbacks. The country gradually became more and more organized by criminal principles, where public service positions were used to extract illegal money streams (such as customs, border positions, tax officers, prosecutors and the infamous GAI road police). Everything was sold for money, and money was expected to continually flow up the hierarchy; the higher up an individual was, the more they were expected to pay upwards. The devastating cynicism of the Soviet system, and the general practice of "double-speak" practiced by everyone in communist times, smoothed the path to creating this system of social organization.

This all occurred against the background of a quickly deteriorating economic situation in the 1990s. While systemic inertia led towards a kind of criminal-patronal system, rulers also needed to worry about the economy. One instinct of policymakers was to pursue closer integration with the countries of the former Soviet Union, particularly Russia; however, such integration was not a feasible way to solve economic problems for many reasons. The other approach was to seek Western help, particularly from the International Monetary Fund (IMF). IMF assistance, however, came with certain obligations regarding economic management. Reforms came in waves. Where Henry Hale rightly sees the cycle of the patronal regimes, the economist also sees an intermittent, but accumulative, process of creating a market economy. In times of grave crisis, the regime engaged the IMF in negotiations, but always with the myopic idea of merely surviving the actual crisis that may cause a loss of popularity and, ultimately, power. As soon as the imminent threat had disappeared, the leadership allowed the construction of local monopolies with renewed vigor, essentially constituting various building blocks of the patronal pyramid. The goal was always twofold: on the one hand, to weather economic and political storms and remain in power; and on the other, to get fabulously rich, in a manner unimaginable in Soviet times, but known from Dallas and other Western media depicting the lives of the super-rich.

Kuchma's reforms in 1994 initially seemed very radical; indeed, Anders Åslund calls them more radical than Yegor Gaidar's original package of reforms in Russia.[12] However by 1995, after only a few months, Kuchma deviated from the liberal tenets of his reforms in his public pronouncements. This was a critical rupture at a point when oligarchic powers had not yet been entrenched. Again, the Polish example could have shown the way for Kuchma. The economy was still in a transitional decline, which could have either strengthened his resolve to continue the radical systemic transition, or alternatively conclude that the problem in fact had been the transition itself, and he needed "industrial policy" to save the Soviet-era industries that were crumbling due to the collapse of the USSR. Nobody offered a strategy that, within the framework of systemic transition, could also have addressed the tremendous loss of industrial culture accumulated in the Soviet industrialization, which had become obsolete in the new (not at all) "free market" conditions. In the absence of a positive vision, the default option was simply to muddle through.

Kuchma's personal inclinations as a former "red director" were very different from what would have been needed to continue radical reforms. He himself was an industrialist who could not accept the idea that some of those heavy industries must be allowed to fail. In that sense, Kuchma epitomized his country, just like Putin with his KGB background epitomizes Russia. None of the "good reformers" had a "red director" leading the country for 10 years. Kuchma's personal power base was drawn from the former military heavy industry in Dnipropetrovsk. He still could not imagine the kind of departure from economic symbiosis with Russia that gradually, but inevitably, would occur. Moreover, he saw his own power base still in the heavily industrial East, with its consequent lobbying powers. For him, strengthening the presidency was a personal power issue, but also a consequence of his conviction that this was the only way to build a viable state in the face of massive communist and socialist opposition in parliament.

Kuchma, at the same time, could see himself as a state builder with some legitimacy. Under his presidency, the national currency was established and consolidated. Economic decline first slowed before, in 1999, growth finally resumed. The country established a relationship with the international financial organizations, the IMF and the World Bank, and also with the major powers of the time, the United States and the European Union.

In his first presidential period, Kuchma consolidated his power by making the political system into a fully presidential one, by essentially coercing the parliament into agreeing to his constitutional "reform" in 1996, strongly influenced by Alyaksandr Lukashenka's success in creating a presidential system in Belarus in 1994. At the same time, in the second half of the 1990s he formed a pact with emerging oligarchs that allowed him to concentrate economic power as well as media control, since the emerging private media scene was heavily controlled by the oligarchs. He essentially established an alliance in which the oligarchs supported his political ambitions to continue to dominate Ukrainian politics, while he provided a "krisha" ("roof" in English, a widely used Russian word for political cover for illegal activities) for them to illegally profit from the country. Establishing a powerful presidency also built a cultural bridge to the previous Soviet system, in which the party's Central Committee had constituted the center of power. The presidency now filled this institutional vacuum left by the Soviet collapse. The ambiguity between formal and informal spheres was also similar: as in the Soviet era, the executive was the government which could be blamed, instead of the party, for any lack of success (particularly in the economy). This is the period in Ukraine, following the Russian lead, of using the emerging oligarchs as the base of presidential power. At the same time as Kuchma's efforts, Russian President Yeltsin used his famous swap of assets for electoral support which helped him win the elections in 1996, but also defined the main oligarchs in the system. The birth of the oligarchy, in symbiosis with the presidency, was simultaneous in the two countries. At the time, the oligarchs were of qualitatively different stock: in Ukraine, there was a much greater emphasis on people with a criminal background, while in Russia the oligarchs were more typically people with a white collar background, predominantly growing out of the late period of the Soviet Communist Party youth organization, the Komsomol.

This navigation between initially radical reform, followed by quickly abandoning it, also worked well for Kuchma in 2000, following his second presidential bid. He took victory in the presidential elections of 1999, despite the continually weak economic situation, and renewed decline as a consequence of the Russian financial crisis in 1998. He won because of the "power vertical" he built in the preceding years, enabling him to manipulate public opinion deviously with the bulk of the media in his hands, while also using administrative resources against his opponents in the 1998 parliamentary elections and the 1999 presidential elections. He ensured that his presidential opponent in the second round run-off would be an unpalatable choice; he was also helped by the fact that the only real heavyweight politician in strongly patriotic Western Ukraine, Viacheslav Chornovil, mysteriously died in a car accident in March 1999, half a year before the presidential elections in which he was supposed to be a candidate. His death was never properly investigated.[13]

Kuchma thus successfully balanced the different risks to his presidency, and in the process built a Ukrainian state in his image. When economic growth finally began to occur under his watch in 2000, it was initially spectacular. In fact, Kuchma appeared powerful enough either to change the constitution to permit him a third presidential term, or to nominate a successor in a way that would have left him in a very influential position.

Essentially Kuchma, unlike his predecessor Kravchuk, methodically constructed the patronal state, using all the means at his disposal. In order to alleviate economic collapse, he worked with the IMF and was able to speak the language of reform. He also created some of the basic attributes of a market economy, established the national currency and ended hyperinflation. At the same time, he was able to work with many of society's ambitious classes: he himself came from the "red director" class, but was able to work with the "young Turks," and also had the stomach to deal with the entrepreneurs of the Donbass and elsewhere of criminal origins. While in 1994 he won on a platform of rehabilitating relationships with Russia and other post-Soviet countries, in the 1999 campaign he was already able to present himself as the candidate of patriotic Western Ukraine, in the absence of any better alternative after the suspicious death of Chornovil. Kuchma was able to rely on the emerging oligarchs from Eastern Ukraine—those from his home base in Dnipropetrovsk, and from the Donbass. What made this relationship easier was that for him—being a former "red director" socialized in the Soviet Union—the idea of making informal deals with new entrepreneurs, including those with dubious backgrounds, was not alien; such alliances were common experiences for economic apparatchiks of the late Soviet era. And Kuchma had the necessary ruthlessness to watch and neutralize those who represented risk for him, such as his onetime prime minister, Pavlo Lazarenko.

What broke this dynamic was the Cassette Scandal or "Kuchmagate," in which recordings of Kuchma apparently ordering a journalist to be kidnapped were leaked by the president's bodyguard, Mykola Melnychenko. In the countries of the former Soviet Union, this scandal stands without parallel. For this reason, many conclude that this was a Russian secret operation that aimed to weaken Kuchma, who was attempting to solidify his relationship with the United States and the European Union. In that sense, the operation was highly successful; paradoxically, however, it also halted Kuchma's evolution towards consolidated authoritarian rule. A strong Ukrainian state with a Western integration model went against the perceived interest of the Russian state elites, who treated Ukraine as a core part of the Russian fabric, of the "Russian world." Under Kuchma, Ukraine continued the pattern developed by Kravchuk of distant and minimal participation in the Commonwealth of Independent States (CIS) integration efforts, driven by Russian hegemonic goals.

If it is true that Russia's interest and tactics towards the near abroad is to create weak political systems which will ultimately fall under Moscow's patronage, it is clear that either of two very different systemic developments in Ukraine would have been very bad news from their imperialistic perspective. First, Ukraine could have constructed a successful, Western-type liberal state. Alternatively, the country could have consolidated the rule of a strongman who built an imperfect nation state from the Western liberal point of view, but strengthened the national idea as well as the technical functions of the state in the long term, making the state both durable and viable. In the early Putin period, this second risk may have seemed even greater than the first.[14] Paradoxically, however, with this Moscow may have contributed in a major way to avoiding the formation of the single-pyramid system. By the time next such risk appeared, the Ukrainian nation was already mature enough to be able to prevent the formation of the mafia tyranny without such outside interference.

Building the single-pyramid system: the Voronin years in Moldova, 2001–2009

Moldova started its independent existence in the most difficult of circumstances. The Soviet market in which it had specialized so deeply had suddenly collapsed, while Europe remained distant, not only geographically but also because of a lack of trade infrastructure. Moldova has only two neighbors, Ukraine and Romania; both had a very poor start to their post-communist existence, among the worst initial performers of the democratic transition. Moreover, the identity of the state was highly disputed. The faraway, isolated country did not get effective assistance from the international organizations or from the European Community during its initial transition. Nobody understood the specificities of the country, and from the IMF on, every organization suggested more or less uniform post-socialist recipes for it.

All this occurred in a relative geopolitical vacuum. While the population in the Visegrád countries naturally gravitated towards the emerging European Union—let us not forget that at the time of the disintegration of the socialist system only a less politically integrative formation, the European Economic Community, existed—in the case of Ukraine and Moldova the interest was less intense. On the other hand, in the 1990s Russia was weak and felt dependent on the West's goodwill. It was only gradually that the world (essentially Europe and the US) became more interested, geopolitically and otherwise, in what is now called the Eastern Neighborhood. The EU only established a diplomatic mission in Moldova in 2005. And Russia, emerging from its post-transition slump fueled by the oil bonanza of the first decade of the new millennium, started to insist ever more assertively on again subordinating the "lost" territories of its former empire.

Isolated Moldova tried its best to be a good pupil, achieving membership in the IMF as well as in the World Trade Organization (WTO) as soon as possible. While its IMF membership was approved around the same time as the other post-Soviet countries in 1992, the country gained the much more demanding WTO membership ahead of most of the CIS in 2001,[15] a remarkable success. It meant that Moldova undertook the first generation of reforms—macroeconomic stabilization, including introducing its own currency, privatization, and trade and price liberalization—in the first half of the 1990s, as international donors expected. Moldova, having had a large agricultural sector in the Soviet period, also needed to transform its agriculture skillfully to make economic gains. USAID recognized this fact early, and provided large scale support in the 1990s through the early 2000s.

All this, however, was not enough to get the population on board for the post-Soviet transition. The country's economy continuously fell until 1999, and nobody had a clear vision of how to build a successful liberal state; international advice was followed, but it was simply not enough to turn the corner. In 2001, the most explicitly nostalgic pro-Soviet party, the Party of Communists of the Republic of Moldova (PCRM), offering safety, stability and a close association with Russia (rather than European or Romanian orientation), gained a constitutional majority in the parliamentary elections. Before the presidency of the PCRM's Vladimir Voronin, Moldova had only modestly advanced in building the patronal system; in particular, as Henry Hale has pointed out, the "divided-executive" nature of the constitutional order slowed down the process.[16] As Moldova is also a smaller, rural country, the usual easy privatization and theft generated less wealth, and thus translated less easily into superior political power. Furthermore, economic reform efforts made oligarchic formation slower.

However, Voronin's strong mandate meant he could easily begin to build a single-pyramid system, in spite of the constitutional obstacles to a strong presidency, as his party, built on a strictly hierarchical structure, enjoyed a constitutional majority in the parliament. First and foremost—somewhat like Putin in Russia—he clipped the wings of the early oligarchs in order to prevent them from limiting his power. At the same time, he also did not create the kind of presidential constitution that Lukashenka in Belarus had instituted after his overwhelming victory in 1994. The most likely reason was that he was afraid to ignite pro-Romanian (or anti-Russian) protests, though these did later materialize in 2003 when he tried to sign an agreement with Putin reuniting Transnistria with Moldova—the so-called Kozak Memorandum—on highly unfavorable terms, that would have locked Moldova into a pro-Russian orientation. The protests, along with Western pressure, led to Voronin's withdrawal from the agreement.[17]

On the basis of his strong electoral mandate and unquestioned power in his party, Voronin developed his own oligarchic clans. From today's perspective, the most skillful of them was Vlad Plahotniuc. However, in the early 2000s, he was not nearly the strongest player around Voronin; in fact, he only worked his way into the president's entourage around 2003. He gained his influence due to a business relationship with Voronin's son that over time proved the strongest mechanism to secure monopolistic access to business assets. For a long time, Voronin maintained a careful balance among his chief businessmen; Plahotniuc only gradually gained predominance among them.

The timing of Voronin's electoral victory was fortunate for him. When he took the helm of Moldova, the country's post-transition economic growth period had just started. This happened in most post-Soviet countries; after the Russian financial crisis of 1998, economic growth resumed following about nine years of economic decline.[18] In a technical sense, this period would have been ideal for further reforms towards a liberal state, putting the country on a more solid long-term growth trajectory. However, the logic of reform and democratic politics did not coincide here: by then, a majority of the population were disillusioned with the goals and slogans of the liberal state, and many simply craved a return to the Soviet Union. Voronin essentially won over the electorate by recognizing this and offering three promises: paying pensions and government salaries on time and in full; reuniting with Russia (and Belarus); and, accordingly, regaining Transnistria, a separatist enclave with very strong ties to Russia.

For Voronin, an important political turning point came in November 2003. Two events simultaneously shaped his international orientation, with major significance for the political system he built in the country. Firstly, he engaged in secret negotiations with Putin over a peace agreement with Transnistria. The resulting Kozak Memorandum gave highly disproportional powers to the Transnistrians relative to their size, while also establishing a Russian military base in the territory. Secondly, and simultaneously, the Rose Revolution occurred in Georgia. This proved to be one of the major factors leading to Voronin's ultimate withdrawal from the Kozak Memorandum. His fear of a similar revolution at home and pressure from the West[19] persuaded him to step back at the last minute from signing the agreement, which would have sold out Moldovan interests to

Moscow. From then on, Voronin half-heartedly pursued a Western orientation. His fundamental cultural predisposition was pro-Russian, but he ruled over a country where part of the population would not agree to move it under Russian patronage in any circumstances. Moreover, he spoiled his burgeoning relationship with Putin, who wanted to score his first great foreign policy victory with this agreement. Voronin's turn was instrumental in sealing his 2005 presidential victory, since many Western and pro-Western leaders helped his campaign, including the president of neighboring Romania, Traian Băsescu. Still, Voronin's Western orientation proved to be a further obstacle to building a consolidated single-pyramid patronal political regime in Moldova.

The centrality of prosecution services in the East European single-pyramid system: Ukraine and Moldova

Political scientists usually downplay the role of prosecution services (and of secret services and tax authorities) in the shaping of the single-pyramid patronal social systems. Without understanding the centrality of these institutions, particularly of prosecution services, it is impossible to understand why and how these systems have emerged. **Under Stalin's Soviet power, prosecution authorities evolved into a central institution of state repression. In the post-Soviet system, the fear factor was seriously reduced, but the privileged legal status of the prosecution service has been instrumental to presidents seeking to cement their dominant power over other contenders in a world of densely intertwined political and private economic power.**

Taras Kuzio traces the core power of the Ukrainian public prosecution service to the Donbass gang, dating from the late Kuchma period until near to the present. Many of the key prosecutors of the Donbass clan started their unsavory careers in the 1980s or later, going on to establish a close relationship to Yanukovych during his years as governor of the Donetsk *oblast*, and to the oligarch Rinat Akhmetov. Svyatoslav Pishkun was twice prosecutor general, while other holders of this post including Hennadiy Vasylyev, Oleksandr Medvedko, Renat Kuzmin and Viktor Pshonka "have been loyal to the Donetsk clan."[20] Kuzio also mentions other key governmental institutions for their capacity to blackmail. Mykola Azarov, core member of the Donetsk clan, was Kuchma's head of State Tax Administration, and later minister of finance for eight years out of ten. As Kuzio says, quoting journalist Jaroslav Koshiw: "He [Azarov] gave Kuchma the impression that the President was making the decisions when actually it was Azarov who controlled the agenda."[21] In the criminal or near criminal world of post-Soviet "elite" politics and society, blackmail, *kompromat* and, as a "positive" incentive, under-the-table payments all play key roles—showing strong continuity with the Soviet times, but in a much less restricted manner. In this, the institution of the public prosecution service was central. In Ukraine, this system had fully evolved during the Kuchma years, while in Moldova it remained less fully formed, as presidential power was much weaker and parliament maintained its importance, until the election of Voronin.

Neither of the two revolutions in Ukraine were able to make fundamental and radical changes in this mafia system.[22] Viktor Yushchenko gained the presidency with the necessary compromise of weakening his own constitutional role. On the other hand, he still had the right to directly appoint the prosecutor general; however, he did not use this prerogative and kept the Donetsk-related Svyatoslav Pishkun in the position. Worse, when Pishkun was finally replaced, he did so on the basis of a deal with his oligarch secretary of the National Security and Defense Council (and current President), Petro Poroshenko. Incredibly, another of the Donetsk clan, Oleksandr Medvedko, took over and controlled the prosecutor's office during the entire period of Yushchenko's presidency. This resulted in complete immunity from prosecution for the people who had created and run the criminal state under Kuchma. The tragedy of the Yushchenko period was that while Prime Minister Yulia Tymoshenko wanted to be tougher with representatives of the previous regime than Yushchenko, her reign was extremely disappointing and ultimately a huge failure in terms of economic governance. Moreover, the rivalry between the president and his prime minister also weakened any chance of reform where it could have fundamentally changed the functioning of the state.

Was this inevitable or was it just bad luck for the country? Yushchenko's ultimate consumption by the system rests on two key factors. Firstly, it points to the strength of the core criminal part of the state, originating in the "wild East" culture of the Donbass region of the 1990s (particularly Donetsk). Secondly, Yushchenko's presidency started with a major compromise between him and the largely criminal oligarchic structures, who were able to weaken the constitutional prerogatives of the presidency ahead of

Yushchenko taking over. However, this in itself could have been a blessing if it established a more stable division of powers. It was pure misfortune that in Tymoshenko the country got a prime minister who had no intention to reform economic regulation. Her ingrained statism saw the use of extensive, arbitrary practices thought to be long forgotten, such as extensive price controls. Yushchenko also disappointed, due to many factors, not least the unfortunate after-effects of his shocking poisoning.

The division of power in this administration led to paralysis and opened the room for the unlikely gradual comeback of Yanukovych, who had been nominated to the presidency after being underestimated by the oligarch sponsor of both Kuchma and Yanukovych, Rinat Akhmetov, and then thought to be a political corpse after the Orange Revolution. Given that the Donbass gang was a more cohesive organization than other oligarchic groups, their Party of Regions was able to offer the only alternative to the fractious Orange group. Furthermore, the strong ethno-nationalist symbolism of the late-era Yushchenko presidency inadvertently helped to consolidate the east of the country under the Donbass-based Party of Regions, despite the fact that neither the culture of the Donbass nor its representatives were at all popular in other large eastern Ukrainian centers such as Kharkiv and Dnipropetrovsk. For much of the East, they simply seemed to be the lesser evil.

The international factor was also of some relevance here. Neither the European Union nor the United States were able to provide either the carrot or the stick of successful influence. Clearly, after the Orange Revolution Ukraine should have been offered security as well through NATO membership and the long-term possibility of EU integration. These needs became ever more pressing after the Russian war in Georgia in 2008. Neither of the two options were offered to Ukraine, which softened their incentive to reform as well as the leverage of the US and Europe over Ukrainian policy. Moreover, at the time nobody understood sufficiently the degree of reform the country required to break out from the system established under Kuchma. The deep systemic character of the distortions of the justice system, particularly the criminal character of the prosecutorial system,[23] were poorly understood outside the country; it took international actors another decade of disappointments to gradually learn this. As such, conditionalities for Ukraine were not sufficiently strict.

While analysts have not realized the core importance of reforming the manner in which justice was provided in these societies, the actors, of course, have been fully aware. As I will discuss later, in the Moldovan case Vlad Plahotniuc became a dominant figure in society because he understood more than others how little traditional politics matters when compared to who controls key power institutions, particularly the public prosecution service.

Georgian reforms under Mikheil Saakashvili: an attempt to break out from the mafia system

Ukraine provides an unfortunate example of a country that squandered a huge chance for the kind of reform that may have taken the country to a Western type of developmental path, to real systemic change. By contrast, a little further East, in a more difficult geographical situation Georgia undertook a genuine, albeit somewhat flawed, effort to follow a Western modernizing path. Its relative success shows how many chances Ukraine had after the Orange Revolution, and it gives us valuable insights into how to overcome the post-Soviet mafia style single-pyramid patronal systems—both from its successes and its shortcomings. In many ways, Ukraine's path to reform began from a more advantageous position, as the Georgian reformers in the last two years working in Ukraine would point out; Georgia had started with criminal structures more deeply integrated into the state (some of which in fact are still active but outside the country, in places like Russia and Germany). In fact, Georgia had by far the most *vory v zakonie*[24] in the decade after the disintegration of the Soviet Union. Moreover, the general educational level and desire to obey the law in Ukraine is perceived by the Georgians with experience of Ukraine to be higher than in Georgia. However, what made the Ukrainian situation more difficult, besides the accidental factors I highlighted above, was the enormous, albeit pluralistic, strength of the oligarchs.

When looking at Georgia, one must consider the big picture: the country spent most of its modern history under Moscow's rule, with only a short period of independence in 1918–21. The fall of the Soviet Union ensured that Georgia became independent again in 1991, essentially like Ukraine and Moldova; however, Georgian national consciousness was much clearer than that of Moldova and Ukraine. At the beginning of Georgia's independent existence, an extreme level of anarchy was prevalent. Law and order was in jeopardy; street crime, shootings and contract murders were commonplace. The country looked extremely disjointed. From this perspective, even Eduard Shevardnadze's rule should be acknowledged for the great progress it made, as it established a degree of stability in a country which was previously at the brink of various civil wars. However, the state worked like most of the CIS countries, with people close to Shevardnadze, including his family members, acquiring large monopolistic economic rights, including in the oil and gas trade. That was changed by the Rose Revolution. In fact, the last quarter century can be seen almost as the continuous success story of constructing the nascent Georgian state. Shevardnadze established it but with large deficiencies, the Saakashvili period cleansed it and launched very liberal economic policies and laws, while the last four years witnessed the consolidation of these gains. Of course, there are many different ways to interpret these twenty-five years, and the jury is still out on whether this successful nation-building will continue.

Against the backdrop of the frenzy of reforms under the towering dominance of President Saakashvili, it is easy to forget that he initially came to power with a delicate coalition. Despite this, he relentlessly pursued his reformist ideals. It was leadership, rather than the circumstances, that mainly explains the difference between the Georgian reforms and the rest of the CIS. In Ukraine, the argument is often made that it was easier for Georgia to reform, as it had a fully presidential political system. In fact, the reform momentum of Yushchenko in 2004 was actually larger than that of Saakashvili. The greatest difference is that Saakashvili used the power he had to launch far-reaching, and in many ways popular, reforms.[25]

The Saakashvili era consisted of two distinct periods. The first one, lasting until the 2007 closure of the Imedi television station, followed by mass protest and violent repression, was characterized by an incredibly energetic and ambitious modernization agenda for the Georgian state. It combined two distinct currents: the genuine and brave fight against organized crime and corruption, and a libertarian drive to shrink the scope and extent of the state.

Significant in this marriage of the two currents was the homecoming of businessman Kakha Bendukidze in the middle of 2004, and the fact that Saakashvili understood and embraced the cohesion between his modernizing agenda and Bendukidze's anti-statist one. This period saw the complete and radical overhaul of state institutions, as well as a radical liberalization of the economy. However, what this period did not produce was the clear separation of executive and judicial power, a key component of the rule-of-law. The authorities were very strict with crime and corruption. Sentences were harsh and the prison population grew. This was crucial to break the expectation of the criminal state's eternal survival; it sent the message that there would be zero tolerance of crime and corruption. Corners were cut so that the goal could be quickly achieved—but this had a long-term price. Indeed, in two important ways, the reforms remained incomplete throughout the entire Saakashvili period. Firstly, the judiciary and the prosecution services were never made independent. The maintenance of the umbilical cord between the justice sector and the state, particularly the president, led to the second restraint on reform: the creation of an arbitrary and excessive repressive apparatus.

Media pluralism suffered after the 2007 Imedi case,[26] where the police used force to disperse a demonstration, then the government ordered the closure of the Imedi television stations and police damaged equipment in their central studio. The media situation suffered a further blow after the war with Russia in the summer of 2008. The government did not tolerate dissent and became increasingly paranoid, seeing the hand of Russia everywhere. Media pluralism was severely reduced during the Saakashvili era as a major limitation on democratic norms.

The period following the war in 2008 is, in general, different from the reformist frenzy of the earlier phase of Saakashvili's rule. On the one hand, the wounded Saakashvili changed from "Misha the reformer" to "Misha the builder." He started large scale popular projects such as the transformation of Batumi, the second largest Georgian city, into an international holiday and entertainment center. This project was successfully accomplished. He also initiated the construction of a new sea port, a project that was abandoned by the new authorities for a period, then recently resurrected. An innovative combination of the visible developments and essential reforms was the creation of the Public Service Halls. These new buildings combine many government services in one heavily digitalized and concentrated location. The buildings themselves are meant to symbolize transparency. In each major city, they were built by a renowned architect and are also meant to be visible landmarks of modernity. These modern architectural landmarks are phenomenally successful: they symbolize the fitting of the ultra-modern into the very ancient in aesthetical terms and, at the same time, symbolize the modernized service state in a spectacular way.

While the merit-oriented "cadre" policy of the first period introduced a large amount of new young talent, from 2008 onward loyalty increasingly came above competence. Often this resulted in talented workers leaving the public service. This change of heart was relative, and even after 2008 many young, Western educated and talented people found their way into the state apparatus, particularly since the salary reform eliminated the traditional disincentive that plagues most of the CIS countries. Still, by then the picture became more mixed, rather than unequivocally reformist and positive.

At the same time, enemies of the Georgian reforms assert that these were abandoned after the Imedi affair and the regime only cared about maintaining its power, which is not accurate. Further critical liberalizations took place in and after 2008 and liberal fiscal principles were enshrined in the constitution at this time. Undoubtedly, however, the reformist vigor lessened and the democratic deficit grew. One area that was not particularly strongly reformed and desperately required an overhaul is non-university level education. This is particularly noteworthy because of the otherwise strong modernization drive of the Saakashvili team.

The sweeping tax reform of 2005–6 was a textbook case of the Laffer curve: lower "marginal" tax rates resulted in greatly increased tax revenues.[27] The tax reform radically simplified the tax system. By eliminating loopholes, it contributed to the elimination of one of the major sources of corruption in the post-Soviet patronal politics, the highly arbitrary tax system. All in all, it was a spectacular success, not leaving any budgetary gaps behind.

Paying taxes has become a question of dignity; previously, doing so had been regarded as an unmanly embarrassment. The first step to the establishment of a taxpaying culture used fear. That is now gone, but the "inertial" positive experience of the habit of paying taxes remains. Tax levels are low and the system is simple. Georgia has four types of taxes, plus excise: personal income tax; profit tax; tax after distributed profit; VAT; and excise on petrol, alcohol and tobacco. The self-employed pay a simplified business tax, and under a turnover of 100,000 lari (about 50,000 USD) do not pay any business tax. In 2007, company social contributions were eliminated, as they were regarded as an anti-employment device.

The Saakashvili government cleaned up the banking system, leading to the kind of development that gave credit to the ambition of making Tbilisi a regional financial center. New regulation was introduced that requires transparent, identifiable owners, independent auditors and supervisory boards. They reduced bureaucracy drastically, unified FX and interest rates, introduced more rigorous capital requirements than the international Basel rules, and liberalized and simplified foreclosure rules. The central bank also radically shrunk: while in 2007 there were still more than one thousand employees in eight central bank branches, by the end of Saakashvili's rule, its branches were eliminated and employment shrunk to three hundred. In the meantime, the assets of the banking sector grew twenty-five-fold.

The economic reforms brought sweeping deregulation that the Western partners didn't always understand, as they lacked appreciation of the context of those reforms. Two very visible measures occurred in 2005–6, when the car and food safety agencies were eliminated, since they did not take care of car and food safety but were purely hotbeds of corruption. The European Union Association Agreement has since mandated the reinstatement of the food safety agency. Famously in 2010, the High Representative of the European Union, Catherine Ashton, publicly stated in Tbilisi that a precondition of the Association Agreement is to establish phytosanitary control in the country. The early shocks of eliminating these dysfunctional, parasitic institutions, as well as other agencies, were often treated as "excessive" and even "lunatic" by international partners. In fact, it was exactly this radicalism that was a core factor in reforms that triggered real—not merely cosmetic—change.

During the Saakashvili period, it became a principle that advocates of a regulation or a supervisory agency must address two key concerns: firstly, that it fulfills a public purpose; and secondly, how it will concretely fulfill that purpose. The starting point was always inherently skeptical—it posed that the Georgian state was overburdened, and thus needed to shrink. In the deregulatory effort, two additional considerations were applied: if the agency is abolished, legislators buy time to review the underlying regulations; and when higher level legal acts (laws) were abolished, bylaws were also eliminated. In addition, in 2007 the guillotine principle was applied, which deliberately cleaned the system of about 1,600 regulatory acts.

In 2009, a constitutional amendment established that taxes can only be increased by referendum. Later, in 2011, the Liberty Act was introduced, adding to the constitution binding rules about the deficit (limited to 3% per year), the public debt and the size of the budget relative to GDP (set at 30%). This second period of the Saakashvili era—the supposed "non-reform period"—also brought about sweeping simplifications for the pharmaceuticals market, such as the elimination of licensing for pharmaceutical products already licensed in major markets. Visa rules were also liberalized: countries with a GDP three times per capita higher than Georgia's obtained an automatic visa waiver for all their citizens. Saakashvili was uniquely capable of selling liberalizing reforms as he saw, and believed in, their popular angle.

A weak point of the reforms was, and has remained, agriculture. The modernizer Saakashvili, and his team, essentially overlooked a sector that still employs 47% of the work force (while 92% of GDP is produced in the three major cities, Tbilisi, Batumi and Kutaisi). At the end of the Soviet Union, agricultural employment stood at 25%, which means that the transitional crisis brought about a degree of de-urbanization, much as in Moldova and Ukraine. It appears that none of these three regimes has yet been able to work out a positive, effective agricultural program.

The 1993 land reform distributed land in a routine manner without any consideration to external factors: everybody got the same size of land in the village, in three different pieces. As a consequence, average land ownership is extremely small, 1.2 hectares, but because it is usually in three separate parts, the land pieces are in fact much smaller than this. There are a couple of thousand sizeable estates; if they are taken out of consideration, the average land holding is below one hectare. However, when the land reform happened back in the early 1990s, it actually saved lives, as Georgia was undergoing a serious food shortage. Thus in the post-communist period, including the Saakashvili era, the land policy de facto played a kind of social policy role.

Besides wine, the farmers specialized in labor-intensive products, like hazelnuts and citrus fruits. Export of both these commodities are sizeable, especially since the Russian market reopened after the Saakashvili era. In the last few years, at European instigation, Georgia has been experimenting with agricultural cooperatives as a way of pooling resources. So far, the results have not been spectacular. Typically a few people in the village create a cooperative to reap the financial benefits, but not much in practical terms so far has changed, and so general opinion about the cooperatives is skeptical. As such, the politically puzzling lack of strategy to address the paradox of relatively modern cities with their service sectors, and very inefficient and obsolete countryside, remains.

Sweeping deregulation of the economy in Georgia was accompanied with state reform that put rooting out corruption at its center. It relied heavily on centralization of power within the public administration. This very unorthodox, completely homegrown "policy mix" worked very well for Georgia insofar as the main target, corruption, was concerned. Indeed, in

Georgia centralization worked so well that for the Georgian reformers it became a dogma, for four reasons. Firstly, they aimed at maximum cleansing of the state. If they delegated systematically to regions and municipalities, they would be unsure of controlling the implementation of the reforms; Saakashvili did delegate, but only within the centralized state. Secondly, he inherited a state that was highly fragmented, to the extent that further disintegration was a risk. This was particularly the case in the province of Adjara, but they could not be certain that other regions would not follow. Thirdly, Georgia is a small state, particularly when compared to Ukraine, where its model has been most intensely tested, although it is also diverse, so a decentralization argument would have been defensible at the time. And fourthly, part of the young Georgian team's deeply seated ethos was to use IT extensively. It helped to centralize many processes, perhaps most predominantly in the Ministry of Internal Affairs, that under Saakashvili became a very powerful, and at the same time very efficiently-run, ministry.

The international aspects of the decentralization dilemma are also important for Georgia, Moldova and Ukraine. Since the disintegration of the Soviet Union, fragmentation of states in the "near abroad" evolved into a conscious Russian policy, with the aim of using parts of these nascent states to blackmail the larger entity back into Russian hands. Thus, policy considerations must take a careful look at the risks of state disintegration. In sum, the Georgian centralization experience brings an important, albeit by no means conclusive, case into the debate on how best to transform the patronal state.

In Saakashvili's Georgia, law enforcement institutions and individuals became very influential, since so much of the new team's success in reforms depended on their work. Many of them, like Eka Zguladze, Eka Gigauri and others were not typical law enforcers: they were young, talented women and men with great creative energy, ambition and self-confidence. Law enforcement, however, later became a source of Saakashvili's political problems, as the excesses of the law enforcement machinery increasingly became unpopular, and much of the population felt them disproportionate.

Saakashvili's early reforms in law enforcement were on two tracks, both responding to popular demand. Firstly, he undertook a complete overhaul of some of the services most visible to the population. He eliminated the infamous GAI street police, whose almost sole activity beforehand had been to stop cars on the streets and extract illegal fines from them, which then flowed upward to their superiors' pockets. The logic was simple: if you didn't agree to the illegal fine, you would get a much larger official fine. This informal system was in place almost everywhere in the non-Baltic post-Soviet space, and persisted in Georgia until the reforms. The system is highly pyramidal: people bought their positions in the mafia-like road police, and on the job they "earned" for themselves, while also supplying a continued money stream up to their superiors. Higher positions would then get bought for higher sums. The "tariffs" would get extremely high, as the cash-flow from this activity is significant. Essentially, the same system also worked in the border guard services, in customs and in the tax services in the same set of countries of the former Soviet Union. Such practices typically reach up to the highest political levels. Saakashvili's reforms eliminated all these criminal pyramids, mainly through radical overhaul, severe fines for offenders, and zero tolerance, but also through offering high salaries as a positive incentive.

For this kind of institutional transformation to work, the salary reform became critical. The Georgian strategy was to replace the old, irremediably corrupt guard in many institutions with new, better educated, younger people. These new recruits needed to receive higher salaries to remain fully motivated, while at the same time no corruption was tolerated. At the top level, Saakashvili's hiring of the most important agents of change proved to be exceptionally successful. He succeeded in creating a faithful top cadre who, for a few years, dedicated their lives to the modernization of their country. As such, everyone in power positions fell in line with the reform strategy. Leadership was critical to the success of the institutional reforms in Georgia.

The salary reform started with the salary supplement system that was run from two funds. One was initiated by George Soros at Saakashvili's request, and co-created and fully managed by my team at the United Nations Development Project (UNDP). The other was more informal, not as transparent as the one managed by the UNDP, and created by contributions from businessmen. These practices were explicable and creative from the start and, together with the fully transparent international salary supplement program, they bridged the time gap until the national budget, now cleansed from corruption, could step in. This came surprisingly quickly. We originally designed the salary supplements to decrease year on year, ending after three years. In reality, they ended after one year, thanks to the criticism from Putin that Saakashvili was "on the payroll of Soros"; the government decided to replace them immediately with budgetary financing.

The whole system of road police and border guards were completely overhauled from the beginning. Saakashvili needed this measure to generate popular support for reform. In the case of the border guards, the conscript system was terminated, and an entirely new personnel was hired with much higher professional and moral expectations. They were well paid professionals, and the whole ethic of the border guards changed with an effect that lasts, very visibly to the traveler, until today. The introduction of the patrol police, which has replaced the road police with a broader mandate, has been also a very popular reform. Like the border guards, their complete overhaul introduced a completely new, uncorrupted ethos. The PR effect was important: they usually look stylish, are generally courteous and people like them. Criminal policing is a highly complex area, where the reforms were more modest than the more visible, and to an extent PR-driven, patrol police reform. These techniques have re-emerged in the Ukrainian reforms, having been mainly promoted by Eka Zguladze, former deputy minister of internal affairs in Georgia who also introduced a patrol police reform as Ukrainian deputy minister of internal affairs in 2014–16.

The most important and complex segment of rule-of-law reforms concerned the judiciary and the public prosecution service. The judiciary went through a sea change after the Rose Revolution. This was seen as absolutely necessary, as even though stability improved under Shevardnadze, Georgian criminal gangs were still very strong. Although the competence of judges and prosecutors improved and cases got managed faster as a consequence of the reforms after 2003, the judiciary did not become independent. Revolutionary centralization here meant direct control over the appointment of judges, to the extent that until 2007 President Saakashvili even chaired the High Council of Judges (HCJ) to oversee radical de-Sovietization of the system. This shows the importance he placed on judicial reform, and how much this reform was about fighting corruption and crime, rather than the full establishment of the rule-of-law. From 2007 the situation evolved, as the number of judges grew in the HCJ and they became a majority there. In other ways too, the government pursued change of the judiciary by rationalizing the system: for instance, the eight district judge positions in Tbilisi were reduced to one. They also invested in the dilapidated court infrastructure by building modern court houses. However, the lack of independence of the judiciary meant that after 2007, as political competition and pressure intensified, the government increasingly took politically sensitive cases to "friendly" judges.

As discussed earlier in this paper, prosecution reform in the post-Soviet patronal state is critical. Saakashvili wanted radical change, but not so radical as to weaken the role of the prosecutors since he wanted to break organized crime, and not cut the umbilical cord of the prosecutorial office to the executive. The core ideology was the fight against corruption, and it had enormous merits, but in the process he left too much of the post-Soviet power of the prokuratura intact. Some reforms went through: the number of prosecutors decreased dramatically, from about 1500 to 450, and general oversight, a typical Soviet relic, was abandoned. But the prosecution service remained centralized and militaristic during the Saakashvili era, and investigative power was not taken away from them. Moreover, Saakashvili used it for his political purposes. While some of the critiques greatly exaggerate the level of arbitrariness of this period, it is true that during the entire Saakashvili era the prokuratura continued to go after businesspeople and, later, after political opponents. The harshness of sentences was also a problem as Georgian society, while first welcoming the crackdown on corruption, which was often in very visible places, soon became concerned about the number of people staying in prison and the length of sentences. Much of the public judged the repressive measures against corruption simply excessive. Moreover, the Ministry of Internal Affairs did not care to reform the appalling Soviet-style conditions in prisons. The introduction of the plea bargain was a good step, but too often it was used to arbitrarily extract confessions of guilt in the hope of avoiding conviction.

At the beginning of the Saakashvili period, businesspeople associated with the previous regime were often put in jail and released after a pledge to pay. At that point, it was purely informal and could even be justified by the urgent financial needs of the new, revolutionary state. This arbitrariness, however, never really ended. At first, it was an understandable deviation from the rule-of-law which was considered to be temporary; later, the Saakashvili team thought they could take shortcuts to reforming the state. And yet even later they needed the dependent institutions to keep power. Paradoxically, the prison drama was instrumental in bringing Saakashvili down—as such, his reluctance to go for full, rather than partial, reform of justice caused his demise.

As for the current government, it has listened to the demands of international actors to free the judiciary and public prosecution institutionally from the influence of the executive. The current Prime Minister Giorgi Kvirikashvili has launched the "third wave" of justice reform, aiming to increase the independence of the judiciary and the prosecution services. However, while preparing the legal base for that independence, in its practical daily work the executive has used its strong political power, consolidated for a further four years during the November 2016 elections, to build up its strong informal influence in these institutions. While the chairman of the High Council of Justice is from the previous governing team, the secretary of the HCJ is drawn from the current executive. Since he has proven more agile, through him the government has gained strong influence. Moreover, the secretary created a milieu of solidarity—one where, however, he can only protect the judges if they cooperate with the government. Still, many judges refuse to yield to political pressure, and are therefore treated by government as people of the "old guard."

While the media environment has improved in the current political cycle, the recent Rustavi 2 TV channel case is testing this record. The case of the old owner, Kibar Khalvashi, reclaiming his stake in the TV channel has been notorious and a recent example of undue governmental political influence. On August 5, 2015, Khalvashi, who had owned Rustavi 2 until 2006, reclaimed his ownership in the television channel, claiming that in 2006 he had been forced into selling it.[28] Since the case is ten years old, the Saakashvili-affiliated opposition regarded it as undue government interference in order to eliminate media freedom ahead of the October 2016 elections. They charged the judge with governmental influence. The case ultimately went to the Supreme Court which "found [the] appeal from Rustavi 2 TV, which is disputing lower courts' ruling ordering transfer of ownership of the broadcaster to its former co-owner, admissible." The international partners of Georgia, namely the US, the EU and international watchdogs, have all weighed in heavily to stop the broadcaster being taken away from its current owners, who have strong links to Saakashvili.[29]

The current government has continued to control the prosecution services as its predecessor did. First, it appointed a highly controversial prosecutor general, Otar Partskhaladze, who had been convicted of a criminal offense in Germany. Partskhaladze also appeared to unduly pressure Ivane Merabishvili, the Saakashvili government's long-running minister of internal affairs and one of its strongest figures, during the latter's detention. When he was removed thanks to international reaction, the minister of justice took over and held the function until the end of 2015. The EU exerted pressure on the government to change this, and according to new legislation, the prokuratura has now been taken out of the control of the MoJ. This is potentially a significant step towards prosecutorial independence.

Overall, the institutional situation of the rule-of-law has still improved since 2012. Here we are witnessing a potentially fortuitous sequence of the Saakashvili government first reorganizing and modernizing the justice sector, and then the current government, under international pressure, making further organizational arrangements towards prosecutorial independence. Nevertheless, the situation is far too fragile to declare victory yet.

An important component of the Georgian reforms under Saakashvili was an ambitious use of technology. Again, they bravely hired young talent from the very beginning, who strove to radically upgrade the IT system, which was, at the time, almost non-existent. IT turned out to be instrumental in the pursuit of centralization of functions, since in a country as small as Georgia, it is easier to manage and use a centralized data system. In the fight against organized crime, IT was a powerful tool in the hands of the reformed police. The pioneering use of IT was also instrumental in improving road safety, and it helped the signature patrol police reform as police enforcement was taken away from the realm of human discretion. They installed an incredible 15,000 traffic enforcement cameras during the "Safe City" campaign. As a consequence, speeding and other traffic violations dramatically dropped. They also tried to design a system that bypassed human discretion in sending out fines. The Ministry of Internal Affairs was another area where IT use was instrumental, as it introduced Police Service Centers offering transparent customer service for auto licenses along the same principles as the Public Service Halls. These centers work quickly and efficiently, using IT extensively; furthermore, drivers' licenses are designed in a transparent way, using computers so that the once universal bribing for licenses can be eliminated. Overall, the effort to move beyond human discretion and introduce transparent procedures wherever possible was a very important core effort of the Georgian reformers.

Many of these reforms became deeply entrenched, either through their popularity, or by the above mentioned constitutional amendments. As such, since Saakashvili's government was replaced by the current regime, not much has been changed.

Overall, the results of the reforms have been spectacular. The economy has grown on average much faster than the rest of the region. The Saakashvili presidency witnessed 6.6 percent real annual growth, in spite of the problems of 2008—a year which saw both war and the severe impact of the international financial crisis. The economy proved to be highly adaptable to the crisis circumstances, and moved back to growth rapidly.[30] Furthermore, the European Bank for Reconstruction and Development (EBRD) projects that economic growth will continue at a higher pace in Georgia than among its neighbors.[31] The state bureaucracy is now of the highest quality among the Eastern Neighborhood countries. Everyday corruption was wiped out in a nation that once was regarded the epitome of corrupt society, that once had combined traditional kinship values with (post-)communist hypocrisy. Much of this survived the democratic change of government in 2012–13, a major indicator of reform sustainability, even if the quality of leadership and governance arguably dropped significantly. The Saakashvili period was characterized by an influx of young talent. The charisma of Saakashvili and Bendukidze resulted in an almost religious cadre of young, talented people with extremely rare creative skills and energies who worked tirelessly to move the country into modernity.

While the overwhelming majority of these extremely talented young people left the scene after Saakashvili's electoral defeat, or some already after his regime turned more authoritarian in 2007–8, the striking fact is that the mid-level bureaucracy and judicial cadre were already almost sufficient to maintain a highly qualified state bureaucracy and justice system. Corruption has not (yet?) reemerged. However, the earlier nepotistic features of prior appointments did soon return. State services are courteous, quick and service oriented. This all seems to have become ingrained in Georgian society in such a way that if it changes, people will likely react strongly. The constitutionally established caps of 2010–12, instituted by the Saakashvili administration, have also ensured that the state does not restart its usual proliferation.[32]

What is often overlooked when examining the Georgian success is the intimate linkage between the crusade against corruption and the relentless pursuit of libertarian ideology. Trying to curb the bloated state apparatus through law enforcement alone would not have sufficed; it had to be accompanied by a very hard-nosed government, slashing away bureaucratic layers that were deemed excess. The ethos was a functioning and small state. It was thought that a poor country with weak state traditions could not afford a Swedish-type welfare and regulatory state; instead, it had to be smaller and simpler. In fact, even the free trade negotiations with the European Union were deemed to be a compromise in the name of geopolitical needs.

Georgia needed the European Union for protection against Russia, but it rightly regarded the regulatory regime imposed on it as excessively bureaucratic and illiberal.

The indices measuring democracy have deteriorated in Georgia after the Rose Revolution, at the same time as sharply improving corruption and general governance and freedom indicators. However, how much these indicators are able to capture reality is also in question, in light of the fact that in 2012 and 2013 a peaceful, election-based transition of power occurred from Saakashvili and his United National Movement (UNM) party to the opposition, a rare phenomenon in the post-Soviet patronal world.

The elections in 2016 strengthened the power of Georgian Dream, the party that unseated Saakashvili and his United National Movement in 2012 and 2013. Georgian Dream won a constitutional majority with fewer votes than the losing UNM had received in 2012. Such an oddity was possible first of all due to the deliberate change of electoral system, bringing in a strong majoritarian component. Georgian Dream won most of the majoritarian districts, and as such, will have the opportunity to consolidate its patronal power in Georgian society during its four year term. It is a particularly fragile situation as the de facto power behind the party is the country's dominant oligarch, Bidzina Ivanishvili. While Ivanishvili exercises his power with a certain amount of restraint, such overwhelming power rarely leaves informal institutions unchanged. To this end, Georgia's gains during the Saakashvili period, creating a modern state in place of a once single-pyramid patronal one, will be tested in the ensuing period.[33]

Finally, it is important to ask why the voters did not vote the modernizing force, UNM, back into power. As I have written above, many reforms were, and have remained, popular. However some, particularly the very strict punishments for violations, brought many people outside of their comfort zones; people who used to live with the combination of traditional family, clan, or geographical affiliation, rather than that of modern Western ethics. Moreover, the fact that the provision of justice throughout the whole Saakashvili period contained an element of political arbitrariness—either towards perceived enemies, or for the purpose of extracting budgetary or political revenues from rich businesspeople—left large chunks of the elite also not wanting Saakashvili back. It can be argued that, towards the end of the campaign period, Saakashvili's strong personal appearance at UNM rallies seems to have been strongly counterproductive. Indeed, it appeared to push many voters towards the "safe bet" of the Georgian

Dream, who have practiced power without the excesses of Saakashvili in the last four years. Worryingly, both tinkering with the election system and manipulating the election results were part of the reason for the *extent* of the Georgian Dream victory.[34]

The next few years will see a severe test of Georgia's socio-political system, due to a combination of less political control by the opposition, and the temporary strength of Russia, whose ambition is to use corruption to curtail the autonomy of its neighboring states. While the Saakashvili reforms were remarkably radical, and many elements of them withstood the next electoral cycle, the newest circumstances may contribute to an erosion of hard-won reforms, rather than completing the journey towards a modern liberal state organization. The posture of the European Union in this period will be important, as the main external actor that can positively influence the direction of the Georgian state in the current geopolitical environment.

Ukrainian and Moldovan travails around the rule-of-law

Successful liberal reforms in Central and Eastern Europe and the Baltic states occurred after revolutionary changes, such as those in Poland after 1989, Georgia following the Rose Revolution, and to some extent in the Czech part of the former Czechoslovakia after the Velvet Revolution. In some countries reform occurred much more slowly and gradually, such as Hungary, which had already undergone some partial economic reform prior to 1989. In Romania, reform took even longer; after the revolution that removed Nicolae Ceaușescu, no radical economic reforms occurred until 1999, to a large extent thanks to international assistance and pressure in a country which chose to follow a Western geopolitical path. Typically, reforms occurred during a window of opportunity, what Balcerowicz so fittingly labelled the "extraordinary politics," if the Western anchor was strong enough—though Romania provides an odd gradualist counterexample to this rule. We must consider the cases of Ukraine and Moldova with open eyes, mindful of the need for a different approach to the dynamics of rule-of-law reforms from those first generation shock-packages. Recent change in these two countries has been extremely complex. It is for the reason of its importance that we will start with Ukraine.

Hope was high in Ukraine after the Orange Revolution, which occurred a year after the Rose Revolution in Georgia. It was too early to understand or use the principles of the Georgian reform experience, even if the sense of solidarity between these countries (and soon also Moldova, an odd companion due to its nominally communist leadership) as well as their most ardent European supporters was high. The fact that the revolution did not translate into ensuing systemic transition had many causes. I want to highlight two that show the strength of the patronal political system, and one that is more incidental.

As systemic analysis is mostly written by political scientists, what typically gets emphasized are the president's failings. These failings are well documented and undeniable. However, in terms of the loss of revolutionary momentum, the missed opportunity for economic reform by Prime Minister Tymoshenko was also of enormous importance. Tymoshenko was not President Yushchenko's first choice for prime minister; he initially wanted Petro Poroshenko, the businessman who lent him critical support throughout the campaign, financing it and giving him airtime on his television channel, 5 Kanal. However, Tymoshenko's charismatic role during the Orange Revolution made her very popular, and Yushchenko felt obliged in front of the public to yield to Tymoshenko's expectations and nominate her.

At the time, Tymoshenko's stance towards the oligarchs seemed more uncompromising than that of Yushchenko; nevertheless, both this, as well as her fixation on popularity ahead of the parliamentary elections the following year, meant that she was quite unwilling to implement radical economic reforms.[35] Hers was a combination of extreme political skills with a total lack of appreciation for workable, let alone reform-oriented, policies. Where she performed better, and where Yushchenko was the main obstacle, was in fighting certain oligarchs. But because of the lack of a common strategy, and the fact that the previous regime, particularly the Donetsk clan, largely held control over the prosecution service, her efforts were fruitless.

It is by now well documented that the post-revolution leadership of Ukraine did not break the ties between the government and systematic corruption, nor did they make institutional reforms that would have weakened the state mechanisms of corruption. To begin with, as part of the negotiated outcome of the protests and political crisis, presidential power was seriously weakened. Even in situations where it nominally remained, Yushchenko essentially allowed the Donetsk clan to continue dominating the prosecutor's office, which was a crucial component of the organized criminality of the state and, conversely, was a very important weapon in the hands of Saakashvili in his crusade to wipe out corruption in Georgia.

The post-Orange Revolution governance situation simply incorporated an unlucky combination of factors. The revolution produced a two-headed hydra, a "divided-executive" situation in Hale's terminology, which even then could have worked, had it not combined the worst characteristics of both Yushchenko and Tymoshenko. Tymoshenko's economic policy was disastrous, while Yushchenko was too eager to make unprincipled compromises with the oligarchs and with the representatives of Kuchma's people.

It is also difficult to draw conclusions from the fact that the post-revolution period weakened the constitutional situation of the presidency. On the one hand, Hale's point that expectations are important in patronal politics is correct here too: with the same (reinstated) constitution, Poroshenko today is a much stronger president than Yushchenko was during his term. Yushchenko was also hindered by the shocking poisoning he had suffered during the election campaign in unclear circumstances; he was visibly less energetic and less willing to engage in conflict than before.

What also must be added is that at the time, while aware of how important reform of the judiciary and the prosecution services was, neither international actors nor civil society representatives gave as much weight to the importance of institutional reform and breaking the power of the oligarchs as we all do now. Tymoshenko did concentrate on the oligarchs, though it is hard to judge from today's perspective if she did it for the right reasons—she did not articulate them—or simply wanted to redistribute power in the system towards herself. The usual assumption is the latter. At the time, the systemic view of Ukraine (or any other post-Soviet state) as a criminal state was not yet present. Significant economic reform, increasing competition in the economy and fixing the big public finance problems, such as incredibly large pension outlays and energy subsidies, could have prolonged the dynamic economic growth that Ukraine experienced in the years before the Orange Revolution. Simultaneously, it could have gradually diminished the role of the oligarchs, particularly the ones based in the Donbass industrial region on the Eastern edge of the country. Instead, incompetent economic management and later internal conflict within the Orange coalition, combined with the devastating effect of the 2008 crisis to Ukraine's economy, brought about an incredible political turn with major systemic consequences. Nobody expected Yanukovych to reemerge. After all, he was humiliated in the 2004 elections, and his patrons, Kuchma and Putin, evidently did not think highly of him. He appeared the least likely candidate to win the presidential elections five years later.

As such, we can conclude that a combination of accidental and systemic factors contributed to missing a very big opportunity to move Ukraine in the direction that a decade and a half earlier, its neighbor, Poland, had taken towards establishing a functioning liberal state.

In Moldova, the leader of the Party of Communists of the Republic of Moldova (PCRM), Vladimir Voronin, had constructed a profound single-pyramid patronal system by 2004. First, in 2001, the PCRM gained a constitutional majority; later, at the 2005 elections, it solidified its position, achieving an absolute majority. In 2004, after the failure of Putin's plan to unite Transnistria with Moldova under Russian patronage, Voronin made a sharp turn towards Europe, and the opportunities for reform seemingly could have improved. However, his geopolitical turn in itself was not indicative of any desire to accomplish radical systemic reform. The European Union's interest in Moldova was remote; it only established a Delegation in Chișinău in October 2005. It created the position of EU Special Representative in March 2005 but the representative's mandate was to deal with the Transnistrian conflict, and to some extent with human rights, not with domestic reform issues.

Voronin's single-pyramid patronal system was ultimately brought down by a combination of factors. Hale emphasizes one: that throughout the whole period, the parliamentary system remained in place, unlike in any other post-Soviet state outside the Baltics. While this is undoubtedly a factor, the answer remains multifaceted. For one, Ukraine had a presidentialist system under Kuchma, yet still, political forces prevented the long-term consolidation of the authoritarian single-pyramid structure. Voronin's communists suffered a significant—albeit relative—setback during the 2007 local elections, where the main opposition party of the time, Alianța Moldova Noastră, gained about twenty percent of the votes and about sixteen percent of the mayoral positions. The Liberal Party's candidate, Dorin Chirtoacă, became mayor of the capital Chișinău. The communists failed to gain an absolute majority at the local elections. While Voronin officially endorsed the idea of European integration in this political cycle, the political style and concomitant value systems did not get close to those in Western Europe. The Moldovan communists did not follow the liberal economic reforms of the successful countries in the region, nor did they satisfy the broader human rights and democratic standards of the European Union.

The communists performed well in the parliamentary elections of April 2009, much better than their performance in the local elections of 2007.

With almost half of the votes, they gained 60 seats in the parliament of 101 members, missing out on the qualified majority necessary to elect the President by just one seat. Surprisingly, over two months' efforts, they could not gain the missing one vote in a very corrupt country, so new elections were held in July where they lost their absolute majority. They still remained the most popular party, but the opposition that had stayed united between the elections now formed a coalition and removed Voronin from power; the Lilliputians ultimately won against the giant Gulliver. Voronin fell from power despite winning an absolute majority in the first parliamentary elections, and still having the largest fraction in the parliament in the second elections. Why?

Voronin, in spite of his opening towards the West, ultimately remained a man of the past in important ways. He felt much more at home with people of the Soviet and post-Soviet culture, including the Russians. Right until the end he wanted to please the Russians, not only because part of his core electorate were Russian speakers. He remained deeply suspicious of the Romanians whom he treated, in line with his Soviet-era indoctrination, as nationalists and irredentists. This bias severely limited his room for maneuver, and the culture of the street protests, which were instrumental for the opposition to maintain their unity and discipline, had a very distinct pro-Romanian character partly as a reaction to Voronin's excesses. Importantly, Moldova has a very specific ethnic complexity, meaning that any political leader trying to move the country either towards Russia or towards Romania would face genuine resistance from the other side. Voronin was ultimately unable to bridge the cultural divide and convince the Romanian-speaking urban electorate that he is also their president. Moreover, among Moldova's Russian speakers, he had to face a lack of enthusiasm from Moscow. Voronin instinctively remained a strong believer in centralized power; he was the master of his small, poor country, a role that came naturally to him. This in itself would not have prevented him becoming a nation and state builder, but his authoritarian style, together with his one-sidedness in nationality policies, ultimately cemented the opposition against him.

His original economic policies were old-fashioned, but he quickly abandoned some of the old communist goals, such as renationalization and reestablishment of the collective farms. However, what he built in its stead was an oligarchic system where no major investment could happen without bribing one of his oligarchs, and without allowing them to maintain some control. Consequently, very little investment came to Moldova, and even less in the productive sectors. Besides, the country was isolated from major markets, so it would have needed a concentrated encouragement of investment. Instead, a local clan system stifled foreign investment. Since the country was in the phase of post-transition recovery, like the other states of the former Soviet empire, Voronin's political stability secured strong economic growth for a time. This coincided with an economic exodus of people from Moldova who, through remittances, contributed to wealth creation in the country—albeit at the huge cost of divided families.

Besides these deep structural problems with Voronin's Soviet-rooted identity and economic policies, his management of the 2009 crisis also contributed critically to his loss of power. After all, he could still carry much of his original power base: the rural population, pensioners and Russian speakers. He carried about half of the votes in April 2009 (almost exactly as in 2001) and still about 45% in the repeat elections of July, in spite of the economic deterioration during the political crisis. Ultimately, his support only marginally diminished.

His major miscalculations occurred between the two elections, in his effort to secure the presidency. Hale puts a lot of emphasis on the Moldovan constitution being parliamentarian. But how, then, can we explain the enormous significance politicians attributed to the election of the president by the parliament during the political crisis of 2009?

In a way, the problem was contrary to what Hale's explanation would suggest. During his eight years as president, Voronin made Moldova a presidential country, regardless of the nuances of its constitution. Foreign actors and institutions tried to explain to the Moldovans that in fact the constitutional role of the president was weak, but nobody believed this to be important. Voronin could have easily secured his candidate's election as president if he had the foresight of agreeing to the election of his popular parliamentary speaker, Marian Lupu. According to this scenario Voronin could have held the position of speaker and, by controlling the communists who had an absolute majority, could have had exercised a significant degree of control. But Voronin didn't trust Lupu; moreover, he himself believed that the situation would remain "presidential" even after he quit. He needed a more docile president of his choosing, but the opposition was able to prevent this from happening. In particular, he was not helped by the fact that his candidate, Zinaida Greceanîi, made some inflammatory comments around which the opposition could galvanize their resistance.[36] There were other alternative candidate choices for Voronin, but they were pushed too hard by Russia's background influence; hence, Voronin did not go for them. From Voronin's perspective, an obvious positive outcome would have arisen under Lupu's presidency and a cooperative situation with his opposition, but he did not have the foresight to pursue this option. Indeed, Voronin was insulting the opposition the night after the elections, when he thought the communists had reached the 61 seat majority which would have made agreement with the opposition unnecessary. This arrogant behavior later backfired, since it became all the more difficult to create a cooperative parliamentary situation for future agreements.

Ultimately, the communists lost power in the two consecutive elections of 2009. Besides Voronin's evident mistakes, and the pro-Romanian and pro-European sentiments of a large part of the opposition, international influence was very important. Russia would not have objected if Voronin had disregarded democratic norms in the elections, but he did not want to rely entirely on the Russians. He tried to continue a balanced international policy, declaring his ultimate goal to be European integration combined with neutrality. But if he wanted to continue European integration, he needed to maintain some minimal democratic elements. The European Union did not look the other way when, prior to the elections, the communists tried to close the main television channel sympathetic to the opposition. Its ultimatum prevented that step.[37] The EU expected free and fair elections. Whereas the April elections were not entirely fair—opposition politicians were harassed and the communists had a media advantage—as the OSCE observer mission stated, the elections did provide genuine political alternatives.[38]

Plahotniuc's climb to power: building a single-pyramid patronal system from the back seat

Moldova's current situation is, in some ways, unprecedented in the rich history of patronal societies and politics in the former Soviet Union and Eastern Europe. Its current de facto ruler, Vlad Plahotniuc, is unelected and holds no official governmental position, giving him very weak levels of legitimacy. It is true that Plahotniuc has taken the title of "executive coordinator" of the ruling coalition, but the public treats this title with disdain, since it is so transparently an effort to legitimize his enormous unofficial power. Below I will describe how this "state capture" by a non-state official has taken place, and the perspectives held by both Plahotniuc and the Moldovan state more broadly.

There are many rumors about Plahotniuc's alleged criminal background, as his early years are not fully accounted for. As I wrote above, he started out in the Voronin regime as an emerging businessman. He grew into the "oligarch" position through clever strategic moves, gaining the personal trust of both Voronin and his son. Over time, he became the main gatekeeper and front for the Voronin family's large business investments, including banks. He also moved closer to Igor Dodon, elected in November 2016 as president. Dodon, a minister of economy during Voronin's rule, helped him acquire the hotel Codru in Chișinău through dubious privatization measures. His business strategy relies heavily on privatizing the cash flows of state companies. These include Moldtelecom, Metalferosa, and the railway company Calea Ferată din Moldova, but also state services such as car plate licenses and even bread production. Through these activities, he reportedly makes around one hundred million dollars of profit every year.[39]

The second tier of business he controls is advertising, through his Casa Media company. He controls 70% of the advertising market, reportedly making about twenty million dollars profit annually. As the Media Power Monitor group notes: "CTC Moldova and Super TV were acquired by the company Real Radio, [a] company owned by Dorin Pavelescu. Mr Pavelescu has business links with Mr Plahotniuc, according to a recent investigation from RISE. Mr Pavelescu is the head of the advertising agency Casa Media Plus, which is headquartered at the same address as General Media Group, Mr Plahotniuc's media conglomerate. General Media Group owns Public TV, Prime TV, Canal 2 and Canal 3."[40]

Moreover, he has over time essentially privatized the Democratic Party of Moldova (PDM). He controls a large chunk of local administrations, between ten and twenty of the thirty-two raion heads. Here, his people are mostly from his earlier business connections. In addition, a few, perhaps three or four, will lend their support to him when necessary. Though the PDM took only 17% of the vote in the last nationwide local elections, it controls about 400 mayoral seats. About 150 of these mayors switched sides from the Liberal Democratic Party of Moldova (PLDM) or the communists.[41]

In government, his concentration of power is overwhelming. Prime Minister Pavel Filip and parliamentary speaker Andrian Candu are very close business associates of Plahotniuc, as are the minister of economy, Octavian Calmîc, and the minister of finance, Octavian Armașu, who also controls tax and customs.⁴² The minister of internal affairs, the Inspector of Police, the Chief of Criminal Police, and the minister of infrastructure, responsible for airports, telecoms, car license plates, documentation and archives are all under his direct influence. The Secretary General of the government, Tudor Copaci, who designed the privatization of Chișinău International Airport, is also a close associate.⁴³

Critical state agencies are also under his control, including the head of customs Vitalie Vrabie, at least three members of the Constitutional Court (including its head), the Supreme Court of Justice, the Court of Appeal, the Council of Magistrates, and, by local estimates, about half of the country's judges. Most critically, he controls the prosecutor general and half of the prosecutors as well as the Center for Combating Economic Crimes and Corruption, plus the Center of Special Investigations that deals with large-scale crime. In addition, he controls the Center for Telecommunications, the two deputy heads of the security services, whose head is seen as passive, and the Center for Competition.

A widely documented case is that of Energokapital, widely assumed to be run by Plahotniuc, as so many state agencies involved in it are directly linked to him. In December 2014, after the Ukrainians stopped delivering electricity to Moldova, the country turned instead to the Transnistrian separatist enclave, but using the kind of intermediary scheme that was also operating in Ukraine. According to documented claims, in the one-and-a-half years since the scheme started, the annual profits sent to offshore accounts total 39 million US dollars. According to the civil investigation, this could not happen without the knowledge of Gazprom.⁴⁴ What makes this scheme particularly noteworthy—otherwise, its scale is smaller than the usual Ukrainian schemes, whose Russian end is also Gazprom—is that it contributes to the preservation of the Transnistrian regime. Electricity is produced from Russian gas, delivered by a 50-50 joint venture of Gazprom and Moldovagaz, to the Transnistrian power station Moldavskaya GRES. The Transnistrians regularly pay less than the required amount, and have gradually accumulated a multibillion dollar debt both to Gazprom and the Moldovan state. For Gazprom, this is a calculated political game to improve Russia's bargaining position in the Transnistrian settlement vis-à-vis Moldova and its Western supporters. However, taking advantage of this with additional intermediaries on the Moldovan end amounts not only to illegally robbing the domestic taxpayers, but also serves to effectively support Russia's geopolitical games in Transnistria.

Plahotniuc organized his departure from the Voronin camp in a masterful, albeit evidently unethical, manner. In the tumultuous spring months of 2009, when Voronin's political power began to slip away, Plahotniuc switched his support to Marian Lupu, the presidential candidate whom Voronin did not want to help into the position. Plahotniuc and Lupu essentially used a failed party (albeit with a considerable tradition), the Democratic Party (PDM), for their new political project. The front was Lupu, who had a strong political reputation at the time, and behind him was the financier Plahotniuc.

Lupu's presidential hopes did not ultimately materialize. His and Plahotniuc's vassal party, the PDM, did not become the strongest in the July 2009 elections. That position was earned by Vlad Filat's Liberal Democratic Party of Moldova. The initial rivalry unfolded around the post of the president, as symbolically that position was regarded, contrary to any constitutional stipulations, as the country's strongman position. The situation unfolded quite differently from how it might in a normal democratic system. Since the communists had an absolute majority in the brief period between the April and July elections, in normal circumstances they could have engaged in negotiation with the opposition and found a compromise presidential candidate for whom that the majority would vote, in exchange for political and policy concessions. As the communists were only one vote short, this would have been a superior solution to simple vote-buying. However, the opposition's fear of Voronin's continuing dominance, along with the lack of democratic culture in Moldova, prevented this from happening.

It was also very difficult then to agree over the presidential vote after the repeat elections in July, where the opposition gained a majority, but one insufficient to elect a president. First, there was the challenge of sitting down with the Communists and finding an agreement. Since in April, the then-opposition forces were uncooperative, it was difficult to now expect cooperative behavior from the communists in return. Moreover, there was a great difference between the two strongmen of the emerging coalition, Filat and Lupu, as both demanded the presidential position.[45] Filat felt entitled to the presidency since his party was the strongest in the coalition; Lupu countered that without him quitting the communists, the opposition would not have a majority. Both treated the presidential position, in spite of what the constitution stipulated, as the main prize.

The international community played an important role in the solution of this double rivalry. First, many took a highly simplistic position of the emerging coalition, assuming that the losing communists were simply representing Moscow's interests, and therefore not demanding the new winners to strictly play by the democratic rules. During the first period of the crisis, it was assumed by the EU and the US that the communists would dissolve the parliament if their president was not elected; however, when the coalition extended the time allowed to elect the president through constitutional gimmicks, the same rigor was no longer applied. Second, the coalition's decision to organize a referendum if the people wanted to elect the president directly, in direct violation of the constitution, was also tolerated by the EU and US, with the Venice Commission's endorsement. Thus, the journey down the slippery slope, ever further from the rule-of-law, began. The EU, the US, the IMF and the Council of Europe had all the opportunity to guide tiny, poor Moldova on the road towards systemic reform, but this failed to happen. The coalition utilized pro-European slogans but showed no real willingness to reform, almost six full years after the highly relevant Georgian experience demonstrated the importance and feasibility of systemic reform.

The issue of electing the president got another twist with an invalid referendum in September 2010.[46] This played into the hands of Filat, who understood before anyone else that the constitution gave him the potential to gain extra power as prime minister; however, he also needed a situation without a legitimately elected president. While he could not openly oppose the referendum, the invalid vote worked out well for him. If the vote was valid, he would have run for the presidency, but this situation suited him better as he was unsure whether he would win the presidential race against Lupu. The other player who gained much from the situation was Plahotniuc—he, in the long run, would actually gain more than Filat. Though it is true that his client, Lupu, didn't get the chance to elevate to the presidency, if Lupu had advanced to the post of president, his sponsor's power would have been more limited. Instead, he could gradually grow politically above Lupu, and, over time, above anyone else in the country.

How could Voronin's chief oligarch, supposedly pro-Russian, become the most powerful man in a coalition that declared itself totally and resolutely anti-Voronin and pro-European, with strong support from the United States and Romania? Over the years, he played a complex game. He saw ahead of others the crumbling of Voronin's empire and quit, together with Lupu, before it collapsed entirely and swept him away. While the July 2009 election results suited his client, Lupu, he still remained the main oligarch of the earlier regime. Reportedly he moved to Romania after the election victory of the opposition coalition, until such a time when he could appoint the prosecutor general of his choice. While in the coalition agreement among the four parties, the Democratic Party did not get to choose the prosecutor general, according to reports, Plahotniuc "bought" this right from the Liberal Democrats' Serafim Urechean and chose someone who would guarantee his personal safety.[47]

Filat's political strategy included a special relationship with the EU and the United States, and a degree of openness towards reforms. His ministers were far more professionally competent and "modern" then the others, who were typically professional rent-seekers. However, Filat himself lacked Saakashvili's reform drive, and there was no Bendukidze-type conceptual reformer in the team either. Filat did have an outstanding diplomatic team, including the Minister of Foreign Affairs and European Integration Iurie Leancă and his chief deputy for European affairs, Natalia Gherman, as well as the other deputy, Andrei Popov, a distinguished activist and diplomat. They could easily oversell the reform drive of the country in Brussels. With the political enthusiasm over a "pro-European" coalition, and the ability of the new leadership's representatives to speak the language of the European and American partners, Moldova became the darling of the Eastern Partnership area countries.

Meanwhile, a reorganized clientelist society was evolving beneath the surface with the dual stewardship of Filat and, increasingly, Plahotniuc. Filat could have played this political game longer, but he weakened himself with an arrogant personal style that caused long-term alienation, even if it helped to subordinate key players in the short term. Some of his party heavyweights began to quit, while he could not win the most reform-minded figures from elsewhere to his side, even if they still saw him as the reformist, as well as Moldovan patriotic, hope. His winning strategy would have incorporated energetic and resolute reforms, with European support for them. While his talk gained much more support in Europe than, for instance, Saakashvili's straightforward style did, it became slowly visible that the substance behind it was minimal. He was successful at pursuing those issues that the Europeans fixated on, such as biometric passports for the visa-free regime, but the EU had no clear view on how the critical reforms and their implementation would occur. The fiction of the European way was maintained for years, and ultimately a great opportunity was wasted. Among the Eastern Partnership countries, Moldova was rewarded with the visa-free regime first, essentially for "good European behavior" based on a very superficial evaluation.[48]

Filat scored better than both his predecessors and the alternatives on another front that was particularly important to Europe and the US. He quickly understood the essence of the European philosophy to the Transnistrian settlement and played along. He tried to build confidence with the erstwhile Transnistrian leader, Igor Smirnov, and when at the end of 2011 the young Yevgeny Shevchuk was surprisingly elected to the leadership position (a presidency unrecognized by the rest of the world) he could continue this policy even more energetically.

A dramatic accident in early 2013 uncovered the real nature of which way the country was heading, as opposed to the fiction put into practice by the country's leadership and perceived by its European admirers. The event was also typical of the nature of politics in Moldova. During a boar hunt attended by the country's top elites, a local businessman, Sorin Paciu, was accidentally killed. The participants tried to cover it up to avoid scandal, but a famously outspoken critic of high level corruption found out, and broadcast the news at a press conference. Since "Plahotniuc's" prosecutor general was also there, Filat saw an opportunity to weaken his rival and remove one of the oligarch-adversary's chief figures. However, he was not expecting that Plahotniuc would have an answer to such a case. He aired highly compromising secretly taped conversations of Filat, and organized a political counterattack. This situation brought the communists out of the political wilderness, as both sides in the conflict played the communist faction, still the largest in parliament, against each other.[49] Thanks to European and American pressure, a compromise was finally crafted, according to which the relatively popular and well regarded Minister of Foreign Affairs and European Integration, Iurie Leancă, took on the role of prime minister, and both Filat and Plahotniuc stepped back. It was hoped[50] that the untainted Leancă would be able to reinvigorate the reformist course.

This did not happen. Instead Filat, who remained the leader of the party, opposed Leancă's genuine plans for reform and barriers against the continued evolution of clientelist power, while Filat and Plahotniuc struck a truce, allowing both men opportunities to advance their oligarchic goals. However, as another dramatic event on October 15, 2015 showed, Plahotniuc made better use of this truce, as he had control over more strategically important levers than Filat in what was, essentially, a turf war between gangsters. When in coalition, they achieved an agreement to replace the prosecutor general with a neutral, jointly agreed nomination. In a dramatic turn of events, the prosecutor general came to the parliament the following day, and instead of announcing his resignation in accord with the coalition agreement, he announced criminal charges against Filat.[51] A secretly prearranged majority voted to strip Filat's immunity, and he was taken away in handcuffs. Soon after, incriminating *kompromat* against Filat was strategically aired, and his trial was organized in secret, in blatant disregard of the rule-of-law and elementary human rights.

At this point, Plahotniuc emerged as the dominant political figure of Moldova, essentially achieving state capture. He won the battle against Filat for several reasons, despite Filat's apparent dominance from 2010. While both were secretive power players, Plahotniuc was better at exploiting the instruments of the post-Soviet patronal or mafia state. He understood the critical importance of the secret services and of the prosecution organization, and he used them unscrupulously to get ahead of his competitors. He treated these as natural instruments of the struggle for power. This is also how he saw the situation when Voronin was in power, when criminal cases were launched against everybody who stood in the way, either economically or politically, of the president. Filat understood the significance of these tools, of course. But he thought that "classical" political tools would be more important for him, particularly after the ousting of Voronin.[52] Furthermore, his political organization, when he built it, was oriented towards modernization and European integration. He disposed of his team gradually, but he was not as effective with the alternative, post-Soviet repertoire of tools as Plahotniuc. Filat was also more heavily scrutinized by the Western partners when it turned out that the reforms which emerged were not as they had been skillfully advertised. Ultimately, Filat neither fully played the reformist game, nor the mafia one.

Plahotniuc's game was more sinister. By the time of his emergence as the major figure in Moldovan politics, he already controlled much of the media, the judiciary, the prosecution service, the police and the secret services. Through these means, his reach within the local authorities is considerable, while his Democratic Party holds many local government positions. He also maintains a confidential relationship with the Romanian government, the nature of which is not known in detail. This keeps a degree of restraint to the European Union's criticism of him.

However, his power is not absolute. First and foremost, he is unpopular, and lacks the legitimacy of an elected politician. He is publicity-shy, an asset when he exercised power from the shadows, first as Voronin's oligarch and then as the sponsor of Lupu. However, as he stepped forward as the most powerful politician, his lack of charisma and public confidence became a major disadvantage. A very large majority of civil society is against both him and the social system he supported, established and ran. Moldovan society became so disappointed by the system, and by the scandals it produced, that for the first time in Moldova's independent existence a protest movement emerged that eschewed geopolitical considerations in favor of domestic issues. These protests emerged in 2015, concentrating on the scandalous privatization of the Chișinău airport, as well as the robbery of the Banca de Economii that had been publicized in 2014.[53] The protests, organized by the emerging civil organization Demnitatea și Adevăr (Dignity and Truth), were the largest since the pro-independence demonstrations in 1989–91.

The protest movement has laid an important obstacle to the degree of Plahotniuc's rule. The movement demanded new parliamentary elections in 2015. And when the Parliament, to a large extent now under Plahotniuc's influence, wanted to install him as prime minister, then president of Moldova, Nicolae Timofti, committed the bravest act of his otherwise controversial tenure by refusing Plahotniuc's candidacy. On one hand Timofti's act was not in line with the letter of the constitution; on the other hand, Plahotniuc's nomination was such a blatant act of corruption by a whole political class, and so much against the popular will of the winter demonstrators, that this nuance was overlooked. Timofti's official communication argued that "The President believes there exist reasonable suspicions that Mr. Vlad Plahotniuc does not have necessary integrity for his nomination as a candidate for Prime Minister," and pointed out that in February 2013 he suffered a no-confidence vote as deputy speaker of the parliament on the grounds that "[h]e was then accused of illegal activities that inflicted damage to the image of the Moldovan Parliament and of the Republic of Moldova."[54]

Following this, the Parliament nominated a close associate of Plahotniuc, Pavel Filip, for the post of prime minister. The Parliament building was stormed by the disappointed protesters, who felt that Plahotniuc's ad hoc coalition was not what they had voted for in the general elections. In order to diminish public anger, Plahotniuc orchestrated another grand deception. The Constitutional Court, which was also obedient to him, ruled on March 4, 2016 that its own decision back in 2000 had been erroneous, and that direct presidential elections had to be held. To show how manipulative and arbitrary this decision was, the Court kept in force a different part of the same ruling that established a minimum age of forty for the president,[55] clearly to exclude the most formidable competitor, the charismatic young mayor of Bălți city, Renato Usatîi.

While he clearly manipulated the sequence of events,[56] as a sign of the limits to his power, Plahotniuc needed to seek major compromises, or the "least damaging" situation, after his prime ministerial appointment was refused. Instead of allowing for parliamentary elections that had been the demand of the protest movement of 2015, he orchestrated a presidential election where he seemingly yielded to European expectations by supporting the candidate with a resolutely anti-corruption program but, through his near total monopoly of the media, he de facto supported the other candidate, Socialist party leader Igor Dodon, who was running on a pro-Russian platform. Dodon indeed won the election, though only by a narrow margin, in spite of his oligarchic support and far greater financial capability. His opponent was a seemingly unlikely candidate, Maia Sandu, who refused oligarchic finances and ran her campaign on a shoestring budget, yet she still gained 48 percent of the vote.[57] While for the time being Plahotniuc controls the political situation, through the figure of Dodon, the "main puppeteer" chose to support a candidate whom he may be unable to control in the long run, due to Dodon's political party machinery and Russian support as well as his political experience. Clearly, Plahotniuc wanted to maneuver himself into a situation where the "West" needed to support him against the "pro-Russian" president.[58] However, this will be a very delicate game without a clear outcome.

This became already apparent during the mayoral elections in the capital city Chișinău in May–June 2018. Here Plahotniuc again played a complex game behind the scenes, yet the electorate chose neither his preferred candidate with strong managerial background, Silvia Radu, nor his second-best choice, the socialist Ion Cioban. The second round of the election was won instead by Andrei Năstase, one of the key figures of the 2015 protests, with 52 percent of the votes.[59] Plahotniuc's court then dutifully—although in a quite unprecedented way—annulled the election results, bringing the relations with the EU to a new low and causing financial support to freeze.

Plahotniuc is the first leader in the post-Soviet space who succeeded to dominate politics while not holding any of the major functions of state.[60] This, along with his massive unpopularity, obviously pose a challenge for him. He will only have a chance of overcoming this challenge if he can show marked improvement of the economic situation and living standards of the people, as well as reducing massive corruption. He has little room for maneuver, like a skier who is forced to slalom between ever more frequent poles.

On the other hand, the opportunities for breaking away from the logic of patronal politics and society are considerable, despite the melancholy in Moldova and the world in general. There is a coalition of purpose between civil society and the country's major Western partners. Furthermore, there is a realization that rule-of-law reforms are one of the key conditions for irreversible systemic change. Plahotniuc critically lacks legitimacy and popularity. If he undertakes the necessary reforms to accelerate economic growth, it means demonopolization of the Moldovan economy and an investment-friendly environment, which would reduce his rent-seeking opportunities; if he does not implement those reforms, he will remain unpopular. Thus the largest current risks for Moldova are a populist politician directing the country towards Russia, or if Plahotniuc, as the chief patron, finds himself in a dead-end, from which the only escape route is moving the country towards the Russian sphere of interest. If Moldova avoids these risks, in the long term its civil society may work out a reform package with real effect. The Georgian experience is very relevant here, as it represented a package that did not cure all the problems of the patronal society, but through its internal logic made a departure from some of its core characteristics. As a more general point, it is difficult in Moldova's geopolitical situation, taking into account its small size, to endure lasting domestic state capture. The long-term risk of a "Russian capture," however, remains real.

In 2015, a very significant chance was wasted. The demonstrations were the first time in Moldova's independent history that the different language communities came together, realized that their main problem was the awful quality of governance, and that they could only address it through acting together for radical reform, regardless of geopolitics. Unfortunately, important external actors, mainly the Romanian and US governments, disagreed: due to their misplaced fear of Russian geopolitical gains, they essentially continued to support mafia rule against the noble aspirations of the people. They still failed to comprehend that the nature of the social system and geopolitical orientation are deeply connected. In this critical moment, the people of Moldova remained alone.

The Donbass clan: mafia within the state rises to the top to create a single-pyramid patronal rule

To understand the Yanukovych phenomenon, one needs to consider several factors, chiefly the difference between various types of emerging oligarchic groups and personalities. In the case of Ukraine (and Russia), analysts generally emphasize three types of such groups. The first is the "red directors" who were in top managerial positions during the collapse of the socialist empire. The second group could be called the Komsomol-types, those who were young members of the nomenklatura during perestroika: open-minded and ideologically flexible, with privileged access to information, regulation and assets during the changes. The tremendous economic and political crisis that preceded the demise of the Soviet Union also pushed these young hopeful people to become capitalist entrepreneurs of sorts. The third group, most infamously, were the criminals.

While people speak about the "Odessa clan," the "Dnipropetrovsk clan," and the "Kharkiv clan," it is only in the case of Donetsk that self-organization of a geographical clan gained such significant momentum and complexity. Taras Kuzio analyses this phenomenon extensively. There are two questions here: firstly, why the criminal oligarchy in Donetsk has been so dominant; and secondly, why have they succeeded over the rest, at least for almost one full presidential cycle.

As to the first question, Donetsk, with its notable mining and metallurgical industries and its relatively less rooted population, as well as its large prison concentration, has, alongside the Crimea and Odessa, a strong criminal tradition. According to Kuzio, unlike in other parts of the country, having a criminal background is not a reason for embarrassment. The importance of criminality did not start with Yanukovych and Rinat Akhmetov. In the 1990s, the criminal leader Akhat Bragin was essentially the Donetsk godfather until his murder in 1995, which remains shrouded in mystery even to this day. Akhmetov was reportedly his assistant, inheriting his pompous residence and the Shakhtar Donetsk football team. The two were also tied by their Tatar origin; Bragin grew the Tatar clan into the strongest mafia organization.

The Donbass, with Donetsk as its most important city and regional center, had some special characteristics that made it one of the least "Ukrainian" parts of the country. In the chaos of the post-World War I period, the region created its own government and did not seek to join either the nascent Ukrainian state or Bolshevik Russia. It was also an above-average victim of Stalinist terror. The influx of Russians to the Donbass was particularly high, partly to replace those who had been killed, but also because of the particularly intense industrialization. In the period of industrialization, the crime level was very high, and the authorities allocated a large proportion of prisons here.

In the Ukrainian independence referendum of 1991, during the collapse of the Soviet Union, the Donbass also voted for an independent Ukraine, albeit in smaller proportions than any other region but the Crimea. However, this was more due to the expectation of a better economic future than any form of patriotism. By 1993 national identity problems were already intense, as the West of Ukraine wanted to distance the country from Russia, whereas the East increasingly felt that the continuous economic malaise was caused by the disintegration of the Soviet Union, which could be remedied by moving closer to Russia. The coal miners' strike in the summer of 1993 contributed significantly to the calling of early presidential elections in 1994, and their subsequent loss by the incumbent President Leonid Kravchuk. From then on, it was clear that controlling the Donbass was of paramount importance for overall political power. The region also accounted for about fifteen percent of Ukraine's total electorate. After the strike, one of the prominent "red directors," the owner of one of the most important mines, Yukhym Zvyahilsky, was appointed acting prime minister.

In the ensuing period, a sharp consolidation of power took place in the Donetsk region, the senior partner among the two regions of the Donbass. The consolidation, true to form, was bloody: the chief criminal, Akhat Bragin, was killed by a bomb in his Shakhtar Donetsk Stadium. One year later, the emerging industrial oligarch of the region, Yevhen Shcherban, was assassinated together with his wife at the Donetsk airport. Shcherban was not exactly a "red director," but a white-collar actor, originally a mining engineer. In the early 1990s, he built up considerable assets in the natural gas industry, and, a year before his assassination, established the Industrial Union Donbass company together with Serhiy Taruta. As its name indicates, the company strived to become the dominant economic force in the region.

There was no independent investigation into these murders, nor into the many more of less prominent actors in the Donbass and national scene. These series of events opened up the opportunity for the Yanukovych–

Akhmetov tandem to rise. Already in 1996 Yanukovych, a twice convicted criminal, was appointed deputy governor of the Donetsk region. Akhmetov took over much of Bragin's assets, and expanded in the coal and metallurgy sectors. The Donetsk clan was also instrumental to President Kuchma, insofar as they provided the necessary votes for him in the highly populated Donbass, but also, their 'business" methods were useful in national politics. Mykola Azarov, who served as loyal prime minister to Yanukovych during his entire presidency, acquired his fame as Kuchma's tax chief who instrumentalized the position to the maximum, both for personal enrichment, but also for using the authority (and blackmailing capacity) of the position to clamp down on political and business opponents.

Kuchma, during his presidency, tried to maintain a balance between the different emerging oligarchic groups. By and large, this tactic was successful, but over time the Donetsk clan gained the upper hand in the oligarchic jostling for position, to the extent that in 2004 Kuchma halfheartedly chose Yanukovych as his presidential candidate. Kuchma's first obvious choice would have been to change the constitution and run for president a third time in 2004, eventually taking on a Putin-type role. At one point, this seemed eminently possible: after all, he presided over a very well-oiled machinery for elections, both presidential and parliamentary. However, the murder of politician and journalist Georgiy Gongadze and the aforementioned Melnychenko tapes severely undermined his authority, both in the emerging civil society and in the West. Yanukovych was a successful prime minister insofar as economic growth was very strong in the first years of the new millennium, to a large extent thanks to the legacy of Yushchenko's short prime ministership in 2000 that saw a flurry of reforms. Yanukovych and Akhmetov organized the Donetsk region, and practically the whole Donbass, into a more or less unified pyramid, which no other oligarchic group has managed to do. Moreover, they "owned" the Party of Regions, a stable political machinery in a country where parties had been in constant flux. Their system of clientele was very tight. Putin, while sometimes showing a degree of contempt towards Yanukovych, put his full weight behind him and openly campaigned for him in 2004. This mattered tremendously to the pro-Russian segments of Ukrainian society. This organizational superiority proved decisive to the unlikely sequence of events which led to Yanukovych winning the presidency in fair and free elections in 2010. He was discredited in 2004, and many in society felt profoundly alienated by his criminal background and style. But with Akhmetov's backing, keeping the Party of Regions a fully operational force, he gradually gained the upper hand in Ukrainian politics once more.

Yanukovych's presidency was the clearest attempt at creating a single-pyramid patronal system (in its highly criminal version) that ultimately failed. While Kuchma's presidency created and shaped the single-pyramid system of Ukraine, Yanukovych's ambition was to make his rule permanent. He fortuitously landed in a kind of power vacuum, created by the huge disappointment with the Orange team. While the most important question is why his bid failed, let us also look at the nature of the system Yanukovych and the Party of Regions developed. After winning the presidential elections, Yanukovych began energetic preparations to make the results irreversible. Internationally, he turned towards Russia. He created with Dmitry Medvedev (or, really, with Putin) a platform for deep inter-governmental cooperation. He agreed to extend the stationing of the Russian navy in the Crimean base of Simferopol until 2047. In a modest exchange, Russia agreed to reduce the price of natural gas for a limited period. On the domestic front, he rapidly centralized power. In a procedurally flawed manner, he changed the constitution and reinstated a presidential regime.[61] He appointed governors mainly from his power base in the Donetsk clan. Moreover, in each region he had his informal "holders" (smotryashchie) who provided a double check that events were progressing as he wished. The predatory nature of the Ukrainian economic system exploded during the Yanukovych presidency. Reports state that he demanded a fifty percent share in successful large companies. Moreover, he used the state's repressive apparatus to clamp down on his political opponents, putting Tymoshenko and the former Minister of Internal Affairs, Yuriy Lutsenko, in prison. During Yanukovych's presidency, there was "order" in the mafia state. People generally knew the bribes required for judges, prosecutors, policemen, tax and customs officers in different situations, and illegal trades. He placed his close associates in key central governmental posts, including Mykola Azarov as prime minister and Viktor Pshonka as prosecutor general (which was, of course, a de facto key governmental function in Ukraine's criminal state). He coopted some key figures of the Yushchenko camp, first and foremost Petro Poroshenko, whom he appointed minister of economic development and trade in 2012.

During the Yanukovych presidency not only he and his son gained enormous economic assets, but his close associate, Akhmetov, according to a Kommersant report, became the richest person in Europe by 2011, with an estimated wealth of thirty billion US dollars. Even if this was not an accurate estimate, on Forbes' list Akhmetov also figured very prominently, with an estimated wealth of sixteen billion dollars.[62]

When examining why this effort to build a stable single pyramid failed, I would start with the international factor. Although Putin was highly instrumental in bringing Yanukovych to power, ultimately the two had very different goals. Putin's goal was to subordinate Ukraine for several reasons. In Russian foreign policy doctrine, for ideological, psychological and practical reasons, Ukraine's subordination was and remains the most important strategic goal. This is a deep-seated identity issue for Russia as an empire, as many analysts have pointed out. Moreover, Russia's whole cultural predisposition is arguably such that it is unable to conduct foreign policy in a classical Western sense. Foreign policy, as the extension of domestic policy, is really about subordination, using the same methods as those used in domestic political conflicts: blackmail, *kompromat*, and false promises. While this is a strong cultural feature of Russian foreign policy, it has increased in significance under Putin's rule as he has incorporated time-honored methods from his KGB past. In the case of Yanukovych, his goals clearly differed from that of Putin: he wanted to have as little as possible constraining his power over his prey—Ukraine.

The most significant factor here is that during his presidency Yanukovych, learning the hard realities of being Putin's associate, moved over time towards trying to accommodate an association agreement with the EU. He needed this for several reasons. First, the Donbass business interests needed the most open markets possible—both European and global—for their metallurgical goods. A free trade agreement, part of the association agreement, was an appropriate tool for this. Second, he needed the EU and the United States as safeguards in his daily tug-of-war against Putin's Russia. Third, an important part of the electorate expected the Ukrainian state to move steadily towards European integration.

Yanukovych's eastern supporters had the reputation of running the state machinery more effectively than the unruly disorder of Yushchenko and Tymoshenko. As such, technical work on the Association Agreement progressed adequately. After the chaotic experience with Yushchenko and Tymoshenko, the EU and the United States had unfortunately increased their tolerance of Yanukovych's lightminded approach to the rule-of-law. Most notably, their reaction to the reinstitution of the pre-Yushchenko constitution, a violation of the law, was distinctly mute. The stumbling block remained the imprisonment of Yulia Tymoshenko, the most visible violation of human rights, which lent itself well to mediatization because of her carefully nurtured public image.

Yanukovych cancelled the Association Agreement in November 2013, under Russian pressure and the promise by Putin of a 15 billion USD loan under favorable conditions, plus again some reduction in price of Russian natural gas deliveries. The harsh reaction from the EU, which negotiated the agreement for many years, was to be expected. As a result, Yanukovych inadvertently established a natural alliance between civil society and the European Union against him. If the Russian posture was different during the Yanukovych years, his quest for long term domination may have been more successful. The international dimension again played an important role in shaping Ukraine's politico-economic system.

This story highlights two other very important factors forming Ukraine's model: namely the economy and civil society. Yanukovych was in such a difficult situation also because he was not able to deliver spectacular economic successes. The Ukrainian economy was particularly vulnerable to the 2008 global crisis that harshly punished the debtor classes. Ukraine was severely indebted, in contrast to Russia, which learnt to manage its debt responsibly after the 1998 financial crisis. Not only was it externally indebted, but its budgetary burden was high, as it redistributed a high percentage of its revenues; for instance, Ukraine's pension outlays were the highest in Europe in terms of proportion to GDP. Thirdly, Yanukovych was in no mood to institute economic reforms that liberated entrepreneurship, nor did he understand their importance. His economic mindset was rooted in socialism's gigantomania, with the key difference that he wanted himself to own most of it. He and his Donetsk gang had no idea of the usefulness of small and medium-size entrepreneurship. His economic success as prime minister in the early 2000s was based on two elements of sheer luck: the post-transition decline reached its nadir, and Chinese demands in the metallurgical markets gave the mainly Donbass-based commodity a significant terms-of-trade gain. Yushchenko's reforms in 2000 also helped, both economically and politically: the Donbass clan was usually less strong in gas and oil trading schemes. As such, its curtailing during Yushchenko's premiership (by his then Deputy Prime Minister Tymoshenko) helped to mitigate an important continuous burden on the economy.[63] In spite of his and the broader Donbass clan's earlier reputation as "good economic managers," Yanukovych did little to put the economy on the right track. Populism and theft, as well as lack of a proper economic philosophy, prevented this, in spite of his regime's somewhat more orderly management.

The other important factor preventing Yanukovych from consolidating his single-pyramid patronal system was the state of civil society. It has evolved in this originally core Soviet state in phases, and in as complex a manner as could be imagined in such a large, diverse society. The Orange Revolution was undoubtedly a very significant experience in multiple ways. First, people realized the capacity of large crowds to make politics, and activists gained experience in organizing large demonstrations. Second, disillusionment with the aftermath of the mass protests in November 2004 were also transformative, as people learned not to give unconditional trust to any politician. Third, by 2013 civil society think tanks were robust, self-confident and better educated. The attention of civil society policy thinking also shifted towards rule-of-law related issues, particularly in the wake of the Euromaidan. The civil society factor is something that not only Putin has difficulty in understanding, but Yanukovych too.

Both Moldova and Ukraine culturally follow the presidential model, even though their constitution distributes power in a semi-parliamentarian way. Russia's example, cultural affinity to the strong man role, and the natural bias of the mafia state all point in this direction. There is a halo around the presidency in these societies, that is difficult but not impossible to dress up on the institutions of the prime minister. Moreover, the president is not the manager of the executive. Instead, he is portrayed as sitting above such managerial posts (in this sense, more akin to a king) distributing either praise or criticism, while being presented by the media as a fatherly figure. Even in meetings he sits behind his pompous desk, rather than on the other side of the table with his fellow politicians.

Post-Euromaidan: Is Ukraine departing from patronal politics and society towards "Europeanness"?

In 2013–14, large parts of Ukrainian society revolted for a second time against a corrupt and unethical elite. This time the revolt held an even stronger geopolitical character, as the protesters claimed that reforms must also mean European orientation: the geopolitical alternatives represent choices of social order. Looking forward, three years after the so-called Revolution of Dignity, analysis is still split if Ukraine is undergoing a transformation from a patronal society towards a liberal state, or if the reforms have only so far scratched the surface. This section argues that breakthrough reforms of the Georgian type, that would start moving the country away from the criminal state model, have yet to occur. My assertion is that, while important partial changes have happened, the fundamental logic underpinning the organized criminal character of the state has not yet altered. Nor has any breakthrough occurred towards the more ambitious goal, establishing a rule-of-law regime independent of the executive power. However, the coalition of civil society and international donors, their understanding of the issues, and the desire to reform, still holds the opportunity for fundamental systemic change, like in Moldova.

In the process, the Poroshenko presidency, without the ugly excesses of the Yanukovych regime, has returned to its default position: it works to advance the business interests and power of the president and his team, and it has strived to nominate people to positions in state enterprises according to the financial interests of the president and his entourage. Poroshenko delayed legislation and constitutional changes establishing the rule-of-law, and fought strongly against the independence of the prosecution service and for unimpressive prosecutor generals, who were not by any standards reformist, and refused to fight crime in an uninhibited manner. After the Euromaidan, the legislature restored the pre-Yanukovych constitution, again with a weakened role for the presidency. The reality of the situation, however, is more complex: the factual role of the presidency is stronger than the letter of the constitution would imply, but the presidency is certainly not as overpowered as in Russia or Belarus, or as it was under Yanukovych. As such, the president was already informally a kind of *primus inter pares* in 2014. In the legislature, even the very reformist MPs thought that "respect" towards the presidency dictated that they should not take a driving role, even though the constitution would have allowed it.

Of course, Poroshenko first had to win the elections, which he did remarkably well, carrying every region in the country. His electoral success was the result of a brilliant balancing act, a skill at which he is extremely accomplished. His legitimacy was strengthened by his prominent role in the critical period of the Euromaidan protests, where he chose the side of the challengers and benefited from it—in spite of his earlier engagement with Yanukovych. On the other hand, he also cultivated a relationship with prominent members of the Yanukovych team, such as Serhiy Lyovochkin and Dmytro Firtash, who was already wanted by the US and was stuck in

Vienna. In the presidential election campaign, Poroshenko visited Firtash in Vienna: it was not a risk-free move, but he calculated accurately that it would ultimately be beneficial to him. The East, and the chief oligarchs, rightly gauged that he would not rock the boat if in power—something they certainly would not have expected of Yulia Tymoshenko.

In this way, in spite of the large number of deaths during the Euromaidan, the whole process remained fundamentally negotiated both externally, involving the Polish and German foreign ministers as well as (indirectly) Putin, and also internally. Among many layers of the revolution, one of the most critical was the rearrangement of powers among the oligarchs of Ukraine. Yanukovych, the representative of the Donbass mafia, had clearly overstretched, and there was a large interest among the other oligarchs and key actors that he leave power. This did not mean, however, that they wanted to change the oligarchic political system established by Kuchma. To the outside observer, this system was clearly dysfunctional, leading to Ukraine becoming the second poorest country in Europe. To a large degree, this contributed to the loss of Crimea and parts of the Donbass, as the homeland did not attract sufficient allegiance from the "least ethnically Ukrainian" parts of the country (after the loss of Crimea) to protect it in the period of the Russian menace.

Clearly, Hale's stress on the importance of political expectations also applies to the regional context. The concept of "Russkiy mir" (Russian world) works also in this area: the demonstration effect of the Russian model is such that the presidential position is afforded particular reverence in the region. Filat was able to counteract this in Moldova because the election of the president was delayed by many years in which period an interim president filled the post, after which the coalition partners settled on a profoundly non-threatening figure. In Ukraine, the expectations for the president to be the strong man of the country helped Poroshenko to grow above his constitutional role relatively quickly. The war also helped to increase his informal power, as defense remains among the president's responsibilities.

Poroshenko took power in a situation when he had to satisfy many external actors. Among them, the American government was particularly important, since in the time of a major Russian aggression Ukraine counted on help from the US and NATO. The European Union was also an important target as the Ukrainian government was hoping for EU financial assistance, the opening up of export markets, as well as diplomatic assistance, and an operational police force in the areas targeted by the Russian forces and their separatist clients in Eastern Ukraine. The Americans, the EU, and the IMF used this leverage from immediately after the Euromaidan to try to convince the Ukrainian government to initiate a decisive anti-corruption drive. However, none of these external players had an appropriately sophisticated reform strategy. The Georgian experts, of course, had a tried and tested one, and they appeared on the scene early on. They had a strong interest in contributing to the Ukrainian reforms, and were hoping for a post-Rose Revolution type of situation in Ukraine to allow rapid breakthrough reforms. Moreover, by the time of the Euromaidan, they had left the Georgian government. The new Georgian leaders were hostile to the politically visible representatives of the Saakashvili government, but even the technicians of the Saakashvili team found the new governing environment back home profoundly unattractive and simply left. For them, the ethos of the modernization reforms was a big part of the story, in very sharp contrast to the new governing team in Georgia, whose main agenda was simply to get rid of Saakashvili and create their own monopoly on power.[64] Saakashvili's experts made themselves available for assistance to the Ukrainian government.

However, their position became entrenched only gradually. When the main anti-corruption legislation was written, the Georgians still played only a minor role. The legislation carried the mark of two things: first, that the Ukrainian political class had changed only modestly in the wake of the Euromaidan; second, that the donors and civil society were still lacking a realistic reform strategy, or, more precisely, had a misconception of what was needed. They generally did not think deeply about the *systemic* character of the problem. They thought that "fighting" corruption meant literally and solely "fighting" against corrupt individuals, as if the problem was only a few bad apples. Oddly, some Georgians came to a similar conclusion that did not emphasize systemic change in their own country, instead focusing excessively on imprisoning oligarchs. This combination of two intentions— one to sabotage the anti-corruption reforms by the new leaders, the other to simply treat it as a "fight"—resulted in the weaknesses of the greatly advertised anti-corruption package in October 2014.[65] It foresaw the establishment of the National Anti-Corruption Bureau of Ukraine, the National Agency for Prevention of Corruption, and a "strategy" in a legislated document: a vague paper with few concrete plans, but rather a list of inconsequential "good intentions." The international actors, with the expert lead of the Council of Europe, also demanded a radical change of the judiciary and the prosecution service, though this was a secondary concern in 2014. The international supporters' understanding of the reforms required had never been as thorough as it was in 2014, but it was still not good enough for cornering a governing elite that wanted the goodwill of the West at any price in the face of Russian aggression, but also wanted to escape truly radical reforms.

Something very similar can be said about civil society. Its organization, professionalism and understanding of the reforms required in Ukraine increased considerably in the years leading up to the Euromaidan. In general, Ukrainian civil society played an incredibly important role both during and after the revolution. During the Euromaidan, its members organized events, provided assistance, and generated and distributed information. After the revolution and during the Russian invasion, when the army was totally unprepared for the menace from the East, they provided volunteer assistance to the army, both financial and in kind. They also formed different types of civic groups, some for the military front, others for helping the overstretched police, itself plagued by rampant corruption and low levels of professionalism, to maintain public order. Some helped the injured and collected money for the families of the deceased. The extent of the Ukrainian active and organized civil society was enormous indeed. Many more organizations emerged to help with formulating reforms and monitoring their implementation.[66] There was an emerging understanding that besides macroeconomic stabilization and technical reforms with major systemic consequences, such as the tax system, the justice sector also needed profound reform. The reformers organized in two major groups. One was the totally civic initiative Reanimation Package of Reforms. The other, initiated by George Soros and accepted by the government and president and supported by the EBRD, were the Strategic Advisory Groups, which placed strategic advisors in a number of ministries, as well as a coordinating unit into the office of the president.

In this period, if conditionalities have been stricter and more precise, breakthrough reforms would not have been impossible, despite the lack of interest from the top leadership. The outcome, however, has been less than satisfactory. Particularly striking to this writer was the lack of consultation by the IMF on its structural reform conditionality—in spite of the fact that the IMF is a relative novice in the area of rule-of-law policy. Conditioning support on structural reforms is absolutely the right thing to do, but it would have helped if this conditionality was based on an expert view. In the absence of such views, the main demand in fighting corruption was the establishment of the National Anti-Corruption Bureau.[67] However, it turned out (as I expected at the time) that there were plenty of ways for the presidency and government to prevent either the emergence or the proper functioning of an effective and truly independent bureau.

Despite the rapidly increasing power of the president in the governing institutions, he could not establish a firm single-pyramid power structure for many reasons. First, the combination of a coalition government—Poroshenko did not have anything close to an absolute majority in the Parliament—with a prime minister from another party, and with different oligarchic alliances, created oligarchic rivalries. Prime Minister Arseniy Yatsenyuk was a partial reformer in some areas, and a follower of the systemic logic of oligarchic alliance in others. Minister of Internal Affairs Arsen Avakov, another strongman of Yatsenyuk's party, was himself something of a smaller regional oligarch. Together, they were able to sustain a somewhat multiple power pyramid, a situation that enabled oligarchs to survive the post-revolutionary situation. Despite this, the Donbass clan lost much of its power due to Yanukovych's fall and Akhmetov losing a large proportion of his wealth to the war and widespread looting.

There was a moment where Akhmetov could have done things differently. Apparently at the instigation of Yulia Tymoshenko, he was also offered the position of Governor of the Donetsk region, but he declined it. In the neighboring Dnipropetrovsk region, the local oligarch Ihor Kolomoyskyi accepted the challenge and took up that region's governorship. During his one year tenure, Kolomoyskyi organized a successful defense of the region with combined police and quasi-military forces, not always following either the letter or the spirit of the rule-of-law. Those, however, were extraordinary times. Should Akhmetov have taken the same approach, Donetsk would probably still be controlled by Ukraine, and Akhmetov himself would be even richer. He would also look much better in the eyes of the Ukrainian public.

Akhmetov lost a considerable part of his wealth through war damage, and the de facto Russian occupation of the city of Donetsk, including many of his assets. As such, an important source of the single-pyramid system eroded with the Euromaidan, and with Akhmetov's hesitation to join the Ukrainian national cause unequivocally. Kolomoyskyi was also unable to outpace his rivals during this period. Although he could advance his business interests through his administrative control of Dnipropetrovsk, his personality was ill-suited to the kind of sophisticated political games required in his position, and he ultimately failed to fully capitalize on it. Moreover, Kolomoyskyi famously lived not in Dnipropetrovsk but in Switzerland, which made it more difficult for him to gain overwhelming support in Kyiv. In fact, using the pretext of his blatant violation of the rule-of-law, Poroshenko removed him as governor in March 2015, in an act characteristic of the president's balancing skills.[68] At the end of 2016, he suffered a further blow with the nationalization of the largest Ukrainian bank, Privatbank, that he owned.[69] The other oligarchs watch, with increasing worry, the president's efforts to expand his and his closest associates' business holdings. They see an imbalance of power which works in no one's interest. What they have not been able to do is create a situation that would assure the stability of assets and positions. Although they could benefit from establishing the rule-of-law together with an amnesty for earlier deeds, they lacked the necessary foresight and have not tabled such initiatives.[70]

Where the reforms have been most successful is in areas related to macroeconomic policy, where the IMF has had the most expertise and leverage. Given that the country is walking on the edge of financial unsustainability, IMF conditionality has been a major factor of systemic evolution. Where immediate macroeconomic concerns prevailed, the IMF was effective in imposing adequate measures. Not only the macroeconomic policy remained tight, but two effectively structural measures were imposed which, at least temporarily, seriously reduced the extent of corruption and rent-syphoning from the state to the private sector. The Ukrainian banking sector has gone through serious consolidation in the last one-and-a-half years. While the banking industry had developed technically since independence, until the current consolidation, it was characterized by large volumes of insider transactions where the owners of banks lent to related companies. This practice was reduced, and a large proportion of those effectively "pocket banks"[71] were closed by the National Bank of Ukraine, that was largely able to maintain its political independence from the executive. It has also managed well the nationalization of the largest bank, Privatbank, with the large systemic risks involved.

The other important macroeconomic achievement under the IMF's watch was the serious reduction of subsidies to the extraction industries. Traditionally, this type of rent-seeking was huge for coal, helping to finance the rise of the Donbass clan, with Akhmetov at its helm. An even larger system-shaping industry was the gas trade, where the Russian leadership played a very significant role. For the Russian leaders, the introduction of an intermediary organization had multiple functions. First, it offered the possibility to siphon off profits from the company to politicians in Russia, simply by adding extra costs between the production expenditures and the sale price to Ukrainian end-users. Conveniently, it also enabled them to influence, or in the case of Firtash, select outright, the middleman through whom they gained an important informal vehicle to influence Ukrainian politics. Thirdly, it served to corrupt the "elites" of the target society for recolonization, allowing the production and collection of *kompromat* on them. As Åslund notes, "for 2012, the International Monetary Fund (IMF) assessed the state energy subsidies at no less than 7.6 percent of GDP. These subsidies are likely to have peaked at 10 percent of GDP in 2014."[72] In political economy terms, this not only channeled public funds to oligarchs, but also increased Ukraine's external dependence (essentially decreasing sovereignty) by keeping wasteful energy consumption in place, since the end-users, corporate and individual alike, received cheap energy resources. This had a profoundly detrimental impact on public finances, the budget and external finances. Ukraine also failed to use its own significant energy resources, such as oil and gas, because of these market distortions. Furthermore, adoption of the necessary technologies was hindered by the negative climate for foreign direct investment in an environment of rampant corruption.

One of the chief conditionalities of the IMF and the European Union for macroeconomic assistance was to increase gas prices to market levels, reduce subsidies, eliminate intermediaries, and introduce competition in the gas trade, ending Naftogaz' monopoly. Of this whole range of reforms, the most immediate and least complex one, though politically difficult, was increasing the prices of gas. Since these efforts coincided with the freefall of international prices for natural gas, the Ukrainian government almost achieved full cost recovery, from an earlier situation when only a fraction of the gas prices were covered. This has immediately resulted in a dramatic decline in energy use, augmented by the effects of war, loss of territory, and a consequent dramatic drop in GDP. This reform, therefore, belongs exactly in the category mentioned above: immediate, with macroeconomic significance, and easy to verify. The country desperately needed the IMF program funds, which totaled 17 billion US dollars, and so acquiesced to this politically difficult decision. However, no substantial reforms have taken place that would undermine the capacity of rent seekers to siphon away massive funds in the future. In July 2016, the government decided to organize the storage and transport facilities of Naftogaz into separate companies, but conveniently the implementation of this decision was postponed indefinitely, ostensibly due to a major international legal dispute with the Russian Gazprom over payments for earlier deliveries. As such, Naftogaz will continue to act as a monopolist ad infinitum, and its level of asset leakage will continue to depend on goodwill as its corporate governance has also not changed since the Euromaidan.[73]

This pattern of reforms in all other areas, important for the kind of systemic change that would lead Ukraine from a power-based, patronal society towards a rule-of-law one, has shown the same characteristics: make changes that give as few concessions to foreign donors and civil society as possible, and definitively avoid changes that make transition towards a rules-based society irreversible. With the macroeconomic situation stabilized, the government needed to deal with deeper rule-of-law issues, improving the investment climate to help address the concern of future economic decline. Major reforms, therefore, were required in the energy sector, the chain of justice provision (judiciary, prosecution services and police) and taxation, including customs. Furthermore, massive deregulation and shrinking of the state could have addressed some of the incentives for corruption. Public administration reform—making it functional and competent, rather than dysfunctional and serving special interests, including those of state officials—and greater transparency of the state sector were on the agenda.[74] These reforms could have improved markedly the investment climate for new investors, rather than the few oligarchs who control much of the state apparatus. They could also help to generate the feeling that the state is no longer a repressive, faceless failure, but a thriving service-oriented institution. While not necessarily all the reforms needed to be implemented fully, a critical mass was required so that its internal logic worked, and its components reinforced each other. In the post-Euromaidan presidential and parliamentary cycle this has not yet happened.[75]

A discussion emerged between civil society, Kyiv analysts and the international partners over the immediate post-Euromaidan period as to which of the two leaders of the coalition were the more "true reformers." The reality is that both of them played by the same old rules. The main difference was that the most immediate reforms, directly impacting the crisis in the macroeconomic situation, were predominantly the prime minister's responsibility. As such, the president's objections to reform became more visible over time, as his apparatus obstructed the dynamic implementation of one of the Euromaidan's main demands: the reform of the judicial system, including public prosecution. The reforms required constitutional changes as well, something the presidential team could easily obstruct, in order to mitigate their impact, by slowing down legislation. In fact, there was no significant reform that the president would even have enthusiastically supported, let alone spearheaded. He was able to get away with this because of his extraordinarily good sense for public relations, both internationally and domestically, plus the goodwill he accumulated for being the commander-of-chief of an army which has weathered Russian military aggression. He is also a cunning dealmaker with other oligarchs.

Concerning corruption, the focus of the international partners and the public was too simplistic and concentrated solely on repression. As such, there was very little attention paid to the regulatory and incentive side of the issue. One of the core problems, visibly, was the conflict of interest of many, but in the case of the president, it required particular attention for the sake of systemic development. Nevertheless, this was completely avoided during the debate over the "anti-corruption package."[76] Transparency of public administration was an area where the Georgians had much experience, and their example could have been followed. After some time, in 2016, an electronic procurement system was introduced which was open and transparent, although initially it only covered a fraction of the procurements.[77] In the ocean of inertia, it was still hailed as a big reform step. Unlike in Georgia, no serious attempt was made to reduce governmental bloat by eliminating agencies and reducing state employment. Similarly, little attention was paid to the obvious fact that in public administration and the justice sector, very low salaries were a key component that had kept the vicious circle of corruption intact by not allowing people to have a decent living; the income from salaries alone was not sufficient for most employees. Even when the Law on the Public Prosecutors' Office— one of the reform laws—prescribed an increase in prosecutors' salaries,[78] the government did not make the necessary budget provisions to cover the increased costs, despite a significant planned reduction of the number of prosecutors that would partially cover the increased wage costs.

This pretending game, mixed with half-reforms, has characterized the whole period since the Euromaidan. Poroshenko invited true reformists to be ministers or deputies on his ticket into the post-Maidan government. Several were foreigners, some from Mikheil Saakashvili's Georgian government, himself included. Over time, however, the president came into conflict with all of them aside from Natalia Jaresko, the American-born minister of finance of Ukrainian origin. Reforms in the area for which the president was directly responsible, most of the "power" sectors, whose reform the entire systemic transition depended on, were basically blocked.

As I wrote earlier, a key tool of the post-Soviet patronal mafia state is a deeply corrupted prosecution service with direct links to the presidency; it is a vital glue that helps bind together the criminal state. A strong recommendation from the Council of Europe, the norm-setting European institution for issues relating to the rule-of-law, was to weaken the legal position of the public prosecution service, loosen its internal hierarchy, and eliminate its quasi power ministry (militarized) status.[79] The president did not find the risk of spearheading prosecutorial reform tolerable. In a world where mutual blackmail, production of *kompromat* and shady deals are standard daily practices, losing control over the prosecution authority is not a voluntary option, since other oligarchs would surely try to exploit it. At the same time, in 2014 there was great pressure on the president and the post-Euromaidan government, from both civil society and the international partners, to go ahead with the reform.

The tactic of derailing it was multifold. First, the Rada adopted a new law that was praised by the international community, including the Venice Commission.[80] Most importantly, the law eliminated the so-called general oversight, the full discretion of public prosecutors to initiate investigation against any individual or institution without justification. It cut investigative powers from the prosecutors and made them more independent from the presidency. It also envisioned a bottom-up reorganization of the prosecutorial office. However, the law itself gave the authorities a six-month grace period for implementation. The authorities, including Prosecutor General Vitaly Yarema, who was there essentially to sabotage the implementation of the law, used this half-year to prepare further delays. He also wanted to change the provisions of the law in parliament (obviously not acting on his own initiative), but rebellion was so strong among the reformers that it forced the president to replace Yarema. In the political clash over Yarema, the opposition also publicized photographs of his luxurious home. This raised bad memories of the notorious prosecutor general of Yanukovych, Viktor Pshonka. Poroshenko could not resist the public pressure to sack Yarema, but he faced more public anger when he appointed another typical representative of the old guard. As an experienced actor in this environment, he knew the risks of appointing a truly independent and reform minded prosecutor. He preferred to accept the loss of political capital and appointed yet another poor candidate, Viktor Shokin, who, instead of undertaking the critically important task of destroying and transforming the institutional monster built by Stalin's repressive state, was mainly there to block any critical reforms.

The way the new prosecutor general did this was by making sure that his two reformer deputies, Vitaliy Kasko and Davit Sakvarelidze, could not do their jobs. Shokin prevented them from investigating corrupt high-ranking prosecutors,[81] and also derailed the reorganization process. Shokin proved to be a reliable gatekeeper. However, the pressure started to mount on the president to fire Shokin as well. Ultimately he did, but he made sure that before leaving office, Shokin fired the two reformers. Once again, his next appointment was controversial, making it clear to everyone that he did not want prosecutorial independence. After Shokin, he appointed Yuriy Lutsenko, a man with a brave political background. More importantly, however, Lutsenko was the head of Poroshenko's parliamentary faction, and thus the opposite of an independent professional. Poroshenko used Lutsenko's earlier brave political stature as his selling point, particularly towards the US and the EU. The Americans were especially involved politically, right up to vice-President Joe Biden, who took a strong personal stake in Ukraine's state building success. Lutsenko's appointment raised a degree of hope. To understand this, we need to remember the Georgian case, where the rule of law was not necessarily followed, yet there was a strong clamp down on crime and corruption. In Ukraine, public expectations concerning progress were closely linked to the punishing of the criminals associated with Yanukovych. This is what Lutsenko promised and what his whole background would, in an optimistic reading, project. However, so far his attitude as prosecutor general has been fully subservient towards the president and the punishments have not come; they do not fit into the president's political plan.

In order to fundamentally reform an organization as rotten as the public prosecution service in Ukraine, legislative change and public-driven campaigns for punishing the most outrageous crimes—such as the particularly grievous cases of theft during the Yanukovych-era or the murder of Euromaidan protesters—were insufficient. What was needed in order to radically change the corporate ethos of the institution was a complete overhaul of the personnel. The old staff had specialized in very different matters than those nominally within the prosecution office's purview. Indeed, during my time working with this body, I heard one of the reformers claim that "these people don't know what investigation is." One of the components of Sakvarelidze's reform strategy, therefore, was to reorganize the body's 18,000 prosecutors from grassroots level. An additional bill also sought to decrease their numbers to 10,000. Sakvarelidze's "bottom-up" reform was eventually blocked, both by the government and by Viktor Shokin from inside. A critical component of protecting the old order was that prosecutors' salaries were kept low, which together with the eroding effect of inflation, made it impossible for them to live honestly on their governmental pay alone. A bill from the Public Prosecutor's Office prescribed a significant increase. However, in breach of the law, the government did not give the necessary budgetary funds for the increase and continued to use the old salary scale. This was even more devastating, as it did not take into account the impact of rampant inflation during the crisis period. Prosecutors were, therefore, deliberately kept in financial dependence on their political-oligarchic masters. Adjusting salaries to a level where professional pride, basic human honesty and job security mean more to the majority than the potential gains from corrupt deals is a key ingredient of a successful reform.

Judges have been even more despised by Ukrainian society than prosecutors. While in the courtroom prosecutors have the power—more than 99 percent of judicial processes initiated by the prosecutor result in the judge handing down a guilty verdict—judges constitute the more direct and visible interface with the public. The Euromaidan demanded a major reform and overhaul of the judicial corps, so that corrupt processes and verdicts could be stopped. While much was formally improved, even during the Yanukovych presidency, in the legislative basis of justice, the problem of corruption was magnified by an overly complicated four-level system. After the Euromaidan, the judiciary became a central subject of bargaining between the executive—in this case definitely the presidency, although Prime Minister Yatsenyuk's party contributes the minister of justice—on one hand and civil society, Western partners and reform-minded legislators, with the deputy speaker Oksana Syroyid spearheading reform efforts, on the other. Her original core professional interest is constitutional law.

One way of meeting the demand of the Euromaidan protesters and the wider public would have been a vetting process by revolutionary organs. Such organs, however, did not emerge. The furthest the government got was the creation of the monitoring, watchdog and advisory organizations that have survived since the revolution. On the other hand, the Rada passed a lustration law after long delays in August 2014,[82] half a year after the government nominated a lustration committee head. This law left a great deal of arbitrary judgment to the internal lustration committees, and in the three most important institutions—the Security Services of Ukraine, the judiciary and the Public Prosecutor's Office—it was easy to block the process. But fundamentally, it did not go anywhere in any of the institutions except, perversely, in the border guard services, which were regarded as the most reformed of the power institutions of Ukraine. The reasons for lustration there were purely political: the presidency wanted to remove the border guards' leadership, and the fact that by law all of them had to be trained in the KGB academy served as a convenient argument. They voluntarily stepped down. The Council of Europe criticized the lustration law as being arbitrary and weakly defined, and asked for revisions at the end of 2014. After this the process slowly died, although the lustration organs continued to nominally function with little effect. Ultimately, the avenue whereby a civilian organization could examine the criminally or politically inexcusable deeds of earlier officials proved to be a dead end, and as time passed by, gathering enough force to instigate radical change became more and more difficult.

The blocking tactics for the reforms in the judiciary were to make the changes piecemeal and slow, and to keep the judges in a strong position in designing the changes. There was a split of opinion among the reformers: some wanted to simply apply the Council of Europe "best practices," while others argued that if no vetting preceded the introduction of real judicial independence, the same corrupt body of judges would not get their own house in order. The Georgians in government, like the other radical reformers, advocated strongly first for cleansing, and then independence for both the prosecution service and the judges; but this was not to happen. This fight for a better judiciary has been going on throughout the post-Euromaidan period. Three waves of legislation followed, and each time the presidency, together with vested interests in the Rada, succeeded in weakening the legislation sufficiently so that no radical improvement occurred in the two interconnecting issues of corruption and dependency on the presidency. The tools of control in this fight have kept the corrupt judges in place,[83] making the process of reform slow, conserving the power of the presidents of district judges, avoiding changes in the appellation courts and keeping some presidential power over judges, holding some prerogatives in appointment, and maintaining a few "temporary" rules until constitutional amendments on decentralization took effect. During this "transitional" period, "the President of Ukraine establishes, reorganizes, and liquidates courts."[84]

A specificity of the Ukrainian situation is that the rulers need to show progress to the public and their Western friends. They are trying to do this in a manner that is not creating truly independent justice. At the same time, the changes may yet prove to be considerable. The constitutional changes of June 2, 2016 have simplified the overcomplicated four-tier structure into three, and decreased the role of the president in judicial appointments. Anti-corruption rules have been tightened and salaries increased to incentivize better behavior. Access to the Constitutional Court has been widened.[85] There has also been some practical follow up. While the ruling elite maintains plenty of guarantees that in sensitive cases, no independent judgment can happen for a long time (particularly while the appellate courts are unreformed), there may be a chance that islands of independence and professionalism can be created for less sensitive cases. Moreover, salary reforms in the judiciary allow for professionally proud judges to do their jobs for an honest salary: they are no longer forced to seek bribes.[86] Still, at the very best, the move towards honest, independent justice has been slowed down tremendously.

Public administration reform is an important component of breaking out of the patronal/mafia state. Here too, a cat-and-mouse game evolved between the government on one hand, and donors and civil society on the other, in the specific areas of civil service and decentralization. In the sphere of public administration, the Georgians in the Ukrainian government had the experience of a radical transformation that had simultaneously shrunk the state apparatus and institutions, while increasing its professionalism and wiping out corruption. In a less innovative way, the European Union also offered a reform blueprint and used the services of SIGMA, the specialized initiative for public administration reform (PAR). Decentralization, at the same time, was a strong demand of the Euromaidan, as Ukraine is a large territory with the paradox of huge theoretical overregulation, only made workable through corruption—and overregulation, of course, serves the exact purposes of corruption. In both the areas of public administration reform and decentralization, the executive prevented fast progress. In the first case it was the parliament, and in the second the presidency, that dragged its feet. The government was not ready to take either the Georgian or the European path, and on the way lost 90 million euros that had been assigned for the implementation of PAR in 2015, that a year later was finally regained.[87]

The decentralization issue was burdened by Russian demands for federalization, so that via the Donbass they could get friendly figures inside the Ukrainian government, and use their veto power to blackmail Ukrainian politicians into submission. The muddied management of the issue within the Ukrainian elite resulted in a political stalemate. An obvious compromise would have been if the government opted for significant decentralization towards the municipalities, while not giving as much power to the regions that would enable them to undermine national security interests. The obstacle on this path was that the municipal net is far too fragmented. The government did not risk initiating a general overhaul of the municipal landscape, but rather incentivized voluntary amalgamation of the municipalities. This process is slowly progressing.[88] The issue of the regional level could have been handled so that the political compromises for the occupied territories, sanctioned in the Minsk agreements,[89] would have been separate from the rest. However, the stalemate that caused clashes and fatalities in front of the parliament on August 31, 2015, was not inconvenient to the president, who would have lost some of his power over the regional bosses if the reforms had gone ahead. The project's opponents, who were afraid of fragmentation, scored a pyrrhic victory, since after the August clashes they could be blamed as uncompromising. This incident set back the process, wrecking yet another aspect of state reform.[90]

President Poroshenko has strengthened one element of his power: over the international corruption scandal of one of his confidantes, Prime Minister Arseniy Yatsenyuk was forced by public opinion to leave. His replacement, Volodymyr Groysman, was a very close associate of the president. Also, in the reshuffle all the reform heavyweights left government. Indeed, even before Yatsenyuk was forced to leave, the respected Lithuanian-born minister of economy, Aivaras Abromavičius, quit.[91] He took his grievances public, accusing Poroshenko's "smotryashchiy" ("overseer," a term originating in organized crime) in parliament and government, Ihor Kononenko, of informally trying to convince him to appoint "questionable individuals" to top positions at state-owned companies, particularly Naftogaz.[92] His fragile coalition disintegrated to the point that the president, who had used his connections to the former government's main supporters extensively since his bid for the presidency, now has to resort to their support in the Rada as well, holding only a slim majority.[93] This is also what happened with the deal over the new government but also with the above mentioned constitutional changes on June 2, 2016.[94] Whereas Poroshenko consolidated his power within his coalition in 2016, this could not change the pluralistic outlook of Ukrainian politics. Groysman proved to be more independent than expected at the time of his appointment, while oligarchic interests in the Rada have forced Poroshenko into repeated compromises. The price of maintaining this political pluralism is nevertheless the delaying of vital reforms, such as liberating land sales.

Perspectives: patronal state, mafia state, or rule-of-law?

This chapter has examined the social system of the three countries between the European Union and Russia that have strong declared aspirations to integrate with the West, meaning the European Union and, in the Ukrainian and Georgian cases, NATO. During the communists' rule, Moldovan society overwhelmingly opted to follow a European path, while today it is roughly equally split. At the same time, it is constitutionally a neutral country, and while support for this is not unanimous, a strong majority certainly feels that this is the best option to preserve peace in the face of an aggressive Russia. Because of the Russian wars against them, Ukrainians and Georgians are overwhelmingly pro-Western, including aspiring to NATO membership.

For each of them, it remains uncertain which social model will materialize in the foreseeable future. In each country, powerful internal mechanisms are working towards consolidating the single-pyramid patronal system, and others are struggling against it. The Russian leadership is trying hard to bring these countries back under its close subordination, including through the use of its extractive industry companies, above all Gazprom, fostering the deeply corrupt—and in fact criminal—oligarchic system. For the elites of these countries, this is a hard choice: in the long run, a patronal political system is incompatible with European integration. A single-pyramid system, including its state capture variants in Moldova and Georgia, carries the risk that it may ultimately push them into Putin's arms. However, the Russian president does not offer any real alternative, as they know that belonging to the Russian integration model corresponds to long term submission to Putin, which large components of civil society and indeed the rulers themselves in each country would deeply resent. The Euromaidan has sent a cautionary message of what the consequences to this could be.

In all three countries, a lack of breakthrough reforms has caused systematic internal conflicts with an urban civil society and population whose expectations of government are approaching Western norms. Reform, therefore, must remain a vital priority. However, since Saakashvili in Georgia, no leader has emerged with a credible breakthrough reform agenda. Indeed, Georgia is the only country within the CIS area[95] that has achieved significant, even if only partial, success in moving the system away from its mafia character. In the Saakashvili era, the new government demolished the state's organized criminal character, even if it still left arbitrariness in the system and the provision of justice remained strongly linked with the executive. The Saakashvili-era experience also helps us to formulate the following dilemma or paradox: one can only break the strong logic of the patronal-mafia system if centralized, near revolutionary power is exercised. However, such power also lends itself to the formation of a new single-pyramid patronal network. Saakashvili was not free from that temptation, although ultimately, thanks partly to encouragement from external partners, he left power in a democratic manner after losing elections. In an optimistic scenario, one may hope that the incompleteness of the Georgian reforms would be gradually addressed by the Georgian Dream governments. On the other hand, the landslide victory of Georgian Dream in 2016 raises questions about the sustainability of Saakashvili-era gains due to weakening checks on the executive.

Geopolitical orientation and social organization in these three countries are deeply interconnected: the more they are able to pursue a European integration pattern, the more likely it is that attributes of a liberal, rules-based state will gradually take root. These factors are mutually reinforcing: the more any of these societies transform, the more likely it is they gravitate towards Europe and the West in general. It is exactly because this transition has not occurred more quickly, that pro-Western integration moves have also been hesitant. This is not to deny that Europe should promote transition much more effectively. The European Union and the United States both badly need to develop a proper change strategy for the countries of the region, particularly those that are eager to integrate with them. Some major structural weaknesses so far have hindered this process. Firstly, the EU needs to differentiate more clearly between state and society. It has conditioned the visa-free travel regime on too many things. While it is completely legitimate to ensure that the countries of the EU are safe from unwelcome visitors and settlers, a whole range of conditions were added that depend on the quality of governance in the countries. Similarly, free trade is a mutually beneficial proposition for both sides, and the best support regime for economic transition. In light of this, the EU's hard negotiation stance on this issue has been misconceptualized. On the other hand, for too long the conditionalities for support were based on half-baked ideas, which reflected the donor countries' home agendas as much as the actual needs of the transition countries. The systemic logic of these societies requires a realistic change strategy; writing laws that only remain on paper helps very little. Moreover, it is deeply unlikely that any society can jump seamlessly from very conservative value systems to the most sophisticated and radical human rights standards. Finally, the EU itself is an overregulated space. Imposing the same excessive regulation in countries with significantly less state capacity and reflexive corruption is a recipe for failure.

The theory of dual transition saw the tasks of building market economies and liberal democracy as a simultaneous dual task. Even in those successful transitioning states which later joined the European Union, the way the task of building the rule-of-law was articulated was weak and not very concrete. Taras Kuzio's article back in 2000 was very important, as for a large number of post-socialist countries—those which newly emerged from the ashes of the Soviet Union and Yugoslavia—it spoke of the challenge of quadruple transition. Here the state-building task, one of the four transitions, may involve the building of effective institutions and provision of the rule-of-law. However, only recently has the attention of international partners been fully focused on the problem of corruption having become the very system itself, as it is often formulated. Moreover, a new problem has emerged on the horizon: the global geopolitical situation seems to be changing radically at the time of writing this paper, and not in the West's favor. Whether the positive influences of the West will survive those changes will have a major impact on the systemic dynamics of the countries in the Eastern Neighborhood of the European Union.

In the best-case scenario, a proper external influence channeling ambitious but realistic change toward a liberal state, combined with similar expectations from the three countries' societies—their young urban component in particular—will sooner or later sweep away the entrenched single pyramid, patronal and mafia nature of the state, replacing it with genuine rule-of-law and a dynamic market economy. Both external influences and civil society activism remain crucial to reform in these three countries, whose societies yearn to belong to the West. These chances are all the better as the single-pyramid state cannot deliver to the young urban classes the kind of economic prosperity seen throughout the modern world.

Notes

[1] Henry E. Hale, *Patronal Politics: Eurasian Regime Dynamics in Comparative Perspective* (New York: Cambridge University Press, 2014); particularly chapters 7 (for Ukraine) and 10 (for Moldova).

[2] Vladimir Dubrovskiy, "The Ukrainian Tax System: Why and How It Should Be Reformed? Part II," *Vox Ukraine*, Jul. 13, 2005, http://voxukraine.org/2015/07/13/the-ukrainian-tax-system-2/.

[3] Vladimir Dubrovskiy, "The Ukrainian Tax System: Why and How It Should be Reformed. Part I," *Vox Ukraine*, Jun. 30, 2005, http://voxukraine.org/2015/06/30/the-ukrainian-tax-system-why-and-how-it-should-be-reformed/.

[4] Taras Kuzio, *Ukraine: Democratization, Corruption, and the New Russian Imperialism* (Santa Barbara, CA: Praeger Security International, 2015), 360–64; and more generally chapters 9 and 10.

[5] Alexander Kupatadze, "'Transitions After Transitions': Coloured Revolutions and Organized Crime in Georgia, Ukraine and Kyrgyzstan" (PhD diss., University of St. Andrews, 2010).

[6] Early extensive descriptions of the dollar-based shadow economy can be found in Pawel Wyczanski, "Kvázi-valutapiac Lengyelországban," *Pénzügyi Szemle*, no. 10 (1984); also Kálmán Mizsei, *Lengyelország: Válságok, Reformpótlékok, Reformok* (Budapest: Közgazdasági és Jogi Könyvkiadó, 1990).

[7] On the early post-Soviet years particularly, see Anders Åslund, *Ukraine: What Went Wrong and How to Fix It* (Washington, DC: Peterson Institute for International Economics, 2015), 61–66.

[8] Andrew Wilson, *The Ukrainians: Unexpected Nation* (New Haven, CT: Yale University Press, 2009), 156–71.

[9] Taras Kuzio and Andrew Wilson, *Ukraine: Perestroika to Independence* (London: MacMillan, 1994), 184–91 and 205.

[10] I will use the term "social" system for the description and dynamics of the system we are discussing, as it is broader than "political," encompassing political institutions, economic institutions and social norms.

[11] Kuzio expands in detail on the specificities of the Donbass in Kuzio, *Ukraine: Democratization, Corruption,* and also in id., *Putin's War against Ukraine: Revolution, Nationalism and Crime* (CreateSpace, 2017), particularly chapter 6.

[12] Anders Åslund, *How Ukraine Became a Market Economy and Democracy* (Washington, DC: Peterson Institute for International Economics, 2009), 71–72.

13 "Chornovil, Viacheslav," Internet Encyclopedia of Ukraine, accessed Jan. 12, 2018, http://www.encyclopediaofukraine.com/display.asp?linkpath=pages%5CC%5CH%5CChornovilViacheslav.htm.
14 Lukashenka is a nuisance to Moscow, but does not represent such a risk to Russian hegemonic aspirations for two reasons: firstly, he is not building a sufficiently strong economy that could be less dependent on Russian gas and oil deliveries; secondly, his authoritarian rule at the outset was based on a strongly pro-Russian premise. So, he locked himself into a strong dependency on Russia's rulers.
15 Ukraine became a WTO member in 2008, while Russia only joined the organization in 2012.
16 Hale, *Patronal Politics*, 375–76.
17 Eugen Tomiuc, "Moldova: Caught Between a Hammer and a Sickle as Anti-Communist Protests Continue," Radio Free Europe/Radio Liberty, Nov. 28, 2003, https://www.rferl.org/a/1105158.html.
18 This was not the case for the Baltic states, whose recovery had started much earlier due to their radical early reforms.
19 William H. Hill, *Russia, the Near Abroad, and the West: Lessons from the Moldova-Transdniestria Conflict* (Washington, DC: Woodrow Wilson Center Press, 2012), 149–53.
20 Kuzio, *Ukraine: Democratization, Corruption*, 346.
21 Ibid.
22 For a systematic typology, see Bálint Magyar, *Post-Communist Mafia State: The Case of Hungary* (Budapest–New York: Central European University Press and Noran Libro, 2016).
23 It also applies to the current author, who initiated a major advisory work for the new president with both international and local involvement from the platform of the United Nations Development Program (UNDP). From the perspective of another decade, our work—while including some novel practical advice—was clearly one-sided. See Blue Ribbon Commission for Ukraine, *Proposals for the President: A New Wave of Reform* (Kyiv: United Nations Development Programme, 2005).
24 This term, from the Russian meaning "thieves in law," refers to the mafia-like members of organized crime syndicates in the post-Soviet states. A detailed analysis of the phenomenon can be found in Kupatadze, *Transitions After Transitions*.
25 For the most detailed account of these reforms, see The World Bank, *Fighting Corruption in Public Services: Chronicling Georgia's Reforms* (Washington, DC: The World Bank, 2012). The account below is based on that study, as well as the personal experiences and interviews of the author. Another able assessment can be found in Larisa Burakova, *Pochemu u Gruzii poluchilos* (Moscow: Alpina Biznis Buks, 2011).
26 "Georgia: Imedi Opposition TV to Return to Airwaves," Radio Free Europe/Radio Liberty, Dec. 4, 2007, http://www.rferl.org/a/1079231.html.
27 Arthur Laffer, *The Laffer Curve: Past, Present, and Future*, The Heritage Foundation, June 1, 2004, https://www.heritage.org/taxes/report/the-laffer-curve-past-present-and-future.

28 An unbiased description of the story can be read here: "Timeline: Rustavi 2 TV Row," Civil Georgia, Nov. 16, 2015, http://www.civil.ge/eng/article.php?id= 28775.
29 "Supreme Court Finds Rustavi 2 TV's Appeal in Ownership Dispute Admissible," Civil Georgia, Sep. 9, 2016, http://civil.ge/eng/article.php?id=29427. See also "Rustavi 2 TV Shareholders Lose Appeal in Ownership Dispute," Civil Georgia, Jun. 10, 2016, http://www.civil.ge/eng/article.php?id=29219.
30 In 2016, Georgia's economy continued to outperform most of its neighbors in the region. ISET's forecast for 4th quarter GDP growth was 4.15%; its GDP growth projection for Georgia was 3.4%. For comparison, the World Bank's June 2016 projections of annual growth for neighboring countries are as follows: Armenia, 1.9%; Azerbaijan, -1.9%; Turkey, 3.5%; Ukraine, 1%; Russia, -1.2%. "March Data Shows Remarkable Stability of Economic Indicators," ISET Policy Institute, May 30, 2016, http://www.iset-pi.ge/index.php/en/gdp-forcast/1402-march-data-shows-remarkable-stability-of-economic-indicators.
31 See "Georgia's 2017–2018 Economic Growth Forecast by EBRD Improved," Ministry of Economy and Sustainable Development of Georgia, November 9, 2017, http://www.economy.ge/?page=news&nw=366&s=ebrdma-saqartvelos-ekonomikuri-zrdis-2017-2018-wlebis-prognozi-gazarda&lang=en.
32 Of course, in a society where the rule-of-law is not ingrained by centuries of development, even constitutional arrangements have a degree of fragility.
33 In fact, anecdotal evidence points to the possible erosion of the modernizing features described above, and a consequent return to the corruption of the past. It is not yet shown in Transparency International's 2017 Corruption Perception Index, the most frequently quoted and followed metric of corruption. Here Georgia's score only deteriorated by one point, and its slide in ranking has also been minimal so far. See "Corruption Perceptions Index 2017," *Transparency International*, last modified February 21, 2018, https://www.transparency.org/news/feature/corruption_perceptions_index_2017#regional.
34 See the OSCE preliminary report on the Georgian elections: "Voting assessed positively in competitive run-off elections in Georgia, although legislative framework lacking, international observers say," *OSCE*, last modified Oct. 31, 2016, https://www.osce.org/odihr/elections/georgia/278091. "'The withdrawal of some candidates between the first and second rounds is a serious issue and the motivation of these withdrawals should be thoroughly analyzed,' said Emanuelis Zingeris, Head of the PACE delegation. 'Legal investigation of the irregularities in the first round must be completed. It goes without saying that allegations, coming from all sides, on irregularities during the second round must be carefully evaluated as well.' The Election Code does not regulate the second round. Aiming to address a few procedural issues the central election commission issued decrees, however, these were adopted late in the process, interpreted the law in a contentious manner, and, at times, contradicted the Election Code."
35 Before the presidential election I, in my capacity as the regional director of UNDP for Europe and the CIS, set up a reform advisory team for the new president, with a mixed membership from the best local and outstanding international experts. During the period when, after the rerun of the presidential election, Yushchenko

was already declared the new president but not yet inaugurated, we had in-depth discussions with all the major players in his entourage. This consisted of about twelve detailed policy discussions; see Blue Ribbon Commission for Ukraine, *Proposals for the President: A New Wave of Reform* (Kyiv: United Nations Development Programme, 2005). The discussion with Yulia Tymoshenko stood out, due to her refusal to heed our advice, that at the time was widely publicized and authoritative. She argued that the government could only implement popular reforms because there are looming parliamentary elections that they needed to win. On another occasion in February 2015, at the beginning of her prime ministerial work, she requested a private meeting with George Soros that I also attended. Both I, and Michael Emerson who was also present , were shocked by the naïveté of the new prime minister's policy ideas. Tymoshenko at the time combined very charismatic leadership qualities, extreme political tactical skills, and an incredible lack of policy intelligence, bound up in intensely provincial ideas about how the world works. Following up on the Blue Ribbon Commission on my side, and the late Boris Nemtsov's high profile personal involvement with the Orange Revolution, we established an advisory group with Nemtsov and Marek Dabrowski. This group faltered for two reasons. First, Tymoshenko was not really interested in policy advice; she perhaps also felt intimidated by Nemtsov's patronizing, "big brother" style. Moreover, after the first policy mistakes, such as the reintroduction of price controls and export restrictions, he publicly scolded the prime minister. But this episode also illustrates that Tymoshenko, though she performed excellently in the Yushchenko government in 2000 when she needed to politically break the monopolies of Kuchma's various oligarchs, completely failed as an economic policy maker due to the lack of policy experience that many of us, including Nemtsov, had.

[36] See "VIDEO. Zinaida Greceanîi: 'Nu regret declarațiile mele din aprilie 2009'," *Agora*, last modified Jun. 25, 2015, http://agora.md/stiri/10323/video--zinaida-greceanii-nu-regret-declaratiile-mele-din-aprilie-2009.

[37] After learning about the decision, I flew to Chișinău in my capacity as European Union Special Representative, and delivered this ultimatum. As the BBC reported, the license of PRO-TV Chisinau was "extended provisionally after a meeting between the EU envoy Kalman Mizsei and Moldovan President Vladimir Voronin, who heads the ruling Party of Communists (PCRM)." See Petru Clej, "'Law is an ass' stunt brings fine," *BBC News*, December 23, 2008, http://news.bbc.co.uk/2/hi/europe/7797698.stm.

[38] "The 5 April 2009 parliamentary elections took place in an overall pluralistic environment and offered voters distinct political alternatives." See "Parliamentary Elections, 5 April 2009," Organization for Security and Co-operation in Europe, http://www.osce.org/node/57994, accessed Jan. 10, 2018. Also referred to in Ellen Barry, "After Protests, Moldovan Opposition Claims Election Fraud," *New York Times*, Apr. 9, 2009, http://www.nytimes.com/2009/04/10/world/europe/10moldova.html?ref=global-home.

[39] "The saga of an oligarch that dreams of becoming a president," *Jurnal.md*, January 6, 2015, https://web.archive.org/web/20150718141958/http://jurnal.md/en/politic/2015/1/6/the-saga-of-an-oligarch-that-dreams-of-becoming-a-president/.

40 "Controversial Businessman Vlad Plahotniuc Buys Two More TV Stations in Moldova," *Media Power Monitor*, Feb. 12, 2016, http://mediapowermonitor.com/content/controversial-businessman-vlad-plahotniuc-buys-two-more-tv-stations-moldova.

41 For the full official results, see "General Local Elections of June 14 and 28, 2015," *E-democracy.md*, http://www.e-democracy.md/en/elections/local/2015/, accessed January 14, 2018.

42 Since the finishing of the manuscript, Armașu became governor of the central bank, having been replaced as minister of finance by Ion Chicu, while Octavian Calmîc was replaced as minister of economy by Chiril Gaburici.

43 For more on Plahotniuc's informal power, see Kamil Całus, "Moldova: from oligarchic pluralism to Plahotniuc's hegemony," Ośrodek Studiów Wschodnich, Apr. 11, 2016, https://www.osw.waw.pl/en/publikacje/osw-commentary/2016-04-11/moldova-oligarchic-pluralism-to-plahotniucs-hegemony.

44 In particular, see Sergiu Tofilat, "Schema Energokapital explicată pe înțelesul tuturor," *Blog de analize economice*, Aug. 3, 2016, https://sergiutofilat.wordpress.com/2016/08/03/schema-energokapital-explicata-pe-intelesul-tuturor/.

45 Here, to some extent, I differ from Hale. In my view, he makes too much of the weak constitutional position of the president. Not only were Lupu and Filat both trying to become president, rather than prime minister, in the April–May stalemate Voronin also acted under the assumption that this is the strongest position in the country. Symbolism has long superseded any constitutional distribution of power.

46 Only 30.29 percent of Moldova's eligible voters cast their ballots, which was lower than the required 33 percent. While 87.8 per cent of those who voted were in favor of direct presidential elections, the referendum thus ended up being invalid. See William E. Crowther, "Second Decade, Second Chance? Parliament, Politics and Democratic Aspirations in Russia, Ukraine and Moldova," in *Post-Communist Parliaments: Change and Stability in the Second Decade*, ed. David M. Olson and Gabriella Ilonszki (London: Routledge, 2011), 51; see also "Results of the Republican Constitutional Referendum of September 5, 2010," http://www.e-democracy.md/en/elections/referendum/2010/results/.

47 "Usatyi reveals how Plahotniuc made Zubco prosecutor general; The oligarch appealed to the help of the thief in law Karamalak in order to intimidate several disobedient deputies," *Jurnal.md*, Oct. 13, 2016, http://www.jurnal.md/en/politic/2016/10/13/usatyi-reveals-how-plahotniuc-made-zubco-prosecutor-general-the-oligarch-appealed-to-the-help-of-the-thief-in-law-karamalak-in-order-to-intimidate-several-disobedient-deputies/.

48 This would not have happened after 2013 when reality gradually set in, both in Brussels and major European capitals. However, I think it is good it happened the way it did: providing a visa-free regime as conditional on regime behavior is a very dubious idea.

49 Kamil Całus, "Vlad Filat: a vote of no confidence in Moldova," *New Eastern Europe*, Mar. 14, 2013, http://neweasterneurope.eu/2013/03/14/vlad-filat-a-vote-of-no-confidence-in-moldova/.

50 Including by this author: see Kálmán Mizsei, "Kalman Mizsei: Restabilirea AIE nu poate fi realizată fără SCHIMBAREA prim-ministrului," HotNews.md, Mar. 12, 2013, http://hotnews.md/articles/view.hot?id=19650.

51 Vladimir Socor, "Moldovan Political Leader Filat Arrested in Intra-Coalition Coup," *Eurasia Daily Monitor* 12, no. 188, Oct. 19, 2015, https://jamestown.org/program/moldovan-political-leader-filat-arrested-in-intra-coalition-coup/.

52 This angle was pointed out to me by Nicu Popescu.

53 On the scandalous scheme that caused the theft of over ten percent of GDP to the Moldovan taxpayers, see Mihai Popșoi, "Anti-Corruption Policy Failure: The Case of Moldova's Billion Dollar Scandal," *Moldovan Politics*, May 19, 2016, accessed May 12, 2018, https://web.archive.org/web/20160521054714/https://moldovanpolitics.com/2016/05/19/anti-corruption-policy-failure-the-case-of-moldovas-billion-dollar-scandal/; also Kenneth Rapoza, "Billion Dollar Theft: In Moldova, One Rich Banker's 'Crime' Has A Nation Doing Time," *Forbes*, Aug. 1, 2016, http://www.forbes.com/sites/kenrapoza/2016/08/01/billion-dollar-theft-in-moldova-one-rich-bankers-crime-has-a-nation-doing-time/#14b163737a4d.

54 "President Timofti Rejects Plahotniuc's Candidacy," Infotag, Jan. 13, 2016, http://www.infotag.md/politics-en/215995/.

55 "Curtea Constituțională a restabilit dreptul cetățenilor de a-și alege Președintele," Curtea Constituțională, Mar. 4, 2016, http://www.constcourt.md/libview.php?l=ro&idc=7&id=759&t=/Prezentare-generala/Serviciul-de-presa/Noutati/Curtea-Constitutionala-a-restabilit-dreptul-cetatenilor-de-a-si-alege-Presedintele. See also Mihai Popșoi, "Controversial Ruling by Moldova's Constitutional Court Reintroduces Direct Presidential Elections," *Eurasia Daily Monitor* 13, no. 46, Mar. 8, 2016, https://jamestown.org/program/controversial-ruling-by-moldovas-constitutional-court-reintroduces-direct-Presidential-elections/.

56 Kamil Całus, "Moldova's tricky reform," *New Eastern Europe*, March 9, 2016, http://neweasterneurope.eu/old_site/articles-and-commentary/1915-moldovas-tricky-reform.

57 Mihai Popșoi, "Russia scores symbolic victory in Moldova's Presidential election," *Eurasia Daily Monitor* 13, no. 182, Nov. 14, 2016, https://jamestown.org/program/russia-scores-symbolic-victory-moldovas-Presidential-election/.

58 Most of the news reporting about the elections used the highly simplistic "pro-Russian" as opposed to "pro-Western" dichotomy to categorize the candidates. See, for instance, Alexander Tanas and Alessandra Prentice, "Pro-Russian candidate triumphs in Moldova Presidential race," *Reuters*, Nov. 13, 2016, http://www.reuters.com/article/us-moldova-election-idUSKBN1380TN.

59 "La Chișinău, mandatul primarului ales nu a fost validat de magistrați:Andrei Năstase va contesta decizia la Curtea de Apel." *Radio Europa Liberă*, June 18, 2018, https://www.europalibera.org/a/29305075.html; and "Moldovan Court Annuls Chisinau Mayoral Election Results," *Radio Free Europe-Radio Liberty*, June 20, 2018, https://www.rferl.org/a/moldovan-court-annuls-chisinau-mayoral-election-results/29305971.html.

60 In the Georgian case, Bidzina Ivanishvili first took the prime minister function, and only after a year started to lead from the background.

61 Tadeusz A. Olszański, "Ukraine's Constitutional Court reinstates Presidential system," Osrodek Studiów Wschodnich, Oct. 6, 2010, https://www.osw.waw.pl/en/publikacje/analyses/2010-10-06/ukraines-constitutional-court-reinstates-Presidential-system.

62 Vlad Lavrov, "Akhmetov flies high on Forbes' richest list," *Kyiv Post*, Mar. 10, 2011, https://www.kyivpost.com/article/content/business/akhmetov-flies-high-on-forbes-richest-list-99496.html.

63 Åslund, *How Ukraine Became a Market Economy*, 138.

64 Here I am not disputing the rightfulness of this agenda: indeed, one can argue that at a certain point, the one-time revolutionary and visionary reformer Saakashvili became a risk to the democratic evolution of the country. I am simply trying to establish the facts.

65 See "Ukraine: parliament passes important laws to tackle corruption," *Kyiv Post*, Oct. 23, 2014, https://www.kyivpost.com/article/content/business-wire/ukraine-parliament-passes-important-laws-to-tackle-corruption-369122.html.

66 For an assessment of civil society after the Euromaidan, see Ukraine: "Nations in Transit 2016," Freedom House, accessed Jan. 15, 2018, https://freedomhouse.org/report/nations-transit/2016/ukraine.

67 "Ukraine: Request for Extended Arrangement under the Extended Fund Facility and Cancellation of Stand-by Arrangement," *IMF Country Report* 15/69, https://www.imf.org/external/pubs/ft/scr/2015/cr1569.pdf: 33.

68 David M. Herszenhorn, "Ukraine President Dismisses Billionaire Ally from Governor's Role," *New York Times*, Mar. 24, 2015, https://www.nytimes.com/2015/03/25/world/europe/ukraine-President-dismisses-billionaire-ally-from-governors-role.html.

69 Roman Olearchyk and Neil Buckley, "Ukraine Nationalizes its Largest Lender," *Financial Times*, Dec. 19, 2016, https://www.ft.com/content/13833aa6-c576-11e6-9043-7e34c07b46ef.

70 Timothy Ash, "Reflections on the Yalta European Strategy Conference in Kyiv," *Kyiv Post*, Sep. 18, 2016, https://www.kyivpost.com/article/opinion/op-ed/timothy-ash-reflections-on-the-yalta-european-strategy-conference-in-kyiv-423153.html.

71 "Pocket banks" are financial institutions that the owners have established with the aim of lending to related economic units. These are typically small, though Privatbank has shown these characteristics in Ukraine, and it was the largest bank before its closure.

72 Anders Åslund, "Securing Ukraine's Energy Sector," *Atlantic Council Global Energy Center and Dinu Patriciu Eurasia Center Issue Brief*, Apr. 2016, http://www.atlanticcouncil.org/images/publications/Securing_Ukraine_s_Energy_Sector_web_0404.pdf.

73 Kenneth Rapoza, "Three Years After Euromaidan, Naftogaz Remains Hostage To Ukrainian Politics," *Forbes*, Dec. 28, 2016, http://www.forbes.com/sites/kenrapoza/2016/12/28/naftogaz-ukraine-euromaidan-russia-poroshenko/#571541843bf0.

74 Decentralization was also a primary demand of the Euromaidan. However, with the occupation of parts of the Donbass, this item became overloaded by the

political interests of the Russians, who pushed for "federalization" of the region, which essentially meant giving veto power to their local clients over important national decisions.

75 Both presidential and parliamentary elections are due in 2019.
76 As the Head of the European Union Advisory Mission for Civilian Security Sector Reform in Ukraine, I consistently tried to draw attention to this elementary aspect of cleaning the system in a country where CoI thinking is totally absent—to no avail. Only in late 2015 was it initially picked up by George Soros, and then to some extent by others. See Kálmán Mizsei, "Ukraine's state reform is a vital national security interest," *Euractiv*, January 19, 2016. https://www.euractiv.com/section/europe-s-east/opinion/ukraine-s-state-reform-is-a-vital-national-security-interest/.
77 Yuriy Bugay, "ProZorro: How a volunteer project led to nation-wide procurement reform in Ukraine," Open Contracting Partnership, Jul. 28, 2016, http://www.open-contracting.org/2016/07/28/prozorro-volunteer-project-led-nation-wide-procurement-reform-ukraine/.
78 "CDL-REF(2014)047-e Law on the Public Prosecutor's Office of Ukraine (Unofficial translation)," Venice Commission, accessed Jan. 17, 2018, http://www.venice.coe.int/webforms/documents/?pdf=CDL-REF(2014)047-e, 37–38.
79 Power ministry is a term rooted in the Soviet (post-Soviet) cultural reality, describing ministries with hierarchical structures which have the ability to coerce. In the cynical world of the Soviet/Russian tradition, this is what ultimately matters. Prosecutors still use their uniform as a way of projecting power—an important psychological attribute of their ability to coerce and thus become corrupted.
80 See, most significantly, "CDL-AD(2013)025-e Joint Opinion on the Draft Law on the Public Prosecutor's Office of Ukraine adopted by the Venice Commission at its 96th Plenary Session (Venice, 11–12 October, 2013)," Venice Commission, accessed Jan. 17, 2018, http://www.venice.coe.int/webforms/documents/?pdf=CDL-AD(2013)025-e.
81 The case of the so-called diamond prosecutors was very famous. On July 5, 2015, a large amount of money, firearms and piles of diamonds were found in the apartments of two high ranking prosecutors. Despite the wide media coverage of the case, the prosecutors were not taken to court and the investigation was halted, since the two knew too much about other high-ranking officials, and could not be pursued without the risk of an avalanche of revelations following. The case since has been blocked. For an account of the sabotage of prosecutorial reform, see Alya Shandra, "How Ukraine's old guard killed the prosecution reform," *Euromaidan Press*, May 14, 2016, http://euromaidanpress.com/2016/05/14/how-ukraines-old-guard-killed-the-prosecution-reform/.
82 "Ukraine's parliament passes law on lustration at third attempt (UPDATE)," *Kyiv Post*, Sep. 16, 2014, https://www.kyivpost.com/article/content/ukraine-politics/ukraines-parliament-passes-law-on-lustration-364873.html.
83 On September 29, 2016, an extraordinary session of the Rada fired nearly twenty judges, as a sign that both the president and the Rada realized the importance of giving some limited concessions to the part of civil society that demands reforms.

84 Olena Makarenko, "Pursuit of Judicial Reform in Ukraine," *Vox Ukraine*, Jun. 29, 2016, http://voxukraine.org/2016/06/29/pursuit-of-judicial-reform-in-ukraine-en/.

85 "Amendments to the Constitution of Ukraine passed: Ukraine takes a major step towards a European System of Justice," CMS Law-Now, Jun. 9, 2016, http://www.cms-lawnow.com/ealerts/2016/06/amendments-to-the-constitution-of-ukraine-passed-ukraine-takes-a-major-step-towards-a-european-system-of-justice.

86 The key current battleground is the reattestation of the Supreme Court judges. On this see Mykhailo Zhernakov, "Will judicial reform survive?" *Ukrayinska Pravda*, Aug. 17, 2016, http://www.pravda.com.ua/eng/columns/2016/08/17/7117997/.

87 See "EU provides €104m to support Ukraine's public administration reform," European Union External Action, Dec. 22, 2016, https://eeas.europa.eu/headquarters/headquarters-homepage/18096/eu-provides-eu104m-support-ukraines-public-administration-reform_en.

88 The latest legislative act to accelerate the process is detailed here (in Ukrainian): "Dobrovil'nomu pryyednannyu hromad buty: Parlament pryjnyav dovhoochikuvanyj zakon," Decentralizaciya v Ukrayini, Feb. 9, 2017, http://decentralization.gov.ua/news/item/id/4264.

89 "Full text of the Minsk agreement," *Financial Times*, February 15, 2015. https://www.ft.com/content/21b8f98e-b2a5-11e4-b234-00144feab7de.

90 On the decentralization issue, the numerous Georgian experts in and around the Ukrainian government have also expressed a skeptical view. Their experience was that, in Georgia, the anti-corruption fight could be successful because power was centralized in the presidency. They also believe in the power of new IT that could help to exercise greater control in the regions than would have earlier been the case.

91 Alec Luhn, "Economic minister's resignation plunges Ukraine into new crisis," *The Guardian*, Feb. 4, 2016, https://www.theguardian.com/world/2016/feb/04/economic-minister-resignation-ukraine-crisis-aivaras-abromavicius.

92 "Ukraine Today: Western ambassadors regret economy minister's resignation," *Kyiv Post*, February 3, 2016, https://www.kyivpost.com/article/content/ukraine-politics/ukraine-today-western-ambassadors-regret-economy-ministers-resignation-407279.html.

93 This means even more corrupt transactions, partially to buy the votes of those who are not in the coalition. See the account of the investigative journalist-turned-MP Serhij Leshhenko (in Russian): Serhij Leshhenko, "Korrupcyonnaya blyzorukost' Vladymyra Hrojsmana," *Ukrayinska Pravda*, Feb. 3, 2017, http://blogs.pravda.com.ua/authors/leschenko/5893b07734e37/.

94 Since finishing the manuscript, much has happened but fully in line with the Ukraine analysis of this chapter. Ahead of the 2019 election season the president has been busy to build the single-pyramid system as a guarantor of his victory at the elections. At the same time his popularity is very low, thus the outcome of the elections is very uncertain.

95 Since the 2008 war, Georgia is no longer a member of the CIS. I am using the term to describe the post-Soviet area, but without the Baltics.

BÁLINT MAGYAR

Parallel System Narratives—Polish and Hungarian regime formations compared
A structuralist essay

The Polish election results of 2015 seem to have brought Hungarian and Polish development into synchronicity again, a congruence that has been apparent many times throughout history. At first glance, it may appear that we are dealing with regimes of an identical nature, especially taking into account the similarities of the authoritarian politics practiced by Jarosław Kaczyński (*Prawo i Sprawiedliwość*, PiS) and Viktor Orbán (*Fiatal Demokraták Szövetsége*, Fidesz), characterized by a tendency to eliminate autonomous social forces and control mechanisms, as well as the application of similar ideological frames.

But beneath the superficial similarities, these attempts are aimed at establishing different types of autocratic regimes—as this paper ultimately concludes. Orbán's regime, which I define as a mafia state, is built on the twin motivations of power centralization and the accumulation of personal and family wealth; the instrument of its power is the adopted political family, freed of the limitations posed by formal institutions. Kaczyński's regime is better described as a conservative-autocratic experiment, driven by ambitions of power and ideological inclinations. The active subject of the Polish experiment in autocracy is the ruling right-wing party, PiS. While the Hungarian regime essentially exploits ideology for pragmatic purposes, the Polish regime is driven by ideology.

The widely-held kindred spirit of Polish and Hungarian people is cemented in historically extant socio-structural parallels, rather than particular historical links. These include the traditionally high proportion within both societies of the middle nobility, the defining role of the feudalistic culture they transmitted, as well as the assimilation of this former nobility into the structure of modern state bureaucracy following the decline in the political and economic influence it previously enjoyed. Their shared historical fates, despite the apparent historical similarities, are based as much in myth as fact. In much of the nineteenth century the lack of sovereignty, the independence struggles against absolutist dynasties, the similarities in the way the nations were formed, the feudal serfdom, and the absence of industrialization were common to both nations. But while Poland, separated into three parts, was almost homogenously Catholic, Hungary, while being predominantly Catholic, had strong, influential Protestant churches as well. While the Protestant churches were more in favor of independence, the Catholics institutionally stood more for loyalty to the ruling house. The Austro-Hungarian compromise of 1867 brought Hungary quasi-sovereignty and half a century of extraordinary economic prosperity. The nationalities comprising the majority of the population, however, also faced many restraints and state-driven efforts of assimilation. World War I concluded very differently for the two countries. Poland regained its territory, independence and sovereignty. Hungary, on the other hand, not only lost two-thirds of its territory and half of its population, but also the middle power status it believed to have as part of the Austro-Hungarian Empire. In addition, it had to pay punishing war reparations and face serious military restrictions. Both countries experienced either perceived or real betrayal by the West (Hungary in 1920, 1947, and 1956; Poland in 1939 and 1945).

A long quarter century after regime change in 1989, the rule of both the PiS and Fidesz seem to display certain characteristics that have their roots in the period between the two World Wars. Although the regimes hallmarked by the figures of Horthy and Piłsudski show a good deal of similarity, there were also a number of structural differences between the two.

Despite the great difference in the roles the two countries played in World War II, both became communist dictatorships integrated into the Soviet sphere of influence after 1945. At the same time, divergent courses of development in the period from 1945 to 1989 are also apparent, and these continue to determine the different attitudes of their societies today.

POLAND | ## HUNGARY

From regaining independent statehood to World War II

At the end of World War I, **an independent, autonomous and sovereign Polish state was established** after a gap of one hundred and twenty-three years. The borders of the new Poland were the result of military conflict, uprisings, and a war fought against the Soviet Russian state. **The Polish political elite and society felt they were victors**, and became defenders of the new European status quo. The new Poland had become a **remarkably heterogeneous state in ethnic and cultural terms**, with no significant number of Polish people outside its borders. Only a small segment of the large Jewish population assimilated, a majority kept apart both socially and culturally.

Paradoxically the **birth of an independent Hungarian state was simultaneously entwined with national trauma**. In the now sovereign Kingdom of Hungary (which happened to be a monarchy without a monarch), brought about by the Peace Treaty of Trianon following the dissolution of the Austro-Hungarian Monarchy, **Hungarian society felt beaten and humiliated**, and strived to change the European status quo. The Little Entente constructed around Hungary with French backing isolated the country internationally. The new Hungary became an **ethnically homogeneous nation state**, but remained heterogeneous denominationally, while a quarter of ethnic Hungarians were stranded in the neighboring successor states.

The formation of the Polish state was closely tied to the figure of Marshal **Józef Piłsudski**, though he did not accept any **formal political office**. The constitution of 1921 was one of the most democratic constitutions in Europe, with the predominance of **legislative power**.

Miklós Horthy's authoritarian regime was limited to the forced path of **grievance politics grounded in Trianon**, with growing power for the Regent. No constitution was ratified in Hungary, and the political praxis shifted weight towards **preponderant executive powers**.

According to Piłsudski's understanding of nationhood, **citizenship consciousness was more important than a sense of national-ethnic belonging** where the relationship of the individual to society

The politics of the **Horthy era** realized the concept of a homogenous nation state (with Schwab and Jewish minorities). In the relationship between the individual and the community **the nation**

POLAND	HUNGARY
was concerned, since Poland was a linguistically and culturally heterogeneous state. Piłsudski's **state (rather than ethnic) nationalism** declined to give a unified ideological image to the nation. He considered loyalty towards the state of prime importance for all ethnicities. Piłsudski's concept of the nation was relatively democratic: **all who are loyal to the state are members of the nation**. Piłsudski's **chief opponents** were the national democrats, composed in part of the **large land-holding aristocracy**, and in part of the petite-bourgeois educated classes with close ties to the Church. At the same time, however, the middle classes themselves were rather weak. Furthermore, the existence of a five-million strong Ukrainian minority, which responded to repression with separatist ambitions, caused quite a problem, destabilizing his premise of the state.	**overshadowed everything**. Horthy's **ethno-nationalism** gave the regime a unified ideological image proclaiming a "Hungarian cultural superiority." The most important factor was not loyalty to the state, but ethnic belonging to the Hungarian state. Though a decisive majority of Hungarian Jewry assimilated, even this did not make it possible for them to win acceptance into the state apparatus, and did not protect them from discrimination, or prevent the ultimate murder of the overwhelming proportion of them during the Holocaust. This was a "controlled democracy," in which it was **always "the nation" that governed**: that is, the **large landholding aristocracy and the landed nobility**. Moreover, the defensive mechanisms of the state-dependent gentry elite only strengthened the closed, feudal nature of the regime.
• The political system was largely in pieces, and due to the **democratic electoral laws not a single party could gain a majority** in the Sejm until 1930. In a system reminiscent of the former Polish "noble republic," governments crumbled one after the other. Society soon became disillusioned with the unstable political system, and Piłsudski took advantage of this in his 1926 coup. Even the communists, forced underground, welcomed this turn.	• Continuing **electoral constraints** and an **open ballot** (unlike anywhere else in Europe) ensured the operation of a **dominant party system overseen by the government parties**, in which marginal roles were afforded to the left, liberal, and until the mid-1930s, extreme right-wing parties. Mandates of a two-thirds majority were frequent (Unified Party 1922: 58%, 1926: 69%, 1931: 64%; Party of National Unity 1935: 69%; Party of Hungarian Life 1939: 73%).

POLAND	HUNGARY
• At the time, Poland still had **the right to strike and freedom of assembly**, along with **independent workers' unions**. The communist party was finally brought to its knees and liquidated not by Piłsudski, but the Comintern under Stalin. The main **opponents of the system were the radicalized and anti-Semitic national democrats** (Camp of Greater Poland, National Party, National Radical Camp). **No anti-Jewish laws were passed** or Jewish wealth expropriated and redistributed after the coup, or under the so-called "rule of the generals" after Piłsudski's death. Still, there were many atrocities committed against Jews during this time, including discriminatory local regulations, the "ghetto seats" for Jews at the universities to which the government turned a blind eye, and attacks on shops and markets. After Piłsudski's death the whole government camp also shifted heavily to the far right.	• In 1922, Prime Minister István Bethlen forced a pact upon the **social democrats. In exchange for official permission to exist, they renounced recruiting** state employees, rail workers, and postal workers, limited their propaganda work among agricultural workers, gave up organizing mass strikes and republican propaganda, desisted from criticism of foreign policy, and took up a moderate opposition stance. The government also took forceful steps against extreme right movements after consolidation, though it itself ultimately swung to the extreme right. At the 1939 elections, however, with the introduction of a secret ballot, the **Arrow Cross Party received 14.3%**. Between 1938 and 1942, **four anti-Jewish laws were passed**. By means of the anti-Jewish laws, Jewish properties were robbed and widely redistributed, without any notable social or agricultural reform.
• Poland was **threatened by Germany from the start**, a danger that became even more stark after Hitler took power. The German-Soviet Treaty of 1922 in Rapallo constantly hung as the Sword of Damocles over Poland. Piłsudski and Foreign Minister Józef Beck **rejected the block policies**, joining neither the Little-Entente	• Hungary **went out of its way to form a good relationship with Germany and Italy from the start. It joined the Anti-Comintern Pact.** This alliance made it possible for Hungary to regain a significant portion of the territory that had been handed to successor states (Upper Hungary in 1938, Northern-Transyl-

POLAND	HUNGARY
nor the Anti-Comintern Pact. Beck's **Intermarium (between-seas) concept** served the purpose of building an alliance of states between the Baltic, Adriatic and Black Seas.	vania in 1940, and South Hungary in 1941). The Country was swept into war alongside the Germans, and attacked the Soviet Union, with catastrophic consequences.
• Following the Soviet-German occupation of Poland in 1939, **armed resistance organizations were immediately formed**. The largest Polish armed opposition organization of World War II, the Home Army, was established, but the communists (People's Guard), the radical national front (National Armed Forces), and even the peasantry (Peasant Battalions) had their own armed units. The leadership of the earlier opposition parties formed the government in exile, which directed resistance at home from Paris, and later London. Two significant uprisings broke out against the Germans: the Ghetto Uprising of 1943, and the Warsaw Uprising of 1944.	• Hungary attacked the Soviet Union as an ally of Germany, and suffered a major defeat there. At the same time, in a Europe mostly under occupation, Hungary formally preserved its independence, with its internal set-up unchanged. **No significant resistance movement formed** within the country: neither against the Horthy regime or the later German occupation of 1944, nor against the discrimination of the Jews or even their later deportation. In October 1944—after an unsuccessful attempt to exit the war—Horthy handed over power to the leader of the Arrow Cross, Ferenc Szálasi.

Absorption into the Soviet empire

Poland came out of World War II victorious, but the Allies—in opposition to Stalin—did not acknowledge the merits of Poland, and they were not allowed to take a seat among the victors. **After they were tried in Moscow, leaders of the Home Army, which leaned towards**	**Hungary came out of the war defeated**, and branded as Germany's last ally, continuing to fight on the side of Germany even at the end of 1944. The prime ministers responsible for the war (Bárdossy, Imrédy) were executed, as

POLAND	HUNGARY
the West, were executed or given life sentences by the Soviets, as were the delegates sent to Poland by the London government in exile.	was Ferenc Szálasi. **Horthy, however, escaped a court trial.**
The new Poland established after the war lost significant territories in the East, but gained huge western territories as "compensation." **The new borders were determined by Stalin's strategic interests.** At the beginning of the war, the Soviet leadership had already made up its mind: if any Poland would be left at the end of the war, **it must have Soviet leanings.** This was the master plan into which the **Katyń massacres** fit, aimed explicitly at the liquidation of the middle-class Polish elite considered to be anti-Soviet.	After the war, Hungary once again lost the territories it had regained through the revisions, territories it only had a chance to keep if it had broken the alliance with Germany in time. **Hungary was not of special importance to the Soviet leadership**, and although it was placed under the oversight of the Allied Control Commission under Marshal Voroshilov, a checked course for democratic development was left open, allowing for political pluralism built on a multi-party system.
The adoption of Polish Stalinism began with the active participation of the NKVD from the last day of the war. Having learned from the Hungarian parliamentary elections of 1945, **free parliamentary elections were not even announced**—with all probability, Stanisław Mikołajczyk's Polish People's Party would have won. The Polish Labor Party established in Moscow formed the government instead in Lublin, and though under Western pressure it was made to appear as a coalition government, the internal ministry and the police remained in communist hands. The West accepted the fact	Hungarian Stalinism began with the "strangling of democracy." The Soviet-type regime had weak internal support. This was proven by the **parliamentary elections of 1945, where the Independent Smallholders Party won a landslide victory of 57%** under the leadership of Zoltán Tildy. The communists were given far greater influence in the coalition government than their mandate. The internal ministry, the political police, and even the economy came under their direction, **making way for the salami tactics, directed first against the Smallholders' Party, and later the rest of the political opposi-**

POLAND	HUNGARY
of Soviet occupation, while a serious **civil and partisan war** was underway in the country, against the Soviets and their Polish followers. Finally, in January 1947, **through electoral fraud** the communists took full control of the country, later merging with the socialist party in December 1948. This was when Gomułka was removed from the post of chairman of the communist party, since he would have wished to incorporate the traditions of independence from the socialist party into the new party program.	tion. Even so, they could only secure **22.2% of the votes in the rigged elections of 1947. Power was nevertheless more and more openly concentrated in their hands, though** the first completely communist government was only formed in December of 1948—after the annexation of the Social Democratic Party by the communists.
After the war, Poland was considered the most important area for Stalin, both in geopolitical and military terms. After the liquidation of the national forces and the de facto division of Germany into two states in 1949, it ceased to be a frontier country, and became simply a military staging area.	Immediately after the war, Hungary did not have any particular strategic significance, since Soviet troops were stationed to its west, in Austria, and Tito's still friendly Yugoslavia neighbored it from the south. From 1948–49 however, with the heightening Soviet-Yugoslav conflict, the strategic importance of the country grew from Moscow's perspective.
In Poland power came to be held by a trio: **Bolesław Bierut, Hilary Minc and Jakub Berman.** All three were "Muscovites," yet while Minc and Berman were of Jewish origin, Bierut was of Catholic peasant stock.	Power came to rest in the grasp of a trio, **Mátyás Rákosi, Ernő Gerő and Mihály Farkas.** All three were "Muscovites" (belonging to the Moscow-based emigré wing of the Party), and of Jewish origin.
In the series of show trials launched in Eastern Europe in 1949, the Polish communist **Władysław Gomułka was marked** for the role of chief accused. However, **Bierut did not show too**	In the series of show trials that began in Eastern Europe in 1949, the Hungarian communist **László Rajk was picked out** for the role of chief accused, and Rákosi, as "Stalin's best pupil" led the

POLAND	HUNGARY
much willingness to organize the trials. Mass executions did, however, occur in the army. Later the trials took an anti-Semitic turn, for which Gomułka no longer fit the description, but he was nevertheless kept under arrest for three years from 1951. **Polish Stalinism** had fewer victims in comparison to the other Eastern European countries. **Attempts to break the Catholic Church were unsuccessful**; in fact, Primate Wyszyński signed an agreement ensuring the Church relative autonomy, though he was under arrest for three years from 1953 onwards without trial. **Collectivization also ran aground.**	way, **having him executed by September 1949**. Hungarian Stalinism became one of the **most repressive regimes** in Eastern Europe. One in ten Hungarians were prosecuted for a variety of charges. The **church was completely broken**, with the Prince Primate, Archbishop of Esztergom, József Mindszenty imprisoned as the result of show trials. In agriculture **a "dekulakization" and a violent, though only partially successful, collectivization was underway.**
After the 20th Congress of the Soviet Communist Party, Bierut's death, and the worker's uprising of Poznań, **Gomułka became the most popular "local" communist**, who was expected to loosen the ties of dependence from the Soviet Union and introduce reforms of the Soviet model to Poland. In October 1956, Khrushchev finally agreed to Gomułka's return, and Stalinism ended with a bloodless revolution. **The Polish Stalinists did not defend their positions, accepted Gomułka's leadership**, and did not begin bloody rear-guard actions. The Soviet defense minister and councilors were sent home.	After the 20th Congress of the Soviet Communist Party, Ernő Gerő became General Secretary of the Hungarian Communist Party instead of Rákosi, while **Imre Nagy became the most popular communist,** though he had been thrown out of the party earlier, and his return raised expectations of loosening ties of dependence from the Soviet Union and a reform of the Soviet model. Following the first Soviet intervention in the aftermath of October 23, 1956, and the bloody response from state security forces, the revolution turned into a freedom struggle. When events got out of control for the Soviets—and the reticent stance of the Americans was taken to mean a continued recognition of the existing status quo—on October 31 they decided to repress the revolution.

1956: The consequences of the two revolutions

POLAND	HUNGARY
In the year following the events of October 1956, further reforms were the subject of hot debate. Polish society felt more than mere sympathy for the Hungarian Revolution—many watched the young people fighting against the Soviets with envy. They also believed that the reforms could be continued, that Gomułka would carry through with the reforms of the Soviet model, and a decentralized, grass-roots, democratic socialism would come into being and take into account the specificities of the Polish nation. Instead, Gomułka progressed in the opposite direction, and in the autumn of 1957 there were protests against him for banning the weekly *Po Prostu*, which supported the reforms.	As Soviet troops repressed the Hungarian Revolution of 1956, around two hundred thousand citizens fled the country. In the course of the reprisals following the Revolution, Imre Nagy, the reform-communist prime minister of the Revolution, and hundreds of its participants were executed. Meanwhile, in spite of the Soviet occupation and reprisals, the new leader János Kádár not only declined to rehabilitate the first line of the earlier Muscovite-Stalinist leadership, but from 1962–63 began to openly distance his economic, social, and cultural policies from the practices of the Rákosi regime, both in word and deed.
After 1956, Gomułka took leadership of an **unbeaten society**:	After 1956, Kádár gained power over **a beaten society**:
• Polish society largely experienced the events of October as a victory; • The leadership of the party was dominated by moderate communist forces, and Gomułka was a rather popular political figure; though officially maintaining the policy, they in fact gave up on the experiment of forcibly collectivizing private farms, but at the same time their modernization was also neglected;	• Hungarian society suffered its third defeat of the twentieth century after November 4, 1956; • Kádár's political circle was composed of representatives of the orthodox communist line, and he was reviled both at home and abroad; • Between 1959 and 1962 agricultural collectivization was completed, followed later by the modernization of agriculture and villages;

POLAND	HUNGARY
• The Catholic Church held onto its integrity and social influence, under the leadership of the earlier imprisoned Cardinal Wyszyński, and at a later stage became a pillar of support to forces critical of the regime.	• The communist regime made the Church its vassal; Archbishop Mindszenty took refuge at the American embassy, and was forced into emigration years later.

Processes of consolidation and deconsolidation from the mid-sixties

The result of the 1956 uprising in Poland was not a society degraded and broken to the extreme. The grounds for negotiation between society and politics were not—as in Hungary—the presence of the Soviet troops, the mass executions, the imprisonments and hundreds of thousands of fleeing émigrés. What followed was not a social compromise based on constant concessions made by a hardline dictatorship, but a **permanent deadlock** between the ruling powers and society. Though the communist party maintained its dominance over society, it could not settle into a mellow sense of security. In order to strengthen its legitimacy, it constantly sought closer relations with the Church. In the Polish socialist system, society moved constantly in a triangle of **resistance-acceptance-participation**, but there was no sharp boundary between these three forms of behavior.

The reprisals following the repression of the Revolution of 1956 made it clear to Hungarian society that there would be no return to either the coalition governments of the period prior to 1948, or the regime that existed between the two world wars. With the acknowledgement of these conditions, there came to exist a new form of unspoken **"social contract,"** a **"compromise"** (or as it was called back then, **consensus**) between the regime and society (including a significant segment of the intelligentsia, and the Church leadership), which developed and functioned until the end of the eighties. Essentially, this compromise meant that so long as citizens did not interfere with politics, the regime would not interfere with their private lives, while also promising citizens increasing, though limited, prosperity. The foundations for this were laid in early 1957, with a large increase of wages for laborers.

POLAND	HUNGARY
The Polish leadership **did not have a socialist "national strategy,"** because it was not able to create the economic foundations for the gradual and predictable improvement of its citizens' living standards. Polish society did not become depoliticized, because it expected further reforms, while the regime took the opposite direction. They turned away from the path of reforms, while the standard of living did not improve, and the cultural freedom that had been secured was also increasingly curtailed. As a result, the first opposition debate circles and critiques appeared already in the sixties. There was also no socialist petite-embourgeoisement such as that in Hungary. A characterization of the period: • The nationalization program for **private farms** was never taken off the agenda. In fact, it existed as a threat throughout; only the time of its execution was continuously delayed by new party decrees. The absence of collectivization did not mean the rehabilitation of the private farms, but merely a hibernation in the state that had preceded collectivization. **Cold collectivization** meant that even if the state could not expropriate the land, or take it into farming collectives, it expropriated the eco-	The Kádár regime's "national strategy" meant that everyone could be a part of the nation so long as they accepted the rules of the game. Yet rather than giving ground to nationalism, this was a strategy of **antinationalist nation-building**. The popular epithets found to describe the "soft" communist dictatorship of the following decades reflect the burgeoning of a depoliticized petite-bourgeoisie: among them **"gulyás communism,"** or **"refrigerator socialism."** In the phrase "the happiest barracks in the socialist camp," on the other hand, there is a reference to the forced social acceptance of geopolitical realities and collusion with power. A characterization of the period: • The communist party proclaimed a new, relatively de-ideologized way of building a relationship with society at its Congress of 1962, stating that "those who are not against us, are with us"; • in education, the system of discrimination on the basis of class of origin ("class alien") was ended; • in agricultural cooperatives—unlike during the collectivization efforts of the fifties—the former semi-rich or rich farmers (kulaks) and their descendants could

POLAND	HUNGARY
nomic environment of the private farms: - it prevented the concentration of estates, which meant that the ownership structure of private farms remained essentially the same from 1945–1970; - it upheld the system of compulsorily submitting produce until 1972; - it continued with the wide use of state-set prices; - the trade in agricultural tools was in state hands, along with curbs on the growth of free market trade. - The Polish leadership—not having a cultural politician of such weight as György Aczél—showed a disinterest in cultural issues: apart from demanding respect for the basic taboos, a relatively free cultural life emerged, with great variety in genres (jazz, beat, rock, abstract art). This intellectual-cultural stratum had become the indirect, or in some cases even direct, opposition to the regime already by the mid-sixties.	advance to leadership positions based on a clear and unequivocal offer from the regime: either you fill the position of a leader in the collective, or you will be stripped of your land and be marginalized. From the mid-sixties onwards, agriculture was provided with large development resources, and the collectives functioned increasingly as independent economic organizations rather than as kolkhozes; - in 1963, amnesty was declared for the majority of political prisoners, putting an end to the period of reprisals; - party leaders sought to demonstrate that there would be no return to the Rákosi-Stalinist period by decommissioning the majority of the pre-1956 hardline state security personnel, transferring them to the spheres of production; - official Marxist-Leninist dogma still held primacy in cultural life, but certain "civic" trends were also accepted. In a cultural policy directed by György Aczél, the politics of the "three Ts" (in Hungarian: *támogatjuk* [support], *tűrjük* [tolerate], and *tiltjuk* [prohibit]) dominated. The system was able to integrate broad swaths of intellectual life placed in the tolerated category, which did not require displays of ideological commitment.

The Gomułka-leadership **had no strategy for modernization**; it neither could, nor desired to substantially change the political system, or the mechanism of economic control. Even though it was clear that further growth of living standards could not continue without a

POLAND	HUNGARY
surge of development in agriculture and modernization of the countryside, since the PZPR (*Polska Zjednoczona Partia Robotnicza*) never had total control over society, any attempt at decentralization and sharing of decision-making authority would have led to further weakening of the establishment. On the other hand, the concentration of estates and modernization of the countryside would have further encouraged the flow of the population to the cities, which was not desirable during an ongoing population boom. This boom had caused between two and three hundred thousand new people to appear on the employment market from the mid-sixties, a cause for great concern. For this reason, the "well tried and tested" program remained in place: a majority of investments went into construction and other large-scale industries that could engage such large labor forces. The establishment did not have the strength to: • vanquish the peasantry, but could prevent the development of peasant farms. By these means it not only caused tensions among the peasantry, but also undermined the foundations of food supplies to the cities; • earn the loyalty of a majority of workers, but meanwhile shut them up in the large state corporations,	In order for the compromise of "don't politicize, but prosper" to become sustainable, a restricted marketization of the economic system had to be carried out under the banner of a **modernization** strategy, that would uphold the monopoly of the state and cooperative property, and not encroach the least bit on the political system. The establishment of the **socialist market economy** and fulfillment of the requirement of continuous growth in living standards was assisted by the introduction, in 1968, of the **New Economic Mechanism** (NEM): • In the field of production and development the role of central organization was reduced, and company independence in decision-making was supported: excepting Yugoslavia, this was the only communist country where the command economy was abolished (**decentralization**); • the price system was reformed, leading to an increase in the range of so-called freely priced products, which contributed to preparing conditions for the market activity of companies (**price liberalization**); • average wage regulation was introduced to the wage system, which made it possible for companies to decide the salaries of employees based on a provided overall fund for wages (**wage liberalization**);

POLAND	HUNGARY
stripping them of any opportunity to earn legal extra income; • win the ideological battle with the Catholic Church. In fact, the Church would ultimately become the most important support for Polish society; • educate the young intelligentsia to become followers of socialism, or even accept it. It did, however, have the means to "reward" the young intelligentsia with prison sentences from time to time.	• an extended system of **secondary manufacturing branches and small farms attached to the cooperatives** developed. The secondary manufacturing branches simultaneously served rural needs for part-time employment and diversification of consumer goods, as well as that of flexible suppliers to the rigid state structure. The over one and a half million backyard farms ensured families comprising both peasants, and industrial laborers working away from home, a stable source of food and income.
In summary, the regime obstructed every social layer from pursuing its own interests, achieving its goals, and fully playing its roles, but on the other hand it could not present a positive vision for the future either. These bleak prospects led to violent action in 1968, when the establishment assaulted the young intelligentsia, and on the pretext of the Arab-Israeli War, started a brutal anti-Semitic campaign with which it drove away most of the remaining people of Jewish origin, mostly intellectuals. Two years later, with the massacre of protesting workers, it also turned the laborers against itself permanently. The regime remained successful in turning the various social layers against one another at this time, but by 1976 it no longer had strength even to achieve this. After the	The New Economic Mechanism was strongly influenced by Polish economists such as Oskar Lange, Michał Kalecki, and Włodzimierz Brus, who had in fact completed the theoretical aspect of the work in Poland, but their ideas had never been realized in practice. The halt called upon the processes of economic reform at the end of the seventies, and a partial withdrawal from some changes already introduced, drove the country into a crisis situation. The **broadening of mechanisms offering means of self-exploitation** served to uphold the compromise based on continuous growth of living standards: within state companies, surreptitious small-scale production (*fusizás*), often during official working hours and using the tools and resources

POLAND	HUNGARY
brutal repression of the summer strikes, the workers and intellectuals found an alliance. In the seventies, the regime tried to dampen social tension through renewed investment in—outdated—large-scale industry, financed by Western loans. While the Hungarians spent their Western loans on maintaining the growth of living standards, Poland used them to bring about outmoded large-scale industrial concerns.	of the company, was legalized by the creation of the so-called economic work partnerships (GMK). The introduction of this form of economic association was prompted by a fear of the spread of the demands of the Polish Solidarity movement. This simultaneously increased the income of the more resourceful workers, while simultaneously reducing the inflexibility of the rigid state companies. But the mid-seventies also gave way to an increasing reliance on Western loans, necessitated by the continuous increase of consumption and the provision of state-subsidized services. Furthermore, these loans also came to be employed to stave off financial bankruptcy, and made the Hungarian economy comparable to a collapsing house of cards.

The social foundations of anti-regime politics, or its absence

The lesson Poland took away from 1956 was that as long as public demands do not challenge the country's position in the Soviet Bloc, it is possible to effect change. At the same time, **the system did not bestow the masses with paths to individual happiness**: it restricted peasants in their role as private farmers, while shutting the labor force up in large state enterprises. Due to the lack of reforms and continuous decline in living standards, the groups that can be considered as the "opposition" already	In Hungary, the reprisals that followed 1956 taught society that resistance to the power establishment was futile, and that they would have to make their lives more comfortable within the framework of the communist system. At the same time, the leadership of the Kádár regime learned from 1956 that a peaceful society could not be sustained through total repression. With the lack of fundamental freedoms, the improvement of living standards and conditions became a necessity. The Kádár consolidation and

POLAND	HUNGARY
appeared by the mid-sixties, with the seventies bringing the masses to radical manifestations of social discontent. - In **1968**, a series of protests by students began; the regime took brutal action against intellectuals. - In **1970**, strikes in Gdańsk protesting drastic hikes in food prices were violently repressed. 44 people were fatally injured, and over a thousand more wounded. Edward Gierek replaced Gomułka at the helm of the party in the aftermath. - In **1976**, protests broke out in a number of cities due to rising food prices; these were brutally repressed by the regime, and many workers were imprisoned. In the aftermath of these events, an organization of intellectuals aiming to help those who suffered repression was established, called the **KOR** (Komitet Obrony Robotników).	"compromise" embodied in part by the constant growth of general consumption established **safety valves for the release of social tensions**, giving those critical of the regime private means of escape through individual accumulation of wealth and other deals within the framework of the system. All of this ruled out mass support for any initiative critical to the regime. Society was immunized to oppositional thinking, so the opposition movements critical of the regime were limited to rather small circles. - In **1968**, a small group of philosophers protested against the occupation of Czechoslovakia. - In **1977**, a few dozen dissident intellectuals acclaimed the formation of the Czechoslovak Charter '77. - In **1979**, approximately 250 individuals, largely intellectuals, signed a petition against the imprisonment of Václav Havel. This event can be considered the first step towards the institutionalization of the anti-communist dissident movement.
The relationship between the radical workers and the system-critical intellectuals was, thereafter, institutionalized and permanent in Poland. The KOR was not merely an aid organization; through a work by **Adam Michnik**, *A New Evolutionism*, it was also ideologically and strategically formative. As	The Hungarian anti-communist dissident movement led by **János Kis** followed the Polish opposition's strategy, without it gaining any form of broader social support. For in Hungary, unlike Poland, the sort of social deadlock arrived at by constant conflict with the regime had never come into existence. So-

POLAND	HUNGARY
such it rejected the dilemma between whether to improve the operation of the system while remaining integrated in it, or to try to overthrow it from outside. Instead it proposed the building of parallel civil structures, thereby also demonstrating that it had understood the geopolitical power situation that kept the communist system in place for the moment, but neither recognized nor legitimized it. The institutions of the parallel society generated by the intellectuals were the so called **flying universities** and **independent publishers**. Both were mass based and multi-centered. By **1980**, the Solidarity movement, growing out of the shipyard of Gdańsk under the leadership of Lech Wałęsa, was no longer just a parallel society, but also an embodiment of a parallel political power. The Solidarity movement was unique in the region, not only for its vast size (ten million members), but also its heterogeneity. It joined individuals and groups of various world views, of different social positions, and was strongly supported by the Catholic Church as well as Pope John Paul II, former archbishop of Kraków. A constellation of this sort was unimaginable in any other socialist country. In the course of the one-and-a-half-year existence of Solidarity, it became clear that this deadlock could not be sustained and would have to go in one direction	ciety, with its peculiar compromise not only tolerated, but accepted the soft dictatorship ruling over it. In the spirit of the adopted Polish strategy, the "flying (underground) universities" and samizdat literature began to spread more quickly with the greater visibility of the Polish Solidarity movement, though it remained always more restricted, single-centered, and with fewer copies in circulation. Though the Hungarian communist party observed the rise of Solidarity with some concern, its fall in 1981 only resulted in a temporary surge of repression against opposition movements. Nonetheless, while avoiding imprisoning dissident intellectuals, every effort was made to impede the logistics of the samizdat publications and the material wellbeing of the few dozen opposition leaders. The contact of the isolated, small opposition movement with the broader "masses" was ensured by Radio Free Europe, which reported on opposition actions and publications. Hungarian society at large did not participate in the system-critical movements and was, at most, an audience. Apart from the system-critical anti-communist dissident movement, from the eighties onwards there were also the environmental protection groups taking action against the dams of Bősnagymaros, who however kept their

POLAND	HUNGARY
or the other. Though Jaruzelski's coup defeated Solidarity at significant cost, it was not able to reinstate the legitimacy of the regime even to its previous level. After the introduction of a state of emergency, the Jaruzelski leadership fell into complete international isolation, at a point when it would have severely required Western loans. On the other hand, the economist intellectuals of Solidarity had had enough of collectivist illusions, and a program promoting liberalization of the economy grew increasingly popular among them. After joining the IMF in 1986, no other course was left open for the leadership of the party either.	criticism within the "paradigm of public policy," without politically challenging the regime. Others involved in politics included the activists of the peace movement Dialogue, who kept their distance from the radical opposition groups, and the Catholic grass-roots community, which came into confrontation with the Catholic Church. The circle of so-called *népi* (folk) writers did not think in system-critical terms either, but wholly in terms of protecting the rights of the Hungarian minority across the border within the system, remaining undecided between joining the opposition and bargaining with the reform communists even in the last third of the eighties. In Hungary, in spite of the economic crisis, few concrete propositions for the transition materialized. A "social market economy" grew to become a popular formula.

1989–1990: the two peaceful, negotiated regime changes of the Eastern Bloc

The demolition of the communist party in the Soviet Union was carried out by the communist party itself, with the leadership of Gorbachev, as a continuation of Perestroika—a process beginning in the second half of the eighties and lasting over many years. In the rest of the East-Central European countries with a hard dictatorship—the GDR, Czechoslovakia, Romania, and Bulgaria—regime change took the form of a sudden break, without negotiations. Among the satellite states of the Soviet sphere of influence, a **negotiated regime change** was only conducted from 1989–90 in the two soft dictatorships of Poland and Hungary, between the ruling communist parties and the actors of the

POLAND	HUNGARY

political opposition. In both countries, the segment of the communist party ready to accede to talks, was the one ready to face reality. In neither country was transition or regime change the aim of these members of the communist party, but rather the legitimization of measures required to deal with the economic crisis made it seem worthwhile to involve an opposition they perceived as weak. Regarding Solidarity, they assumed that seven years after the state of emergency, it would not be capable of the show of force it had in 1980–81. The Hungarian democratic opposition lacked broad social support. One must add that these events did not unfold simultaneously in the two countries, but the Hungarians (both the reform communists and the opposition) followed the Polish developments. The adoption of the form of roundtable talks and then the results of the semi-free Polish elections, along with the Soviet response to them, showed that regime change had become a real possibility.

In Poland, it was the broadly supported Solidarity, as the pioneer of the process and a movement gathering actors critical of the system, who negotiated with the regime—with the mediation of the Catholic Church. Peaceful transition and regime change was meanwhile guaranteed by a conditionally free electoral system, which ensured the Polish communist party and its allies retained power in the Sejm, while fully opening the reinstated Senate to free political competition. This is where the first semi-free elections of the eastern bloc took place in the summer of 1989. Solidarity set out to win 35% of the mandates in the Sejm, and the seats in the Senate under the name of Citizens' Committee. Though neither the PZPR, nor Solidarity, believed that the latter could win a landslide victory, this did in fact occur. In the two-round election system Soli-	The program of the democratic opposition in 1987, the "Social Contract," still represented the Polish strategy of power sharing. However, after the international thaw and transformation in Poland, the opposition parties established in 1988 brought about the Opposition Roundtable in the spring of 1989, unifying the opposition for talks with the communist party to ensure a peaceful transition. But the Hungarian opposition parties, lacking real links with the masses, represented the various trends in the opposition intellectual elite. The two most significant formations were: the Hungarian Democratic Forum (MDF), grouped around the népi (folk) writers and representing a popular, national and Christian ideology with a conservative identity; and the Alliance of Free Democrats (SZDSZ), which had grown out of the anti-communist dissi-

POLAND	HUNGARY
darity won everything it could. Solidarity, therefore, ran for the elections as a unified but heterogeneous movement, with the existing internal differences only bringing about permanent divisions after the elections.	dent movement, with a Western orientation and a leftist, liberal approach that represented radical system-criticism. In this case, therefore, the differentiation and institutionalization of opposition forces with different ideological foundations had concluded even before free elections were held.
Following the elections, Solidarity succeeded in splitting earlier followers of PZPR, the Democratic Party, and the United People's Party away from the alliance, which made coalition formation necessary. Adam Michnik came up with a proposal: "we will delegate the prime minister, and you delegate the president." Thus, in exchange for Jaruzelski being elected president by a majority of one vote in the Sejm and the Senate, in September 1989, Tadeusz Mazow-	In the course of the negotiations, the reform communists no longer had the chance to ensure themselves a guaranteed powerbase unaffected by political competition, as the Polish Sejm did. Instead, they aimed to create a semi-strong presidential position with similar authority vested in it. A separate deal between the MDF and the reform communists was forestalled by a referen-

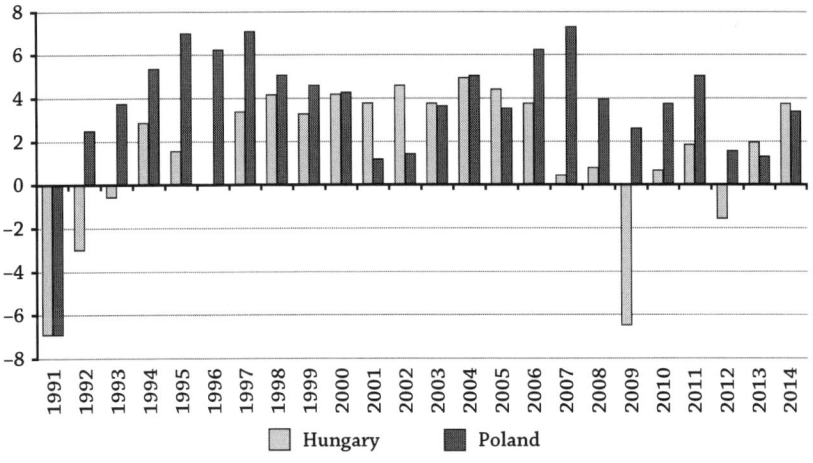

Figure 19.1: *The intersecting cycles of economic growth in Poland and Hungary (in percentage of annual growth of GDP)*

POLAND	HUNGARY
iecki became the first non-communist prime minister in the region since 1947. After the elections, a number of parties emerged out of the Solidarity Movement, while Solidarity began to function as a real labor union.	dum at the end of 1989 initiated by the SZDSZ, that preceded the first free elections in the spring of 1990 and resulted in the victory of the MDF, leading to the formation of the national-Christian coalition.

Hungary 2010, Poland 2015: the second regime changes

The first time Viktor Orbán came to power, in 1998, he summed up his goals in his party's campaign slogan: "More than change of government, less than change of regime." The PiS, led by the Kaczyński brothers, voiced a similar demand from 2005. Orbán's government remained for one full term, while Jarosław Kaczyński's stayed for less than two years. Their return to power took place eight years later. Orbán defined Fidesz's return to power in 2010 as a ballot box revolution, and his government as a second change of regime, while Kaczyński also made claims of regime change on a similar scale upon his return to power in 2015. They consider themselves the keepers of a tradition of Polish-Hungarian historical friendship. Poland symbolically supported the pro-government demonstrations in Budapest expressing loyalty to Orbán (called the "peace marches") by transporting Polish PiS activists to Hungary for the occasion, and Orbán also ensures the new Polish government of his solidarity through exercising his veto against any EU sanctions which threaten it. In spite of the similar ideological models and political language, however, the immediate antecedents of these governments and their natures are quite different.

Antecedents: the electoral defeat of the Polish government parties and the collapse of the third Hungarian republic

• The concept of "welfare regime change," used with predilection in Hungary, is **unknown** in Poland. Three right-wing, or center-right, governments carried out **shock**	• The coalition between the former reform-communist MSZP (Hungarian Socialist Party) and the liberal SZDSZ that came to power in 2002, following the program of "welfare re-

POLAND	HUNGARY
therapy reforms, which had a social cost that cannot be dismissed. The first shock therapy program was initiated by the finance minister of the Mazowiecki government, Leszek Balcerowicz, in 1990, which helped complete a relatively quick switch from a state socialist shortage economy to market competition based on private ownership. The second round of shock therapy is attributed to the Buzek government (1997–2001), in which Balcerowicz was deputy minister and finance minister. Significant reforms were introduced in four major fields: education, pensions, public administration, and healthcare. Finally, under the first PiS government (2005–2007), new radical changes were introduced in the battle against corruption, for lustration, and to "clean up" the secret services. • The leading politicians and intellectuals-experts of the PiS, in government between 2005 and 2007, and the Civil Platform, in government from 2007–2015, all followed in the footsteps of the Mazowiecki and Buzek administrations. **The Polish right wing has believed in the free market and capitalism right from the start.** They have not changed these fundamental principles even after both the Mazowiecki and the Buzek governments suffered huge electoral defeats.	gime change" declared by the Socialist Party, went on a spending spree that the economy could not afford: it raised the wages of public employees by fifty percent, introduced an extra month's pension for December, and various social benefits were also raised significantly. The program could not be made sustainable even with a growth in debts, and so the policies of halfheartedly and necessarily accepted austerity began. In contrast to the logic of the Kádár consolidation—in which the harsh reprisals and sanctions once applied were followed by the politics of continuous, incrementally introduced little "rewards," concessions and improvements in living standards—in this case the one-time boost in welfare spending, which would be forgotten in a few months, was followed by a constant policy of austerity. This undermined faith in the future of the government and its credibility. • The reform of large social welfare systems also stalled, partly because its implementation would have required the support of two-thirds of the parliament, and partly because Fidesz's so-called "welfare referendum" of 2008 excluded the institutional introduction of market elements in health-care and education. In its aftermath, the government coalition fell apart, and the following

POLAND	HUNGARY
- Following the failure of the first PiS government, the coalition of the center-right Civil Platform and the agrarian—ideologically nationalistic, economically slightly left-leaning—Polish People's Party formed a government in 2007. **The politics of the government led by Donald Tusk was calm and predictable.** The Polish economy was in full swing; even in the worst year of the economic crisis (2009), it could still produce growth of 1.8%. By 2010 this figure was 3.9%, and in 2011 had risen to 4.5%. Tusk's defeat was due to the fact that significant social groups were left out of this prosperity: notably those in small cities, villages, and the eastern regions. - The World Bank's "Doing Business 2015" index ranked Poland in 32nd place. This means that **conditions for investors are constantly improving** in Poland; indeed, they are the best among the East-Central European members of the European Union. Thanks to EU funds directed to Poland, more than 160,000 projects have been successfully completed in the period between 2004 and 2013. **The huge infrastructural development is highly apparent.** Poland can avail itself of **120 billion euros** of the EU budget from 2013–2020, the greatest total value among all the EU member states.	two years up to the 2010 elections passed with a minority government. - A few months after the electoral victory of the MSZP-SZDSZ coalition in 2006, a speech given by Ferenc Gyurcsány to the MSZP faction became public: in it, he admitted the manipulation of budget deficit figures in a statement paraphrasing the slogan of 1956 ("we lied morning, noon and night"), causing an irreparable breach of confidence. The violent anti-government protests that erupted in the aftermath, and the police reaction to them, were merely the prelude to a period of **cold civil war**—which composed the essence of Fidesz's politics in opposition. - Fidesz's strategy of cold civil war in opposition replaced the necessary consensus that had been built into the constitutional order with a politics of bribery and liquidation. On the one hand, they did not support systemic reforms requiring a two-thirds majority in the national assembly, whatever compromises they may have included; on the other, when it came to the election of heads or members of the institutional control mechanisms of liberal democracy, they either approved the appointment of their own nominee only, or paralyzed the operation of the institution by withdrawing their cooperation.

POLAND	HUNGARY
• Poland has achieved significant prestige in international politics as well, primarily on account of its **consistent commitment to a Euro-Atlantic alliance**, and stable, predictable governance. In 2014, Prime Minister Donald Tusk was elected to lead the European Council. Jarosław Kaczyński personally congratulated him on his appointment. • In 2015, **the defeat of the PO-PSL government surprised many, but it bequeathed a prosperous economy and an internationally respected Poland** to the incoming PiS administration.	• Going beyond the—at times justly critical—tenor and norms of political battles until then, they used character assassination and the influence of the prosecutor's office to paint government politicians in diabolical colors. • Initially, the erosion of any ability to govern, followed by the governing parties' loss of credibility and paralysis, revelatory cases of corruption, the economic crisis of 2008, as well as the political climate of cold civil war, finally brought about **the collapse of the third republic in Hungary**.

The effect of different electoral systems on the concentration of power and the extent of regime conversion

- The regional list electoral system results in a relatively proportional distribution of mandates. The PiS won the 2015 elections with 37.6%, gaining a 51% majority in the Sejm. The results were distorted in favor of PiS, as the United Left did not win any mandates despite achieving 7.6% of the vote; as such, if the SLD had appeared on the ballot alone, the PiS would not even have a majority in the Sejm. In 2011, the Civil Platform won the elections with 45% of the mandates, after gaining 39.2% of the total vote. Neverthe-

- The mixed election system effective in Hungary until 2011 (a single chamber parliament of 386 seats, filled by 176 representatives elected from single-member constituencies, a minimum of 58 mandates from the national list and a maximum of 152 seats from the regional lists) made it possible for Fidesz to secure a two-thirds majority in Parliament with only 52.7% of the vote in 2010, providing it with practically **unlimited political power**. On the one hand, it could rewrite the Constitution alone (which it did in 2011, amending it

POLAND	HUNGARY
less, even with this distorted distribution of the mandates, the PiS was only capable of a simple change of government, and **not a complete appropriation of political power**. A change of constitution (requiring, unlike in the Hungarian system, the support not of two-thirds of all the members of parliament, but only of those present for the vote) would have required extreme manipulation. Appointments in the institutions of political control, however, do not require a two-thirds consensus, and the limits for changes are set instead by the fixed terms of their appointment. At the same time—not having the cardinal Acts that can only be changed by two-thirds of the parliament—it has more leeway in introducing broader changes to the system, though all such changes can be just as easily undone by a new government. • Changes to Polish electoral law, along the lines of the Hungarian ones, are not allowed by the constitution, which demands proportionality. Moreover, PiS already enjoys a comfortable majority in the Sejm, and a switch to a mixed election system (individual and list) would in any case have unpredictable con-	multiple times since as its political needs dictated), and could easily pass any legislation. On the other hand, it was able to directly appoint the heads and other officials of institutions meant to serve as balances of power in a liberal democracy (Constitutional Court, Media Authority, National Council of Justice, election overseeing bodies and so on) without any need for consensus with the opposition, simply installing its own cadres. Moreover, the terms in office for numerous positions were unrealistically extended: the Chief Prosecutor, along with the President and members of the Media Council have terms of 9 years, while the President and Vice-President of the State Audit Office of Hungary are appointed for terms of 12 years each. Therefore, the systemic changes wrought by the Fidesz government are virtually irrevocable even after the government is defeated, since the currently scattered opposition would be unable to gain a two thirds majority, but the people appointed by Fidesz will remain in their positions even after any change in government. • Through changes to the electoral law (increasing the disproportionality of the system, redrawing single-member constituencies, introducing a shorter time-period for the collection of signatures required to stand

Parallel System Narratives—Polish and Hungarian regime

POLAND	HUNGARY
sequences. Since it is impossible to change the proportionality of the electoral system, power machinations are limited mainly to a state-owned public media. • The legal system and the PiS' lack of a two-thirds majority prevent any change to the constitution, and by extension, the overthrow of democratic institutions. As such, the new regime turns to **open violation of the constitution**, or modifies the old institutions in such a way as to be able to give positions to its own cadres (as demonstrated, for example, by the current alteration of the court system and the media). Yet these laws cannot be cemented across governmental terms.	for elections, establishing a one-round election system (that forces opposition parties to form a coalition prior to the elections), giving ethnic Hungarians outside Hungary the right to vote, and so on) by 2014 Fidesz could secure a two-thirds majority in Parliament with only 44.9% of the votes. The parliamentary majority was only lost later, as a result of defeats in by-elections. • The two-thirds majority Fidesz secured in Parliament allowed it to conduct a **constitutional coup** through the new Constitution and its continuous amendments. If new laws it had passed were declared unconstitutional by the Constitutional Court, then rather than adjusting the laws to the Constitution, it adjusted the Constitution to the laws.

Various attempts to dispense with liberal democracy: attempted Polish conservative autocracy vs. established Hungarian mafia state

• Kaczyński's politics is motivated by **power and ideology**: the concentration of power goes hand in hand with the goal of achieving hegemony of the "Christian nationalist" value system, which is not to be confused with the value system of Christian democracy. • The regime is more driven by **ideology**, and its "inconsistencies" do	• Orbán's politics is motivated by **power and wealth**: the concentration of power and the accumulation of wealth in the political family. • The system is not ideologically driven, its approach to ideology is utilitar-

POLAND	HUNGARY
not mean a multitude of 180 degree turns, as in the case of Hungary. As conceived by Jarosław Kaczyński, the state and the Catholic Church operate in concert ("the Church is an organic component of being Polish.") It follows from this that **the liberal value system built on the autonomy of the individual is viewed as an enemy**, since the interests of the Polish collective nation are seen as higher than the interests of the individual. At the same time, the regime still **endorses free market competition and respect for the freedom of enterprise**, because it considers the collectivist economy a "communist invention" that destroyed Poland. It should be noted here that the majority of Polish society also rejects collectivism. • They wish to break with the values of liberal democracy, but at the same time, they take the break with the communist legacy seriously.	ian. Its ideological "coherence" is not achieved by the representation of a definite value system. Its ideological "consistency" is ensured through its use of ideological frames that fit with the patterns of enacted power tied to the patriarchal head of the family. Naturally, it follows that **the liberal value system built on the autonomy of the individual is considered an enemy**. But it only picks and chooses from the leftwing-collectivist values with caution. When necessary, it relies on the frames of social populism. It pragmatically uses conservative, collectivist values ("God, fatherland, family"), which can be attached to **a centralized chain of command built on a patron-client network of vassalage** (for example, respect for the sanctity of private property—which could be considered conservative—is alien to it.) • Under the guise of breaking with the communist legacy, they actually want to do away with the values of liberal democracy.

The divergent approaches of the two autocratic tendencies to ideology (namely ideology driven vs. ideology utilizing) do not, in the meantime, exclude the possibility of the **common ideological frames** they use being closely related:
- they define their administrations not as changes of government, but as changes of regime;
- accordingly, they distance themselves from the regime change of a quarter century ago, and interpret the history of the peaceful, negotiated

POLAND	HUNGARY

change of regimes as a deal between elites, concluded over the heads of society at large. Moreover, they attempt to use this to legitimize the necessity for the actual regime change they represent;
- the new constitutive legislation also serves to distance their new autocratic regimes, on a symbolic level, from the repudiated legacy of the regime change. This is true of Poland even though the country had formally ratified a new constitution in 1997;
- by "nation" they mean a community of people committed to an ideology rather than autonomous citizens, a concept which they use to create a basis of legitimacy and an argument for excluding citizens critical of their regime from the nation, painting them as representatives of alien interests;
- they share a particular form of Euro-skepticism, and continue a "national freedom struggle against the Brussels dictatorship" on the basis of historicized grievance politics, while continuing to expect EU resources. This behavior is no less than the realization of a rent-seeking policy on an international scale, without moral qualms;
- fear and suspicion of refugees, migrants and aliens is exceptionally high in both countries, which populist politics easily transforms into active xenophobia.

The similarities between these ideological frames only demonstrate that they are equally adaptable to the needs of two different types of autocratic regimes.

POLAND	HUNGARY
• The actual decision-making remains **centered within the framework of formal institutions** in Poland. Kaczyński occupies the peak of the power pyramid as the president of the PiS. The prime minister, the ministers of defense, and the secret services are the vice-presidents of the party. The leaders of the Sejm and the Senate, as well as other ministers, are members of the presi-	• **Real political and economic decision making is removed from the world of legally defined, formalized organizations and social control.** Important decisions are not made within the formalized, legitimate framework of parties, government, parliament, or fora of mutual consultation. These institutions are merely the transmission belts of decisions made outside them, trans-

POLAND	HUNGARY
dency of the party. The PiS is a **centralized** party, serving as a center of power. Anyone with real power must, first and foremost, be found an appropriate position in the party hierarchy, and fill a function in public office through this position. This form of organization is focused on the concentration of power, applied using the classical instruments of autocratic systems. A twenty-four member government, made up by ministers with real competencies, operates this system, unlike in the Hungarian case, where governance is concentrated in a few top ministries.	ferring them into the sphere of legality. The transformation of Fidesz as a party went through the following shifts: alternative movement, Western-oriented party, centralized party (excluding representatives of rival trajectories within the party), vassal party (the party president has the legally arraigned prerogative to appoint candidates for membership of parliament and mayoral seats), and finally **transmission belt party** (filling up the leading bodies with insignificant stooges, while they cease to be actual decision-making fora).
• Relationships in the power structure—unlike in the clan-like mafia state, with its ruling structure stretched beyond the formal offices of public authority—are not consecrated as "family" or "blood" ties. **Party political nepotism** means the distribution of state-political, and state-commercial, media positions and sinecures among the party's own cadres. To facilitate this, they have lowered the professional requirements to fill certain positions. Meanwhile, there are no oligarchs, stooges, or advisors around Kaczyński who have significant influence on the decisions of the party president. Even demands coming from the Church (for instance, the complete ban on abortions) are not	• The decision-making "organ" of the informally exercised power is the **adopted political family**, or rather its topmost reaches composed of a score of members. This cannot be compared either to the former Soviet nomenclature, the "politburo," or the formalized, transparent, accountable institutional system of modern democracies. The members of the "chief patron's court" are the ministers attached to the pater familias/prime minister (Antal Rogán, János Lázár), the minister of the interior, the oligarchs or stooges, and advisors. This narrow center of power broadens in concentric circles, with the inclusion of formal public offices of authority, positions in the private sector of the economy, and

POLAND	HUNGARY
necessarily unconditionally supported by PiS. • **State dirigist control** is being established: a sweeping away of the Civic Platform is underway, meaning the purge-like replacement of those appointed by the previous government to positions in administration, public services and the state corporate sector. However, the regime is not able to spread beyond the spheres of state administration, state institutions, and state corporations. There are areas of social autonomy that, for the moment, it cannot reach. • Kaczyński's anti-corruption stance is not motivated by any intent to centrally expropriate corruption. **The war on corruption lies behind the party name, Law and Justice, as well.** Lech Kaczyński, the now deceased brother of the current party president, had been minister of justice in the Buzek government when he was confronted with the extent of corruption and vast role of the old-type secret service networks. This was what gave the twins the impetus to form the PiS after the fall of the Buzek administration. • **In its first term** (2005–2007) **the PiS moved towards combatting corruption**, introducing a new lustration law in 2006, establishing an Anti-Corruption Bureau, and disbanding the Military Intelligence	individuals whose position is difficult to ascertain. • With the eradication of individual and institutional autonomies based on equality before the law, **a system of patron-client relations** is being built: shaping civilians into clients dependent on individual political decisions. This is not accomplished with the homogeneously repressive instruments of classical dictatorship, but a wealth of forms suitable to the requirements of "democratic legitimation." • The Orbán regime does not fight corruption, but monopolizes it through centralization. In its case, we are not speaking about state capture, but the capture of the oligarchs. Corruption does not work against the state, but **the state itself works as a criminal organization**. The mafia state is simply the privatized form of the parasite state. • **Politically selective law enforcement**, as practiced in the mafia state, ensures loyalty to the adopted political family. The Governmental Control Office, the State Audit Office, the tax authorities and the Prosecutor's Office are not neutral, impartial institutions taking action against illegal activity, but actors

POLAND	HUNGARY
Agency. At the time, these acts were also supported by the Civil Platform, and with the exception of the 2006 lustration law, they are still effective today. Kaczyński even used the Anti-Corruption Bureau against his own coalition partners, exposing his coalition ally, Andrzej Leppert. Paradoxically his own government fell as a result. • To date, there is no evidence that the PiS would seek to replace the economic elite, to expropriate, redistribute, and channel private property into its own fields of interest. Yet the unification of the posts of minister of justice and chief prosecutor is not an encouraging sign, since this measure will make prosecutions more readily subject to political orders. Nonetheless, there is no sign in Poland that law enforcement authorities might act as protectors of economic interests close to the regime. • PiS is preparing to withdraw the public education reform that was introduced at the end of the nineties (the shift, in particular, from an 8+4-year educational system to a 6+3+3-year system has resulted in East-Central Europe's only lasting educational success, through extending the period in which basic competencies are taught). Its goal, it would seem, is boosting the position of the Church colleges in comparison	integrated into the criminal organization in government. They operate not under the law, but under the political and economic interests of Viktor Orbán: when required, they are part of the Fidesz campaign machine, or the concealers of economic crimes committed by central command. • The regime not only occupies positions of public authority, and manipulates the sphere of politics, but acquires family wealth through the replacement of the leading economic elite and its methodical stripping of properties. The essence of the mafia state is that **the adopted political family accumulates wealth through the bloodless instruments of state coercion.** This centrally directed activity as a criminal organization involves the concerted operation of Parliament, government, the tax authorities, the Governmental Control Office, the Prosecutor's Office, and the police. Traditional corruption is suppressed: it is not state officials who are offered bribes, but the state criminal organization that takes protection money. The fortunes of the political family are piled up by the stooges and oligarchs belonging to the internal circle, laundering it through means supported by the

POLAND	HUNGARY
to the secularized schools of public education. • Loyal members of the power pyramid are **rewarded with office, not wealth**. Kaczyński lives alone in a rented apartment in Warsaw in extremely **austere** conditions. His wealth declaration shows that he had to borrow money from a friend in order to adapt his home to meet his ailing mother's medical needs, and then to create a small memorial to her after her death. Since its formation, the PiS has campaigned under the slogan of "the inexpensive state," and to date, no costly prestige investments can be tied to it. The president of the party is, in any case, weary of public appearances, and rarely appears in the media.	state, and the introduction of offshore companies. • **The new elite brandishes its wealth** unabashedly. The godfather/prime minister builds a football stadium in the neighborhood of his country house, transferring billions into his football foundation, while his family piles up land and fortunes through stooges, buying palaces and country mansions. He will soon move into the royal castle in Buda. The visible wealth of the stooges and oligarchs who can be tied to him is in excess of 110 billion forints (350 million euro). The amounts siphoned off to members of the political family are on the scale of millions–billions, and the public revelation of such acts is an unremarkable, everyday occurrence.

The difference between the two autocratic experiments' foreign policy

• Kaczyński's **relationship with Germany is ambivalent**. During the PiS's first term in government, he fostered good relations with Angela Merkel; these relations developed further during the governance of the Civil Platform. Merkel's support was likely necessary for Donald Tusk to become the President of the European Council. On the other hand, many historical grievances	• Orbán **is not fighting Germany, he is fighting Merkel**, and he looks for allies in this struggle even among members of her party. The slogan "Give Hungarians respect," used in a major billboard campaign, expresses how offended he was at not being shown the respect he believes he deserves in the Western world. His critique is not ideologically based; it is merely revenge for the lack of

POLAND	HUNGARY
are deeply engrained in Kaczyński (his father fought in the Warsaw Uprising, and he was born in 1949 in a city leveled to the ground by the Germans). In his opinion, German capital should play a larger role in the revival of Poland. Once in a while, the politicians of the PiS bring up these historical debts they believe the Germans owe.	respect demonstrated towards the godfather, and is a means to position himself, rather than his country. Meanwhile, he acknowledges that Germany is Hungary's number one economic partner, with which it cannot engage in an economic battle.
• **Kaczyński is unflinching in his commitment to the Atlantic Alliance**. He considers the USA and NATO the chief guarantors of Polish independence and sovereignty. The country's first PiS foreign minister, Witold Waszczykowski, is an American university educated individual who had worked in Geneva and at the Brussels office of NATO. His successor, Jacek Czaputowicz, has a similar orientation. It is one of the main aims of the PiS to allow NATO to establish permanent bases in Poland, achieved partially at the 2016 NATO Summit in Warsaw. In addition, he continues to work on Poland being added to the NATO Nuclear Sharing program, thereby further increasing the security of the country.	• Orbán has **ejected all politicians and diplomats committed to the Atlantic Alliance** from his foreign affairs team. There is no Atlantic commitment, only bargains with the USA and NATO. With regard to Hungary's NATO obligations, they are met at the lowest possible level, merely to prevent the USA taking a stronger line against the autocratic regime in Hungary. This, of course, does not stop government propaganda from publicizing all sorts of anti-Hungarian conspiracy theories, among them stories of secret societies controlling the world, international banking offensives, sabotage by George Soros—adding to all of this a splash of anti-Semitism for good measure.
• One of the cornerstones of Polish foreign policy—irrespective of the government—is that Russia is a threat to Poland at all times. The Polish people believe that **dependence on Russian energy has a political**	• The program of **Eastern Opening** in Hungarian foreign policy aims to secure socially unchecked, freely expendable resources for the adopted political family through its connections to Putin and other autocrats.

POLAND

cost, and so every effort must be made to avoid it. Poland carries on expansive commercial activities with the countries of the Far East, but business does not signify political legitimacy for any anti-democratic regime. The current PiS government takes up the cause of any country or people fighting against Russia (Ukraine, Chechnya, Georgia), and supports maintaining the sovereignty of the Baltic states by every means it has at its disposal, as well as Ukraine's intent to distance itself from Russia. Accordingly, Warsaw usually criticizes the West for not fully backing these causes.

- Kaczyński's **opposition to Brussels is motivated by a repositioning of Poland's status within the EU**. But this does not mean Warsaw has any intent to leave the EU. Quite the opposite: Poland would like to have more of a say in matters, **and wishes to be in the mainstream of the EU**. Naturally, it needs allies to achieve this, and Warsaw has recognized that the **Visegrád Four** (V4) are not strong enough for it to achieve its aims. This is why it has resurrected Piłsudski's concept of the Intermarium introduced between the two World Wars, which would have joined the countries of the East-Central European region, stretching from the Baltic Sea to the Adriatic and the Black Sea.

HUNGARY

This, it must be added, is not classical commerce, for the chief merchandise is Hungary's disloyalty to the EU, for which the adopted political family gains financial favors. Russian gas-diplomacy, the renovation of the Paks Nuclear Power Plant, and other similar deals put Hungary in an obliged, dependent position in exchange for private benefit. It is not the countries and nations, but the autocrats between whom the Eastern Opening serves to create an intimate, familial atmosphere. Fidesz tries to present its position of staying within the EU while opening towards the East as bridging East and West. In reality, however, its position mostly involves doing "family" business with the East, while blackmailing the West.

- To strengthen its position against Brussels, Orbán seeks allies in the framework of the **Visegrád Four**. With a collective stance opposed to Brussels' strategy for dealing with the refugee crisis in the form of compulsory relocation quotas, he also tries at the same time to turn it into a stronger community with a stronger bargaining position. Such a group would offer protection and support to the other participants in cases where, citing a democracy deficit, Brussels wished to take measures against moves toward autoc-

POLAND	HUNGARY
Kaczyński would not envisage such an alliance to win protection and support against Brussels' claims of a democratic deficit, but rather to have its status as a regional middle power within the EU recognized. It was no coincidence that Poland took a middling, wavering position on the compulsory quota system for the placement of asylum seekers, since it did not want to antagonize Brussels and Berlin in this matter. • Various organizations within the EU reacted strongly—even threatening to activate Article 7 of the Lisbon Treaty—to those political changes orchestrated by Kaczyński, which were aimed at a concentration of power and violated the constitution. This surprised the government, and compelled it to partial retreat. The amplification of the nationalist ideological strain is not part of a larger strategy, but a spontaneous reaction to the criticism aimed at his government.	racy within the EU. In the case of the V4, Orbán insists on a role as leader: if not for Hungary, then for himself. His personal ambition reaches beyond the intent to bring about this regional community of shared interests: he wants to be the provider of a model and a program opposed to the community of values that comprises the EU. At the same time, Hungarian foreign policy is either wholly "deaf" to the Polish initiatives—mainly because they also have an anti-Russian component—or simply cherry-picks those elements that could be useful for its propaganda. • Orbán's **"Europe of Nations"** program is simply a demand for a new relationship with the EU: to make sure that the EU maintains the transfer of convergence funds, while at the same time securing the autonomy necessary for the building up of "national democracies," that is, autocracies.

Chances of a restoration of liberal democracy: party structure

- **Polish party structure has been in constant motion since the regime change:** some parties disappeared, while other new organizations formed. PiS, which won the 2015 elections, had only formed in 2001.

- After the electoral victory of Fidesz in the 2010 elections, the **party structure that had been stable since the regime change**—even rigid, in a certain sense—**collapsed**. The two large parties emerging from the re-

POLAND	HUNGARY
This does not, however, mean that a large number of new faces made it into the political mainstream. Jarosław Kaczyński is one of the longest currently active politicians, already being actively involved in the opposition movement in the seventies. Typically, though parties may have failed or been discredited, this has been less true of their politicians. Only the leftist successor party seems to be disappearing from the political stage, both in organizational and personal terms. Clearly, however, new arrivals are taking their place. • **In spite of constant change, Polish political life can basically be divided into two sides:** the Christian-nationalist and the liberal-conservative sides. In the last fifteen years, this has meant a division between PiS and PO. The former usually call the latter leftists, or "communists"—without foundation. The third side could be the disappearing old left, and the new left now in formation. Characteristically, however, neither the **PiS, nor the PO, occupies the central arena of power**, despite the fact that for a long while it seemed like the PO would be able to do so. **The PiS**—though it holds itself the only ideologically legitimate representative of the nation—is not	gime change, the national conservative MDF and liberal SZDSZ, disintegrated. The socialist party split into two: the legal successor MSZP, an eclectic party with its politics grounded in inherited relationships rather than common principles, and the social-liberal Democratic Coalition (DK), led by the former prime minister Ferenc Gyurcsány. However, both parties held on to the discredited personal makeup of the party's figureheads. A new left-wing green party, LMP (Politics Can be Different), was elected to parliament, but also later split in two, producing PM (Dialogue for Hungary). They now compete, along with another minor party formed after 2010, Együtt, for the votes of the left-wing electorate who won't vote for MSZP or DK. • **A three-party system** replaces the two-party system that preceded 2010. Fidesz managed to occupy what Orbán has termed a **"central arena of power"** (*centrális erőtér*), referring to its dominance in the political arena, rather than its position on the political spectrum. Jobbik, an ideology-driven, extreme-right radical party is positioned to its right, while the divided socialist and liberal parties are to its left. This party alignment rather resembles the situation under the Horthy regime, where the

POLAND	HUNGARY
holding the center ground, but is positioned on the extreme right. **Even organizationally it integrates the extreme right-radical formations**, individuals and voters.	government party in the center also constantly saturated **elements of extreme-right ideology** in order to hold the right-wing camp together. **While Fidesz** largely absorbs the ideological frames and language of the radical right in order to keep its support base, **it does not integrate the voters of the extreme right.**
• The PiS does not dominate the right-wing political field, since the PO is still a major party of the liberal-conservative **right**. Moreover, not only did Nowoczesna, a **new liberal party** make it into parliament in 2015, but its support has grown a great deal since. The forces of the civil middle-ground, therefore, have a serious, institutionalized power and base in Poland. Besides them, another stable presence is the Polish People's Party (PSL), which gains its main support among the strata of provincial officials and civil servants.	• Since 2010 there has been **neither a moderate center right party, nor a liberal party that could be taken seriously** in Hungary. Therefore, voters disillusioned by Fidesz, which commands most of the right, do not have a natural party environment where they could find representation on the right of the political ground without the mafia state elements. Therefore, their break with Fidesz would also have to mean a break with their right-wing values. This, however, is not a viable option for them, since it would mean much more than simply changing party preferences.
• The **electoral list system** does not exclude the possibility of defeating PiS even without a united opposition. Since PiS is considered unsuitable for coalition by most of the political parties, if it is unable to secure more than half of the mandate alone, it will conceivably lose its chance to form a government.	• The one-round, **disproportional election system** would only allow for the replacement of Fidesz through elections if the multitude of opposition parties—which justly see each other as unsuitable, and exclude one-another based on values and voter base—would form an electoral alliance. This is what ensures Fidesz its stability in power, although its popularity rises and falls.
• In Poland, the governing party cannot bring opposition parties into a position where they depend on the	

POLAND	HUNGARY
governing party, and either openly or latently become its vassals. If a political party is discredited, another is immediately formed in its place.	• In the mafia state, politicians are stigmatized and criminalized, **while opposition parties are marginalized or domesticated**.

The municipal hinterland for the protection of liberal democracy

- Since 2015, not only the capital and the major cities, but even the majority of rural municipalities in Poland are under the leadership of opposition forces. As such, it is impossible to administratively limit the influence of the parties, or to take away the financial independence of its followers; there are significant obstacles to forcing them into positions dependent on the government.

  Due to Poland's size and heterogeneity, there is an extraordinarily strong regional consciousness, which manifests itself in political choices as well. In the northern, western, and Silesian metropolises of the country, a majority of the electorate supports the liberal-conservative camp, and the plebeian-populist PiS finds it very hard to address them. The clerks of the rural towns in the east also prefer to vote for the PSL. Moreover, the next municipal elections will only be in 2018, which means the PiS is forced to govern

- In contrast to Fidesz's 1998–2002 term in government, by 2010 practically the whole of the municipal sector had come under the influence of Fidesz. This made it impossible for the municipalities to form a sort of hinterland, or base, for the parties of the democratic opposition. Fidesz openly socializes the electorate to expect that if they do not elect a leadership loyal to the government, they will be divesting themselves of all central and EU development resources. Moreover, municipalities also depend on the central budget for a decisive majority of their current revenue. Meanwhile, the vassal status of mayors dependent on Orbán has made it possible for the municipalities to be stripped of their education and healthcare institutions without opposition, even as their free handling of their budgets has been curtailed. As a result, the municipalities have become essentially custodians, extensions of the power of government. Political and

POLAND	HUNGARY
against the strong tide of oppositional municipal governments.	cultural life is heavily centered on Budapest, and the few cities numbering between one to two hundred thousand have never played an independent role of political consequence for the whole country.

The chances of an independent media

POLAND	HUNGARY
• The PiS had made efforts to bring public media under party control as early as the end of 2005. With minor amendments, the same law was in effect while the PO was in government. As such, the public media, though not a government mouthpiece, nevertheless tailored its broadcasts according to the values of the PO. • In line with the Hungarian model, the PiS set its sights on the creation of a one-party media authority, so it is to be expected that they will try to redistribute radio frequency concessions as well. • According to the government program of the PiS, the next step will be to establish a centralized organ through merging the former National Radio and Television Committee, the Office of Electronic Communications, and the Office of Competition and Consumer Protection. • The two largest Polish commercial TV broadcasters (TVN and Polsat)	• With the Media Act passed in 2010, the media, which had been under multi-party control until then, was placed under the jurisdiction of one party, meaning that public radio, television, and the central news agency essentially became unchecked propaganda tools of Fidesz. • In redistributing frequencies, the one-party media authority serves frequency owners loyal to the government, and throws owners of frequencies who are not committed to the government out of the media market. • With the establishment of the National Office of Communications, the communications tasks of the public sector and the public procurement of state advertisement were centralized, allowing the state to fundamentally limit the freedom of the media market. • Fidesz has made attempts to gather two major commercial television channels (RTL Klub and TV2) into its own circle of clients using the

POLAND	HUNGARY
are in the hands of committed liberal democrats. The TVN Agency belongs to the international TVN Group, which is currently the largest advertising company in Poland. Until now there has been no attempt to force them out of the market.	tools of state coercion. In the case of TV2, its efforts were successful: the acquisition by one of Orbán's stooges was made possible through a state loan, and the repayment of the loan is assisted by the provision of state advertisements.

Civil resistance and the political parties

- Civil movements challenging the anti-democratic actions of the PiS-led government manifest themselves in regular demonstrations, bringing tens of thousands, or occasionally over a hundred thousand, protesters out on the streets. Their moves to protect liberal democracy and the constitution are fundamentally of a **political and system-critical nature**, since they are usually organized by the urban middle class and intellectuals. Actions to protect collective interests usually belong to the sphere of labor unions in Poland. But since the union with the largest membership and a reach across sectors, Solidarity, is bound closely to the PiS both politically and ideologically, it is unlikely to be willing to continue the hard line it took in the protection of collective interests under earlier administrations. Nevertheless, it is possible that the good economic results of earlier years may

- Most of the civil demonstrations called against the actions of the Fidesz government were about **protecting collective interests,** or of a **government-critical** nature, and altogether failed to culminate in a nationwide political movement that would formulate a general critique of the system itself. Generally, the protests concerned harm to personal material interests: the withdrawal of early retirement pensions, the nationalization of private pension funds, the situation of people with foreign currency loans, the nationalization of tobacco shops, the redistribution of state land leases, or the losses caused by the brokerage scandals. A partial exception to this rule were the mass actions in response to the elimination of autonomy in public and higher education; nonetheless, these movements also remained within the paradigm of government criticism. Two govern-

POLAND	HUNGARY
allow the government to turn to the politics of distribution. • During the renewed waves of demonstration, the **KOD (Committee for the Defense of Democracy)** was formed, evoking the traditions of the organization formed by dissident intellectuals in the mid-seventies, the KOR (Workers' Defense Committee). On the part of the current opposition movements, this **signifies an open commitment to the regime-changing traditions** of the past, and places current actions against the government in this positive historical tradition. KOD was the announcer and organizer of the latest mass demonstrations; it tries to function not only as an umbrella organization, but also focuses on building an extensive, largely rural network. • The huge demonstration by democratic forces in June was already supported by **three former presidents of the republic** (Lech Wałęsa, Aleksander Kwaśniewski and Bronisław Komorowski). Komorowski established his own institute after he left office, with its chief aim being the preservation and support of the achievements won after the change of regime. At the same time, KOD **invited the Polish opposition parties** to ally with it, cooperating to protect democracy.	ment initiatives with an impact on middle-class lifestyle and consumer habits were withdrawn in the face of massive popular opposition. The ban on shops opening on Sundays lasted little over a year, while the planned introduction of an internet tax was dropped altogether after mass demonstrations. The flash-mob demonstrations bringing tens of thousands of people onto the streets were not brought into existence by old civil organizations or political parties, and the spontaneous mobilizations were not able to institutionalize or produce leading opposition figures. • The majority of the demonstrations were critical of the entire postcommunist period, and **did not reach back to the regime-changing traditions of the anti-communist dissident movement**. In paradoxical unison with the government ideology, they considered the 1989 regime change itself a deal concluded by the elites, bypassing society at large. This may of course be a consequence of the fact that the Hungarian anti-communist dissident movement—unlike the Polish example—continued in the liberal party (SZDSZ), both in terms of the individual actors and its institutionalized form. With its loss of credibility and ultimate disappearance, it virtually

POLAND	HUNGARY
Most opposition parties joined this call, though the PO has kept its distance thus far. KOD was also supported in its call for an alliance of the opposition by the fact that although the right-of-center PO lost the elections, it was not discredited, while other opposition parties, such as the liberal Nowoczesna, are growing in popularity. • The institutionalization of the civil movement and its promising cooperation with the political parties of the opposition is extending the resistance movement and its institutional base, countering the PiS with a dynamism that shows no sign of slowing.	blocked any route of return to the traditions of democratic opposition. • **László Sólyom**, the Fidesz-supported president of the republic between 2005 and 2010, and one of the leading legislators of the constitutive establishment of the change of regimes, **remained detached from movements critical of the government**, aside from a few small gestures. • As the left-wing parties of the democratic opposition had largely been discredited, and its new, green parties were insignificant, a trap formed for the new civil movements. Cooperation with these parties would place them into a quarantine with no perspective, while a refusal to cooperate isolates them from the base of minimal, but extant, active, system-critical voters. At the same time, the civil resistance mobilized from time to time is also unable to constitute a new party, because their aims are always focused on a single issue, rather than against the system as a whole. • The wavering, self-extinguishing futurelessness of the movements after 2010 resulted neither in the institutionalization and stabilization of civil movements as political forces of consequence, nor the renewal of the parties in democratic opposition.

In summary

- The chances of the **conservative Polish attempt at building an autocracy** being defeated are strong even under the current democratic institutional framework. This is ensured by a number of factors: the proportional electoral system, which constitutionally prevents excessive power concentration; the social traditions of resistance to authority; the civil movement building on these traditions; the existence of moderate right and liberal parties constituting the main part of the opposition forces; PiS being forced onto the extreme right of the political spectrum; the political diversity offered by municipal governments; and the strong media platforms for freedom of expression. At the same time, the possibility of a Hungarian scenario unfolding in Poland is also prevented by the very character of the PiS, its personal composition, principles, and program, as well as the tradition and actuality of the Polish right. In its current form, the PiS is not capable of following the Hungarian model; that is, many circumstances and components are missing for it to do so.
- Conversely, the chances of overcoming the **Hungarian mafia state** within the framework of the given institutional system are far more limited. Factors preventing the supplanting of the mafia state include: the disproportional and manipulative electoral system that makes election fraud a real possibility; a lack of social traditions of resistance to authority; the historical culture of individual, detached bargaining with the regimes in power; the lack of a moderate right-wing or liberal party for any voters abandoning Fidesz; the central position of Fidesz in the tripartite political field; the uniformity of the political-institutional map, since the municipalities have integrated into the ruling system; as well as the elimination or ghettoization of spaces for freedom of expression. All of this will likely result in a continued decline in the chances of a change of government through free elections and the re-establishment of liberal democracy in Hungary. Hungary is on a calamitous track towards the course of development undergone by former Soviet republics after the end of communism, reaching the point of no-return, where electoral possibilities for change have been exhausted, and only vibrant revolutions following rigged elections made it possible for the reigning regimes to fall.

(I am much indebted for constructive and critical advice to Attila Ara-Kovács, András Bozóky, András Domány, Csilla Frank, Góralczyk Bogdan, András Kardos, Márton Kozák, László Lengyel, Maziarski Wojciech, Iván Pető, Sobolewska Elżbieta, and János Széky.)

Translation by Bálint Bethlenfalvy

List of Contributors

Sarah Chayes, author of *Thieves of State: Why Corruption Threatens Global Security* (2015).

Oleksandr Fisun, Professor of Political Science and Department Head at the V.N. Karazin Kharkiv National University in Ukraine

Henry E. Hale, Professor, George Washington University

Miklós Haraszti, Hungarian writer, human rights advocate, fellow at the Center for Media, Data and Society, Central European University

Andrei Kazakevich, Institute of Political Studies, Palitychnaya Sfera, Belarus; Vytautas Magnus University, Lithuania

János Kornai, Professor Emeritus at Harvard University and Corvinus University of Budapest

Bálint Magyar, Hungarian sociologist and liberal politician

Nándor László Magyari, Sociology Department of the Babes-Bolyai University, Cluj, Romania

Mikhail Minakov, Kennan Institute, Woodrow Wilson Center for International Scholars

Dumitru Minzarari, Department of Political Science at the University of Michigan-Ann Arbor

Kálmán Mizsei, Department of Economics, Central European University

Nikolay Petrov, Faculty of Social Sciences / School of Political Science, Moscow

Alexei Pikulik, Institute for Russian and Eurasian Studies, Uppsala University

Uladzimir Rouda, Professor of Political Science, European Humanities University, Belarus

Andrey Ryabov, Russian Academy of Sciences' Institute of World Economy and International Relations

Zoltán Sz. Bíró, Senior Research Fellow Institute of History, Research Centre for the Humanities of Hungarian Academy of Sciences in Budapest

Ilja Viktorov, researcher at the Department of Economic History and International Relations, Stockholm University.

Index

A

Abramovich, Roman, 198
Abromavičius, Aivaras, 598
Acemoglu, Daron, 36
Aczél, György, 623
Adjara, 552
Adly, Amr Ismail, 494
adopted political family, 13, 15, 112, 114, 117–19, 121–27, 129–30, 134–35, 137–39, 142–43, 145, 147–50, 152, 156, 164–70, 172, 184, 213, 219, 232, 250, 253–54, 258–261, 265–67, 269–70, 289, 463–65, 472, 475, 477, 479–80, 482, 611, 640–45, 637
Afghanistan, 512, 515, 519, 524, 526n13, 529, fig. B.7
Africa, 11, 29, 76, 79–80, 520, 528n37
Akayev, Askar, 429
Akhmetov, Rinat, 236–38, 543, 545, 577
al-Assad, Bashar, 511
Albania, 61, 99, 105, 108, 115, 474, 528n31
Aliyev, Heydar, 336, 518, figs. A.3, A.8
Aliyev, Ilham, 336, 510–11, 516–17, 523, 661–63, figs. A.5, A.8

Aliyev, Mehriban (Pashayev), 510, 517–18, figs. A.1, A.8
America, *see* Latin America; United States
Amirov, Said, 205
Amur Oblast, 185
Andropov, Yuriy, 41, 222
anti-capitalist sentiments, 24, 54
anti-corruption
    agencies, 187, 192–93, 209, 249, 282, 289, 296, 311, 514, 586, 588, 641–42
    campaigns, 109, 138, 172, 252, 293–94, 301, 360, 586, fig. B.1
    cases, 207
    industry, 277, 295–96
    legislation, 586, 592
    policies of, 109, 138, 278, 296, 301, 303, 304, 508–10, 586, 592, 597
    rhetoric, 252, 294, 360, 514, 586, 641
    struggle against, 294
Arab Spring, 100, 372, 374, 388, 507
Arendt, Hannah, 42
Argentina, 61
Armașu, Octavian, 567
Armenia, 105, 108, 115, 336, 369n8, 421, 423, 427–28, 474, 604n30, fig. A.7

Ashton, Catherine, 550
Asia, 29, 76, 79–80, 303, 415, 528n37
  East, 174n5. *See also* Central Asia
Åslund, Anders, 536, 590
Atambayev, Almazbek, 511, figs. B.1,
  B.4
authoritarianism, 5, 56, 181, 386, 391,
    403, 425, 428
  authoritarian leaders, 357, 405, 425,
    427–28, 430, 564
  competitive, 353, 373
  hybrid, 249
  move away from, 389, 392, 405–6,
    431
  move toward, 212, 239, 242, 253,
    267, 356, 359, 372–73, 426–27,
    429, 539, 563
  neo-authoritarian, 374, 376
  pluralistic, 233, 241
  populist, 353
  Russian, 213, 376, 385
  smart, 390
  theory of, 6, 7, 9, 76, 80, 389, 392
  "weak," 6
autocracy, 44–45, 48, 55–56, 58, 102,
    108, 400, 483, 611
  autocratic leaders, 39–40, 62, 122,
    129, 398
  capitalist, 11, 60–61
  move away from 389, 405, 493, 499,
    654
  move toward, 43, 46, 49, 61, 100,
    103, 145, 250, 491, 499, 637–38,
    646
  post-communist, 13, 102, 109,
    113–14, 117, 126–38, 142–44, 146,
    148, 153–57, 166–69, 171–72, 250,
    489
  theory of, 6, 11, 36–41, 47–48, 56,
    107, 113–14, 133–34, 638–43
Avakov, Arsen, 588
Aven, Petr, 198
Azarov, Mykola, 237, 543–44, 579–80
Azerbaijan, 58, 100, 105, 108, 115,
    314n77, 336, 358, 374, 376, 421,
    423, 426–28, 474, 508, 510–11,
    513, 515–18, 520–21, 523, 528n32,
    604n30, figs. A.1–8, C.3

B

Bakiyev, Kurmanbek, 429
Balcerowicz, Leszek, 534, 560, 633
Bălți, 575
Baltic states, 44, 49, 98–99, 102,
    271n10, 434n13, 489, 532–33, 535,
    553, 560, 603n18, 645
Banerjee, Abhijit V., 393
Bárdossy, László, 616
Băsescu, Traian, 302, 306n22, 307n28,
    309n38, 310n49, 311n79, 543
Bashkortostan, 184, 451
Bashneft, 184–85, 189, 450–53
Bastrykin, Alexander, 198
Batumi, 548, 551
Baturina, Yelena, 184
Baumol, William J., 36
Beck, Józef, 615–16
Belarus, 14–15, 92, 105, 108, 115, 131,
    158, 231, 233, 247–70, 271n10,
    353–58, 361, 363–65, 367–68,
    369n8, 378, 421, 423, 427–28,
    474, 489–93, 495–97, 499, 502–3,
    504n2, 537, 541–42, 584
Belavezha Accords, 284
Belgorod Oblast, 204
Below, Georg von, 78
Belyaninov, Andrey, 183, 209
Belykh, Nikita, 183, 206
Ben Ali, Zine el-Abidine, 513, 518,
    527n33, 528n25
Bendix, Reinhard, 79
Bendukidze, Kakha, 547, 558, 571
Berezovsky, Boris, 150, 387, 440
Berman, Jakub, 618
Bertelsmann report, 50–51
Bethlen, István, 615
Biden, Joe, 594
Bierut, Bolesław, 618–19
Blanc, Louis, 23
Bogdankevich, Stanislav, 255
Bogoliubov, Gennadii, 234, 235

Bohle, Dorothee, 36
Boiko, Volodymyr, 237
Boiko, Yuriy, 237
Borodin, Andrey, 184, 450, 452
Bortnikov, Alexander, 198–99
Bortnikov, Denis, 201
Bragin, Akhat, 577–79
Bratsk, Irkutsk Oblast, 205
Brazil, 507
Brechalov, Alexander, 194
Brezhnev, Leonid, 41, 181, 222, 224–25, 226, 263
bribery, 8, 27, 87, 142, 146, 170, 280, 287, 301–2, 305n11, 452, 476, 477–78, 507, 515, 518–19, 523, 525, 533, 580, 597, 634, 642, figs. A.1, A.8, B.1, B.8, C.1, C.8
Britain, 63, fig. A.5. See also United Kingdom
Brus, Włodzimierz, 625
Brussels, 57, 571, 606n48, 639, 644–46
Bruszt, László, 494
Bukharin, Nikolai, 221
Bulgaria, 49, 98–99, 103, 105, 108, 115, 303, 474, 629
bureaucracy
  dictatorship of (*byurokratura*), 208
  neopatrimonial, 87–88, 90
  patrimonial, 87
  party, 88
  sovereign, 208
  state, 11, 88, 132, 250, 269–70
  in Georgia, 549, 558
  in Belarus, 250, 259, 262–63, 270, 354, 359, 366–67
  in Romania, 304
  in Russia, 187, 208, 331, 438, 441, 445, 451
Buzek, Jerzy, 633, 641
Bykov, Anatoly, 205

C

Calmîc, Octavian, 567
Cambodia, 45–46
Candu, Andrian, 567, fig. C.1

capitalism, 42, 52–54, 59, 155, 166, 417, 489, 633
  crony, 53, 110, 512
  clannish, 420, 423–25
  political, 85–86
  rent-based, 426, 432
  state, 52, 417, 427, 491, 493
  theory of, 11, 23–36, 42, 52, 63, 86
  transition to, 31–32, 36, 46, 59, 155, 419–20, 438, 453
capitalismization, 490–91
cartel agreements, 76
Castro, Fidel, 32
Caucasus, 474. See also North Caucasus; South Caucasus
Ceaușescu, Nicolae, 25, 278, 560
censorship, 45, 371–75, 377–83
  quasi-democratic state, 15, 373–74
Central Asia, 99–100, 102–3, 109, 126, 128, 159, 165, 249, 261, 348, 358, 398, 420–21, 423, 427, 475–76, fig. B.7
Central Europe. See under Europe
centralization, 32, 40, 59, 91, 129, 139, 145, 164, 169–72, 185, 192, 196, 211, 255, 418, 427, 466, 471, 475, 551–52, 554, 557, 564, 611, 640, 641, 650
Chaika, Artem, 201
Chaika, Igor, 190, 201
Chaika, Yury, 198, 199
charisma, 56, 430, 558, 561, 574–75, 605
charismatic rulership, 79–80, 430
Chávez, Hugo, 365
Chayes, Sarah, 16, 657
Chechnya, 204, 645
Chekist, 182, 185, 187, 197, 200, 204, 447, 457n28, 458n29
Chemezov, Sergey, 198, 199, 211
Cherkesov, Viktor, 446–47
Chernivtsi, 236
Chernomyrdin, Viktor, 319, 328
chief patron. See under patrons
China, 22, 42, 44–46, 58, 67n36, 108, 174n5, 254, 268, 354, 373–74, 380, 398, 406, figs. B.4, B.8

Chişinău, 563, 567–68, 574–75, 605n37
Chornovil, Viacheslav, 538–39
Churchill, Winston, 25, 40, 56
Churov, Vladimir, 343
Cioloş, Dacian, 522
clans, 13, 82, 87–88, 125–27, 137, 144, 205, 217–43, 372, 423, 426, 535, 577–83
clan state, 13–14, 137, 140–41, 217–18, 241–42
clientelism, 53, 82, 89, 91, 110, 199, 278, 288–92, 294, 299–300, 430–31, 433, 465, 571–72, 579
Clinton, Bill, 373
Commonwealth of Independent States (CIS), 248, 257, 539, 541, 549, 600, 610n95
communism
  national, 228–29, 247, 278
  patrimonial, 98, 104
  reform, 24, 228, 620, 629, 631–32
  theory of, 13, 23–24, 65n5, 104, 114, 117, 121, 156
  transition from, 5, 11, 85, 97, 98, 100, 103, 117, 152, 157, 159, 220, 228, 373, 534, 629
  See also under dictatorship
communist parties, 27, 29, 32, 45, 66n19, 97, 120, 123, 129, 130–31, 135, 153, 221, 228, 324–25, 340, 357, 417, 629
competing-(multi-)pyramid system, 9–10, 12, 14–15, 112, 115, 117, 162–63, 211, 218, 233, 239, 288, 292–94, 296, 299, 492–93, 503
Copaci, Tudor, 568
corporate raiding (*reiderstvo*), 16, 157, 161–65, 232, 238, 270, 437–455
  black raiding, 161–62 164, 441–42
  gray raiding, 161–64, 442
  white raiding, 161–65
Council of Europe, 142, 461, 523, 570, 586, 593, 596, fig. A.6
crime,
  corporate, 141, 162–63
  governmental, 141
  organized, 103, 138–40, 142, 162, 170, 172, 189, 205, 208, 238, 308n31, 313n69, 421, 424, 456n15, 463, 517–18, 534, 547, 555, 557, 598, 600, 603n24, figs. A.2, C.4
  organizational, 141
  state, 140–41, 162–63, 462
  speech, 378
  white-collar, 141, 276, 300
Crimea, 179, 186–87, 189, 191–95, 199, 209, 236, 240, 252, 258, 345, 534, 577–78, 580, 585
criminal state, 114, 140–44, 164, 462–64, 473, 477, 533, 544, 548, 562, 580, 584, 593, 641–42
criminalization, 132, 149, 172, 204, 378–80, 454, 649
Croatia, 99, 105, 108, 115, 474
Cuba, 30, 32, 44, 46, 67n24
Czaputowicz, Jacek, 644
Czech Republic, 99, 105, 108, 115, 159, 474, 476, 560, figs. A.5, A.8
Czechoslovakia, 532, 560, 627, 629

D

Dadin, Ildar, 186
Dagestan, 205
Dahl, Robert, 37, 426
De Gaulle, Charles, 56
democracy, 5–6, 8–11, 13, 25, 36–50, 55–56, 58, 61, 63, 76, 88, 97–109, 132–33, 218, 280–81, 371–72, 375, 389, 499
  authoritarian, 110
  bourgeois, 49
  controlled, 107, 614
  electoral, 133, 448, 464
  defective, 249
  delegative, 204
  façade/staged, 130, 390
  gentry, 247
  illiberal democracy, 47, 70n51, 101, 107, 289, 297–98, 372, 374, 482–83
  liberal/Western, 13, 43, 58, 60–61, 77, 97, 98, 100, 102, 104, 106, 107,

109–114, 117, 119–23, 127–28, 133, 135–36, 143–44, 151, 154, 156–58, 161, 165–66, 171–72, 217, 295, 298, 319, 338, 371–72, 376–77, 379, 483, 498, 601, 634, 636–37, 646, 651, 654
  majoritarian, 110, 373
  move away from, 49, 51, 60, 230, 373, 638
  move towards, 49, 389, 405, 420, 429, 433, 491
  national, 646
  neopatrimonial, 12, 92
  oligarchic democracy, 84
  partial, 107, 491
  patronal, 109, 131, 133–34, 239, 242
  people's democracy,
  sovereign, 340
  transitional, 275
  weak, 6
deprivatization, 152, 166–67, 169, 189
  See also nationalization
Deripaska, Oleg, 184
despotism, 58, 416
dictatorship, 11, 25–26, 36–42, 44–48, 50–51, 56, 58–60, 63, 83, 107–9, 112, 114, 130–33, 155, 208, 303, 372, 381, 415, 464, 482–83, 639, 641
  bureaucratic, 208
  communicational, 382
  communist, 13, 41, 48–49, 97–98, 220, 278, 612, 621–22,
  Nazi, 41
  personalistic, 265
  "soft", 622, 628–29
Dmitriev, Vladimir, 209
Dnipropetrovsk, 222–25, 227, 231, 234–36, 240, 242, 537, 539, 545, 577, 588, 589
Dobkin, Mikhail, 237
Dod, Yevgeny, 209
Dodon, Igor, 567, 575
Donbas (Donbass), 224, 230, 240, 534–35, 539, 543–45, 562, 577–79, 581–82, 585, 589, 598, 602n11, 608n47

Donetsk (Stalino), 223–24, 227, 230–31, 234–38, 240, 242, 244n21, 535, 543–44, 561, 577–80, 582, 588
Dubrovskiy, Vladimir, 531, 533
Duflo, Esther, 393
Durov, Pavel, 401
Duskin, Eric, 223
Duverger, Maurice, 258

E

East Germany, 29, 49, 67n36, 99, 105, 382, 396
East-Central Europe. *See under* Europe
Easterly, William, 393
Eastern Europe. *See under* Europe
economy
  command, 156–57, 159, 166, 466, 452–53, 466, 624
  informal, 304
  liberalization of, 248, 547, 551, 629
  market, 52, 97, 156–57, 217, 226, 229, 251, 420, 432, 438, 463, 491, 500, 536, 538, 602, 638
  political, 65, 511, 520, 590
  relational, 156, 157, 161
  relation to politics, 36, 44, 46, 52, 90, 123, 155
  shadow, 226, 534
  shortage, 26–27, 29, 59, 152, 475, 534, 633
  state control over, 14, 35, 165–66, 185, 255, 353, 356, 404–7, 416, 418, 420, 423, 447, 490
  state socialist mixed (social market), 24, 490–91, 498–99, 501–2, 624, 629
  surplus, 26–27
Egypt, 100, 511–12
Eisenstadt, Shmuel, 80–81, 90
Elbe-Saale, 98
elections, 38, 50, 90, 183, 372, 381, 426–27
  contested, 133–35, 319, 329, 333–34, 337, 341, 346, 556, 560, 566, 575

free, 123, 132–35, 283, 319–20, 323–24, 326, 333–34, 361, 579, 630, 654
  regulation of, 55, 319–21
  in Belarus 248, 249, 259, 264–65, 267, 355, 359, 361–62, 365
  in Georgia 559–60
  in Hungary 55, 60, 127, 154, 617–18, 631, 634, 635–37, 648, 654
  in Moldova 563–66, 569, 575
  in Poland 49, 617–18, 630–31, 635–37, 648
  in Romania 283, 294–95, 302
  in Russia 183, 187, 193, 202, 319–48, 385, 538
  in Ukraine 229, 230–31, 327, 331, 339, 562, 584–85
elites, 87, 99, 117–27, 140, 180–87, 195–97, 201, 205–12, 219, 425, 544, 643
  atomization of, 196, 199, 249
  autonomous, 119–21, 135
  communist, 120, 123
  consolidation of, 15, 76, 89–91, 76, 134–35, 183, 195–97, 202, 204–7, 243, 263, 300, 332, 358, 389, 429, 447, 590
  contest among, 76, 91, 206–7, 229, 428, 492, 446, 448, 455, 502, 512
  economic, 87, 90, 120, 122, 447, 463, 512, 642
  "nationalization" of, 183, 187, 209, 211
  networks of, 9, 137, 199, 219, 229–30, 445, 447, 455
  nomenklatura, 121, 123, 180–81
  political, 120, 179, 120, 122, 196, 202, 207, 333, 341, 358, 364, 367, 373, 379, 388–89, 398, 449, 451, 463, 475, 479, 613
  regional, 185, 202, 204–7, 225, 227, 229, 236, 330, 332, 365
  ruling, 85, 110, 114–18, 120–22, 126–27, 136–37, 143, 155, 157–58, 204, 249–50, 263, 269, 379, 391, 397, 426–27, 430, 433, 587, 597

Soviet, 15, 91, 205, 221, 242, 422, 531
  structure of, 195–202, 229–300, 358
  sub/partial, 85, 91, 120–21, 123–24
el-Sisi, Abdel Fattah, 512
Engels, Saratov Oblast, 205
Erdoğan, Recep Tayyip, 378, 382
Estonia, 5, 105, 108–9, 115, 474, 476
Ethiopia, 79, 519
Eurasia, 5, 7, 16, 75–76, 108, 112, 189, 218–19, 254–55
Euromaidan, 165, 239, 240, 430, 583–88, 591–97, 600, 608
Europe, 5, 11, 57–58, 89, 98–99, 104, 247–48, 250, 255, 265, 416, 490, 497, 519, 532, 540, 545, 563, 566, 571–72, 580, 582–83, 585, 600, 613–14, 616, 646
  Central, 76, 84, 158, 395, 532
  Central and Eastern, 76, 128, 248, 491, 514, 532, 560
  East-Central, 7, 16, 49, 91, 98, 278, 395, 532, 629, 634, 642, 645
  Eastern, 91, 97, 107, 128, 257, 268, 353–54, 531, 543, 566, 618–19
  Northern, 65n8
  Southern, 76, 84, 91
  South-East, 303
  Western, 57, 65n8, 84, 98, 99, 532, 563. *See also* European Union
European Union (EU), 57, 102, 106, 170, 434
  anti-democratic tendencies within, 55, 57, 113, 632, 645–46
  integration of new member states into, 98, 102–3, 128, 167, 295, 354, 434, 474, 601, 634, 645–46, 684
  funds provided by, 53, 57, 467, 475, 522, 524, 634, 639, 646, 649, figs., B.6, B.8
  relations to post-Soviet states, 103, 121, 252, 254, 258, 474, 502, 508, 510, 522, 537, 539–40, 545, 550, 556, 558–60, 563, 566, 570–71, 573, 575, 581–82, 585, 586, 590, 594, 597, 599–601, 638

F

Farber, Ilya, 186
Farkas, Mihály, 618
Filat, Vladimir (Vlad), 50, 569–73, 585, 606n45, fig. C.1
Filip, Pavel, 567, 574
Firtash, Dmytro, 584–85, 590
Fisun, Oleksandr, 11–12, 14, 657
Fokin, Vitold, 227
Foucault, Michel, 287
Fradkov, Mikhail, 209, 215n27
Fradkov, Pavel, 199, 201
Fradkov, Petr, 201
Franco, Francisco, 26
Freedom House, 50–51, 71, 265, 296
Fridinsky, Sergey, 210
Friedrichs, David O., 141
front men, 14, 112, 144, 154, 473, 480–81. *See also* stooges
FSB (Federal Security Service of the Russian Federation), 185, 195–97, 200, 202, 207, 401, 442, 446–47
Fursenko, Andrey, 198–199

G

Gaidar, Yegor, 323–24, 326, 330, 536
Gans-Morse, Jordan, 454, 458n36
Garancsi, István, 472, 473, 481, 486n8
Gayzer, Vyacheslav, 183, 208
Gdańsk, 627–28
Gelman, Vladimir, 262
Gentelev, Alexander, 440
Georgia, 6, 12, 44, 92, 105, 108, 113, 115, 357–58, 376, 385, 388, 421–22, 427, 429, 432–33, 435n30, 474, 490, 532–33, 542, 545–61, 570, 576, 584, 586, 592, 594, 598–600, 604n30, 610n90, 645, fig. A.7
Germany, 25–26, 35, 39, 42, 63, 67, 222, 320, 546, 556, 615–18, 643, 644, fig. B.6. *See also* East Germany
Gerő, Ernő, 618–19
Gherman, Natalia, 571

Gierek, Edward, 627
Gierke, Otto von, 78
Gigauri, Eka, 552
godfather, 54, 289, 292, 300, 302, 577, 643, 644
Golikova, Tatyana, 198
Gomułka, Władysław, 618–20, 623, 627
Gongadze, Georgiy, 579
Grabow, Karsten, 127
Granovetter, Mark, 395
Greceanîi, Zinaida, 565
Gref, Herman, 198
Greskovits, Béla, 36
Grotius, Hugo, 77
Groysman, Volodymyr, 598–99
Guatemala, 507, 511
Gupta, Akhil, 285
Gurr, Ted, 394
Gusinsky, Vladimir, 387
Gyurcsány, Ferenc, 634, 647

H

Hale, Henry E., 99, 112–13, 134–35, 218–20, 230, 241–42, 275, 280, 311n54, 386, 492, 532, 536, 541, 562–63, 565, 585, 657
Hall, Peter A., 35
Haller, Karl Ludwig von, 77
Haraszti, Miklós, 15, 657
Havel, Václav, 627
Hawking, Stephen, 280
Hegel, Georg Wilhelm Friedrich, 50
Hitler, Adolf, 25–26, 39, 42, 615
Hobbes, Thomas, 77
Hofmeister, Wilhelm, 127
Honduras, 507
Hong Kong, 45, 681
Horthy, Miklós, 26, 62, 612–14, 616, 617, 647
hostile takeover, 157, 161, 437, 439, 442–44, 446
Howard, Marc, 132
Hungary, 11–12, 15–16, 22, 25–26, 33, 41, 49, 51–52, 54–62, 99, 103,

105, 108–9, 113–16, 120, 123, 124, 127, 131, 153, 159, 165, 179, 260–61, 263, 270, 275, 280, 289, 295, 297–304, 314, 320, 372–74, 376, 382, 461, 463, 473–80, 482, 484–85, 507, 532–33, 560, 612–54
Huntington, Samuel P., 22, 37, 48–49, 57, 76
Hurenko, Stanislav, 227, 299
hybrid regimes, 6, 58–59, 61, 76, 104, 107, 110, 179, 183, 249, 280, 289, 291, 300, 373, 415, 476, 498–502

I

illiberal democracy, 47, 70n51, 101, 107, 289, 297–98, 372, 374, 482–83
illiberal regimes, 372–82, 559
Imrédy, Béla, 616
Inglehart, Ronald, 100–101, 409n31
International Monetary Fund (IMF), 528, 536–38, 540–41, 570, 586–90, 629, figs. C.6, C.8
Iran, 354, 374, 380
Iraq, 507, 512, 515
Irkutsk Oblast, 202, 205
Islamic State (ISIS), 58, 507, 515
Italy, 54, 138, 528n31, 615, fig. C.4
Ivanishvili, Bidzina, 422, 559, 607n60
Ivanov, Sergey, 197, 198, 200, 201, 209
Ivanov, Viktor, 196, 197, 200, 209
Ivashkevich, Viktor, 256
Ivashko, Volodymyr, 227

J

Jaresko, Natalia, 593
Jaruzelski, Wojciech, 629, 631
Jellinek, Georg, 78
John Paul II, 628

K

Kaczyński, Jarosław, 611, 632, 635, 637–47
Kaczyński, Lech, 632, 641

Kádár, János, 25, 41, 620, 622, 626, 633
Kadyrov, Ramzan, 198, 204
Kalecki, Michał, 625
Kamenev, Lev, 221
Kamenshchik, Dmitry, 188
Karbalevich, Valery, 252
Karelo-Finnish Soviet Socialist Republic, 222
Karimov, Islam, 348
Karimova, Gulnara, 518
Karklins, Rasma, 280
Karl, Terry L., 499
Kasko, Vitaliy, 594
Kasyanov, Mikhail, 334
Katyń, 617
Kazakevich, Andrei, 15, 657
Kazakhstan, 58, 99–100, 105, 108, 115, 126, 252, 369n8, 374, 376, 423, 426–28, 438, 475, figs. B.3, B.8
Kazanets, Ivan, 227
Kebich, Vyacheslav (Vyachaslau), 248–51, 254, 258, 358–59
Kemerovo Oblast, 204
Khalvashi, Kibar, 556
Kharkiv, 223, 227, 231, 236–37, 244n20, 545, 577
Kherson, 240
Khmelnytskyi Oblast, 236
Khodorkovsky, Mikhail, 150, 186, 213n7, 387, 441, 449–50, 452, 458n36
Khoroshavin, Alexandr, 183, 208
Khrushchev, Nikita, 226, 619
Kirill, Patriarch of Moscow, 198
Kiriyenko, Sergey, 192, 210
Kirov Oblast, 206
Kirovograd Oblast, 224, 240
Kis, János, 72n63, 627
Kiselyov, Tikhon (Tikhan Kisialyou), 358
Kivalov, Sergii, 237
kleptocracy, 13, 16, 110, 449, 515, 521, 523–24
    networks of, 508–10, 512–16, 518–20, 523, figs. A.1, A.8, B.1, B.2, B.4, B.8, C.1, C.4, C.5

structure of, figs. A.1–8, B.1–8, C.1–8
systems of, 382, 511, 521, 523
kleptocratic state, 143–44, 171, 382, 491, 493
Kliuyev, Andriy, 237
Knuth, Magen, 247
Kocharian, Robert, 428
Kochnev, Dmitry, 200
Kolesnikov, Borys, 236–37
Kolomoyskyi, Ihor, 234, 235, 240, 588–89
Komi Republic, 185, 205–6, 208
Komorowski, Bronisław, 652
Kopecký, Petr, 290
Kornai, János, 10–12, 15, 108–9, 155, 657
Koryak Autonomous Okrug, 185
Koshiw, Jaroslav, 544
Kostin, Andrey, 198
Kötcse, 55
Kovalchuk, Boris, 199, 201
Kovalchuk, Mikhail, 199
Kovalchuk, Yury, 198, 215n23
Kozak, Dmitry, 198
Kozhemyako, Oleg, 185
Kozhin, Vladimir, 196–97, 209
Kraków, 628
Krasnodar Krai, 204
Krasnoyarsk Krai, 185, 205
Kravchuk, Leonid, 228–31, 534, 538–39, 578
Kryshtanovskaya, Olga, 125
Kuchma, Leonid, 91, 165, 230–35, 239, 429, 534–39, 543–45, 562–63, 579–80, 585, 605n35
Kudrin, Alexei, 191, 198
Kuran, Timur, 395
Kushchevskaya, 204
Kutaisi, 551
Kuwait, 355
Kuzio, Taras, 84, 534–35, 543, 544, 577, 601
Kuzmin, Renat, 543
Kvirikashvili, Giorgi, 555
Kwaśniewski, Aleksander, 652
Kyiv, 223–24, 228–29, 234–35, 239–40, 589, 591

Kyrgyzstan, 44n45, 92, 100, 105, 108, 115, 126, 257, 358, 369n8, 376, 388, 420, 423, 427, 429, 475, 490, 508–9, 511–13, 518–19, figs. B.1–8
kompromat, 172–73, 544, 573, 581, 590, 593
Kozak Memorandum, 541–42

L

Lange, Oskar, 625
Laos, 45–46
Latin America, 26, 29, 76, 80, 84, 91, 424, 507, 519
Latvia, 105, 108, 115, 357, 474, 476, figs. B.5, C.6
Lavrov, Sergey, 198
Lázár, János, 640
Lazarenko, Pavlo, 234–35, 539
Leancă, Iurie, 571–72
Lebanon, 507
Lebedev, Vyacheslav, 203
Leipzig, 396, 397
Leitha, 98
Lenin, Vladimir, 412
Leningrad, 222, 379. See also St. Petersburg
Leninism, 45, 268, 623
Leppert, Andrzej, 642
Levitsky, Steven, 6, 260, 271n10
Libya, 102
Likhachev, Alexey, 210
Linz, Juan, 250, 269
Litan, Robert E., 36
Lithuania, 105, 108, 115, 247, 357–58, 474, 476, 598
Lohmann, Susanne, 396–97
London, 235, 450, 524, 616–17, fig. A.5
Lublin, 617
Lukashenka, Alyaksandr, (Alexander), 15, 132, 231, 233, 248–63, 265–71, 356, 359–63, 366, 368, 378, 490, 537, 541, 603n14
Lupu, Marian, 565–66, 569–70, 574, 606n45
Lutsenko, Yuriy, 580, 594

Luzhkov, Yuriy, 184, 330, 450
Lviv, 236
Lyashko, Oleksandr, 227
Lysenko, Mikhail, 205
Lytvyn, Volodymyr, 339

M

Macedonia, 99, 105, 108, 115, 474
Machiavelli, Niccolò, 36
Magocsi, Paul R., 222
Magyar, Bálint, 12–16, 54, 179, 218–20, 242, 275, 280, 297, 372, 387, 401, 492, 657
Magyari, Nándor, László, 15, 657
Mahdavy, Hossein, 495–96
Makarkin, Alexei, 196
Makhachkala, 205
Malaysia, 507, fig. A.5
Mao Zedong, 49
Markus, Stanislav, 448
Marx, Karl, 23, 24, 63
Marxism, 24, 65n5, 268, 623
Masherov, Pyotr (Piotr Masherau), 357
Maslow, Abraham, 403
Masol, Vitalii, 227
Matviyenko, Sergey, 201
Matviyenko, Valentina, 198
Mazowiecki, Tadeusz, 633
Mazurov, Kiril (Kiryl Mazurau), 358
McAdam, Doug, 398
McAllister, Ian, 248
McConnell, Mitch, 519
media, 15, 24, 50 120–22, 354, 371–83, 650–51, 654
    mass, 9, 285, 321, 397, 431, 511
    fake, 382–83
    governance, 371–78, 381–82
    online, 264, 378–79, 380–81, 383, 397
    pluralism, 241, 283, 371, 375–77, 381–82, 548
    regional, 438
    social, 376, 379, 381, 512
    state-owned, 6, 15, 251, 258, 263, 269, 321, 374, 377, 382, 482, 637
    access to, 132–34, 264, 312, 333, 375, 485
    control over, 15, 354, 371–80, 382, 433, 514, 537, 573, 575, 650
    restrictions of, 55, 132, 207, 295, 378–83, 482, 556, 650,
    and corruption, 238, 242, 276–77, 279–85, 288, 290, 294–96, 304–5, 306n22, 307n27, 379
    See also censorship
Medvedev, Dmitry, 196–98, 330, 334, 340, 342–43, 438, 451, 580
Medvedko, Oleksandr, 543–44
Melville, A. Yu., 425
Merabishvili, Ivane, 556
Merkel, Angela, 643
Merkushkin, Nikolay, 185
Mészáros, Lőrinc, 472–73, 481, 486n8
Michnik, Adam, 251, 627, 631
Mihalisko, Kathleen, 251
Mikołajczyk, Stanisław, 617
Miller, Alexei, 198, 211
Minakov, Mikhail, 14, 657
Minc, Hilary, 618
Minchenko, Yevgeny, 199, 201
Mindszenty, József, 619, 621
Minsk, 260, 262, 358, 598
Minzarari, Dumitru, 16, 657
Mironyuk, M. G., 425
Mises, Ludwig von, 23
Mizsei, Kálmán, 9, 15, 605n37, 657
Mlodinow, Leonard, 280
Mohl, Robert von, 78
Moldova, 16, 44, 92, 103, 105, 108–9, 115–16, 130, 358, 385, 421, 423, 427, 429, 430, 433, 435n30, 474, 490, 507–8, 510–14, 517, 519–20, 522–23, 528n31, 531–34, 540–44, 546, 55–52, 560–61, 563–74, 576, 583–85, 599, 606n46, 607n53, figs. C.1–8
Mongolia, 49, 61, 382
Mordovia, 185
Moscow Oblast, 201, 208, 443
Moscow Princedom, 416, 418

Moscow, 179, 182–84, 190, 193, 203, 206, 211, 213n7, 214n19, 224, 228, 236, 251–52, 337–38, 341, 344, 346, 385, 442–43, 450–51, 458n37, 496, 539–40, 543, 546, 564, 570, 603n14, 616–18, 658, fig. B.6
Mubarak, Gamal, 512
Mubarak, Hosni, 512
Munck, Gerardo, 249
Mungiu-Pippidi, Alina, 286, 296, 298, 304
Murov, Andrey, 199, 201
Murov, Yevgeny, 196–97, 200, 209, 215n25
mafia state, 13–16, 54, 111–12, 118, 136–46, 149–53, 155, 164–65, 169–70, 172, 179, 204, 217, 219, 239–42, 247, 250, 254, 258–61, 265, 267, 269–70, 275, 280, 283, 288–90, 292–93, 297–301, 303–4, 371, 373, 382, 387, 461–63, 465, 467, 472–73, 476–77, 480, 482–85, 573, 580, 583, 593, 597, 599, 611, 637, 640–42, 648–49, 654
minigarch, 13, 150, 154
moguls, 289, 291, 297, 303, 306n22

N

Nabiullina, Elvira, 198
Nagorno-Karabakh, 523, fig. A.7
Nagy, Imre, 619–20
Naryshkin, Sergey, 198, 209
Năstase, Adrian, 291, 310n51, 312n59
Năstase, Andrei, 575
National Anti-Corruption Bureau of Ukraine, 586, 588
National Anticorruption Center, Moldova, 514, fig. C.2
National Anticorruption Directorate (DNA), Romania, 277, 281–83, 288, 302, 307–8, 311, 313–14
nationalization, 66n15, 94n25, 157, 166–69, 453, 463, 589, 622, 651, 676
 of corruption, 138
 of the elite, 183, 187, 209, 211

 See also deprivatization; patrimonialization; renationalization
Nauru, 355
Navalny, Alexei, 186
Nazi dictatorship, 26, 41, 73n69, 223
neo-nomenklatura, 15, 126–27, 179–82, 212
neopatrimonial(ism), 11, 12, 14, 75, 77, 79–91, 111, 127, 218
 democracy, 12, 92
 See also under bureaucracy
Nicaragua, 30, 378
Nigeria, 515, 518, 526n13, 528n24, 529n47
nomenklatura, 13, 48, 85, 118–21, 123, 129, 131, 135, 137, 151, 155, 160, 179–84, 205, 212, 213n3, 220–22, 225, 227, 232, 242, 356–61, 364, 368, 417–24, 427, 431, 439, 577, 640
 economic, 418
 secret service, 103, 126–27
 See also neo-nomenklatura
North Caucasus, 189, 192, 194, 214n12
North Korea, 29, 31, 33, 45, 108, 174
Northern Tyumen, 187
Novosibirsk Oblast, 185
Nureyev, Rustem, 423–24

O

Oberschall, Anthony, 398
Odesa (Odessa), 236–37, 240, 534, 577
Offe, Claus, 103
oligarchs, 13, 54, 124, 146–147, 150–54, 162, 165–66, 184, 207, 220, 233–34, 238, 250, 255, 270, 289, 291–93, 297, 300, 303, 371, 377, 382, 386–88, 390, 440–42, 445–46, 449–50, 462–63, 472–73, 492, 500, 536–46, 559, 561–62, 564, 567, 570, 572, 574–79, 585–86, 588–593, 595, 599, 640–43
 types of, 148–50, 238
 state capture by, 150, 169, 297, 379, 382, 461, 467, 532
 subjugated, 147, 163, 641
 See also minigarch; moguls; poligarch

oligarchy, 353, 428, 538, 577
  competing, 424, 426–29, 491–92
  national, 299–300
  oligarchic anarchy, 103, 148, 164–65
  oligarchic capitalism, 36
  oligarchic democracy, 84
  oligarchic neopatrimonialism, 91
  oligarchic republic, 217, 231
Olson, Mancur, 419
Oman, 355
Orange Revolution, 165, 209, 239–40, 339, 346, 491, 545–46, 560–62, 583, 605n35
Orbán, Viktor, 22–23, 55–59, 61–62, 70n51, 73n71, 127, 154, 165, 179, 297, 300, 303–4, 310n49, 314n77, 373, 382, 472–73, 480–81, 486n8, 611, 632, 637, 641–47, 649, 651
Organization for Security and Cooperation in Europe (OSCE), 249, 265, 333, 337, 373, 566
Ortega, Daniel, 378
Orttung, Robert, 377

P

Paciu, Sorin, 572
Pakistan, 254, 512
Palermo Protocols, 142
Pannonia, 98
Parfenchikov, Artur, 210
Partskhaladze, Otar, 556
party of power, 14, 87–90, 249, 258–60, 269–70, 331–32, 334–37, 339–40, 342–43, 346
patrimonial(ism), 11, 14, 77–79, 81–83, 85–87, 89–90, 99, 111, 157, 167, 218, 430–31, 433, 464
  communism, 98, 104
  See also under bureaucracy
patrimonialization, 79, 93n11, 157, 167. *See also* deprivatization; renationalization
patron's court, 118, 123–25, 135, 142–43, 292, 640

patronal democracy, 109, 131, 133–34, 239, 242
patronal networks, 8–10, 12, 14–15, 87–91, 99, 104–5, 109, 111–18, 121–23, 127–129, 131, 134–35, 137–38, 144–45, 149–150, 152, 157, 163–64, 166, 169, 172–73, 183, 218–19, 229, 233, 239–42, 293–94, 298–99, 466, 473, 475, 477, 563, 600, 638
patronal parties, 127–131, 136
patronal politics, 9–13, 16, 112–13, 218–20, 275, 280, 311n54, 549, 562, 576, 583
patronal regime, 124, 532, 536, 541, 543, 559, 561, 577, 580
patronal servant, 145, 154
patronal society, 566, 576, 584, 591
patronal state, 13, 137, 217, 241, 531–32, 538, 552, 555, 573, 593, 597, 599, 601
patronalism, 8–12, 99, 105, 109, 115–16, 218–20, 267, 269, 298, 386
  nomenklatura based, 227
  clan based, 233, 235–36
patron-client relations, 53, 82–83, 85–91, 104, 109–14, 131, 137, 146–84, 217–18, 265–66, 292, 294, 299–300, 347, 401, 464, 479, 482, 631
patrons, 10, 15, 82, 152, 218, 220, 239, 302, 303, 448, 450, 453, 562
  chief, 9, 13, 16, 112, 116, 118–19, 123–24, 126, 129–32, 135, 138–39, 142, 145, 150, 153–55, 162, 164–65, 170–71, 173, 179, 184, 255, 292, 472, 475, 479–80, 576, 640
  clan, 89, 220, 235
  See also subpatrons
Patrushev, Andrey, 201
Patrushev, Dmitry, 201
Patrushev, Nikolay, 196, 198, 199
Pazniak, Zianon, 250–51
Peron, Juan, 61
Persian Gulf, 355
Petrov, Nikolay, 15, 657

Philippines, 314n77, 374
Pidhornyi, Mykola, 227
Pikulik, Alexei, 14, 657
Piłsudski, Józef, 612–15, 645
Pinchuk, Victor, 234–35
Pipes, Richard, 221, 416
Pishkun, Svyatoslav, 543–44
Plahotniuc, Vladimir, 510–11, 514, 522–23, 529n45, 542, 546, 566, 567–76, figs. C.1, C.2, C.4, C.6, C.7
Plokhoi, Oleg, 209
Podillia, 236
Poland, 15, 26, 29, 49, 67n36, 99, 105, 108, 115, 159, 247, 264, 372, 374, 439, 453, 474, 476, 532, 534, 535–36, 560, 563, 611–54
Polányi, Karl, 24
poligarch, 13, 124, 144–45, 151, 153, 154, 170, 220, 225, 234, 237, 238, 240, 245n36, 300, 463
political family. *See* adopted political family
Poltava Oblast, 223
Ponta, Victor, 291, 307n29, 311n52, 313n66
Popov, Andrei, 571
populism, 24, 60, 92, 169, 207, 249, 251–55, 260–62, 269–70, 353, 372–73, 382–83, 427, 507, 576, 582, 638–39, 649
Poroshenko, Petro, 347, 544, 561–62, 580, 584–85, 588–89, 592–94, 598–99
Potanin, Vladimir, 184
power&ownership (*vlast'-sobstvennost'*), 16, 123, 152, 156–57, 161, 415–33
Pribaltika, 222
prikhvatizatsiya, 157–58, 165–66
Primakov, Yevgeny, 330
Privalov, Alexandr, 446
privatization, 102–3, 123, 148, 157–61, 165, 167–68, 221, 238, 242, 255–56, 353, 368, 418, 423, 437–46, 451–46, 455, 462, 475, 532–33, 535, 541, 567–68, 574

of the state, 89, 113, 144, 462
See also reprivatization; *prikhvatizatsiya*
Proudhon, Pierre-Joseph, 23
Pshonka, Viktor, 543, 580, 593
Pskov Oblast, 201
Pufendorf, Samuel, 77
Pussy Riot, 186
Putin, Vladimir, 15, 22–23, 42, 67n37, 125–26, 131, 164, 179–83, 186, 188–89, 195–202, 204, 207–8, 211, 213, 214n19, 250, 253–54, 257–58, 321, 325, 327, 330–34, 336, 339–40, 342, 344–45, 376, 382, 386–87, 438, 442, 445–47, 450–51, 454, 458n37, 493, 537, 540–43, 553, 562–63, 579–83, 585, 599, 644
pyramid systems. *See* competing-(multi-)pyramid system; single-pyramid system

R

Radkov, Alyaksandr, 258
Rajk, László, 618
Rakhimov, Murtaza, 184, 451
Rakhimov, Ural, 451
Rákosi, Mátyás, 618–20, 623
Razvozzhayev, Leonid, 388
reiderstvo. See corporate raiding
renationalization, 157, 166–69, 377, 451–53, 564
rentier state, 14, 490, 493, 495–97
rent-seeking, 11–12, 84–85, 90–91, 95n29, 105, 143–44, 152, 170–72, 472, 492, 494, 496, 498–503, 533, 571, 589, 639
regime, 14, 489–93
state, 143, 171
reprivatization, 53, 166–68, 297, 377
See also privatization
Reymer, Alexander, 208–9
Robinson, James A., 36
Roessler, Philip, 132
Rogán, Antal, 640
Rojansky, Matthew, 448

Romania, 15, 25, 29, 98–99, 102, 105, 108, 115, 275, 278–80, 282–86, 288–91, 295–304, 311n52, 312n61, 314n80, 474, 507, 522, 540, 543, 560, 564, 570–71, 573, 576, 629, figs. C.6, C.8
Romodanovsky, Konstantin, 200, 209
Roosevelt, Franklin D., 56
Rose Revolution, 421, 542, 547, 554, 559–60, 586
Rotenberg, Arkady, 198
Rotenberg, Igor, 190
Rotenberg, Roman, 201
Roth, Guenther, 79–81
Rouda, Uladzimir, 14–15, 658
Rubezhnoi, Alexei, 200
Rubik, Ernő, 33
Rubinov, Anatoly, 259
Runov, Anton, 423–24
Russia, 5, 12, 14–16, 32, 42–43, 54, 58, 91–92, 98, 103, 105, 108, 115, 117–18, 125–26, 130–31, 150, 161, 164, 179, 183, 187–88, 190–93, 195, 199, 201, 204, 206–7, 212–15, 229, 231–33, 236, 240, 248, 250–54, 257–59, 261, 263, 266, 270, 297, 319–20, 322–28, 330–48, 354, 357, 365, 369n8, 374, 376, 379–80, 382, 385–90, 393, 399–401, 405–7, 411n61, 415–20, 422–29, 433, 437–42, 445–55, 457n28, 458, 459n47, 474, 475, 489–97, 500, 502–3, 507, 519–20, 533, 535–42, 546, 548, 559–60, 564, 566, 568, 576–78, 580–85, 587–88, 590, 599, 603n15, 604n30, 613, 644, 645, figs. A.6, B.4, B.5, C.5, C.7.
See also Soviet Union
Ryabov, Andrey, 16, 658
Rybak, Volodymyr, 236–37
Rybkin, Ivan, 328–29

S

Saakashvili, Mikheil, 429, 546–61, 571, 586, 592, 600, 608n64
Sachs, Jeffrey, 534
Saint-Simon, Henri de, 23
Sakhalin Oblast, 185, 205–6, 208
Sakvarelidze, Davit, 594–95
Sakwa, Richard, 387, 458n36
Samara, 185
Sandu, Maia, 575
Sapronov, Timofei, 221
Saratov Oblast, 205
Scherlis, Gerardo, 290
Schramm, Carl J., 36
Schumpeter, Joseph, 23, 37, 50
Sechin, Igor, 198, 211–12, 452
Sechin, Ivan, 201
Serbia, 99, 105, 108, 115, 376, 474
Serdyukov, Anatoly, 183, 206–7, 209
Sergun, Igor, 201
Sergun, Olga, 201
Sevastopol, 187, 497
Shamalov, Yury, 201
Shcherban, Yevhen, 578
Shcherbytsky, Volodymyr, 225, 227
Shelest, Petro, 227
Sherzai, Gul Agha, 519
Shestakov, Ilya, 201
Shevardnadze, Eduard, 429, 547, 554
Shevchuk, Yevgeny, 572
Shkolov, Yevgeny, 198, 199, 209
Shokin, Viktor, 594–95
Shoygu, Sergey, 198, 199, 201, 211
Shushkevich, Stanislav, 251
Shuvalov, Igor, 198
Siberia, 222, 444, 451
siloviki, 184–85, 196, 198, 199, 200, 203, 407, 445–47, 449, 452–54
Siluanov, Anton, 198
Simferopol, 580
Simicska, Lajos, 472–73
Singapore, 58, 374, fig. A.5
single-pyramid system, 9, 10, 12–16, 40, 87, 109, 111–12, 114–18, 121–24, 126–27, 130–31, 135, 150, 152–53, 157, 162–65, 169, 219, 231, 239, 275, 288, 293–95, 300–1, 466, 473, 475, 503, 540–41, 543, 546, 559, 563, 566, 577, 580–81, 583, 588, 599–602, 610

Slovakia, 105, 108, 115, 303, 474, 476
Slovenia, 99, 105, 108–9, 113, 115, 474, 476
Smirnov, Igor, 572
Smirnov, Ivan, 221
Smith, Adam, 495
Sobyanin, Alexander, 323
Sobyanin, Sergey, 198, 211
Sólyom, László, 653
Somalia, 512
Soros, George, 553, 587, 605n35, 609n76, 644
Soskice, David, 35
South Africa, 507, 681
South Caucasus, 421
South Korea, 507
Southern Europe. See under Europe
Soviet Union (USSR), 24–25, 29, 43, 49, 63, 75–76, 84, 98–99, 102, 119, 130, 217, 220–21, 223–25, 228–29, 248, 253, 260, 266, 268, 271n10, 319–20, 325, 356–58, 361, 369n8, 382, 407, 415, 417–22, 424, 432, 441, 453, 474, 489, 496, 504n2, 510, 531, 533, 536, 539, 542, 546, 551–53, 566, 577–78, 601, 616, 619, 629. See also Russia
Spain, 26, 522
Spengler, Oswald, 63
St. Petersburg, 32, 126, 186, 192, 197, 201, 204, 214n19, 215n27, 346. See also Leningrad
Stalin, Joseph (Iosif Dzhugashvili), 25, 41–42, 67n37, 129, 179–82, 197, 205, 221, 223, 225, 379, 543, 594, 615–18
Stalino (Donets'k), 223, 224
state, 10, 13, 35, 52–53, 77, 84, 103, 136–43, 162, 285, 297, 416, 430, 492
   apparatus, 52, 88–89, 159, 169, 187, 206, 269, 331, 441, 446, 448, 454, 549, 558, 591, 597, 614
   authoritarian, 385, 389–90, 392, 394, 403–5
   constitutional, 114
   democratic, 91, 241, 247, 261, 400, 403, 405
   feudal, 111, 118
   gangster, 143
   ideology, 267–78, 269
   modern, 79, 80, 81, 86, 91, 145, 559, 560
   parasite, 144, 462, 641
   predatory, 143–44, 164, 172
   resource, 143
   welfare, 24, 65n8, 143
   See also criminal state; clan state; mafia state
state capture, 54, 77, 92, 139–40, 163, 169, 297, 301, 372–73, 461–62, 466–90, 494, 500, 532, 566, 573, 576, 599, 641
   partial, 140, 162–63, 468, 471, 473, 476–77, 508
   party, 477
state socialism, 94n25, 258, 490–91, 498–99, 501–2, 633
Statkevich, Nikolai, 249
Stavropol Province, 222
Stepan, Alfred, 250, 269
stooges, 14, 112, 138, 144–45, 151, 154, 220, 238, 307n28, 309n36, 382, 464, 481, 640, 642–43, 651
   economic, 151, 153
   political, 130, 151–54
   See also front men
Stukal, D. K., 425
subpatrons, 116, 119, 170, 466, 476
Sugrobov, Denis, 183, 208
Sukhovolsky, Vladislav, 323
sultanism, 14, 83, 91, 111, 249–50, 254, 268–70, 353
Sumy Oblast, 223
Surkov, Vladislav, 207
Suslov, Mikhail, 222
Sverdlovsk Oblast, 208, 456n16
Syria, 102, 512
Syroyid, Oksana, 595
Szálasi, Ferenc, 616–17

T

Taiwan, 45, 522
Tajikistan, 45, 91, 100, 105, 108, 115, 126, 369n8, 420, 423, 427–28, 475, figs. B.7, B.8
Tarrow, Sidney, 396
Taruta, Serhiy, 578
Tatarstan, 204
Tbilisi, 549, 550–51, 554, fig. A.6
Thailand, 355, 512
Theobald, Robin, 82
Tiborcz, István, 472–73
Tildy, Zoltán, 617
Timchenko, Gennady, 198
Timofti, Nicolae, 511, 574
Tishchenko, Alexander, 208
Tokarev, Nikolay, 198
Tolokonsky, Viktor, 185
Tolstoy, Leo, 489
Torlopov, Vladimir, 208
Tóth, István János, 466
Toynbee, Arnold, 63
Transnistria, 523, 541–42, 563, 568, 572, fig. C.7
Transparency International, 276, 296, 476, 604
Trotsky, Leon, 221, 419
Trump, Donald, 70n57, 383n1, 507, 517, 519
Tullock, Gordon, 398, 492
Tunisia, 511, 513, 518, 526n13, 527n20
Turchak, Anatoly, 201
Turchak, Andrey, 201
Turkey, 102, 314n77, 374, 382, 520, 604n30, figs. A.3, A.5, A.6, A.8, B.6, B.8, C.4
Turkmenistan, 44–45, 91, 100, 105, 108–9, 115, 126, 130, 158, 256, 348, 420, 423, 426–28, 475, 490
Tusk, Donald, 634–35, 643
Tuvalu, 355
Tymoshenko, Yulia, 234, 238–39, 544–45, 561–62, 580–82, 585, 588, 605n35

U

Udaltsov, Sergei, 388
Uganda, 355, 374
Ukraine, 6, 12, 14, 16, 44, 91–92, 103, 105, 108–9, 115–16, 164–65, 180, 190, 209, 217–36, 239–42, 248, 251–52, 254, 258, 266, 327, 331, 339, 344, 346–48, 357, 376, 379, 385, 388, 422–23, 425, 427, 429–33, 435n30, 438, 448–49, 474, 489–91, 492n93, 495–97, 500, 502–3, 504n2, 507, 511, 519, 523, 531–40, 543–47, 551–52, 560–63, 568, 577–83, 585–91, 594, 596–97, 604n30, 645, fig. C.7
Ulyukayev, Alexey, 183, 191, 208–9, 452–53
United Kingdom (UK), 25, 60, 444, 450, 517, figs. A.6, A.8, B.5, B.8, C.5. *See also* Britain
United States (US), 35, 54, 57, 60, 70n70, 88, 138, 234, 252, 254, 295, 309n38, 327, 354, 371, 378, 381, 383, 388, 393, 507, 519–20, 522, 537, 539, 540, 545, 556, 570–72, 576, 581, 584–86, 594, 600, 619, 621, 644, figs. A.5–6, A.8, B.6–8, C.5–8
Urechean, Serafim, 571
Usatîi, Renato, 575
Usmanov, Alisher, 198–99
Ustinov, Anton, 201
Uzbekistan, 91, 100, 105, 108, 115, 126, 130, 158, 256, 348, 420, 423, 427–28, 475, 490, 518, 526n13, fig. B.8

V

Vajna, Andy, 481, 486n8
Vasylyev, Hennadiy, 543
Venezuela, 354, 365, 374, 502
Vienna, 585

Vietnam, 40, 45, 46, 61, 108, 174n5
Viktorov, Ilja, 16, 658
Vinnytsia Oblast, 236
Visegrád countries, 540, 645–46
Viskuli, 248
Volchik, Vyacheslav, 416, 424
Volkov, Alexandr, 446
Volkov, Vadim, 442, 446
Volodin, Vyacheslav, 198, 209
Voloshin, Alexandr, 334
Vorobyov, Andrey, 201
Vorobyov, Yury, 201
Voronin, Vladimir, 540–44, 563–67, 569–70, 573–74, 605n37, 606n45
Voroshilov, Kliment, 617
Voslensky, Mikhail, 417
Vrabie, Vitalie, 568

W

Wałęsa, Lech, 628, 652
Walker, Christopher, 377
Warsaw, 616, 643–45
Waszczykowski, Witold, 644
Way, Lucan A., 3, 260, 271n10
Weber, Max, 9, 11, 14, 24, 39, 41, 65n12, 77–79, 83, 85–87, 95n28–29, 105, 110–11, 136, 144–46, 153, 249, 281, 286, 466
Wedel, Janine R., 140
Weimar republic, 39, 41, 73n69
Welzel, Christian, 100–101
Western Europe. *See under* Europe
White, Stephen, 248
Wilson, Andrew, 535
Woodruff, David, 439, 453
World Bank, 133, 255, 296, 389, 400, 474, 537, 634, figs. B.8, C.8
Wyszyński, Stefan, 619, 621

X

xenophobia, 58, 70n17, 382, 639

Y

Yakunin, Vladimir, 196–97, 209
Yanukovych, Oleksandr, 237
Yanukovych, Viktor, 164–65, 233, 236–40, 339, 340, 347, 429–30, 519, 543, 545, 562, 577–85, 588, 593–95
Yarema, Vitaly, 593
Yatsenyuk, Arseniy, 588, 595, 598
Yavlinsky, Grigory, 257, 329, 330, 334, 338
Yeltsin, Boris, 91, 131, 180, 182, 196, 207, 214n18, 231, 253, 319–20, 322–23, 327, 330–31, 334, 342, 386, 390, 439, 441, 445–46, 453, 491, 493, 538
Yevtushenkov, Vladimir, 183–85, 450–52, 459n41
Yugoslavia, 98, 388, 531, 601, 618, 624
Yushchenko, Viktor, 239, 245n36, 339, 544–45, 547, 561–62, 579–82, 604–5n35

Z

Zakaria, Fareed, 70n51, 373
Zakharchenko, Dmitry, 208
Zaporizhzhia Oblast, 224, 240
Zguladze, Eka, 552, 554
Zhirinovsky, Vladimir, 323–25, 334–35, 341
Zinoviev, Grigory, 221
Zolotov, Viktor, 198–200, 209
Zorkin, Valery, 203
Zvyahilsky, Yukhym, 230, 236–37, 578
Zyuganov, Gennady, 322, 325, 330, 334